LABOR ECONOMICS:

Theory, Evidence, and Policy

THIRD EDITION

BELTON M. FLEISHER
Ohio State University

THOMAS J. KNIESNER
University of North Carolina

PRENTICE-HALL, INC., *Englewood Cliffs, New Jersey* 07632

Library of Congress Cataloging in Publication Data

FLEISHER, BELTON M.
  Labor economics.

  Includes bibliographies and index.
  1. Labor economics. I. Kniesner, Thomas J. II. Title.
HD4901.F47 1984   331   83-15997
ISBN 0-13-517417-1

Editorial/production supervision and
  interior design: Sonia Meyer
Cover design: Mark Berghash, 20/20 Services, Inc.
Manufacturing buyer: Ed O'Dougherty

Printed in the United States of America

10 9 8 7 6 5 4 3 2 1

ISBN 0-13-517417-1

Prentice-Hall International, Inc., *London*
Prentice-Hall of Australia Pty. Limited, *Sydney*
Editora Prentice-Hall do Brasil, Ltda., *Rio de Janeiro*
Prentice-Hall Canada Inc., *Toronto*
Prentice-Hall of India Private Limited, *New Delhi*
Prentice-Hall of Japan, Inc., *Tokyo*
Prentice-Hall of Southeast Asia Pte. Ltd., *Singapore*
Whitehall Books Limited, *Wellington, New Zealand*

TO H. GREGG LEWIS

AND MELVIN W. REDER

CONTENTS

PREFACE

The third edition of *Labor Economics* contains much new material. In addition, every chapter has been extensively revised in order to enhance the *accessibility* of the material to students with limited backgrounds in economics. We believe we have increased the readability of the text without sacrificing rigorous analysis of labor market theory, applications to social policy, or in-depth empirical analysis of labor markets. Besides a streamlined exposition, there have been the following significant changes and additions:

1. Increased use of "starred" (*) sections, containing more technical material that can be skipped without loss of continuity, so that the instructor can more easily adapt assigned readings to the level of students' backgrounds and to course objectives.
2. Extensive analyses of topics neglected in the second edition, including compensation and discrimination in labor markets.
3. More extensive end-of-chapter exercises and questions.

Our goal, as in earlier editions, has been to integrate modern neoclassical labor market theory, policy applications, and evidence in a single text. We have aimed to help the student develop a set of tools that will be useful *after* the course has been completed. Toward this end, much emphasis has been placed on a problem-solving approach—the use of economic analysis to develop sensible views of current issues. The end-of-chapter exercises are designed to further the development of these skills. In presenting evidence, we discuss problems of measurement in labor economics and try to help the student evaluate how well data currently gathered correspond to variables in our theoretical analysis. Chapter 2 (extensively revised) is devoted entirely to a survey of measurement problems in economics. It gives the student enough information to read the remainder of the text intelligently, even without previous courses in statistical procedures.

We have organized the third edition into five general parts. In Part I we develop the concept of labor economics as a science. In Part II we consider the labor market under competitive conditions, and in Part III under conditions that interfere with competition. Part IV presents the material on the labor market in the long run: investment in human capital. Part V deals with some labor market aspects of economic welfare: real wages, compensation, discrimination, unemployment, and inflation.

Within each chapter a basic theoretical framework is first developed, then examined for its implications about human behavior. Some of the behavioral implications are interesting in their own right; many produce a basis for sound economic policy. Finally, the best evidence available concerning the validity of the theory is presented and discussed.

We feel that the approach we have adopted helps to promote responsible and informed citizenship through liberal education. Because government is increasingly using the advice of social scientists to help design social programs, it is important that citizens understand scientific methods and the criteria that can help them choose among alternative outcomes. This way, they are more likely to support policies that will promote desired social ends most efficiently.

Acknowledgments

Our greatest debt is to the numerous scholars whose attempts to relate economic theory to the world around us have resulted in the articles, dissertations, monographs, and books that provide the basis for much of this text. We are extremely grateful to the reviewers whom Prentice-Hall has asked to comment on all or part of the third edition. Their comments have been of great help. We hope that when we have decided not to follow their advice, our reviewers do not interpret these difficult decisions as reflecting lack of appreciation for their time and effort. The following is an alphabetical list of the scholars who have helped us: Steven G. Allen, Ann Bartel, Donald J. Cymrot, Evangelos Falaris, Henry S. Farber, Masanori Hashimoto, David Lilien, Richard W. Moore, Randall Olsen, Frank P. Stafford, and George W. Thomas. We are particularly grateful to Nicholas M. Kiefer and Mark R. Killingsworth for their review of all, or major segments, of the manuscript and to W. Kip Viscusi and Solomon W. Polachek for their intensive reviews of individual parts of the book.

Gary Ferrier, Roger Lagunoff, and Gary Margeson provided excellent research assistance, and Betsey Pierce typed much of the first draft. Once again Jeanette White typed the final draft with her customary speed and accuracy.

1

AN INTRODUCTION
TO THE FIELD
OF LABOR ECONOMICS

A. Educational objectives
  1. To introduce the general way in which economists conceptualize labor market issues
  2. To examine why labor is a special branch of economics
  3. To see why labor economics is a subject worth studying

B. Labor economics as a science (p. 2)
  1. Science is a systematic study of a topic leading to the discovery of regular patterns of behavior (p. 2)
  2. Stages of scientific analysis (p. 2)
     a. Developing a conceptual framework for analyzing an issue
     b. Formulating a hypothesis
     c. Testing a hypothesis
     d. Evaluating results

C. Why labor is a special branch of economics (p. 5)
  1. Labor is a factor of production (p. 5)
     a. Labor is a key ingredient in the production of nearly every commodity
     b. An input-output table for society is a conceptual framework for viewing labor's role as a factor of production
  2. Labor is a source of income (p. 10)
     a. Payments to labor are about three-fourths of national income in the United States
     b. The circular flow of income
  3. Labor is a human resource (p. 11)
     a. Is it proper to subject labor to a logical quantitative analysis similar to that of markets for commodities or financial assets?
     b. Labor is a unique factor of production because it is physically inseparable from its owner, and formal lifetime contracts (slavery) are illegal

D. Why study labor economics? (p. 12)

E. Organization of analysis (p. 14)

LABOR ECONOMICS AS A SCIENCE

This chapter will show you how economists think through a labor market issue. The economists' approach is not the only one that has merit; we might also concern ourselves with the employers' or the workers' viewpoints. We take the economists' approach, however, because this book emphasizes labor economics *as a science*.

Stages of Scientific Analysis

Science refers to a systematic study leading to discovery of regular patterns of behavior. To understand science in general and labor economics in particular, we need to answer two questions: (1) What events lead to a scientific discovery? and (2) How do we know one when we see one? The answers are the same in labor economics as in other sciences, and we can best see them by discussing the stages of discovery scientists go through when attempting to advance the state of knowledge.

Stage 1: Developing a conceptual framework.   The first stage of analysis in any science is the conceptualization of the basic principles governing behavior in a particular area. In the case of labor economics, economists conceptualize the decision processes of households and firms with respect to their labor market behavior. This involves postulating a behavioral goal for each decision maker, such as profit maximization or utility maximization, then examining how this goal and the environment surrounding the decision maker should lead, for example, to decisions of how much labor to demand or supply.

You have already performed this type of activity in your course on principles of economics when you studied the supply of output by a profit-maximizing competitive firm. There you examined how a firm with the goal of maximizing its profit was led to produce a particular level of output. The firm's output decision was determined by its economic environment, which was characterized by (1) a fixed product price, (2) fixed prices of its inputs, plus (3) a given state of technology for producing the product.

In labor economics we apply similar kinds of representations of decision makers, known as **models,** to examine theoretically the linkage between the economic environment of firms and households and their decisions governing the quantity and quality of work they will supply and demand. As we said before, all science begins with this stage of discovery. Astronomers attempt to create a physical model of the solar system. Aeronautical engineers seek to develop the principles of aerodynamics. Physicists concern themselves with the general relationships between bodies in motion. At this stage the language and logic of a science are developed.

Stage 2: Hypothesis formulation. Scientists develop conceptual frameworks for one primary purpose—to formulate hypotheses describing behavior. A **hypothesis** is a prediction as to how a body or an organism (decision maker) will respond when stimulated. It is really nothing more than a prediction in the form of an if-then statement. Probably the most basic hypothesis from labor economics is that if a profit-maximizing firm suddenly faces a higher wage rate, then it will desire to purchase less labor. Notice that we have made a prediction based on a conceptual framework of the demand for labor by a profit-maximizing firm.

There are four key properties that scientists attempt to give their hypotheses. The first is that they must involve events that are important or interesting. An example of an extremely important hypothesis from physics is that if an object, such as a ball, is dropped from above the ground, it will fall to the ground. This is certainly important for anyone who may fall from a building. Another clearly important hypothesis is that if a Boeing 747 attempts to fly, it will be successful. Thousands of travelers each year certainly believe (and test) this hypothesis when they board flights to London from New York.

A second key property of a hypothesis is that it must be the result of logic. By this we mean that it has been systematically developed from the behavioral implications of the conceptual framework in stage 1. In other words, a hypothesis should follow from rigorous deduction of initial postulates or assumptions describing how decisions are made or how bodies or organisms interact. Notice that this is much different from simply getting "hot flashes" about the future, such as in fortune telling. Limiting ourselves to predictions derived logically from a conceptual framework is valuable because it saves us from wasting time on outlandish ideas. For example, if we were to ignore the principles of physics developed in stage 1, we could formulate the hypothesis that if a lead ball were dropped from the top of the World Trade Center in New York, it would shoot upward through outer space and hit Mars. There are actually an infinite number of hypotheses we might formulate if we were to bypass the first stage of discovery: development of a conceptual framework.

A third key property of a hypothesis is that it must be testable. Thus, it must relate to observable events. To hypothesize that when two unicorns mate they will produce a human offspring is fairly useless, because a unicorn is a mythical animal. For a hypothesis to be of any use to us we must be able to test it, and a hypothesis can be tested only against observations of behavior or outcomes.

The fourth key property of a hypothesis is that it can sometimes be incorrect. This is a way of stating that a *definition* is *not* a hypothesis. For example, it is *not* a hypothesis to say that if we are in Columbus, Ohio, then we are west of New York City and east of Los Angeles. There is no way that this statement could ever be false, because its truth depends only on the definitions of *east* and *west*. On the other hand, the statement that a lead ball dropped from the top of a tall building will fall to the ground *is* a hypothesis. Even though it is almost impossible to imagine an event (such as a wind of 10,000 miles per hour) that might render the hypothesis a false predictor of a lead ball's behavior when dropped, the only way to discover whether the hypothesis is correct is to conduct an experiment and actually let the ball drop. The point is that a hypothesis is *much more* than a definition. It represents a stimulus-response pattern that can be checked against reality and has the *possibility* of not being true.

Stage 3: Hypothesis testing.   Eventually, scientists test their hypotheses. Confronting hypotheses with data from either a controlled experiment or a survey is a crucial stage in scientific discovery. Remember that scientists want to discover regular patterns of behavior. Throughout this book we will be developing and discussing hypotheses concerning how various events influence labor supply, labor demand, wages, working conditions, employment, and unemployment—for example: (1) if the minimum wage is increased, then employment opportunities will be reduced; (2) if job safety standards in the form of OSHA are introduced, then jobs will become safer; (3) if unemployment compensation is increased, then the unemployment rate will rise.

In many sciences, such as physics or chemistry, hypotheses are tested with controlled experiments. Because economics deals for the most part with *human* subjects, behavioral implications derived from economics are examined through the use of survey data. Economists gather data on the behavior of decision makers and see whether that behavior fits the stimulus-response pattern expected from their hypothesis. The data economists use and the way they study stimulus-response patterns with data are the topic of Chapter 2. Because of the very nature of certain economic variables and the requirement that they be examined through survey data, the measurement of economic variables takes on a special importance; this is also discussed in some detail in Chapter 2.

Stage 4: Evaluation of results.   If a scientist finds that the expected relationship between a stimulus and response is *repeatedly* observed, then that hypothesis is said to be confirmed. If this is not the case, then the researcher returns to stage 1 and reconceptualizes. In the case of economics, an economist would reconceptualize the decision process of firms or households. The process of scientific discovery then begins anew.

The state of knowledge in a scientific field is really just its collection of confirmed hypotheses. It is possible, though, that many of the confirmed hypotheses are only *qualitative* in nature. An example from economics would be the hypothesis that fluctuations in either government spending or the growth rate of the money stock cause business cycles. Economists are pretty sure that this is the case, but they do not have much to say about the *timing* or *severity* of business cycles. This situation has a number of analogues in the physical sciences. Meteorologists know what causes rain but not exactly *when* it will rain. Geologists have difficulty predicting when earthquakes or volcanic eruptions will occur. The more numerous the confirmed, *quantitative* hypotheses are that characterize a scientific field, the more well developed that science is said to be. A quantitative hypothesis provides us not only with the *direction* of a response but also its *magnitude*. Physicists are quite sure of the time it will take for a ten-pound ball dropped from 1,000 feet to hit the ground. In the case of labor economics, economists are reasonably comfortable with the conclusion that an extra year of schooling will raise lifetime earning power, on average, by about 4 to 8 percent after inflation.

Table 1-1 summarizes the stages of scientific discovery and provides some examples from labor economics. Notice that part of the table is blank. To make sure you understand the stages of discovery, fill in the blank boxes with some examples from your favorite natural science. If you do not have a favorite one, we suggest you try astronomy. Most people are familiar with the movement of the planets and their implications for day and night or the seasons. After you have done this, proceed to the next section, where we explain why labor is a *special* branch of economics.

WHY LABOR IS A SPECIAL BRANCH OF ECONOMICS

Most universities have a special course devoted to the economics of labor. Why? After all, we can think of many economic topics that do not merit their own course. Why labor? The answer lies in three key dimensions of labor: (1) labor is a factor of production, (2) labor is a human resource, and (3) labor is the major source of income in most countries. It is useful to elaborate on each of these in turn.

Labor Is a Factor of Production

Labor is an essential ingredient in the production of nearly every commodity, along with other productive resources such as wood, steel, petroleum products, and electricity. Of course, few productive factors are used in their pure states. By the time they enter the production process, they have usually gone through several stages of refinement. A farmer will grade, fertilize, and contour the land on which he will plant seeds. Iron ore must be discovered, mined, and transported to the steel mills. Water must be piped to the factory that wants it. Labor is a highly refined resource, and it appears

TABLE 1-1 Stages of Scientific Discovery with Examples from Labor Economics

	Field of Discovery
Stage of Discovery	*Labor Economics*
(1) Development of a Conceptual Framework	Conceptualization of the decision process of households (firms) with respect to labor market behavior. *(Example:* Firms are conceptualized as choosing their labor forces according to a desire to maximize their profits in consideration of the wages they must pay and the prices of their products.)
(2) Hypothesis Formulation	Formulation of a statement (prediction) of how certain economic variables are related. *(Example:* If Congress increases the minimum wage, then firms will hire fewer unskilled workers.)

(3) Hypothesis Testing	Use of data from an experiment or a survey to examine statistically whether the expected relationship between economic variables holds. (*Example*: Use data collected by the Bureau of Labor Statistics to compare, ceteris paribus, the employment of unskilled workers across industries before and after a minimum wage increase.)
(4) Evaluation of Results	If the expected relationship between economic variables is repeatedly observed, then the hypothesis is said to be confirmed. If the hypothesis is not confirmed, return to step (1), reconceptualize the decision process, and start again. (*Example*: Minimum wage laws have repeatedly been shown to reduce the job opportunities of the unskilled.)

in many varieties. Few of us enter the labor force before our sixteenth birthday. By that time, we have all been fed, clothed, educated, doctored, tested, and moved, so that even the most basic unskilled worker has been, in a sense, produced by an intricate process.

To help us see how labor enters the production of an entire economy, look at Table 1-2, which is an **input-output table.** It contains six numbered and lettered rows and six similar columns. Each number represents an industry, such as agriculture or steel, that combines factors of production and semifinished commodities to produce other commodities. The rows lettered L and K represent the factors of production labor and capital. The columns labeled C and G represent two sectors of the economy that purchase the goods and services produced by industries 1, 2, 3, and 4 and purchase some of the factor services, L and K. The sectors C and G are a household sector and a government sector. To make the table as simple as possible we ignore any purchases by foreign countries.

The rows of the input-output table represent the sales of the four industries and the two factors of production; the columns indicate who made the purchases. Thus, if we look across row 1 from left to right, we observe the output of industry 1 used by itself in further production, the output of industry 1 used by industries 2 through 4 in their production, and the output of 1 that is sold to households as consumption or to the government. Similarly, if we glance down column 1, we observe the consumption by industry 1 of its own output, the consumption of industry 1 of the output of industries 2

TABLE 1-2   Input-Output Table

Product or Factor Service Purchased

Output or Factor Service Sold

	1	2	3	4	C	G
1	X_{11}	X_{12}	X_{13}	X_{14}	X_{1C}	X_{1G}
2	X_{21}	X_{22}	X_{23}	X_{24}	X_{2C}	X_{2G}
3	X_{31}	X_{32}	X_{33}	X_{34}	X_{3C}	X_{3G}
4	X_{41}	X_{42}	X_{43}	X_{44}	X_{4C}	X_{4G}
L	X_{L1}	X_{L2}	X_{L3}	X_{L4}	X_{LC}	X_{LG}
K	X_{K1}	X_{K2}	X_{K3}	X_{K4}	X_{KC}	X_{KG}

Note: $X_{ij} \equiv$ Sales of industry i to industry j; thus X_{12} represents the *output* of industry 1 sold to industry 2; X_{1C} represents the output of industry 1 sold to households; X_{L1} represents purchases of labor by industry 1. [i = a row, j = a column.]

through 4, and the purchases by industry 1 of the basic factors, capital and labor. It may seem strange to you that the basic factors of production, K and L, are also purchased by households and governments. Such purchases simply reflect the use of labor as domestic service in households and as secretarial and other services in government. Minicomputers and word processors are examples of capital equipment purchased by both households and governments.

Table 1-2 is your first exposure in labor economics to a conceptual framework. In this regard, an input-output table is useful for understanding the role labor plays as a factor of production. Input-output tables also play an important role in the public policy process because they show the number of jobs created per dollar's worth of output sold by an industry. For example, Federal government economists used input-output tables to calculate the employment effects of the highway construction program mandated by the Surface Transportation Act of 1982. In general, input-output tables for the United States have been constructed by the Bureau of Labor Statistics (BLS) to indicate the jobs created by $1 million of output sales in various industries. Table 1-3 presents some employment effects for selected industries derived from their input-output tables.

TABLE 1-3   Employment Effects of Output Sales in Selected Industries, 1981

Industry	Direct Employment Effect of $1 Million of Sales	Total Employment Effect of $1 Million of Sales
Construction of single family dwellings	23 full-time jobs	45 full-time jobs
Construction of industrial buildings	19	40
Physicians' and dentists' services	22	32
Railroad transportation	16	27
Hotels and lodging	71	83

Source: Bureau of Labor Statistics

The data in Table 1-3 are estimates of the number of full-time jobs created in an industry per $1 million of sales in 1981. Notice that two employment effects are listed. The **direct employment effect** refers to the jobs created within the industry. The **total employment** effect accounts for the fact that when an industry sells output it also buys inputs other than labor. However, these other inputs are themselves produced with labor. So, when $1 million is spent on the construction of industrial buildings, 19 jobs are created for workers to build these buildings. Since workers also help to produce the glass and steel used in the construction of the buildings, the total employment effect of $1 million of new industrial construction is 40 jobs. The difference between the total and direct employment effects is the **indirect employment effect.** In the case of industrial construction, 21 jobs are created in subsidiary industries. Why do you think that the employment effects are so large in hotels and lodgings? What economic policy implications do you see in the data of Table 1-3?

Labor Is a Source of Income

Although all factors of production are directly or indirectly owned by households and their individual members, labor is the factor most widely owned. By this we mean that sales of labor services produce approximately 75 percent of the total revenue from sales of factors of production of all types. Put differently, wages, salaries, and the wage component of self-employment income produce about 75 percent of national income in the United States.

In your first economics course you were undoubtedly introduced to a circular flow diagram such as Figure 1-1. Such diagrams are designed to help us think of labor as a source of income as well as a factor of production. In part, households decide where and how much to work based on the income they can expect from that work, as well as the income they can expect from the sales of the services of other factors of production they might own. At the same time, their tastes for how to spend their incomes also play a role in deciding both how much and where to work. So, income determines and is determined by the allocation of labor among alternative uses, including the possibility of using labor totally within the household sector.

In the inner ring of the circular flow diagram in Figure 1-1 we see sales of goods and services by firms to households and the resulting payments made by households to firms. Figure 1-1 is extremely simple and has no explicit role for the government sector. If you like, you may think of government as a firm that sells goods and services to households in exchange for tax revenues. In any event, there is also an outer ring that indicates payments by producing units to households for providing the services of their labor and the other factors of production they own. Each sale of labor is

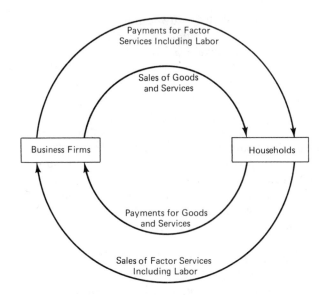

FIGURE 1-1. The circular flow of purchases and payments

made with respect to not only a specific amount of work but also the characteristics of the employer, occupation, and industry in which the worker will be employed. Business firms, governments included, compete to obtain the services of workers. Members of households make decisions concerning where to sell their labor services and how much to sell. At the same time, they determine their command over the output of the business sector because they are determining their incomes.

The relationships depicted in Figure 1-1 are basic to the study of labor economics. One important dimension of labor as a factor of production is submerged in the simplicity of Figure 1-1, the allocation of labor *within* the household sector. These within-household decisions, which involve time spent in schooling, child care, and so on, are crucial determinants of *future* income and are carefully studied in the chapters to follow. Moreover, we should emphasize the fact that labor is a *human* resource. This has played a crucial role in the development of the field of labor economics. It also helps to explain why labor is a special field within economics.

Labor Is a Human Resource

Some of you may feel that labor, being a *human* resource, cannot properly be subjected to the logical, quantitative analysis economists use to analyze the markets for agricultural goods or financial assets. Such an objection is probably based on a misconception of the role of economic analysis in developing scientific knowledge. An examination of labor's role in an economic system is more complicated, however, because it is a human resource. Individuals do not always act as if they were maximizing an easily represented goal, such as money income. Where you work and the nature of your job may be as important as how much you earn. These considerations mean that good labor market theory is difficult to develop, but *not* that it is undesirable. If anything, formal theory becomes even more crucial as organized thinking becomes more difficult. Insights, intuition, and knowledge of the world around us are indispensable ingredients in developing theory that is relevant to today's problems. They are by no means substitutes for such theory, though. Labor economics has developed as a field of investigation because much special knowledge is necessary to formulate useful hypotheses concerning labor markets. It would be inaccurate to say that it has developed because a scientific approach to the study of labor is not a useful one.

Labor is also a unique factor of production because it is physically inseparable from its owner. As a result, nonmonetary issues are much more important in decisions surrounding the allocation of labor than they are with almost anything else in a person's life. For instance, if you owned a truck rental service, you would probably not care all that much if your trucks were driven in cold climates or in smoky air, except insofar as this affected your ability to rent the trucks in the future. You certainly would not care as much as if you were making a decision where you yourself would work. As a rule, individuals do not have to live or work where their financial and physical capital are. However, they have to be in the place where they perform their labor services.

Because labor is physically inseparable from human beings, we have outlawed certain types of contracts between buyers and sellers of labor that are perfectly legitimate between buyers and sellers of almost any other resource. For example, we cannot buy or sell the labor of a person indefinitely. Slavery and indentured servitude are against the law in the United States and most other nations. This has important implications for labor market processes that take place over long periods—notably education and training. Who pays for the training or education of an individual is related to who has the ability to collect the benefits of that training. We will explore this issue in later chapters when we develop the theory of investment in human capital.

WHY STUDY LABOR ECONOMICS?

The preceding section has pointed out why labor is a special, and important, branch of economics. Still, why should you want to study labor economics? Probably the most important reason is that it provides a useful basis for evaluating alternative social policies.

As a citizen and a voter you will want to develop informed judgments concerning labor market policies. For example, should you favor a special minimum wage for youth? Should you be in favor of more free education? Should the activities of labor unions be restricted or encouraged? Is affirmative action legislation sufficient for reducing labor market discrimination, or should legislation requiring equal pay for comparable work be introduced? Scientific knowledge of how labor markets work will help you to decide how to answer such questions. Knowledge of labor economics also will allow you to make economic sense out of a newspaper or magazine story and be able to choose intelligently among politicians advocating alternative approaches to economic problems. While our approach to labor market issues in this text is a scientific one, one of our main goals is certainly to think clearly where labor market policies are concerned.

Of course, the economic policies you prefer will depend in part upon your personal judgment as to what social goals are desirable. This text cannot provide the answers to **normative** questions such as whether incomes *should be* more equally distributed or whether the unemployed individuals *should* receive expanded unemployment compensation benefits. There is no more a consensus on these issues than there is concerning the desirability of abortions or of prayers in public schools. Although normative questions are quite important, their solutions are not a part of scientific labor economics. Your text can, though, help you to identify the kinds of policy actions that will be effective in achieving certain outcomes for society. We will answer questions such as whether additional schooling improves the incomes of the poor. This type of issue requires scientific knowledge and is known as a **positive** question. Everyone with analytical training in labor economics should reach a similar answer to a positive question. The difference between normative and positive questions involves the issue of **equity** versus **efficiency.** Although it is scientifically possible to determine whether society is obtaining the maximum output from its set of resources (using them efficiently), whether those resources are used in a way that is fair to the members of society (equitable) is a philosophical issue.

In this course we will derive many **behavioral theorems** (hypotheses about human behavior) and use them to analyze public policy. There are a number of reasons why we will direct most of our attention to the *positive* dimensions of public policy. One is that we will be able to reach conclusions on scientific grounds. Second, all our lives we have been bombarded with the normative aspects of issues, those frequent discussions of good versus evil. It is time to even things out a little. Even more important if you wish to make statements (reach conclusions) concerning what government policy *should be,* you must accompany those statements with suggestions for their implementation. It is not enough to say that government should foster lower unemployment or racial and sexual equality in wages. You must also make a recommendation as to *how* this is to be done. Consider the issue of unemployment. Should unemployment insurance benefits be reduced as a way of lowering the unemployment rate? Should wage subsidies be paid to employers who hire more labor?

The point is that positive analysis is *necessary* for normative analysis. In order to make good policy it is necessary to have an idea whether or not the policy being suggested will have the intended effect. In later chapters we will see that many well-intentioned policy goals have not been met. Others have been totally contradicted, because what on the surface seemed to be an appropriate policy prescription was exactly the opposite. Often this has been the result of policymakers' lack of familiarity with the subtleties of labor market economics. In the next section we will preview some of the many policy issues to which we will apply our labor economic insights.

ORGANIZATION OF ANALYSIS

Each topic we examine will be analyzed in three steps paralleling the stages of scientific discovery summarized in Table 1-1. First, we try to understand the theoretical analysis economists have developed for examining the topic. Next, we take our theoretical analysis and use it to expand our knowledge of how individuals interact with their environment. This may well be the most important step, because it provides a basis for understanding and formulating sound economic policy. In particular, policy changes the environment conditioning peoples' decisions and, through this, their behavior. Once we understand the link between individuals' environment and their decisions, we can link government policy to human behavior. This relationship is depicted in Figure 1-2. It is important to realize that in the United States, public policy primarily affects behavior by changing the environment that conditions individuals' decisions. There is, however, another, less often used avenue. It is an attempt to change individuals' goals or their tastes and preferences. An example would be campaigns to induce people to use less energy by turning their thermostats up in the summer and down in the winter, appealing to their sense of fair play or guilt. Another example is the public ad campaign to help eliminate forest fires. Attempting to change people's values is a much less common policy in the United States than, say, passing tax and criminal laws that make it costly or financially rewarding to behave in a certain way.

In our discussions of public policy we will always be after the same two facts. First, we will attempt to see who is helped by the particular policy being suggested. Second, we will attempt to see who is hurt or who pays the bill for the particular public policy. By doing both of these we present a *balanced, scientific* view of the policy process and its outcome. Whether or not policy will be or has been adopted always boils down to politics, but policy should be discussed in light of the special insights economic analysis

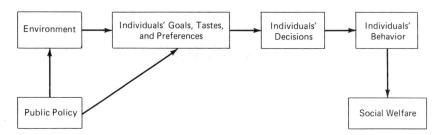

FIGURE 1-2. The avenues through which public policy influences social welfare in the United States

can provide. For example, we will see that the cost of social security is basically unrelated to who legally must pay the social security tax. We will see why society bases college scholarships on both need and ability. We will discuss whether recent health and safety regulation, OSHA, actually has any effect on work-related injuries. We will see that not all unemployment is socially undesirable. Again, it is important to emphasize that economics is at its best when it provides subtle insights that seem to go against common sense.

After we have developed a theoretical framework and then used it to analyze the behavioral implications of changes in the economic environment, our third step in each topic will be to see whether available data confirm that the world works the way economists say it does. An important thing you can take with you from this book is a sense of economists' confidence in their own view of things. In some areas their conclusions are strong and empirically well verified; in others, their analysis needs much more refinement. In any event, the third stage in each of our discussions completes the parallel with the stages of scientific discovery summarized in Table 1-1.

In the chapters that follow you will be confronted with numerous uses of diagrams, tests of hypotheses, and applications of policy. We hope that all this not only *shows you* how economists think but also teaches you to think as an economist when the situation merits. We encourage you to use the tools you learn to identify the social welfare effects of programs you read about in the newspaper or hear about from your friends. Not only will this help you see the relevance of the tools we will be presenting here, but it will also help you to develop a useful lifetime skill—the ability to use economic analysis to get a deeper understanding of labor market issues.

2

MEASUREMENT
IN LABOR ECONOMICS

A. Educational objectives
1. To introduce you to important sources of labor market data
2. To outline some difficulties in measuring theoretical variables, particularly wages, employment, and unemployment, in available data sets
3. To provide a brief introduction to regression analysis, the economist's favorite empirical tool

B. Sources and interpretation of labor market data (p. 17)
1. Some important and widely used data sets (p. 17)
2. Measuring the quantity of labor (p. 18)
   a. Employment
   b. Hours
   c. Quality of labor
   d. Unemployment
3. Interpreting data on wage rates (p. 25)
   a. Fringe benefits
   b. The time period: permanent and transitory wages

C. Using theory and data to understand labor markets (p. 27)
1. The role of theory (p. 28)
2. Economic hypotheses and human behavior (p. 31)
*3. Understanding regression analysis (p. 35)
   a. Brief review of logarithms and other common algebraic forms
   b. An example

---

* Represents more technical material that may be skipped without loss of continuity.

This chapter is designed to help you understand the chapters that follow. Our aim is to provide you with a basic knowledge of how economic theory is used to understand economic "facts," how the facts are measured, and how the two are related to each other in scientific analysis. We live in a world in which we rely increasingly on scientific knowledge and expertise as guides in choosing among policy alternatives. Therefore, even though few of you who read this book will choose to become social scientists, a rudimentary knowledge of scientific tools and the labor market data to which they are applied will prove useful in your future careers and to you as concerned citizens.

SOURCES AND INTERPRETATION
OF LABOR MARKET DATA: OVERVIEW

In studying the economics of labor markets, terms such as **wage rates, quantity of labor, employment,** and **unemployment** are crucial variables. We first develop a theory of the relationship among these variables, and then we explore how theory helps us to understand observed behavior. Making the connection between theory and "fact" will be much more rewarding if you understand how these variables are measured and some of the problems involved. It may seem unnecessary to you to dwell on these details—everyone knows what a wage rate is, or an hour of work, you may think. As we go on, however, we believe you will see that it is not always so easy to match the variables of our theories to the data we can obtain.

Many sources of data are used in the study of labor markets. All, however, fall into one of two important categories: (1) answers to questions asked of households, and (2) answers to questions asked of business firms. In the first category are data sources such as the decennial population census of the United States, the Current Population Surveys conducted monthly by the U.S. Census Bureau, and surveys conducted by nongovernment research organizations.[1] In the second category are data sources such as the Census Bureau's *Census of Manufactures* and the monthly *Employment and Earnings* surveys of the U.S. Department of Labor.[2]

---

[1] For a more complete description of United States government household surveys, see Bureau of Labor Statistics, *Handbook of Labor Statistics,* Technical Notes. Three widely used bodies of data produced by nongovernment agencies are the National Longitudinal Surveys of the Center for Human Resource Research at The Ohio State University, the Survey of Working Conditions, the Quality of Employment Survey, and the Panel Study of Income Dynamics, all of The University of Michigan Survey Research Center. The first and fourth are so-called panel surveys, in that they follow a particular group of individuals over a number of years. See Herbert S. Parnes et al., *The Pre-Retirement Years: A Longitudinal Study of the Labor Market Experience of Men,* Vol. 1 (Washington, D.C.: U.S. Department of Labor, Manpower Administration, 1970); James N. Morgan et al., *Productive Americans: A Study of How Individuals Contribute to Economic Progress* (Ann Arbor: Survey Research Center, University of Michigan, 1966); and James N. Morgan, ed., *Five Thousand American Families—Patterns of Economic Progress* (Ann Arbor: Survey Research Center, University of Michigan, 1974).

[2] For a description of the establishment surveys (surveys of business firms), see one of the monthly issues of U.S. Department of Labor, Bureau of Labor Statistics, *Employment and Earnings.*

These data sources differ in the kinds of information they provide. Household surveys provide answers to questions about whether household members were working, looking for work, attending school, and so on, during the calendar week prior to the date of the survey. Using answers to such questions, we can estimate the size of the labor force. The labor force consists of all persons 16 years of age and over who were working or who were unemployed (where "unemployed" implies availability for work). Household surveys are also used to gather information about dual job holders, earnings and other income of family members, hours worked, family size, and other information important for studying labor force behavior.

Data gathered from firms also provide information about wage rates. Because this information is readily obtainable from the firms' financial records, wage data gathered from firms are likely to be more accurate than those gathered from household surveys. Such hard-to-remember items as paid vacation time, withholding taxes, social security payments, fringe benefits, insurance premiums, and the like are recorded better there. However, if one wishes to relate wage rates or earnings to the personal and family characteristics of persons receiving them, it is almost impossible to do this on the basis of firms' records alone. In addition, data gathered from firms provide information about the volume of labor turnover (quits and layoffs), the combinations of labor of different degrees of skill used in production and nonproduction activities, and so on.

It is beyond our scope to evaluate the many data sources used in the study of labor markets, but we will point out in the next few paragraphs some important problems in measuring widely discussed concepts. In many instances, available data do not conform neatly to the economic concepts we would like to measure. While a well-formulated theory will provide information on the ideal way to measure economic variables, considerations of cost, protection of personal privacy, or political expediency may hinder gathering perfectly appropriate data. Relating the available information to the concepts of economic theory is a difficult and essential branch of what we call **econometrics,** the application of statistical methods to the study of economic data and problems.

MEASURING THE QUANTITY OF LABOR

When studying labor markets, one of our most important tasks will be to specify the quantity of labor and the units in which it is measured. We might speak of *employee-hours*—work units of constant quality. Although we begin our study of the theory of labor markets as if we could easily measure homogeneous employee-hours of labor, such measurement in fact is seldom easy. Let us look at a few of the problems of measuring the quantity of labor in the context of the total size of the labor force.

The Amount of Employed Labor

Most people would agree that the labor force should include the amount of available labor resources in the economy. The advantages of alternative labor force measures can be understood only in the context of a theory of the labor market. Figure 2-1 represents an extremely simple but useful theory. It shows the supply and demand for labor in the economy; on the horizontal axis is measured the quantity of labor of uniform quality in hours per period of time (employee-hours per time period), and on the vertical axis the wage rate for labor of uniform quality. Later on, we will see why the demand curve has a negative slope, and we will also see that the supply curve may not be upward sloping; but Figure 2-1 as it stands is sufficient to demonstrate some important problems of measuring the quantity of labor resources. In its simplest form, the theory implies that the wage rate and the level of employment are determined at the intersection of the supply and demand curves [$L(1)$ and $L(2)$ correspond to such points of intersection]; the employment level so determined is a so-called equilibrium value.

In a very important sense, the current official measure of the labor force in the United States corresponds largely to an equilibrium value of employment such as $L(1)$ or $L(2)$ in Figure 2-1. This is because the most important component of the official measure of the labor force is the number of people who are actually working. An important problem of measuring labor resources by a magnitude such as $L(1)$ or $L(2)$ is that it depends on the demand for labor as well as the supply. There would be no problem if the supply curve of labor were vertical (completely inelastic and insensitive to

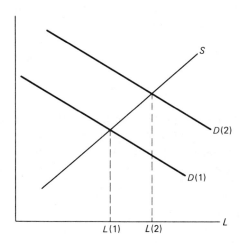

FIGURE 2-1. Labor demand, supply, and employment

demand). But in general it is not, and thus the volume of employment does not tell us how much labor could be drawn upon in the case of, say, a war or other national emergency; neither does it tell us how many persons might be put to work if the demand for labor in private industry were to grow.

Employment data for the United States are gathered from household surveys as follows: The total number classified as employed are all persons aged 16 years and over who answer survey questions in such a way as to indicate that they were working or had a job from which they were temporarily absent during the survey week. Table 2-1 shows the actual questions asked monthly of a sample of the United States' population, whose answers are subsequently adjusted according to statistical procedures to yield an estimate of the number that would have been obtained if everyone in the United States had been interviewed. (Not every person about whom answers are obtained is interviewed personally; often questions about several family members are answered by only one respondent.) Persons classified as **employed** are those whose answer to question 19 is that they were working most of the prior week, or whose answer to question 20 is "Yes" (that they worked at all during the prior week), or who were classified as "with a job but not at work." This last category includes those who answered "Yes" to question 21 and who were absent for reasons 1 through 4 in question 21A. Also included are persons who worked 15 hours or more as unpaid workers in a family business or firm.

One way out of the problem that measured employment depends on demand conditions would be to measure the total population, rather than $L(1)$ or $L(2)$. But then, should we count the ill, the very young, the aged, and those in school? We cannot avoid evaluating the population's labor force potential according to some more or less arbitrary criteria, and we may find no better measure of potential or maximum labor force than to observe the employment behavior of the economy during periods of high labor demand.

Hours of Employment

Now we consider the problem of adding the dimension hours to the measurement of employment. Again, economic theory is an invaluable aid. According to economic theory, the number of hours worked depends on labor supply and demand, the number of hours supplied responding either positively or negatively to changes in demand. If we use a market criterion for measuring labor force hours as we do for measuring the number of workers in the labor force, then hours actually worked measures hours in the labor force. But does hours actually worked reflect the number of hours individuals desire to supply? The answer depends on one's view of how labor markets function. Although there are people who complain about not being able to get enough overtime hours and others who wish they could

TABLE 2-1 Facsimile of Current Labor Force Status Section of Current Population Survey

work a shorter workweek, we believe the market criterion represents a reasonable approach to measuring our labor force in terms of hours.

But, given the market criterion, how do we find out how many hours people work? In many cases, we may obtain the information from employers. This is actually done by the government, and one of the principal sources of data on hours worked is provided by the answers to monthly questionnaires sent to employers of a large number of the economy's workers. Monthly surveys of the population also provide information about hours of work, in the answers given by people who worked or by their relatives. Apart from the statistical problems of sampling, which are of a rather technical nature and probably introduce few serious errors into our presently available measures of labor hours, rather important errors may arise simply because of our inability to find out from respondents exactly what their behavior has been, even in the recent past. The problems are serious enough when it is necessary to ask an employee who is paid by the hour how many hours he or she worked in the previous week; the respondent may have worked overtime hours and forgotten, or may neglect to report a temporarily shortened workweek. Even worse, interviewers may be forced to ask crucial questions of one family member about the labor force behavior of all persons living in that household. Still worse, the self-employed and many salaried workers probably cannot accurately define when they are working and when they are not. Questions 20A through 20E in Table 2-1 show the painstaking procedure used by interviewers to find out how many hours were worked during the survey week. Notice that it is virtually impossible to discern from the answers whether anyone who worked 35 hours or more was working more or less than he or she desired. It is possible, however, to get some idea of whether respondents who worked less than 35 hours did so voluntarily. Presumably, the ideal measure of employee-hours would reflect the hours workers voluntarily would work under given labor market conditions.[3]

The Quality of Labor

The problem of measuring labor quality is so serious that at present no official measure of the labor force allows for quality variation. However, economic theory does suggest ways in which labor quality might be measured. If we adopt the view that "labor is what labor does," then labor force members can be weighted by their contribution to production or output (see Chapter 3) to calculate aggregate labor force measures. Since wages represent a measure of workers' contribution to output in monetary terms, wage rates provide a means of measuring the labor force that reflects variations in quality as well as in the number of workers and hours worked. That is, one hour worked at $10 represents approximately twice as much labor, quality adjusted, as one hour at $5. Lacking sufficient wage data, we might try to account for the variation in labor quality that is associated with underlying conditions generally believed to affect it and that may be more or less easily measured.

One such characteristic is the educational level of the labor force. If we observe labor force hours declining but the average educational level of workers rising, we have reason to suspect that labor resources are declining

---

[3] The Panel Study of Income Dynamics, for example, contains questions designed to measure discrepancies between actual and desired hours of work.

less rapidly than the simple hours figure indicates. Other readily observable correlates of labor quality are age and experience; perhaps slightly more difficult to observe is health. Thus, if we observe that since 1900 the proportion of the population in the labor force has risen, while hours worked per week have declined, education has risen, more women (who have less labor force experience on average than men) are working, a higher proportion of youths are in school, and a higher proportion of the elderly are retired (although a higher proportion of the population is elderly), may we conclude that labor force quality has risen or fallen? Although there is no easy answer to this question, there is perhaps a presumption that it has risen, the principal impetus having been increased educational attainment and health of workers.

Still another dimension of labor force quality, generally unreported in official statistics but certainly not unnoticed by employers, is the intensity of work effort. As work hours have fallen over the year, it is not unreasonable to suppose that the intensity of work effort has increased, since workers do not tire as much on the job. Surely work effort varies widely among different nations and cultures. It is an interesting and important component of labor force quality, the measurement of which would lend much to our knowledge of the economy's human resources.[4]

The Unemployed Component of the Labor Force

We have so far assumed that the labor force can be measured, however imprecisely, by counting the number of people at work. However, there are always persons who are on layoff from their jobs, who have lost their jobs and who are looking for work, who have quit their jobs and are looking for new work, and who are entering or reentering the labor force but have not yet found a job. These people constitute the **unemployed,** and the unemployed are by official definition a part of the labor force. All the problems of measuring the employed labor force apply to the unemployed as well. Moreover, the problems associated with inferring from the answers of nonworking respondents whether they are unemployed or out of the labor force merit special attention.

Consider first a simple definition of unemployment suggested by economic theory. In Figure 2-2 we see a diagrammatic description of a labor market in which the wage rate is higher than the level that would equate demand and supply. Consequently, $L(1)$ units of labor are demanded and $L(2) > L(1)$ supplied. $L(2) - L(1)$ represents an excess supply of labor (there could just as well be an excess demand if the wage were less than equilib-

---

[4] For an analysis of this topic, see Gary S. Becker, "A Theory of the Production and Allocation of Effort," Working Paper No. 184, National Bureau of Economic Research (Cambridge, Mass.: National Bureau of Economic Research, 1977).

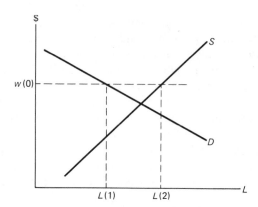

FIGURE 2-2. Labor demand, supply, employment, and unemployment

rium). Thus, at the going wage, $w(0)$, $L(2) - L(1)$ persons are unemployed. This is a conceivable theoretical definition of unemployment, which, as we will see in Chapter 12, is much too simple. It associates unemployment with an excess supply of labor, whereas information and adjustment costs in labor markets assure that there will always be some workers seeking employment even when supply and demand are equal to each other. Figure 2-2 is simply inadequate to deal with the concept of unemployment. We will not deal here with the difficult question of what level of unemployment is associated with no excess demand or supply of labor (the so-called full employment level of unemployment). Rather, we will confine ourselves to the equally difficult problem of how we decide when someone who is not working is counted as part of the labor force.

In practice, measuring the unemployed component of the labor force relies on two major criteria: (1) an unemployed person must be *available* for work and (2), if not on layoff and awaiting recall, must be actively seeking work, or must have sought work in the last four weeks.[5] Thus, the unemployed must have answered questions 19 and 20 of Table 2-1 that they did not work last week, and question 22 affirmatively. For those who are not on layoff, the requirement that an unemployed person be actively seeking work corresponds to a commonsense definition of unemployment. However, the Current Population Survey does not inquire into the conditions under which a respondent would actually accept a job. Perhaps most important, no attempt is made to discover whether a job seeker requires or expects a rate of pay so high that no reasonable employer would offer a job to such a person. Consider a coal miner who is laid off due to mechanization and who cannot find another job as a coal miner. Suppose he had been earning $15 per hour,

---

[5] BLS, *Handbook of Labor Statistics,* Technical Notes.

but because of his age, previous training, and so on, the best job he can find now will pay only $6; or perhaps the job would necessitate his moving away from his old home. Now, if the miner does not realize this—after all, a decline in one's market worth is not easy to accept or easy to discover in a short period of time—he may turn down or not look for jobs that pay less than, say, $10 per hour. In fact, if and when he discovers that he can find work only at $6, he may choose to retire from the labor force if he is an older worker—or he may decide to do the best he can with part-time work or welfare. Thus, while the miner would probably be classified as officially unemployed, there would be good reason for classifying him as out of the labor force instead, because if he had full information he probably would stop looking for work and would not take a job if offered one.

The implication for our measurement of the labor force is clear: To the extent that individuals have an incorrect perception of their going wage rates and would change their behavior if they had full information, we probably do not estimate unemployment and the size of the labor force correctly. (This is not to say that persons such as the hypothetical coal miner should not be classified as unemployed for purposes of determining the allocation of unemployment compensation, aid to depressed areas, and so on.) Furthermore, when unemployed workers do stop looking for work and are thus counted as out of the labor force, we should recognize that they might be productive workers and labor force members if they had information about jobs unknown to them, perhaps in other regions of the country.

The Interpretation of Wage Rate Data

An individual's (real) **wage rate** is the value of market goods that can be purchased for an hour's work. From the firm's point of view, the (real) wage it must pay is the value of output that must be turned over to a worker for each hour of work. The wage rate is an important element in economic theory both because it represents an inducement to work and because it represents the cost to business firms of hiring labor. However, many aspects of the inducement to work and of the cost of hiring labor are not represented by the wage rates recorded in the various sources of wage data.

Fringe Benefits and Costs

A substantial proportion of today's jobs involve not only an hourly rate of pay, but also payments into private pension funds, health plans, social security, unemployment insurance schemes, and the like. In Chapter 11 you will see that these **fringe benefits** account for about 15 percent of a typical worker's compensation in the United States. To what extent do wage supplements represent additional inducements to workers and additional costs to employers?

From the employer's point of view, a dollar contributed to social security, a private pension fund, or a health insurance program is a cost of production. Thus, in measuring the relationship between wage rates and a firm's hiring decisions, all the costs of labor should be measured, not just the wage rate paid directly to the worker. When measures of the cost of fringe benefits are not available, the question arises of how big an error is made by ignoring fringes. This question can be answered only in the context of a particular study. In general the amount of fringe benefits is positively related to nominal wage rates. The importance of nonwage benefits and their role in the labor market are dealt with in Chapter 11.

The time period.   So far we have spoken of the wage rate almost as if it were given to each person for all time. Later on however, we will learn that time plays an important role in many labor market decisions and therefore an important role in the measurement of labor market variables. Suppose, for instance, that we want to estimate the labor supply behavior of families of farm workers and that in areas where farm wage rates are persistently relatively high, we expect to observe fewer wives and children of farm workers in the labor force than elsewhere. But, since harvests vary from year to year and from place to place, we should also expect to find that hourly wage rates are unusually high where crops are unusually good, and vice versa. Since an increase in the wage rate that is expected to be temporary will not have a significant effect on a family's view of its normal level of income, when crops are unusually good we should not expect to observe much labor force withdrawal of women and children, and men may work even more than usual, since it pays to supply labor when the wage rate is highest.

Another problem in measuring wage rates that is due to the role of time in economic behavior arises from the importance of certain kinds of on-the-job training. In addition to formal and informal training programs, much on-the-job training takes the form of learning by doing. Whatever form on-the-job training takes, it is expected to have the effect of raising future productivity and earnings, so workers are willing to pay for it. That workers are willing to pay is suggested by the relatively low wage rates of apprentices, physicians in residency, and the like. That is, training is paid for in many cases by accepting a wage lower than productivity in order to compensate employers for providing training. Whatever the nature of the training process, investment affects typical age-earnings profiles of many kinds of workers.

Several years after leaving college, as you will learn in Chapter 9, college graduates earn little more than do high school graduates of similar age. However, early career wage differentials do not reflect the value of on-the-job training being acquired. The amount is substantial, and greater than that acquired by high school graduates. That is, the earnings figures reflect the willingness of workers to accept lower initial wages in return for training and other experiences that are expected to yield higher earning power later in life. The low *reported* earnings in earlier years therefore understate *total* earnings because the value of much of the training being acquired is not included.

The point here is not to develop a theory of on-the-job training, but rather to indicate that the relationship between the wage rate and, say, hours worked per week may be seriously obscured by faulty measurement of the wage rate. If the payment "in kind" that reflects payment for being in a job that allows some kind of training or learning to take place is ignored, the measured wage rate will reflect only money earnings; this will result in an underestimate of the real wage rate, and the underestimation may be very large for young workers with a great deal of education.

Workers not paid by the hour. In many cases, it is necessary to convert observed payments for labor services to a common time basis. For instance, if the hourly wage rate is the standard measure, the payments made to workers paid by the week, month, or year must be converted to an hourly figure. This is a straightforward procedure if the hours worked per week, month, or year are known. However, measurement errors in estimating hours worked will cause related errors in the calculation of hourly wages. These errors can have an important effect on estimated behavioral relationships. For example, if hours worked are overestimated, the calculated *hourly* rate of pay for a worker paid by the week will be too small. If this hourly rate of pay calculation is used to estimate a labor supply curve, a wage observation that is too low will be matched with an hour's observation that is too high, and the resulting estimate of labor supply will be biased. The reverse is also true. If hours of work are underestimated, the corresponding hourly rate of pay calculation will be too large. Such calculations could lead us to believe that when wages rise, hours of work decline, even if there were no relationship between these two variables.

The problem is probably most serious in studying the behavior of professional workers and the self-employed. Here it is not only difficult to measure hourly wage rates, but it is also not clear that the marginal contribution to income of an hour's extra work is anywhere near equal to average hourly earnings. At this point it is probably best only to point out the problem without suggesting possible solutions.

USING ECONOMIC THEORY AND DATA
TO UNDERSTAND LABOR MARKETS

Throughout this text we proceed as follows: (1) a labor economics topic is introduced; (2) the topic is simplified and defined by means of economic theory and hypotheses; (3) usually, the theory is applied to some aspect of economic policy or used to interpret labor market behavior of particular interest; (4) the theory or hypothesis is tested, or its quantitative properties are estimated with labor market data.

The Role of Theory

As soon as we mention the words *theory* or *hypothesis,* many readers will feel threatened by the prospect of having to read the remainder of this text. This is unfortunate, because theory is a *simplifying* device, not something that makes economics more difficult than it would otherwise be. It is true that economic theory is at times difficult (although we have set off the more difficult parts in special optional sections of the text); *without* theory, however, understanding labor markets would be *impossible.* The world around us is far too complex to comprehend without the invaluable assistance provided by a theoretical framework. We hope this section will help relieve the fears of those readers who *do* feel threatened by the need to use theory to understand the world around us.

Another objection sometimes raised against the use of economic theory by some people is that it is based on "unrealistic" assumptions. For example, we frequently assume that buyers (firms) and sellers (households) of labor operate in competitive markets in which they cannot individually affect wages or product prices by their activities. These assumptions are attempts to focus on the crucial aspects of economic behavior and to ignore others in the name of simplicity. There is little question that they are strictly true only in a small fraction of the cases to which the theory is applied. However, theory based on more realistic assumptions about how buyers and sellers directly affect the prices and wages they face would be more complex. A more complete, realistic theory is more difficult to develop and use. For the additional cost to be worthwhile, the theory must yield more or better implications about the behavior under investigation.

Most of the discussions in this text deal with *hypotheses* derived from a basic theoretical framework. In the next few paragraphs we will show how a specific hypothesis is interpreted and used, so that readers can more easily make their way through the remainder of the book. Some readers will find this material very elementary. They do not have to review what is essentially a set of basic math concepts and can go on to the next section on the use of statistical analysis in economics.

Components of hypotheses.   Our example is based on the demand for labor. A labor demand curve is a hypothesis derived from a more basic theory. For example, the most commonly used theory is that of an economy in which firms and households are competitive—free to enter all markets to either buy or sell goods or services over whose prices they have no direct control. An important hypothesis derived from this theory will have to do with a profit-maximizing firm's demand for labor. For the sake of illustration, suppose that the hypothesis is as follows: the quantity of labor demanded by the firm depends on the firm's output level, its capital stock (available machinery, equipment, and buildings), and the wage rate the firm must pay for labor of a given quality. It is usually more convenient to express the hypothesis algebraically or geometrically. The algebraic expression can be general or specific. A general formulation of the labor demand hypothesis would be explicit enough to indicate the *direction* (sign) of the relationships implied by the hypothesis. An explicit formulation would indicate the actual mathematical form more precisely and, in a few cases, might even contain numbers denoting the quantitative magnitudes involved.

Equation (2-1) is a general algebraic expression for a skeletal version of the labor demand hypothesis stated above:

$$L = D(w, Q) \qquad \textbf{(2-1)}$$

where $L \equiv$ the quantity of labor demanded per period of time

$w \equiv$ the market hourly wage rate

$Q \equiv$ the firm's output level per period of time

and the letter D denotes a functional relationship indicating that the quantity on the left of the equal sign depends on the right-hand variables.

Before going on, it might be a good idea to review an important concept—the distinction between the **equality sign (=)** and the **identity sign (≡).** Both of these are used repeatedly from here on, and life will be much easier for those who understand the difference between them. The equality sign (=) denotes a relationship of *equivalence* that is true only when certain conditions implied by the theory hold. For example, the demand for labor by a *government* enterprise (which is *not* assumed to maximize profit) would not in general by represented by equation (2-1), because additional variables might belong inside the parentheses on the right-hand side of the equation, and the magnitudes of the explicit demand equation would almost certainly be different. The identity sign (≡), however, denotes equivalence under all circumstances. For example, in your courses in economics principles you learned that national income, *by definition,* can be divided into three components in a simple macroeconomic framework, namely consumption expenditures, savings, and taxes, or

$$Y \equiv C + S + T \qquad \textbf{(2-2)}$$

Definition (2-2) is *always* true in *any* economy at *any* time, because it is nothing more than an exhaustive categorization of all income received. Another set of categories divides *expenditures* on national income into consumption, investment, and government categories as follows:

$$Y \equiv C + I + G \qquad \textbf{(2-3)}$$

Subtracting *identity* (2-3) from *identity* (2-2) yields a third *identity:*

$$I + G \equiv S + T \tag{2-4}$$

The *identity* (2-4) should not be confused with the *equation*

$$I(P) + G = S(P) + T \tag{2-5}$$

where the (P) denotes *planned* magnitudes, and which holds *only* when the macroeconomy is in equilibrium (all plans to buy and sell are realized).

Economic theory *may* imply what the specific form of equation (2-1) will look like. Usually our theories are not complex enough, however, and specific formulations of hypotheses are approximations. Here is an example of a very simple specific approximation to equation (2-1):

$$L = \alpha(0) + \alpha(1)w + \alpha(2)Q, \qquad \alpha(1) < 0, \ \alpha(2) > 0 \tag{2-6}$$

Equation (2-6) is a *linear* equation (because it can be represented by a straight line as in Figure 2-3). Moreover, since the basic hypothesis (2-1) does not include nonlabor inputs, such as capital, that influence the demand for labor, it is understood that it *holds true only for given values of nonlabor inputs in production.* In general equation (2-6) is specified *ceteris paribus*— other things equal. If any of the conditions held constant change, then equation (2-6) will no longer hold. In addition to nonlabor inputs, other things that

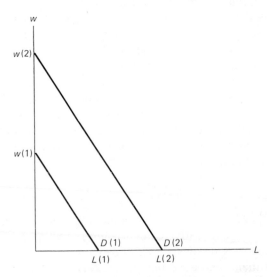

FIGURE 2-3. Geometric representation of equation (2-6)

would change (2-6) if they were altered include the assumptions of the theory used to derive equation (2-1), including the profit motive and the competitive structure of the industry.

The specific hypothesis equation (2-6) can also be expressed geometrically, as shown in Figure 2-3. Figure 2-3 shows the relationship between L and w defined by equation (2-6) for two different values of Q, $Q(1)$ and $Q(2)$. *Both* of these labor demand curves are drawn holding constant the firm's use of nonlabor inputs. If output (Q) should grow beyond $Q(2)$, the demand curve will lie to the right of $D(2)$. The intercepts, $w(1)$, $w(2)$, $L(1)$, and $L(2)$ in Figure 2-3, can be found by "solving" equation (2-6) for either L when $w = 0$ or w when $L = 0$, then inserting $Q(1)$ and $Q(2)$ for Q. For example,

$$L(1) = \alpha(0) + \alpha(2) \cdot Q(1) \tag{2-7}$$

and

$$w(2) = \frac{\alpha(0) + \alpha(2) \cdot Q(2)}{-\alpha(1)} \tag{2-8}$$

Remember, $\alpha(1)$ is a negative number, so $w(2)$ is positive. The slope of both $D(1)$ and $D(2)$ is $\alpha(1)$, which represents the hypothesis that as the wage rises, the quantity of labor demanded will fall, and $\alpha(2)$ tells us how far D is expected to shift to the right for each unit that output increases.

An even more explicit formulation of (2-1) replaces the coefficients $\alpha(0)$, $\alpha(1)$, and $\alpha(2)$ with actual numbers—for example,

$$L = 1,500 - 520w + 100Q \tag{2-9}$$

With equation (2-7), it is possible to substitute actual values of w and Q to hypothesize exactly how many units of labor the firm will demand. For example, suppose $w = \$5$ per hour and $Q = 1,000$ units. Then, we hypothesize that the number of units of labor demanded will equal $1,500 - 2,600 + 100,000 = 97,400$. If the wage rate *increases* to $10 per hour, we hypothesize that the quantity of labor demanded (Q remaining unchanged) will *fall* by 2,600 units. If output grows by 100 units (w remaining unchanged), L is expected to rise by 10,000 units.

Economic Hypotheses and Human Behavior

Hypotheses such as Figure 2-3 and equations (2-6) and (2-9) imply that economic behavior will correspond *exactly* to a mathematical formula. In using theory and hypotheses to understand the economy, however, we recognize that mathematical formulas and equations are at best only *approximations* to actual behavior. For several reasons it is generally not possible to develop hypotheses that correspond to human behavior exactly. One reason is that it is not usually possible to account for all variables affecting economic decisions. While we can *assume* "other things equal," probably no two individuals or firms confronted with the same prices, incomes, and so on will decide to purchase or sell *exactly* the same quantities of some good or service. They can be expected to differ in *unobserved* conditions such as their tastes, production processes, family circumstances, and so on, in ways that contribute to variation in behavior, given identical values of *observed* variables.

Statistical and econometric analysis has been developed to bridge the gap between *exact* hypotheses and the *inexact* behavior that hypotheses attempt to describe or explain. What econometric research frequently involves is that a specific formulation of an economic relationship is assumed to hold in a form such as equation (2-6). Then, statistical techniques are used to estimate the magnitudes of the coefficients of the relationship [the αs in equation (2-6)], yielding an equation like (2-9). The statistical procedures used by economists and other social scientists allow us to make use of the *law of averages* in analyzing data. Using labor demand as an example, we can illustrate what statistical analysis does. Suppose that, in order to study labor demand, we want to relate the quantity of labor demanded by various firms to the wage rates they pay, but that each firm is affected by unknown factors such as bad weather, a strike, or a fire in a plant. It can be shown, using statistical analysis, that we are justified in relating the quantity of labor employed by each of a large number of firms to the wage rate that those firms pay, *if* the following condition holds: *The other variables affecting employment, which we do not observe, do not vary systematically with wage rates.* In statistical jargon, we say that these omitted variables must be uncorrelated with, or randomly related to, the observed variables that are hypothesized to influence demand (for example, the wage rate).

There are many ways in which the effects of omitted random variables may be taken into consideration in studying economic behavior. All of them, however, involve some kind of averaging. Averaging works if the omitted variables, such as the bad weather that affects one of the firms in our labor demand example, are random, because their influence on the behavior being studied averages out to zero—it cancels out—over a large number of observations. This is where the law of averages, or to be more precise, the **law of large numbers,** plays a crucial role. One of the most common and best-known applications of the law of large numbers is in the business world. Insurance companies can accurately predict death rates as a simple function of age for large groups of people, even though it is impossible to predict exactly when any individual in good health will die. Another example is the ability of banks to meet their daily demands for cash even though they never have enough on hand to pay off all their depositors at once.

The way averaging would work in a very simple study of labor demand

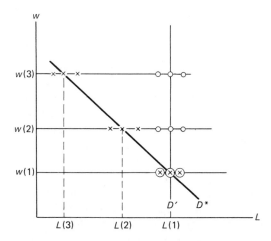

FIGURE 2-4. Estimating a demand curve

is shown in Figure 2-4. Suppose we have data obtained from observing nine firms, each of which pays one of three possible wage rates. Each firm accepts the wage it must pay as given and can hire all the labor it wants at that wage. In terms of economic analysis, we say that each firm faces one of three infinitely elastic labor supply curves at wage rate $w(1)$, $w(2)$, or $w(3)$. These firms are located, perhaps, in different geographical areas with different labor market conditions. Nevertheless, they are alike in all other *known* respects and therefore we assume that each firm's labor demand can be approximated with the same equation, which we would like to *estimate* from the data available. Other variables beside the wage rate determine the quantity of labor demanded by each firm, but we cannot observe these variables and believe them to be *uncorrelated* (randomly associated) with wage rates. Therefore, we hold the **maintained hypothesis** (assumption) that the omitted variables in our demand study are uncorrelated with the included independent variable (the wage rate), and we conclude that averaging the quantity of labor the firms demand at each of the three wage rates will provide an *unbiased estimate* of their labor demand curve.

The quantities of labor demanded by the nine firms in our study are denoted by the xs in Figure 2-4. Each x represents the quantity of labor demanded by one of the firms at one of the three wage rates. By averaging the three xs at wage rate $w(3)$, the three at wage $w(2)$, and the three at $w(1)$, we determine the average quantity of labor demanded at each of the three wage rates [$L(1)$, $L(2)$, and $L(3)$] and draw the estimated demand curve D^* through these three points, since we assume the demand curve is a straight line.

The simple averaging procedure we have described is a legitimate method for estimating a demand curve under very simple conditions. In practice, however, we may have hundreds of observations rather than nine, and we may wish to estimate simultaneously the influence not only of the wage rate, but of other observed conditions, such as the rate of interest, the price of raw materials, the presence of unions, or the existence of right-to-work laws. Fortunately, statisticians, and modern computers have given us the means to use large numbers of observations and variables in estimated economic relationships. The most common technique for these tasks is **regression analysis.**[6] Regression analysis is a mathematical procedure for estimating a line such as D^*. The procedure possesses desirable mathematical properties, provided that the maintained hypothesis regarding the randomness of omitted variables is correct. If D^* were estimated by means of regression analysis, the following statement would be true: (1) D^* would pass through the mean quantity of labor demanded and the mean of the three wage rates; and (2) the sum of the squared differences (deviations) of each quantity of labor from the estimated demand curve D^* would be as small as possible.

Empirical work using regression analysis is presented frequently throughout this book, and we will give a brief guide to interpreting regression results in this chapter. First, though, we need to describe the pitfalls in using an averaging device such as regression analysis when the unobserved or omitted variables are correlated with the variables whose influence on some form of economic behavior is being investigated. Suppose, in the example above, that the reason some firms must pay higher wage rates than others is that they face unusually strong labor unions. Moreover, suppose that the unions that are strong enough to win especially favorable contracts with employers are also successful in negotiating featherbedding agreements, in which the firms are required to maintain on the payroll employees they do not want. Imagine that these excess quantities of labor are represented in Figure 2-4 by the horizontal distance between the circles, or os, and the xs. That is, the circles represent the actual quantities of labor employed by our nine firms, even though they would prefer to hire the quantities represented by the xs, given the wage rates they must pay. With the featherbedding agreements, *we do not observe the xs*. Rather, we observe only the os. The labor demand curve of economic theory is represented by the xs, however. Now, if we knew about the peculiar nature of the collective bargaining contract for each firm, we could subtract the quantity $o - x$ from the observed employment of each firm and estimate the labor demand curve in which we are interested, D^*. But if we are ignorant of these contracts, we are in a situation in which an omitted variable is *not* randomly correlated with the observed independent variable (the wage rate). You can see in

---

[6] See, for example, the discussion of regression analysis in Jan Kmenta, *Elements of Econometrics* (New York: Macmillan, 1971).

Figure 2-4 that the omitted variable, excess employment, is greatest in those firms paying the highest wage rates.

In other words, the omitted variable in this case is positively correlated with the wage rate. Thus, if we assume randomness when we observe the os instead of the xs, our averaging procedure will make us believe that the true demand curve for labor is D' instead of D^*. Since D^* represents the firms' desired quantities of labor, it is an unbiased estimate of the true labor demand curve, whereas D' is a *biased* estimate of the true demand curve. If we believed that D' was the true demand curve, and if someone asked us what would happen, say, if a union won an especially large wage increase or if Congress raised the minimum wage by a substantial amount, we would answer that employment would be unchanged. This would be unfortunate, because our prediction of the employment effects of these two events would be based on our ignorance of the fact that featherbedding affected the quantities of labor employed by the firms in our sample. In fact, employment would decline if either of these events took place unless firms were prevented from exerting free choice in hiring their preferred number of workers. The bias resulting from omitted variables can be avoided by explicitly recognizing their influence and including an appropriate variable representing it in a regression equation. For example, a variable representing union strength could be included in the example cited above.

Understanding Regression Equations*

Since regression analysis is used so frequently in this text, it would be a good idea to make sure you have a rudimentary understanding of how to interpret the results of estimated regression equations. Regression equations are interpreted in much the same way as equations (2-6) and (2-9). The basic characteristic of the regression equations we will use in this book is that they are all *linear* regressions. (The demand curve in Figure 2-4 is *linear* in that it is a straight line.) Therefore, understanding the properties of linear equations is a necessary step in understanding the results of regression equations. You may at first jump to the conclusion that regression analysis is of limited value because it confines us to demand curves, supply curves, and other economic relationships that are straight lines or their multidimensional equivalents (linear hyperplanes). This is only partly true, however, since regression analysis allows us to use a number of nonlinear forms that can be *translated* into linear forms, such as quadratics (square terms), logarithms, and more. One reason why regression equations are only *approximations* to actual human behavior is that only relatively simple mathematical formulations can be used without incurring very high computational costs. This will become clearer to you as we go on.

For a change of pace, we will illustrate some ways to use regression analysis with an example that does not come from labor economics. Suppose we want to estimate the demand curve for carrots. A consumer survey of 10,000 individuals provides the data we need on the price of carrots, quantity consumed per week,

---

* This section contains more technical material that may be skipped without loss of continuity. If you skip, go to page 44.

income levels, and other variables that may influence carrot demand. Our first approximation to the carrot demand equation will be a demand function of the form

$$c = \alpha(0) + \alpha(1)p + \alpha(2)y \qquad \text{(2-10)}$$

where $c \equiv$ quantity of carrots consumed per week in pounds
$p \equiv$ the price per pound of carrots in dollars
$y \equiv$ family income (in thousands of dollars per year).[7]

We hypothesize that $\alpha(1) < 0$ and $\alpha(2) > 0$; that is, as price rises, the quantity of carrots demanded falls, and carrot consumption rises with income. Equation (2-10) can be graphed just as equation (2-6) is in Figure 2-3.

After estimating the values of $\alpha(0)$, $\alpha(1)$, and $\alpha(2)$, we will be interested in seeing whether the hypotheses that $\alpha(1) < 0$ and $\alpha(2) > 0$ hold true. We may also be interested in how much the quantity of carrots demanded changes when p or y changes. Some simple calculus will be very helpful for this. The change in c when p changes (holding y constant) is the **partial derivative** of c with respect to p, $\partial c/\partial p = \alpha(1)$. The change in c when y changes (holding p constant) is $\partial c/\partial y = \alpha(2)$. We are now ready to estimate the carrot demand function by means of regression analysis. Our regression will provide us with numerical estimates of the coefficients of equation (2-10), $\alpha(0)$, $\alpha(1)$, and $\alpha(2)$. It will also give us estimates of the **standard errors** of $\alpha(1)$ and $\alpha(2)$ and the **coefficient of determination** for the entire regression equation. Since the latter two concepts have not yet been mentioned, we will consider them now before going on.

The standard error of an estimated regression coefficient is a measure of the *reliability* with which the true value of the coefficient has been estimated. The individuals in our sample do not behave exactly in accordance with equation (2-10). Rather, a number of unknown factors cause seemingly identical individuals to consume different quantities of carrots, given price and income. Thus, if we were to plot points on a graph representing the relationship between c and p for individuals who had the same value of y, the points would not all fall on the same straight line, just as the xs in Figure 2-4 lie on either side of the estimated demand curve D^*. The scatter of the xs makes it difficult to estimate the slope of the line that best "fits" the data. A large value of the estimated standard errors relative to the estimated values of the αs tells us that we cannot be very confident in the values of the αs we have estimated. A common way of measuring the size of standard error relative to its α is to calculate the ratio $\alpha/S = t$, where S is the standard error of a particular regression coefficient, α is the coefficient, and t is called a **_t_ ratio.** When t equals two or more, we can be reasonably confident that the estimate of α is **statistically significant**—that is, it is a good estimate. As t becomes smaller, we have less confidence in the quality of the information provided by our regression estimates. When t is less than 1 (when S is larger than α), we have little confidence that there is a relationship between the variables.

The **coefficient of determination,** R^2, is a measure of the overall "explanatory power" of the regression equation. It measures the proportion of the overall variation in the dependent variable that is explained by the estimated regression equation. In the simple bivariate case of Figure 2-4[8] the unexplained variation in the dependent variable can be seen as the horizontal distance between the xs and the estimated

---

[7] When there is more than one variable on the right-hand side of an equation, we refer to the estimation technique as *multiple* regression.
[8] When the relationship is bivariate—for example, $Y = a + bx$—the square root of R^2 is the correlation coefficient between y and x, usually written as r.

demand curve D^*. (Actually, R^2 depends on the *square* of these distances.) If all the xs lay *exactly* on D^*, R^2 would equal 1. For a very poor fit, R^2 approaches zero.

It cannot be overemphasized that a low R^2 does not mean that the economic theory or hypothesis being investigated is false or useless. It is possible for regression analysis to yield both a low R^2 and relatively high t ratios at the same time. This is often the case when the sample on which the estimated regression equation is based consists of *individuals* instead of *average* figures for various *groups* of individuals. Thus, in our carrot demand equation, we want to explain the carrot consumption of 10,000 individual consumers. What a combination of a low R^2 and high t ratios would tell us is that we have a good idea of how the right-hand, or independent, variables influence the behavior of the left-hand, or dependent, variable, but that behavior is affected by many other forces as well. Thus, although we could not use our estimated regression to predict the carrot consumption of any particular individual with a high degree of accuracy, we could use the results to predict what would happen, on the average, to the quantity of carrots demanded by a large group of similar individuals if the price of carrots or personal incomes should change.

Here are some make-believe results of estimating equation (2-10) by means of regression analysis.

$$c = 0.5 - 0.5p + 0.25y, \qquad R^2 = 0.40 \qquad \textbf{(2-11)}$$
$$(0.2) \quad (4.1) \quad (5.2)$$

The t ratios, shown in parentheses below their estimated regression coefficients, indicate that the estimated values of $\alpha(1)$ and $\alpha(2)$ are significant—that is, we can be reasonably confident how price and income affect carrot demand. The R^2 tells us that 40 percent of the variation in carrot consumption can be accounted for by variation in p and y when they are multiplied by their respective regression coefficients as shown in (2-11). To show that you understand what we have done so far, calculate carrot demand for $p = \$1$ per pound and $y = \$10,000$ per year. (Remember that y is measured in *thousands* of dollars.) What will happen if p rises by $\$0.50$ and income falls by $\$5,000$ per year?

Suppose that we are not satisfied with the straight-line relationship implied by equation (2-10). For example, we may not like the fact that (2-10) permits the possibility of $c < 0$ if $y > 0$. Or we may suspect that the true demand curve is not a straight line. We therefore experiment with one of the several nonlinear equations that can be *transformed* into a linear equation and is therefore suitable for our purposes. Probably the most frequently used transformation involves the use of *logarithms* (logs). While most readers are familiar with logs and other algebraic forms, many will not be, and we want to remind them of what logs mean, how they are used, and why they are so popular with economists.

Very brief review of logarithms and other commonly used algebraic forms. It is easiest to begin by defining what is known as a *common logarithm*. The common logarithm of any given number is the power to which the number 10 must be raised to equal that number. For example, since $100 = 10^2$, the logarithm of 100 equals 2, or log 100 = 2. Unless specified to the contrary, however, we will always mean *natural logarithms* whether we use the expression "log" or "ln" to denote the logarithm of a number. The natural logarithm of any number is the power to which the number e (approximately 2.7182818) must be raised in order to equal the given number. In general, $X \equiv e^{\ln X}$. The reason for using natural logs is that we are interested in certain *general properties* of logs that are easier to talk about when using logs to the base e. Common logs are easier to use only when certain types of calculations are made without a calculator. Now that everyone has access to inexpensive calculators, there is little to be gained by not using natural logarithms. Just to satisfy your curiosity, however, here are a few approximate numerical values of natural logs:

$$\ln 100 = 4.605$$
$$\ln 10 = 2.303$$
$$\ln 1{,}253 = 7.133$$
$$\ln 0.156 = -1.858$$
$$\ln 1 = 0$$
$$\ln 0 \text{ is undefined}$$

The log of 1 to *any* base is always zero, because $1 \equiv X^0$, where X takes on any value. The log of zero is undefined, because the equation $0 = X^n$ holds only for $X = 0$, and zero raised to *any* power equals zero.

Logs are popular because of two properties: (1) they permit us to express *multiplicative* relationships, which often make good sense in economic analysis, as *linear* relationships; and (2) they have interpretations in calculus that correspond to the common economic concepts of *elasticity* and *growth rates*. These properties are summarized in Tables 2-2 and 2-3.

Before summarizing the interpretations of log relationships in calculus, we want to show how a logarithmic equation is transformed into a linear equation and mention a few other commonly used transformations. From Table 2-2 you should easily be able to see that if we respecify equation (2-10) as

$$c = \alpha(0) p^{\alpha(1)} y^{\alpha(2)} \tag{2-12}$$

we can make it linear by expressing both sides in logs as

$$\log c = \log \alpha(0) + \alpha(1) \log p + \alpha(2) \log y \tag{2-13}$$

Equation (2-12) is nonlinear, because its graph is not a straight line or linear plane. For example, the graph of $c = \alpha(0)p^{\alpha(1)}$ is shown in Figure 2-5 for $\alpha(1) = -0.5$ and $\alpha(0) = 5$. Prove to yourself that this equation can be linearized by constructing your own graph with $\log c$ on the vertical axis and $\log p$ on the horizontal axis. Then plot values of $\log c = \log 5 - 0.5 \log p$ on the graph. You will obtain a straight line.

Another common nonlinear equation and its linear transformation are

$$c = e^{\alpha(0)+\alpha(1)p+\alpha(2)y} \tag{2-14}$$
$$\log c = \alpha(0) + \alpha(1)p + \alpha(2)y \tag{2-15}$$

Figure 2-5 shows the graph of $c = e^{3-0.5p}$. Can you graph $\log c = 3 - 0.5p$ to show it is a straight line?

**TABLE 2-2   Some
Properties of Logarithms**

$\log XY \equiv \log X + \log Y$
$\log X/Y \equiv \log X - \log Y$
$\log X^Y \equiv Y \log X$
*$\log e^X \equiv X$
$\log 1 \equiv 0$

* Applies only to natural logarithms.

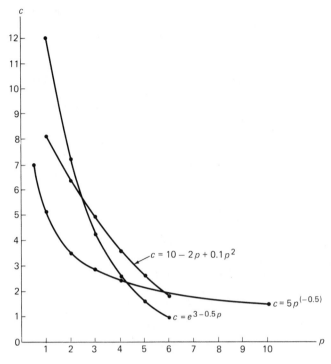

FIGURE 2-5. Graphic representation of some common nonlinear equations

Not all nonlinear equations that have simple linear transformations involve logs. For example, there is the *quadratic* expression

$$c = \alpha(0) + \alpha(1)p + \alpha(2)p^2 + \alpha(3)y + \alpha(4)y^2 \tag{2-16}$$

which is linear in higher powers of p and y. That is, you should think of p^2 and y^2 as separate variables, which could just as well be defined $x \equiv p^2$ and $z \equiv y^2$. Then (2-16) would be a linear equation with the variables p, $x \equiv p^2$, y, and $z \equiv y^2$ on the right side. Figure 2-5 shows the graph of $c = 10 - p + 0.1p^2$.

Finally, we want to introduce you to an extensively useful device called a **dummy variable.** Dummy variables are quite useful when a relationship contains variables that are categorical rather than continuous. For example, we may be interested in behavioral differences between men and women, northern residents and southern residents, black persons and white persons, or subgroups of three or more categories such as high school dropouts, college graduates, and individuals with graduate training. The way to deal with categorical differences in behavior is through the use of dummy variables.

If, for example, we can identify a group of consumers who prefer more carrots than others do, *other things equal,* we might alter equation (2-10) as follows:

$$c \equiv \alpha(0) + \alpha(1)p + \alpha(2)y + \alpha(3)d \tag{2-17}$$

where $d \equiv$ a dummy variable $= 1$ for carrot lovers, $= 0$ for normal people.

The estimated value of $\alpha(3)$ tells us by how much the carrot demand function *shifts up* [or down, if $\alpha(3)$ is negative] if the consumer is a carrot lover. Since $d = 1$ for carrot lovers, another way to think of the dummy variable technique is as follows. For carrot lovers, the constant term of equation (2-11) is $\alpha(0) + \alpha(3)$. For normal people the constant term is $\alpha(0)$. To make sure you understand the use of dummy variables, add a dummy variable d to equation (2-11) whose coefficient $\alpha(3) = 1.0$. Graph this equation for both carrot lovers and normal people.

Table 2-3 shows some useful relationships from calculus for the types of relationships shown in equations (2-12) through (2-17).

TABLE 2-3   Calculus Relationships for Equations (2-11) through (2-16)

If
$$c = \alpha(0)p^{\alpha(1)}y^{\alpha(2)}$$

$$\frac{\partial c}{\partial p} = \alpha(0)\alpha(1)p^{\alpha(1)-1}y^{\alpha(2)} = \frac{\alpha(1)c}{p}$$

$$\frac{\partial c}{\partial y} = \alpha(0)p^{\alpha(1)}y^{\alpha(2)-1} = \frac{\alpha(2)c}{y}$$

$$\log c = \log \alpha(0) + \alpha(1) \log p + \alpha(2) \log y$$

$$\frac{\partial \log c}{\partial \log p} = \alpha(1) = \frac{\partial c}{\partial p}\frac{p}{c} \equiv \text{elasticity of } c \text{ with respect to } p$$

and so on.*

If
$$c = e^{\alpha(0)+\alpha(1)p+\alpha(2)y}$$

$$\frac{\partial c}{\partial p} = c\alpha(1), \quad \text{and so on*}$$

$$\log c = \alpha(0) + \alpha(1)p + \alpha(2)y$$

$$\frac{\partial \log c}{\partial p} = \alpha(1) = \frac{\partial c}{\partial p}\frac{1}{c} \equiv \text{rate of growth of } c \text{ with respect to } p$$

and so on.*

If
$$c = \alpha(0) + \alpha(1)p + \alpha(2)p^2 + \alpha(3)y + \alpha4(y)^2$$

$$\frac{\partial c}{\partial p} = \alpha(1) + 2\alpha(2)p$$

and so on.*

If
$c = \alpha(0) + \alpha(1)p + \alpha(2)y + \alpha(3)d$, where $d = 1$ for one group of individuals (called group A) and $d = 0$ for all others (called group B), then

$c(A) - c(B) = \alpha(3)$, *other things equal.*

---

* You should be able to complete the table with respect to the remaining variables.

An example of the demand for carrots.   Suppose we believe the demand for carrots can best be approximated by a *constant elasticity* demand function. This would be specified as indicated by equations (2-12) and (2-13). Table 2-3 shows why these are called *constant elasticity* demand equations. The coefficient $\alpha(1)$ is the elasticity of demand for carrots with respect to the price of carrots, and $\alpha(2)$ is the income elasticity of demand for carrots.

Since we desire to do an excellent job in estimating carrot demand, we will take advantage of additional information contained in our consumer survey on the personal characteristics of consumers that we believe may be associated with their tastes for carrots, and we decide to make use of a dummy variable.

To show how dummy variables will help us estimate an accurate demand function for carrots, it will be easier if we first go back to equation (2-11). Suppose we modify equation (2-11) as follows:

$$c = \alpha(0) + \alpha(1)p + \alpha(2)y + \alpha(3)B \qquad \textbf{(2-10*)}$$

where $B \equiv$ a dummy variable $= 1$ if the carrot consumer has ears over three inches long, pink eyes, and white fur, $= 0$ otherwise.

Suppose that when (2-10*) is estimated, we find that

$$c = 0.4 - 0.4p + 0.26y + 8.0B, \qquad R^2 = .51$$
$$\quad (0.1) \quad (5.0) \quad (6.0) \quad (12.1)$$

where the numbers in parentheses are t-ratios.

The coefficient of B is large and statistically significant. What does it tell us? If a carrot consumer has furry ears, $B = 1$, and if not, $B = 0$. Thus, multiplying B by its regression coefficient, we see that for consumers who pay the same price, p, and receive the same income, y, carrot consumption will be 8.0 pounds per week more for furry consumers than for their nonfurry counterparts. Now, let us apply the dummy variable concept to equation (2-12) and elaborate on its interpretation in greater detail. Modifying equation (2-12) to include the dummy variable B gives us:

$$c = \alpha(0)p^{\alpha(1)}y^{\alpha(2)}e^{\alpha(3)B} \qquad \textbf{(2-18)}$$

where $e \equiv$ base of natural logarithms
$B \equiv$ (as before) a dummy variable $= 1$ if the carrot consumer has long ears, pink eyes, and white fur, $= 0$ otherwise.

Taking logs of both sides of (2-18) yields

$$\log c = \alpha(0) + \alpha(1) \log p + \alpha(2) \log y + \alpha(3)B \qquad \textbf{(2-19)}$$

Suppose that (2-19) when estimated yields

$$\log c = 1.1 - 2.2 \log p + 1.5 \log y + 2.3B, \qquad R^2 = 0.68 \qquad \textbf{(2-19')}$$
$$\quad (2.1) \quad (5.2) \qquad (4.1) \qquad (50.1)$$

where, as before, the numbers in parentheses are t-ratios.

Evidently, changing functional form and adding the individual characteristic dummy variable B have further improved our regression's explanatory power. How do we interpret equation (2-19')? The coefficient of $\log p$ is the *price elasticity of demand* for carrots. The coefficient of $\log y$ is the *income elasticity of demand*. What will happen to carrot consumption if p and y both rise by 10 percent? What is carrot consumption if income is zero?

What does the coefficient of the dummy variable B tell us? Recall once again the value that B takes on for the two kinds of individuals it represents. If a carrot consumer has long, furry ears, $B = 1$. If not, $B = 0$. Thus, multiplying B by its regression coefficient, we see that for furry-eared consumers, the log of carrot consumption is 2.3 more than for their furless, short-eared counterparts. Consider two typical carrot consumers, one furry, one nonfurry, who have *identical values* of p and y equal to p^* and y^*, respectively. Denoting furry carrot consumption as $c(f)$ and nonfurry carrot consumption as $c(n)$, equation (2-19') tells us that

$$\log c(f) - \log c(n) = [1.1 - 2.2 \log p^* + 1.5 \log y^* + 2.3B]$$
$$- [1.1 - 2.2 \log p^* + 1.5 \log y^*]$$
$$= 2.3$$

since $B = 0$ for nonfurry consumers. From Table 2-3 we know that

$$\log c(f) - \log c(n) \equiv \log \frac{c(f)}{c(n)}$$

Thus, carrot consumption of furry and nonfurry carrot crunchers can be compared by calculating the *antilog* of log $c(f)/c(n)$. This is the number for which 2.3, the coefficient of B, is the natural logarithm. The antilog of 2.3 is 9.97. Therefore, we conclude that, other things equal, furry types demand almost 10 times as many carrots as others. Since this is in accord with our prior knowledge of carrot consumers, we are inclined to accept this result as reasonable, our confidence being increased by B's t-ratio, which is very high. To make sure that you fully understand this example, calculate the quantity of carrots demanded by a furry-eared consumer with an annual income of $8,000 when the price of carrots is $0.50 a pound.

This concludes our brief discussion of measurement and quantitative methods in labor economics. As you read the remainder of this text, we hope you will remember that there is no way to evaluate statistical results without reference to an economic theory that explains how the variables are thought to be related and the kinds of estimates that are acceptable evidence. There is much room for judgment and experience in interpreting the results of empirical investigations, and reasonable and competent economists can and do disagree on whether a given theory or hypothesis has been confirmed or rejected or whether it is useful in helping to understand the world around us. At many points we have had to use our best judgment in interpreting empirical studies of labor markets, and other economists may well have wished to use the results of different empirical investigations, or to interpret results somewhat differently. The important thing for you will be not so much to read and believe as to read and understand.

REFERENCES AND SELECTED READINGS

BECKER, GARY S., *A Theory of the Production and Allocation of Effort,* Working Paper No. 184, National Bureau of Economic Research. Cambridge, Mass.: National Bureau of Economic Research, 1977.

INTRILIGATOR, MICHAEL D., *Econometric Models, Techniques, and Applications.* Englewood Cliffs, N.J.: Prentice-Hall, Inc., 1978.

KMENTA, JAN, *Elements of Econometrics.* New York: Macmillan, 1971.

MORGAN, JAMES N., ED., *Five Thousand American Families—Patterns of Economic Progress.* Ann Arbor: Survey Research Center, University of Michigan, 1974.

————, *Productive Americans: A Study of How Individuals Contribute to Economic Progress.* Ann Arbor: Survey Research Center, University of Michigan, 1966.

PARNES, HERBERT S., *The Pre-Retirement Years: A Longitudinal Study of the Labor Market Experience of Men,* Vol. 1. Washington, D.C.: U.S. Department of Labor, Manpower Administration, 1970.

PINDYCK, ROBERT S., AND DANIEL L. ROBINFELD, *Econometric Models and Economic Forecasts,* 2d ed. New York: McGraw-Hill, 1981.

U.S. DEPARTMENT OF LABOR, BUREAU OF LABOR STATISTICS, *Employment and Earnings* (published monthly).

————, *Handbook of Labor Statistics.* Washington, D.C.: U.S. Government Printing Office, Bulletin 2070, December 1980.

EXERCISES

1. Without using any graphs or algebra explain:
   (a) Function
   (b) Hypothesis
   (c) Regression analysis

2. Explain how the three concepts in question 1 are related in economic analysis. Specifically, how do economists use all three when they analyze a topic? Support your answer with specific reference to equation (2-10) in the text.

*3. Consider equation (2-10) of this chapter.
   (a) Suppose that you expect carrot consumption to vary by the sex of the consumer, ceteris paribus. How would you change the mathematical form of (2-10) to allow for this possibility? How would you use your respecified equation to test this hypothesis?
   (b) Suppose that you expect the impact of carrot price on the quantity of carrots demanded to vary by income level. How would you change (2-10) to permit this possibility? How would you use your respecified equation to test this hypothesis?
   (c) Suppose that you expect the effect of extra income on carrot consumption to vary by income level. How would you change (2-10) to allow this as a possibility? How would you use your respecified equation to test this hypothesis?

---

* More technical exercise.

3

THE DEMAND
FOR LABOR
IN COMPETITIVE
MARKETS

A. Educational objectives

1. To establish the general qualitative relationship between firms' desired amounts of labor and the wage rate per unit of labor services
2. To identify the influence of various environmental disturbances or governmental policies on the quantities of labor firms wish to purchase
3. To illustrate techniques for verifying and quantifying the expected downward-sloping demand curve for labor

B. The firm's labor demand curve when its capital input is fixed (p. 46)

1. A simple introduction (p. 46)
2. A deeper look at the firm's demand for labor (p. 49)
3. The marginal product of labor (p. 54)

C. The demand curve for labor when the firm adjusts its nonlabor inputs (p. 60)

1. Isoexpenditure lines and the firm's optimal (cost-minimizing) input combination for a given level of output (p. 60)
2. Cost minimization (p. 62)
3. The expansion path (p. 65)
4. Profit maximization and labor demand (p. 66)
5. The relationship between the competitive firm's labor demand curves when capital is fixed versus variable: comparison of relative slopes (p. 68)
*6. A deeper look at labor demand (p. 72)

D. The demand for labor by a competitive industry (p. 75)

1. The role of industry composition (p. 76)
2. Applications (p. 77)
   a. The effect of minimum wage legislation on employment and earnings: the role of elasticity of demand
   b. Determinants of the elasticity of labor demand: Marshall's rules
   c. Shifts in labor demand caused by change in other factor prices
3. Relaxing the profit-maximization assumption: nonprofit firms and public sector employers (p. 84)
   a. Labor demand in the public sector

---

* Represents more technical material that may be skipped without loss of continuity.

Labor demand is usually referred to as a **derived demand.** That is, *it stems from the demand for commodities that labor helps to produce.* Have you ever been to a fast-food restaurant like McDonald's, and upon completion of your meal wondered whether you should leave the trash on the table or clean up after yourself? On the one hand you hated the thought of leaving a mess, but on the other hand you worried about taking the job away from some deserving teenager or senior citizen. If you answer yes, then you are already well on your way to understanding the general principle that the demand for labor depends upon or is derived from the demand for final output. In the situation above, the more hamburgers sold, the greater the quantity of wrappers left on the tables and the more teenagers hired to clean up.

The general framework used to analyze the demand for labor has four components, or assumptions that we must specify: (1) the firm's *technology,* describing the relationship between its inputs of productive factors such as labor, machinery, or raw materials and its output; (2) the economic environment in the markets where firms purchase their inputs, such as competitive or noncompetitive; (3) the degree of competition in the firm's output markets; and (4) the firm's goals—profit maximization being the typical goal assumed. In this chapter we begin by analyzing the profit-maximizing firm's demand for labor when both input and product markets are competitive and the firm's technology is given. After we derive the labor demand curve under these conditions, we will see how changing the assumptions surrounding the theory change the nature of the demand curve developed from it.

The basic decision-making unit in determining the demand for labor is the *firm.* We will assume initially that each firm's demand for labor is based on its desire to reap the largest possible profit. In order to maximize profit, a firm must accomplish two related goals: (1) it must produce each quantity of output at a cost that is the lowest attainable for that quantity; (2) the output level chosen must be neither too large nor too small. Any event that causes a firm to change its profit-maximizing output will cause the quantity of labor demanded to move in the same direction. It is a bit more complex to analyze how the firm's demand for labor relates to goal 1—cost minimization. We

---

* Represents more technical material that may be skipped without loss of continuity.

turn first to an analysis of the impact of the firm's output decision on its demand for labor.

The next section presents a formal analysis of the implications for labor demand that follow from the assumption that firms attempt to maximize their profits. The purpose of this theory is to help us—students of labor force behavior—to understand labor markets systematically. It is not designed to describe how actual firms go about minimizing input costs or deciding how much output to produce. Firms and their managers may or may not use mathematical techniques to accomplish their goals. Nevertheless, whether or not they survive in a competitive world depends on firms' abilities to produce at lowest cost and choose their scale of operations correctly, either through trial and error or more sophisticated means. The theory that follows is the economist's way of attempting to systematically analyze how this behavior determines the demand for labor.

THE COMPETITIVE FIRM'S LABOR DEMAND CURVE WHEN CAPITAL IS FIXED

A Simple Introduction

The firm's demands for labor and other inputs are derived from consumers' demand for the firm's output. Our perception of the relationship between the output and input sides of the firm's operations will be greatly enhanced if we take a little time to review the elementary theory of the competitive firm and industry.

In competition, each firm is assumed to behave as if it has no direct control over the price at which its output is sold or the prices it must pay for factor inputs. It is, therefore, a **price-taker** in both input and output markets. Figure 3-1 shows a competitive industry and one of the (identical) firms in the industry. We assume, for convenience, that the industry is in long-term equilibrium, with price being equal to minimum average total cost for each firm.

In Figure 3-1, panel (b) shows how the industry equilibrium price $P(0)$ and quantity $Q(0)$ are determined by industry supply $S(P)$ and demand $D(P)$. A representative firm in the industry is depicted in panel (a). Each firm takes the industry price $P(0)$ as given and chooses its profit-maximizing output. As you will recall, when each firm maximizes profit, not only must it adopt production techniques that make the costs as low as possible, but it must also choose the profit-maximizing output. At this output, shown as $Q(0)$, marginal cost (MC) will equal marginal revenue (MR). For a competitive, price-taking firm marginal revenue is the equilibrium market price $P(0)$. Therefore, when a competitive firm maximizes profit, the following condition holds in equilibrium:

$$P \equiv MR = MC \qquad (3\text{-}1)$$

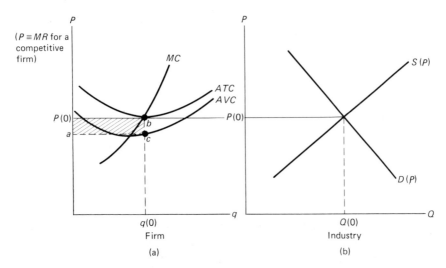

FIGURE 3-1. Equilibrium price and output in a competitive industry

We begin our analysis of the firm's demand for labor by considering the simple case in which only the input of labor is adjusted to changing market conditions. Throughout this chapter we will simplify our view of the firm's production decisions by assuming that it uses only two inputs—labor (L) and capital (K) (for example, machinery and buildings and natural resources). There is good reason to believe that a firm will generally be quite cautious in adjusting its capital input. Generally, investment in new plant and equipment is a relatively expensive undertaking. This fact is apparent in many events affecting the business world.

For example, in 1978 the price of TV advertising time was rising rapidly, causing many advertisers to switch to magazine ads. The consequent increase in the derived demand for paper caused price increases, but little expansion in the capacity of paper mills. The reason the mill owners gave was that capacity expansion is very costly, and they were unsure that the increased demand for paper would persist.[1] The same considerations would affect a firm's decision on how to respond to a change in wage rates. Only after it becomes clear that a wage change will persist will a firm alter its physical plant and equipment to adapt to the new economic environment.

Thus, in beginning our analysis of the demand for labor, we hold constant the competitive firm's input of capital services. With capital inputs fixed, the firm's average variable cost (AVC) consists entirely of labor costs. *You should now see that, with labor the only variable input, the firm's output decision goes hand in hand with its decision on how much labor to hire.*

Let us explore in greater detail the implications of the last paragraph for the firm's labor demand. The price of a unit of labor is the wage rate (w).

---

[1] "Paper Shortage Hits Magazines," *Wall Street Journal,* January 26, 1978, p. 1.

Therefore, in Figure 3-1, the firm's AVC curve can also be defined as the wage rate multiplied by the quantity of labor used in production, or

$$AVC \equiv \frac{wL}{q} \tag{3-2}$$

Since marginal cost is, by definition, the change in variable cost required to produce one more unit of output, marginal cost can be defined in terms of the wage rate and the additional amount of labor required to produce one additional unit of output:

$$MC \equiv w \cdot MIL \tag{3-3}$$

where *MIL* is a **marginal input of labor,** the amount required to produce one more unit of output. (That is, $MIL \equiv \Delta L/\Delta q$ when $\Delta q = 1$.)

The firm's labor demand curve provides an answer to the question: How will the firm's use of labor change when the wage rate changes? Therefore, in order to derive the firm's labor demand curve, we examine what happens when the wage rate changes. Remember, the firm is a *price-taker* in its input markets as well as in its output markets. For example, suppose the firm in Figure 3-1 is a manufacturer of women's dresses located in Miami, Florida. A political crisis on a Caribbean island results in a wave of migration to Miami, and the firm can now hire workers at considerably lower wages than in the past. In terms of definitions (3-2) and (3-3) a reduction in w implies a drop in MC and AVC (and, of course, average total cost, ATC). These changes for the firm are shown in Figure 3-2. The wage decline causes

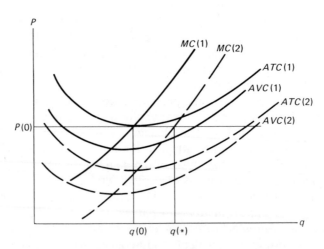

FIGURE 3-2. The firm's response to a reduction in costs caused by a falling wage rate

all the firm's cost curves to shift downward from $ATC(1)$, $AVC(1)$, and $MC(1)$ to $ATC(2)$, $AVC(2)$, and $MC(2)$, respectively. Since only *this firm* has experienced a decline in the wage it must pay, the *industry's* supply and demand conditions remain essentially unaffected. Therefore, the firm can enlarge its profit by increasing output from $q(0)$ to $q(*)$. Because marginal cost has shifted down, $P(0)$ is equal to the firm's marginal cost $MC(2)$ at output $q(*)$, which lies to the right of (is larger than) output $q(0)$.

We can now summarize the firm's adjustments in terms of its demand curve for labor. In Figure 3-3, the firm initially had faced the labor supply curve $S(1)$, which indicates that the firm was a price-taker in the labor market, paying wage rate $w(1)$. Given $w(1)$ and output price $P(0)$, the firm maximized its profit by producing output level $q(0)$ with the quantity of labor inputs $L(0)$. The influx of immigrants caused the firm's labor supply curve to shift downward from $S(1)$ to $S(2)$ and the wage rate from $w(1)$ to $w(2)$. The firm now found that profit maximization required increasing output to $q(*)$ and its labor input to $L(*)$. In response to a decline in the wage, the firm has increased the quantity of labor used. *In general, the firm's demand for labor slopes downward with respect to the wage rate.* This is shown by the downward-sloping labor demand curve d in Figure 3-3.

A Deeper Look at the Firm's Demand for Labor

We have shown how the firm's demand for labor is intimately linked to its profit-maximizing output decision. We will now analyze this connection between a firm's output and factor demand in greater detail. The connection between a firm's output and factor demands is governed by the technical

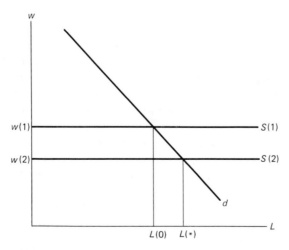

FIGURE 3-3. The firm's demand curve for labor when capital is fixed

(engineering) relationship between its inputs and product called its **production function.** Suppose once again that a firm uses only two inputs in its production process—labor of a given quality and capital such as machinery, buildings, and natural resources. Its production function describes precisely, in mathematical terms, how each possible combination of labor and capital is related to the output maximum obtainable with that input combination.

The firm's production function.   A general algebraic expression of a firm's production function is

$$q = f(L, K) \tag{3-4}$$

where $q \equiv$ the *flow* of output per unit of time

$\quad L \equiv$ the number of units of labor (for example, workers $\times$ hours worked) used during the same time period

$\quad K \equiv$ the number of units of capital (for example, machine-hours) used during the time period

$f(L, K) \equiv$ algebraic expression describes how L and K are combined to produce q.

For example, q might stand for the amount of automobile production per week, L the total hours of labor used on the assembly line during the week, and K the number of hours assembly-line equipment is used multiplied by the number of units of machinery.

A numerical example will help you see how a production function relates output to the inputs used. One of the simplest production functions can be written down as

$$q = (LK)^{0.45} \tag{3-5}$$

This particular production function tells us that if one unit each of labor and capital are employed, output (q) will equal $(1 \times 1)^{0.45}$, or one unit. However, if each input is doubled to two units, output will grow only to $(2 \times 2)^{0.45}$, or 1.87 units. If inputs double again to four, output grows only to 3.48 units. Therefore we say that this production function exhibits **decreasing returns to scale.** Each firm in a competitive market must eventually reach a size where it faces decreasing returns to scale. Decreasing returns implies that inputs and, therefore, production cost grow proportionally more rapidly than output. If this were not the case, there would be no limit to the size of each firm. The number of firms in each market would tend to diminish and competition would disappear. To see if you understand the concept of decreasing returns to scale, prove to yourself, using a numerical example, that the production function $q = (LK)^{0.5} \equiv L^{0.5}K^{0.5}$ exhibits constant returns to scale. Can you write down a production function that exhibits increasing returns to scale?

What does such a production function imply about a firm's cost? Does it increase more or less rapidly than output? Why?

One of the most important items of information provided by a firm's production function is the various ways in which a given level of output can be produced with different combinations of the inputs L and K. We can use the production function of equation (3-2) as an example of this important economic principle. In order to discover the range of input combinations capable of producing a given amount of output, we simply express (3-5) in a different way so that either K or L becomes the variable on the left-hand side of the equation. For example, we can solve (3-2) for L as follows:

$$L = \frac{q^{1/0.45}}{K} \qquad\qquad (3\text{-}6)$$

By arbitrarily setting output (q) equal to some given amount (10 units, for instance), equation (3-5) becomes a function relating L and K, showing all the combinations of the two inputs that will yield that level of output. There is an infinite number of input combinations that will work. Table 3-1 shows some of them for three levels of output—10, 20, and 50 units. These input combinations are graphed in Figure 3-4.

An important feature of Table 3-1 is that it clearly shows decreasing returns to scale. Suppose the firm is producing 10 units of output using 10 units of K and 16.7 units of L. If it wishes to double output to 20 units it can do so, but *more than* twice as many resources are needed. For example, if double the amount of K is used (20 units), 2.3 times as much L is required (38.9 units compared to 16.7 units). If output is quintupled, and the input of K increased fivefold (to 50), L must increase by a factor of 7.1 to 119 units.

TABLE 3-1   Some Combinations of L and K Capable of Producing 10 Units of Output (q), 20 Units of Output, and 50 Units of Output Given that $q = (LK)^{0.45}$

	Amount of L Required to Produce		
Amount of K	10 Units of Output	20 Units of Output	50 Units of Output
1	166.7	778.4	5963
5	33.4	155.7	1193
10	16.7	77.8	596
20	8.3	38.9	298
25	6.7	31.3	239
35	4.8	22.2	170
50	3.3	15.6	119
70	2.4	11.1	85

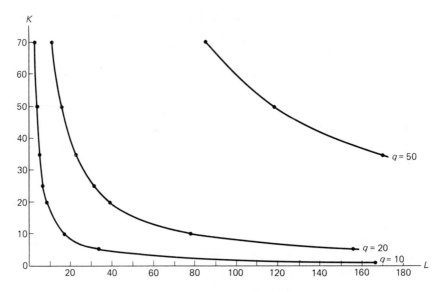

FIGURE 3-4. Some input and output combinations for production function
$q = (LK)^{0.45}$

A second important feature of the numerical example is perhaps seen
more clearly in Figure 3-4. Each of the input combinations capable of producing a given level of output lies on a downward-sloping curved line known
as an **isoquant.** Three isoquants, or equal-quantity lines, are shown in Figure
3-4. Each isoquant represents combinations of K and L that produce a certain level of output within a given time period. There is one isoquant for each
level of output the firm is capable of producing, three of which are shown in
Figure 3-4.

Let us now go on to illustrate how the isoquant map of a typical firm's
production function looks. A generalized view of a firm's production function is shown in Figure 3-5. Once again, we show three out of the infinite
number of the firm's isoquants. This isoquant map, in contrast to that of
Figure 3-4, shows that portions of isoquants may be positively sloped. However, only the negatively sloped (downward from left to right) portions of the
isoquants are relevant to the firm's production decisions. The isoquant labeled 100 in Figure 3-5, for example, indicates that a weekly output of 100
widgets may be produced with 6 units of L and 10 units of K (point T) per
week or with 11 of L and 6 of K per week (point S). Notice that point R also
lies on the isoquant 100. While *technologically* feasible, it will not be chosen
by the competitive firm if labor services have a positive price, because R is
more expensive than the input combination at point S. To generalize, combinations of K and L along an isoquant above where it becomes vertical or to

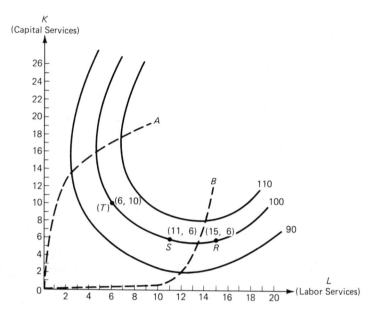

FIGURE 3-5. A general view of the production function

the right of where it becomes horizontal cost more than another input combination along the same isoquant and may therefore be ignored. The dashed lines *OA* and *OB* in Figure 3-5 are called **ridge lines** and delimit the region where production will occur. (In subsequent figures the portions of the isoquants outside the ridge lines are eliminated.) Remember that there are many levels of production possible and that each is represented by a different isoquant, so that Figure 3-5 would be very messy were we to attempt to depict completely the production process for all possible output levels. To keep our example manageable, Figure 3-5 and the geometrical representations of production that follow show only a few isoquants.

Here are some very important general properties of isoquants. First, a given input combination is associated with only *one* level of output—isoquants do not intersect. (To prove that isoquants do not intersect, construct a counterexample by drawing a diagram in which the isoquants cross each other. It should be clear that wherever one of the isoquants lies above the other, the portion that is above is irrelevant, because the firm can obtain the same output with fewer of both inputs by going to the lower isoquant.) The most important characteristics of isoquants, however, are that in general they are *negatively sloped* and *convex* to the origin (as in Figures 3-4 and 3-5). The *negative slopes* represent the **principle of substitution,** which means that when either factor is reduced, the other must be increased for output to be held constant. The slope of an isoquant at a point describes the firm's ability to substitute factors for one another while holding output constant. If the slope were minus 1/3, for example, three units of labor would need to be added if capital were to be reduced by one unit. Economists call the absolute value of the slope of an isoquant the **marginal rate of technical substitution (MRTS)** between factors. *Convexity* means that along each isoquant the amount of L necessary to compensate for one less unit of K grows as L/K grows.

The production function as illustrated in Figures 3-4 and 3-5 conveys one of the most important ideas in economics: *A given level of output can be produced in alternative ways.* There are numerous examples of this. In heavily populated Asian countries, crops are produced on little land with a great deal of labor. In contrast, in California, where labor is very expensive, similar crops such as rice are produced with relatively large amounts of land and machinery. In business offices, accounting can be done with many bookkeepers working with adding machines or with only a few individuals using sophisticated computers. Thus, the existence of a production function implies that a firm must choose among alternative input blends.[2] How a firm makes such choices determines its demand for labor. To go from the firm's production function to its demand for labor, however, we must first know its input purchase options.

THE COMPETITIVE FIRM'S INPUT PURCHASE OPTIONS
AND THE MARGINAL PRODUCT OF LABOR

In competition, the prices a firm must pay for its inputs are established by forces outside its control—the interaction of supply and demand in the factor markets.[3] Each competitive firm feels (correctly) that it may purchase as many units of K or L as it wants without affecting their respective prices. Under competitive conditions, then, the supply curve of L or K to the firm is horizontal (perfectly elastic) at the market price. Such a labor supply curve

---

[2] Because this chapter is devoted to the demand for labor by *firms,* we limit our discussions of production to that context. The concept of a production function, though, describes any individual's or group's ability to transform inputs into output. In Chapter 4 we discuss the household's production of commodities such as meals with the inputs of goods purchased in the market and time of family members. A recent article, Solomon W. Polachek, Thomas J. Kniesner, and Henrick J. Harwood, "Educational Production Functions," *The Journal of Educational Statistics,* 3:3 (Autumn 1978), 209–31, presents estimates of the mathematical relation between an individual student's study time, class attendance, college board score, and grade on a midterm exam in a macro principles of economics course. For the mathematically trained reader, we offer the following activity: Take the estimates presented in the above article and offer to sell some first-year macro principles students estimates of the amount of time each of them must study in order to achieve grades of A on their first midterm, given intended class attendance and college board score. Ten percent of all profits from this activity must be paid as royalties to Polachek, Kniesner, and Harwood, who accept no responsibility for poor predictions.

[3] The concept of a labor market is formally developed in Chapter 5.

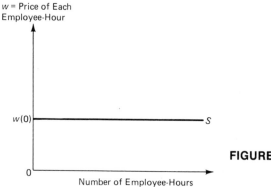

w = Price of Each
Employee-Hour

w(0)

S

0

Number of Employee-Hours

FIGURE 3-6. The supply curve
of labor to the
competitive firm

is depicted in Figure 3-6, whose vertical axis measures the dollar price of one hour of labor services and whose horizontal axis measures employee-hours per week. The labor supply schedule is parallel to the horizontal axis, indicating that the firm will obtain no labor if it offers a wage less than $w(0)$ but can purchase as much as it wants at $w(0)$. The supply curves of other inputs would be drawn similarly.

We are once again in a position to establish a competitive firm's demand curve for labor when its capital input is fixed. Assume that the firm can now hire workers at considerably lower wage rates than in the recent past. It had been producing 90 dresses per day with 6 units of K and 6 of L (point R in Figure 3-7). Now that the firm's cost of production has dropped, it has an incentive to expand output. With capital services unchanging at 6 units, the firm will adjust by adding labor only, moving out along the **expansion path** indicated by the horizontal line going through point R. The horizontal line, or ray, going from zero output outward to the right at an input of 6 units of capital is called an expansion path because it describes how inputs must change as output expands (or contracts). By how much will dress production and labor input grow? As you know, the firm will increase its profit if it expands output (q) whenever the value of additional production is greater than its cost. The value to the firm of additional production is equal to the extra output (Δq) multiplied by its price. Since the price of output is also beyond the control of a competitive firm, the crucial determinant of its demand for labor will be the behavior of output as additional labor is added to its fixed capital input.

Economists call the addition to output that stems from a small increase in labor services (capital fixed) the **marginal physical product of labor (MPPL).** Symbolically, using the Greek letter Δ to denote a smaller change, $MPPL \equiv \Delta q/\Delta L$. We can see labor's marginal physical product by examining the isoquants in Figure 3-7 along the expansion path. Points on this line

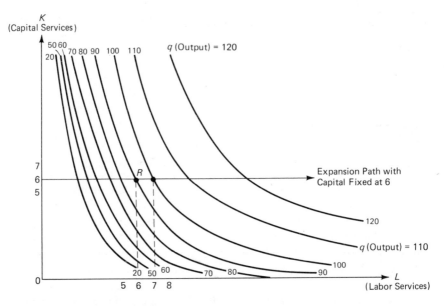

FIGURE 3-7. The production function and expansion path with K fixed at 6

represent the levels of output that correspond to various inputs of L with K fixed at 6 horsepower-hours per week. Differences between the output levels represented by the isoquants show the change in output attributable to adding labor inputs. Notice that as we move outward along the expansion path (increasing L/K), progressively larger inputs of L must be added to raise production by a given amount, since going from left to right each isoquant represents 10 more dresses. This is called **diminishing marginal physical productivity.**

Let us put aside temporarily the hypothetical dressmaker of Figure 3-7 and make sure we understand the concept of diminishing marginal physical productivity of labor. Consider a farmer with 100 acres of land. If he tries to do all the farming, he will be handicapped by the fact that he can be in only one place at a time. But if he hires a helper, the output of the farm may more than double, because some specialization will be possible. Moreover, if there is a hole in the fence at the same time there is a leak in the roof of the barn, both emergencies can be taken care of at once; the resources of the farm will be employed more flexibly. This increasing efficiency of labor may continue as our farmer hires a second, third, or even a fourth helper. As the number of workers on the farm grows, however, the marginal physical product of labor must eventually fall. At some point, the farmer will have so many helpers that an additional one will be idle most of the time waiting for supervision or to use machinery, as well as getting in the way of other workers.

The marginal physical product of labor for our hypothetical dress-manufacturing firm is shown in Figure 3-8. Units of labor are measured on the horizontal axis, just as in Figure 3-7. The curve labeled *MPPL* is drawn by plotting the *changes* in output (differences between the isoquants) along the expansion path in Figure 3-7 against the corresponding initial amounts of labor. For instance, the marginal product of adding the seventh unit of labor is 10. This is plotted against 6 units of labor in Figure 3-5. Also shown is the firm's **average physical product of labor (APPL).** The *APPL* of labor is simply the total output divided by total amount of labor. (*APPL* is what newspaper stories mean when they loosely refer to **productivity.**) At 6 units of labor, *APPL* in our example is $90 \div 6 = 15$. The *APPL* curve in Figure 3-8 is drawn by plotting Q/L along the expansion path in Figure 3-7 against the corresponding amounts of L.

Since we want to see how the firm adjusts its output and labor input in order to maximize profit, it will be helpful to convert *APPL* and *MPPL* into value terms. Because the competitive firm can sell as much output as it wishes at the going price, on which its own actions have a negligible influence, it is a simple task to convert the relations in Figure 3-8 into value terms. We need only multiply the firm's *MPPL* and *APPL* schedules by the market price (*P*) of output to find the **value of marginal product of labor (VMPL)** and the **value of average product of labor (VAPL).** *VMPL* is the change in total revenue (ΔTR) the firm obtains if it adds one more unit of labor. *VAPL* is simply total revenue divided by the total quantity of labor used, or the average value produced by a unit of labor. Since we are multiplying by a constant, the *VMPL* and *VAPL* schedules have the same general shapes as *MPPL* and *APPL*, respectively; they are shown in Figure 3-9.

In Figure 3-9, suppose the labor supply curve is *S*, indicating that the firm can hire as much labor as it would like at a wage rate of $w(0) = \$6$. How

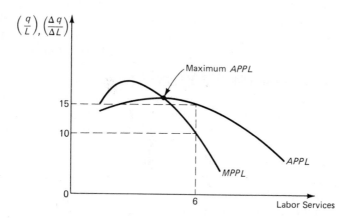

FIGURE 3-8. Marginal physical product of labor and average physical product of labor

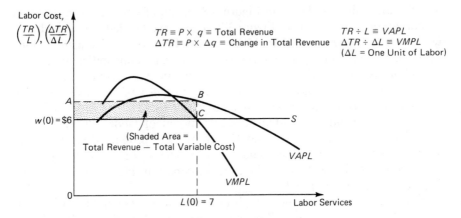

FIGURE 3-9. Value of marginal product of labor and value of average product of labor

much labor will the firm hire? Remember equation (3-1), which states that a firm maximizes its profit by producing up to the point where marginal cost (*MC*) equals marginal revenue (*MR*), and that in competition marginal revenue equals product price (*P*). Equivalently, the firm will hire labor, the only variable factor of production in this example, until the marginal cost of labor, which is the wage rate, is equal to the marginal revenue it creates or *VMPL*. Expressed algebraically, the *firm's profit-maximizing hiring policy* is to find the level of labor where

$$w = VMPL \equiv P \cdot MPPL \qquad \qquad \textbf{(3-7)}$$

This occurs in Figure 3-9 at point *C*. At a wage of \$6, profit is maximized by hiring 7 units of labor. Symbolically, the profit-maximizing quantity of labor is *L*(0). [If the firm maximizes profit when *w* = \$6 by hiring 7 units of labor, what must be the value of *P*, the market price of a dress? *Hint:* See equation (3-7).]

It is easy to demonstrate that the firm's profit-maximizing *output* policy is equivalent to its profit-maximizing *hiring* policy. We need only show that (3-1) and (3-7) say the same thing. In Figure 3-7, *MPPL* at an input of 6*K* and 6*L* equals 10 dresses. The amount of additional labor required to produce just one more dress—a marginal input of labor—is the reciprocal of its marginal physical product. That is, $MIL \equiv 1/MPPL$. Therefore, it would take approximately $\frac{1}{10}$ additional unit of labor to raise output from 90 to 91 dresses. In equation (3-3) we have already seen that $MC \equiv w \cdot MIL$; that is, a marginal input of labor multiplied by the wage rate is the cost in dollars of one more unit of output. Consequently, all we must do to relate *MC* to

MPPL in terms of dollars is to multiply 1/*MPPL* by *w*, obtaining *w*/*MPPL* ≡ *MC*. For example, if *w* = $6, the marginal cost of producing the 91st dress is $0.60. We may thus rewrite equation (3-1) as

$$P = \frac{w}{MPPL} \tag{3-8}$$

Equation (3-8), which is equivalent to (3-1), can be transformed into (3-7) by multiplying both sides by *MPPL*. Thus, when *K* is fixed, the condition under which a firm will maximize its profit in the hiring of labor is identical to that under which it will maximize its profit in the production of output. Over most of its range, the firm's *VMPL* schedule is its demand curve for labor when capital is fixed. A labor demand curve answers the question: *How much labor will the firm wish to hire at various wage rates?* As long as it pays the firm to operate at all, the *VMPL* curve answers this question; therefore it is the firm's labor demand curve when capital is fixed.

Remember from basic economics that a firm will stay in business so long as total revenue does not fall below total variable cost. [In Figure 3-1, this means the firm will continue to operate so long as *P*(0) exceeds minimum *AVC*.] In Figure 3-9, the firm hires *L*(0) units of labor at wage rate *w*(0) = $6. The value of average product of labor is *A*, and the total revenue is, by definition, *A* × *L*(0), or the area of the rectangle 0*ABL*(0). (Can you explain why?) Similarly, total variable cost is *L*(0) × *w*(0), or the area of the rectangle 0*w*(0)*CL*(0). The amount by which total revenue exceeds total variable cost when the firm maximizes its profits for *w*(0) is represented, then, by *w*(0)*ABC*. [Go back and look at Figure 3-1 once again. The area *w*(0)*ABC* in Figure 3-9 corresponds to the shaded area *aP*(0)*bc* in Figure 3-1(a). Can you see why?] It is possible to construct such a rectangle for any profit-maximizing output *greater* than the output corresponding to maximum *VAPL*. When the wage rate equals maximum *VAPL*, however, the rectangle representing the excess of total revenue over total variable cost vanishes. [Similarly the area *aP*(0)*bc* in Figure 3-1, panel (a), vanishes when the wage rate increases to the level that causes minimum *AVC* to equal *P*(0).] Thus, when the wage rate is less than or equal to maximum *VAPL*, the firm will maximize its profit (minimize its loss) by hiring labor up to the point where *w* = *VMPL*.[4] Should the wage rate rise above *VAPL*, however, the firm will lose the least by not producing at all. *Hence, the VMPL curve below maximum VAPL is the firm's demand-for-labor schedule when capital is fixed.*

---

[4] Remember that profit (π) is the difference between total revenue (*TR*) and total cost (*TC*), and that *TC* has two components: *w* · *L* plus payments to other (fixed) factors. Even if *TR* − *w* · *L* is positive, profit may still be negative (the firm is losing money). The firm will continue to produce when π is negative so long as its losses are reduced by the act of production or if (*TR* − *w* · *L* > 0).

Here is a summary of the key results just developed. First, when capital is held constant, the firm's demand curve for labor is downward-sloping. Owing to diminishing marginal physical productivity, the profit-maximizing firm will purchase additional labor if and only if the wage rate falls, all other things remaining unchanged. Second, underlying the inverse relationship between the wage and the competitive firm's demand for labor services are (1) the state of technology, or the production function represented in the isoquant map; (2) a given price of final output; and (3) a particular level of capital service. A change in *any* of these three will disturb *VMPL* and *VAPL* and, therefore, shift the firm's labor demand curve. The interrelationship between technology and labor usage is what underlies most popular arguments concerning the labor market effects of automation. The effect of a change in product price on the demand for labor by a competitive firm will become obvious in our subsequent analysis of the demand for labor by a competitive industry. For now, we go on to examine the firm's demand for labor when it adjusts its use of capital services as well.

THE DEMAND CURVE FOR LABOR
WHEN THE FIRM ADJUSTS CAPITAL

To recap: when the firm does not adjust its input of capital, there is only one way to change output—add more labor or use less of it. Therefore, there is a simple correspondence among the price of labor, the cost of production, the quantity of output produced, and the amount of labor demanded by the firm. To preview: when the firm adjusts its inputs of *both* labor and capital, the labor demand relationship is more complex. The process we are now trying to understand has *two* aspects. *First,* the firm must find which of the many possible combinations of L and K minimizes the cost of each level of production. *Second,* the firm must choose the level of production that maximizes profit, given output price P, the wage w, the price of capital services r, and technology, as reflected in the production function. When we have finished analyzing the firm's demand for labor when it can also adjust its capital input, we will compare the demand curve for capital variable to the demand curve for capital fixed.

The Firm's Input Purchase Options

We now examine the demand for labor by a competitive firm when a wage change is considered sufficiently permanent to warrant adjustment of labor and capital services. The initial step is to represent the firm's input purchase options on the same graph as the production function. In the production diagram, we measure physical quantities of factors along the axes; at first glance there appears to be no place to represent the inputs in monetary terms. However, if we know the dollar prices of the services of machinery and labor, we have the necessary information.

Suppose that the wage rate paid to a unit of labor services, w, is \$1 and the price of a unit of capital services, r, is \$2; then the relative price of labor is $w/r = \frac{1}{2}$. That is, if the firm decides not to purchase some additional L but to purchase instead more K, it can get $\frac{1}{2}$ unit of capital for every unit of labor services it, in a sense, gives up. In general, the relative price of labor tells us how the firm can implicitly trade L for K when purchasing these two inputs. Note that in competition the *dollar prices* of labor and capital do not depend on how much of either factor the firm buys. Thus the *relative price* of labor is independent of input purchases as well.

Three sets of purchase options when the relative price of labor is $\frac{1}{2}$ are represented in Figure 3-10. The line nearest the origin shows all combinations of K and L that can be obtained for \$10, such as $8L$ and $1K$, $6L$ and $2K$, or $4L$ and $3K$. The next highest line shows the amounts that can be obtained for exactly \$20, such as $16L$ and $2K$, $12L$ and $4K$, and so on. Note that the absolute value of the slope of each line, $|\Delta K/\Delta L|$, is equal to the price of labor relative to the price of capital, $w/r = \frac{1}{2}$. Since each line represents a fixed number of dollars spent on the two factor inputs, they are called **isoexpenditure lines** (also called **isocost lines**). Isoexpenditure lines are straight and

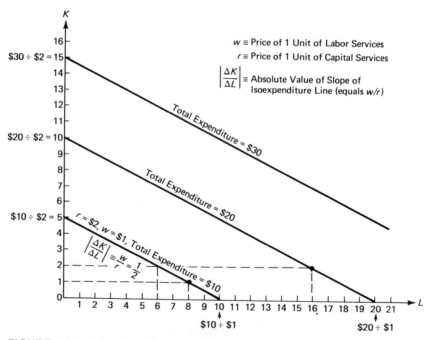

FIGURE 3-10. A family of isoexpenditure lines

parallel, since the relative price of labor is beyond the control of a competitive firm. You should see that if the price of labor were to rise to $2 and the price of capital remained unchanged, the isoexpenditure lines in Figure 3-10 would become *steeper*. Their slope would change from $w/r = \frac{1}{2}$ to $w/r = 1$. Given the level of expenditures on both L and K, for every unit of K *not* bought, only *one* more unit of L could now be purchased instead of two when $w/r = 1$.

Cost Minimization

Where there is only one variable factor (labor variable, capital fixed), cost minimization does not require special attention. There is only one possible way to produce each level of output. However, when all points on an isoquant are feasible production methods, the firm must minimize the cost of production at *whatever* level of output is selected if it is to maximize its profits. To see how a firm minimizes cost by comparing input purchase options with production possibilities, an isoquant and isoexpenditure lines have been brought together in Figure 3-11. Suppose the firm wishes to produce 100 units of output as cheaply as possible. It would be technologically feasible for the firm to produce 100 units of output with the combination of $4K$ and $4L$ at point T, which represents an expenditure of $12. The competitive firm will not select point T, however, because it can produce these 100 units for less than $12. Starting at point T, the firm can reduce production cost by substituting L for K until it reaches point R, indicating 2 units of K and 6 units of L, where the isoquant and the isoexpenditure line $10 are tangent (just touch). No other combination of K and L produces 100 units

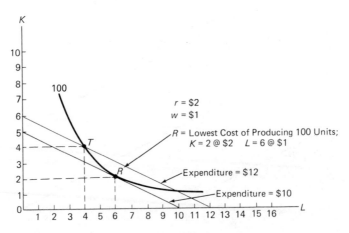

FIGURE 3-11. Least-cost method of producing 100 units

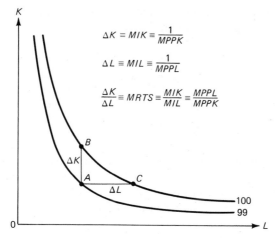

FIGURE 3-12. Definitions of *MRTS*, *MI*, and *MPP*

and costs less than $10.[5] In general, the firm minimizes the cost of a given level of output by producing at a point where an isoexpenditure line is *tangent to* (just touches) an isoquant.[6]

A look at Figure 3-12 provides deeper insight into the economic meaning of the tangency least-cost position. Point *B* on isoquant 100 lies directly above point *A* on isoquant 99. They differ by one unit of output and by just enough *K*, (ΔK), to account for the difference in production (*L* is the same at both *A* and *B*). Now compare points *A* and *C*. They differ by just enough *L*, (ΔL), to account for one unit of output. The line segment $\overline{AB}$ represents a concept already encountered, a marginal input of *K* (*MIK*) (see page 48). Analogously, $\overline{AC}$ is a marginal input of *L* (*MIL*). Thus, we may think of the absolute value of the slope of isoquant 100 as *MIK/MIL*.[7] To generalize, the slope of an isoquant is the ratio of the marginal inputs of the factors, or

$$\frac{\Delta K}{\Delta L} \text{ (isoquant)} \equiv \frac{MIK}{MIL} \qquad (3\text{-}9)$$

---

[5] Notice that 100 is also the highest level of output that can be achieved by spending $10 on factors of production.

[6] There is, of course, an exception: the case where an isoquant and isoexpenditure line intersect at one of the axes. You should be able to show that when this occurs, the least-cost method of production uses only one of the two inputs. This case, called a corner solution, is possible only if the isoquants intersect an axis. Corner solutions are precluded if some small amount of each factor is required in production.

[7] Reference to the slope of either an isoquant or an isoexpenditure line is to the *absolute* value of the slope.

We have also seen (page 48) that the marginal input of a factor is the reciprocal of its marginal product. Therefore,

$$\frac{MIK}{MIL} \equiv \frac{MPPL}{MPPK} \qquad (3\text{-}9')$$

and

$$\frac{\Delta K}{\Delta L} \text{ (isoquant)} \equiv \frac{MPPL}{MPPK} \qquad (3\text{-}10)$$

Equations (3-9) through (3-10) tell us that the marginal rate of technical substitution may be thought of as either the ratio of marginal inputs or the ratio of marginal physical products. Recall, however, that the slope of an isoexpenditure line is the relative price of labor:

$$\frac{\Delta K}{\Delta L} \text{ (isoexpenditure line)} \equiv \frac{w}{r} \qquad (3\text{-}11)$$

Since at a point of tangency between an isoexpenditure line and an isoquant their slopes are equal, equations (3-10) and (3-11) yield as the condition for cost minimization

$$\frac{w}{r} = \frac{MPPL}{MPPK} \qquad (3\text{-}12)$$

With a slight amount of manipulation, the economic sense of (3-12) will become apparent. Divide both sides of the equation by w and multiply both sides by $MPPK$, yielding as an equivalent expression

$$\frac{1}{r} \cdot MPPK = \frac{1}{w} \cdot MPPL \qquad (3\text{-}13)$$

The term $1/r$ represents the amount of K that can be purchased for \$1. Similarly, $1/w$ is the amount of L that can be purchased for \$1. *Equation (3-12) indicates, then, that when cost is minimized, the last dollar spent on K must increase output by the same amount as the last dollar spent on L.* Go back and look at Figure 3-11. At point T, too much is being spent on K and too little on L. This is so because in moving from T to R, expenditure on K is reduced by \$4 ($2K \times \$2$), while expenditure on L is increased by only \$2 ($2L \times \$1$), and output is unchanged. Since at point T, $MPPK/r < MPPL/w$, the firm can reduce its expenditure on K and spend *less* than the amount released on L, while maintaining output at 100. As more L is used, $MPPL$ falls, and as less K is used, $MPPK$ rises. (Why?) The firm continues to substitute L for K, reducing the cost of production, until the changes in

MPPK and *MPPL* create the condition defined by (3-13). Once point *R* is reached, additional cost saving is not possible if output is to be maintained at 100.

To test your understanding of cost minimization, see how well you understand the following example. Ever since the development of high-fructose corn syrup by the Japanese in the early 1970s, corn-based sweetener has vied with cane or beet sugar (sucrose) as an important ingredient in jams, jellies, and soft drinks. Construct a diagram with sucrose on one axis and corn syrup on the other. Show how an increase in the price of sucrose will cause manufacturers to substitute corn syrup for sucrose in producing, say, strawberry jam. In general, the sweeteners in jam, jelly, and soft drinks are not 100 percent corn syrup. Show under what circumstances a firm might use either sucrose only or corn sweetener only. Would this require that sucrose and corn syrup be perfect substitutes?

Finally, a warning is necessary: Do not confuse cost minimization with profit maximization! Although equation (3-12) describes what is required to minimize the cost of any *particular* output, there are *many* possible levels of production. At only *one* level of output will the firm also maximize profit! Cost minimization is *necessary* but not *sufficient* for profit maximization.

The Expansion Path

In order to relate cost minimization to labor demand when labor *and* capital are variable, we must again derive the firm's *expansion path*. (Go back to page 55 to see the firm's expansion path when only labor is variable.) Figure 3-13 illustrates a set of isoquants and a set of isoexpenditure lines tangent to them. For any given set values of the wage rate *w*, the price of capital *r*, and technology, there is one combination of *K* and *L* that is the cheapest way of producing each possible level of output *q*. In Figure 3-13 we show three output levels q_1, q_2, and q_3, which can be produced most cheaply by input combinations $L(1)$, $K(1)$; $L(2)$, $K(2)$; and $L(3)$, $K(3)$, respectively. These least-cost (L, K) combinations define the firm's expansion path. For simplicity, the expansion path in Figure 3-13, line $\overline{0A}$, is drawn as a straight line. Its upward slope means that increases in output require increases in the input of *both L* and *K*. Since the expansion path is a straight line, as output grows, the ratio *L/K* does not change.

The expansion path defines the way a firm adjusts its inputs as output grows or contracts. If the firm shown in Figure 3-13 should experience an increase in the demand for its output, it will move outward along path $\overline{0A}$, increasing its demand for both *L* and *K* in fixed proportions. If $\overline{0A}$ were flatter, the amount of *L* used would be larger relative to the amount of *K* used for each level of output. Nevertheless, as long as $\overline{0A}$ is a straight line, any change in output (say, *n* percent), will always change the amounts of *L* and *K* used by the same percentage as output has changed. Thus, if you were

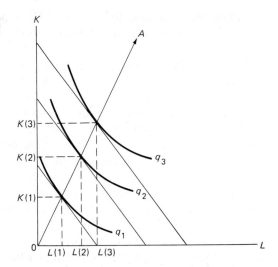

FIGURE 3-13. The firm's expansion path
(capital variable)

working for a firm whose expansion path is flatter than $\overline{0A}$ and the firm's output expanded, the demand for *your* labor services would grow no faster, proportionately, than if you worked for the firm as depicted in Figure 3-13.

Profit Maximization

We have shown that when the firm minimizes its cost of production for any level of output, it will choose an input combination defined by the expansion path. Producing at the lowest cost is a necessary condition for profit maximization. Once again, maximizing profit requires choosing the correct level of output. The profit-maximizing output level in Figure 3-13 will give us *one point* on the firm's labor demand curve, since Figure 3-13 is constructed for a *given* wage, as well as r and price of output.

Just as in Figure 3-1, when the firm described in Figure 3-13 maximizes its profit it will choose an output level suit that $MC = P$. We have assumed that the production function is of such a form that the distance between successive isoquants gets larger as the firm moves outward along the expansion path $\overline{0A}$. This implies that the marginal inputs of both K and L grow larger as output increases. Thus, the additional cost of additional output, MC, is growing as output gets larger. To refresh your memory, Figure 3-14 shows the firm's marginal cost curve, which depends on the values of w and r and on the firm's technology used to derive the expansion path in Figure 3-13. Since MC increases as output grows, MC will eventually be equal to the price of output that the firm takes as given.

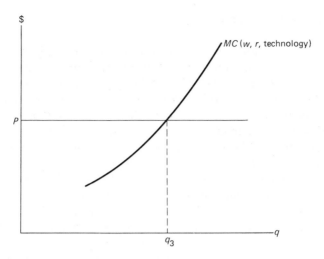

FIGURE 3-14. The firm's marginal cost, given *w, r,*
and its technology

Suppose that $MC = P$ at output level q_3. Then, the firm maximizes its profit, given w, r, and its technology, by producing output level q_3, employing $K(3)$ units of capital and $L(3)$ units of labor. In other words, the firm demands $L(3)$ units of labor when the wage rate equals w, the value on which expansion path $\overline{0A}$ is based, *given r* and the firm's technology. This point on the firm's labor demand curve is depicted in Figure 3-15.

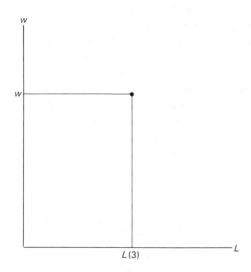

FIGURE 3-15. One point on the
firm's labor
demand curve

The Labor Demand Curve

Now that we have derived one point on the competitive firm's labor demand curve, we are in a position to derive the rest of the demand function. We do this by allowing the wage rate w to vary, holding constant the price of capital services r, the price of output P, and the firm's technology as reflected in its production function. In Figure 3-16(a) the firm is maximizing its profit at point a on expansion path $\overline{0A}$, producing q_3 units of output with $L(3)$ units of labor and $K(3)$ units of capital as in Figure 3-13. The wage rate now designated $w(1)$ is equal to the wage rate on which Figure 3-13 is based. In Figure 3-16(b) we show the firm's marginal cost curve $MC(w(1), r)$, the market price of output, and the firm's profit-maximizing output q_3. Assume that the firm's total expenditure on L and K is equal to $\$Y$. Therefore, the firm is on the isoexpenditure line intersecting the K axis at Y/r and the L axis at $Y/w(1)$. You should see that Y/r and $Y/w(1)$ are the maximum amounts of K and L, respectively, that the firm can purchase for $\$Y$, given the input prices r and $w(1)$.

Now let the wage rate fall from $w(1)$ to $w(2)$. *This results in a counterclockwise shift of the firm's isoexpenditure lines.* In particular, the isoexpenditure line intersecting the K axis at Y/r now intersects the L axis at $Y/w(2)$, indicating that given the amount of K purchased, more L can now be bought for $\$Y$, because the price of L has declined. It is also true that so long as some L is used, more K can be bought (given the quantity of L purchased).

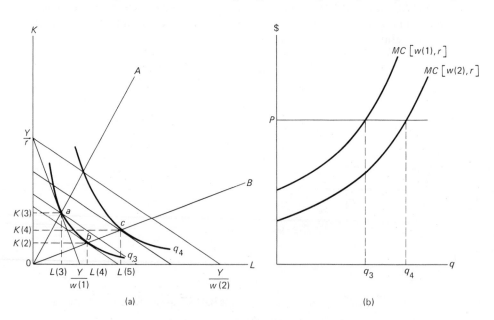

FIGURE 3-16. The firm's response to a decline in the wage rate

Since r is unchanged, the isoexpenditure line still intersects the K axis at Y/r units of K. The decline in the *relative* price of labor is denoted by the flattening, or counterclockwise shift, of the isoexpenditure lines. Their slope has fallen from $r/w(1)$ to $r/w(2)$.

The firm, which was in equilibrium at point a, is no longer maximizing its profit. There are two reasons for this. First, the output q_3 is no longer produced most cheaply at point a. Because the expansion path has shifted from $\overline{0A}$ to $\overline{0B}$, q_3 can be produced most cheaply at point b, using $K(2)$ units of capital (less than before) and $L(4)$ units of labor (more than before). Note that the isoexpenditure line now tangent to q_3 at b intersects the K axis *below* Y/r, indicating that less than $\$Y$ need now be spent to produce q_3, and that this amount is even less than needed to produce q_3 with the input combination $L(3)$, $K(3)$. The fact that cost is lower at b than at a is shown by the position of the isoexpenditure line reflecting the lower wage $w(2)$ passing through a. It lies above the isoexpenditure line passing through b.

The second reason the firm is no longer in equilibrium is shown in Figure 3-16(b). Marginal cost is now lower than before, and the profit-maximizing output, given industry price P, is now larger than before. The firm maximizes profit by *expanding* output from q_3 to q_4.

We are now in a position to add a second point to the labor demand curve we began in Figure 3-15. We do so in Figure 3-17. When the wage rate declines from $w(1)$ to $w(2)$, holding constant r and the firm's technology, the quantity of labor demanded grows from $L(3)$ to $L(5)$. In general, as the wage falls, the quantity of labor demanded grows. It is useful to think of the firm's adjustment from $L(3)$ to $L(5)$ as occurring in two steps. The first step is

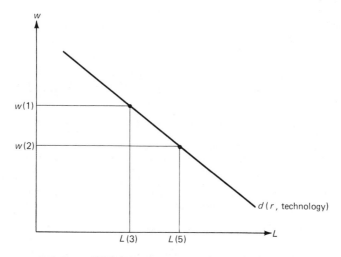

FIGURE 3-17. The firm's labor demand curve when it adjusts capital

depicted in Figure 3-16 by the shift from point *a* to point *b*. Since this adjustment involves substituting labor for capital in response to the decline in the relative price of labor w/r, it is called the **substitution effect** of a change in the relative price of *L*. The substitution effect implies that even if a firm did not change its output, a change in relative input prices would lead it to change its input *mix* so as to increase *L* and decrease *K* whenever w/r decreases.[8] Thus, even if the firm in Figure 3-16 were regulated by the government and could not increase its output except by permission of the regulatory agency, the substitution effect would assume that the firm would use more labor in response to a fall in the wage rate.

The second adjustment the firm makes is to increase output because production cost has fallen while product price has not. Consequently, the firm proceeds northeast along expansion path $\overline{OB}$ from point *b* to point *c*, where *MC* once again equals *P* as shown in Figure 3-16. This movement, using *more* of both *L* and *K*, is called the **scale effect** of the decline in the wage rate from $w(1)$ to $w(2)$.

Comparison of labor demand curves.   In Figure 3-18 we compare the firm's labor demand curve when it does not adjust capital to its demand curve where *both* labor and capital are adjusted when the wage rate changes. In other words, we are comparing the firm's labor demand curve in Figure 3-17 with that in Figure 3-3. Essentially, we want to answer the following questions: (1) How does *VMPL* shift when the firm adjusts capital? (2) Is the elasticity of demand for labor greater when the firm's capital input is fixed at, say, $K(3)$, so that *VMPL* $(K3)$ is the relevant labor demand curve, or is the elasticity greater after capital is adjusted to, say $K(4)$ as in Figures 3-16 and 3-17? [9]

In general the answers to these questions are as follows. (1) When the firm can adjust both its labor and capital inputs, the quantity of *capital* demanded may either *decrease* or *increase* in response to a decline in the wage rate. It all depends on whether the *scale* effect is large or small relative to the substitution effect. When the quantity of capital $K(4)$ in Figure 3-16 is

---

[8] A standardized measure of the substitution effect is known as the elasticity of substitution (σ), which is defined as the percent change in (K/L) due to a 1 percent change in the slope of an isoquant (marginal rate of technical substitution), which in equilibrium equals the slope of an isoexpenditure line (w/r). In Figure 3-16, σ is the percentage difference in the slope of rays $\overline{OA}$ and $\overline{OB}$, divided by the percentage difference in the slopes of isoquant q_3 at points *a* and *b*. Simply put, σ reflects the curvature of an isoquant. The easier it is to substitute labor (capital) for capital (labor), the greater is the value of σ and the more like a downward-sloping straight line is the isoquant. Perfect substitution is said to exist when the elasticity of substitution "goes to" infinity. At the other end of the spectrum is a production function whose isoquants are right angles ($\sigma = 0$), indicating that capital and labor must be used in fixed proportions if waste is to be avoided.

[9] Remember: The *elasticity* of a demand curve is the percentage change in quantity demanded divided by the percentage change in the price (wage rate). See equation (3-23) and Table 2-3 for mathematical formulations.

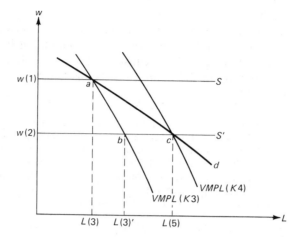

FIGURE 3-18. The firm's labor demand with capital variable compared to its labor demand with capital fixed

less than the quantity $K(3)$, we say that L and K are **gross substitutes.** When $K(4)$ is greater than $K(3)$, we say L and K are **gross complements.** (2) *Regardless* of whether more capital or less capital is used to produce output q_4— that is, regardless of whether $K(4)$ is greater or less than $K(3)$—$VMPL(K4)$ will lie to the right of $VMPL(K3)$, and the elasticity of demand for labor when capital is variable will be greater than when capital is fixed. This is because when L and K are gross complements, an increase in K will cause $VMPL$ to increase. When L and K are gross substitutes, a decrease in K will cause $VMPL$ to increase. Suppose you were a producer of machinery used to harvest tomatoes. If new legislation greatly increased the number of Mexican farm workers who can work in this country, would you be better off if harvesting equipment were a *substitute* or a *complement* for farm labor? Which relationship do you think actually holds true? Why?

Figure 3-18 shows how we compare the firm's labor demand curves in the capital-fixed and capital-variable cases. *It is extremely important to know that the demand curve for labor slopes downward with respect to w,* but *why should we care whether the elasticity of demand for labor is greater when the firm adjusts capital than when it does not?* One example of why this is an extremely important proposition applies to labor unions. A principal goal of labor unions is to increase the wages of their members. However, they are constrained in their wage demands by the employer's tendency to reduce the amount of labor hired when wages go up. What Figure 3-18 shows is that a union wage strategy that *initially* appears to result in only a small reduction in jobs for union workers will *eventually* result in larger job losses. Over time, employers will find it profitable to adjust capital inputs in ways that will lead to greater job losses than the union experienced at first. This *lagged* effect of wage increases on employment can result in a serious reduction in the size of union membership. Can you think of anything besides firms' adjustment of capital that is likely to cause the long-term effects of a wage increase on the reduction in the quantity of labor demanded to be greater than the initial effect?

A deeper look at the labor demand curve.*   It will help to solidify understanding of the firm's labor demand to extend the algebraic presentation of the demand for labor with fixed K. There we demonstrated that the profit-maximizing competitive firm hires labor up to the point where $VMPL$ equals w. When *all* inputs are adjusted, profit maximization requires that the value of marginal product of *each* factor equal that factor's price. This can be shown with a little algebra. By definition, the cost-minimization condition in equation (3-12) is the same as

$$\frac{w}{r} = \frac{MIK}{MIL} \tag{3-14}$$

Cross-multiplication of this equation yields

$$w \cdot MIL = r \cdot MIK \tag{3-15}$$

Equation (3-15) provides an important additional interpretation of equation (3-12): When cost is minimized, a one-unit increase in output is equally expensive, whether a marginal input of L or K is used. In other words, when the firm is minimizing the cost of a given output,

$$MC = w \cdot MIL \tag{3-16}$$

and

$$MC = r \cdot MIK \tag{3-17}$$

Since we know that the profit-maximizing competitive firm chooses output so that marginal cost equals product price, equations (3-16) and (3-17) are equivalent to

$$P = w \cdot MIL \tag{3-18}$$

and

$$P = r \cdot MIK \tag{3-19}$$

respectively. (Remember: $w \cdot MIL$ and $r \cdot MIK$ are the marginal costs of expanding output by increasing L only or K only.) Finally, divide both sides of (3-18) by MIL and both sides of (3-19) by MIK, yielding

$$w = \frac{P}{MIL} \equiv P \cdot MPPL \equiv VMPL \tag{3-20}$$

and

$$r = \frac{P}{MIK} \equiv P \cdot MPPK \equiv VMPK \tag{3-21}$$

Thus, profit maximization does require that *each* factor's price equals its *VMP*.

---

* This section contains more technical material that may be skipped without loss of continuity. If you skip, go to p. 75.

A second goal of this section is to provide a more rigorous demonstration that the labor demand curve with capital fixed is less elastic than the labor demand curve when the firm adjusts its capital input as well. It will help a lot if, while you follow the analysis, you look at both Figures 3-18 and 3-19, which show the same adjustment process two different ways. We want to answer the following questions: (1) When the firm can adjust both its capital and labor inputs, how does VMPL shift as the firm adjusts the quantity of capital? (2) Is the elasticity of demand for labor greater when the firm's capital input is fixed and VMPL[K(3)] is the relevant labor demand curve, or is the elasticity greater when capital is adjusted to minimize production cost? To answer these questions, suppose the firm initially adjusts to a decline in the wage rate from $w(1)$ to $w(2)$ by moving along VMPL[K(3)] from point a to point b. This change in the quantity of labor demanded is shown in both Figures 3-18 and 3-19.

In Figure 3-18 the firm, confronted with wage $w(1)$, maximizes profit at point a on VMPL(K3). This curve is so labeled because it is drawn conditional on the firm's capital input, $K(3)$. Since the profit-maximizing firm satisfies both equations (3-20) and (3-21), there is implicitly another diagram representing the VMP of capital, which would be labeled VMPK(L3) if we were to draw it. This curve would show the firm demanding $K(3)$ units of capital at price r, given the labor input $L(3)$. You should draw the diagram showing this demand for capital to make sure you understand the firm's input decisions.

Subsequently, when the firm decides that the change in labor supply conditions will persist long enough to warrant adjusting capital inputs, it will move from point b to some point c along the expansion path associated with the lower price of labor $w(2)$. There are two possibilities: (1) L and K are gross complements; the scale effect will dominate the substitution effect and the firm will use more capital as in Figure 3-19(a). (2) L and K are gross substitutes; the substitution effect will dominate, and the firm will end up using less capital as in Figure 3-19(b). In the diagram of the demand for capital services that you have drawn for yourself, the adjustment shown in Figure 3-19(a) is associated with a *rightward* shift in the VMP curve for capital. At the fixed price of capital r, the firm demands more capital services $K(4)$ because the increase in the quantity of labor from $L(3)$ to $L(4)$ has *raised* the marginal product of capital. The adjustment in Figure 3-19(b), on the other hand, is associated with a *leftward* shift in the VMP curve for capital. At the fixed price of capital r, the firm demands *less* capital services because the increase in the quantity of labor from $L(3)$ to $L(4)$ has *lowered* the marginal product of capital.

It will help you understand this analysis if you note that in Figure 3-19(a), the gross complement case, point b *must* lie to the *right* of the new expansion path 0B. The reason is this: point c represents profit maximization ($MC = P$) when the firm adjusts *both* L and K. Therefore, MC must be *less* than P at point b'. Since the firm can get to point b' without adjusting its use of K, and since $MC < P$ at b', it will pay the firm to increase output beyond that indicated by the isoquant passing through b', even holding K fixed. Thus, even with K fixed, the firm will increase output to a point beyond the new expansion path when L and K are gross complements. At point b, $VMPK > r$, since the increase in L raises the marginal product of K. Therefore, when it adjusts capital, the firm will move *upward* (toward 0B) from point b in panel (a). We can now answer question (1) asked earlier.

The answer to question (1) is as follows. It can be shown mathematically (usually in advanced economic theory courses) that when capital and labor are gross complements, an *increase* in the quantity of capital, as in Figure 3-19(a), results in an *increase* in the marginal product of labor. When capital and labor are gross substitutes, however, a *reduction* in the quantity of capital, as in Figure 3-19(b), increases the marginal product of labor. Thus, in Figure 3-18, VMPL(K4) will *always* lie to the

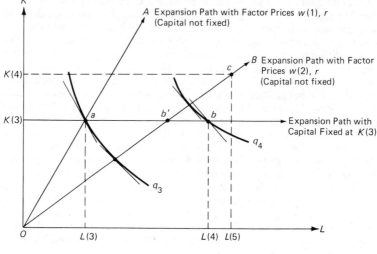

(a) Gross Complements

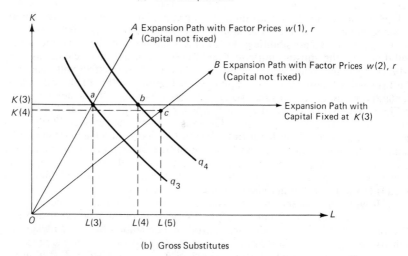

(b) Gross Substitutes

FIGURE 3-19. The firm's adjustment to a decline in the wage rate, holding constant the price of capital.

right of $VMPL(K3)$. It is also clearly cheaper in Figure 3-19(b), to produce output level q_4 along the expansion path $0B$ than it is at point b. Therefore, when the wage rate falls, the quantity of labor demanded at wage rate $w(2)$ after the firm adjusts its capital inputs, $L(5)$, will *always* exceed $L(3)$, the quantity of labor demanded when capital is fixed. It follows that the answer to question (2) is, the labor demand curve with variable capital is *more elastic* than the labor demand curve conditional on a fixed input of capital by the firm.

In general, the firm's labor demand curve when the firm adjusts capital is

$$L = l(w, r, P; \text{technology}) \tag{3-22}$$

which says that the number of units of labor services a competitive firm wishes to purchase depends upon the wage rate, the prices of other inputs, the price of final output, and the firm's technology. A change in either the price of other inputs or that of output will shift the entire demand curve for labor. So will a change in the production function.

To summarize what we have learned in this section: We have shown more rigorously that when the firm adjusts its inputs of *both* L and K to a change in a factor price, it does so in such a way as to minimize the cost of production with the new price(s). We have also demonstrated more rigorously the reason why, when the firm adjusts both inputs, its labor demand curve is more elastic than when capital is fixed.

THE DEMAND FOR LABOR
BY A COMPETITIVE INDUSTRY

A **competitive industry** is a collection of firms, each of which is too small to have any noticeable effect on the prices of output and factors of production. In deriving an industry's demand for labor schedule, we are tempted simply to add up the firm's demand curves. In order to examine the issue of what happens to the desired amount of labor services by an industry as the wage changes, think of what would happen if labor supply conditions changed for an entire industry. If, for example, there were a decline in the wage rate, we know that each firm will use more labor per unit of machinery (substitution effect) and expand production (scale effect) because it will pay to produce more at the going price of output. But will the selling price of output remain unchanged? NO! Although each competitive firm faces a fixed price for its output, an industry does not. As all firms simultaneously attempt to sell more output due to the decline in the price of labor, they as a group will be able to do so only if the price of output falls, inducing consumers to purchase greater quantities. As equation (3-7) shows, the decline in product price will disturb the individual firms' demand curves for labor because their value of marginal product of labor schedules will shift downward. (Why?) As a result, the labor demand schedule of a competitive industry will generally be steeper than the sum of the demand curves of the individual firms. The truth and importance of this fact will become clearer as we develop a numerical example in Figure 3-20.

Assume that we have a competitive industry composed of five identical firms. Figure 3-20(a) depicts one of the firms. At output price $P(1)$ each will hire the amount of labor that equates the value of marginal product of labor $VMPL(P1)$ with w. If, for example, the wage rate were \$5, each firm would hire 10 workers. Industry demand is point B in panel Figure 3-20(b), 50 workers. What would happen if the wage fell to \$2.50? If product price

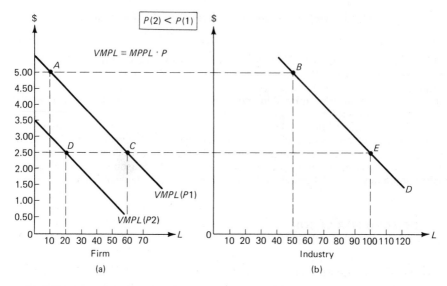

FIGURE 3-20. Derivation of the demand for labor by a competitive industry with five firms

remained unchanged at $P(1)$ when all firms simultaneously expand output, industry demand for labor would be 300 workers, or five times the number of workers demanded by each firm at point C on $VMPL(P1)$. Instead product price falls to $P(2)$ as the industry increases production, and each firm's value of marginal product of labor schedule shifts downward to $VMPL(P2)$. At a wage of $2.50, each firm ultimately purchases 20 units of L and the industry 100 units [point E in Figure 3-20(b)]. Instead of an increase in labor demanded from 50 to 300 workers as the wage rate falls from $5 to $2.50, which would be the case if industry demand were simply the sum of firms' demands, industry demand increases to only 100 workers. Owing to the feedback effect of a decline in product price, the quantity of labor demanded by the *industry* doubles rather than increases by a factor of 6. Thus, *when the number of firms is fixed,* the industry labor demand schedule is made up of points like B and E and the quantity of labor demanded is less responsive to wage changes than the sum of labor demanded by each competitive firm, all other things being equal.

The Role of Industry Composition

The preceding analysis of the demand for labor by a competitive industry ignores what happens to labor demand as firms enter or leave the industry. This is an important omission, because the circumstances surrounding production by an industry may be quite different from those for a firm.

Essentially, the firm's demand curve for a productive factor must slope downward for the same reason that competitive firms must remain small relative to the size of the industry—diseconomies of scale lead to costs increasing proportionately more rapidly than output. Once the firm moves to a new expansion path, the value of marginal product is eventually made equal to marginal factor cost for each input (marginal cost is brought to equality with marginal revenue) as the firm moves northeastward along the path, because we assume that at least one factor (entrepreneurship?) is fixed in amount for each firm and ultimately limits size. As a result, if there were a decline in the wage that must be paid by an *individual firm,* the firm would be prevented from expanding to take over the entire industry by inherent limits to its size—limits that act primarily to lower the marginal productivities of all variable factors as the firm expands. An *industry,* however, may expand output in two ways: (1) Initially, each firm may expand its output. (2) Eventually, new firms may enter the industry if existing firms earn positive economic profits. If the new firms that enter as demand grows are as efficient as the old firms, the only limits on industry growth are demand for output and supplies of variable inputs. If the industry is small, or does not use highly specialized inputs, demand is the only limiting factor.

Thus, the *demand for final output* limits the size of a competitive industry and its demand for inputs, while *diseconomies of scale* (increasing production costs) limit size and input demand of individual firms making up the industry. Since a competitive industry may experience constant, rather than increasing, costs as output expands and new firms are free to enter, diseconomies do not necessarily restrict the industry's demand for labor. In contrast to the situation where the number of firms in the industry is fixed, when the number of firms in the industry is variable, it is ambiguous, a priori, whether the industry's demand for labor is more or less sensitive to wage changes than each of its component firms. The outcome depends on how steeply the industry's output demand curve slopes downward compared to how rapidly each firm's marginal cost rises when output grows. The most important aspect of our analysis of the competitive industry's demand for labor, however, is that in general it is negatively sloped. In Chapter 7 we examine in detail the importance of this for trade unions. Now we can see that the inverse relationship between wages and employment also has important implications for economic policy.

The Demand for Labor
by a Competitive Industry: Applications

Now that we have derived the competitive industry's demand curve for labor, it would be a good idea to see how we can apply it to understand the behavior of the labor market. In the first example, we use the demand curve to analyze the potential effects of a controversial labor market policy—the

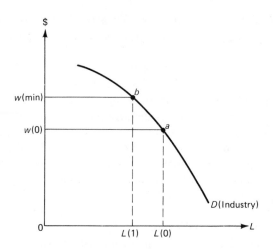

FIGURE 3-21. The effect of a minimum wage
on employment

minimum wage. Since 1938, the federal Fair Labor Standards Act has mandated that many (nowadays most) employers cannot hire workers below a
minimum wage rate. The basic federal minimum wage is now $3.35 per hour.
Many states have minimum wage laws that outdate federal legislation. The
basic intent of minimum wage legislation is to increase the ability of low-
wage workers to earn a living. Other, less altruistic, goals motivate supporters of minimum wage rates as well, and these may explain, as well as or
better than the motive to raise the earnings of low-wage workers, why we
have such legislation.[10] For purposes of the present discussion, however, we
concentrate on what demand theory tells us about whether establishing a
minimum wage can in fact increase the earnings of poor workers.

Consider Figure 3-21, which depicts the labor demand curve for a
particular industry in which the unregulated market wage would be $w(0)$ and
the quantity of labor demanded $L(0)$. What is the effect on the earnings of
workers in this industry if it is decided that $w(0)$ is too low and a minimum
wage established at $w(\text{min})$? Will workers in this industry be helped or
harmed?

In answering this question, the first thing to notice is that the theory of
labor demand predicts employers will respond to imposition of the minimum
wage by reducing the total quantity of labor employed (the number of workers times average hours of work) from $L(0)$ to $L(1)$. Those workers who
retain employment clearly earn more per hour of work than previously, but

---

[10] See, for example, Belton M. Fleisher, *Minimum Wage Regulation in the United States*
(Washington, D.C.: National Chamber Foundation, 1983), and Chapter 7.

other workers may lose their jobs and become worse off, or work hours may be cut back for all workers. To make our problem as simple as possible (which forces us to ignore many important effects of minimum wages), suppose that employers do not discharge any employees, but reach their goal of hiring less labor by reducing the work hours of all employees equally so that $L(1)$ total hours of labor are hired.

As a first approximation to deciding whether workers will be hurt or helped by the imposing of a minimum wage on the industry, as represented in Figure 3-21, we will decide that workers are helped if their earnings rise and harmed if they decline. The direction in which earnings move in response to establishing a minimum wage depends on the elasticity of demand for labor (ε) between points a and b on demand curve D. The (arc) elasticity of demand for labor is defined as[11]

$$\varepsilon \equiv \frac{\dfrac{\Delta L}{L}}{\dfrac{\Delta w}{w}} \qquad \text{(3-23)}$$

Whether earnings rise or fall is determined by the magnitude of the proportionate decline in labor hired that results when the minimum wage is increased by the fraction $\Delta w/w$. This is seen by multiplying both sides of (3-23) by $\Delta w/w$, the percentage change in the wage between $w(\min)$ and $w(0)$, obtaining

$$\frac{\Delta L}{L} = \varepsilon \cdot \frac{\Delta w}{w} \qquad \text{(3-24)}$$

Since total earnings of workers subject to the minimum wage law equal $L \times W$, if the proportionate *decline* in employment is larger in magnitude than the percentage *increase* in the wage rate, earnings will fall; if the decline in employment is proportionately less than the increase in the wage, earnings will rise. Thus, the answer to the question about the impact of a minimum wage on earnings depends on whether ε, the elasticity of demand for labor in this industry, exceeds or falls short of unity (1) in absolute value.

If the absolute value of $\varepsilon > 1$, earnings will fall when the wage rate is increased from $w(0)$ to $w(\min)$. This can be seen somewhat more formally by noting in Figure 3-21 that the change in earnings is the difference between two rectangles whose areas are $[L(0) - L(1)] \times w(0)$ and $[w(\min) - w(0)] \times$

---

[11] *Arc* elasticity refers to a movement from one point on a curve to another, nonadjacent point. *Point* elasticity refers to only one point on the curve. The formula for point elasticity is $\varepsilon = (dL/L)/(dw/w)$, as in Table 2.3.

$L(1)$, or, using the "Δ" notation, $\Delta L \times w(0)$ and $\Delta w \times L(0)$, respectively. Defining the change in earnings as ΔE, we have

$$\Delta E \equiv \Delta L \cdot w(0) + \Delta w \cdot L(0) \tag{3-25}$$

where ΔL is opposite in sign to ΔW, because the demand curve is negatively sloped. From definition (3-23) we can substitute for ΔL, obtaining

$$\Delta E \equiv \varepsilon \cdot L(0) \frac{\Delta w}{w(0)} \cdot w(0) + \Delta w \cdot L(0) \tag{3-26}$$

which simplifies to

$$\Delta E = L(0) \cdot \Delta w(\varepsilon + 1) \tag{3-27}$$

Since $L(0)$ and Δw are positive numbers, ΔE will be positive if $\varepsilon + 1$ is positive. Because the labor demand curve D slopes downward, ε is a negative number, and it is clear ΔE is positive if, and only if, the *absolute value* of ε is less than unity—that is, $-1 < \varepsilon < 0$.

A word of caution.   The preceding application of the labor demand curve used the concept of *elasticity* to show the usefulness of demand theory in analyzing public policy toward the labor market. *Extreme caution* is called for in using such applications. For example, in deciding whether the minimum wage helps workers on the basis of whether the elasticity of demand is less than one in absolute value, we made the following explicit and implicit assumptions: (1) reductions in employment or hours of work are shared equally among all workers; and (2) employers do not adjust working conditions (other than hours of work) or fringe benefits to offset increased hourly wage costs. When these assumptions do not hold, the analysis of the effects of minimum wages becomes more complex.

A useful approach to evaluating the impact of minimum wage legislation on affected workers' well-being would involve using the best available estimates of labor demand elasticity. However, it would also recognize that not all workers are alike in the eyes of their employers. In response to imposition of a minimum wage, employers will not only reduce the amount of labor used, but probably they will scrutinize their workers carefully and lay off those whose performance is least satisfactory. Some workers who were acceptable at wage $w(0)$ may not be employable at $w(\min)$. Moreover, the higher wage that employers are now required to pay is likely to induce additional workers to offer their services. Older workers with more labor force experience and who are less likely to quit their jobs will replace younger workers. Workers who do not have as much education, training, intelligence, good looks, or other favorable characteristics are much less likely to share in the benefits of minimum wage legislation than those with greater ability or acquired skills. Indeed, disadvantaged workers are likely to be harmed if wages are forced up to the point where employers no longer find it worthwhile to hire them.[12] Evaluating minimum wage legislation requires that the tendency of workers at the low end of the "desirability" scale to lose out to those whose qualities make them more valuable to employers be considered an important criterion of policy, along with the overall degree of disemployment implied by the magnitude of the elasticity of demand for labor.

Determinants of the Elasticity of Demand for Labor: Marshall's Rules

From the above discussion, it should be apparent that the elasticity of demand for labor is an important and useful concept with many applications. In addition to helping us understand the implications of minimum wage rates for the economic well-being of low-wage workers, demand elasticity describes the tradeoff between higher wage rates and reduced employment faced by labor unions. Thus, in Chapter 7 you will see that it is in the best interests of union members to reduce the elasticity of demand for their services, and the discussion below should give you some hints on how lowering demand elasticity might be accomplished. Another use of the elasticity concept is to gain insight into the effect of a change in immigration policy on the wage rates of American workers. If we were to eliminate all immigration barriers, how much would the wage rates of low-skilled American workers be reduced as Mexican laborers entered the country in increased numbers?

Economic theory suggests four factors that influence the elasticity of demand for labor: (1) the ease of substituting other inputs for labor in the production process (a formal measure of substitutability is called the *elasticity of substitution*); (2) the elasticity of demand for final output; (3) the importance of labor in total production cost; and (4) the elasticity of supply of other inputs. The greater is any of these factors, the greater is the elasticity of demand for labor. Developed by the famous economist Alfred Marshall, the relationships between the elasticity of demand for labor and these four factors are known as **Marshall's rules.**[13]

---

[12] For documentation of such impacts of minimum wages, see "Rise in Minimum Wage Spurs Some Firms to Cut Work Hours and Hiring of Youth," *Wall Street Journal,* August 15, 1978.

[13] Probably the best formal treatment of Marshall's rules is the appendix to Chapter 6 of J. R. Hicks, *Theory of Wages,* 2d ed. (London: Macmillan, 1964), pp. 241–47. Hicks proves that factors 1, 2, and 4 are unambiguously positively related to labor demand elasticity in the case of a competitive industry with a production function exhibiting constant returns to scale in two inputs, labor and capital. Hicks also identifies an exception to Marshall's third rule, the positive relation between the share of labor cost in total production cost and the elasticity of demand for labor. For a nice verbal explanation of the "economic logic" behind Marshall's rules, see Albert Rees, *The Economics of Trade Unions,* rev. ed. (Chicago: University of Chicago Press, 1977), pp. 66–69.

While it is mathematically too difficult to derive Marshall's rules formally, a few words should help you grasp their validity intuitively. The basic idea to remember is that the demand for any factor is based on two crucial adjustments each firm makes in response to a change in the price of labor— (1) *substitution* of a relatively less costly factor for relatively more expensive factors and (2) expansion or contraction of the *scale* of output. Clearly, the greater the degree of substitutability among factors (as measured by the distance each firm's expansion path moves in response to a change in the price of a factor), the greater the substitution influence on labor demand elasticity will be. To see this, look at Figure 3-16 again. The greater the ease with which L and K can be substituted for each other, the flatter will the isoquants be, and the greater the distance between expansion path 0A and 0B.

If the quantity of an industry's output demanded by purchasers changes a great deal when output price changes, then the greater will be the scale influence on the elasticity of derived labor demand. In Figure 3-20, in an industry with a relatively elastic demand, P(2) will not be very much less than P(1). Therefore, VMPL(P2) will not lie very far to the left of VMPL(P1), and in panel (b), point E will lie relatively far to the right of point B.

If a productive factor constitutes a large proportion of total production cost, then a given change in its price will have a relatively large impact on production cost. That is, each firm's AVC, ATC, and MC will shift by a relatively large amount when a factor price changes. The larger the shift in each firm's cost curves, the greater will be the effect on output price for any given industry demand curve, and the greater will be the change in the quantity of output demanded. Hence, there will be a relatively large scale effect on factor demand.

Finally, when each firm adjusts its demand for, say, capital, in response to a change in the price of labor, the price of capital may change.[14] For example, if the price of labor has fallen for all the firms in an industry, the demand for capital may either increase or decrease (see pages 72–75). If the supply function of capital to the industry is upward-sloping, the price of capital will rise if more capital is demanded and fall if the demand for capital shifts to the left. Either of these changes in the price of capital will affect the quantity of labor demanded. It can be shown mathematically that such change in the price of capital will *always* reduce the elasticity of demand for labor *regardless* of whether, as a result of a decline in labor's wage, the demand curve for capital shifts to the right or to the left.

---

[14] Up to this point we have developed the demand for labor, assuming that the *prices* of other productive factors are constant. That is, we have assumed that the *supply curves* of other factors are infinitely elastic. It is equally valid to derive the labor demand curve assuming that the supply curves of other factors are unchanging but not infinitely elastic. Remember that we are dealing with a competitive *industry*. An upward-sloping factor supply curve to the industry is consistent with a completely elastic supply curve facing each individual *firm*.

Another Application: Shifts in the Demand Curve for Labor

We have derived an industry's demand curve for labor under clearly specified circumstances. If any of these circumstances change, then the demand curve will be altered. For example, we assumed that the state of the supply of other productive factors does not change. Here we briefly analyze the effects of a shift in the supply of another factor on the demand curve for labor. To make the analysis as simple as possible, suppose the supply curve of a nonlabor factor of production to an industry is infinitely elastic, as in Figure 3-22, implying that this industry is an unimportant (small) user relative to the size of the market for the factor. Thus changes in the industry's demand for the factor will not have a noticeable effect on factor price. In Figure 3-22, a factor of production, K, is available to an industry at a price $r(0)$. Given the demand curve, $K(0)$ units of K are used in production. The question we now address is: What would happen to the *demand* curve for *labor,* should the *supply* curve of K shift upward or downward? We will answer this question using the following example.

Meet the "steel collar" workers.   In recent years, new developments in the technology of computers have made it possible to use industrial robots in relatively complicated kinds of manufacturing assembly and fabrication tasks. This new technology can be characterized as a reduction in the price of capital relative to labor, as it now costs less to install a machine to spray-paint an auto or weld a joint than in the past, while wage rates have not declined. Union leaders are worried that the demand curve for labor will

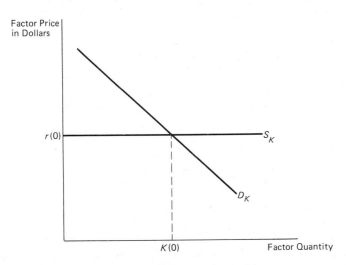

FIGURE 3-22. Infinitely elastic factor supply

decline as a result of the introduction of these new machines. They seem to believe that the reduced price of capital will cause employers to replace blue collar workers with so-called steel collar workers. Employers agree that substitution of capital for labor will occur, but they argue that the reduced production costs they can achieve with new methods will enable them to expand sales sufficiently so that more workers will be hired. In our terminology, employers claim that labor and capital are gross complements while unions argue that they are gross substitutes. These two possibilities are shown graphically in Figure 3-23. What variables will be crucial in determining who is correct? You should be able to answer this question based on your understanding of the determinants of the demand for labor.

Relaxing the Profit-Maximization Goal: Nonprofit Firms and the Government Sector

When any of the conditions specified in deriving the labor demand curve are changed, we should expect the demand curve to be altered as well. We now take a brief look at the demand for labor when the employer's goal is no longer profit maximization. Two such types of employers are (a) "nonprofit" firms and (b) government. When employers have goals other than profit maximization, is it still true that more labor is demanded at lower wages than at higher wages? If so, is the elasticity of demand likely to be larger or smaller in absolute value? The next paragraphs suggest some answers to these questions.

The demand for labor by nonprofit firms. In market economies, resources are allocated through a variety of firms in addition to *for-profit* firms. One type of firm not treated so far includes productive enterprises organized

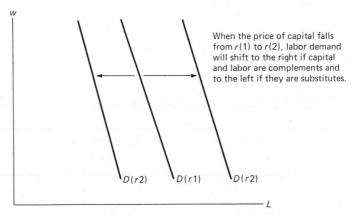

FIGURE 3-23. Labor demand shifts in response to a decrease in the price of capital

around the *nonprofit* principle—usually because such status permits the firms to avoid many taxes they would otherwise have to pay.

For a variety of reasons, society may wish to encourage the use of certain goods and services by awarding firms that produce them tax-exempt status, provided that these firms do not earn profits exceeding specified amounts. In general, very little is yet known about the economic importance of such institutions. We can, however, cite examples of the wide variety of services that they provide. The research and educational activities of The Ford Foundation and private universities, such as Harvard University, are outputs of the private nonprofit sector. It is difficult to attend college and not have some contact with the nonprofit Educational Testing Service. In the ever-growing health-care industry, *for-profit* hospitals play only a minor role.[15]

An interesting topic, and one that economists have only recently attempted to address, is how the demand for labor by a nonprofit firm differs, if at all, from the demand for labor by an otherwise similar profit-maximizing competitive firm. This has important implications for such issues as the cyclic fluctuations in salaries and employment of university faculties and the formation of unions by nonprofessional hospital employees. One of the most careful theoretical examinations of the nonprofit firm is that of Richard Freeman, and we now sketch out some aspects of his work. It is important to remember that we analyze the case where the two types of firms (nonprofit and profit maximizing) have the *same* production functions, operating efficiencies, and (fixed) market prices of inputs and outputs. This permits us to isolate differences in labor demand that stem from the zero-profit restriction, at the expense of neglecting differences due to the particular goals of or reasons for the existence of the nonprofit firm.

To identify some of the differences in labor demand schedules of nonprofit and for-profit firms, we examine the situation where the two types of firms produce a single output during a period of time that is too short for their inputs of capital services to be adjusted. We further simplify our discussion by ignoring any revenues received from gifts or subsidies. Finally, we must specify in detail the objectives of the two firm-types we wish to compare. As usual, we treat the profit-maximizing competitive firm, confronted with a fixed price of output and a fixed wage, as choosing the amount of labor that generates the greatest difference between total revenue and total cost; this includes shutting down whenever the wage bill exceeds total revenue. The nonprofit competitive firm will be assumed to maximize output subject to the constraint that it equates total revenue to total cost whenever profit is *potentially* positive and minimizes its financial losses otherwise.

---

[15] For example, in recent years for-profit hospitals employed less than 5 percent of the total personnel in nongovernmental short-term hospitals. See *Statistical Abstract of the United States,* 1979, p. 112.

We already know that the profit-maximizing firm's labor demand schedule is the portion of its *VMPL* curve that lies below value of average product of labor. The nonprofit firm's labor demand schedule is most easily understood if we first examine the situation where positive potential profit exists and then the situation where only potential losses exist. Profit is defined as

$$\Pi \equiv Pq - wL - F \tag{3-28}$$

where $\Pi \equiv$ profit

$P \equiv$ (fixed) product price

$q \equiv$ output

$w \equiv$ (fixed) wage rate

$L \equiv$ quantity of labor

$F \equiv$ fixed costs (expenditures on plant, equipment, and so on).

Figure 3-24 shows the firm's *VAPL* and *VMPL* curves along with a curve showing *VAPL* less fixed costs per unit of labor. From our earlier discussion of the firm's demand for labor (with capital fixed), you should recall that the firm will shut down if w is greater than maximum *VAPL* and earns zero economic profit if $(VAPL - w) \times L$ equals fixed cost. Formally, potential profit is positive if

$$VAPL - \frac{F}{L} > w \tag{3-29}$$

Therefore, potential profit is positive if w lies below the curve labeled *VAPL* $- F/L$ in Figure 3-24.

For wage rates where Π is *potentially* positive, the nonprofit firm achieves $\Pi = 0$ by choosing L such that

$$Pq = wL + F \tag{3-30}$$

or

$$w = \frac{Pq}{L} - \frac{F}{L} \tag{3-31}$$

Notice that the firm term on the right-hand side of (3-31) is *VAPL*. Thus, for values of w associated with potentially positive profit [w less than $w(1)$ in Figure 3-24], the nonprofit firm chooses its labor input so as to equate $(VAPL - F/L)$ to w. In Figure 3-24, then, the segment of $(VAPL - F/L)$ to the right of B represents one portion of the labor demand schedule of the nonprofit firm. By contrast, a *profit-maximizing* firm would demand labor such that $w = VMPL$, which is less labor than along *VAPL* $- F/L$.

Two aspects of the demand for labor when profit is potentially positive

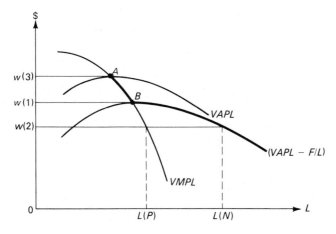

FIGURE 3-24. The demand for labor by a nonprofit firm

are readily apparent. First, the nonprofit firm uses *more* labor than the profit-maximizing firm. At a wage of $w(2)$, for example, the nonprofit firm employs $[L(N) - L(P)]$ more units of labor than the for-profit firm. Second, the demand for labor by the nonprofit firm is *more* elastic (flatter) than the demand for labor by the profit-maximizing firm. But what are the two respective labor demand schedules when wage rates *exceed* $w(1)$? For values of w exceeding $w(1)$ in Figure 3-24, the inequality (3-29) is reversed, and potential profit is always *negative*. Therefore, the nonprofit firm can only expect to minimize its losses, just as a for-profit firm, and it will hire labor up to the amount where $w = VMPL$. The demand curve for both for-profit and nonprofit firms is $VMPL$ when the wage rate is between $w(1)$ and $w(0)$, and both firms go out of business when the wage exceeds $w(0)$.

To summarize, when potential profit is positive, a nonprofit firm should exhibit greater employment variation in response to a particular wage rate change than a for-profit firm, ceteris paribus. Under no circumstances should the labor demand schedule of the nonprofit firm be *less* elastic than that of the profit-maximization firm, other things equal.

The demand for labor in the public sector. The demand for labor by government agencies is more difficult to analyze than that of profit-maximizing or nonprofit firms, because the ability of government employers to maintain themselves does not depend directly on their success in selling output for revenue. Indeed a classic rationale for government's providing any good or service is that markets are not efficient providers of goods or services in cases where it is impractical to exclude consumers or users who do not pay. A common example is military protection. The cost of protecting a country from invasion is largely independent of the number of consumers of protection, the citizens, and to protect one citizen from invasion is hardly less costly than protecting a much larger number. Because military protection must be provided for everyone or no one at all, *individual* citizens have no incentive to pay if they are not required by law to do so. This is not to say that governments never engage in activities that cannot be undertaken efficiently by private, for-profit firms. Indeed, there are many examples of such parallels—state-owned liquor stores, state-owned workers' compensation insurance systems, government agencies that deliver parcels, and, in other Western countries, state-owned banks, auto manufacturers, and steel companies. However, the general ability of governments to raise taxes and to transfer receipts among various programs insulates most of their activities from the need to pay all costs from sales-generated revenues or voluntary donations and thus affects governments' demands for all inputs, including labor.

Despite their tax-raising powers, governments do face constraints. They are clearly motivated to maintain themselves in office. In a democratic society this requires obtaining an adequate number of votes. Votes will not be forthcoming if a sufficient number of citizens are dissatisfied with the output of government services or the cost of providing these services as reflected in service price or taxes. Moreover, the services provided by government that can influence voting behavior include the quantity and type of labor hired and the wages paid, as well as what labor produces. Private firms (either profit or nonprofit) typically do not find themselves in this position.[16]

One implication that follows from the preceding discussion is that it may be inappropriate to consider government's demand for labor in this chapter, which deals with employers who are price-takers in both input markets and product markets. To the extent governments participate only in those activities where private firms could not effectively charge *individual consumers* for services or goods provided or where they have created monopoly power for themselves by restricting private firms from entering, say, the retail liquor business, governments can be viewed as product market monopolists, not price-takers. Even so, state and local governments are not immune from competitive pressures in product markets, since citizens can "vote with their feet" by leaving communities where the output-tax mix is inferior and moving to those that better match their desires.[17] Moreover, if we view *political parties* or *coalitions* as competing among themselves for

---

[16] An exception would be symphony, opera, art, and charitable foundations whose directors and prominent staff acquire social prestige and contribute money in return. For a theoretical analysis of the public sector's demand for labor, see Melvin W. Reder, "Labor in the Public and Nonprofit Sectors," ed. Daniel S. Hamermesh (Princeton, N.J.: Princeton University Press, 1975), pp. 1–48.

[17] A seminal paper on this topic is Charles Tiebout, "A Pure Theory of Local Expenditures," *Journal of Political Economy,* 64 (October 1956), pp. 416–24.

the right to manage government's provision of services, then competition takes place through elections, even if not through conventional market forces.

The main lesson to be drawn from the last few paragraphs is that, as complex as analysis of a profit-maximizing competitive industry's demand for labor may appear, it is even more difficult to develop a systematic discussion of governmental behavior. Perhaps the most crucial difference between government and private employers arises from the dependence of votes on whom is hired and at what wages. If a private firm does not minimize production costs, competition will eventually do it in. By contrast, a governmental agency that vigorously pursues cost minimization is likely to incur the wrath of labor unions and other special interest groups within the labor force. A decline in demand for its output or an influx of new labor services would likely lead a private firm to seek wage concessions from the labor unions it deals with, to replace high cost labor with low wage workers, or to lay off a number of employees. By contrast, governments are less likely to risk losing votes by offending powerful employee groups they deal with directly or by appearing exploitative to labor and the public at large. Governments are likely to include the vote-generating capacity of individual workers as an addition to their conventional value in production of output when making hiring or layoff decisions. Thus, other things equal, a government is more likely to hire and less likely to discharge an inefficient worker (measured by conventional *VMP*) than is a private employer. This is the glue that helps hold political "machines" together. Nevertheless, governments will lose votes to the extent taxes or deficits are raised with no perceived increase in the value of governmental services provided, other things equal.

All things considered, it would be extremely surprising if the government's demand for labor were not a negative function of the wage rate. Even governments must economize on inputs that become relatively more expensive. Because of governments' sensitivity to their need to maintain political support, however, the degree and rapidity with which the quantity of labor demanded is reduced as labor costs rise is likely to be smaller than in the private sector of the economy. Thus, we expect that the elasticity of demand for labor by governments is likely to be smaller than that in the private sector.

If this suspicion is correct, it bears important implications for the effect of public employee unions on wages. As we show in Chapter 7, a principal determinant of a union's bargaining strength is the employment loss that occurs when wages are increased. If labor demand elasticities for public sector workers are low, then unions bargaining with government employers will have especially great power to extract wage increases for their members.

Before going on to discuss empirical evidence on labor demand, it would be a good idea to review briefly some of the factors that cause labor

TABLE 3-2   Factors That Cause Labor Demand to Shift

Factor Affecting Labor Demand	Direction of Shift in Labor Demand (Change in Quantity of Labor Demanded at a Given Wage Rate)
1. Increase in price of a gross complement	Decline
2. Increase in price of a gross substitute	Increase
3. Increase in demand for final output	Increase
4. Changing firm's status from "for-profit" to nonprofit	No shift or increase

demand curves to shift. Therefore, you should examine Table 3-2 and try to recall why the factors listed cause labor demand to shift. If the reasons are not clear in your mind, it would be a good idea to review briefly before going on to the next section.

EVIDENCE ON THE DEMAND FOR LABOR

Economic theory implies unequivocally that the demand curve for labor is a negative function of the wage rate. Important economic policy and collective bargaining strategy questions hinge on the degree to which the quantity of labor demanded falls when wages rise, other things equal. Only empirical investigation can determine the magnitude of the elasticity of demand for labor. Estimating labor demand curves is a highly technical aspect of empirical studies in economics, and we cannot present an in-depth analysis of research in this area. However, the following material should give you an idea of the results of attempts to arrive at quantitative knowledge of the elasticity of labor demand in several sectors of the economy.

The Elasticity of Demand for Low-Wage Workers

One important reason for measuring the elasticity of labor demand is to know whether imposing a minimum wage is likely to raise the average earnings of workers covered by the law. As we discussed previously, this is a very rough guide to whether minimum wage legislation constitutes good or bad economic policy. If the elasticity of demand for covered workers exceeds 1 in absolute value, then their average earnings as well as employment opportunities will fall when a minimum wage is imposed or increased.

Numerous studies have provided estimates of how much the quantity of low-wage workers falls when the minimum wage is raised. What is tricky about work in this area is to isolate the demand for only those workers whose market rate of pay would be less than the minimum wage if there were no legal minimum. Sufficiently detailed information to permit one to estimate the elasticity of demand for these low-wage workers is seldom available, and approximations are usually necessary. One approach is to estimate the demand for labor in *low-wage industries*. Even in these industries many workers earn more than the minimum. For example in March 1964, six months after the basic federal minimum wage was increased to $1.25 per hour, only 23 percent of workers in four low-wage manufacturing industries (tobacco, textiles, apparel, and leather) in the lowest-wage region of the United States (the South) earned $1.30 per hour or less. Probably the lowest-paid group of workers covered by federal minimum wage legislation are nontipped restaurant employees. In October 1966, six months before minimum wage legislation was first extended to cover these workers, only 18 percent of covered nontipped workers in the South received less than $1.00 per hour (the minimum wage effective April 1967), while 71 percent received over $1.05.[18]

In addition to the difficulty of measuring the effect of minimum wage increases on the demand for directly affected workers when data on employment of these workers are inadequate, there is a general problem that involves controlling for the simultaneous influence of forces influencing the demand for low-wage labor other than the increase in the minimum wage. Labor demand theory implies that an increase in the minimum wage will result in lower employment, *other things equal*. In a growing economy with periodic business fluctuations, such as in the United States and other countries, there is a tendency for both employment and wage rates in most industries to increase over time—faster in some years and less rapidly in others. Therefore, if an increase in the minimum wage is followed by an increase rather than a decline in employment, the theory of labor demand is not necessarily refuted. Long-term trends and business-cycle effects must be statistically eliminated before an adequate test of labor demand theory can be carried out. The theory implies only that *when the minimum wage increases in relation to the level of wages that would have prevailed in the absence of the minimum, the quantity of labor demanded will rise less rapidly or fall more rapidly than would have otherwise occurred*. This important and basic principle of empirical research is frequently overlooked or conveniently ignored. A glaring example is a statement by former Secretary of Labor F. Ray Marshall. He said that since teenage employment grew after the 1978 increases in the minimum wage, the minimum wage therefore had not reduced labor market opportunities for youth.[19] To see what is fallacious about Secretary Marshall's conclusion, review Table 3-2 and then draw a

---

[18] U.S. Department of Labor, Wage and Hour and Public Contracts Division, *Eating and Drinking Places* (Washington, D.C.: Government Printing Office, 1968), Table 3.

[19] "Higher Labor's Price," *Wall Street Journal,* August 15, 1978.

diagram of the demand for labor similar to Figure 3-21. Show the simultaneous effects on the quantity of labor demanded of (a) an increase in the minimum wage and (b) an increase in the demand curve for final output. What is the net effect on employment?

Whether a study of minimum wage effects has adequately controlled for other influences on labor demand is frequently subject to debate among equally qualified researchers. This is true not only in minimum wage studies but in much empirical work in economics, and not only in economics but in all other social and natural scientific disciplines as well. Before you conclude that the practice of economic research is more art than science compared to other areas of knowledge, think for a moment of the arguments surrounding such medical research as the effect of marijuana smoking on the probability of developing genetic defects in your children or the difficulty scientists have in predicting long-term weather trends. The problems in these areas are similar to those faced by economists: laboratory experiments are difficult or of limited use and reflect the influence of a multitude of forces in addition to those whose effects we wish to measure. These other forces may be unknown or difficult to measure precisely. Thus, research conclusions are subject to challenge and revision as alternative approaches are tried and contradictory research results emerge.

There are estimates of the sensitivity of the demand for low-wage labor to increases in the minimum wage based on studies that appear to be reasonably well designed, considering all the difficulties enumerated above. One such study was published by Albert Zucker in 1973. Zucker examined employment in seven low-wage United States manufacturing industries: confectionery products, tobacco, men's and boys' furnishings, girls' and children's outerwear, fertilizers, and footwear. These industries were selected because they occupied the lowest portion of the wage distribution in United States manufacturing. The period over which employment was studied started in the last quarter of 1947 and ended in the last quarter of 1966; it encompassed increases in the minimum wage from $0.40 per hour to $1.25 per hour. The average hourly rate of pay for production workers in these industries was less than $1.10 in 1949.

Zucker assumed that had the minimum wage not increased, the average rate of pay and employment in the seven low-wage industries included in his study would have behaved in a pattern that bears a fixed relationship to the other, higher-wage manufacturing industries. That is, the trend of economic growth and short-term fluctuations due to the business cycle would have been reflected in the low-wage industries' employment and pay proportionately to their impact on the rest of manufacturing. After accounting for the long-term growth in employment that would have occurred in the absence of increases in the minimum wage and for fluctuations in employment over the business cycle, Zucker's study implies that every 1 percent increase in the minimum wage probably resulted in more than a 1 percent decline in the total employment of covered workers measured as the number of workers times their average hours of work.[20]

A study published by George E. Tauchen in 1981 used a procedure similar to Zucker's to estimate the effect of minimum wages on employment, rather than on total hours, in the tobacco, textiles, apparel, and leather industries over the period 1949–74. He estimated an elasticity of total industry employment demanded with respect to average industry wages that had an absolute value of well in excess of unity (about 1.6), once again implying that the elasticity of demand for low-wage workers is substantial and that the average earnings of these workers falls when the minimum wage is raised.

In 1961, minimum wage legislation was extended to retail trade, where, because average hourly earnings are much lower than in manufacturing, the disemployment effects of a legislated wage floor would be expected to be more severe than in the typical manufacturing industry. Fleisher studied the impact of minimum wages on employment in retail trade and found that the reduction in total hours of work attributable to the minimum wage, other things equal, implies an elasticity of demand for low-wage workers of about minus two—probably larger than in low-wage manufacturing. Finally, John M. Peterson estimates that about one-third of the total reduction in work hours attributable to minimum wages has occurred in retail trade. This is interesting because in 1970 retail trade accounted for only about 15 percent of total employment in the United States.

The Elasticity of Demand for Labor in United States Manufacturing

In 1980, Kim B. Clark and Richard B. Freeman of Harvard University published a study measuring the elasticity of demand for labor in all United States manufacturing industries. They estimated the relationship between employment, both number of workers and total hours, and two factor prices—average hourly earnings and the price of capital services. In their study, Clark and Freeman estimated the influence of these two factor prices, holding constant the level of output and the effects of unmeasured variables that change steadily over time ("trend" variables). This is a generally accepted procedure for holding other things equal in studies of the demand for

---

[20] Zucker found the elasticity of total hours of *all workers* demanded with respect to the *average* wage to be approximately minus one. Since low-wage workers directly affected by the minimum wage constitute only a fraction of total employment, and because firms will substitute high-wage workers for low-wage workers after the minimum is raised, the proportionate decline in total labor hired will be less than the decline in the total hours of work demanded only from low-wage employees. On the other hand, the proportional increase in the average wage paid to all workers will be smaller than the proportional increase in the minimum wage. George E. Tauchen shows that the net effect of the failure to measure the employment and wages of low-wage workers directly is to underestimate the elasticity of demand for low wage workers. See his "Some Evidence on Cross-Sector Effects of the Minimum Wage," *Journal of Political Economy,* June 1981, pp. 527–47.

labor. You should recognize that by treating sales as an independent influence on labor demand, Clark and Freeman are able to estimate only the *substitution effects* of changes in wage rates and the price of capital on the quantity of labor demanded. Using a number of different statistical techniques, they derive labor demand and elasticities in the neighborhood of 0.5.

   A deeper look at Clark and Freeman's study.* It is worth looking more closely at one of the approaches taken by Clark and Freeman in their study of the elasticity of demand for manufacturing labor. In their approach it is recognized that firms do not instantaneously reach their new level of desired employment when there is a change in factor prices. The *desired* level of employment that they would like to have is assumed to be

$$\log L_t^* = \alpha(0) + \alpha(1) \log w_t + \alpha(2) \log r_t + \alpha(3) \log S_t + \alpha(4) T \qquad \textbf{(3-32)}$$

where $L_t^* \equiv$ desired production worker employment in manufacturing
  $w_t \equiv$ average hourly earnings
  $r_t \equiv$ the cost of capital services
  $S_t \equiv$ shipments of manufactured goods
  $T \equiv$ trend variable (= 1 in the first quarter of 1956 through 107 in the third quarter of 1977)
  $t \equiv$ index denoting the quarter in which data are measured (1 through 107— see T above).

It is further assumed that the process by which firms adjust toward their desired employment levels can be described by the equation

$$\log L_t - \log L_{t-1} = \lambda(\log L_t^* - \log L_{t-1}), \qquad 0 < \lambda < 1 \qquad \textbf{(3-33)}$$

where L_t = actual employment in the tth quarter. Equation (3-33) implies that firms try to make up a fraction of the difference between their actual and desired employment between any two quarter-year time periods. Substituting equation (3-32) into (3-33) for L_t^* yields

$$\frac{1}{\lambda} \log L_t - \frac{1-\lambda}{\lambda} \log L_{t-1} = \alpha(0) + \alpha(1) \log w_t + \alpha(2) \log r_t$$
$$+ \alpha(3) \log S_t + \alpha(1) T \qquad \textbf{(3-34)}$$

Multiplying through by λ and subtracting $(1 - \lambda) \log L_{t-1}$ from both sides gives us one of the labor demand equations estimated by Clark and Freeman:

$$\log L_t = \lambda\alpha(0) + \lambda\alpha(1) \log w_t + \lambda\alpha(2) \log r_t + \lambda\alpha(3) \log S_t \qquad \textbf{(3-35)}$$
$$+ \lambda\alpha(4)T + (1 - \lambda) \log L_{t-1}$$

   Since the partial derivative of $\log L_t^*$ with respect to $\log w_t$ in equation (3-32), $\partial \log L_t / \partial \log w_t = \alpha(1)$, is the same as

$$\frac{\partial L_t}{\partial w_t} \frac{w_t}{L_t}$$

or the elasticity of demand for labor, holding constant the other variables in the equation, we can obtain the estimated elasticity of demand if we divide the estimated

---

* This section contains more technical material that may be skipped without loss of continuity.
If you skip, go to p. 95.

coefficient of log w_t in equation (3-35) by one minus the estimated coefficient of log L_{t-1}. Estimating equation (3-35) by means of regression analysis, Clark and Freeman obtained

$$L_t = -0.052 - 0.285w_t + 0.056\dot{r}_t + 0.583S_t$$
$$\quad (0.098) \quad (0.039) \quad (0.019) \quad (0.033)$$
$$\quad -0.003T + 0.421L_{t-1}, \quad R^2 = 0.99$$
$$\quad (0.0002) \quad (0.037)$$

(3-36)

where the numbers in parentheses are standard errors. (You may wish to review at this point the discussion of regression equations in Chapter 2.) Dividing the coefficients of w, r, and S by $(1 - 0.421)$ provides us with the following estimated relationships:

1. The elasticity of demand for labor with respect to the wage rate equals -0.49, output and other variables constant.
2. The elasticity of demand for labor with respect to the price of capital services is $+0.096$, output and other variables constant.
3. When sales grow by 1 percent, the demand for labor grows by an equal amount if the prices of labor and capital and other variables do not change.
4. If L_t^*, desired employment, is not equal to L_{t-1}, actual employment last quarter, 57.9 percent of the difference is made up between last quarter and the present quarter.

(Why do you think the coefficient of T is negative?)

Clark and Freeman's estimate of the elasticity of demand for manufacturing workers is lower than estimates of the elasticity of demand for low-wage labor in low-wage industries, discussed above. Still, it is a fairly large number in terms of the magnitude of the change in the total amount of labor that would occur in response to an exogenous change in wages—say due to collective bargaining. This is especially so when it is remembered that employment changes associated with adjustments in *output* levels would occur *in addition* to a one-half percent decline in employment per 1 percent increase in wage rates due to substitution of capital for labor. To gain some idea of how large the *total* adjustment in labor input would be, consider the following "guesstimate." The share of payroll in total cost in manufacturing was approximately 0.45 in 1976.[21] Thus a 1 percent increase in average wage rates would cause production cost—and output price—to rise by about 0.45 percent. If the elasticity of demand for manufacturing production is 1.0, which is probably a reasonable assumption, the resulting decline in the quantity of output demanded would be 0.45 percent. Thus the *total* decline in the quantity of labor demanded in response to a 1 percent increase in wages would be about 0.5 percent (substitution effect) plus 0.45 percent scale effect, or close to 1 percent.

The Demand for Labor by Nonprofit and Government Employers

Relatively little is known about the elasticity of demand for labor by nonprofit firms or by government. Freeman has examined the demand for labor by institutions of higher education using a fairly complex model of faculty demand, salary adjustment, and supply. His study includes public as well as private nonprofit colleges and universities over the period 1920–70.

---

[21] *Statistical Abstract of the United States*, 1979, p. 797.

TABLE 3-3   Selected Estimates of Labor Demand Elasticities

Industry or Labor Force Group and Study Where Estimate Appears	Elasticity (Absolute Value)
Minimum-wage workers in low-wage manufacturing:	
Zucker (1973)	At least 1.0
Tauchen (1981)	About 1.6
Minimum-wage workers in retail trade:	
Fleisher (1981)	About 2.0
Production workers in manufacturing:	About 0.92 (including
Clark and Freeman (1980)	scale effect)
Institutions of higher education:	
Freeman (1973)	Between 0.4 and 0.7
State and local government employees:	
Ehrenberg (1973)	
Police	Between 0.01 and 0.35
Public welfare workers	Between 0.33 and 1.13

He finds that the demand for faculty declines in response to increases in salaries, and he estimates that the absolute value of elasticity of demand is between 0.4 and 0.7. These estimates are somewhat smaller than those for the private, for-profit industries presented above. The tenure system and the tendency to upgrade faculty quality when markets are depressed, rather than increase quantity, may account for these relatively small magnitudes. This means that it may not be appropriate to use data for college faculty to test the hypothesis that nonprofit firms' labor demand is likely to be more elastic than that of for-profit firms.

The demand for state and local government employees has been estimated by Ronald Ehrenberg over the years 1958–69 for ten categories of government activities. His method involved establishing the relationship between the number of full-time equivalent employees in each category (education, highway, public welfare, and so on) to their rates of pay corrected for inflation, holding constant the level of each state's total employment budget for state and local employees[22] and a small list of other variables that varies among government categories. (For example, the proportion of young people in the population is held constant in estimating the demand for education employees with respect to their wage rates.) Ehrenberg found that the elasticity of demand for public employees is negative (employment falls as wages

---

[22] Technically, the *predicted* value of the budget was used to avoid feedback from employment to the budget that would result in biased results.

rise) and considerably less than one in all categories except public welfare. The estimated elasticities range from between 0.01 and 0.35 for police to between 0.33 and 1.13 for public welfare workers. Ehrenberg's estimates of labor demand elasticities for public employees lend support to the idea, developed above, that public sector employees' labor demand elasticities are likely to be smaller than those of private, for-profit firms.

Labor markets are far too complex to allow us to summarize the responsiveness of the quantity of labor demanded to changes in wage rates. Table 3-3 lists the labor demand elasticities cited as examples in this section. These estimates provide a sample indicating roughly the range of elasticities that has been reported by researchers.

*FRONTIERS OF LABOR DEMAND ANALYSIS

Up to now, we have studied the effect of changes in the prices of factors of production on the quantity of labor demanded. Wage rates and other factor prices have been viewed from the individual firm's point of view—determined by forces of demand supply beyond its direct control. Technically, we have assumed that firms adjust to *exogenously* determined factor prices, *exogenous* meaning that these prices are generated *outside* the firm's control. The analytical framework we have used is based on the concept of a production function, an algebraic relationship between a firm's inputs and output. In this section we adopt the useful fiction (assumption) that the entire economy can be viewed as a single "firm" with a well-defined production function. Moreover, we turn the theory of derived demand on its head, so to speak, by viewing changes in factor prices as being determined *endogenously* in response to *exogenous* shifts in factor quantities. From the viewpoint of the entire economy, events such as major changes in population and labor force size, as well as investment in new capital, generate shifts in factor supplies that interact with factor demand curves to determine factor price.

At the most fundamental level, it is incorrect to treat many shifts in aggregate (economywide) factor supplies as determining, but not determined by, factor prices. However, to develop a *general equilibrium* approach that explains factor supplies, demands, and prices simultaneously is too complex a task for this text. Fortunately, we can make significant progress in understanding the aggregate labor market by assuming that factor supplies affect productivity and factor prices but are not affected by them. In doing this, we pay the cost of some degree of inaccuracy, but we benefit by gaining some understanding of two important topics relating to the economic well-being of the work force: (1) causes of productivity growth and (2) the effect of changes in the quantity of one type of labor (for example, young high school graduates) on the productivity and earning power of other labor force groups (for example, older college grads).

Factor Growth, Factor Proportions, and Productivity Growth

Figure 3-25 reintroduces what is by now a familiar concept, part of a production function, which we now assume refers to an entire economy. The two solid lines are isoquants, which show how various combinations of labor and capital can be

---

* This section contains more technical material that may be skipped without loss of continuity. If you skip, go to p. 103.

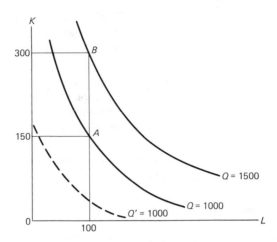

FIGURE 3-25. A production function for the economy

used to produce the economy's total production (*Q*) as measured, say, by gross national product. At point *A*, for example, 100 units of labor are combined with 150 units of capital to produce gross national product (GNP) of 1,000.

The average physical product of labor in this economy is a commonly used measure of productivity, $Q/L = 10$. There are 100 units of output produced for each worker. This measure of productivity is related to general economic well-being, since in a market economy output will be divided among households on the basis of their ownership of the productive resources, labor and capital, and the marginal products of these factors. Most households provide both labor and capital to business firms in return for the income derived. Thus, if average GNP per worker rises, so will average household income.

What are some causes of changes in labor productivity as measured by Q/L? Historically, one of the most important has been investment in physical capital in the form of new plant and equipment. Suppose households save part of their incomes and buy shares or bonds from business firms that use this saving to invest in additional capital. In Figure 3-25, if the capital stock, *K*, thus increases to 300 (point *B*), GNP will rise to 1,500, and labor productivity Q/L will become 150, half again as large as before.

The idea that an increase in the quantity of capital can cause an increase in the productivity of labor should not be new to you. In deriving the demand curve for labor when the firm adjusts its inputs of both labor and capital, we saw how the marginal product of labor (*MPPL*) shifts when the input of capital services changes. For individual *firms* we could not specify whether an increase in capital would cause the *MPPL* curve to shift to the right (increase) or to the left (decrease). This was because each firm is assumed to be ultimately limited in the amount it can produce by diseconomies of scale, or increasing production cost per unit of output, as production grows. Thus, an increase in the scale of operations accompanying an increase in capital could lower the marginal and average product of labor. While this could theoretically be true of the entire economy, too, the overwhelming weight of evidence on the relationship between the amount of capital and labor productivity in the United States and throughout the world supports the view that increases in the amount of capital relative to labor raise labor productivity.

Before going on to discuss other possible causes of changes in labor productivity, it will be helpful to introduce a more formal method for discussing and measuring the concepts that are important in productivity analysis. The basic concept is the production function, as we have already seen. A formal, algebraic representation of the production function that has received wide application in economics is the Cobb-Douglas function:[23]

$$Q = \alpha L^{\beta} K^{1-\beta} \qquad (3\text{-}37)$$

where $Q \equiv$ output
$\quad L \equiv$ input of labor services
$\quad K \equiv$ input of capital services.

The parameter β is assumed to be greater than zero and less than 1. While this function may seem complex or a little intimidating at first glance, it is in reality rather simple, and it is very easy to use to illustrate our discussion of productivity. For example, the most commonly used measure of productivity, output per unit of labor, takes on the following form with a Cobb-Douglas production function:

$$\frac{Q}{L} = \frac{\alpha L^{\beta} K^{1-\beta}}{L} = \alpha \left(\frac{K}{L}\right)^{1-\beta} \qquad (3\text{-}38)$$

Since $0 < \beta < 1$, labor productivity clearly increases when K does, holding L constant. It should also be easy for you to see that the *marginal* physical product of labor is

$$MPPL = \alpha\beta \left(\frac{K}{L}\right)^{1-\beta} \qquad (3\text{-}39)$$

which is also a positive function of K, holding L constant.

Another cause of changes in labor productivity is a change in the *quality* of labor. Suppose that because the labor force is becoming better educated or older and more experienced, a typical worker today is 10 percent more productive than a year ago. This amounts to saying that one worker working one hour today produces as much as a worker used to produce in one hour and six minutes. To see how this improvement in worker quality affects our usual measure of productivity, suppose that we measure productivity this year and compare our measurement with productivity last year, assuming that the quantity of work hours and the quantity of capital services used have not changed. Using the numbers (0) and (1) to denote last year and this year, the ratio of productivity this year compared to last year can be expressed as $Q(1)/L(1) \div Q(0)/L(0)$. From equation (3-37) we can see that increasing the *effective* input of labor between last year and this year by 10 percent will result in output equal to

$$Q(1) = \alpha[1.1L(0)]^{\beta}K(0)^{1-\beta} = 1.1^{\beta}\alpha L(0)^{\beta}K(0)^{1-\beta} = 1.1^{\beta}Q(0) \qquad (3\text{-}40)$$

Thus, if we calculate productivity in terms of the "raw" quantity of labor, the ratio of productivity this year to that of last year would turn out to be

$$\frac{Q(1)}{L(0)} \div \frac{Q(0)}{L(0)} = 1.1^{\beta}Q(0) \div Q(0) = 1.1^{\beta} \qquad (3\text{-}41)$$

---

[23] C. W. Cobb and Paul A. Douglas, "A Theory of Production," *American Economic Review*, 18 (May 1928), pp. 139–65.

Equation (3-41) shows that when labor quality improves, productivity as conventionally measured will increase. If you understand this example, you should be able to show that a 10 percent improvement in the quality of *capital* between last year and this will lead to a ratio of this year's labor productivity to that of last year's amounting to $1.1^{1-\beta}$.

Still another cause of productivity change can be attributed to what is often called improvements in technology. We are constantly discovering new ways of using labor and capital, which are frequently embodied in inventions and innovations applied to production processes that increase the efficiency of *both* labor and capital. For example, the invention of the transistor and, later, the integrated circuit has increased both labor and capital productivity in computation over a millionfold. When such technological advances increase the marginal products of labor and capital by the same proportion, it is sometimes convenient to show their influence via an increase in the efficiency parameter, α, of equation (3-37), and a symmetrical, inward shift of the isoquants in Figure 3-25, such as from $Q = 1,000$ to $Q' = 1,000$. It is clear from equation (3-38) that an increase in α will cause productivity, Q/L, to increase proportionately.

It is very important to note that increases in productivity are usually not simply accidents. Rather, they almost always are the result of an expenditure of resources on such activities as research and development of new production techniques, education, training, reallocation of resources from less rewarding to more rewarding uses, and so on. Thus, the transistor was not "discovered" in the way John Sutter stumbled on a gold nugget in his California mill stream. It resulted from a well-designed and costly research program. Consequently, an increase in measures of productivity attributed simply to an increase in the value of the efficiency parameter tell us little or nothing about the *causes* of productivity growth unless we can explain why efficiency has improved. Indeed, that is what interesting and useful studies of productivity attempt to do.

Although all economists recognize the need to *account for* as well as simply *report* or measure productivity increases, some researchers believe it is misleading not to treat *all* changes in productivity as changes in effective inputs.[24] These economists would prefer to include as arguments (right-hand variables) in the production function *all* inputs, such as the quality as well as quantity of labor and capital, research and development expenditures, and so on with the aim of measuring their contributions to output directly rather than indirectly through changes in productivity. To show how these two approaches complement each other, suppose that there is a 10 percent improvement in the quality of *both* labor and capital between last year and this year. From the development of equations (3-40) and (3-41) you should see that this will lead to a conventionally measured ratio of productivity this year to that of last year equal to $1.1^{\beta+1-\beta} = 1.1$, which amounts to the same thing as a 10 percent increase in the efficiency parameter α. Either the increase in productivity as reflected in $\alpha(1) = 1.1\alpha(0)$ must be accounted for in terms of improved labor and capital inputs, or we can include effective labor and capital measures directly in the production function, obtaining

$$Q(1) = 1.1Q(0) = \alpha[1.1L(0)]^{\beta}[1.1K(0)]^{1-\beta} \qquad \textbf{(3-42)}$$

with α and β constants, not changing over time. Both approaches recognize that in the end, unexplained productivity growth is no more than a measure of our ignorance of the causes of economic progress.

---

[24] An easy-to-read summary of this dispute is contained in Mark Perlman, "One Man's Baedeker to Productivity Growth Discussions," *Contemporary Economic Problems 1979* (Washington, D.C.: American Enterprise Institute, 1979), pp. 79–116.

TABLE 3-4

1. Annual Percentage Rate of Change in Real Gross Product Per Capita, United States:

1800–1888	1855–1890	1889–1919	1919–1948	1948–1973
1.1	1.6	2.1	1.8	2.3

2. Annual Percentage Rate of Change in Real Gross Product Per Unit of Labor, United States:

1929–1948	1948–1966	1966–1973	1973–1978
0.3	3.5	2.1	1.1

Source: John W. Kendrick, "Productivity Trends and the Recent Slow-down," in *Contemporary Economic Problems 1979* (Washington, D.C.: American Enterprise Institute, 1979), Tables 1 and 4.

Application: Productivity growth in the United States and international comparisons. Over the years, real gross product per unit of labor has grown considerably in the United States as well as in other nations. Nevertheless, productivity growth has fluctuated sharply over time and has been much higher in some countries than in others. In many industrial countries over the past thirty years, productivity has grown more rapidly than in the United States. It is important to remember that we are talking here about productivity *growth*, not *levels*. In terms of productivity levels as measured by national output per person employed, the United States remains above other nations, but the margin of productive superiority has narrowed considerably. For example, in 1950 real product per employed person was only 15.6 percent as high in Japan as in the United States and 85.0 percent as high in Canada. By 1979, Canada's productivity had risen to 92.1 percent of that in the United States, while Japan's had grown over fourfold *relative* to that in the United States, to 68.4 percent.[25] An examination of Table 3-4 shows that productivity growth in the United States has slowed down in recent years. Nevertheless, United States productivity growth is still higher than it has been during some periods in the past.

A great deal of discussion has centered on the relative performance of the United States and Japanese economies, because of the remarkable difference in their productivity growth rates in recent years. Over the period 1960–73 productivity in the United States and Japan grew at a rate of 3.1 and 9.9 percent per year, respectively. Between 1973 and 1979, average annual growth slowed down to 1.1 percent in the United States and 1.9 percent in Japan.[26] To what extent can differences in the rate of investment in physical plant and equipment and in changes in the quality of capital and labor account for these remarkably different growth rates? What accounts for the remainder? Painstaking research by several economists provides some answers to these questions.

For technical reasons, we will not delve into the details of these studies but simply summarize their major results. The single most important difference between the United States and Japanese economies has been in the rate of investment in new plant and equipment. Between 1960 and 1973 the annual rate of growth of plant and equipment was about two and one-half to three times greater in Japan than in the

[25] John W. Kendrick, "International Comparisons of Recent Productivity Trends," in *Essays in Contemporary Economic Problems* (Washington, D.C.: American Enterprise Institute, 1981), pp. 125–70.

[26] Kendrick, "International Comparisons," Table 7.

United States.[27] If we ignore the fact that new capital equipment embodies technological change—the results of past research and development expenditures—to a
much greater extent than old plant and machines do, the more rapid increase in the
capital-to-labor ratio in Japan accounts for about one-third of its higher productivity
growth compared to the United States.[28]

Labor quality changes over time, as does the quality of capital. The two most
important determinants of what might be called the *effective* amount of labor, compared to a simple count of labor-hours, are probably education and training. The
number of years a typical worker has attended school has grown over the years, both
in Japan and the United States. This has tended to increase labor quality in both
countries at about the same rate. Changes in the age-sex composition of the labor
force can affect labor quality in either direction. In the United States during the
1960–73 period, two major changes in the age-sex composition of the labor force
tended to lower the average productivity of an hour's work, other things equal. One
of these changes we have already discussed—the increase in the proportion of married women in the labor force. Since the average woman entering the labor force has
less labor force experience at any age than the average man, her productivity (and
pay) is likely to be less. This statement holds quite apart from any question of sex
discrimination, which may or may not enlarge male-female wage differences or account for part of the difference between the labor force participation of men and
women. The other change in the United States labor force resulted from the postwar
baby boom. Starting in about 1963, these young workers began entering the labor
force, depressing the average level of experience. These two changes in the United
States labor force together resulted in a 0.3 percent average annual *decline* of labor
productivity over the 1960–73 period. In Japan, by contrast, changes in the age-sex
composition of the work force resulted in a 0.1 percent average annual increase in
productivity over the same years.[29]

Much of the remaining difference in productivity growth between the United
States and Japan over the 1960–73 period can be attributed to advances in knowledge
and applications of innovations associated with investment in new capital equipment. It appears that only about one-fourth of the difference remains unaccounted
for in terms of the major influences discussed above.[30]

Between 1973 and 1979 average annual productivity growth was much lower in
both Japan and the United States than it had been during the preceding thirteen
years—3.8 percent in Japan and 1.1 percent in the United States compared to 9.9
percent and 3.1 percent, respectively, during the earlier period. Probably the two
most important changes accounting for the sharp decline in productivity growth were
(1) a much lower rate of investment in new capital in both countries and (2) the sharp
increase in world oil prices, which caused some existing capital to become much
costlier to operate and which probably made investment projects that would have
been undertaken unprofitable.[31] Increasingly stringent environmental and safety regulations have probably also reduced the productivity of new investment, as conventionally measured, as well as its profitability.

---

[27] Kendrick, "International Comparisons," Table 1, and L. R. Christensen, D. Cummings, and
D. W. Jorgenson, "Economic Growth, 1947–73: An International Comparison," in John W.
Kendrick and Beatrice N. Vaccara, *New Developments in Productivity Measurement and
Analysis* (Chicago: University of Chicago Press, 1980), Table 11-13.
[28] Kendrick, "International Comparisons," Table 7.
[29] *Ibid.*
[30] *Ibid.*
[31] *Ibid.* and Christensen, Cummings, and Jorgenson, "Economic Growth, 1947–73."

Studies of productivity and productivity growth show that the production function is an extremely useful tool in helping us to understand many aspects of this crucially important economic process. It should be emphasized, however, that application of the production function concept to analyze productivity is most helpful in understanding the *proximate* causes of productivity growth. It is important to know what these are—increases in the capital/labor ratio, improvements in labor quality, and so on. Nevertheless, even if *all* productivity growth could be accounted for in these terms, fundamental questions still would need answering. These include why investment in new physical capital varies among nations and over time, and why research and development expenditures fluctuate and differ from economy to economy. Tentative answers to these questions have been proposed. As suggested above, environmental concerns and occupational safety regulations have probably reduced investment profitability in recent years. Solving these puzzles is a fascinating challenge to on-going economic research.

CONCLUSION

In this chapter we have examined the linkage between the demand for output, the production process, and the demand for labor under competitive conditions. We began our analysis by considering the situation in which a single competitive firm, facing fixed prices for its inputs and output, can adjust production only through purchases of labor services. In this case, the firm maximizes its profit by hiring the quantity of labor that equates the wage rate to the value of the marginal product of labor. More important, the value of the marginal product of labor schedule serves as the firm's labor demand curve and is downward-sloping because of the diminishing marginal physical productivity of labor.

Next, we analyzed the demand for labor by a competitive firm when it is able to adjust its inputs of labor *and* capital services. This means that a given level of output can be produced in a variety of ways, and that to maximize its profit, the competitive firm must first establish the cost-minimizing combination of inputs for its various possible levels of production. The firm's cost-minimizing input combinations are summarized by its *expansion path*. To choose the optimal (profit-maximizing) amount of labor, the firm locates that point on its expansion path where marginal cost of production equals marginal revenue. To fix this process in your mind, it may be easier if you think of the firm that has experienced a wage-rate change as first moving to a new expansion path, which is known as the *substitution effect* of a wage change, and then moving along the new expansion path until marginal revenue again equals marginal cost, which is known as the *scale effect* of a wage change. Although the analysis of the effect of a wage change on the quantity of labor demanded is more complex when capital is variable, in general the firm hires less labor at higher wage rates, and the demand schedule is more elastic (flatter) than in the case where labor is the only variable input. This difference has important implications for the employment impact of union-induced wage increases, for example.

An extremely important conclusion developed in this chapter is that the demand for labor by a competitive *industry*, while downward-sloping, is more complex than the simple sum of the individual firms' demand schedules, owing to feedback effects of price changes in the market for final output as industry production expands or contracts. Another important result is that a competitive industry's labor demand elasticity depends on whether the number of firms in the industry is fixed or variable. As a result, we cannot reach a general conclusion as to whether the industry demand for labor is more or less elastic than the demand curves of its component firms, although the key result that industry demand for labor is inversely related to the wage rate is preserved. Next we applied the theory of the demand for labor by a competitive industry by examining the impact of legal minimum wage rates on employment and workers' earnings. We noted that, depending on the elasticity of demand and whether all workers have the opportunity to share in employment at the minimum wage, such legislation may make low-wage workers worse off, contrary to the intent of legislation. In another application, we examined the effects of changes in the prices of other factors on shifts in the demand for labor.

Finally, we relaxed the assumption that employers maximize their profits but retained the assumption that they purchase labor in competitive markets. Doing this allowed us to examine the demand for labor by nonprofit firms and by government employers. Although governments sometimes can be classified as noncompetitive in their "product" markets, we have chosen to treat governments' demand for labor in this chapter rather than in Chapter 6. While relaxation of the profit-maximization assumption changes our expectation of the magnitude of the elasticity of labor demand, it does not affect the important implication that when wages rise, employment will fall.

Next we summarized several studies that report empirical estimates of the elasticity of demand for labor. There is quite a bit of evidence that the elasticity of demand for low-wage workers—those who are directly affected by minimum wage legislation—is high enough to make it likely that their average earnings are reduced rather than raised. This is very important evidence concerning this controversial labor legislation. We also discussed empirical evidence on the elasticity of demand for all production labor in manufacturing and on the elasticity of demand for labor by nonprofit and government employers.

Finally, we turned the theory of labor demand on its head, so to speak, and examined the impact of changes in factor quantities on labor productivity and on relative wages of workers who differ in their age and years of schooling. We showed that the concept of an aggregate production function for the entire economy is a useful framework for understanding economy-wide changes in labor productivity and the labor market effects of swings in birth rates and the acquired schooling of workers. We were also able to explain some important differences in productivity growth between the United States and Japan.

REFERENCES AND SELECTED READING

BAILY, MARTIN NEIL, "Productivity in a Changing World," *Brookings Bulletin,* 18 (Summer 1981), 1–4.

BERGER, MARK C., "The Effects of Labor Force Composition on Earnings and Earnings Growth," Ph.D. dissertation, Ohio State University, 1981.

CHRISTENSEN, LAURITS, R., DIANE CUMMINGS, AND DALE W. JORGENSON, "Economic Growth: 1947–73: An International Comparison," in *New Developments in Productivity Measurement and Analysis,* ed. John W. Kendrick and Beatrice N. Vaccara. Chicago: University of Chicago Press, 1980.

————, AND L. J. LAU, "Transcendental Logarithmic Production Frontiers," *Review of Economics and Statistics,* 60:1 (February 1973), 28–45.

CLARK, KIM B., AND RICHARD B. FREEMAN, "How Elastic is the Demand for Labor?" *Review of Economics and Statistics,* 62:4 (November 1980), 509–20.

COBB, C. W., AND PAUL A. DOUGLAS, "A Theory of Production," *American Economic Review,* 18:3 (May 1928), 139–65.

"Deepening Troubles In Puerto Rico," *New York Times,* February 15, 1976, Business and Finance Section.

EHRENBERG, RONALD, "The Demand for State and Local Government Employees," *American Economic Review,* 63:3 (June 1973), 366–79.

————, *Fringe Benefits and Overtime Behavior.* Lexington, Mass.: D. C. Heath & Company, 1971, pp. 5–22.

FERGUSON, C. E., *The Neoclassical Theory of Production and Distribution.* Cambridge, Eng.: Cambridge University Press, 1969, Chaps. 6, 9.

FLEISHER, BELTON M., *Minimum Wage Regulation in Retail Trade.* Washington, D.C.: American Enterprise Institute, 1983.

————, *Minimum Wage Regulation in the United States.* Washington, D.C.: National Chamber Foundation, 1983.

FREEMAN, RICHARD B., "The Demand for Labor in a Nonprofit Market: University Faculty," in *Labor in the Public and Nonprofit Sectors,* ed. Daniel S. Hamermesh, Princeton, N.J.: Princeton University Press, 1975.

————, *The Over-educated American.* New York: Academic Press, 1976.

————, "Overinvestment in College Training?" *Journal of Human Resources,* 10:3 (Summer 1975), 287–311.

GRANT, JAMES, "Labor Substitution in U.S. Manufacturing," Ph.D. dissertation, Michigan State University, 1979.

————, AND DANIEL S. HAMERMESH, "Labor Market Competition Among Youths, White Women and Others," *Review of Economics and Statistics,* 63:3 (August 1981), 354–60.

HAMERMESH, DANIEL S., "Econometric Studies of Labor Demand and Their Application to Policy Analysis," *Journal of Human Resources,* 11:4 (Fall 1976), 507–25.

HICKS, J. R., *Theory of Wages,* 2d ed. London: Macmillan, 1964.

"Higher Pay's Price," *The Wall Street Journal,* August 15, 1978, p. 48.

KENDRICK, JOHN W., "International Comparisons of Recent Productivity Trends," in *Essays in Contemporary Economic Problems*. Washington, D.C.: American Enterprise Institute, 1981.

NELSON, RICHARD R., "Research on Productivity Growth and Differences," *Journal of Economic Literature,* 19:3 (September 1981), 1029–64.

OI, WALTER W. "Labor as a Quasi-Fixed Factor," *Journal of Political Economy,* 70:6 (December 1962), 538–55.

"Paper Shortage Hits Magazines," *The Wall Street Journal,* January 26, 1978, p. 1.

PAULY, MARK, AND MICHAEL REDISCH, "The Not-for-Profit Hospital as a Physician's Cooperative," *American Economic Review,* 63:1 (March 1973), 87–99.

PERLMAN, MARK, "One Man's Baedeker to Productivity Growth Discussions," *Contemporary Economic Problems 1979*. Washington, D.C.: American Enterprise Institute, 1979.

PETERSON, JOHN M., *Minimum Wages: Measures and Industry Effects*. Washington, D.C.: American Enterprise Institute, 1981.

POLACHEK, SOLOMON W., THOMAS J. KNIESNER, AND HENRICK J. HARWOOD, "Educational Production Functions," *The Journal of Educational Statistics,* 3:3 (Autumn 1978), 209–31.

REDER, MELVIN W., "The Theory of Employment and Wages in the Public Sector," in *Labor in the Public and Nonprofit Sectors,* ed. Daniel S. Hamermesh. Princeton, N.J.: Princeton University Press, 1975.

REES, ALBERT, *The Economics of Trade Unions,* rev. ed. Chicago: University of Chicago Press, 1977.

ROSEN, SHERWIN, "Short-Run Employment on Class-I Railroads in the U.S., 1947–1963," *Econometrica,* 36:3–4 (July–October 1968), 511–29.

"Steel-Collar Jobs," *The Wall Street Journal,* October 26, 1981, p. 1.

"Sweet Competition: New Corn Derivative Challenges Big Sugar as a Shake-Out Looms," *The Wall Street Journal,* November 2, 1976.

TAUCHEN, GEORGE E., "Some Evidence on Cross-Sector Effects of the Minimum Wage," *Journal of Political Economy,* 89:3 (June 1981), 529–47.

TIEBOUT, CHARLES, "A Pure Theory of Local Expenditures," *Journal of Political Economy,* 64:5 (October 1956), 416–24.

U.S. BUREAU OF THE CENSUS. *Statistical Abstract of the United States*. Washington, D.C.: Government Printing Office, 1979.

U.S. BUREAU OF LABOR STATISTICS. *Handbook of Labor Statistics*. Washington, D.C.: Government Printing Office, 1980.

U.S. DEPARTMENT OF LABOR, WAGE AND HOUR AND PUBLIC CONTRACTS DIVISION, *Eating and Drinking Places*. Washington, D.C.: Government Printing Office, 1968.

WEISBROD, BURTON A., "Private Goods, Collective Goods: The Role of the Non-Profit Sector," *The Economics of Non-Proprietary Organizations,* supplemental to volume II, ed. Kenneth Clarkson and Donald Martin; *Research in Law and Economics,* ed. Richard O. Zerbe. Greenwich, Conn.: JAI Press, 1980.

WELCH, FINIS, "Effects of Cohort Size on Earnings: The Baby Boom Babies: Finan-
    CIAL BUST," *Journal of Political Economy,* 87:5, part 2 (October 1979),
    S65–S97.
ZUCKER, ALBERT, "Minimum Wages and the Long-Run Elasticity of Demand for
    Low-Wage Labor," *Quarterly Journal of Economics,* 87:2 (May 1973),
    267–77.

EXERCISES

Choose whether each of statements 1, 2, and 3 is *true, false,* or *uncertain* (whether
true or false depends on unspecified circumstances). Justify your answer. Your
justification is the most important part of your answer.

1. The United States tomato-growing industry has become highly mechanized in the
   past few years. This is an example, in the theory of factor demand, of the substitution effect dominating the scale effect.
2. An increase in the minimum wage will make workers who are covered by the
   minimum wage better off, provided the elasticity of demand for their labor is
   greater than one in absolute value.
3. A competitive industry's factor demand curve is a simple aggregate of the labor
   demand curves of the firms in the industry.
4. The Pretty Puppy Palace (3P) grooms dogs. The 3P has a fixed capital input and
   uses only one variable input, labor. Moreover, 3P sells its output and purchases
   labor under competitive conditions. You are given the following information
   about 3P's operation.

L	Q	MPPL	VMPL
0	0	—	—
1	10	10	5
2		15	
3	45		10
4	60		
5	72		6
6		10	
7	90		
8			
9	100	4	
10	102	2	1

where

$$L \equiv \text{units of labor}$$
$$Q \equiv \text{number of dogs groomed}$$
$$MPPL \equiv \text{marginal physical product of labor}$$
$$VMPL \equiv \text{value of marginal product of labor.}$$

(a) How many dogs are groomed when 6 units of labor are employed?
(b) What is the marginal physical product of the seventh unit of labor?
(c) What is the price of having a dog groomed by 3P?
(d) What is the value of marginal product of the eighth unit of labor?
(e) Suppose that the competitive wage is $6 and that at this wage 3P hires 5
    workers. Calculate 3P's gross profit (total revenue minus total labor cost).

5. (a) In your own words, and without using any graphs or equations, explain why the demand for labor by a profit-maximizing competitive firm with a fixed capital input is downward-sloping. Be sure to define the concept of a labor demand curve in your answer and be very very brief. Of what relevance for economic policy is the fact that the labor demand curve slopes downward?

   (b) At a wage of \$50/day (per worker) a competitive firm has a total daily labor cost of \$150,000. Suppose that if the wage were to rise to \$75/day per worker the firm would continue to spend \$150,000 each day on labor. What is this firm's elasticity of demand for labor? Give a specific numerical value and explain briefly how you got it. What are the policy implications of your answer?

   (c) A competitive industry currently pays a wage of \$3 per hour. The slope of its labor demand curve is $-5,000$. The government wants to set a minimum wage in excess of \$3 but is concerned over the lost employment opportunities it will cause for these workers. Suppose that the government wants to set the highest minimum wage it can subject to the condition that no more than 1,250 jobs are lost as a result. What minimum wage will it set? Give a specific numerical answer and briefly explain how you got it.

*6. A government agency uses capital and labor to produce a service. The agency purchases K and L in competitive markets at fixed prices r and w, respectively. The agency's goal is to maximize the production of its service subject to its fixed budget constraint.

   (a) Depict graphically the agency's choice of capital and labor.
   Suppose that the agency is assigned L_0 workers by a government employment program. The agency does not have to pay those workers, and they are perfect substitutes for the workers it normally hires.

   (b) Depict graphically the agency's new choice of capital and labor. What happens to the amount of labor the agency *hires*?

   (c) Suppose that instead of being assigned the free workers, the agency was given a budget increase of wL_0, an amount exactly enough to hire the L_0 workers itself. Depict graphically the agency's new choice of capital and labor. Will the impact of the extra budget on labor *hired* be the same as in (b)?

   (d) Of what practical value to politicians are the answers to (b) and (c)?

---

* Denotes a more difficult exercise.

4

LABOR SUPPLY:
Individual Behavior
in the Short Run

A. Educational objectives
1. To establish the qualitative relationship between the individual's desired quantity of market work and the hourly wage and nonemployment income
2. To identify the influence of various environmental disturbances and government policies (including taxation) on the desired amount of market work
3. To discuss evidence bearing on labor force participation and hours of work; to explain major trends in labor force participation and hours of work

B. A simple introduction:
The supply of labor and the demand for leisure (p. 111)

C. A deeper look at labor supply decisions (p. 113)
1. The utility function (p. 113)
2. The budget constraint (p. 117)
3. The decision whether or not to work (p. 118)
4. Hours of work—income and substitution effects (p. 124)
    a. Application of the income and substitution effects: A negative income tax
    b. What does the labor supply curve look like?
    c. Relaxing some assumptions: Permanent versus transitory changes in the wage rate
    d. Fixed costs of getting to work

D. Evidence on labor supply (p. 137)
1. The facts on labor supply in the United States (p. 138)
2. Understanding labor supply behavior (p. 140)
3. The negative income tax experiments: Results from Seattle and Denver (p. 142).
4. Experimental studies with animal subjects (p. 147)
5. Labor supply studies with nonexperimental data (p. 150)
    a. Adult men and women with an application to tax effects on labor supply
    b. Why has the male labor force been shrinking?
    c. The "full-time" workweek
6. Labor supply functions derived (p. 161)

E. Frontiers of labor economics: The new home economics (p. 162)

F. Conclusion (p. 166)

In the study of labor supply, the family plays a pivotal role, much like that of a firm, deciding how to use its limited resources in the best way to achieve its goals. The decision we focus on when analyzing labor supply is how the family allocates its available time between the labor market and other uses. When time is sold to employers in exchange for income, we say that labor is supplied, or that market work is performed. Of course, the family also uses some of its time in a wide variety of *nonmarket* activities, including child care, personal health maintenance, and amusements. In addition, time may be spent in school that yields no money income at the moment but influences the amount that can be earned in the future. As a result, it would be perfectly correct if this chapter's title were "The Household's Allocation of Time" rather than "Family Labor Supply." In fact, the general framework to analyze family labor supply is almost the same as that used in the theory of consumption and the demand for goods and services.[1]

We will begin, as we did in Chapter 3, by specifying the three basic components or assumptions of labor supply (or household time allocation) theory: (1) the *family's utility function,* which describes how the household's nonmarket time (which for convenience we will call **leisure**) and market goods consumed affect the family's economic well-being; (2) the *economic environment,* which describes the markets where the household sells its labor to firms and purchases goods and services; and (3) the *family's goals.* In this chapter we will analyze family labor supply decisions where family members (a) seek to maximize utility and (b) have no control over either the prices they must pay for goods and services or the wage rate they are paid. Just as in the analysis of labor demand, if any of the assumptions surrounding the theory of labor supply change, the implications about labor supply behavior will also change.

The process by which individual family members decide how much of their time to supply to the labor market is doubtless very complex. That is, a husband may consider his wife's wage rate, his **nonlabor income,**[2] his expected duties in the home, and the attitudes of the community, his wife, and his children in deciding when, where, and how much to work in the labor force. We may think of the wife, children, and other family members as making decisions similarly. While it is important to emphasize that each family member's labor supply decision is reached via a simultaneous process in which all members' decisions are made, to incorporate all the important variables in a first approach to the theory of labor supply would make the analysis unnecessarily complicated. Therefore, we will assume that an individual decides how much labor to supply in light of his tasks and preferences

---

[1] This insight is found in a classic article by Lionel Robbins, "On the Elasticity of Demand for Income in Terms of Effort," *Economica,* 10 (June 1930), 123–29.

[2] Income due to rent, dividends, interest, capital gains, and payments from other family members and public and private welfare agencies. In general, nonlabor income is all the income an individual has to spend *outside of his own labor market earnings.*

for leisure versus consumption, his earning power, and nonlabor income. We allow for the possibility that part of the individual's nonlabor income may come from other family members and that he may take into account other family members' needs when choosing what goods and services to buy.[3]

A SIMPLE INTRODUCTION

It is just as valid to view the allocation of an individual's time from the point of view of the *demand* for leisure as from the point of view of the *supply* of labor. It will help us to understand the more complex analysis of the next section if we first use the theory of demand taught in earlier economics courses to develop a simple leisure demand or labor supply curve. Demand curves answer the question, "What happens to the quantity demanded when the price of a good changes, other things equal?" Here the good in question is leisure time measured in hours, and its price is the opportunity cost of using an additional hour in some way other than market work. This opportunity cost is, of course, the pay that would be received for an additional hour of work outside the household—**the market wage.**

In demand theory, income and tastes (the utility function) as well as the market wage determine the quantity demanded. But how can we take income as fixed for someone who is deciding how much leisure to demand and labor to supply? Isn't income determined by the amount worked? The way out of this problem is to take a more fundamental view of what is meant by income. An individual can obviously alter his or her income by adjusting labor supply, but there is still a constraint on the amount earned or spent. Ultimately, no one can consume more than the spending power he can command from (1) nonlabor income sources and (2) earning power. The amount each individual can earn is limited by the most basic constraint we each face—the amount of time available—and the wage rate. So, the quantity of leisure an individual demands depends on the fixed amount of time available, the wage rate, and nonlabor income.

Consider someone who wishes to decide how to allocate 168 hours per week (24 × 7) between leisure and market work, given a wage rate of w per hour and nonemployment income v. Suppose that up to now 118 hours have been demanded for home use, and 50 = (168 − 118) hours have therefore been devoted to market work. This yields earnings, y, equal to $50w$ per week, and total income, i, equal to $(50w + v)$ per week. Now let the worker unexpectedly receive a raise to w' per hour. What happens to the number of

[3] For further examination of household decision making see Gary S. Becker, "A Theory of Social Interactions," *Journal of Political Economy,* 82:6 (November–December 1974), 1063–94, and Marjorie B. McElroy and Mary Jean Horney, "Nash-Bargained Household Decisions: Toward a Generalization of the Theory of Demand," *International Economic Review,* 22:2 (June 1981), 333–50.

leisure hours demanded? Two opposing forces are at work. (1) The opportunity cost of leisure has risen. Each additional hour *not* worked reduces earnings by \$$w'$, which is \$$(w' - w)$ greater than before. (2) The worker is now financially better off. There is now more income available to spend on both consumption and leisure.

The two forces we have just listed that are set into motion by a wage increase have opposite effects on how much leisure an individual wants. The increase in the opportunity cost of leisure time motivates the worker to use less time outside the labor market and to reduce the quantity of leisure demanded. On the other hand, the increase in potential income tends to have the opposite effect. The higher wage also means that it is possible for the worker to increase consumption of *both* market goods and leisure. For example, in response to a wage increase from \$4 to \$5.50 per hour, the quantity of leisure demanded might rise, despite its higher price, to 128 hours from 118 hours per week. Market work would fall, then, to 40 hours from 50 hours per week while earnings and consumption of market goods would be \$20 (= \$220 − \$200) greater than before. Thus, the individual's leisure demand curve could well be *upward*-sloping, as in Figure 4-1(a). Because labor supply is the difference between total time available and leisure consumed, this means that the labor supply curve is *downward*-sloping, as in Figure 4-1(b).

Notice that these are not like the demand and supply curves you are used to seeing. While economic theory does not *necessarily* imply that the leisure demand curve will be upward-sloping, the fact that we all possess the

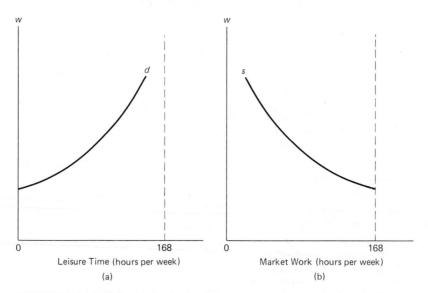

FIGURE 4-1. Possible leisure demand and labor supply curves for an individual

power to allocate our time among alternative uses implies that an increase in the price of leisure makes us better off, and an upward-sloping leisure demand curve is therefore not at all unlikely.

Perhaps you are still a bit troubled by the fact that an individual's demand curve for a commodity such as food is downward-sloping while the demand for leisure can be upward-sloping. The difference lies in how changes in the prices of the two respective items affect purchasing power. Consider first an increase in the price of food. The price increase not only makes food relatively more expensive but also lowers the individual's real income, because the price of an important item in the budget has risen. Both of these lead the individual to buy less food when its price rises. Now consider an increase in the wage. The wage increase raises the relative price of leisure *and* raises the individual's real income, because earnings are the major source of income for most people. Thus, the wage increase has opposing influences on leisure consumption. The higher price of leisure makes people want less of it, but the greater real income stemming from a wage increase tends to make them want more of everything, including leisure. The leisure demand curve will be downward- or upward-sloping, depending upon how the individual evaluates these two conflicting influences. In the next section we take a deeper look at individuals' leisure demand and labor supply schedules.

A DEEPER LOOK AT LABOR SUPPLY DECISIONS

The Utility Function

Imagine that an individual's goal is to achieve the greatest possible satisfaction from the limited resources he or she has available. The individual is a price-taker in the market where goods and services are purchased as well as the market where labor services are sold. Basically, the individual's resources are defined by the amount of time available, the value of time when sold or supplied to the market, and the individual's ability to purchase market goods and services even if no market work is performed. In the short run, an individual cannot alter the market wage rate he can earn in the labor market. In the long run, however, as we show in Chapters 8 and 9, schooling and training are important activities affecting individual earning power. The ways in which the individual's resources can be combined to provide satisfaction are formally represented by a **utility function.**

From what has been said so far, it should be easy to see that the only reason time is supplied to the labor market is in order to obtain wages, or employment income, to buy market goods. Unfortunately, when time is traded for income it can no longer be used for other purposes. Therefore, a decision maker has to balance a desire for goods against the wish to use time in nonmarket activities. The utility function tells us how economic well-being **(utility)** is related to various combinations of market goods (or the equivalent real income) and time used in nonmarket activities. For convenience, we will often refer to all the nonmarket uses of time as leisure, even though it is obvious that many, if not most, of the things people do other than work at market jobs, such as caring for children, cooking, fixing up the house, and so on, are not always fun.

We can write the utility function in a form analogous to the production function, equation (3-4), as follows:

$$U = u(g, h) \qquad\qquad \textbf{(4-1)}$$

where $U \equiv$ the level of utility or economic well-being
$g \equiv$ units of market goods
$h \equiv$ hours of "leisure."

In equation (4-1), $u(\cdot)$ is a mathematical relationship that translates (maps) flows of two commodities, goods and hours of leisure, into utility per period of time.

Figure 4-2 shows a typical utility function relating economic well-being to the levels of market goods and leisure used by a representative individual. The horizontal axis measures the number of hours in a given period of time used in nonmarket activities of all sorts, including caring for children and doing things with other family members. The vertical axis measures the

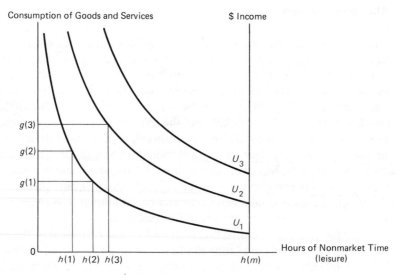

FIGURE 4-2. A typical utility function

consumption of market goods and services of all sorts per time period. Remember that individuals generally live in families, and they will therefore take other family members' needs and feelings into account when choosing what particular goods and services to purchase. The number of hours per period of time is strictly limited. There are, for example, 168 hours in a week. The maximum usable nonmarket time is denoted on the horizontal axis of Figure 4-2 by the amount $h(m)$. The quantity of market goods and services is measured along the vertical axis. Assuming that the prices of various goods do not change over the time period, we can also measure consumption in terms of total income spent on goods and services. This equivalent monetary measure of consumption is shown on the vertical line on the right-hand side of Figure 4-2, going through $h(m)$. Be careful to note that the amount of work gets smaller as the amount of nonmarket time being measured on the horizontal axis gets larger. The number of hours of labor supplied to the market is equal to $h(m)$ *minus* the amount of nonmarket time used by the individual. An increase in the use, or consumption, of goods and nonmarket time is assumed to result in an increase in the individual's utility.

The utility function consists of a set of negatively sloped, convex lines called **indifference curves,** such as U_1, U_2, and U_3 in Figure 4-2.[4] Each indifference curve represents a constant level of utility, or satisfaction. The farther a curve lies from the origin, the higher the level of utility it represents. Along each indifference curve, the various combinations of hours and consumption all yield the same satisfaction. Thus, the individual is *indifferent* between the consumption-leisure combinations denoted by any two points along a particular curve in Figure 4-2. As a result, we might have named the indifference curves *iso-utility curves*. In Figure 4-2, the combination of consumption level $g(1)$ and leisure time $h(2)$ yields satisfaction equal to the combination $g(2)$ and $h(1)$. If, however, the individual consumes $g(3)$ and has nonmarket time $h(3)$, this yields more satisfaction than either of the first two combinations.

The most important characteristics of the indifference curves are their slope and their shape. Their negative slope implies that it is possible to hold the level of utility constant while substituting hours for goods. Thus, the negative slope implies a substitutability of nonmarket time for the consumption of goods and services. A term often applied to the slope of an indifference curve is the **marginal rate of substitution (MRS)** between consumption

---

[4] The numbers attached to indifference curves are important only for ranking the curves in order. Note that each indifference curve in Figure 4-2 is numbered, with the numbers increasing as we move outward from the origin toward the northeast. This implies higher levels of satisfaction as consumption increases. However, the numbers attached to the indifference curves are not unique. We may use *any* set of numbers that fulfills the condition that as we move toward the northeast, the numbers get larger. It does not matter whether we measure successively higher utility levels as 1, 2, 3; 1.1, 1.2, 1.3; 100, 200, 300, and so on.

and leisure. The term "marginal" denotes the rate at which a small amount of hours can be substituted for a small amount of goods, with utility still held constant. The convex shape of the indifference curves implies imperfect substitutability between hours and goods. If hours and goods were perfect substitutes, then the *MRS* would be the same, no matter what combination of hours and goods was being consumed. The indifference curves would be straight lines in this case. The **principle of imperfect substitutability** implies that though the individual can maintain a constant level of utility by trading time for goods, and vice versa, the greater the amount of nonmarket time relative to goods and services consumed, the greater the marginal (additional) amount of hours required to compensate for giving up a marginal amount of goods. Clearly, this relationship works in the opposite direction too. The greater the ratio of goods and services consumed to hours of leisure, the greater is the *marginal* amount of consumption required to compensate someone for giving up a marginal amount of leisure hours.

Soon we will elaborate on the fact that a decision maker can choose to forego market income, or dollars, in return for having more time available for nonmarket activities. The *MRS* measures the individual's willingness to do so. Thus, it is often useful to think of the *MRS* as a kind of "wage rate." The market wage rate, after all, is the price at which a unit of time can be sold to the labor market—it represents the additional dollar amount of goods someone can obtain if one hour of leisure is foregone. The *MRS*, on the other hand, represents the dollar amount of market goods the decision maker is willing to give up, or "pay," in order to avoid selling an hour of time to the labor market. Thus, *MRS* represents the value, in terms of goods and services or equivalent dollars, someone places on using a small additional amount of time in nonmarket activities. For this reason, we shall often refer to the *MRS*, the slope of an indifference curve, as the **home wage rate.** The *MRS* at the particular point where an indifference curve intersects the vertical line through $h(m)$ is of special interest. Since it is impossible for the decision maker to allocate more than $h(m)$ hours to nonmarket activities, the home wage at a point such as the intersection of U_1, U_2, or U_3 with $h(m)$ tells us how much the family decision maker would be willing to pay in order to buy an additional hour of time, if it could be obtained.

Before going on, we want to emphasize that the utility function, as well as the budget constraint introduced in the next section, are *economists' tools* for systematically analyzing the labor supply decision. No one out there in the so-called real world needs to actually draw an indifference map in order for us to analyze behavior as if people really did draw them. The individuals who are making the decisions are "groping around" for what is best for them and probably find it through trial and error. The diagrams we use are the analyst's orderly way of describing how individuals' decisions are reflected in observed behavior—labor supply in particular.

Consumption Opportunities: The Budget Constraint

Obviously, if utility increases with the nonmarket time and goods and services consumed, utility maximization implies proceeding indefinitely far upward and to the right or northeast on the utility map—consuming an infinite amount of goods and leisure hours. There are, however, constraints that prohibit someone from consuming infinite quantities of these. First, time is strictly limited to 168 hours per week. This is a basic constraint. Second, individuals cannot generally dictate the terms at which their labor services are sold to the market. We assume people sell their time as labor services in a competitive market. Thus, there is a fixed, market-determined wage rate at which their time can be exchanged for dollars. Finally, while the individual's nonlabor sources of income such as interest, dividends, rent, government welfare payments, financial help from other family members, and the like may permit the purchase of some market goods even if no work is performed, the amount of such nonemployment income is surely limited.

Individuals are prevented from consuming unlimited quantities of goods and hours because only limited amounts of hours and income are available to them. These limitations are summarized in the **budget constraint** that defines the individual's **consumption opportunities.** Figure 4-3 shows a representative budget constraint. As in Figure 4-2, consumption is measured along the vertical axis, and hours of nonmarket time (hours *not* worked for pay) are measured along the horizontal axis. The line parallel to the vertical axis and intersecting point $h(m)$ measures the dollar equivalent of market goods, or income. Given the level of nonemployment income $v(1)$ and the amount of market goods that can be bought with the pay for an hour's work, the budget constraint is the line connecting $v(1)$ and $g(1)$. Notice that $g(1) = i(f)$ is the amount of goods that could be obtained if all *available* hours were

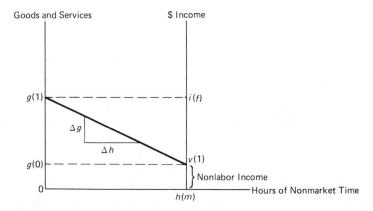

FIGURE 4-3. A typical budget constraint

sold in the market. [A good way to view $h(m)$ is total time less the number of hours required to maintain productivity through proper sleep, recreation, and the like.] Economists sometimes refer to the quantity $g(i)$ or $i(f)$ as **full income.**

It may help you to understand labor supply analysis if you bear in mind that the budget constraint has *three* properties. Each one defines an economic limitation faced by the individual represented. They are (1) the slope of the budget constraint, (2) its height, and (3) its length from left to right. The absolute value of the slope of the budget constraint in Figure 4-3 is $\Delta g/\Delta h = [g(1) - g(0)]/h(m)$ and represents the **market wage rate.** The market wage rate is depicted as a constant independent of the number of hours worked because we have assumed that individual workers have no direct control over the rate of exchange between their time and market goods (earnings). The market wage that the individual cares about is the *real wage,* which can change either because money (paycheck) wages change or because the price level changes. The height of the budget constraint is most easily measured by its intercept with the vertical line through $h(m)$, $v(1)$ or nonemployment income. Nonemployment income is, by definition, independent of the current work-leisure decision. The right-to-left length of the budget constraint represents the amount of time in the decision period (that is, 24 hours per day, 168 hours per week, 8,760 hours per year). You will soon see that we are interested in how a change in any of the three basic properties of the budget constraint affects labor supply—particularly the effects of changes in the slope and height of the budget constraint. We will also explore the effect of a change in the *effective* amount of time available (the right-left dimension of the budget constraint) on labor supply.

The Goal of Utility Maximization and the Decision Whether or Not to Work

We assume that the decision maker wishes to obtain the greatest amount of utility, given the budget constraint. Let us see what this implies for the decision whether or not to work at all.

The individual's problem is to get to the highest indifference curve allowed by the budget constraint. In analyzing the decision whether or not to work at all, focus on the point $v(1)$ in Figure 4-4, where the budget constraint and indifference curve U_2 intersect at $h(m)$ hours of nonmarket time. Point $v(1)$ is obviously a possible choice, as is point a, since both lie on the budget constraint and thus are contained in the set of available opportunities. Given how the indifference curves have been drawn, it should be apparent that the greatest level of utility will be attained if *no market work is performed*—that is, if this person does not participate in the labor market. Point a, while

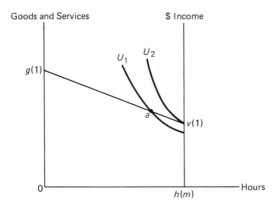

FIGURE 4-4. Utility maximization: No work

attainable, lies on indifference curve U_1, which indicates lower economic well-being than U_2, the indifference curve through $v(1)$. Clearly, the closer a point lies to $g(1)$, the lower would be the indifference curve going through the budget constraint at the point. Figure 4-4 shows that *if the indifference curve that intersects the budget constraint at the point indicating zero hours of market work $h(m)$ is steeper than the budget constraint at that point, then the greatest level of economic well-being is achieved by not participating in market work at all.*

The preceding paragraph demonstrated that given the budget constraint and indifference curves as we have drawn them, the necessary and sufficient condition for not selling any hours to the labor market is that the *MRS* between market goods and time exceeds the market wage rate at the point where no market work is performed. Perhaps this crucial aspect of the decision whether or not to work will be more meaningful if we recall that the *MRS* is also called the *home wage rate*. The condition that the *MRS* be greater than the market wage is the same thing as saying that the home wage exceeds the market wage. This means that the amount of income the decision maker would be willing to sacrifice if only one more hour of time could be earned exceeds the amount of income that could be obtained if one hour of time were given up (sold) to the market. That is to say, the individual's valuation of an additional hour of time (when the maximum amount is being consumed) is greater than the market's evaluation of that time. Under these circumstances, *more* time would be bought for use in *nonmarket* activities if that were possible, and it therefore makes obvious sense not to sell any.

In Figure 4-5 the indifference curves are drawn in such a way as to show the situation when the decision to work in the market will enable the individual to reach a higher level of utility than the decision not to work.

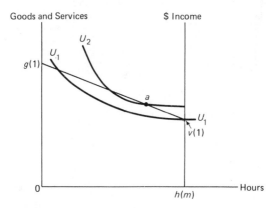

FIGURE 4-5. Utility maximization: Work

Again, both points $v(1)$ and a represent feasible situations, since both lie on the budget constraint. Now, however, if a is chosen, the level of economic well-being will be represented by indifference curve U_2, which lies above the indifference curve associated with a decision not to work at all, U_1. Figure 4-5 shows the converse of Figure 4-3: *If the indifference curve passing through the budget constraint at h(m) is less steep than the budget constraint at that point, then the greatest level of economic well-being is achieved by selling some time to the labor market.* The decision maker chooses to sell some time to the labor market when the *MRS* between market goods and nonmarket time (at zero hours of work) is less than the market wage. In other words, if the home wage rate is less than the market wage rate, the individual values his time (when no work is performed) less than the market values his time, and it pays him to sell time in return for the income that can be obtained.

Those individuals who perform some market work in our economy (or who are actively seeking work) are called **labor force participants,** and the proportion of labor force participants in the total population is called the **labor force participation rate.** Economists and policymakers are often interested in the labor force participation rate and its determinants, because labor force participation is necessary in order to obtain sufficient market income for most persons to lead a reasonably comfortable life. Moreover, the labor force participation rates of various subsets of the population—married women, older persons, and teenagers—provides information about how men and women specialize in obtaining market income and in performing child care and other kinds of work in the home, how older persons fare in providing for their material desires, and how youth allocate their time between current market work and preparation for future economic well-being through formal education. Therefore, we will spend some time analyzing how changes in the budget constraint affect the labor force participation decision, given the individual's utility function.

Participation and the market wage rate.   Reexamine Figures 4-4 and 4-5. You will recall that someone will participate in the labor force if, and only if, his or her home wage is less than the available market wage at the point on the budget constraint corresponding to an allocation of $h(m)$ hours to nonmarket activity. This relationship between the home and market wage rates is recounted in Figure 4-6. Note that since we have assumed the budget constraints are straight lines, the market wage along constraint $v(1)g(1)$ is measured by $[g(1) - g(0)]/h(m)$. Along $v(1)g(2)$, the market wage is $[g(2) - g(0)]/h(m)$ and is clearly greater, because $[g(2) - g(1)] > 0$. The *MRS* along indifference curve U_1 at point $v(1)$ is greater than $[g(1) - g(0)]/h(m)$ but less than $[g(2) - g(0)]/h(m)$. Thus, at the lower wage the person depicted in Figure 4-6 desires no market work. An increase in the wage rate to $[g(2) - g(0)]/h(m)$ causes the individual to enter the labor force, however. As the market wage increases, it will eventually reach a value where an individual who was initially a nonparticipant in the labor force becomes indifferent between working and not working. At this value, called the **reservation wage rate,** the budget constraint is *tangent to* (just touches) the indifference curve at $h(m)$ hours. Clearly, *a sufficiently large increase in the market wage, holding nonemployment income constant at some level such as $v(1)$, will make the market wage exceed the home wage. At this point, an individual who had been allocating all available hours to nonmarket activities will enter the labor force.*

It should be apparent that all other things being equal, an increase in the wage would never cause someone who is now working to stop working.

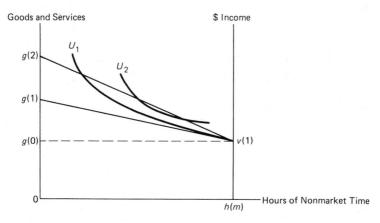

FIGURE 4-6. The effect of a wage change on labor force
            participation

Why? The condition for labor force participation is that the market wage exceeds the reservation wage at $v(1)$. If the market wage is greater than the reservation wage at $v(1)$, further increases in the market wage can only widen this inequality, never reduce it. To summarize, our theory implies that labor force participation and the market wage rate rise and fall together.

Participation and nonemployment income. The budget constraint is determined not only by the market wage rate (its slope), but also by the level of nonemployment income, which is measured by the height at which the constraint intersects the vertical lines through $h(m)$. This is how we examine the effect of changes in nonemployment income on labor force participation, holding the market wage rate constant. The shift in the budget constraint in Figure 4-7 depicts an increase in nonemployment income from $v(1)$ to $v(2)$. Notice that the wage remains constant at $[g(1) - g(0)]/h(m) = [g(3) - g(2)]/h(m)$.

In order to analyze the effect of changes in nonemployment income, we need to make a further assumption about the utility function. We need to know what happens to the value of hours in terms of market goods as utility increases, holding hours of leisure unchanged. We will assume that hours of nonmarket time is a **normal commodity,** meaning that the amount of income (goods) someone is willing to give up in order to consume an additional hour of time in nonmarket activities rises as utility increases, the consumption of hours remaining unchanged. The increase in utility due to greater and greater amounts of nonlabor income, the consumption of hours held constant, can be traced out along the vertical income line through $h(m)$. The normality assumption is reflected in the increasing steepness of the indifference curves at $h(m)$ hours, as the levels of utility and nonlabor income rise. Thus, indifference curve U_2 is steeper at $h(m)$ hours and nonemployment income $v(2)$ than is indifference curve U_1, which is associated with nonemployment income level $v(1)$. In other words, the assumption that leisure is a normal commodity means that the reservation wage rate rises as utility increases. *If we assume that nonmarket time is a normal commodity, then a sufficiently large increase in nonemployment income will cause a working individual to leave the labor force.*

Thus, in Figure 4-7, the individual is a labor force participant at market wage $[g(1) - g(0)]/h(m)$ and nonemployment income $v(1)$. An increase in nonemployment income from $v(1)$ to $v(2)$, however, causes the individual to become a nonparticipant. As nonemployment income rises, the value of the reservation wage rate rises, while the market wage obtainable remains unchanged. Eventually, the reservation wage exceeds the obtainable market wage, and the greatest economic well-being is attained by performing no market work.

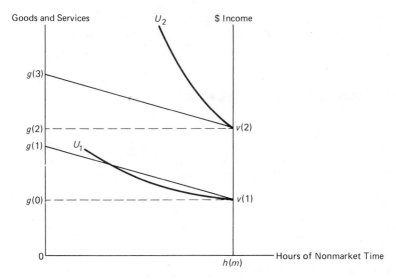

FIGURE 4-7. The effect of a change in nonemployment income on labor force participation

The two changes in the budget constraint we have just considered both affect economic well-being in the same direction. However, they have opposite effects on labor force participation. An increase in the market wage rate and an increase in nonemployment income both make it possible to consume more market goods and (for labor force participants) to allocate more hours to nonmarket activities. When the market wage rises, however, it becomes more lucrative to sell hours to the labor market in exchange for income, and thus labor force participation becomes more likely. Alternatively, as utility rises owing to an increase in nonemployment income, the reservation wage rate increases. As a result, labor force participation becomes less likely when nonemployment income grows, other things equal.

In order to make sure you understand the analysis of labor force participation, we would like you to construct a diagram like Figure 4-7, showing the effects of welfare laws, such as Aid to the Families with Dependent Children, the Federal Food Stamp Program, and the like. Essentially, these programs pay a minimum level of income or its equivalent in food stamps, subsidized housing, medical care, and so on to the head of a family, depending on family size and composition. However, the nonemployment income paid to the family head is reduced by a substantial amount for each dollar the family members earn through market work. This *implicit tax* on market earnings is sometimes dollar for dollar—even *exceeding* 100 percent on occasion. In the diagram you draw, show how the basic welfare payment shifts the budget constraint up or down. Show how the "takeback," or implicit tax on earnings affects the slope of the budget constraint. What are the combined effects of these two changes on labor force participation?

UTILITY MAXIMIZATION: HOURS OF WORK

In this section we analyze the number of market work hours desired by an individual who has decided to participate in the labor force. Analyzing the hours-of-work decision requires a somewhat more precise understanding of the relationship between the indifference curves and the budget constraint implied by utility maximization. In order to see how the decision maker maximizes utility given the budget constraint, start at $v(1)$ in Figure 4-8 and proceed toward $g(1)$ until the highest indifference curve is reached. This will be at point b, where utility is maximized by consuming $h(0)$ hours and $g(0)$ goods such that the budget constraint is tangent to an indifference curve. Point b also represents a choice of $i(0)$ income, $i(0) - v(1)$ of which represents wage income $y(0)$. Hours of work equal $h(m) - h(0)$. It follows from the assumed shape of the budget constraint and the indifference curves that there is one, and only one, point such as b.

Suppose the decision maker decided on a combination of goods and nonmarket hours corresponding to point c, which does not represent a point of tangency between $v(1)g(1)$ and an indifference curve. The indifference curve passing through c is U_1, representing a lower level of utility than U_2, the curve that passes through b. It is clear that at c, consumption possibili-

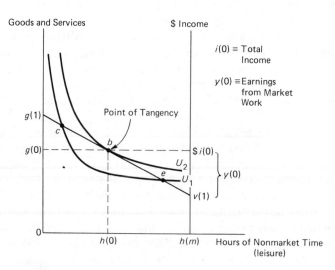

FIGURE 4-8. Utility maximization and hours of work

ties are such that by giving up some goods and consuming more hours, the decision maker can increase utility. This will be true until the consumption combination represented by point *b* is obtained. Obviously, the same argument would apply in reverse if the initial point chosen were *e*, where "too many" hours and "too few" goods would be consumed.

Let us express the condition of utility maximization more formally. Recall that the absolute value of the slope of the budget constraint is the market wage rate, which we now represent by the symbol $w(m)$. This means that along a budget constraint

$$\frac{\Delta g}{\Delta h} \equiv w(m) \qquad\qquad \textbf{(4-2)}$$

The slope of an indifference curve, on the other hand, represents the home wage rate, $w(h)$. Thus, along an indifference curve

$$\text{slope of indifference curve (absolute value)} \equiv MRS \equiv w(h) \qquad \textbf{(4-3)}$$

The tangency condition of utility maximization can therefore be expressed concisely with a few symbols. Specifically, utility is maximized when the slope of the budget constraint is equal to the slope of the indifference curve having a point in common with the budget constraint. At this point[5]

$$w(m) = w(h) \qquad\qquad \textbf{(4-4)}$$

At a point like *c* in Figure 4-8, $w(h) > w(m)$. This is to say, the value the individual places on an additional hour of time allocated to leisure exceeds the income that must be sacrificed if one less hour is devoted to market work. Thus, *c* represents too much market work and too little time devoted to nonmarket activities to produce utility maximization. Similarly, at *e*, $w(m) > w(h)$, or the home wage is less than the market wage. Since the amount of income the family is willing to sacrifice in order to use one more hour in the home is less than the labor income that can be earned by selling the hour to the labor market, utility maximization requires increasing the number of hours of market work.

The Supply of Hours of Work

We have just seen that once the decision has been made to participate in the labor force, the number of hours of work are chosen to achieve the greatest level of economic well-being consistent with the time and income constraints faced by the individual. The **supply schedule** of hours of work

---

[5] As we have seen, for nonparticipants, $w(m) < w(h)$ when utility is maximized.

tells us how this optimal number of hours is affected by changes in the wage rate and nonemployment income. Ultimately we will concentrate on the relationship between hours of work and the market wage rate. First, however, we analyze the influence of a change in nonemployment income, holding the market wage constant.

In order to analyze the effect of a change in nonemployment income on hours of work, we proceed in the same way as we did in studying the influence of nonemployment income on labor force participation. We assume that leisure is a normal commodity, meaning that the amount of income (goods) someone is willing to give up in order to consume an additional hour of time in nonmarket activities rises with utility, hours of leisure remaining unchanged. In other words, the home wage rises as utility increases.

For example, in Figure 4-9, if nonemployment income is $v(1)$ and the market wage is $[g(1) - v(1)]/h(m)$, utility maximization implies choosing to work $h(m) - h(0)$ hours in return for $\$[i(0) - v(i)]$ of market income. Now, suppose nonemployment income rises to $v(2)$, or still higher to $v(3)$, but the market wage remains unchanged. Along budget constraints $v(2)g(2)$ and $v(3)g(3)$ it is still clearly possible to choose $h(0)$ hours of leisure. However, the indifference curves U_2 and U_3 passing through $h(0)$ hours along these higher constraints are *steeper* than U_1 at $h(0)$ hours. Along the constraints $v(2)g(2)$ and $v(3)g(3)$, then, neither U_2 nor U_3 is the highest indifference curve attainable. When nonemployment income is $v(3)$ and $h(m) - h(0)$ hours of work are chosen, the home wage rate exceeds the market wage rate. Fewer hours should be worked and more devoted to nonmarket activity. The value $h(m) - h(1)$ represents the utility-maximizing number of market work hours after nonemployment income has risen to $v(3)$, the wage rate along $g(3)v(3)$ remaining equal to that along $g(1)v(1)$. *Thus, the assumption*

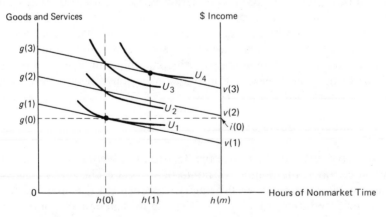

FIGURE 4-9. The effect of a change in nonlabor income hours of work

that nonmarket time is a normal commodity implies that hours of work fall when nonemployment income rises and the market wage rate remains the same.

The way Figure 4-9 is drawn, goods and services and leisure are normal commodities. Successively higher levels of nonlabor income raise the maximum utility attainable, and the points of tangency between the indifference curves and budget constraints rise upward and to the right (northeast). The consumption of leisure and goods and services increases. Although we have assumed that the individual consumes more of these as utility rises, there is nothing in economic theory requiring this to happen. Nevertheless, the assumption of an upward-sloping utility-consumption path for the individual has intuitive appeal. One can imagine cases in which either goods or leisure hours would be an inferior commodity.[6] If goods were an inferior commodity, the utility-consumption path would slope toward the southeast; if leisure hours were inferior, toward the northwest. However, with broad commodity groups, the assumption of a northeasterly sloping utility-consumption path seems reasonable.

The aspect of the supply of hours of work on which we want to focus most of our attention is the relationship between hours of work and the market wage rate. The effect of a change in the market wage on hours of work chosen is shown in Figures 4-10 and 4-11. A change in the wage rate is represented by a change in the slope of the budget constraint. Thus, to examine the effect of a change in the wage rate with nonlabor income unchanged, we rotate a budget constraint about the point on the vertical line going through $h(m)$. As the budget constraint is rotated clockwise, the wage rate increases. Figures 4-10 and 4-11 show two budget constraints, each depicting a different wage rate, but the same nonlabor income.[7] The wage rate is lower along the constraint $h(m)g(1)$ than along $h(m)g(2)$. The point of utility maximization is a along $h(m)g(1)$ and b along $h(m)g(2)$. Note that b may lie either to the right or to the left of a. We cannot predict from economic theory whether an increase in the wage rate will result in a larger or a smaller amount of labor being supplied by a utility-maximizing individual. The case of a reduction in labor supplied is shown in Figure 4-10; an increase is shown in Figure 4-11. (Recall that an increase in the wage rate can never reduce labor force participation to zero hours.)

What lies behind the ambiguity concerning the effect of a change in the wage rate on the change in the amount of labor supplied? We can see the answer more clearly in Figure 4-12. Note that by increasing the wage rate, the individual is moved to a higher indifference curve. This means, of course, that when the wage rate increases, someone is better off. In Figure

---

[6] No study known to us suggests that such a case has been observed.
[7] For convenience, nonlabor income is set equal to zero in Figures 4-10 and 4-11.

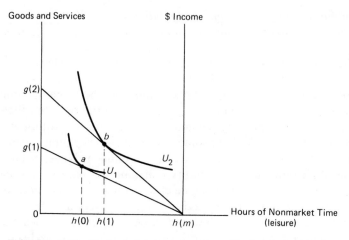

FIGURE 4-10. Reduced labor supply with increased wage
rate

4-12 we note that indifference curve U_2, the highest achievable after the
budget constraint rotates from $h(m)g(1)$ to $h(m)g(2)$, lies above U_1, the previously highest attainable indifference curve. (We assume that b lies to the
northeast of a.) Now, we could also increase the individual's welfare to U_2
without increasing the wage rate by increasing nonlabor income just enough
to compensate not having the wage increased. In other words, imagine placing the individual on budget constraint $v(1)g(3)$, which is *parallel* to
$h(m)g(1)$, but tangent to indifference curve U_2 (at c). Here $v(1)$ represents

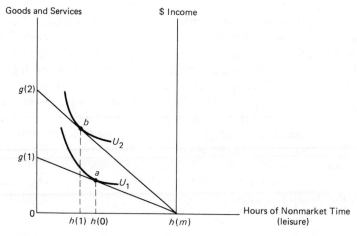

FIGURE 4-11. Increased labor supply with a rise in the wage
rate

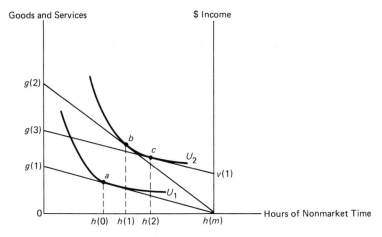

FIGURE 4-12. The substitution and income effects of a wage change

just enough nonlabor income to compensate the individual for not receiving a wage rate increase. Note that since $v(1)g(3)$ is parallel to $h(m)g(1)$, the wage rates along the two constraints are the *same*.

But what would be the difference in behavior if the budget constraint were $v(1)g(3)$ rather than $h(m)g(2)$? Along $h(m)g(2)$, $h(m) - h(1)$ hours are worked and $h(1)$ hours of leisure are consumed, whereas along $v(1)g(3)$ only $h(m) - h(2)$ hours would be worked, while $h(2)$ leisure hours would be consumed. The implication is that if we were to raise the individual to U_2 by increasing nonlabor income rather than the wage rate, the incentive to work would be decreased. On the other hand, keeping someone on indifference curve U_2 while changing the budget constraint will cause hours of work to change in the same direction as the wage rate. Theoretically this *must* happen because of the negative slope of the indifference curve. The difference in the number of hours worked along U_2 at the two different wage rates, $h(2) - h(1)$, is called the **substitution effect** of a change in the budget constraint from $h(m)g(1)$ to $h(m)g(2)$.[8] When the individual moves from U_1 to U_2 by means of a change in nonlabor income only, consumption of hours rises from $h(0)$ to $h(2)$, and hours worked falls by $h(2) - h(0)$. This is called the **income effect** of the change in the budget constraint from $h(m)g(1)$ to $h(m)g(2)$.

The initial change in the budget constraint from $h(m)g(1)$ to $h(m)g(2)$ causes the individual to change the consumption of hours from $h(0)$ to $h(1)$.

---

[8] Alternatively, we could lower the wage rate from $h(m)g(2)$ to $h(m)g(1)$ and measure the substitution effect on U_1. For small changes in the budget constraint, there is a negligible difference in these two ways of measuring the substitution effect.

Because an increase in the wage rate is in one respect similar to an increase in nonlabor income, the change from $h(0)$ to $h(1)$ can be broken down into two components: (1) $h(2) - h(0)$, the change in leisure due to the change in the level of utility, holding the wage rate constant, called the income effect, and (2) $h(1) - h(2)$, the change in leisure due to the change in the wage rate, holding the level of utility constant, called the substitution effect.

To summarize, *the substitution effect says that the individual will "buy" less leisure as it becomes relatively more expensive due to a wage increase and buy more leisure as it becomes relatively less expensive due to a wage reduction. The income effect says that a wage increase makes the individual richer so that he or she buys more leisure, and that a wage reduction makes the individual poorer so that he or she buys less leisure.* Thus, the total effect of a change in the wage rate on labor supplied in Figure 4-12 is $h(1) - h(0)$, which equals $h(2) - h(0)$, the income effect, plus $h(1) - h(2)$, the substitution effect.[9]

The important point to remember from this section is that the income and substitution effects have opposite influences on hours worked. As a result, economic theory implies that *hours worked may either rise or fall as the result of an increase in the wage rate, and the issue may be resolved only by empirical investigation.*

Application of the income and substitution effects: A negative income tax   Some readers may suspect that all this discussion of income and substitution effects is important only to labor economists, who are afraid of letting people think their subject is too simple and have therefore invented these concepts as a "make-work" project. In fact, the income and substitution effects are extremely important parts of economics. They are very valuable in helping us understand labor supply behavior and the effects of various government policies. One very important application is to understand the effects of income-maintenance programs on the amount people work. A particular income-maintenance program that has received a great deal of discussion, and about which we will have more to say later in this chapter, is the so-called **negative income tax.** The way a simple negative income tax program would work is described precisely in Figure 4-13.

In Figure 4-13 we describe the situation of an individual worker who in the absence of a negative income tax-type income-maintenance program would face labor market opportunities described by the constraint $h(m)g(1)$. For simplicity, we will ignore the income tax we are all used to (the "positive" income tax). Therefore, the slope of the constraint, $g(1) \div h(m)$, measures how much each hour of market work adds to actual real take-home

---

[9] As an exercise, do a similar decomposition of the total wage effect into an income effect and a substitution effect for the individual depicted in Figure 4-11.

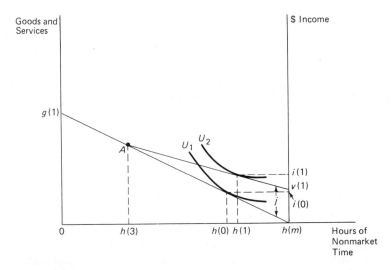

FIGURE 4-13. The effect of a negative income tax on labor supply

earnings. This individual chooses to work $h(m) - h(0)$ hours, reaching indifference curve U_1 and receiving an income, all from earnings, equal to $\$i(0)$.

Suppose that an income of $\$i(0)$ per month is below the level that society defines as poverty and that a law is passed guaranteeing everyone a monthly payment of $\$j$, so that income will *never* be less than $\$v(1)$. Thus, to someone who earns nothing, the government will pay $\$j = \$v(1)$. However, for every dollar earned, the government reduces this income transfer by $\$0.50$. In other words, low-income individuals receive a "negative tax" payment from the government of $\$j \le \$v(1)$. Since j falls by $\$0.50$ for every $\$1$ increase in earnings, labor market income is essentially taxed at a rate of 50 percent, so that the payment from the government *falls* as earnings *rise*—the negative income tax law changes the effective budget constraint from the line $h(m)g(1)$ to the kinked line $v(1)Ag(1)$. Point A is the **breakeven point** (or **breakeven income**) where the negative income tax payment j has become zero.

One great controversy surrounding negative income tax proposals concerns their effect on work incentives. The income and substitution effects tell us that for the *working* poor who do not participate in other welfare programs, a negative income tax will clearly reduce work incentives. It should be clear to you that an individual who reaches indifference curve U_1 before the negative income tax program will be induced by *both* the income and substitution effects of the negative income tax to *reduce* work hours. The fact that constraint $v(1)Ag(1)$ lies above constraint $h(m)g(1)$ at $h(0)$ hours of leisure means there is an *income effect* to reduce work hours.

The fact that the effective wage rate along the $v(1)A$ portion of $v(1)Ag(1)$ is only one-half that along $h(m)g(1)$ means that there is also a substitution effect to reduce work hours. Thus, we show this person reducing work by $h(1) - h(0)$ hours following introduction of a negative income tax transfer program. At $h(m) - h(1)$ hours of work total income equals $\$i(1)$ and includes a negative income tax payment of

$$\$j = \$v(1) - \frac{g(1)}{h(m)} [h(m) - h(1)] \times 0.5$$

Whether $h(1) - h(0)$, the reduction in work hours, is small or large can be determined only by empirical study. We discuss evidence on the likely work disincentive effects below.

Before ending this discussion, we must emphasize that we have treated only the impact on the *working* poor. Many individuals who receive income transfers, housing subsidies, food stamps, and so on are already affected by a *combination* of income-maintenance programs, which, when the "positive" income tax and social security tax are added in, implicitly tax earnings at rates equal to or even exceeding 100 percent, inducing a very strong work disincentive. Replacing such transfer programs with a negative income tax would almost certainly increase work incentives for persons who benefit from current welfare schemes.

What does the supply curve of work hours look like?   Many economists agree that for adult workers who hold full-time jobs in the United States, the labor supply curve looks like that drawn in Figure 4-1(b) (p. 112). The supply curve in Figure 4-1 is drawn with respect to a *given* level of nonlabor income. If nonlabor income were to increase, the assumption that leisure is normal means that *s* would shift to the left, with fewer work hours offered at each wage rate. Note that when the labor supply curve is negatively sloped with respect to the wage rate, this does not necessarily imply that as the wage rate increases, earned income declines. Whether earned income rises or falls as wage rate increases depends on the elasticity of the labor supply curve. If that elasticity is algebraically greater than -1, then income rises as the wage rate rises, even if hours of work decline.

Relaxing some assumptions: Permanent versus transitory changes in the wage rate.   So far we have implicitly assumed that when an individual's wage rate changes, it is viewed as a permanent change—one generating a new wage that is expected to persist indefinitely. Thus, the income effect of a change in the wage rate is commensurate with the income effect of a change in nonlabor income. By contrast, suppose a worker is offered the opportunity of working overtime hours for a few weeks at a *temporarily* higher rate of pay. In this case, the effect on the worker's long-term expected income is relatively small. Even though weekly income may rise considerably for a while, the increase has to be treated in the context of normal income in the absence of overtime work (and in the context of whatever nonlabor income may accrue to the worker). For example, a three-week period of overtime work may generate $500 extra income. If normal earnings equal $400 per week, this would represent a 41 percent increase in income over three weeks, but only 2.5 percent over a year and only 0.025 percent over a ten-year horizon.

The key point in all of this is that the income effect of a wage rate change that is expected to be temporary—that is, what economists often call a **transitory change in the wage rate**—is theoretically much smaller than the income effect of a **permanent (persistent) wage rate change.** On the other hand, the effect of such a change in the wage rate on the price of hours relative to market goods is *independent* of whether the change in the wage rate is permanent or transitory. Thus, for transitory wage rate changes, the substitution effect is much more likely to dominate the income effect than is the case for permanent wage changes. An example of this point is that if we accept the existence of a backward-bending labor supply curve as the principal explanation of the long-term decline in hours of work per week (this is discussed further on pp. 158–161), we may be troubled by the fact that over short periods of time when unemployment is relatively low, and wage rates (including overtime premiums) are relatively high, workers tend to work relatively long hours. The difference between the effects of permanent and transitory wage rate changes helps account for this.

Fixed costs of getting to work. A labor supply curve showing hours of work continuously falling as the wage rate rises is only one of several possibilities. Theoretically, it is difficult to rule out a more general view of labor supply such as shown in Figure 4-14, in which at the *reservation wage rate,* $\bar{\omega}$, a very small number of hours is supplied to the labor market. At levels of nonlabor income that are high enough to support life without working, it seems reasonable that the hours an individual desires to work at the reservation wage, the **reservation hours of work**, will be only slightly greater than zero. In this case, the number of hours worked would rise with the wage to, say $l(1)$ at wage $w(1)$, and only then (if ever) begin to fall along the backward-bending portion of the labor supply curve s. However, we do *not* observe individuals working, say, only 10 minutes a week. Workweeks as short as 8 hours or less are relatively rare. In this section we introduce the concept of the **fixed cost of holding a job.** We show that this provides a basis for understanding why, when a worker receives a rate of pay that is only slightly larger than the reservation wage, his or her reservation hours will typically be a significant lump of time. The result is that much of the upward-sloping

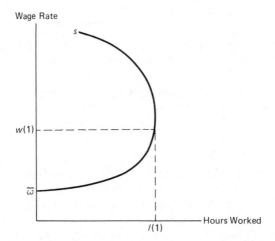

FIGURE 4-14. A more general labor supply curve

portion of supply curve s in Figure 4-14 is not observed in data on hours of work in the United States.[10]

In general, it is costly to hold a job, even though earnings clearly make it worthwhile for job holders to bear these costs. *Money* costs must be incurred to pay for transportation to work, suitable clothing, meals away from home, and perhaps babysitting services. *Time* costs are also incurred, if for no other reason than that few persons live "in back of the shop" any more, and considerable time is frequently required to travel from home to job.

The fixed time cost of working is depicted in Figure 4-15 as a *shortening* in the left-right length of the budget constraint caused by a leftward shift of the vertical line through $h(m)$ whenever work hours are positive. If the individual described by Figure 4-15 performs no market work, then $h(m)$ hours are available for leisure activities. However, if any time is supplied to the market, $h(m) - h^*(m)$ hours must be used for non-wage-earning, non-leisure activities, such as commuting. *Effective* time available to use in leisure or at work is reduced to $h^*(m)$ hours in the case where some market work is performed.

If there were *no* fixed time cost of market work, then this individual's budget constraint would be the line $v(1)g(3)$. With a fixed time cost, the budget constraint is the kinked line $v(1)ag(1)$. This latter budget constraint is

---

[10] This discussion is based on John Cogan, "Labor Supply with Time and Money Costs of Participation" (Santa Monica, Calif.: Rand Corporation, 1976), and "Labor Supply with Costs of Labor Market Entry," in James P. Smith, ed., *Female Labor Supply: Theory and Estimation* (Princeton, N.J.: Princeton University Press, 1980).

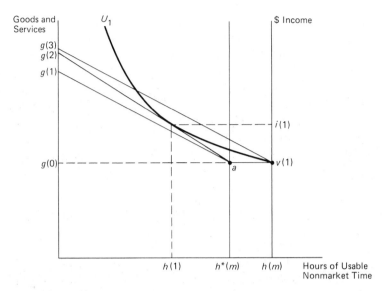

FIGURE 4-15. Fixed time cost of a job and reservation work hours

horizontal between $v(1)$ and a, indicating that the fixed job time cost contributes nothing to earnings. Since nothing happens to the wage, it has the same slope between a and $g(1)$ as constraint $v(1)g(3)$. Now consider an individual whose indifference curve through the $h(m)$ line at $v(1)$ is U_1. This individual would definitely be a labor force participant if there were no fixed time cost. (Why?) However, since U_1 lies above the constraint $v(1)ag(1)$, we can see that he or she will not supply any hours of work if $h(m) - h^*(m)$ hours must be used as the fixed time costs necessary to hold a job.

Finally, suppose the wage rate is raised from $[g(1) - g(0)] \div h^*(m)$ per hour of work to $[g(2) - g(0)] \div h^*(m)$. At the higher wage, this individual becomes indifferent between (a) entering the labor force, working $h^*(m) - h(1)$ hours for a total income of $\$i(1)$, and (b) devoting $h(m)$ hours to household activities while receiving an income of $\$v(1)$. Thus, $[g(2) - g(0)] \div h^*(m)$ is the individual's reservation wage, given $\$v(1)$ nonlabor income and $h(m) - h^*(m)$ fixed time cost of holding a job.

The major implication of all this is that the decision maker's reservation work hours equal $h^*(m) - h(1)$, which is substantially greater than zero. The individual either performs no market work at all or enters the labor force at a significant number of hours per week.

What do you think will happen to the reservation wage rate and the hours a person will work if there should occur an *exogenous increase* in the fixed time cost of holding a job, other things equal? For example, there could be an increase in traffic congestion requiring longer commuting time, or the government could pass a law lowering the speed limit from 55 to 40 miles per hour. (By an exogenous increase in time cost we mean a change that is not the direct result of the worker's own decision. For example, moving to a more distant suburb would *not* be an *exogenous* increase in commuting time.) The effects of such a change are shown in Figure 4-16, which has been changed, compared to Figure 4-15, to show the following: (1) the fixed time job cost has risen from $h(m) - h^*(m)$ hours to $h(m) - h^{**}(m)$ hours, and (2) the individual depicted in Figure 4-16 has a wage higher than his reservation wage, even after commuting time increases.

Two things are apparent in Figure 4-16: (1) an increase in fixed time job cost raises the reservation wage; and (2) an increase in such costs reduces hours actually worked. Effect 2 is apparent, because income declines from $\$i(2)$ to $\$i(1)$ as the budget constraint shifts leftward from $v(1)ag(3)$ to $v(1)bg(2)$. Since these two constraints are parallel, indicating the same wage rate, income falls only because hours of work are reduced. Notice that hours of leisure *also* decline, from $h(2)$ to $h(3)$ hours. The reduction in *both* hours of work and leisure, as well as in income earned, will always occur so long as both goods and leisure are normal commodities. Can you see why this is so?

It is also apparent in Figure 4-16 that *reservation* hours of work have risen with increased commuting time costs, even though hours actually worked have declined. The distance along the horizontal axis, $h^*(m) - h(1)$, is clearly smaller than the distance $h^{**}(m) - h(3)$. For simplicity, we have

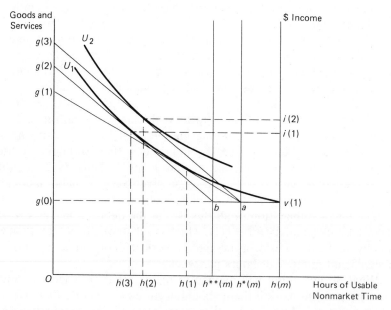

FIGURE 4-16. The effect of an increase in the fixed time cost of a job on the reservation wage rate and on hours of work

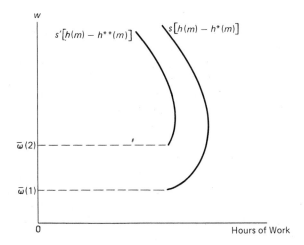

FIGURE 4-17. The effect of an increase in
the fixed time cost of a job on
the labor supply schedule.

constructed Figure 4-16 so that after commuting time has increased, time
actually worked [$h^{**}(m) - h(3)$ hours] is just equal to reservation hours. If
the fixed time cost of holding a job were to rise further, this person would
remain in the labor force only if the wage rate were to rise also.

Figure 4-17 summarizes the impact of an exogenous increase in the
fixed time cost of a job. The supply curve $s[h(m) - h^*(m)]$ represents the
situation with the initial time cost. When the time cost rises to $h(m) - h^{**}(m)$
hours, the reservation wage rises from $\bar{\omega}(1)$ to $\bar{\omega}(2)$, and the supply curve
shifts to the left. We also show that reservation hours of work may rise when
the time cost rises. The leftward shift in the labor supply schedule implies
that not only will the labor force be reduced in size, but also those who
remain will work fewer hours. The reduction in hours of work stems from
the fact that the reduction in total usable time (due to higher time costs of
holding a job) is shared between reductions in leisure *and* work. However,
the *net* reduction in the supply of labor will cause wage rates to rise for the
labor market as a whole. (Why?) In light of this, what effect do you think
more commuting time, say, will have on labor force participation and hours
of work *in the long term?*

EVIDENCE ON LABOR SUPPLY

In this section we examine some of the most important features and trends of
labor supply in the United States and relate them to the economic theory of
labor supply developed earlier. We also show how interpreting labor supply

data in terms of labor supply theory can help us to gain insights into the labor supply effects of various economic programs and policies such as income and social security taxes and income maintenance programs. By and large, we will confine ourselves to the short-run theory of labor supply. This means that we do not incorporate in any great detail decisions about the accumulation of human capital—education, training, and so on. Ultimately, decisions about whether to work and how many hours to supply to the market cannot be isolated from decisions concerning the accumulation of human capital. An individual's choice of which age to begin market work in earnest is connected to decisions about education and training, and the amount of investment in human capital in turn depends upon anticipated lifetime labor supply. Thus, where necessary, we will incorporate schooling and other long-run variables in the analysis of labor supply, even though a deep look at investment in human capital must wait until Chapters 8 and 9.

The Facts of Labor Supply in the United States

It will help focus attention on the interesting and important features of labor supply if we first present an overview of basic trends in labor force participation and hours of work in the United States.

The concept of labor force participation deals with the labor supply in a categorical sense. Specifically, in discussing labor force participation we treat the question of whether an individual offers any hours at all to the labor market. By official definition, any individual who worked at least one hour or was unemployed during the survey week is considered to participate in the labor force. The proportion of a group who participate in the labor force at any moment of time is the group's **labor force participation rate.** As Table 4-1 shows, the steady-to-gradually-rising proportion of the population performing some market work masks sharp increases and precipitous declines for various age and sex groups. The composition of the United States labor force has changed markedly over the course of the twentieth century. Comparing 1980 to 1900, a far higher proportion of married women and a much smaller proportion of teenagers and older men participate in the labor force. There has also been somewhat of a decline in the labor force participation rate of middle-aged men. Although this change has been smaller than those for the other groups mentioned, it is worthy of attention, because it signals a significant change in the principal source of income for the affected families. As of 1980, in over 15 percent of husband-wife families whose husband was between 45 and 64 years old, the husband was a nonparticipant in the labor force.

Once the choice to perform some market work has been made, the labor supply decision involves choosing the desired number of hours. When hours of work data are examined, it becomes clear that the decline in weekly hours of work, at least through the first half of the century, was quite dra-

TABLE 4-1 Labor Force Participation Rates, 1900–1980 (percent)

Year	Total Civilian Labor Force[a]	Married Women Total	Married Women 20–24 Years	Married Women 35–54 Years	Men 14–19 Years	Men 18–19 Years	Married Men 45–64 Years	Men 45–64 Years	Men 65 Years and Over
1900	50.2	5.6	—	—	61.1	—	—	90.3	63.1
1920	50.3	9.0	—	—	52.6	—	—	90.7	56.6
1930	49.5	11.7	—	—	41.1	—	—	91.0	54.0
1940	52.9	15.7	—	—	34.4	—	—	88.7	41.2
1948	—	22.0	24.9	19.4	—	79.9	—	—	46.8
1949	—	22.5	24.5	20.6	—	—	94.3	—	46.9
1950	59.2	23.8	28.5	21.8	—	—	92.8	89.3	45.8
1960	59.4	30.5	30.0	34.2	—	79.0	93.0	—	33.1
1970	60.4	40.8	47.4	44.1	35.8	69.9	91.6	—	26.8
1979	63.7	49.4	61.2	46.8	—	—	84.7	82.7	20.0
1980	63.8	50.2	60.2	47.2	—	73.2	84.9	82.2	19.1

[a] 1900–1930, the labor force was measured to include persons 10 years and older; 1940–1960, 14 years and older; 1970–, 16 years and older.

Sources: (1) 1900–1940, *Historical Statistics of the United States, Colonial Times to 1970*, Part 1, Series D11, D35, D60; 1948 and later, *Employment and Training Report of the President*, 1981, Tables A-3, A-5, B-3. (2) For 14- to 19-year old men, Clarence D. Long, *The Labor Force Under Changing Income and Employment* (Princeton, N.J.: Princeton University Press, 1958), Table A-2 (1900–1950) and *U.S. Census of Population, 1970*, Employment States and Work Experience, Subject Reports PC(2)-6A, Table 1.

matic. Table 4-2 lists the average weekly hours of work in three representative industries—manufacturing, building trades, and retail trade.[11] It also shows the economywide data for nonagricultural industries since 1950 and for what is known as the standard (full-time) workweek during 1890–1950. These series all confirm a substantial decline in average weekly hours of work through 1940. The pattern is less clear since then. Average weekly hours have continued to decline, but those seeking a shorter workweek have not found employment uniformly across industry groups. They are concentrated mainly in retail trade and (not shown) the service industries.

Understanding labor supply behavior.   It is probably fair to say that the empirical study of labor supply behavior has received more attention than most other topics studied by economists, particularly over the past 25 years. While much has been learned, many puzzles remain.[12] There are at least two standards against which empirical studies can be judged; a truly satisfactory investigation would produce results that achieve high marks when evaluated against both of them. (1) The results should be consistent with, or help us to understand, the major features of labor supply behavior, such as the trends described in Tables 4-1 and 4-2. (2) The results should be consistent with the theory of labor supply developed earlier in this chapter. Unfortunately, many empirical examinations of labor supply data do not meet these tests, and our discussion cannot possibly go into the technical depth or great length that a comprehensive evaluation requires.[13] In what follows we will try to give you an overview of a few major studies and relate them to some important features of labor supply behavior and policy issues.

From a purely research point of view, the ideal way to study labor supply behavior would be to observe individuals' reactions to changes in their wages, nonemployment income, tax rates, fixed costs of holding a job, and so on, in circumstances that allow us to be sure that our observations are not contaminated by events over which we have no control and which we may not observe. This would require placing human beings in a laboratory environment. Because such an environment would impose unacceptable restrictions on freedom of action and in general result in a miserable life for experimental subjects, truly controlled experiments in the social sciences are quite rare. Social sciences are not unique in this constraint on empirical work. The medical sciences face very similar problems in assessing the

---

[11] In 1960, these industries accounted for the following proportions of production workers in nonagricultural industries of the United States: manufacturing, 22.3 percent; building trades as represented by contract construction, 5.0 percent; retail trade, 15.5 percent. *Statistical Abstract of the United States,* 1980, Table 692.

[12] We are indebted to Mark R. Killingsworth for letting us read his manuscript, *Labor Supply* (Cambridge: Cambridge University Press, 1983). For additional comprehensive views of recent labor supply literature see the first three articles in Ronald G. Ehrenberg, ed., *Research in Labor Economics,* Vol. 4 (Greenwich, Conn.: JAI Press, 1981).

[13] See Killingsworth, *Labor Supply,* for a major effort in this direction.

TABLE 4-2   Average Weekly Hours in Manufacturing and Selected Nonmanufacturing Industries, 1890–1981

	(1)	(2)		(3)		(4)	(5)
				Building Trades			
	All	Manufac-		and Building			Hours in
	Nonagricultural	turing		Construction		Retail	Standard
Year	Establishments	a	b	a	b	Trade	Workweek
1890		62.2		51.3			
1895		62.3		50.3			66
1896		62.1					
1897		61.9					
1898		62.2					
1899		62.1					
1900		62.1		48.3			62
1905		61.1		46.1			
1910		53.5		45.2			57
1915		58.2		44.8			
1920		53.5	47.4	43.8			53
1925		52.2	44.5	43.9			
1930			42.1				52
1935			36.6		30.1		
1940			38.1		33.1	43.2	43
1945			43.4		39.0	40.9	
1946			40.4		38.1	41.6	
1950	39.8		40.5		37.4	40.0	41
1955			40.7		37.1	39.0	
1959			40.3		37.0	38.2	
1960	38.6		39.7		36.7	38.0	
1967					37.7	35.3	
1968					37.4	34.7	
1969						34.2	
1970	37.1		39.2*		37.4*	33.8**	
1975			39.5*		36.6*	32.4**	
1979			40.2*		37.0*	30.7**	
1980	35.3		39.7*			30.2**	
1981	35.3		40.1*				

* 1975–1981 data from *Statistical Abstract of the United States*, 1981, Table 666.
** 1975–1980 data from *Employment and Training Report of the President*, 1981, Table C-4.

Sources: Column (1)—*Handbook of Labor Statistics*, 1980, Table 84, and *Statistical Abstract of the United States*, 1981, Table 666. Columns (2)–(4)—*Historical Statistics of the United States, Colonial Times to 1970*: (2a)—Series D 769 (data from employer payrolls); (2b)—Series D 803 (production workers); this series may be understated because large firms are oversampled; (3a)—Series D 774 (union hours); (3b)—Series D 78 (nonsupervisory workers, building construction); (4)—Series D-884. Column (5)—Clarence D. Long, *The Labor Force Under Changing Income and Employment*, National Bureau of Economic Research (Princeton, N.J.: Princeton University Press, 1958), p. 272.

effect of, say, obesity or smoking on health. Often it is necessary to compare the health and longevity of one group of individuals who are, for example, overweight with another who are thinner. It is difficult to be *sure* that because the overweight group tends to die younger, getting fat persons to lose weight will actually increase their lifespans. Other, unobserved factors may be involved. Thus, it is possible for interested groups, such as tobacco growers and cigarette manufacturers, to argue that the bad effects of smoking on health have not been "proven."

Although in a few cases human labor supply behavior has been studied under experimental-type conditions, most studies are based on nonexperimental data in which the behavior of *different* individuals or groups is used to infer how a given individual would respond to, say, a change in his or her wage rate. We will discuss the results of both experimental and nonexperimental studies below so that you can form an opinion on their relative strengths and weaknesses and gain an understanding of the kinds of knowledge they provide. We will organize much of the discussion of empirical labor supply studies around the behavior of those groups that have exhibited significant changes in their labor force behavior over time and that make up very important components of our labor force—adult men and married women.

Experimental studies of labor supply behavior: Income-maintenance experiments.   During the 1960s there developed a growing concern over the complex and numerous welfare programs aimed at alleviating poverty. A great deal of discussion over welfare reform followed. A leading idea was to replace many existing programs with a single scheme that would provide money to those below a given income level, with the basic grant being reduced as earnings increased, but at a rate far less than 100 percent. The goal of such a negative income tax (NIT) would be to reduce poverty while maintaining work incentives. The analytical framework for discussing the work incentive effects of an NIT has been presented above on pages 130–132.

Much of the argument over whether an NIT would be a good idea centered on the magnitude of the work disincentives that would be induced among those who would be eligible but who would not be supported by existing income-maintenance programs such as Aid to Families with Dependent Children (AFDC) and Food Stamps. It was argued by many interested parties that existing knowledge of the magnitude of these disincentives, based on quantitative estimates of labor supply using data from nationwide surveys such as the decennial *Census of Population,* was unreliable because of the difficulty of knowing whether wage and nonemployment income variables reflected genuinely exogenous differences in household budget constraints. It was therefore proposed that the federal government finance experiments in which the labor supply of selected families who would be eligible to receive specially designed NIT support would be compared to the labor supply of similar families who were members of a statistical control group. Conceptually, this is similar to medical studies in which some individuals are randomly assigned specific treatments for an illness, while members of a control group are assigned a placebo. Several NIT experiments were conducted over the period 1968–78.[14] Their results provide unusual data for studying labor supply behavior. Considerable improvement in experimental design occurred as researchers learned from the earlier experimental studies. Thus, we can learn most by examining data from the later studies—the **Seattle and Denver Income Maintenance Experiments (SIME-DIME).** These are the longest-duration, largest, and most comprehensive of the negative income tax experiments.

We should note first that probably the most widely accepted facts to be learned are: (1) such experiments are not the hoped-for panacea for the problems of unobserved influences on labor supply behavior; and (2) the statistical techniques for analyzing the data must be just as complex as those required to deal properly with nonexperimental data.[15] For example, in a truly controlled NIT experiment, the influence of all other income-maintenance programs would be eliminated, so that the behavior of neither the subjects given the NIT "treatment" nor the controls who receive none would be affected by other types of income maintenance. However, it is an unacceptable, and probably unenforceable, restriction on individual freedom to prevent experimental subjects from applying for nonexperimental transfers when it is in their interest to do so.

Another complication is created by the difficulty in knowing what an experimental subject's income and work behavior *would have been* in the absence of the experiment. The only information on this question, which is crucial for measuring the change in labor supply that results from the NIT, is hours of work before the "dose" of NIT is administered. Consider two individuals who have identical incomes, work hours, and wage rates when observed just before going on the NIT program. In terms of Figure 4-13 (p. 131), suppose that both individuals would work $h(m) - h(0)$ hours for $\$i(0)$ income before the program, so that both would supposedly respond to the change in the budget constraint from $h(m)g(1)$ to $v(1)Ag(1)$ in the same manner. However, suppose in reality that only one has the set of indifference curves graphed in Figure 4-13 and the other is an "income lover." The income lover has an indifference curve that is tangent to $h(m)g(1)$ in the region *between* A and $g(1)$, and he or she was only *temporarily* working $h(m) - h(0)$ hours.[16] This individual's *normal* hours of work *exceed* $h(m) - h(3)$ hours, and, if hours of work return to normal after the experimental NIT

---

[14] Keeley, *Labor Supply,* p. 109.
[15] Keeley, *Labor Supply,* chap. 5, and Killingsworth, *Labor Supply,* chap. 6.
[16] Perhaps immediately prior to the NIT experiment things were "slow" at work, and these individuals had been temporarily put on "short hours."

is introduced, then the individual will be located to the left of point A, and his or her apparent response to the NIT will be considerably different than that of the "leisure lover."

This is *not* to imply, though, that the NIT *cannot* affect the income-loving person's supply of labor. Whether there is an adjustment of the income lover's normal work hours depends on whether or not the income lover's indifference curve that is tangent to the budget constraint between A and $g(1)$ passes *under* the $v(1)A$ segment of the constraint. If so, he or she will adjust work hours and receive an NIT grant. If not, no adjustment will occur. Thus, one type of individual—the one with the indifference curves graphed in Figure 4-13—is almost certain to receive an NIT grant and to reduce work hours after the NIT is introduced. Alternatively, the income lover may *increase* work hours and receive no NIT grant, even though he or she would be eligible if work hours remained low.

To summarize, an income lover who is not in the control group and is temporarily located to the right of point A on constraint $h(m)g(1)$ will be *eligible* for the NIT program when it is introduced. He or she may elect *not* to receive a grant, though, because doing so would require moving to the $v(1)A$ segment of the NIT constraint instead of to a point to the left of A.

How are the diverse responses of income lovers and leisure lovers to be analyzed, if the researcher wants to estimate the effects of an NIT on work behavior or the income and substitution effects of an exogenous shift in the budget constraint from $h(m)g(1)$ to $v(1)Ag(1)$? The existence of a control group in the NIT experiments helps answer this question. The control group will also be expected to include income lovers. Some of the income lovers in the control group will also be working temporarily short hours just before the initial availability of the NIT treatment, and some of them will shortly return to normal hours of work. Others will be working normal hours both before and after the NIT is introduced. Thus, by comparing the average adjustment of work hours of experimental subjects, who are eligible for the NIT treatment, with control subjects who by definition are not eligible, the average response to a given NIT can be estimated. If the eligible experimental subjects and the controls are randomly selected from the population, then the experimental results can be "blown up," or extrapolated to the population at large. If, as was actually the case in all the NIT experiments, the subjects were *not* randomly selected (for budgetary reasons), extrapolation to the population at large is more difficult, but still possible.

It is very important to recognize that while the existence of the control group makes it possible to estimate the *average* work response to a *given* NIT program [as measured by the level of $v(1)$ and the steepness of the budget line $v(1)A$ compared to $h(m)g(1)$ in Figure 4-13], more detailed information on labor supply is desirable, including an estimate of the income and substitution effects. This information has a number of valuable uses. (1) It is required if the results of given NIT experiments are to be applied to alternative programs with *different* basic support levels [$v(1)$] and implicit tax rates [the comparative slopes of $v(1)A$ and $h(m)g(1)$]. (2) This information is necessary when Congress wishes to know the work disincentive effects of a wide variety of NIT specifications. (3) It is also necessary to test the reliability of empirical results by how well they correspond with the behavioral implications of the theory of labor supply. Given the statistical problems described in the preceding few paragraphs, extracting such information from NIT experimental data is as complex a task as dealing with nonexperimental data.

Still another problem with the NIT experiments is their *temporary* nature. Because experimental subjects know that the program will last only, say, three, five, or eight years, their response to "treatment" will probably not be the same as if the NIT were expected to be permanent.[17] A review of pages 132–133 will help you see why a temporary experiment may yield misleading predictions of the effects of a permanent program.

A large body of published research results based on the NIT experiments has been accumulated by researchers.[18] From the preceding discussion, you should now realize that researchers hope for two important types of information from these experiments: (1) an estimate of the income and substitution effects of an NIT-induced change in an individual's budget constraint and (2) the estimated budgetary cost of alternative NITs compared with that of existing income-maintenance programs, particularly AFDC and food stamps. As in nonexperimental research, the statistical findings from the NIT experiments are highly sensitive to the statistical procedure used. Thus, the *average* research result from an *experimental* NIT may not be a very reliable indicator of the impact of an *actual* NIT. This should be borne in mind when we discuss the quantitative estimates based on the NIT experiments.

On average, statistical studies of the SIME-DIME data imply that husbands, wives, and female family heads would all reduce their work hours in response to the *income* effect of an NIT. We will analyze this income effect in terms of Figure 4-13. Imagine providing enough nonemployment income to enable an individual who had been earning $i(0)$ on constraint $h(m)g(1)$ to reach the point at which indifference curve U_2 is tangent to constraint $v(1)A$. As a result, the individual could then receive $i(1)$ and consume $h(1)$ leisure hours, although the wage rate remains unchanged. This can be visualized by drawing a line *parallel* to $h(m)g(1)$ *through* the point where U_2 is tangent to constraint $v(1)A$. Please take a piece of paper, copy Figure 4-13, and draw in this line. The individual described in Figure 4-13 would still be able to receive $i(1)$ total income and enjoy $h(1)$ of leisure along the constraint you

---

[17] For an analysis of *how* the responses are likely to differ, see Keely, *Labor Supply,* pp. 143–46.
[18] See Keeley, *Labor Supply,* chap. 5.

have drawn, but probably would not choose to do so. He or she would choose more leisure than $h(0)$, but less than $h(1)$ hours, because the price of leisure is higher on the imaginary budget line you have just drawn than along $h(m)g(1)$. The SIME-DIME results suggest that for each 1.0 percent increase in i obtainable at $h(m) - h(1)$ hours of work (the wage rate held constant) the average decline in work hours is 0.21 percent for husbands, 0.24 percent for wives, and 0.24 percent for single female household heads.[19] Put differently, if $\$i(1)$ is 10 percent greater than $\$i(0)$, the amount of work along the new budget line you have drawn in Figure 4-13 will be between 2.1 percent and 2.4 percent hours lower than $h(m) - h(0)$. This is the *income effect* of an NIT expressed in elasticity terms.

It is also true that NIT lowers the price of leisure, because an individual's benefit payments are reduced by some proportion of earnings. This is denoted by the relative flatness of the constraint $v(1)A$ compared to $h(m)g(1)$. The individual described in the figure you have just drawn will increase leisure hours all the way to $h(1)$. The substitution effect of an NIT is the *difference* between the quantity of leisure you have drawn in your picture and $h(1)$. The SIME-DIME results imply a substitution elasticity of 0.12 for husbands, 0.24 for wives, and 0.17 for single female household heads. This suggests that the *additional* reduction in hours of work, starting from the amount of work implied by the parallel upward shift of the budget constraint you drew in your copy of Figure 4-13, would be 6 percent for husbands, 12 percent for wives, and 8.5 percent for single female household heads. These results are for an NIT program that implicitly taxes earnings at a rate of 50 percent, a fairly modest rate for an NIT. Why do you think the estimated substitution elasticity for married women is larger than that for either husbands or single female heads of households?

The SIME-DIME program tested the effects of a basic support (v) equal to 0.9 times the official poverty level, 1.20 times the poverty level, and 1.4 times the poverty level. Paired with these were implicit tax rates on earnings equal to 50 percent and 70 percent. The results of the experiment have been used to estimate the net cost to the United States Treasury of alternative NITs compared to the AFDC and food stamp programs. This is an important question and one that is impossible to resolve on the basis of economic theory alone. Once again referring to Figure 4-13, we can see the inherent conflict between an adequate basic support level (v), a moderate rate of taxation (relatively small reduction in budget-line steepness), and program cost. Given the level of v, reducing the rate of taxation by increasing the steepness of budget constraint $v(1)A$ increases work incentives. However, it increases the number of income-loving persons who can raise their incomes by accepting an NIT payment. As the $v(1)A$ constraint gets steeper, given $v(1)$, point A moves leftward. This increases the number

---

[19] Keeley, *Labor Supply,* p. 168.

of potential NIT recipients. The SIME-DIME results were used to estimate the net outcome of these offsetting effects on husband-wife and female-headed families who are *not* currently receiving AFDC or food stamps plus the effects on families who currently receive such aid. The work incentives of the latter group would be enhanced by replacing food stamps and AFDC with a typical NIT.

The SIME-DIME results were extrapolated to basic support levels of both 50 and 75 percent of the official poverty level. (According to 1980 data supplied by the U.S. Department of Health and Human Services, maximum AFDC plus food stamps for a family of four ranged from 49 percent of the poverty level in Mississippi to 98 percent in California.) From this it was found that an NIT with basic support set at 50 percent of the poverty level and an implicit tax rate of 50 percent should *reduce* income-maintenance costs by a magnitude equal to about 30 percent of the amounts spent on AFDC and food stamps in 1974.[20] *Increasing* the tax rate to 70 percent further *reduced* costs, so that an amount equal to 40 percent of AFDC and food stamps expenditures would be saved. Increasing the basic support level would substantially increase program costs and result in a net increase in income-maintenance expenditures compared to AFDC and food stamps. For example, even with a 70 percent tax rate, NIT grants paid would nearly double if the basic support level were raised from 50 percent of the poverty level to 75 percent. Income-maintenance expenditures would amount to nearly 25 percent more ($2.2 billion in 1974 prices) than 1974 AFDC-food stamp expenditures. When interpreting these predictions you should bear in mind that they are subject to the same criticisms as are the estimates of labor supply responses discussed above. Although they may be the best estimates of NIT program costs available, a considerable amount of uncertainty is attached to them, and they should be used with caution.

Experimental studies with animal subjects.   It cannot be overemphasized that a repeated theme in empirical research on labor supply is the testing of estimated labor supply functions against the theoretical concept of the substitution effect. One reason is that economists would like to know whether the most important implication of labor supply theory holds up to empirical verification. Another reason is that economists wish to use the substitution effect as a criterion of the validity, or reliability, of particular sets of empirical results. Thus economists are frequently in the awkward position of assuming that the substitution effect is a reliable criterion of the validity of an empirical study while at the same time testing whether the substitution effect is a valid hypothesis describing economic behavior. If we could only be *sure* that the substitution-effect hypothesis stands up to empir-

---

[20] Michael C. Keeley et al., "The Labor Supply Effects and Costs of Alternative Negative Income Tax Programs," *Journal of Human Resources,* 13 (Winter 1978), 3–36.

ical verification, then we would be on much safer ground using it as a criterion of empirical results. What is needed is the truly controlled experiment
testing the implications of labor supply theory. However, as we have seen,
such experiments are probably not achievable with human beings as subjects.[21] Therefore, some social scientists have tested the substitution effect
implication of labor supply theory in controlled experimental situations using laboratory animals as subjects.[22]

Here is a brief description of how a recent animal experiment worked,
and what its results suggest about labor supply choices. The experiment[23] is
of particular interest because it tests the basic propositions of economic
theory concerning the income-leisure tradeoff and labor supply choices.
In this experiment, male white Carneaux pigeons with no previous experimental history were placed in specially designed cages. The pigeons were
paid incomes in the form of mixed pigeon grains received as a wage in return
for pecking a button. Their opportunity sets, or budget constraints, were like
those depicted in Figure 4-18(a). Grains were also freely delivered on a
random basis without pecking. The wage rate was raised by lowering the
average number of pecks required to obtain a given payoff of pigeon grains.
The amount of time taken to complete a peck is about the same for all
pigeons. Thus, it can be treated as a constant, and the number of button
pecks per day is a good measure of how much time a pigeon spends working.
Nonemployment income was raised by providing increased amounts of free
grains, as indicated by v in Figure 4-18.

Wage rates were set at nine different values, ranging from an average
of 0.5 grain payoffs per 100 pecks up to an average of 8 payoffs. The experiment is illustrated in Figure 4-18(a) for two wage rates. The constraint $\overline{0X}$
depicts a wage rate of 1 payoff/100 pecks and $\overline{0Y}$ a wage of 2 payoffs/100
pecks. In both cases, with no free income, $v = 0$, the pigeons were given
several days to adjust to each constraint. For example, we illustrate the
average behavior of four subjects along constraint $\overline{0X}$ at point A, showing
that after becoming accustomed to constraint $\overline{0X}$, they each worked approximately 4,500 pecks/day, on average, earning an income of approximately 45
payoffs.

---

[21] A type of experiment that uses human beings in a more controlled environment (fewer
unobserved effects on behavior permitted) than the NIT experiments, but still less of a controlled environment than experiments with animal subjects, involves **token economies.** Here
human subjects perform tasks in return for token money that can be exchanged for various
commodities. Token-economy experiments are fairly limited because of legal restrictions. For
example, it would usually be considered inhumane to subject humans to stressfully low income
so that they were on the border of malnutrition. Token-economy experimental results have
generally been favorable to the substitution-effect hypothesis. See Raymond Battalio, John H.
Kagel, et al., "A Test of Consumer Demand Theory Using Observations of Individual Consumer Purchases," *Western Economic Journal,* 11 (December 1973), 411–27.
[22] Raymond C. Battalio, L. Green, and John H. Kagel, "Income Leisure Tradeoffs of Animal
Workers," *American Economic Review,* 71 (September 1981), 621–33.
[23] Battalio, Green, and Kagel, "Income-Leisure Tradeoffs."

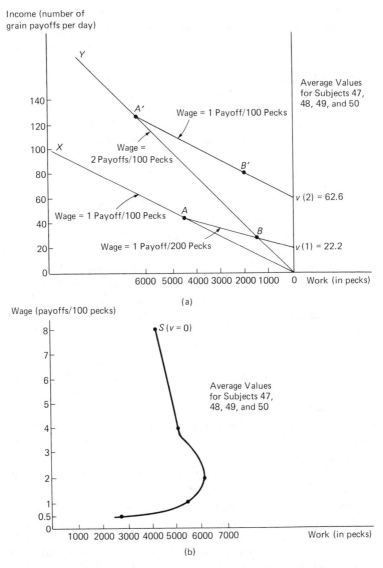

FIGURE 4-18. A test of labor supply theory with pigeons as subjects (a) Substitution effect, (b) Labor supply (in pecks per day)

To test the substitution-effect hypothesis, the pigeons were then provided with an opportunity set defined by constraint $v(1)AX$. This was accomplished by halving the wage rate to 0.5 payoffs/100 pecks and providing free income equal to one-half that earned at point A. Thus, the pigeons could reach point A once again, achieving the same real income as before. Since A

was originally chosen, or preferred, to any point to the left on $\overline{OX}$, the substitution-effect hypothesis would be contradicted by the pigeons' subsequently choosing to work more than they did at point A, after their budget constraint was changed to $v(1)AX$. On average, the pigeons in the experiment *reduced* work effort to approximately 1,500 pecks per day (point B), as implied by the substitution hypothesis.

The same experiment was performed at each initial wage rate, 0.5 through 8 payoffs/100 pecks. In all cases the hypothesis that with real income held constant, the supply of labor is a positive function of the wage rate, was strongly supported.

Points A, A', and the comparable points on constraints defining higher wage rates provide information on the labor supply of pigeons with nonemployment income equal to zero. The average labor supply for the four subjects whose behavior is illustrated in Figure 4-18(a) is represented in Figure 4-18(b). Evidently, pigeons exhibit a backward-bending supply of labor. At lower wage rates, labor supply increases, reaches a maximum, and then declines at higher wage rates. Between the lowest wage of 0.5 payoff/100 pecks and the wage of 2 payoffs/100 pecks, labor supply increased by about 3,500 pecks/day, gradually falling at higher wages. A simple set of calculations shows that average income earned continued to rise as wage rates increased.

Do these results generalize to human beings? What do you think?

Labor supply studies using nonexperimental data: Adult men and women, with an application to the effect of progressive income taxation on labor supply.   By far the majority of empirical labor supply studies have used nonexperimental data from various surveys—the Decennial Census, Current Population Survey (CPS), University of Michigan Panel Study of Income Dynamics (PSID), and Ohio State University's National Longitudinal Surveys (NLS) being the most commonly used data sets. In the next few pages we will summarize the results of a few of these studies. The studies surveyed have been selected because they represent extremely skillful use of statistical and theoretical techniques to overcome the problems inherent in interpreting the results of the uncontrolled "nonexperiments" or because they provide persuasive explanations of important trends and features of labor supply behavior.

The most ambitious of these studies is by Jerry A. Hausman, who incorporates the major complications mentioned or discussed in this chapter in estimating the labor supply of husbands, wives, and unmarried female heads of households.[24] These complications include the following: (1) estimating labor force participation and hours of work decisions simultaneously

---

[24] "Labor Supply," in Henry J. Aaron and Joseph A. Pechman, *How Taxes Affect Economic Behavior* (Washington, D.C.: The Brookings Institution, 1981), pp. 27–72.

(How do you measure the wage rate of someone who is out of the labor force?), (2) incorporating the effect of fixed costs of holding a job (Hausman focuses on the *money* costs of a job rather than the time costs, but the impact on reservation work hours is similar); (3) the effect of existing income-maintenance programs as reflected particularly in Aid to Families of Dependent Children (AFDC); (4) the impact of progressive income taxation and Social Security taxation on labor supply; and (5) allowing for individual variation in tastes for income (goods) versus leisure. Needless to say, carrying out this set of complicated tasks requires sophisticated and complex statistical techniques that go far beyond the scope of this text to explain. Therefore, we will emphasize the basic assumptions Hausman made to estimate labor supply functions and some important features of his results.

Figure 4-19 illustrates some of the complications introduced by the factors Hausman considered in his research. The budget constraint $v(0)X$ is similar to that used to analyze labor supply decisions earlier in this chapter. The individual represented in Figure 4-19 receives nonemployment income of $\$v(0)$, which may include AFDC payments, and a market wage rate equal to the slope of $v(0)X$. However, if this individual performs some market work, the effective budget constraint becomes $v(1)ABCDg(1)$. The fixed money cost of holding a job affects the constraint in exactly the same way as

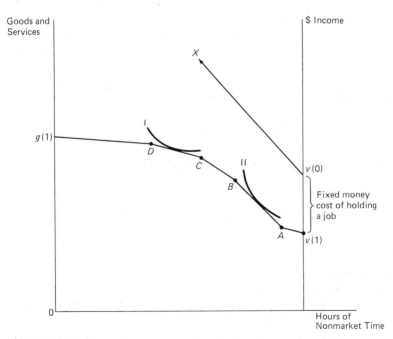

FIGURE 4-19. A budget constraint reflecting fixed money cost of labor force participation, AFDC, and progressive income taxation

a decline in nonemployment income equal to $[v(0) - v(1)]$. The segment $v(1)A$ reflects the implicit 67 percent tax on earnings due to reductions in AFDC payments. The segment AB reflects the lowest positive income tax bracket and the segment BC the next lowest bracket. As earnings rise and AFDC payments fall to zero at point A, the effective marginal tax on earnings falls. At point B the progressive income tax causes marginal tax rates to rise and the effective wage rate to fall. Higher brackets are reached at points C and D. (Hausman actually used twelve tax brackets in his study.) Figure 4-19 shows how an individual's effective (posttax) wage rate is partly determined by hours of work when there is a progressive income tax. If the budget constraint were $v(0)X$, an "income lover" (represented by indifference curve I) would face the same wage rate as a "leisure lover" (represented by indifference curve II). However, when $v(1)ABCDg(1)$ is the relevant constraint, they face different effective wage rates, even though their employers pay them the same amount per hour. The income lover is in a higher income tax bracket than the leisure lover. Consequently, his or her marginal net wage (take-home pay) is *lower* than that of the leisure lover.

In order to simplify his analysis considerably, Hausman assumed that in husband-wife families, labor supply decisions are made sequentially, with the husband being considered the principal earner. It would be theoretically more appropriate, but considerably more complex, to treat husband-wife labor supply decisions as simultaneously determined. In a framework incorporating simultaneous decision making, an increase in the wife's wage would create not only an income effect on the husband's labor supply, but also a pure price (cross-substitution) effect akin to the substitution effect on her own hours of work. This price effect would tend to increase the husband's hours of work if husband and wife's leisure time are complements and reduce it if they are substitutes. (Can you interpret what this means in "common-sense" terms?) Similarly, a change in the husband's wage would create an income and a pure price effect, influencing the wife's hours of work.

Rather than incorporate the complexities just discussed, Hausman opted for a simpler approach. He chose to treat the husband's earnings as part of nonemployment income from the wife's point of view and assumed that the husband's hours of work are determined on the basis of only his own wage rate and the family's nonemployment income, *excluding* the wife's earnings. An important implication of this set of assumptions is that the wife's after-tax wage rate for her *first* hour of work is $w(w)(1 - t)$, where $w(w)$ is her wage rate before taxes and t is the tax bracket applicable to the *husband's last dollar earned*. Thus, in Hausman's study, the value to the family of the payoff for an additional hour of the wife's work is considerably smaller than it would be if the wife were the family's sole earner.

Hausman estimated labor supply functions using PSID data for 1,085 married men and women in 1975. In Hausman's data, the husbands were between 25 and 55 years of age and not farmers, self-employed, or severely disabled. He estimated that the elasticity of hours of labor supplied with respect to the market rate of pay is, on average, about zero.[25] This does *not* imply that husbands' supply of labor is insensitive to changes in their budget constraints—only that for a wage change, holding nonemployment income constant, the income and substitution effects approximately cancel each other. These separate effects were estimated by Hausman to be rather large. One important implication of these estimates is that a negative income tax, which *raises* nonemployment income while *lowering* the effective wage rate, would have a sizable effect on hours of work. One of Hausman's more interesting results is that compared to a situation with *no* taxes, federal income taxes reduced by 8 percent the labor supplied by an average husband.

His results for wives are also interesting. Hausman estimates that the elasticity of a wife's work hours with respect to her hourly wage, holding nonemployment income constant, is rather large—about 0.92 for full-time workers. It is even larger for women who work less than full time. Although his study was not intended to provide an explanation of the rising labor force participation of married women, its results can be helpful in understanding the upward trend.

Hausman's treatment of wives as secondary workers led him to specify the husband's earnings as the wife's nonemployment income. Therefore, his estimates make it possible to answer the question: how would an equiproportionate increase in husbands' and wives' wage rates over time (which is a fairly good approximation to their actual historical trends) affect wives' labor supply? The answer depends on the elasticity of wives' labor supply with respect to their own wage rates and with respect to their husbands' wage rates. Hausman's results imply that the elasticity of wives' labor supply with respect to their husbands' wage rates is opposite in sign to and about two-thirds as large as the elasticity of wives' labor supply with respect to their own wage rates. Thus, given the 0.95 own-wage elasticity mentioned above, a 1 percent increase in *both* husbands' and wives' wage rates would lead to an increase in wives' labor force participation of about (0.95 − 0.63) = 0.32 percent. Thus, the wives' labor supply equation estimated by Hausman is broadly consistent with the historical upward trend in the labor force participation of married women.

The larger own-wage elasticity of wives' labor supply also implies that, for them, there is a relatively large work disincentive built into the existing system of progressive income taxes. On average, Hausman estimates that wives' labor supply is reduced by 18.2 percent compared to a situation with no tax at all.[26] This is about three times as large as the impact of the income tax on husbands' labor supply.

---

[25] The elasticity estimates for Hausman's study are reported in Killingsworth, *Labor Supply,* Table 4.2.

[26] Jerry A. Hausman, "Income and Payroll Tax Policy and Labor Supply," in Lawrence H. Meyer, ed., *The Supply-Side Effects of Economic Policy* (St. Louis: Center for the Study of American Business, Washington University, 1981), pp. 173–202.

The major cause of the progressive income tax's substantial work disincentives is the high tax rates that apply to the earnings received by families in the upper income brackets. Hausman estimates the impact of two types of tax reform on labor supply, tax revenues, and average tax rates (total taxes paid divided by income).[27] The first tax reform is a version of the Kemp-Roth proposal in which the progressive tax structure is retained, but all tax rates are reduced by the same proportion. In particular, Hausman considers 10 percent and 30 percent reductions. It is conceivable that such a reduction in tax rates would increase labor supply so much that tax revenues to the government would not fall as a result of the lower tax rates. Hausman estimates that a 30 percent across-the-board tax cut would raise the labor supply of husbands by about 2.7 percent and that of wives by about 9.4 percent. Despite "supply-side" arguments to the contrary, these increases would not be sufficient to avoid a reduction in tax revenue, which would fall by about 20 percent.

The second kind of tax reform would replace the existing progressive tax structure with a **linear income tax** that yields the same revenue as the present tax structure. A linear tax structure would tax all incomes at the same proportional rate, with an exemption to reduce or eliminate the taxes paid by low-income families. The advantage of this tax system is that it avoids the progressively higher marginal rate of taxation that causes the budget constraint in Figure 4-19 to become flatter as income rises. Instead, the budget constraint would have only one kink in it—at the income level that is the maximum amount exempt from taxation. From that point on, the slope of the budget constraint would be constant, and flatter than the non-taxed portion of the constraint by the tax rate. This is depicted in Figure 4-20. Then, nonemployment income is $v(0)$, and the amount of income exempt from taxation is $i(0)$. The effective (net) wage rate is w up to $h(m) - h(*)$ hours of work, and the net wage falls to $w(1 - t)$ for all work hours in excess of $h(m) - h(*)$.

Hausman estimated that if $4,000 per family were exempt from income taxation, a tax rate of 20.7 percent would yield the same tax revenues as the existing tax system. This would represent a significant increase in labor supply—particularly at higher income levels—compared to the current system of income taxation. The labor supply of husbands would be about 7 percent larger than under the current system, and that of wives about 20 percent larger. These increases are so great that the average taxes paid *as a percent of earnings* would be smaller at *all* income levels than under the present progressive tax structure. (Remember that this would occur with *no* reduction in tax revenues.)

More evidence from nonexperimental data: Why has the labor force of adult men been getting smaller? In our discussion of Hausman's study of

---

[27] *Ibid.*

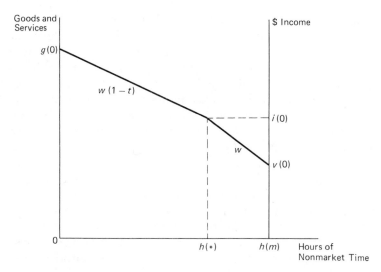

FIGURE 4-20. The budget constraint when there is a linear income tax

the labor supply of married men and women, we noted that his estimates for married women are broadly consistent with the historic increase in their labor force participation. What about trends in the labor supply of men? Hausman's estimate of the labor supply of married men implies that as wage rates increase over time, the quantity of market work supplied will remain roughly constant. Yet, as Table 4-1 shows, over the past thirty years there has been a significant *decline* in the labor force participation rate of married men who are in the middle to late years of their working lives. It is true that the ten-percentage-point decline in labor force participation that occurred between 1949 and 1979 is not as dramatic as the postwar doubling of the labor force participation of married women. However, the fact that married men less than 65 years old have almost always been the principal earners in their families makes this labor force change worth understanding. To what can we ascribe the two-and-one-half-fold increase in the proportion of married men who are labor force *nonparticipants*? What variables, not included in Hausman's study, are responsible? Can the decline in labor force participation be explained in terms of the labor supply theory developed in this chapter?

Poor health has commonly been cited as a reason for early retirement by men under 65. In a recent article Donald Parsons notes that in 1957, social security benefits that had previously been payable only to individuals who were at least 65 years old were made available to those who could prove that a long-term health or physical problem prevented them from engaging in any significant market work.[28] Until 1961, the lower age limit for these social security disability payments was 50. This restriction was relaxed in 1961, further enlarging the number of eligible recipients. Parsons hypothesizes that a significant number of beneficiaries under this plan have health problems that are not 100 percent disabling and that permit certain kinds of work to be performed. As a result, the existence of social security benefits for those who can persuade program administrators that they qualify as disabled may have encouraged many individuals to try to qualify who would instead work if no benefits were available.[29]

The receipt of significant work-related income is used as prima facie evidence that a disability does *not* exist. This means that the earnings of persons whose health is bad enough to qualify for support, but not so bad that work is impossible, are implicitly taxed at a very high rate by the social security disability program. Clearly, those who stand to gain the most by becoming eligible are individuals whose pre-eligibility earnings are relatively small because their market wage is low. Thus, it is not surprising that nonparticipation has grown much more rapidly for men with an eighth-grade education or less than for those who graduated from high school or attended college.[30]

*A detailed analysis of Parsons' study.** In order to assess the impact of social security disability benefits on labor force participation, Parsons estimated the following labor force participation regression equation for approximately 5,000 individual males 45–59 years old in 1966:[31]

$$LFP = 1.25 - 0.00148 \frac{SSB}{w} + 0.000089 \frac{WEL}{w} - 0.152 \, UR$$
$$(5.62) \phantom{0.00148 \frac{SSB}{w}} (0.23) \phantom{0.000089 \frac{WEL}{w}} (5.48)$$
$$- 0.0045 \, AGE - 0.259 \, MORT \, 66\text{--}67 - 0.139 \, MORT \, 67\text{--}68$$
$$(5.44) (8.20) (4.73)$$
$$- 0.174 \, MORT \, 68\text{--}69 - 0.142 \, MORT \, 69\text{--}71 - 0.110 \, MORT \, 71\text{--}73$$
$$(7.09) (5.66)$$
$$- 0.048 \, MORT \, 73\text{--}75 - 0.021 \, MORT \, 75\text{--}76$$
$$(2.56) (0.86)$$

(4-5)

---

[28] Donald O. Parsons, "The Decline in Male Labor Force Participation," *Journal of Political Economy,* 88 (February 1980), 117–34.

[29] During the early years of the program, earning as little as $100 a month was acceptable proof of ability to work (Parsons, "The Decline in Male Labor Force Participation," p. 124). Currently, the limit is $240 per month. Smaller amounts will place an applicant in a "questionable" status.

[30] Parsons, "The Decline in Male Labor Force Participation," p. 121.

* This section contains more technical material that may be skipped without loss of continuity. If you skip, go to page 158.

[31] See Parsons, *ibid.* and "Racial Trends in Male Labor Force Participation," *American Economic Review,* 70 (December 1980), 911–20. Equation (4-12) is not found in exactly the same form in either paper. It was kindly provided by Parsons. We are reporting here a linear probability equation which, although not as appropriate econometrically as those in the cited papers, is somewhat easier to interpret. It does not yield substantially different results than the equations reported by Parsons. The data are for 4,887 men in the 1966 National Longitudinal Survey of Men.

where the numbers in parentheses are t values and

$LFP \equiv$ a dummy variable $= 1$ if the individual was in the labor force during the week surveyed in 1966, and $= 0$ if not in the labor force

$SSB \equiv$ potential monthly social security disability benefits if the individual should qualify as disabled

$w \equiv$ the individual's hourly wage rate

$WEL \equiv$ a measure of state welfare generosity (average general assistance plus AFDC paid in each state per family below the poverty line of \$3,000 in 1966

$UR \equiv$ fraction of year the individual was unemployed in 1965

$MORT \equiv$ a set of dummy variables $= 1$ if the individual died in the years indicated, which are after the survey was conducted in 1966, and $= 0$ if he did not die

$AGE \equiv$ age in years.

Since evidence of poor health is necessary to qualify for social security disability, Parsons used data on whether the men in the sample died in subsequent years as an indicator of health status in 1966. Obviously, a person who died shortly after the 1966 survey was likely to have been in poorer health than someone who lived ten or more years longer.

The interpretation of equation (4-5) is as follows. Because the dependent variable is equal to 0 for nonparticipants and 1 for participants, the coefficients of equation (4-5) represent the effect of a unit change in the respective independent variable on the *probability* of labor force participation for an individual in 1966. Thus, the coefficient of SSB/w tells us that a one-unit increase in the ratio of potential benefits to the hourly wage (about a 2 percent increase in the ratio's mean value) *lowers the probability* of labor force participation by 0.15 percent for an individual and the *labor force participation rate* of a group of identical individuals by the same amount, other things being equal. An individual who died within a year of the 1966 survey ($MORT\ 66\text{–}67$) was almost 26 percent less likely to have participated in the labor force in 1966 than a typical individual who was still alive in 1976, other things equal. Parsons also showed[32] that when the variables (1) SSB/w and (2) SSB/w multiplied by an index based on the $MORT$ variables were used in the *same* equation, the coefficient of SSB/w times $MORT$ indicates a much larger negative impact on LFP than SSB/w alone. This clearly shows that health problems and social security interact to reduce the labor force participation of low-wage workers. The interpretation of the other coefficients of equation (4-5) is similar to that for the coefficients of SSB/w and $MORT\ 66\text{–}67$ and generally supports both the theory of labor force participation and Parsons' hypothesis about social security benefits' impact on labor force participation.

In order to test the power of equation (4-5) to explain the increasing fraction of 45- to 59-year-old men who are nonparticipants, Parsons calculated the economy-wide counterparts of the variables in the equation for each year from 1948 through 1976. He then multiplied each variable in a year by its coefficient in equation (4-5) in order to derive a predicted value of labor force participation for this group of men for the United States. (It might be more accurate to refer to this procedure as "postdicting" or "backcasting" labor force participation of the past.) Subtracting this predicted value from 100 percent yields the predicted value of labor force nonparticipation for each year 1948–76. The predicted values match the actual values quite closely and account for nearly all the growth in nonparticipation. Parsons also found that the relatively severe decline in the labor force participation of black men is also well explained by the influence of social security disability benefits. Because blacks

---

[32] "The Decline in Male Labor Force Participation."

earn lower wage rates than whites, social security benefits make leaving the labor force an attractive alternative for a higher proportion of blacks than whites.[33]

Before concluding our discussion of the decline in male labor force participation, we should emphasize that the ability of equation (4-5) to backcast actual male labor force participation over time between 1948 and 1976 does not by itself prove that the major reason for the decline has been the increased availability and generosity of social security benefits. Other variables in equation (4-5) may be doing the work. For example, equation (4-5) might provide a good explanation of past trends if the health of the population had deteriorated, without any change being attributable to changes in SSB/w. Indeed, the fraction of men in this age group who received social security disability benefits—a possible indicator of bad health—nearly quadrupled between 1960 and 1978.[34] The reason we can reject deteriorating health as an explanation is that a more objective indicator of health condition—mortality—implies a significant *improvement* in health. In particular, mortality *declined* by more than one-fourth over the period studied.[35] Indeed, Parsons' hypothesis implies that we would observe an increase in the proportion of men receiving social security benefits, not because of worsening health, but because of the increasing ratio of potential benefits to wages. Moreover, this has occurred in conjunction with declining labor force participation.[36] Thus, we can be fairly confident that the increasing fraction of men not in the labor force can be explained in terms of their response to changing monetary incentives to qualify as disabled, as opposed to a secular deterioration in health status.

Why has the "full-time" workweek stopped shrinking?   Given Hausman's findings that the labor supply of married men is insensitive to variations in their wage rates, it would not be surprising that the length of the workweek in most industries has remained almost constant during the past forty years (see Table 4-2). However, if we accept this stability as explainable in terms of Hausman's results, we are left with the puzzle of explaining why the workweek declined so steadily during the early part of this century.

Before going on to answer this question, we should consider some possible objections to viewing changes in average weekly hours of work simply as adjustments to rising wage rates along a fixed labor supply curve. Put differently, to what extent is it reasonable to suppose that observed work hours represent only the utility-maximizing choices of individuals responding to their wage rates, given their nonemployment income and tastes for goods versus leisure?[37] After all, is it not likely that the length of the workweek also represents employer preferences, technological constraints, collective bargaining, and wages and hours legislation?

To be sure, employer preferences and technological constraints may be

---

[33] "Racial Trends in Male Labor Force Participation."
[34] Unpublished research provided by Donald Parsons.
[35] "The Decline in Male Labor Force Participation," p. 132.
[36] "The Male Labor Force Participation Decision: Health, Reported Health, and Economic Incentives," *Economica,* 49 (February 1982), 81–91.
[37] For a clear statement of this view and possible objections to it, see H. G. Lewis, "Hours of Work and Hours of Leisure," *Proceedings of the Ninth Annual Winter Meeting, The Industrial Relations Research Association,* December 1956, pp. 196–206.

important in some occupations, and it would certainly be inefficient for employers to have work forces composed of personnel who at any moment of time work different numbers of hours per week at their own discretion and who change the number of hours worked at will. Employers are also unlikely to ignore the extra hiring and training costs that result when more workers are required to offset a declining workweek. Thus, labor *demand* as well as *supply* may influence observed hours of work. As we will see, employers' interests may well have influenced the length of the average workweek of full-time workers in the second half of this century.

As far as wages and hours legislation is concerned, however, the federal Fair Labor Standards Act (FLSA), requiring an overtime premium for work hours exceeding 40 per week, did not become effective until 1938. Hours of work in most industries fell substantially throughout the early part of this century and cannot therefore be attributed to FLSA. A similar argument applies to the effects of trade unions, which did not cover an important proportion of the labor force until after most of this century's decline in the length of the workweek had already occurred.

Thomas Kniesner[38] has attempted to solve the puzzle of the halt in the decline of the full-time workweek. His solution demonstrates the importance of distinguishing between short-run and long-run labor supply decisions. As we pointed out earlier, the labor supply theory presented in this chapter is essentially a short-run theory, explaining the response of labor force participation and hours of work to changes in the market wage rate. By distinguishing between short run and long run, we mean that wage changes caused by worker decisions to acquire additional schooling or training influence work-leisure choices in a different way than do wage changes caused by exogenous increases in the demand for labor of a given quality.[39] Why? One reason is that individuals who increase their market earning power through further schooling are already expressing a commitment to market work. This should lead us to expect that for a given wage rate, workers with greater schooling will probably work longer hours than other workers. Moreover, jobs typically held by comparatively well-educated workers are traditionally relatively pleasant, in that working conditions are better, the tasks more interesting, and so on. This would also increase hours of market work, all other

---

[38] "The Full-Time Workweek in the United States, 1900–1970," *Industrial and Labor Relations Review,* 3:1 (October 1976), 3–15; and "The Full-Time Workweek in the United States, 1900–1970: Revisions and Some Extensions," *Industrial and Labor Relations Review,* 33:3 (April 1980), 385–89.

[39] Please keep in mind that the distinction between long run and short run does not necessarily denote a distinction between long and short periods of time. A long-run decision simply involves a choice that affects an individual over a longer, rather than a shorter, time period. Thus, the decision to complete high school will affect the course of someone's entire life. On the other hand, rising wage rates over a long period of time, such as thirty years, may or may not have anything to do with decisions workers have made in the past to acquire schooling or training, although such wage increases will probably affect short-run decisions on desired hours of work and labor force participation.

things being equal. Since Hausman did not consider the influence of education on labor supply in his research on men, his estimate of the relationship between the amount of labor supplied and wage rates probably reflects the influence of education on both wages and labor supply. If additional schooling raises *both* wage rates and hours of work, neglect of the influence of education would bias upward the estimated effect of the wage rate on work hours. Since Hausman estimated the elasticity of hours of work with respect to wage rates as nearly zero, the actual effect of a wage increase, holding schooling constant, may well be negative.

Schooling also affects the relationship between wage rates and work hours from the demand side of the labor market. As we mentioned above, employers do not view a reduction in hours of work per employee as cost-less, because more workers must be employed to obtain the same number of total work hours. As we will see in Chapter 9, employers tend to invest more money in searching for and training better-educated workers. Therefore, as employees' schooling increases, so does employers' resistance to a reduced workweek. This means that as workers acquire more years of schooling, they are likely to find they are offered higher wage rates, but they will also find that these higher rates of pay are more readily obtained if they are willing to work more rather than fewer hours of work per week.

Thus, when wage rate increases are due to rising schooling levels, we should expect there to be a different association with hours of work than when the increases are attributable to a rising amount of physical capital per worker. Kniesner found that schooling is indeed important in accounting for the leveling off in the length of the manufacturing workweek after 1940. Between 1910 and 1940, median years of schooling completed by persons age 25 and over rose from 8.1 to 8.6. This represents a rate of increase of about 0.2 percent per year in level of schooling. The median level of schooling soared to 12 years by 1970, an annual rate of increase of 1.1 percent during 1940–70. At the same time, the rate of growth of real wage rates also accelerated, but not by nearly as much. Between 1910 and 1940, the average real hourly wage rate in manufacturing rose by about 2.6 percent annually, while between 1940 and 1960 the annual rate of growth was about 3.0 percent.[40] Thus, the relative influence of schooling on hours of work may well have increased over the years.

When the influences of schooling, wife's earning power, and unemployment rates on hours of work are held constant, Kniesner estimates an elasticity of weekly hours of work with respect to real hourly earnings in manufacturing of −0.5; this relationship holds for years both before and after 1940. Since an additional year of schooling is estimated to increase the average workweek by one hour, the approximately four-year increase in median years of schooling since 1940 has substantially offset the effect of

---

[40] Thomas J. Kniesner, "Recent Behavior of the 'Full-Time' Workweek in the U.S." (Unpublished Ph.D. dissertation, The Ohio State University, 1974), Appendix A.

rising hourly wage rates. Kniesner finds that, had there not been the acceleration in years of schooling completed among members of the labor force, the full-time workweek in manufacturing would probably have continued to decline after 1940 about as rapidly, in percentage terms, as it did before 1940.

Labor Supply Functions Derived

What happens to the quantity of labor supplied when there is an increase in wage rates? The answer is represented by the labor supply curve. As we have seen, derivation of the labor supply curve depends upon what other variables are being held constant when the wage rate changes and in which population group we are interested. The labor supply curve also depends on whether we are examining the effect of economywide variation in wage rates or changes in only one industry or local labor market. Here, we will summarize briefly what theory and evidence on the short-run labor supply tell us about the relationship between market wage rates and the quantity of market work offered by individuals.

The economywide labor supply.   When there is a change in the economywide average rate of pay for market work, two types of labor supply responses are elicited. There will be changes in decisions regarding whether to engage in any market work at all, and those individuals already participating in the labor force may wish to adjust their work hours. The major source of variation in labor force participation over time in the United States has come from married women, who have substantially increased their labor force participation in response to historically rising wage rates. However, rising wage rates also imply higher levels of family income. In response to this latter change, to the availability of social security benefits, and to the taxation of earnings implicit in the way social security benefits are determined, the participation of older workers has declined.[41] The net effect of rising wage rates on the labor force participation of the economy at large, then, has been a significant increase in the proportion of the population engaged in labor market activity. Over the last century, the total labor force participation rate has risen by about 20 percentage points.[42] At the same time, the length of the workweek of full-time workers has declined (through World War II). The net change in the proportion of total available time the United States population has chosen to commit to the labor market is largely the outcome of these two opposing trends. Another factor is that the additional workers in the labor force—mainly married women—are much more likely to hold part-time jobs than are men.[43]

---

[41] See Michael D. Hurd and Michael J. Boskin, "The Effect of Social Security on Retirement in the Early 1970's," Working Paper No. 659 (Cambridge, Mass.: National Bureau of Economic Research, 1981).

[42] See sources of Table 4-1.

[43] *Handbook of Labor Statistics,* 1980, Table 48.

To summarize: through the first 40 or 50 years of this century, while the full-time workweek was falling, the population as a whole responded to increased wage rates by reducing the fraction of available time spent in market work—a downward-sloping supply curve. Since then, the economy-wide labor supply curve has been more nearly vertical and perhaps even upward-sloping, as the labor force participation of married women has accelerated while average work hours have fallen significantly only in the service and retail trade industries (probably reflecting the influx of female workers to these jobs). One reason for this difference in the shape of the aggregate labor supply function is the growing importance of schooling in determining real wage increases that we noted earlier.

The labor supply to industries and local labor markets.   The labor supply response to a change in the average wage rate in a single industry or labor market *is not the same as that in the economy as a whole.* The principal reason for this difference lies in the variables that are being held constant when analyzing the labor supply decision. In the case of the economywide labor supply, we focus on variation in the price of leisure while assuming no change in the relative attractiveness of employment in alternative industries or locations. Now we focus on what happens when the wage rate in a single industry or location changes, *wages elsewhere in the economy remaining unchanged.* The labor supply decision in this case involves choosing *where* to work much more than *whether* or *how much.* Given the quality of working conditions (other than rate of pay), it is clearly in a worker's interest to obtain the highest possible wage rate. *Therefore, the labor supply curve to an industry or local labor market should be positively related to the wage rate.* Since changing jobs from one industry or local market to another involves costs that may be substantial, the supply of labor to industries and localities has a significant long-run aspect. Mobility of workers between labor markets is discussed in Chapters 5 and 9.

FRONTIERS OF LABOR SUPPLY ANALYSIS: THE NEW HOME ECONOMICS

Throughout this chapter we have approached labor supply as the choice between market work and "leisure," recognizing that this distinction, although useful as a first approximation, hides much of economic interest. Economists have recently begun to look beneath the surface of the concept of leisure and explore how nonmarket activities contribute to economic well-being. One might say that the emphasis on the role of time out of the labor force constitutes an invasion by economists into the realm of home economics. The essence of this **new home economics** is to place the family as an economic entity on a par with the firm, whereas traditionally the family is viewed as deriving utility from the consumption of time and market goods. The new approach recognizes that neither time nor market goods are consumed by themselves. Hours of nonmarket time are not enjoyable without goods, and all goods require time to consume. Thus, the household is viewed as a firm that combines time and goods inputs into "commodities" which it both produces and consumes.[44] Time is required both as an input in the commodity production process and to trade in the labor market for the other essential input—market goods. Labor supply is therefore determined as the outcome of decisions on which commodities to produce, how many to produce, and how to produce them.

Although it may seem contrived at first to view the household as a firm, it is, once you think about it, not really strange at all. Food (raw materials) and time are combined by the household to produce *home-cooked meals*. In a more complex process, food, shopping time, preparation time, and mealtime are combined in the household to produce the commodity *nutrition*. Time and market goods (tickets) are combined to yield the commodity, *attending a baseball game*. Numerous parental uses of time are combined with market goods such as clothing, food, schooling, medical services, and the time of children to produce *child quality*. Young adults use their time and schooling to enhance their future earning power by producing *human capital* (see Chapter 8). It is intuitively appealing, then, to view the family as deriving utility from the commodities produced in the home with the inputs of time and market goods. The quantity of market labor supplied by individual family members is still viewed as the complement to the quantity demanded for use in the household. The advantage of the household production approach over the simpler theory of labor supply developed earlier in this chapter is that it facilitates the systematic study of a wide variety of household activities and labor supply. Since economists feel that it is possible to understand production technology better than tastes for goods versus leisure, the production approach allows us to explain a wide spectrum of behavior (including aspects of labor supply) with fewer special assumptions about tastes.

Unfortunately, the gain in understanding the intricate relationship among consumption, production, and labor supply activities is not achieved without cost. That cost is a somewhat more complex theory than when consumption activities and labor supply are viewed as unconnected processes. Thus, the outline of some of the basic features of the household production approach will not be as extensive as we would like it to be. In the next few paragraphs we will develop some interesting topics dealt with in the study of household production and relate them to individuals' labor supply decisions.

A Simple View of Home Production and Market Work

We present here a relatively simple approach, developed by Reuben Gronau,[45] to the complex relationships among leisure, home production, and market labor supply. The essential feature of Gronau's approach is a distinction between work at home and leisure. Work at home involves the production of *home goods or services*. Since home goods are equivalent to *market goods,* the decision whether to produce goods or services in the home or to purchase them in the market depends on which method is cheaper. Gronau distinguishes intuitively between work at home and leisure by noting that if the cost were low enough, one would hire another person to

---

[44] Four names closely associated with the new home economics are Gary S. Becker, Kelvin J. Lancaster, Robert T. Michael, and Reuben Gronau. See Becker's "A Theory of the Allocation of Time," *The Economic Journal,* 75 (1965), 493–517; Lancaster's "A New Approach to Consumer Theory," *Journal of Political Economy,* 74 (1966), 132–57; Michael and Becker, "On the New Theory of Consumer Behavior," *The Swedish Journal of Economics,* 75 (1973), 378–96; and Gronau's "Leisure Time, Home Production, and Market Work," *Journal of Political Economy,* 85 (December 1977), 1099–1124.

[45] "Leisure, Home Production, and Market Work."

produce home goods, whereas leisure is almost impossible to enjoy through a surrogate. The total available amount of time is best viewed, then, as being divided three ways, instead of only two as we have assumed up to now.

Gronau's approach to the allocation of time is fairly similar to that developed earlier in this chapter. Given a goal of utility maximization, the individual's time is allocated between leisure and goods production in a way that equates the *MRS* between goods and leisure (the home wage rate) to the marginal product of work. This is depicted in Figure 4-21 for two different individuals, a "leisure lover," whose indifference curves are denoted by Arabic numerals (1, 2) and a "goods lover," whose indifference curves are denoted by Roman numerals (I, II, III). Both individuals are assumed to have the same ability to produce goods, as indicated by the **transformation curve** $H(m)g(0)$, whose slope represents the marginal productivity of time in goods production. In particular, moving one hour to the *left* in Figure 4-21 represents sacrificing one hour of leisure in return for an increment of goods. The market wage is indicated by the slope of the straight line that is tangent to $H(m)g(0)$ and intersects point $g'(0)$ on the goods axis.

It clearly does not pay to produce additional goods in the home after the marginal productivity of time in home production falls below the market wage rate. [This occurs after $H(m) - H(N)$ hours are devoted to producing goods in the home

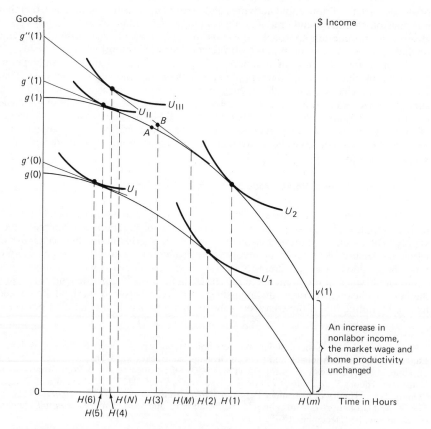

FIGURE 4-21. Leisure, home production, and market work

along curve $H(m)g(0)$. Be sure you can explain why this is so.] Therefore, each individual's *budget constraint* includes only the portion of the transformation curve that represents a marginal productivity greater than the market wage rate. This means that each individual's effective budget constraint is the curve $H(m)g'(0)$. Given the budget constraint $H(m)g'(0)$, the leisure-loving individual will devote $H(m) - H(2)$ hours of time to work in the home, $H(2)$ hours to leisure, and none to market work. The goods-loving person will supply $H(N) - H(6)$ hours to the labor market, consume $H(6)$ hours of leisure, and work $H(m) - H(N)$ hours in the home.

An increase in nonemployment income will increase leisure consumption of both the goods lover and the leisure lover. However, the impact on work in the home will depend on whether or not an individual participates in the labor force. In Figure 4-21, an increase in nonemployment income is depicted by a parallel upward shift of the transformation curve to $v(1)g(1)$ and the budget constraint to $v(1)g'(1)$. In response to a $v(1)$ increase in nonemployment income, the leisure lover increases leisure consumption and reduces home work time by $H(1) - H(2)$ hours, while the goods lover increases leisure by reducing market work time by $H(5) - H(6)$ hours. [Remember that in our graph home production occurs in the region $H(m)$ to $H(N)$.]

Now consider the effect of increasing the wage rate. This is illustrated along transformation curve $v(1)g(1)$, where an increase in the market wage changes the budget constraint from $v(1)g'(1)$ to $v(1)g''(1)$. The leisure lover is not affected by this unless $H(M)$ hours falls to the right of $H(1)$ hours. Then the leisure lover will enter the labor market. The goods lover is definitely affected. In the case depicted, the income effect outweighs the substitution effect, and market work falls by $H(4) - H(5)$ hours.

The preceding discussion helps in understanding the allocation of time by married couples. Wives typically face lower market wage rates than their husbands. Among other things, this may be due to differing desires to specialize in home versus market work, leading to different types of schooling, training, and job experience, or to labor market discrimination (see Chapter 10). Thus, even with the same tastes for leisure versus work, wives are less likely to participate in the labor force in the United States than their husbands. Gronau's model of market work, home work, and leisure leads to the prediction that for the roughly 50 percent of wives who do not engage in market work, an increase in their nonemployment income (as measured by their husband's wage or family nonemployment income) will lead to a reduction in their home work. In the case of wives who are labor force participants, an increase in nonemployment income will reduce *only* their market work, so long as they remain in the labor force.

Gronau was able to test these hypotheses about husbands' and wives' allocation of time using **time budget** data available from the University of Michigan's Panel Study of Income Dynamics. These data measure how individuals allocate their non-labor market time. Gronau estimated the impact of the husband's wage and family nonemployment income on wives' time allocation for those who worked in the market and for those who did not. These effects were estimated holding constant the wife's age, education, her expected market wage, number of children, house size, and her husband's education. For working wives in 1972, a $1 increase in the husband's hourly wage reduced her market work by 152 hours per year, on average, and increased her leisure by 137 hours per year. An increase in nonemployment income of $2,000 per year lowered a working wife's market work by 120 hours per year and raised her leisure time by 80 hours. By contrast, work at home was not significantly affected. For nonworking wives, a $1 increase in the husband's hourly wage reduced home work by a small, but statistically significant amount—16 hours per year. An increase in family nonemployment income of $2,000 per year reduced home work by an average of 88 hours per year, also statistically significant.

An important application to the allocation of wives' time is the effect of a wage increase on market work. Suppose, for example, a nonworking wife in Figure 4-21 allocates her time along constraint $H(m)g'(1)$, at point A. This means that she consumes between $H(N)$ and $H(M)$ leisure hours and devotes the remainder of her time to work in the home. An increase in her wage that makes her constraint become $H(m)g''(1)$ will cause her to enter the labor force. However, even if utility maximization causes her to increase her leisure by moving to point B on $H(m)g''(1)$, her market work will increase from zero hours to $H(M) - H(3)$ hours. Now consider a woman who is *already* working, but perhaps less than full time, say $H(N) - H(5)$ hours, because she also works $H(m) - H(N)$ hours at home. She can also increase her leisure time *and* market work as her wage rises by reducing her home work by $H(M) - H(N)$ hours. The point to remember in all of this is that wives are more likely than husbands to increase their market work hours in response to a wage increase because of their ability to substitute market work for home work. This implication concerning the relative responsiveness of husbands' and wives' hours of market work to wage rate changes is supported by Hausman's research reported earlier in this chapter, as well as that of many other economists.

Still another application of the new home economics, as represented in Figure 4-21, is that it provides a clearer meaning of the value of time spent in home production. One important aspect of this is that our measures of gross national product would be significantly increased if we counted home production *as well as* the production that occurs in the marketplace. Moreover, economists are frequently asked to testify in court cases to help evaluate the economic loss to a family whose wife and mother has been killed or injured in an accident. What is the economic value of the family's loss in this case? Can it be measured by using the wage rate of hired domestic help? If the wife worked in the market, then we know that the value the family placed on her last hour spent in home production was equal to her market wage. Because of the diminishing marginal product of the transformation curves in Figure 4-21, we know that the total value of a wife's home production *exceeds* the product of her wage rate times hours of work in the home. Consequently, multiplying the amount of time a woman spent in home work by her market wage yields an *underestimate* of the value of home goods she produced. Reuben Gronau has developed estimates of the value of wives' home production. He reports that in 1973, the value of wives' work in the home exceeded 60 percent of a typical family's income before taxes and 70 percent after taxes.[46]

CONCLUSION

We began this chapter by noting that the supply of labor can also be viewed as the demand for leisure time. We then presented the theory of labor supply in two parts: labor force participation and hours of work. We focused attention on two variables that determine an individual's budget constraint— nonemployment income and the wage rate. The rate at which the individual is willing to substitute leisure time for market goods, or income, is defined to be the home wage rate. Utility maximization requires that the home wage rate be equal to or greater than the market wage. We subsequently intro-

---

[46] "Home Production—A Forgotten Industry," *Review of Economics and Statistics,* 62:3 (August 1980), 408–16.

duced a complication that also makes labor supply theory more realistic—a fixed cost of holding a job. We were thus able to see why a working individual's work hours are unlikely to fall in a range near zero.

Two of the most important applications of labor supply theory are to the effects of income-maintenance programs and taxation on hours of work and labor force participation. The income and substitution effects of a change in the market wage help clarify the impact of taxes and income-maintenance programs on work incentives. Experimental NIT programs have helped us to obtain evidence on the work disincentives and program costs of alternative combinations of basic income grants and implicit taxation on earnings. They also have taught us much about how difficult it is to develop adequately controlled experiments with human subjects.

We briefly discussed an animal experiment (with pigeons) that lends strong support to the validity of the substitution-effect hypothesis. We also noted that pigeons evidently have a backward-bending labor supply curve, implying that at higher wage rates, the income effect dominates the substitution effect.

Labor supply research based on nonexperimental data is broadly consistent with the historic increase in the labor force participation of married women and provides an explanation of the recent decline in the labor force participation of mature males. Social security benefits and progressive income taxation have both reduced labor supply by lowering effective (after-tax) wage rates. Replacing our present income tax rate structure with a proportional or flat rate tax on incomes would result in substantially increased work incentives and could still be consistent with exempting low-income families from taxation. Nonexperimental labor supply research has also led to an understanding of factors influencing the length of the full-time workweek in the United States.

Finally, the "Frontiers" section introduced a formal analysis of the allocation of time between work in the market, work in the home, and leisure. We saw that the "new home economics" provides insights into the reasons for the difference in husbands' and wives' labor supply responses to wage increases. It also leads to hypotheses about the allocation of home time that can be tested with budget data, and it provides a guide for measuring the value of time used in production in the home.

REFERENCES AND SELECTED READING

Barnett, William A., *Consumer Demand and Labor Supply*. Amsterdam, New York, and Oxford: North-Holland Publishing Co., 1981.

Battalio, Raymond C., and John H. Kagel, et al., "Experimental Studies of Consumer Demand Behavior Using Laboratory Animals," *Economic Inquiry*, 13 (March 1975), 22–38.

———— AND L. GREEN, "Income Leisure Tradeoffs of Animal Workers," *American Economic Review,* 71 (September 1981), 621–33.

———— et al., "A Test of Consumer Demand Theory Using Observations of Individual Consumer Purchases," *Western Economic Journal,* 11 (December 1973), 411–12.

BECKER, GARY S., "A Theory of the Allocation of Time," *The Economic Journal,* 75 (1965), 493–517.

————, "A Theory of Social Interactions," *Journal of Political Economy,* 82 (November 1974), 1063–94.

COGAN, JOHN, *Labor Supply with Time and Money Costs of Participation.* Santa Monica, Calif.: Rand Corporation, 1976.

————, "Labor Supply with Fixed Costs of Labor Market Entry," in James P. Smith, ed., *Female Labor Supply: Theory and Estimation.* Princeton, N.J.: Princeton University Press, 1980.

EASTERLIN, RICHARD A., *Population, Labor Force, and Long Swings in Economic Growth.* New York and London: National Bureau of Economic Research, 1964.

EHRENBERG, RONALD G., ed., *Research in Labor Economics,* Vol. 4. Greenwich, Conn.: JAI Press, 1981.

GRONAU, REUBEN, "Leisure Time, Home Production, and Market Work," *Journal of Political Economy,* 85 (December 1977), 1099–1124.

————, "Home Production—A Forgotten Industry," *Review of Economics and Statistics,* 62:2 (August 1980), 408–16.

HAUSMAN, JERRY A., "Income and Payroll Tax Policy and Labor Supply," *The Supply-Side Effects of Economic Policy.* ed. Laurence H. Meyer. St. Louis: Center for the Study of American Business, Washington University, 1981, 173–202.

————, "Labor Supply," in Henry J. Aaron and Joseph A. Pechman, eds., *How Taxes Affect Economic Behavior.* Washington, D.C.: The Brookings Institution, 1981.

HECKMAN, JAMES J., AND THOMAS E. MCCURDY, "New Methods for Estimating Labor Supply Functions, A Survey," *Research in Labor Economics,* 4 (1981).

HURD, MICHAEL D., AND MICHAEL J. BOSKIN, *The Effect of Social Security on Retirement in the Early 1970's,* Working Paper No. 659. Cambridge, Mass.: National Bureau of Economic Research, 1981.

KEELEY, MICHAEL C., "The Labor Supply Effects and Costs of Alternative Negative Income Tax Programs," *Journal of Human Resources,* 13 (Winter 1978), 3–36.

————, *Labor Supply and Public Policy.* New York: Academic Press, 1981.

KILLINGSWORTH, MARK R., *Labor Supply.* Cambridge, Mass.: Cambridge University Press, 1983.

KNIESNER, THOMAS, "The Full-Time Workweek in the United States, 1900–1970," *Industrial and Labor Relations Review,* 30:1 (October 1976), 3–15.

————, "Recent Behavior of the 'Full-Time' Work Week in the U.S.," Ph.D. dissertation, The Ohio State University, 1974.

————, "The Full-Time Workweek in the United States, 1900–1970: Revisions and Some Extensions," 33:3 (April 1980), 385–89.

LANCASTER, KELVIN J., "A New Approach to Consumer Theory," *Journal of Political Economy,* 74 (1966), 132–57.

LEWIS, H. G., "Hours of Work and Hours of Leisure," *Proceedings,* Ninth Annual Winter Meeting, The Industrial Relations Research Association (December 1956), 195–206.

LONG, CLARENCE D., *The Labor Force Under Changing Income and Employment.* Princeton, N.J.: Princeton University Press, 1958.

MACHLOWITZ, MARILYN, *Workaholics.* New York: Mentor Books, 1980.

MCELROY, MARJORIE B., AND MARY JEAN HORNEY, "Nash-Bargained Household Decisions: Toward a Generalization of the Theory of Demand," *International Economic Review,* 22:2 (June 1981), 333–50.

MICHAEL, ROBERT T., AND GARY S. BECKER, "On the New Theory of Consumer Behavior," *The Swedish Journal of Economics,* 75 (1973), 378–96.

PARSONS, DONALD O., "The Decline in Male Labor Force Participation," *Journal of Political Economy,* 88 (February 1980), 117–34.

————, "The Male Labor Force Participation Decision: Health, Reported Health, and Economic Incentives," *Economica,* 49 (February 1982), 81–91.

————, "Racial Trends in Male Labor Force Participation," *American Economic Review,* 70 (December 1980), 911–20.

ROBBINS, LIONEL, "On the Elasticity of Demand for Income in Terms of Effort," *Economica,* 10 (June 1930), 123–29.

U.S. BUREAU OF THE CENSUS, *Historical Statistics of the United States, Colonial Times to 1970.*

————, *Statistical Abstract of the United States,* 1980.

U.S. Census 1970 of Population, Subject Reports: Employment States and Work Experience.

U.S. DEPARTMENT OF LABOR, BUREAU OF LABOR STATISTICS, *Handbook of Labor Statistics,* 1980.

U.S. DEPARTMENT OF LABOR, EMPLOYMENT AND TRAINING ADMINISTRATION, *Employment and Training Report of the President,* 1980.

EXERCISES

Choose whether each of the statements 1–4 is *True, False,* or *Uncertain* (whether true or false depends on unspecified circumstances). Justify your answer. Your justification is the most important part of your answer.

1. An important feature common to both the theory of labor demand and that of labor supply is that *both* labor demand and supply functions can be "bitonic" (both negatively and positively sloped with respect to the wage rate).

2. The end of the "baby boom" in the late 1960s can be easily understood as the result of the continuous increase in the labor force participation of married women.

3. The income effect of an exogenous wage increase on labor force participation may well be different in sign than the income effect of an exogeneous wage increase on hours of work.

4. Suppose each individual has the option of working either exactly 40 hours a week or not at all. Under these conditions, the labor supply schedule (of hours) may be backward-bending.

5. John is a *utility-maximizing prime-aged male* who has *no nonlabor income*. Leisure is a normal good for John.
   (a) Graphically depict and explain his choice of market goods and leisure.
   (b) Show what would happen to these choices if he were to get some nonlabor income.
   (c) Show what would happen to these choices if his wage rate were to increase.

6. Consider two welfare programs: (1) one that supplements (increases) the wage rates of the poor and (2) one that supplements the nonlabor incomes of the poor in a way that leads them to have the *same* level of utility as under the first welfare program. Put differently, the two respective welfare programs are structured so that both increase the utility of a recipient by the same amount. Thus, potential beneficiaries are indifferent between the two programs.
   (a) What are the labor supply effects of each program? Which one leads the poor to work more? Explain your answer carefully and support it graphically. Be sure to use the concepts of income and substitution effects in your answer.
   (b) Assuming that the two programs are equally costly to administer, which is more expensive for the taxpayers? Explain and support your answer graphically.

*7. In her book, *Workaholics*,† Marilyn Machlowitz examines the lives of people who work "all the time."
   (a) Use the indifference curve-budget constraint diagram you learned in this chapter to depict a workaholic. Be careful.
   (b) Suppose employers decide that workaholism is hazardous to an employee's health and take steps to discourage it. In particular, employees are required to take vacations from their jobs. How effective will this be in reducing the incidence of workaholism? Be as complete as possible and support your answer graphically.

---

* Denotes a more difficult exercise.
† New York: Mentor Books, 1980.

5

THE INTERACTION
OF SUPPLY AND DEMAND
IN COMPETITIVE LABOR MARKETS

A. Educational objectives
  1. To analyze how the forces of labor supply and demand interact in competitive labor markets to determine workers' economic welfare
  2. To determine how exogenous changes in the variables that underlie the labor supply and demand schedules disturb wages, employment, and working conditions

B. The concept of a labor market (p. 172)

C. Equilibrium in a single competitive labor market (p. 172)
  1. Definition of equilibrium (p. 173)
  2. Comparative statics analysis (p. 173)
     a. Exogenous events shifting labor supply or demand schedules.
     b. Qualitative effects of supply and demand shifts on equilibrium wages and employment
     c. Application: Who pays for social security?

D. Multimarket equilibrium (p. 180)
  1. Forces promoting multimarket equilibrium (p. 180)
  2. Economic efficiency (p. 182)
     a. Definition
     b. Economic efficiency, equity, and social welfare
  3. Do United States labor markets tend toward equilibrium? (p. 185)

E. Frontiers of labor economics:
  Supply lags, expectations and dynamic equilibrium (p. 186)
  1. Introduction to the "cobweb" model (p. 186)
  *2. An application to the market for lawyers (p. 190)

F. Conclusion (p. 191)

---

* Represents more technical material that can be skipped without loss of continuity.

In this chapter we apply the knowledge gained in Chapters 3 and 4 to analyze how the forces of supply and demand interact in competitive labor markets to determine wages and employment. Moreover, we are interested in understanding how exogenous changes in factors that underlie labor supply and demand disturb these schedules and thus workers' economic welfare, especially since many such disturbances are the result of government policy. Before we can proceed, however, it is important to elaborate briefly on the somewhat nebulous concept of a labor market, given the central role it plays in the analysis to follow.

It probably seems odd at first to think about a market for *labor*. Most of us have seen pictures of the New York Stock Exchange in action, but who has been to a slave auction? Fortunately, the concept of a labor market need not mislead us as to how economic factors affect workers' economic welfare. It is best to think of a market as a convenient abstraction that economists use to organize ideas. We do something similar in casual conversation when we refer to such intangibles as "the civil rights movement," "women's liberation," or "the democratic process." The point here is that a labor market is really the "place" in economic theory where supply and demand interact. As a result, a market is an extremely flexible analytical tool to have at our disposal, and economists have used it to study regions (the labor market of Chicago), industries (the labor market for production workers in manufacturing), and occupations (the labor market for lawyers). So, the criterion we will use to evaluate the scientific value of the concept of a labor market is not how well it represents an observable economic institution, but whether it helps us to formulate an economic analysis that provides us with reasonably accurate and useful insights into phenomena we seek to understand.

EQUILIBRIUM IN A SINGLE COMPETITIVE LABOR MARKET

In order to understand how the forces of supply and demand determine wage rates and employment, we will discuss a single competitive labor market in which the number of workers and the number of firms is fixed. Premium wage rates for overtime work will be ignored. Moreover, firms will be assumed to be indifferent to the number of employees versus hours of work per employee, so that the quantity of labor they desire to hire (and workers wish to supply) may be represented simply by total employee-hours. Our hypothetical labor market is depicted in Figure 5-1 by a labor supply curve (S) and a labor demand curve (D). Remember that in a competitive labor market there are numerous firms and individuals. The labor demand curve represents the total number of labor-hours firms desire to purchase at various wage rates, allowing for feedback effects from the market for final output. D is downward-sloping for the reasons discussed in Chapter 3. The supply

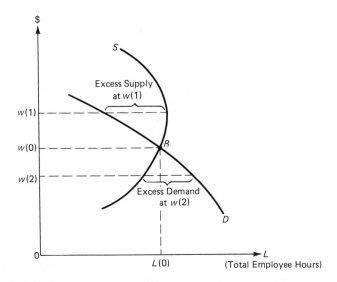

FIGURE 5-1. Labor market equilibrium

curve of labor indicates the total number of hours workers wish to sell at each wage rate. For the set of workers pictured in Figure 5-1, rising income levels are eventually accompanied by an increased desire to spend time in home production (leisure), so that the labor supply curve bends backward.[1]

Where S and D intersect (point R) denotes the **market-clearing** or **equilibrium combination of w and L.** The labor market is said to be cleared at wage rate $w(0)$ because the amount of labor workers desire to sell matches the amount employers desire to purchase. At a wage rate higher than $w(0)$, say $w(1)$, workers are frustrated in the sense that they wish to sell more labor than firms are willing to buy. At a wage rate below $w(0)$, say $w(2)$, firms are frustrated in their attempts to purchase labor. The intersection of supply and demand is a labor market equilibrium because it represents a satisfactory transaction for both groups.

Comparative Statics Analysis of a Labor Market

Probably the most important use of a supply and demand model is to generate predictions of how exogenous events influence wages and employment. Suppose that the supply of labor increases and demand remains unchanged. What do we expect to happen to the market wage rate and the

[1] If we were to measure the quantity of labor by the *number* of workers, could S be backward-bending?

TABLE 5-1   Events That Shift Labor Supply or Demand Curves

Events That Shift an Individual's Labor Supply Curve

1. Change in nonlabor income
2. Change in wage or earnings of other family members
3. Change in household productivity
4. Change in distaste for market work
5. Change in goal of utility maximization to a different goal

Events That Shift a Firm's Labor Demand Curve

1. Change in technology
2. Change in the price of final output
3. Change in price (quantity) of other productive factors
4. Change in goal of profit maximization to a different goal

quantity of labor services firms hire? Economists answer this question by comparing the initial labor market equilibrium point with the equilibrium point after supply has shifted. Such a comparison is known as **comparative statics analysis.**[2]

In general, changes in the environment surrounding the "actors" in a labor market are responsible for shifts in supply or demand curves. For example, we know from Chapter 4 that a market labor supply function indicates workers' desired hours of work at various wage rates, *given their nonemployment income.* Were some to receive windfalls, say from winning lottery tickets, they would very likely spend part of that newly acquired income on leisure, and the market labor supply function would shift to the left. Alternatively, the market demand curve for labor is a sum of the value of marginal product schedules of individual firms. If technology suddenly changed so as to make workers more productive, the resulting increase in firms' marginal physical productivity schedules would lead to a shift in market labor demand.[3] Table 5-1 lists some events that shift supply or demand schedules.

Having identified some factors that disturb labor supply and demand curves, we can fairly simply link these events to their effects on the equilibrium wage and quantity of labor. To do so, we assume that the market for

---

[2] In comparative statics analysis we look at the labor market in *equilibrium* and at how wage rates and employment differs at alternative equilibriums. By contrast, *dynamic* analysis looks at the paths taken by labor market variables *between* equilibrium points. The "Frontiers" section of this chapter presents an example of dynamic analysis.

[3] When workers become more productive, fewer are needed to produce a given level of output. Therefore, when an improvement in technology causes productivity to increase, we cannot say in advance whether the labor demand curve will shift right or left. It will shift right if the lowered production cost and output price arising from increased labor productivity lead to a sufficiently large increase in the quantity of output demanded.

labor is initially in equilibrium and will achieve equilibrium following the environmental shifts under examination. The predicted impact of a set of events, then, is obtained by comparing the labor market equilibrium point before and after their occurrence. You should be able to show, for example, that an increase in the value of marginal product of labor will increase both w and L if labor supply is upward-sloping. The predicted labor market impacts of various combinations of supply and demand shifts when the supply curve is upward-sloping are summarized in Table 5-2. Notice that when only one of the two curves is displaced, we obtain unambiguous qualitative predictions for the changes in w and L. If exogenous events disturb both S and D, however, we can predict the change in only one of the two variables without information as to the relative magnitudes of the shifts. Which of the entries in Table 5-2 will be different if the labor supply curve is backward-bending? Which will differ if S is vertical?

Application: Who Pays for Social Security?

The relatively simple tool of comparative statics analysis is useful in examining the labor market impact of a wide variety of government programs. Over the past several years Congress has been concerned with maintaining the solvency of the social security system. The problem has arisen mainly because of falling birth rates and increasing life expectancy. In particular, the proportion of the United States population over 65 is expected to grow over the next fifty years or so, while the proportion in the prime working age group declines. Either social security benefits must be lowered within the next few decades, or some way must be found to finance the anticipated increase in benefit payments. The latter solution requires a transfer of funds from general tax revenues or an increase in the payroll tax that is currently the source of revenue for social security retirement benefits. Although Congress decided in 1977 to increase taxes, there was considerable

TABLE 5-2   The Qualitative Effects of Market Supply and Demand Curve Shifts on Labor Market Equilibrium*

	Supply Increases	Supply Decreases	Supply Unchanged
Demand Increases	$\Delta w \gtreqless 0$ $\Delta L > 0$	$\Delta w > 0$ $\Delta L \gtreqless 0$	$\Delta w > 0$ $\Delta L > 0$
Demand Decreases	$\Delta w < 0$ $\Delta L \gtreqless 0$	$\Delta w \lesseqgtr 0$ $\Delta L < 0$	$\Delta w < 0$ $\Delta L < 0$
Demand Unchanged	$\Delta w < 0$ $\Delta L > 0$	$\Delta w > 0$ $\Delta L < 0$	$\Delta w = 0$ $\Delta L = 0$

* The labor supply curve is assumed to be upward-sloping.

disagreement about whether the increased taxes should be levied on employers or workers. The arguments in favor of levying the tax on employers rest on the belief that they can better afford it. Alternatively, arguments in favor of levying the tax (or part of it) on employees rest on the feeling that the eventual recipients of social security benefits should bear the financial responsibility. You may be surprised to learn that the theory of supply and demand in competitive labor markets implies that Congress has very little power over the incidence of, or who actually pays, the taxes that finance social security benefits. No matter who "writes the checks," employers or employees, the true tax burden is dependent on the forces of supply and demand.

In this example, we examine the impact of social security on work incentives *before* individuals become eligible to receive benefits. During the years when workers are too young to receive social security retirement benefits, they build up credit based on the amount they earn each year up to a maximum amount. For example, the 1983 schedule of benefits indicates that the maximum social security benefit payable to an individual after age 65 will depend on how much he or she earned, up to $32,000, during the preceding 35 years in which the highest income was earned. This schedule applies to persons born in 1960 or later. However, there is also a minimum benefit payable to anyone who receives at least a minimum level of earnings in at least a minimum number of years after 1960 and before age 65. These maximum and minimum social security benefit levels mean that to a large extent, the social security retirement system is more realistically viewed as a program that transfers income from working-age individuals to retired and semiretired members of the population. A majority of the working population can expect to be eligible to receive social security payments if they retire after age 62 or 65, but the amount of benefits they receive will to a significant extent be independent of how much they have earned. Equally important, the level of funds available to pay social security benefits depends on the total amount paid into the system by both employers and their employees, but not on the division of the tax between them.

The preceding discussion suggests that, as a first approximation, it is reasonable to assume that most workers believe they can increase or reduce the amount they earn within a fairly broad range without affecting the social security retirement benefits they will eventually be eligible to receive. Paying social security (or, more precisely, Federal Insurance Contribution Act) taxes is the price of participating in a game whose payoff will depend more on the relative political power of old versus young members of the population in future years than on the contributions made while one is working.[4] Thus the amount paid in is viewed as a tax on earnings upon which no direct benefit depends. It goes without saying that employers whose payrolls are

---

[4] We thank Mark Killingsworth for emphasizing this point to us.

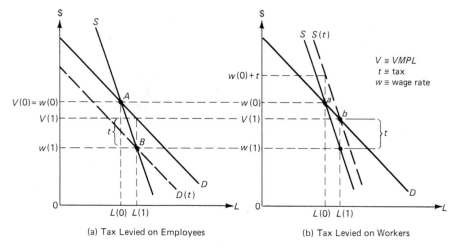

FIGURE 5-2. The supply and demand for labor and the incidence of a specific tax

taxed by the government to help support the social security system do not perceive an offsetting benefit in the form of profit-generating revenues.

We can now proceed to analyze the impact of the social security tax, and who legally pays it, on labor demand and supply. The impact depends crucially on the shape of the labor demand and supply curves. To begin, suppose that the economy's labor supply curve is negatively sloped as in Figure 5-2. To review briefly, recall the discussion of individual labor supply in Chapter 4. It is not at all unlikely that individual workers, if rising wages make them better off, will choose to spend some of their increased real income on leisure. When the amount of labor supplied to the economy declines as wage rates increase, the economy's labor supply curve will be negatively sloped, as in Figure 5-2.[5]

In Figure 5-2(a) we depict the impact of a law that requires *employers* to pay the entire contribution to the social security system. To make the analysis simple, we assume that the law levies a tax of t dollars per hour of labor on employers.[6] If there were no tax, the demand for labor would be curve D, reflecting employers' view of the marginal productivity of their

---

[5] Be careful in working through this example to note that when the supply curve is negatively sloped, it *must* be steeper than the demand curve. If not, an excess supply of labor would cause wage rates to rise, not fall, and an excess *demand* would cause wages to fall. This would mean that, once disturbed, equilibrium would never be regained, and there would be no stable equilibrium values of w and L.

[6] In reality, the tax imposed by Congress is not a specific (fixed dollar per unit of labor) tax, but rather proportional to wages paid, with a ceiling on total payments. To take these facts into account would complicate the analysis significantly while leaving the basic conclusion unchanged.

employees, *VMPL*. With demand curve *D*, employers would maximize profits at point *A* by hiring *L*(0) units of labor at an equilibrium wage *w*(0) = *VMPL*(0). From the employers' point of view, the requirement that they pay a tax of *t* dollars per unit of labor is exactly the same as if *VMPL* had been reduced by *t* dollars, causing a downward shift in the labor demand curve. Thus, after the tax is imposed, employers behave as if their labor demand curve were *D*(*t*) rather than *D*. The gap between *D* and *D*(*t*) is exactly equal to the tax, *t* dollars per unit of labor. Given curve *D*(*t*), an excess supply of labor exists at wage *w*(0). This excess supply causes the wage rate to fall from *w*(0) to *w*(1). Firms now maximize their profits at point *B*, hiring *L*(1) units of labor. Given the labor supply curve *S*, *L*(1) units of labor represents the quantity supplied at *w*(1), so labor market equilibrium has been restored.

What has imposition of the social security tax on employers done to the labor market? It has caused a chain of events analogous to what would have happened had there been a decline in the marginal product of labor. Comparing the new situation with the old, the excess supply of labor at *w*(0) has forced the wage rate to decline. Because the labor supply curve is *negatively sloped,* a decline in the wage rate causes the quantity of labor supplied to *increase*. (Why?) Consequently, a new labor market equilibrium is not reached until the wage rate has fallen sufficiently to induce employers to *increase* the amount of labor used, despite the downward shift in the labor demand schedules. In other words, they move to the right along curve *D*(*t*) so far that *L*(1) is actually larger than *L*(0). In order for this adjustment to occur, the wage reduction *w*(0) − *w*(1) must *exceed* the tax imposed, *t*. Workers are clearly worse off than before the tax was imposed. Paradoxically, even though employers "write the check" for taxes, workers actually pay it. Technically, we say that the **incidence** of the tax is on workers. Their wage rates decline after the tax is imposed by an amount that *exceeds* the tax rate *t*.

To fully understand how imposition of the tax affects the labor market, it is important to distinguish between the *actual* level of *VMPL* and employers' *net VMPL*, which reflects the payment of the tax. From *society's* point of view, worker productivity is still reflected in curve *D*, not *D*(*t*). Thus at the new level of employment, *VMPL* is now *V*(1), less than the initial level *w*(0), not because *D* has shifted downward, but simply because employment has increased. (Why does an increase in employment cause *VMPL* to fall?) The difference *w*(0) − *V*(1) measures the decline in *VMPL* attributable to increased employment. Whereas *VMPL* and the wage were equal to *w*(0) before the tax was imposed, this is no longer so. The tax has driven a "wedge" between *w* and *VMPL* precisely equal to *t* dollars per unit of labor. Thus, in Figure 5-2(a), after all adjustments to the tax have occurred, workers' paychecks reflect a wage rate equal to *w*(1) dollars per hour; employers receive *V*(1) dollars for the incremental output attributable to using the last unit of labor, but they net only *V*(1) − *t* = *w*(1) after paying the tax. They are better off than they were originally, because the full cost of a unit of labor (including taxes) is lower than it was. However, workers earn less than before: their wage has fallen by *more* than *t* dollars per hour, because reaching the new labor market equilibrium requires that the quantity of labor employed increase, causing *VMPL* to decline.

Figure 5-2(b) shows what happens if the same tax is legally imposed on workers rather than their employers. At point *a*, which is the pretax equilibrium situation, workers recognize that after the tax is levied on them, their *take-home* pay falls from $w(0)$ to $w(0) - t$. Because labor supply is determined by take-home pay, workers will now supply $L(0)$ hours of work only if their employers raise their before-tax pay to $w(0) + t$ dollars per hour. That is to say, their entire labor supply schedule shifts *upward* by exactly *t* dollars, from curve *S* to $S(t)$. The chain of events that follows this upward shift in *S* is identical to that which follows a downward shift in *D* to $D(t)$, because at $w(0)$ an excess supply of labor is created which does not disappear until employment increases to $L(1)$. This new equilibrium is denoted as point *b*, where once again *VMPL* has declined to $V(1)$. Workers' paychecks show their *gross* pay to equal $V(1)$, but their take-home pay is $V(1) - t = w(1)$, just as in the case where the tax is levied on employers. So, we see that the effect on employers' profits and workers' take-home pay is identical, no matter who Congress intended to bear the burden of the social security tax.

The result that the market wage declines by more than *t*, the amount of the tax, follows from the negatively sloped labor supply curve. When the labor supply schedule has either zero or positive elasticity, the incidence of the tax is somewhat different. Figure 5-3 illustrates the case in which Con-

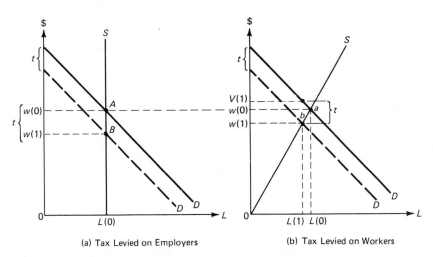

(a) Tax Levied on Employers

(b) Tax Levied on Workers

FIGURE 5-3. The incidence of a specific tax when labor supply has a non-negative slope

gress imposes the tax on employers. In (a) the supply curve is vertical; in (b) it is upward-sloping.[7] Once again, when employers realize they must pay a tax of $t per unit of labor in addition to the wage, the labor demand curve shifts downward by distance t. When the quantity of labor supplied is independent of the wage [Figure 5-3(a)], employers' labor cost remains at $w(0)$ per unit of labor, but the net wage received by workers falls to $w(1) = w(0) - t$. Thus, when the labor supply schedule exhibits zero elasticity, the tax is paid entirely by workers. (Why?)

In Figure 5-3(b) the labor supply curve is *positively* sloped. When workers find that employers are willing to hire $L(0)$ units of labor only if the wage falls to $w(0) - t$, they *reduce* the quantity of labor they supply. Thus, at $w(0)$ there is an *excess supply* of labor. The new market equilibrium is at point b, where a unit of labor now costs employers $V(1)$. This consists of $w(1)$ in workers' take-home pay plus t dollars' tax. When the labor supply curve is upward-sloping and the tax is levied on employers, the tendency for the wage to fall is offset by a reduction in employment from $L(0)$ to $L(1)$ and the resulting increase in the value of the marginal product of labor from $w(0)$ to $V(1)$. Since $w(0) - w(1)$ is less than t, the tax in this case is borne by *both* employers and employees. Workers pay part of a tax meant by Congress for employers alone. Under what circumstances would the incidence of the tax be entirely on employers?

MULTIMARKET EQUILIBRIUM

From our analysis of a single competitive market for labor, we know that an equilibrium wage rate will persist so long as there is no economic incentive for firms or individuals to alter their behavior. For example, in the labor market represented by Figure 5-1, if $w(0)$ is such that employers can increase their profits by purchasing labor elsewhere (equilibrium wages in other markets are lower than $w[0]$) or if workers can increase their economic welfare by seeking employment elsewhere (equilibrium wages in other markets exceed $w[0]$), then $w(0)$ will not be the long-term equilibrium. Suppose we ignore for simplicity the fact that search by employers or employees can be quite time-consuming and costly. In this case, all labor markets will be in equilibrium, and there will be multimarket equilibrium, when the wage rate of a given type of labor is the same in all alternative employments of given (nonwage) characteristics. When there is wage inequality among labor markets, excess supplies will occur in markets where wages are high and excess demands in those where wages are low. The resulting frustrations on the

---

[7] We leave as an exercise the case in which supply has a nonnegative slope and the tax is levied on workers.

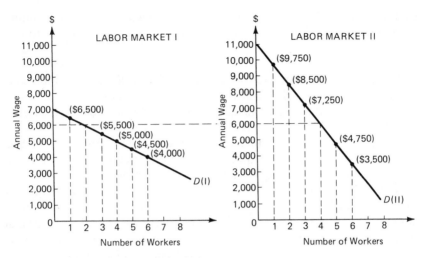

FIGURE 5-4. Multimarket equilibrium

parts of buyers and sellers of labor will cause wage rates to move toward their long-term, multimarket equilibrium values.

In order that we may see more clearly how the forces of supply and demand lead to equal wage rates across labor markets, let us consider the example of an economy composed of two competitive labor markets (for example, geographical regions). The curves labeled $D(I)$ and $D(II)$ in Figure 5-4 represent the demand schedules for labor by firms in markets I and II, respectively. Our sample economy has a total labor force of six identical (equally productive) workers, and jobs are alike in both regions in the sense that each employer offers the same work week, fringe benefits, and working conditions. Finally, we will assume that there is insufficient time for firms to build or rent new plants, so that only workers may move between regions, and that wage information is readily available and migration costless.

Suppose five individuals are initially located in market I and one in market II. This distribution of workers generates temporary market clearing wages of $4,500 in I and $9,750 in II. Remember, however, that all five workers in market I are just as talented as the one in market II and that news of the higher wages in market II will eventually spread. As soon as one of the workers in market I realizes that his or her economic welfare can be improved through relocation, the distribution of workers becomes two in market II and four in market I. The increased quantity of labor in II and the decreased quantity of labor in I narrows the equilibrium wage gap to $8,500 versus $5,000. Workers will continue to migrate from market I to market II as long as they can gain from the move. The flow stops when market I has a labor force of two workers and market II a labor force of four workers. At this point, multimarket equilibrium occurs as both markets clear at an annual wage of $6,000, and there is no economic incentive for any worker to relocate.[8,9]

Speed of adjustment.   Labor markets typically do not adjust to changing supply and demand schedules as rapidly as markets for commodities and other factors of production. Consider the markets for financial assets. Since information about alternatives is widespread and transaction costs small, prices adjust rapidly to disturbances, and interregional differences in price behavior are rare. Markets for grain, beef, pork, and cotton also behave this way. By comparison, the adjustment of labor markets is sluggish indeed. However, in evaluating the adjustment of labor markets to equilibrium, it is necessary to examine the causes of sluggish adjustment as well as the nature of alternative methods for eliminating them. (The role played by labor market adjustments to changing demand and supply conditions in the determination of unemployment and inflation rates is treated in Chapter 12.)

Economic efficiency.   When competitive multimarket equilibrium is achieved, the value of the marginal product of labor is equal to its wage rate, and the wage rate for labor of a given quality is the same in each market.[10] Therefore, the value of the marginal product of labor is the same everywhere. This equality of *VMPL* in alternative employments leads to what is called **economic efficiency,** which means that society obtains the largest possible output (national income) from its available quantities of resources.

To understand how multimarket equilibrium in a competitive economy generates economic efficiency, let us return to our fictional economy of Figure 5-4. When there were five workers in market I and one worker in market II, *VMPL* was $4,500 in I and $9,750 in II. The ensuing relocation of one worker lowered output in market I and increased output in market II such that society's total value of production (income) increased by approximately $4,000. (Can you explain why?) You should verify the results that total production increases until multimarket equilibrium is achieved and that any distribution of workers other than two in market I and four in market II is associated with a lower total income for society. Similarly, if in the United States, labor's *VMP* in the manufacture of autos were to exceed labor's *VMP* in the manufacture of pants, say, the movement of labor "from pants to autos" would increase national income. Migration of workers would continue, and total output would increase, until the incentive was eliminated.

---

[8] "Overshooting" may also occur. Too many workers may move to market II at first, so that multimarket equilibrium requires some to return to market I. Can you cite a real-world example of such return migration?

[9] A formal analysis of the individual's decision to migrate is presented in Chapter 9.

[10] Multimarket equilibrium will produce "equalizing" wage differences for workers of a given quality if job characteristics differ. A discussion of equalizing wage differences occurs in Chapter 11.

This fact is important because it means that barriers to the mobility of workers between labor markets, such as discrimination, trade unions, or license requirements, impose a cost on society in the form of reduced aggregate income.

The concept of multimarket equilibrium and economic efficiency is not confined to a single, national economy. It applies internationally as well. Migration between nations, such as the immense waves of population moving from Europe (and Asia) to the United States before World War I, was motivated by a large *VMPL* and wage gap between the United States and the immigrants' homelands. Today, tremendous pressure exists for population to move to the United States from Mexico and some Caribbean countries. These population movements also tend to increase the combined output of the source and receiving areas, although they are resisted by workers in the United States who fear their wages will be reduced through competition with foreign workers. Restrictions on immigration to the United States create an additional incentive for owners of capital to invest in countries with abundant labor supplies. This migration of capital tends to raise *VMPK* in the United States and lower it in the countries where the investment occurs. What is United States labor's interest in the immigration of capital? Would you expect United States labor to favor laws restricting immigration of capital just as labor resists free immigration of foreign workers?

Economic efficiency, equity, and social welfare.   When an economy attains economic efficiency, production occurs somewhere along its **production possibility frontier (PPF)**. Consider a simple economy in which only two goods are produced—manufactured goods (*M*) and farm goods (*F*). The characteristic of economic efficiency *and* the *PPF* is as follows: when production occurs on the *PPF*, if more *F* is desired, it is necessary to give up some *M*. This principle is illustrated in Figure 5-5, where $\bar{F}$ and $\bar{M}$ are the maximum amounts of farm goods and manufactured goods, respectively, this economy can produce, given its resources and technology. An allocation of resources that allows the economy to reach point *A*, producing $F(1)$ units of farm goods and $M(1)$ units of manufactured goods, is not efficient, because available resources and technology would permit point *B* to be reached, with output of goods equal to $F(2) > F(1)$ and $M(2) > M(1)$.

Economic efficiency is not the only criterion by which an economy is judged, however. A second criterion is **equity**—how *fairly* output is divided among members of society. To see this more clearly, examine Figure 5-6. Think of the circle in Figure 5-6 as a pie representing an economically efficient output of *M* and *F*, such as denoted by *B* in Figure 5-5. This economy's output of *M* and *F* is divided between the workers in its two industries as indicated, with manufacturing workers (who we assume are more numerous) receiving a larger piece of the pie than farm workers. Suppose that there are so many more manufacturing workers than farm workers that each man-

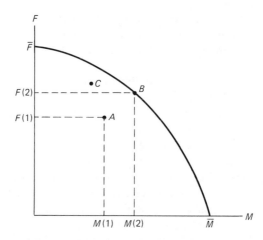

FIGURE 5-5. Economic efficiency and the production possibility frontier

ufacturing worker's individual piece of pie is smaller than that accruing to each farm worker. If the voters in this society decide that the existing division of output is unfair, or inequitable, they may vote to establish a legal minimum wage, higher than the market wage, for manufacturing workers.

To see the effect of a minimum wage in the manufacturing sector, go back to Figure 5-4 and relabel industry I F and industry II M. Let the horizontal axis measure the number of workers in thousands, and assume an efficient allocation of labor—2,000 F workers and 4,000 M workers. Suppose a minimum wage of \$7,250 is imposed on M workers only. M employers will react by reducing M employment until the $VMPL$ of M workers, $VMPL(M)$, rises to \$7,250. This will require laying off 1,000 workers. Assuming that the

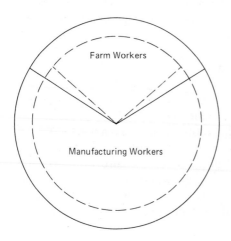

FIGURE 5-6. Dividing the economy's output between farm workers and manufacturing workers

only way these workers can live is to work (that is, their labor supply elasticity is zero), they will all seek employment as F workers, lowering $VMPL(F)$ to $5,500. The resulting economic inefficiency is shown in Figure 5-5 as a movement from point B to point C, representing more F production and less M production, *inside* the *PPF*. In Figure 5-6 the inefficiency is shown as a reduction in the size of the pie to the area marked by the dashed lines. Even if manufacturing workers now have a bigger *share* of the pie (as the dashed lines indicate), they are not necessarily better off, because economic inefficiency has made the pie smaller. Farm workers will be worse off, because they have a smaller share of a smaller pie.

Since the total value of output is reduced by the minimum wage, at least one group of workers *must* be made worse off, but society may decide that a smaller "pie" is a reasonable price to pay if manufacturing workers end up better off than they were. Formally, we say that **social welfare** *may* be increased at the same time that economic efficiency is reduced. Remember, however, that attempts to improve social welfare, if they involve devices such as taxes, subsidies, minimum wages, and so on, are very likely to reduce efficiency and *may* make the intended beneficiaries worse off rather than better off, contrary to the desired result. There is much evidence that minimum wages in the United States have indeed had such an undesired impact on low-wage workers.

Do United States Labor Markets Tend Toward Equilibrium?

If the analysis of multimarket equilibrium presented above is correct, then there ought to be a tendency for workers to leave industries and regions where wages are low and move to jobs where they can earn higher rates of pay. At the same time, owners of capital will find it more profitable to invest in low-wage regions, raising labor demand there. *Other conditions remaining unchanged,* geographic and industrial mobility should reduce wage differentials for workers of similar attributes. A more detailed analysis of geographic mobility in Chapter 9 emphasizes that it is too simplistic to view any and all regional or interindustry wage differentials as reflecting labor market disequilibrium. A moment's thought will certainly suggest that a move to a higher-paying job in another city, where housing costs, heating or cooling costs, and taxes are significantly higher as well as wages would not necessarily result in a higher real income. Such mobility is not implied by the multimarket equilibrium concept, because other conditions are *not* the same.

Moreover, even if living costs were equal among regions, movement of workers toward higher-paying jobs, and capital toward low-wage workers, will not *eliminate* wage differentials if the economy is repeatedly shocked by changes that cause wages to diverge—for example, the growth of new industries (such as computers), the decline of old ones, or the discovery of new resources (such as oil in Alaska). Even though there are many reasons why we may not observe similar workers receiving exactly the same rate of pay for performing the same task in different labor markets, it would be nice to know whether the simple theory of multimarket equilibrium provides any help at all in understanding how labor markets work.[11] After all, it is an easy theory to understand, and few variables are required.

Several major features of labor markets do appear to be described reasonably well by a simple competitive model. Some examples that illustrate this for the United States are contained in a valuable, older study by Melvin W. Reder.[12] Casual evidence suggests that the competitive model is still helpful today. For example, one of the simplest "predictions" of the competitive model of multimarket equilibrium is that regional wage differentials will tend to disappear over time (other things equal, as we emphasized above). A movement toward regional *income* equality, due in part to regional labor mobility's reducing regional *wage* differentials, does seem to characterize the United States over the last twenty years or more. For example, in 1960, per capita incomes in the Pacific region averaged 20 percent more than the national mean, while southerners received about 20 percent less than the average for the entire nation. These differences have become gradually smaller, so that by 1980, persons living in the Pacific states received only about 10 percent more than the national average, and those in the South only a bit more than 10 percent less. A significant fraction of this remaining differential was probably due to regional differences in the cost of living.[13]

FRONTIERS OF LABOR ECONOMICS: SUPPLY LAGS, EXPECTATIONS, AND DYNAMIC EQUILIBRIUM

In discussing equilibrium in competitive labor markets we have implicitly assumed that labor supply decisions, once made, are immediately implemented. Workers are treated as instantly providing the various quantities of labor denoted by their labor supply schedule. For a number of reasons this may not be a reasonable representation of behavior. Workers often need time to get ready for a job. Babysitters may have to be hired or arrangements made with the rest of the family. Relocation or additional training are sometimes necessary. Such activities are time-consuming and will lead to a lag between the moment when work decisions are made and when they are carried out. In this section we formally examine the situation where labor ap-

---

[11] An interesting and valuable analysis of the empirical validity of a simple competitive labor market hypothesis is developed by Melvin W. Reder in "Wage Differentials: Theory and Measurement," in A. Gregg Lewis, ed., *Aspects of Labor Economics* (Princeton, N.J.: Princeton University Press, 1962), pp. 257–311.

[12] *Ibid.*

[13] See "Income Differences Between Regions Narrow as a Result of Mobility, More Women at Work," *Wall Street Journal,* March 4, 1982. For a more technical discussion of regional wage differentials see Don Bellante, "The North-South Differential and the Migration of Homogeneous Labor," *American Economic Review,* 69 (March 1979), 166–75.

pears on the market sometime *after* supply decisions are made. As a result, workers must *anticipate* their eventual market wage rate when planning their labor market behavior. This leads to some interesting implications concerning movements in wages and employment following a labor market disturbance. Moreover, the concepts of equilibrium and stability take on new meanings.

We will now assume that workers train, relocate, or make any other transactions necessary for work *one* period before their labor is offered for sale.[14] In addition, once workers have made such arrangements, they are committed to particular amounts of labor. For example, once someone has contracted for the services of a daycare center, joined a carpool, and purchased enough clothes so as to be able to work 40 hours per week, we assume that he or she will in fact offer that many hours to the labor market. This means that individuals must decide how much to work *before* they know what their wage rates will actually be. Thus, when making decisions about schooling, training, where to work, and so on, they need to predict their market wage rates. We will assume that workers formulate wage rate predictions in a very simple (naive) manner: next period's wage is expected to be the *same* as this period's wage. This is nothing more than a simple prediction mechanism that says, "Tomorrow will look like today." In this situation the supply curve of labor relates the market wage rate in a given period, $w(t)$, to the quantity of labor supplied in the following period, $L(t + 1)$. To remind ourselves of this, we shall denote the supply curve of labor by $S(t + 1, wt)$.

All that we need in order to complete our model of the labor market are descriptions of the demand curve and the market clearing process. As before, we will assume that firms make instantaneous production and employment decisions so that the labor demand curve relates the amount of labor firms *currently* desire to the current wage rate (wt). Finally, once workers commit themselves to a particular amount of work, the market wage rate is equal to what firms are willing to pay for that quantity of labor. In other words, once workers (implicitly) decide how much labor to offer through their choices of preparatory activities, they "take whatever pay they can get." We shall see that this produces time paths for w and L where equilibrium values do not necessarily (and perhaps never) occur at the intersection of supply and demand.

Suppose that Figure 5-7 depicts the labor market for computer designers initially in equilibrium (supply and demand intersect) at point $S(0)$ with wage $w(0)$ and quantity of labor $L(0)$. An exogenous event now occurs, such as the invention of the integrated circuit that shifts the demand schedule to $D'(wt)$. Since the quantity of labor workers supply immediately after demand shifts depends upon their *anticipated* wage rate, they continue to offer $L(0)$, indicated by point $D(1)$. This is so because when decisions are being made, workers expect the wage rate $w(0)$ to also prevail during period 1. As point $D(1)$ indicates, however, their actual wage rate in period 1, $w(1)$, will be above $w(0)$. Remember that once workers decide how much labor they wish to sell, the equilibrium wage is what firms are willing to pay for that much labor.[15] Thus, the market wage rate will increase to $w(1)$, as point $D(1)$ shows. The increased quantity of labor that employers demand leads to a rise in the market wage rate. Notice that period 1's equilibrium combination of wage and employment [$w(1)$, $L(0)$] does not occur at the intersection of supply and demand schedules, but that the labor market is cleared in period 1, as neither firms nor workers are frus-

---

[14] A lag of one period may appear at first to be unnecessarily restrictive. Remember, though, that a period is a *general* concept that does not correspond to a particular length of time.

[15] Once workers have decided to supply $L(0)$, the labor supply curve is effectively vertical through that point.

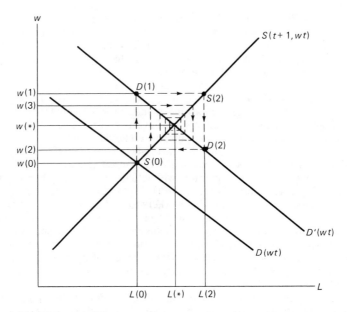

FIGURE 5-7. Stable dynamic equilibrium

trated. Individuals achieve their desired level of employment and firms are "on" their labor demand schedule.

Our scenario does not end here, though, because the higher wage leads workers to increase their quantity of labor in period 2 to $L(2)$, as indicated by point $S(2)$. This results in an equilibrium wage of $w(2)$, as denoted by point $D(2)$. Note that while $w(2)$ is less than $w(1)$, it exceeds the initial wage rate, $w(0)$. Figure 5-8 traces out the time path of the equilibrium wage for the first seven periods in the labor market represented by Figure 5-7. Two facts are important. First, the wage rate oscillates around $w(*)$. Second, the oscillations become smaller over time. If we were to continue to track the market wage rate, it would eventually reach a *stationary* equi-

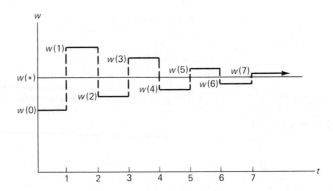

FIGURE 5-8. Time path of the wage rate

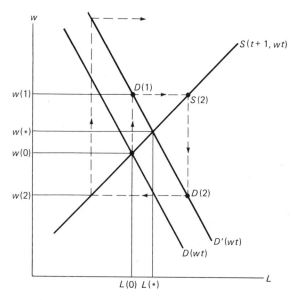

FIGURE 5-9. Unstable dynamic equilibrium

librium value of $w(*)$. This may be seen from the pattern of dashed arrows, which indicate the movement of w and L toward w^* and L^*, respectively, in Figure 5-7. Because this pattern resembles a spider's web, diagrams such as Figures 5-7 and 5-8 are sometimes referred to as **cobweb** diagrams.

A moving equilibrium followed by eventual stationarity of wages and employment is, of course, not the only possible situation if a labor market is characterized by a supply lag. Figures 5-9 and 5-10 depict a market in which w and L will also oscillate, but instead of eventually converging to $w(*)$ and $L(*)$, they move successively farther and farther away. In this case we say that the labor market exhibits *explosive* oscillations as opposed to the *damped* oscillations of Figure 5-7. It is interesting that in *both* the damped and explosive cases the demand curves are downward-sloping and the supply curves upward-sloping. Whether a long-run stationary equilibrium ever occurs depends upon the *relative absolute values* of the slopes of supply and demand. Further examination of Figures 5-7 and 5-9 will verify the general result that convergence to a constant equilibrium results when the absolute value of the slope of the demand schedule is *less than* the absolute value of the slope of the supply schedule.[16]

What have we learned from our examination of a labor market where workers require time to implement their supply decisions? First, we have broadened our conception of equilibrium to permit the possibility of moving or *dynamic* equilibrium. In contrast to comparative statics analyses where we examine the general directions of changes in w and L following labor market disturbances, we have considered here in some detail the period-to-period adjustments in wages and employment. Second, we established the conditions under which w and L will eventually become station-

---

[16] This condition also holds true when supply and demand are both downward-sloping. An important difference exists in the latter case, however. Try showing what happens when S and D are negatively inclined.

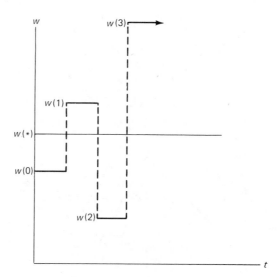

FIGURE 5-10. Time path of wage rate

ary. We saw that a labor market could be *dynamically unstable* [never reach $w(*)$ and L^*] even though demand is negatively sloped and supply positively sloped. This result should be compared to our earlier discussion of stability of a static equilibrium. Finally, remember that we have examined supply lags where workers' wage expectations are formulated in an extremely simple way. If individuals utilize a more sophisticated prediction mechanism, the adjustment patterns of wages and employment will differ from those identified in this section.

*An Application to the Market for Lawyers

Cobweb models have proved quite useful in analyzing the variation over time in the salaries of a number of different occupations where training requirements create supply lags. To conclude our discussion we will briefly summarize an application to the labor market for lawyers, based on research reported by Richard B. Freeman. Freeman noted that the supply of new lawyers has exhibited a cyclical pattern, suggesting that decisions to enroll in law school and to remain in school through graduation are strongly influenced by current salary levels for new lawyers. If the salaries of young attorneys are determined by the demand for legal services and the number of current law degree recipients, then a cobweb-type model of the market for lawyers could explain the observed fluctuating pattern of the number of law school graduates as well as fluctuations in the relative salaries of young lawyers.

Freeman used data for the years 1949–71 to estimate three equations encompassing law school entry and graduation decisions as well as salary determination. He took several approaches to estimating these equations, some of them using rather advanced techniques. Therefore, we present here only a partial summary of his results, which, nevertheless, provides a good idea of how the market for new lawyers

---

* This section is somewhat more technical and may be skipped without loss of continuity. If you skip, go to the concluding section of the chapter.

functions. The simplest equation used to explain the number of students entering law school was estimated to be

$$\log LENT = 6.45 + 2.25 \log LSAL - 1.84 \log ASAL, \qquad R^2 = 0.55 \quad \textbf{(5-1)}$$
$$\qquad\qquad\quad (0.82) \qquad\qquad\quad (1.04)$$

where the numbers in parentheses are standard errors and

$LENT \equiv$ the number of first-year law school enrollees

$LSAL \equiv$ the annual salaries of young attorneys deflated by the Consumer Price Index

$ASAL \equiv$ annual salaries of full-time workers deflated by the Consumer Price Index.

Equation (5-1) tells us that a 1 percent increase in young lawyers' salaries leads to a 2.25 percent increase in the number of law school entrants, holding constant alternative salaries. (What is the effect of a 1 percent increase in alternative earnings, holding constant young lawyers' salaries?)

The second equation estimated by Freeman showed that the number of law school *graduates* is strongly influenced by the number of entrants three years earlier and is somewhat influenced by $LSAL$ (positively) and $ASAL$ (negatively). The third equation represents the demand for young attorneys and shows that, holding constant the level of demand for legal services, the elasticity of salaries with respect to the number of law school graduates is between -0.10 and -0.13. (Do the elasticities of demand and supply satisfy the conditions for a stable dynamic equilibrium described in the last section?) By a chain of substitutions, Freeman shows how the structure of the model represented by these three equations leads to a cobweb-type fluctuation in the number of law school enrollments, with peaks in enrollment followed by troughs every three or four years.

CONCLUSION

The concept of a market is central to all economic analysis. In this chapter we examined in detail a labor market under competitive conditions and the circumstances under which a unique wage-employment transaction, satisfactory to both households and firms, occurs. Our knowledge of the underpinnings of labor supply and demand gained in Chapters 3 and 4 enabled us to predict the labor market influence of changes in the environment and to gain some insights into one economic aspect of a particular public policy, the incidence of the social security tax.

An economy is really composed of *many* labor markets. When competitive conditions apply, a wage rate for labor of a given type will persist in a labor market only if it is the same as wages elsewhere. Wage inequalities between labor markets will lead workers to leave employment in relatively low-wage markets and seek employment in relatively high-wage markets. This migration pattern promotes equality of wages, since only when there is equal pay in alternative markets is there no financial incentive to relocate. An important implication of this worker mobility pattern is that it leads to *economic efficiency:* the maximization of production with society's available resources. A related point is that institutions such as a minimum wage that inhibit the forces of competitive general equilibrium impose a cost on society in the form of reduced consumption of goods and services. It is impossible to conclude on scientific grounds, however, that such institutions are undesirable whenever they alter the *distribution* of income.

We ended the chapter with an introduction to the important problem of labor market dynamics. There we showed theoretically that if labor supply decisions respond to wages with a one-period lag, fluctuations in both wages and the quantity of labor employed will occur before equilibrium is reached. Even a simple cobweb model of the type developed in this chapter has real-world applications, as an analysis of the market for young lawyers demonstrates.

REFERENCES AND SELECTED READING

BALLANTE, DON, "The North-South Differential and the Migration of Homogeneous Labor," *American Economic Review,* 69:1 (March 1979), 166–75.

FLEISHER, BELTON M., *Minimum Wage Regulation in the United States.* Washington, D.C.: National Chamber Foundation, 1982.

FREEMAN, RICHARD B., "A Cobweb Model of the Starting Salary of New Engineers," *Industrial and Labor Relations Review,* 29:1 (January 1976), 236–48.

———, "Legal Cobwebs: A Recursive Model of the Market for New Lawyers," *Review of Economics and Statistics,* 57 (May 1975), 171–80.

"Income Differences Between Regions Narrow as a Result of Mobility, More Women at Work," *The Wall Street Journal,* March 4, 1982.

REDER, MELVIN W., "Wage Differentials: Theory and Measurement," in *Aspects of Labor Economics,* ed. H. Gregg Lewis. Princeton, N.J.: Princeton University Press, 1962.

SIOW, ALOYSIUS, "A Structural Cobweb Model of Occupational Choice," Columbia University Department of Economics Working Paper No. 103. New York: Columbia University Department of Economics, 1981.

EXERCISES

Choose whether statements 1 and 2 are *True, False,* or *Uncertain* (whether true or false depends on unspecified circumstances). Justify your answer. Your justification is the most important part of your answer.

1. If Congress wishes to increase social security tax payments with minimal effect on workers' take-home pay, it is important to specify that employers pay the tax.

2. If the market labor supply curve is negatively sloped, stability requires that it be steeper than the market labor demand curve.

3. The following are the labor supply and demand schedules for a particular labor market.

Labor Demand Schedule		Labor Supply Schedule	
Daily Wage	Quantity of Labor Demanded	Daily Wage	Quantity of Labor Supplied
$60	0	0	0
55	500	$ 5	500
50	1,000	10	1,000
45	1,500	15	1,500
40	2,000	20	2,000
35	2,500	25	2,500
30	3,000	30	3,000
25	3,500	35	3,500
20	4,000	40	4,000
15	4,500	45	4,500
10	5,000	50	5,000
5	5,500	55	5,500

(a) What is the equilibrium wage? Explain how you arrived at your answer. Suppose now that Congress levies a tax on workers of $10 per unit of labor supplied. Specifically, they must "mail in checks" (have withheld from their pay) $10 for each unit of labor they sell.

(b) What is the new equilibrium wage? Explain carefully.

(c) Who *actually* pays the tax of $10 per unit of labor? Be as *complete* as possible in your answer.

(d) What is the *total* tax revenue collected by the government? Explain carefully.

(e) On the whole, have workers been made better off or worse off? Be as *complete* as possible in your answer.

4. A recent newspaper article points out that San Francisco has the most physicians per capita of any United States city, yet the average income of physicians there is among the highest in the United States. How can this be? Aren't wages supposed to be relatively low when labor is relatively plentiful? Explain the forces responsible for the seeming paradox. Support your answer with the appropriate graphs.

*5. A society is composed of six identical workers, each of whom wants a job at any wage and, of course, prefers higher to lower wages. There are two industries in our example society, A and B. This society used to be in competitive equilibrium, but Industry B recently became unionized while Industry A remained nonunion. Industry A currently hires five workers at a wage of $10 each, and Industry B currently hires one worker at a wage of $12. Finally, both industries have fixed capital and linear labor demand schedules with slopes of −1. Based on this information:

(a) Calculate this society's current value of GNP. Explain carefully.

(b) Calculate the reduction in GNP suffered by this society when Industry B became unionized. Explain carefully.

(c) Without using any graphs or symbols, explain *briefly* why unionism or anything else that creates unequal wages for identical workers (such as discrimination or a minimum wage law) reduces GNP.

(d) Create an algebraic formula for the GNP loss (in this society) that requires only *currently observable* information to evaluate.

(e) Explain briefly why the GNP loss being discussed is a socially undesirable aspect of unionism.

---

* Indicates a more difficult exercise.

6

THE LABOR MARKET
WHEN BUYERS
ARE NONCOMPETITIVE

---

* Indicates more technical material that may be skipped without loss of continuity.

Our analysis of wages and employment to this point has concentrated on the interactions between households and firms in competitive labor and product markets. In these situations, an individual buyer or seller of labor services is unable to affect wage rates or the prices of final products. In this chapter we study markets where labor is demanded by various types of *noncompetitive* firms. Specifically, we discuss the cases where a good or service is produced by a single firm or where labor services are purchased by a single employer. The economic theory of wages and employment is the same for competitive and noncompetitive labor markets in the sense that equilibrium is determined by the forces of supply and demand, with marginal productivity of labor the key factor determining the amount of labor services demanded. So, we need only generalize some of the concepts learned in Chapter 3 to examine labor markets in which firms are noncompetitive.

Our discussions will focus on two important questions: (1) How do equilibrium wage-employment combinations differ from the competitive case? (2) How do the labor market effects of public policy perhaps differ from the competitive situation?

PRODUCT MARKET MONOPOLY

A firm is a **monopolist** when it is the *only seller* of a good or service. The most obvious real-life examples of product market monopolists are the public utilities. Only rarely are consumers able to choose their local telephone, gas, or electric companies. In the case of public utilities, the monopoly is usually caused by the ability of a single firm to supply enough output for the entire market more cheaply than when many firms are producing. The reason is the substantial fixed costs involved in a local public utility. Once the enormously expensive citywide network of wires or pipes has been created, however, it is relatively cheap to add an extra customer to this network. This means that one firm can produce output for additional customers much more cheaply than a second firm, which would also have to establish a second network of pipes or wires. In this situation, monopolies are typically referred to as **natural monopolies.**

There are other reasons for monopolies, of course. A firm may exercise complete control over an input necessary to manufacture a product. A classic example from the industrial organization literature is the virtually complete control Alcoa once held over the supply of bauxite, a necessary input in the production of aluminum. As a result, there was a period during which Alcoa was basically a monopoly producer of aluminum. Alternatively, a producer may hold a government franchise giving it the exclusive rights to the production and distribution of a good or service. The U.S. Army is a good example. Except for perhaps the mafia, who else sells protection on a national scale? Finally, monopoly may stem from a patent on a product or the process involved in its manufacture. Can you name an example of this?

The Demand for Labor by a Monopolist
When Capital Is Fixed

In Chapter 3 we saw that when a competitive firm is unable to adjust its input of capital services, it hires the amount of labor services that equates the value of marginal product of labor (*VMPL*) to the wage rate. This made the *VMPL* schedule its labor demand curve. The profit-maximizing monopolist also employs labor up to the point where the last unit hired increases production cost and sales revenue by equal amounts. Once we have found something analogous to *VMPL* for a monopolist, we will have also found its demand for labor during a period of time too short for capital to be adjusted.

Unlike the competitive firm, which has no control over product price, the monopolist determines price by its output decision. Remember that because a monopoly firm is the only seller of a good or a service, it is also the *industry*. Therefore, the demand curve for the monopolist's output is the market demand schedule, which is downward-sloping. As additional units are offered for sale, the price the monopolist can charge must decline. This means that when calculating the value of an additional unit of labor services, the monopolist knows that (1) it will have more output to sell and (2) it will sell (all) its output for less per unit.[1] In the case of monopoly, the change in total revenue due to a small change in labor services is known as the **marginal revenue product of labor (*MRPL*)**. A numerical example should help us understand the sense of the terminology and illustrate that *MRPL* will generally be the monopolist's labor demand curve.

In Table 6-1, column (2) lists the levels of output (*Q*) associated with various amounts of labor (*L*) for a Cobb-Douglas type production function where capital is fixed. In this production function, output is an exponentially weighted average of capital and labor. (See Chapter 3 and the first footnote in Table 6-1.) The demand curve for the monopolist's output is assumed to be linear, and column (4) displays the prices (*p*) associated with the output values in column (2). Notice that as *L* is increased from 1 to 2 units, *Q* rises from 10 to 17, and price falls from \$180 to \$166. Column (6), which displays marginal revenue (*MR*), tells us that each of the 11th through 17th units increases total revenue by an average of only \$146. Although units 11 to 17 will sell for \$166 apiece, units 1 to 10 will now each sell for \$14 less. So *MRPL*, the extra revenue created by an additional unit of labor services, is equal to \$1,022. Because the demand curve for the monopolist's output is negatively sloped, *MRPL* is *less than p* times the marginal physical product of labor (*MPPL*). The importance of this will soon become apparent. Finally, we see that the numbers in column (7) are also equal to marginal physical product of labor times marginal revenue. Can you now guess the origin of the name *marginal revenue product of labor*? Aren't economists clever?

---

[1] We will assume for simplicity that the monopolist is unable to discriminate with respect to price.

TABLE 6-1   Derivation of a Monopolist's Marginal Revenue Product of Labor Schedule

(1) ←Production Function→ L	(2) Q*	(3) MPPL	(4) p†	(5) TR	(6) MR	(7) MRPL
0	0	—	—	—	—	—
1	10	10	$180	$1,800	$180	$1,800
2	17	7	166	2,822	146	1,022
3	23	6	154	3,542	120	720
4	28	5	144	4,032	98	490
5	33	5	134	4,422	78	390
6	38	5	124	4,712	58	290
7	43	5	114	4,902	38	190
8	48	5	104	4,992	18	90
9	52	4	96	4,992	0	0
10	56	4	88	4,928	−16	−64

$L \equiv$ units of labor services

$Q \equiv$ units of output

$MPPL \equiv$ marginal physical product of labor $\left(\dfrac{\Delta Q}{\Delta L}\right)$

$p \equiv$ product price

$TR \equiv$ total revenue $(P \cdot Q)$

$MR \equiv$ marginal revenue $\left(\dfrac{\Delta TR}{\Delta Q}\right)$

$MRPL \equiv$ marginal revenue product of labor $\left(\dfrac{\Delta TR}{\Delta L}\right) \equiv (MR \cdot MPPL)$

* Output produced according to the production function, $Q = K^{\alpha}L^{\beta}$, where $K \equiv$ capital services = 10,000, $\alpha = 0.25$, and $\beta = 0.75$. Output has been rounded to the nearest even unit.
† Price is obtained from the demand curve for output $Q = c - dp$, where p = price, $c = 100$, and $d = 0.5$, so that $p = (Q - 100)/-0.5$.

Having just identified the economic benefits of some extra labor, we now need to consider the monopolist's cost of additional units of L. A number of situations can exist. A monopolist may be one of only a few firms that demand workers' services in a labor market. Later in this chapter we examine the extreme case where a monopolist is the *only* demander of labor. Alternatively, a monopolist may compete for employees with *many* other firms, both competitive and monopolistic. In a large city, for example, the public utility monopolies compete with numerous private corporations, small businesses, and government agencies for secretaries, janitors, and middle managers. This is the situation we will now discuss—wages and employment where a monopolist competes for labor with many other firms.

In a competitive labor market, no one firm, whether a competitor or a monopolist in its output market, purchases enough L to influence the equilibrium wage rate. The supply curve of labor to the monopolist in this case looks similar to that of a competitive firm—perfectly elastic (horizontal) at the prevailing wage rate. This situation is depicted in Figure 6-1, where the monopolist can purchase as much labor as it desires at wage $w(0)$. What remains to be shown is that $MRPL$ is the monopolist's labor demand schedule. To do this, all we must show is that when confronted with a particular (constant) wage rate, the monopolist maximizes profit by hiring the amount of labor that equates the marginal revenue product of labor to that wage.

Every profit-maximizing firm chooses its output so that marginal revenue (MR) equals marginal cost (MC). With a tiny bit of algebra it is easily shown that this decision rule is equivalent to choosing L so that $MRPL = w$. Remember that marginal cost is defined as the change in a firm's total cost (TC) due to a small change in its output (Q). Denoting the change in a variable by Δ, we have

$$MC \equiv \frac{\Delta TC}{\Delta Q} \qquad (6\text{-}1)$$

Total cost (TC) includes expenditures for the services of capital and labor,

$$TC = wL + cK \qquad (6\text{-}2)$$

where $c \equiv$ price of a unit of capital services, and $K \equiv$ quantity of capital services. Since we are considering the situation in which capital is fixed,

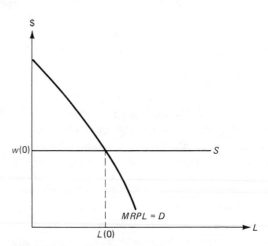

FIGURE 6-1. The labor demand schedule for a monopolist when capital is fixed and labor services are purchased in a competitive labor market

only labor costs change when the firm adjusts its production, or

$$MC \equiv \frac{\Delta TC}{\Delta Q} = w \frac{\Delta L}{\Delta Q} = w \frac{1}{MPPL} \qquad (6\text{-}3)$$

Utilizing (6-3), when marginal cost equals marginal revenue,

$$w \frac{1}{MPPL} = MR$$

or

$$w = (MPPL \cdot MR) \equiv MRPL \qquad (6\text{-}4)$$

So, when confronted with a given wage rate, the monopolist maximizes profit by hiring that amount of labor services which equates labor's marginal revenue product to w. MRPL, therefore, is the monopolist's labor demand schedule when it hires labor in a competitive labor market. In Figure 6-1, the firm will hire $L(0)$ units of labor.

Application: The effects of various taxes on the monopolist's labor demand schedule. Let us examine how the demand for labor by a monopolist is affected by two different taxes: (1) a lump-sum tax, and (2) a sales tax. Although not readily apparent, the effects of both taxes are quite easy to analyze. A lump-sum tax means that the monopolist's net profit becomes $\Pi - Y$ where Y dollars must be paid to the taxing agency whether or not production occurs, and Π is the monopolist's profit. Because $\Pi - Y$ is maximized where gross profit (Π) is maximized, the lump-sum tax does not affect the monopolist's labor demand schedule. The tax is identical to a fixed cost, and we already know that fixed costs affect the level of profit but not the choice of how much labor to use (see Chapter 3).

Here is something to think about. No one likes monopolists and everyone wants to see poverty eradicated. If a lump-sum tax has no impact on the monopolist's labor input and, therefore, its output, why not impose huge lump-sum taxes on the monopolists in the United States as a way of raising revenue to eliminate poverty? Can you think of any flaws in this idea?

We know that in the absence of taxation, the profit-maximizing monopolist hires that amount of labor where the wage rate equals the marginal physical product of labor times marginal revenue. A **sales tax** means that when additional dollars of sales revenue are generated, the firm may keep $(1 - m) \cdot 100$ percent of each dollar, where m is the (constant) tax rate on the revenue. So, the monopolist's *net* marginal revenue is $(1 - m)MR$, and profit is maximized when the net marginal revenue product of labor equals the wage rate, or when

$$(1 - m)(MR) \cdot (MPPL) \equiv (1 - m)MRPL = w \qquad (6\text{-}5)$$

Figure 6-2 illustrates the labor demand schedules of a monopolist before and after the tax when *MRPL* is linear and $m = 0.5$. Notice that at every point D' is *halfway* between D and the horizontal axis. This means that any given wage, a monopolist will demand less labor as the result of the tax. In general, the sales tax reduces the quantity of labor demanded to that which would be desired at a wage equal to $w/(1 - m)$. As an exercise, draw your own graphs and see how D and D' are related for various values of m and shapes of *MRPL*.

The Demand for Labor by a Monopolist When It Adjusts Capital

In Figure 6-3, $MRPL(K1)$ represents a monopolist's marginal revenue product of labor for a particular amount of capital, $K1$. When confronted with labor supply curve S, profit is maximized by employing $L(1)$ units of labor. The question we seek to answer in this section is this: What happens to the quantity of labor employed when the wage rate changes and the monopolist is free to adjust its input of capital?

Consider what happens if the market labor supply schedule increases, leading to a lower wage, $w(2)$, in Figure 6-3. If capital were fixed at $K1$, the monopolist would increase its labor input to $L(2)$. (Why?) The decline in the wage rate, however, has lowered the price of labor services relative to capital services and reduced the cost of production in general. The first of these leads the firm to minimize the cost of any given output, a necessary condition for profit maximization, by using a smaller capital-to-labor ratio.

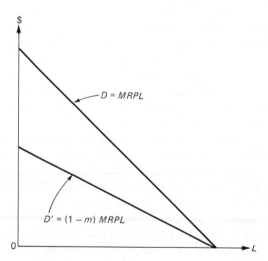

FIGURE 6-2. The effect of a sales tax on a monopolist's demand for labor

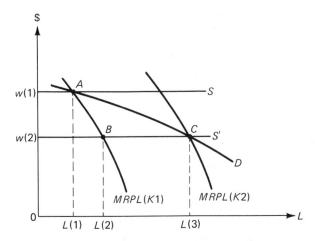

FIGURE 6-3. A monopolist's labor demand
curve when it adjusts capital

We have called this the *substitution effect* of a decline in the wage. In
addition, we know that the monopolist will expand production by using more
of *both* capital and labor. This is the *output effect* of a decline in the wage
rate. As in the competitive case, *MPPL* shifts to the right with the change in
K. This is also depicted in Figure 6-3. The monopolist's labor demand schedule, *D*, connects points like *A* and *C* and is flatter (more elastic) than if
capital cannot be adjusted. So, whether competitive or monopolistic in its
market for output, with fixed or variable capital, the profit-maximizing firm's
labor demand schedule is downward-sloping.

The Market Labor Demand Schedule When Some or All
Firms Are Monopolists

It is possible to have a competitive labor market where *all* the buyers of
labor are product market monopolists, each for a different product. In such a
situation the derivation of market labor demand is actually less complex than
when all the firms are competitive in their output markets. Since a monopolist is also an industry, its labor demand schedule *already* reflects the fact
that product price declines with industry output. So, when only monopolists
compete for workers' services, the labor demand schedule simply plots out
the sum of the quantities of labor desired by each monopolist at the various
wage rates. Formally stated, *the market demand curve is the horizontal sum
of the monopolists' labor demand curves*. It follows directly that when both
monopolistic and competitive industries purchase labor in the same market,
the demand schedule is the sum of the individual industries' demand curves.

Wage and Employment Differentials
Between Monopolies and Competitive Industries

At this point it should be obvious that equilibrium wage and employment are determined by the interaction of supply and demand, whether buyers of labor are competitors, monopolists, or a blend of the two. We now utilize our newly acquired insight into the demand for labor by a monopolist to compare wages and employment in competitive labor markets where some or all buyers are product market monopolists versus competitive labor markets where *only* competitive industries purchase labor services.

We know that each point on a competitive industry's labor demand curve reflects the value of the marginal product of labor, which is the product of the price of output and the marginal physical product of labor. When an industry is a monopolist, however, it maximizes profit by hiring labor so that the wage rate equals the marginal revenue product of labor, which is the product of marginal revenue and marginal physical product of labor. Given the same production functions and demand curves for final output, a monopolist's labor demand schedule will lie below that of a competitive industry because marginal revenue is less than price.

Figure 6-4 illustrates the market labor demand schedules for two groups of industries. The curve labeled $D(C)$ represents the horizontal sum of the labor demand schedules of n identical competitive industries. $D(M)$, labeled the monopolistic demand curve, is derived from the same group as $D(C)$ except that at least one of the competitive industries has been replaced by a monopolist. Notice that in labor markets where monopolies are present, less labor will be demanded. This is simply the result of the fact that monopolies make their profits by restricting output to less than the competitive level and in the process hire less labor. Moreover, if the labor supply curve has any degree of inelasticity, so that it is upward-sloping, both equilibrium wage and employment will be lower than if all industries were competitive. Economists refer to the wage differential $w(C) - w(M)$ caused by the presence of a product market monopoly as **monopolistic exploitation.**

One subtlety is worth noting at this point. In the United States, monopolies are often regulated by the government or face a threat of regulation. This means that an unregulated monopolist may find it desirable to reduce its profits to avoid regulation in the future. One way to do this is to pay a wage higher than $w(M)$ in Figure 6-4. These higher wages may not only be paid in cash but may also take the form of company country clubs, running tracks, and gymnasiums.[2]

At this stage it would be nice to end with a concise statement on the

---

[2] See Armen Alchian and Rubin Kessel, "Competition, Monopoly, and the Pursuit of Pecuniary Gain," in H. G. Lewis, ed., *Aspects of Labor Economics* (Princeton, N.J.: Princeton University Press, 1962).

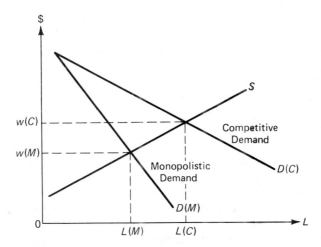

FIGURE 6-4. Competitive and monopolistic labor demand schedules

incidence of monopoly in the United States and the evidence on the differentials in wages between monopoly and competitive industries, ceteris paribus. However, to quote a noted authority on industrial organization, F. M. Scherer, "It is futile to attempt a quantitative summary of how much structural monopoly power exists in the whole of the American economy."[3] Scherer does speculate, though, that no more than 5 or 6 percent of the gross national product seems to be produced under conditions approaching pure monopoly. As a result of the difficulties involved in measuring monopoly power, there are relatively few studies of how the structure of the output market affects wages. What evidence there is seems to be mixed. In particular, there is no clear-cut conclusion to be drawn from the research in this area as to whether monopolies pay lower wages for a given type of worker.[4]

MONOPSONY

Thus far our discussion of the demand for labor in a noncompetitive environment has considered the situation where an individual firm cannot affect the prices of its inputs. Sometimes only a few firms purchase labor, so that one employer's actions will disturb the equilibrium wage rate. The name for this situation is **oligopsony.** In the next two sections we examine a particular

[3] *Industrial Market Structure and Economic Performance,* 2d ed. (Chicago: Rand McNally College Publishing Company, 1980), p. 67.
[4] See Leonard W. Weiss, "Concentration and Labor Earnings," *American Economic Review,* 56:1 (March 1966), 96–117, and Ronald G. Ehrenberg, *The Regulatory Process in Labor Earnings* (New York: Academic Press, 1979).

oligopsonistic labor market, called **monopsony,** where there is only *one* effective buyer of labor.

Although it has been declining in importance, the so-called company town is probably what comes to mind for most of us when picturing a monopsonistic labor market. Alternatively, such a market structure may stem from an agreement by employers not to compete with each other for workers. For example, the three universities in the Research Triangle area of North Carolina—Duke University, North Carolina State University, and the University of North Carolina at Chapel Hill—have an informal agreement not to try to hire faculty members away from each other. Historically, the major professional sports in the United States have operated under a system where experienced athletes were subject to contracts that deny players the privilege of voluntarily quitting one employer and obtaining a job with a rival team. The end of this section is devoted to an examination of the prevalence of monopsony in the United States in general, and to a discussion of one monopsony in particular—professional baseball during the 1960s. But first, we must understand how a monopsonistic labor market works.

The Role of the Labor Supply Schedule

Because a monopsonist is the only buyer of labor, its labor supply schedule is that of the labor market itself. For simplicity we will consider a situation in which workers are equally capable and where hours of work per employee do not vary. In this case the labor supply function relates wage rates to the number of persons seeking employment. We know from Chapter 4 that when quantity of labor is measured as the *number* of workers, the market labor supply schedule is upward-sloping. To see how this fact plays a key role in a profit-maximizing monopsonist's choice of how much labor to use, it is helpful to examine a hypothetical labor supply schedule such as that displayed in Table 6-2. Columns (1) and (2) list how many individuals are willing to work at various hourly wage rates. The monopsony employer's total cost per hour at different quantities of labor (TCL) is presented in column (3). It is the product of the numbers in the first two columns. Notice that we have here a *nondiscriminating* monopsonist, one that pays all its workers an identical wage rate because they are equally capable. Finally, column (4) indicates the marginal cost of labor (MCL) associated with the supply schedule in columns (1) and (2). It represents the increase in labor cost associated with an additional unit of labor.

Notice that MCL rises with L and exceeds w. Moreover, the difference between the two grows with L. When the monopsonist in Table 6-2 hires one worker, for example, it must pay an hourly wage rate of $5, which leads to a total labor cost per hour of $5. In order to expand its labor force to two employees, however, it must increase w to $5.50. In the absence of any wage discrimination, the monopsonist will pay *both* workers $5.50 per hour. Thus,

TABLE 6-2   Derivation of a Monopsonist's Marginal Cost of Labor Schedule

Labor Supply Schedule			
(1) ⟵————————————⟶	(2)	(3)	(4)
L	w	TCL	MCL
1	$5.00	$ 5	$ 5
2	5.50	11	6
3	6.00	18	7
4	6.50	26	8
5	7.00	35	9
6	7.50	45	10
7	8.00	56	11
8	8.50	68	12
9	9.00	81	13
10	9.50	95	14

$L \equiv$ units of labor services (number of employees)

$w \equiv$ hourly wage rate

$TCL =$ total cost of labor per hour $\equiv (w \cdot L)$

$MCL \equiv$ marginal cost of labor per hour $\equiv$ $\left(\dfrac{\Delta TCL}{\Delta L}\right)$

the cost per hour of adding a second worker is $6. Remember that if the firm in Table 6-2 were a competitor, w would be fixed at $5, so that the marginal cost of expanding to a work force of 2 would be $5 per hour. Because the monopsonist must raise w to $5.50 to attract a second worker, its marginal cost of labor is $5.50, the second worker's hourly wage *plus* $0.50, the wage increase for the first worker. Whenever an additional worker is hired in Table 6-2, w increases by $0.50, and all existing employees, therefore, receive $0.50 more per hour. The result is that the larger is a monopsonist's work force, the larger is the *difference* between its current wage and its cost of adding a worker. More workers will be receiving raises to keep their wages in line with the higher wage necessary to attract a new employee.

To emphasize the relation between *MCL* and the labor supply function, we have taken the ones in Table 6-2 and graphed them in Figure 6-5. Again, the important things to notice are that *MCL* is positively sloped and that it lies above *S*. In our numerical example, the slope of *MCL* is twice that of *S*. Whenever L increases by one worker, the market wage rate increases by $0.50 and the marginal cost of labor by $1.[5]

---

[5] Whenever S is upward-sloping and linear, *MCL* is also linear with a slope *twice* that of S. To see this, let S be described by the general linear equation, $w = a + bL$, where a and b are positive constants. From this, $TCL \equiv wL = aL + bL^2$, and $MCL \equiv \Delta TCL/\Delta L = a + 2bL$.

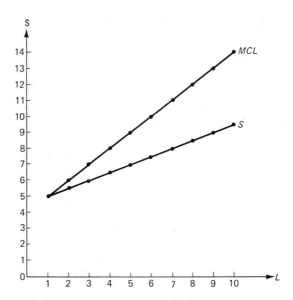

FIGURE 6-5. The labor supply and marginal cost of labor schedules from Table 6-2

The "Demand" for Labor by a Monopsonist When Capital Is Fixed

There is an old joke about a parrot who knew economics: it just kept squawking, "Marginal cost equals marginal benefit." At the risk of being put in a cage, then, we offer the following: a profit-maximizing monopsonist hires the quantity of labor that equates the marginal cost of labor to the marginal dollar benefit of labor. Notice that this is the decision rule followed by *any* profit-maximizing firm in deciding how much labor to hire. In this section we examine the case of a monopsonist that is also a product market monopolist unable to adjust its input of physical capital. This provides us with important background for our empirical analysis of major league baseball. It is important to realize that a monopsonist may also be a competitor in its output market. An example would be a textile mill in a small southern town. While the mill may be the only employer in town, textiles are sold in national and international markets that are quite competitive.

When a monopsonist is also a product market monopolist, it maximizes profit by hiring that amount of labor which equates *MCL* to the marginal revenue product of labor. This is illustrated in Figure 6-6, where $L(0)$ units of labor generate maximum profit. Remember that because only one firm is purchasing workers' services, $L(0)$ is also total market employment. What is the equilibrium wage associated with $L(0)$ in Figure 6-6? Once a profit-

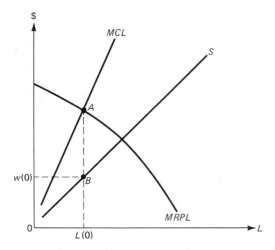

FIGURE 6-6. Equilibrium wage and employment for a monopsonist that is a product market monopolist

maximizing monopsonist has determined its optimal amount of labor, it pays the wage rate on S associated with $L(0)$. A wage lower than $w(0)$ will fail to elicit the optimal number of workers, and a wage higher than $w(0)$ is unnecessary.

Some subtle dimensions of monopsony. There are two subtle dimensions of monopsonies that you may find interesting. First, *all* firms have some degree of monopsony power.[6] Suppose, for example, there has recently been an increase in demand in a competitive labor market so that there is now an excess demand for labor at the currently prevailing wage, $w(0)$. Supervisors will ask workers for longer hours, and personnel managers will attempt to hire new employees at a faster rate. Firms will eventually find that wages will have to be increased in order to obtain their desired amounts of labor. The wage these competitive firms pay will eventually rise to its new equilibrium level; call it $w(1)$. Only at $w(1)$ can competitive firms be said to face a fixed wage in the sense that they have no trouble finding enough labor to meet their needs.

A second subtle aspect of monopsony is that a monopsonist does *not* have a labor demand schedule as customarily defined. To see this, remember that a firm purchasing workers' services in a competitive labor market faces a fixed wage rate. In this situation, MCL is constant at the particular wage rate in question, and the firm's marginal dollar benefit of labor schedule ($VPML$ or $MRPL$) indicates its de-

---

* This section contains more technical material that may be skipped without loss of continuity. If you skip, go to p. 208.
6 See Martin N. Baily, "Dynamic Monopsony and Structural Change," *American Economic Review,* 65:2 (June 1975), 338–49.

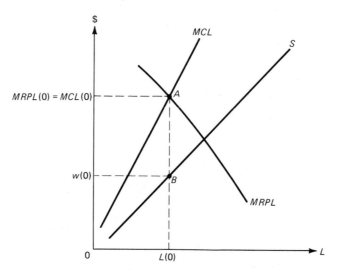

FIGURE 6-7. Monopsonistic exploitation

sired amount of labor services. By considering various constant values of w, we trace out *VMPL* as the competitive firm's labor demand schedule and *MRPL* as the monopolist's labor demand schedule. A monopsony, however, does not face a constant wage, but rather a *menu* of wage rates; each w is associated with a *different L* through the labor supply curve, S. Moreover, S implies a particular upward-sloping *MCL*. When paired with the monopsonist's marginal dollar benefit of labor curve, this marginal cost of labor schedule determines the equilibrium wage-employment combination—for example, $w(0)$ and $L(0)$ in Figure 6-6. Only if the marginal cost of labor *schedule* shifts will the monopsonist change L and therefore w. What we are saying is that *no individual curve* in Figure 6-6 provides the information furnished by a labor demand schedule. This lack of a labor demand schedule for a monopsony is analogous to the lack of an output supply curve for a monopoly producer.

Application: Monopsonistic Exploitation and the Effect of Minimum Wage Legislation on It

Figure 6-7 depicts the equilibrium wage and employment in a monopsonistic labor market. Employment level $L(0)$ equates the monopsonists' marginal cost of labor to its marginal revenue product of labor. Having chosen this level of employment, the monopsonist then offers the wage that obtains $L(0)$ at minimum cost. This process generates an equilibrium wage of $w(0)$ in Figure 6-7. Notice, though, that workers are paid *less* than their marginal value to the firm. This aspect of a monopsonistic labor market is known as **monopsonistic exploitation** and can be measured by the vertical

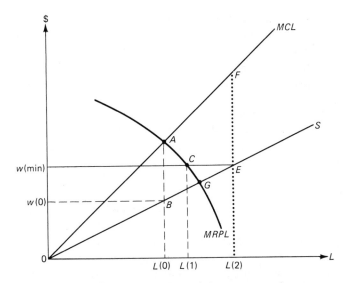

FIGURE 6-8. The effect of a minimum wage law on a monopsonistic labor market

distance AB,[7] which is equal to $MRPL(0) - w(0)$. This is an *upper bound* estimate of monopsonistic exploitation, and alternative measures have been suggested. We will utilize this measure because it is probably the most readily observable and because it has been used to compute estimates of monopsonistic exploitation in professional baseball, which we discuss at the end of this chapter. With this in mind, let us examine a minimum wage law as a device for eliminating monopsonistic exploitation.

Consider once again a monopsonistic labor market where the firm is a monopolist in its output market. This situation is depicted in Figure 6-8. The profit-maximizing amount of labor is determined at point A, which implies equilibrium employment of $L(0)$. Workers demand, and receive, a market wage of $w(0)$ for supplying this amount of labor. The issue we wish to address is whether the monopsonistic exploitation, AB, can be reduced or eliminated by a minimum wage.

Suppose that a minimum wage equal to $w(min)$ is imposed on the labor market depicted in Figure 6-8. $w(min)$ must, of course, exceed $w(0)$ to be effective. To see how equilibrium wage and employment are affected, we must first discuss how a minimum law changes the market labor supply curve. To the left of point E, the supply curve becomes a horizontal line at

[7] See J. P. Gould and C. E. Ferguson, *Microeconomic Theory,* 5th ed. (Homewood, Ill.: Richard D. Irwin, Inc., 1980), pp. 399–401.

the value w(min), since workers are prevented from offering their services for less than the minimum wage. Remember, though, that workers require a wage rate in excess of w(min) to be willing to supply amounts of labor in excess of L(2), so that the market supply curve follows S to the right of E. Thus, the supply curve of labor to the monopsonist becomes the kinked line w(min)ES.

To establish the new equilibrium wage and employment we need the marginal cost of labor schedule associated with the labor supply schedule w(min)ES. For amounts of labor less than or equal to L(2), the cost of an additional unit of labor is also w(min), because whenever the wage is constant it is also the cost of an additional unit of labor. When the quantity of labor exceeds L(2), the marginal cost of labor is again given by MCL, because supply curve S is again in effect. So, when a minimum wage of w(min) is imposed on the monopsonist in Figure 6-8, its marginal cost of labor follows w(min)E, then jumps up to F, and then follows MCL again.

Faced with this new marginal cost of labor schedule, the monopsonist again hires the amount of labor that equates its marginal revenue product of labor to its marginal cost of labor. This now occurs at point C in Figure 6-8, where the resulting equilibrium employment and wage combination becomes w(min) and L(1). Notice that monopsonistic exploitation has now been eliminated. In contrast to the effect of a minimum wage in a competitive labor market, workers have been made *unambiguously* better off. The imposition of the minimum wage on the monopsony in Figure 6-8 has raised market wage *and* employment. The improvement in workers' welfare stems from the fact that the minimum wage makes the monopsonist face a constant price of labor, much like a competitor. As a result the monopsonist pays a wage that is more like a competitive wage.

You should prove to yourself that a minimum wage between w(0) and A will increase both the wage and employment above their monopsonistic values, w(0) and L(0). In addition, you should be able to show that if the minimum wage is placed where $MRPL$ intersects S, this maximizes employment. Finally, prove to yourself that a minimum wage set at the point where MCL equals $MRPL$ maximizes the wage subject to a constraint that employment is not reduced below its monopsonistic level. Finally, for some real fun set the minimum wage in Figure 6-8 to something between w(0) and the wage where $S = MRPL$. What is the wage-employment combination in this case?

The point of this section so far has been to show that a minimum wage can unambiguously improve workers' economic welfare by increasing both employment and the rate of pay when the employer is a monopsonist. This need not be the case, though. For example, if the minimum wage is set too high, such as a wage above A, employment will then be *less than* L(0). Moreover, there are a number of caveats concerning the *practicability* of using minimum wage legislation to eliminate monopsonistic exploitation. They are:[8]

1. The minimum wage must not be set too high, otherwise it will reduce employment. Thus, accurate estimates of labor supply and *MRPL* schedules are required.
2. The minimum wage must vary with occupation.
3. The minimum wage must vary among labor markets.
4. The minimum wage must be adjusted regularly over time.

In short, a national, uniform minimum wage that is changed infrequently does not satisfy these conditions and will not be much help in eliminating monopsonistic exploitation.

This completes our theoretical examination of a monopsonistic labor market. In the interest of brevity we will not consider a monopsony that is able to vary both capital and labor services. If we did, we would find that the basic results are quite similar to those for the competitive firm discussed in Chapter 3 and the monopoly firm discussed earlier in this chapter. In particular, the profit-maximizing monopsonist also chooses K and L so that an additional dollar spent on K increases output by the same amount as an additional dollar spent on L. What sets a monopsony apart from the other two situations is that as the monopsonist adjusts its input mix, input prices change, and this has to be taken into account.[9] Rather than explore the subtleties of monopsony any further, let us now turn our attention to a more important topic—evidence concerning the prevalence of monopsony power in the United States.

Evidence on the Incidence of Monopsony in the United States

The prevalence of monopsony is an important economic issue. If labor markets are largely monopsonistic, this might serve as a justification for minimum wage legislation or for pro-union legislation. We will see in Chapter 7 that collective bargaining can produce an outcome very much like that of a minimum wage law. Alternatively, if labor markets are largely competitive, minimum wages or unions are less likely to offer the possibility for a *definite* improvement in workers' economic well-being. Although far from

[8] George Stigler, "The Economics of Minimum Wage Legislation," *American Economic Review*, 36:3 (June 1946), 360–61.
[9] For elaboration see Gould and Ferguson, *Microeconomic Theory,* pp. 396–99.

recent, a study by Robert Bunting still represents the most careful empirical examination to date of the extent of monopsony in the United States.[10]

Bunting analyzed data on the degree of employer concentration at the county level during 1948. By concentration we mean the fraction of the total labor force hired by the largest employers. Before we summarize Bunting's results, it is important to discuss the relationship between employer concentration and monopsony power.

Remember that monopsony is really a theoretical abstraction that is rarely *formally* observed. How many labor markets do you know that have *exactly* one employer? Can you imagine a group of employers ever admitting they collude to keep wages down? We surely cannot. A readily observable, quantifiable characteristic of a labor market is **employer concentration.** Concentration is said to be high when a few firms hire a large fraction of the labor force in an area and is said to be low when no one firm or small group of firms employs a substantial portion of the labor force. A key assumption underlying Bunting's research is that the degree of monopsony power in a labor market is positively related to employer concentration. Let us elaborate somewhat on this presumed relationship.

Consider a local labor market where employers purchase labor services of a certain type. Employers will face a relatively elastic supply of labor if workers have an appreciable number of jobs available outside this local labor market. In this situation there will be little economic gain to local employers from colluding to try to keep wages low. Monopsonistic activity can only really be profitable when what we have called the local labor market is basically the *complete* market for the workers in question, in the sense that it encompasses *all* employment opportunities they perceive as reasonable. Suppose that we identify a local labor market in which the elasticity of labor supply to firms is low, thus presenting the *potential* for monopsonistic exploitation. We still must remember that monopsonistic exploitation requires collective action by employers, and this should be more difficult the greater the number of firms involved. (If you have ever served on a committee you will know what we mean.) So, a necessary, but not sufficient, condition for labor market monopsony is that such collusive efforts be reasonably easy to arrange and to police. What Bunting does by examining employer concentration is to find labor markets where the *potential* for monopsonistic exploitation is present. Remember, highly concentrated labor markets do not *necessarily* mean monopsonistic exploitation. One can have effective competition

---

[10] Robert L. Bunting, *Employer Concentration in Local Labor Markets* (Chapel Hill, N.C.: University of North Carolina Press, 1962). A summary of Bunting's findings is contained in John F. Burton, Jr., Lee K. Benham, William M. Vaughn III, and Robert J. Flanagan, eds., *Readings in Labor Market Analysis* (New York: Holt, Rinehart, and Winston, 1971), pp. 132–39.

with only a few employers. However, monopsonistic exploitation probably cannot exist *without* a high degree of employer concentration.

Bunting uses three measures of employer concentration: **CR1,** the percentage of workers in a local labor market employed by the largest single employer; **CR4,** the percentage of workers employed by the four largest employers; and **CR10,** the percentage of workers employed by the ten largest employers. Bunting calculated these three measures of concentration for 1,774 local labor markets in 1948, where local labor markets were defined as single counties or small clusters of relatively homogeneous counties. The 1,774 areas studied encompassed about 93 percent of the United States labor force. His basic findings indicate that employer concentration, and thus the potential for monopsonistic exploitation, was really quite low. Less than 10 percent of all workers were employed in labor markets where CR10 exceeded 50 percent, and less than 4 percent of all workers were employed in labor markets where CR1 exceeded 50 percent. Even though Bunting's data are approximately 30 years old, we feel confident that monopsony is not widespread today. Modern roads and relatively cheap used automobiles make workers quite mobile, so that the company town is largely a thing of the past. Employer collusion also does not seem to be widespread except in the case of professional sports, a topic we examine in the next section.

FRONTIERS OF LABOR ECONOMICS:
PAY AND PERFORMANCE IN PROFESSIONAL BASEBALL

Although we have little reason to believe that United States labor markets are largely monopsonistic, in certain cases employers have clearly engaged in collective activities that reduced wage rates below competitive levels. An especially interesting situation was that of major league baseball during the late 1960s. Research by Gerald Scully attempts to measure monopsonistic exploitation due to the institutional structure of the professional baseball industry in the United States at that time.[11] Before we can discuss Scully's findings, we need to understand the peculiar characteristics of the baseball players' labor market in 1968–69.

Since 1964 there has been an amateur players draft in professional baseball. When a player is drafted by a team, he has an option whether or not to sign. If a player does not sign with the team who has drafted him, he must wait, sometimes several years, until he is eligible for another draft. Until rather recently, a player who agreed to play for a team signed a standardized one year renewable contract. The contract contained a provision known as the **reserve clause,** which granted the renewability exclusively to the team's owner. Except for a restriction limiting the reduction in a player's salary from year to year, the standard baseball contract gave a team's owner virtually complete control over a player's future in major league baseball. Scully points out that upon expiration of a player's contract, the *owner's* options were numerous. The owner could renew the contract, terminate the contract,

[11] Gerald W. Scully, "Pay and Performance in Professional Baseball," *American Economic Review,* 64:6 (December 1974), 915–30.

or sell or trade the player to another team. Until recently, sale or trade meant a transfer of exclusive control over a player's services to another team's owner. In contrast, a player had a much more limited set of options, once an owner chose to renew his contract. The player could immediately accept the owner's terms or try to negotiate an improvement by threatening to retire. Once the owner's final offer had been made, however, the player had to accept or give up playing major league baseball.

It should be fairly obvious that the internal organization of the baseball industry during the late 1960s probably had a big effect on players' salaries. By limiting a player to negotiation with his current team, the reserve clause prevented him from voluntarily moving to another team where his services might be valued more highly. This restriction on mobility effectively granted monopsony power to a team's owner, and Scully examines whether or not this *in fact* led to a divergence between players' salaries and their marginal values to their teams. Because baseball teams are granted exclusive rights to play in a geographic area, and the entry of new teams is restricted, an individual team functioned as a monopoly producer of major league baseball in an area. In this case, marginal revenue product represents the value of a player to a particular team.

*Calculating a Baseball Player's Marginal Revenue Product

A player's marginal *physical* product may best be viewed as the additional output he contributes to his team. His marginal *revenue* product is the revenue created for the team by that performance. Specifically, a player contributes to his team's win/loss record, and through this, to his team's gate receipts and broadcast revenues. Equation (1) in Table 6-3 is Scully's regression estimate of a baseball team's *victory production function*. From this, an estimate of a player's marginal physical product may be computed. The dependent variable expresses a team's output as a three-digit number. In particular, it is a team's win-loss percentage times 1,000. Scully's data cover two seasons, 1968 and 1969. Of course, economic theory provides neither a list of all the arguments nor the particular mathematical form of this equation. The linear version displayed in Table 6-3 simplifies estimation but does not allow for diminishing marginal physical productivities. Put differently, inputs are forced to have constant marginal physical productivities. Based on previous research into players' salaries, Scully chose to represent the hitting input by *team slugging average*, a measure of average total base production per time at bat. The pitching input is measured in this equation by the team's *strikeout-to-walk ratio* expressed as a three-digit number. Also included in equation (1) are *NL*, a dummy variable whose coefficient will reflect differences in the quality of play between the American and National Leagues, and the dummy variables *CONT* and *OUT*, which capture differences in "team spirit." In particular, it was expected that teams in the thick of a pennant race should play better baseball, while teams out of the running should play poorer baseball. The regression coefficients in equation (1) are straightforward to interpret. Try interpreting the coefficients of *CONT, OUT,* and *NL* yourself, for example.

When using the results of equation (1) to calculate a player's marginal physical product, Scully makes the assumption that team performance is the sum of individual players' performances. Because each team has approximately 8 regular pitchers and 12 regular hitters, an *average pitcher* (one with a strikeout-walk ratio of 2.00) contrib-

---

* This section contains more technical material that may be skipped without loss of continuity. If you skip, go to p. 218.

TABLE 6-3   Output and Revenue Regressions for Major League Baseball, 1968–69*

Production-of-Team-Victories Regression

(1) $PCTWIN$ = 37.24 + 0.92 TSA + 0.90 TSW − 38.57 NL + 43.78 $CONT$
  (.39)   (4.37)   (5.92)   (−4.03)   (3.77)
  − 75.68 OUT; R^2 = 0.88; N = 44
  (6.17)

Team-Revenue Regression

(2) $REVENUE$ = − 1,735,890 + 10,330 $PCTWIN$ + 494,585 $SMSA70$
  (−1.69)   (6.64)   (4.61)
  + 512 $MARGA$ + 580,913 NL − 762,248 STD
  (4.28)   (1.84)   (2.42)
  − 58,523 $BBPCT$; R^2 = 0.75; N = 43†
  (3.13)

Definitions:

Variables in the Team-Victories Regression	
$PCTWIN$ ≡	[(games won/games played) · 1,000]
TSA ≡	team slugging average = [(total bases/official at bats) · 1,000]
TSW ≡	team strikeout–walk ratio = [(total opposing players struck out/total opposing players walked) · 100]
NL ≡	dummy variable (= 1 if team in National League; = 0 if in American League)
$CONT$ ≡	dummy variable (= 1 if team was less than five games out of first place at the season's end; = 0 otherwise)
OUT ≡	dummy variable (= 1 if team was more than 20 games out of first place at the season's end; = 0 otherwise)

Variables in the Team-Revenue Regression	
$REVENUE$ ≡	home game attendance revenue plus revenue from broadcasting rights
$SMSA70$ ≡	1970 population size of team's Standard Metropolitan Statistical Area
$MARGA$ ≡	variable designed to capture interteam differences in the "intensity of fan interest;" in particular, $MARGA$ is the coefficient of $PCTWIN$ in a regression of a team's attendance on $PCTWIN$ and other variables with data for 1957–71
STD ≡	dummy variable (= 1 for older stadium located in poor neighborhood with limited parking facilities; = 0 otherwise)
$BBPCT$ ≡	percentage of team's players who were black

---

* T-values are in parentheses.

† Since $MARGA$ could not be calculated for Seattle, only 43 observations were employed in the $REVENUE$ regression (2).

Source: Gerald W. Scully, "Pay and Performance in Major League Baseball," *American Economic Review*, 64:6 (December 1974), 919, 920, 926, 927.

utes about 25 points (0.125 · 200) to his team's strikeout-to-walk ratio (*TSW*). An average hitter (one with a slugging average of .340) contributes approximately 28.3 points (0.0833 · 340) to TSA, his team's slugging average. Thus, the marginal physical product of an average pitcher is approximately 25 (victory) points and the marginal physical product of an average hitter is about 28.3 (victory) points. To obtain the economic value of an average player to a professional baseball team we simply need multiply their marginal physical products by marginal revenue. The regression denoted as (2) in Table 6-3 provides the information necessary.

Equation (2) of Table 6-3 expresses income from the sales of ticket and broadcast rights as a linear function of team victories (*PCTWIN*) and other variables.[12] Because a team is granted an exclusive right to play in an area, it is likely that the population of this geographical area is a factor in that team's ability to generate revenue. Scully represents this aspect of the baseball product market empirically by the variable *SMSA70*, the population of a team's Standard Metropolitan Statistical Area in 1970. Equation (2) also yields estimates of how team racial composition and stadium quality affect *REVENUE*. How do we interpret the coefficients of *BBPCT* and *STD?*

Scully's variable representing intensity of fan interest (*MARGA*) in equation (2) requires some elaboration. It is possible that even if two teams play in similar-sized areas, revenues will differ between them because the people in one of the two locations like baseball better. To allow for this possibility, Scully first ran a separate regression (not shown) for each team with time-series data for 1957–71, where attendance is the dependent variable and *PCTWIN* is one of the independent variables. The *coefficient* of *PCTWIN* in each of these time-series regressions became a team's *MARGA* in regression (2). *MARGA* ranged from 603 to 5,819 and represents the differential effect of winning on attendance across cities, one possible index of fan interest in baseball.

Because we wish to calculate marginal revenue, the coefficient of *PCTWIN* in regression (2) is the one of interest. It indicates that a 0.001 increase in the proportion of games won in 1968–69 led to a $10,330 increase in revenue. This result, along with the marginal physical products of an average hitter and an average pitcher calculated above, may be used to calculate players' marginal revenue products. You should be able to show that the marginal revenue product for an average pitcher during 1968–69 was approximately $232,425 and the marginal revenue product of an average hitter was about $268,963. Column (1) of Table 6-4 lists various performance levels for pitchers and hitters. Column (2) presents marginal revenue product calculations for these performance levels from the technique just described. Remember that these marginal revenue product estimates are for 1968–69; similar estimates for today would probably be about three times larger.

Scully's production-of-victories regression presented in Table 6-3 does not hold nonplayer inputs constant. As a result, the marginal revenue product estimates in column (2) of Table 6-4 could be biased upward. Under what conditions would this occur? Attempts to incorporate other factors of production, such as managerial quality, into a victories regression did not suggest an important role for such nonplayer inputs, however, Moreover, the estimates presented in column (2) of Table 6-4 are best thought of as *gross* marginal revenue products, because they are unadjusted for any player development costs or payments to nonplayer inputs. So, when com-

---

[12] Additional regressions that permitted *diminishing* marginal revenue indicated that the hypothesis of *constant* marginal revenue could not be rejected. See Scully, "Pay and Performance," p. 919, fn. 6. It should also be noted that regression (2) has embedded in it the assumption that player performance does not *directly* affect a team's revenue. It is assumed to have only an indirect effect through *PCTWIN*. Why might a player's performance have a direct effect on a team's revenue?

TABLE 6-4   Marginal Revenue Products, Expected Salaries, and Rates
of Monopsonistic Exploitation in Major League Baseball, 1968–69

	(1) Performance	(2) Gross Marginal Revenue Product*	(3) Expected Salary†	(4) Rates of Monopsonistic Exploitation
		Hitters		X
	270	$213,800	$31,700	0.85
	330	261,400	39,300	0.85
SA	390	308,900	47,000	0.85
	450	356,400	54,800	0.85
Star	510	403,900	62,700	0.84
performance	570	451,400	70,600	0.84
		Pitchers		
	160	$185,900	$31,100	0.83
	200	232,400	37,200	0.84
SW	240	278,900	43,100	0.85
	280	325,400	48,800	0.85
Star	320	371,900	54,400	0.85
performance	360	418,400	59,800	0.86

Definitions:
$SA \equiv$ lifetime slugging average (total bases/official at bats times 100)
$SW \equiv$ lifetime strikeout-to-walk ratio times 100
$X \equiv [(2) - (3)]/(2)$

* Calculated using the appropriate value of SA (or SW) along with the regression coefficients of TSA or TSW in regression (1) of Table 6-3 and the regression coefficient of PCTWIN in regression (2) of Table 6-3. Each pitcher is assumed to comprise 12.5 percent of team pitching, and each hitter is assumed to comprise 8.33 percent of team hitting.

† In order to calculate expected salaries, Scully first ran regressions with data for *individual* pitchers and hitters in 1968–69. The logarithm of observed salary was regressed on the logarithms of career performance, contribution to team pitching (or hitting) input, years of major league experience, and variables that capture the franchise's revenue-generating potential. The coefficients from these regressions were used to create the expected (predicted) salary figures in Table 6-4 by varying SA or SW and setting all other variables equal to their sample mean values.

Source: Gerald W. Scully, "Pay and Performance in Major League Baseball," *American Economic Review*, 64:6 (December 1974), 923.

pared with player salary figures, the data in column (2) suggest an *upper boundary* to the amount of monopsonistic exploitation in the professional baseball industry during the 1960s.

*Estimates of Player Exploitation in Major League Baseball

Column (4) of Table 6-4 tells us the difference between a certain quality player's gross marginal revenue product and his expected salary, expressed as a fraction

---

* This section contains more technical material that may be skipped without loss of continuity. If you skip, go to page 218.

of gross marginal revenue product. Notice that, by definition, the rate of monopsonistic exploitation in column (4) will vary between 0 and 1. A value for X of 0 means that a player is being paid his marginal revenue product. The closer is X to 1.0, the greater is the degree of player exploitation. The data of column (4) indicate that players' salaries averaged only about 15 percent of their gross marginal revenue products.

Pay in Major League Baseball: Postscript

Even though Scully's research suggests significant monoposonistic exploitation in major league baseball during the late 1960s, when the reserve clause was in force, players' salaries far exceeded the median earnings of even the most highly skilled occupational groupings. As a result, it was quite difficult for major league baseball players in particular and professional athletes in general to generate legal and popular support for their fight against "low" wages.[13] In the mid 1970s, though, the key source of monopsonistic exploitation in professional baseball, the reserve clause, was weakened. The institutional structure of the baseball labor market changed to permit limited competition for the services of a player whose contract had expired. In particular, a player with six or more years of major league experience was permitted to become a free agent. A draft was held for the negotiating rights to these players, and as many as 14 teams could secure the right to bid for a particular free agent's services.

The key implication of this section has been that the reserve clause led to a gap between the value of a player's services and his wage. Thus, when competition is permitted for players' services, we expect greater equality of lifetime wages and lifetime value of a player's services to a major league baseball team. Casual evidence from the sports pages concerning the multiyear, multimillion-dollar contracts signed in the recent past by players such as Dave Winfield suggest that competition for players' services has indeed raised their salaries relative to their value to their teams.[14]

CONCLUSION

In this chapter we have examined the demand for labor by firms that face prices of output or labor services that vary with the quantity sold or amount hired. Whenever possible, we have attempted to compare the equilibrium wage-employment combinations in such settings to those under competitive conditions. In the process we were able to identify certain cases where the effect of public policy differed markedly from the competitive case. No

---

[13] For a satirical view of this problem see Jim Murray, "Can You Help, Karl Marx?" *Los Angeles Times* (March 5, 1973), Sec. 4, p. 2 [reprinted in Belton M. Fleisher and Thomas J. Kniesner, *Labor Economics,* 2d ed. (Englewood Cliffs, N.J.: Prentice-Hall, Inc., 1980), p. 212].
[14] For further reading on the baseball players' labor market, see Joseph W. Hunt, Jr., and Kenneth A. Lewis, "Dominance, Recontracting, and the Reserve Clause: Major League Baseball," *American Economic Review,* 66:5 (December 1976), 936–42; and George Daly and William J. Moore, "Externalities, Property Rights, and the Allocation of Reserves in Professional Baseball," *Economic Inquiry,* 20:1 (January 1981), 77–95; and Donald J. Cymrot, "Migration Trends and Earnings of Free Agents in Major League Baseball," Working Paper, No. 82-12, Department of Economics, Miami University, Oxford, Ohio, February 1982.

matter what type of noncompetitive labor market we examined, though, labor supply and labor productivity schedules played the key roles in determining employment and workers' incomes.

In contrast to a competitive firm, a monopolist helps to determine the price of its output. This means that the demand curve for labor by a monopolist, while negatively inclined, may also have it purchasing less labor at any given wage than an identical competitive industry. So, in labor markets where some or all firms are monopolists in their product markets, wages may tend to be lower than in labor markets where all firms are competitive in their product markets.

Monopsony is a labor market where there is effectively only one buyer of labor. This leads to the outcome that less labor is purchased and wage rates are lower than when many buyers compete for employees. An interesting aspect of monopsony is the possibility for a minimum wage rate to make workers unambiguously better off. The practicability of such a public policy is open to serious doubt, however. More importantly, monopsony does not appear to be a widespread phenomenon in the United States, but rather specific to a few industries. An interesting example is major league baseball before the 1970s. We noted that in the late 1960s, major league baseball players' salaries were only about 15 percent of their gross marginal revenue products.

REFERENCES AND SELECTED READING

ALCHIAN, ARMEN, AND REUBEN KESSEL, "Competition, Monopoly, and the Pursuit of Pecuniary Gain," in H. G. Lewis, ed., *Aspects of Labor Economics*. Princeton, N.J.: Princeton University Press, 1962.

BAILY, MARTIN N., "Dynamic Monopsony and Structural Change," *American Economic Review*, 65:3 (June 1975), 338–49.

BUNTING, ROBERT L., *Employer Concentration in Local Labor Markets:* Chapel Hill, N.C.: University of North Carolina Press, 1962.

———, "Employer Concentration in Local Labor Markets," in John F. Burton, Jr., et al., *Readings in Labor Market Analysis*. New York: Holt, Rinehart, and Winston, 1971, pp. 132–39.

CYMROT, DONALD J., "Migration Trends and Earnings of Free Agents in Major League Baseball," Working Paper No. 82-12, Department of Economics, Miami University, Oxford, Ohio, February 1982.

DALY, GEORGE, AND WILLIAM J. MOORE, "Externalities, Property Rights, and the Allocation of Resources in Professional Baseball," *Economic Inquiry*, 19:1 (January 1981), 77–95.

FERGUSON, C. E., The *Neoclassical Theory of Production and Distribution* (London and New York: Cambridge University Press, 1969), Chaps. 6 and 9.

GOULD, J. P., AND C. E. FERGUSON, *Microeconomic Theory,* 5th ed. Homewood, Ill.: Richard D. Irwin, 1980, pp. 396–401.

HUNT, JOSEPH W., JR., AND KENNETH A. LEWIS, "Dominance, Recontracting, and the Reserve Clause: Major League Baseball," *American Economic Review,* 66:5 (December 1976), 936–43.

MAURICE, S. CHARLES, "Monopsony and the Effect of an Externally Imposed Minimum Wage," *Southern Economic Journal,* 41:2 (October 1974), 283–87.

ROTTENBERG, SIMON, "The Baseball Players' Labor Market," *Journal of Political Economy,* June 1956, 242–58.

SCHERER, F. M., *Industrial Market Structure and Economic Performance,* 2d ed. Chicago: Rand McNally, 1980.

SCULLY, GERALD W., "Pay and Performance in Professional Baseball," *American Economic Review,* 64:6 (December 1974), 915–30.

STIGLER, GEORGE J., "The Economics of Minimum Wage Legislation," *American Economic Review,* 36:3 (June 1946), 360–61.

EXERCISES

Choose whether statements 1 and 2 are *True, False,* or *Uncertain* (whether true or false depends on unspecified circumstances). Justify your answer. Your justification is the most important part of your answer.

1. The effect of a minimum wage on employment is likely to be greater when employers are monopsonists than in competitive labor markets.

2. A monopolistic firm's demand curve for labor is identical to its *VMPL* curve.

3. Can *monopolistic* exploitation be eliminated by minimum wage legislation? Be sure to support your answer with the appropriate graph(s) and to explain carefully what is meant by monopolistic exploitation.

4. The chart below provides information on teams in the Eastern Division of the American League. Included are predictions made by Jimmy the Swede of team slugging averages (*TSA*) and team strikeout/walk ratios (*TSW*) for the upcoming season.

Team	Population in Millions (*PM*)	Index of Fan Interest (*FI*)	*TSA* (*predicted*)	*TSW* (*predicted*)
Baltimore	2.1	3	0.389	2.9
Boston	3.9	8	0.440	2.4
Cleveland	2.9	6	0.360	1.8
Detroit	4.7	5	0.300	2.1
Milwaukee	1.5	4	0.320	2.0
New York	7.2	7	0.420	2.8

Recent estimates of the determination of a team's percentage of games (*PCTWIN*) and a team's revenue (*REVENUE*) yield (1) $PCTWIN = 0.90\ TSA + 0.085\ TSW$; (2) $REVENUE = 12,500\ (PCTWIN \times 1,000) + 15,500\ (PCTWIN \times PM) + 450,000\ PM + 25,000\ FI$.

a. Based upon Jimmy's predictions of *TSA* and *TSW*, predict the order of finish in the Eastern Division.

b. Calculate the expected revenue for each team.

c. Consider the following predictions of players' performances.

Player	Team	Slugging Average	Fraction of Total Team at Bats	Expected Salary
Bobby Beene	Boston	0.520	0.08	$470,263
Larry Lager	Milwaukee	0.380	0.10	428,295
Billy Bialy	New York	0.400	0.07	317,812
Kenny Crabb	Baltimore	0.390	0.11	483,882

Calculate the gross marginal revenue product for each player. Compare your results to each player's expected salary. What can be concluded from your comparison concerning the structure of the labor market for these players' services?

*5. Graphically depict a *profit-maximizing* monopsonist's optimal wage-employment combination in the situation where capital is fixed. (You may ignore variation in hours of work per employee and treat the labor input as simply the number of workers.) Suppose, now, that the monopsonist can wage-discriminate, that is, pay *each* worker a *different* wage. What wage will it choose to pay each worker? What is its new equilibrium employment? Has the monopsonist experienced an increase in profit as the result of its ability to wage-discriminate? Support your answers with specific references to your graph.

---

* Indicates a more difficult exercise.

7

THE LABOR MARKET WHEN SELLERS ARE NONCOMPETITIVE: The Economics of Unions

A. **Educational objectives**
1. To illustrate the many ways that unions affect the economy
2. To examine data on the historical trends and current extent of union membership in the United States
3. To identify the effects of unions on the economic well-being of society in general and the distribution of well-being among particular subgroups within society

B. **Union activities (p. 223)**
1. Collective bargaining and strikes (p. 224)
   a. The free collective bargaining process
   b. Free collective bargaining and strikes: Evidence
   c. Arbitration
   d. Postscript: Givebacks
2. Activities that reduce the supply of labor (p. 238)
   a. Political support of restrictions on immigration
   b. Political support of occupational licensing
3. Activities that increase the demand for labor (p. 243)
   a. Political support of import quotas or tariffs
   b. Political support of minimum wage laws
4. Activities that make the demand for labor less elastic (p. 245)
5. Featherbedding (p. 247)

C. **Union membership (p. 249)**
1. A model of the supply and demand for union services (p. 250)
   a. The demand for unionism
   *b. Aside: The elasticity of demand for labor, the individual's tastes and preferences, and the decision to join a union
   c. The supply of union services
   d. The equilibrium amount of unionism
2. Union membership in the United States over time (p. 254)
   a. 1900–1953
   b. 1953–1978
3. Right-to-work laws and differences in unionism among states (p. 260)
4. Public employee unionism (p. 263)

Throughout this book we seek to understand how the interactions between firms and households in labor markets lead to a particular level of economic well-being for society and to differences in well-being among groups within society. We also seek to understand the effects of various public policies. The last two chapters suggest that whether employers are competitive or noncompetitive plays a key role in determining wages and employment and in conditioning the labor market influence of public policy. Our analysis of labor markets in the short term is incomplete until we consider the situation where *sellers* are noncompetitive. In this chapter we examine the labor market when workers act in concert, forming a union to represent their mutual interests.

Historically, collective bargaining and strikes have been controversial because of their impact not only on employers but also on consumers and workers not directly involved in the collective bargaining process. The controversy has largely been eliminated in the United States by legislation that provides a fairly clear and stable set of guidelines establishing the rights of the parties involved both directly and indirectly in the collective bargaining process. Some friction still exists. The so-called right-to-work laws, however, continue to be a controversial political issue, and the legality of union activities by government employees is subject to much debate, some of it quite heated. We will see that economic analysis has much to say about these and other important aspects of American unionism.

UNION ACTIVITIES

It is reasonably clear that unions attempt to increase the economic welfare of their members. In our discussion of unions we will largely focus on the wage rate as an indicator of the economic welfare of workers. We will utilize a

---

* Indicates more technical material that may be skipped without loss of continuity.

comprehensive definition of the wage rate, one that includes the value of fringe benefits, paid holidays and vacations, rest periods, and safe working conditions. Remember that all of these have calculable monetary equivalents as far as employers and employees are concerned. Considering them as part of the wage rate, let us develop a manageable yet reasonably comprehensive analysis of unionism. Our first step toward this goal is a discussion of union activities. We will see that some are obvious, such as strikes, but that others are much less so and perhaps go generally unnoticed.

Collective Bargaining and Strikes

Bargaining, backed by a threat of a strike, is the primary way in which unions attempt to raise wages above their competitive levels. Figure 7-1 describes a competitive firm initially in equilibrium with wage and employment $w(0)$ and $L(0)$, respectively. The idea behind collective bargaining is that workers, through their union, threaten the firm with a strike if it does not agree to a higher wage, say $w(1)$. If workers are willing to endure a strike that is long enough to impose severe costs on the firm in the form of lost sales revenue, the employer may find it optimal to accept the higher wage and avoid or end the strike. Of course, the higher wage means that employment will eventually be reduced to $L(1)$.

Remember, however, that a competitive firm earns just enough revenue to pay each factor of production its reservation price. If some of its plant and equipment is fixed and must be paid anyway, a competitive firm might be willing to accept a wage higher than the going rate rather than shut down. In response to a union's threat to strike and withhold labor altogether, in the process forcing it to cease operating for an extended period of time, a com-

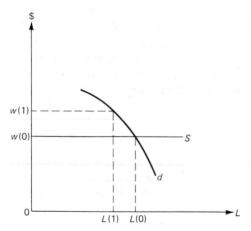

FIGURE 7-1. The impact of collective bargaining on a firm's wage and employment

petitive firm would be willing to pay the higher wage demanded by the union. It would do this so long as it could keep variable cost per unit of output below its fixed selling price. Assume that wage rate $w(1)$ in Figure 7-1 would permit the firm to cover its variable labor costs and stay in business. Thus, the firm would accept this wage rather than endure a costly shutdown due to a strike. Although the firm would eventually not replace its plant and equipment if it could not earn a normal rate of return on them, it would minimize any short-term losses by staying in business.

To the extent that a union has organized many competitive firms or the entire industry, its effectiveness in negotiating higher wages is increased. This is true because output price is fixed for any one competitive firm. As a result, a wage increase puts that firm at a cost disadvantage with respect to the rest of the firms in the industry. In the long term the firm cannot effectively compete with the others who pay the lower, nonunion wage rate. Should *all* the workers in the industry be represented by the union, though, a wage increase will not put any of the firms at such a disadvantage. Increased cost of production will be passed on to the consumers of the product in the form of a higher price. This is one reason why unions desire to grow and represent as many workers as possible—their effectiveness is increased when they represent a greater proportion of an industry's workers.

The impact of collective bargaining on wages and employment described in Figure 7-1 will also hold for a monopoly, because it too has a downward-sloping labor demand curve. The only situation in which there may not be an employment loss is where the union is bargaining with a monopsony.

With these facts in mind, let us turn our attention to the nitty-gritty of the bargaining process.

Any analysis of the collective bargaining process must touch upon five aspects of the behavior of the parties involved: (1) the union's preferred outcome, (2) the dynamics of the union's wage demands during the course of negotiations, (3) the employer's preferred outcome, (4) the dynamics of the employer's wage offers during the course of negotiations, and (5) the details of any third-party involvement in the negotiations. These factors determine whether or not there will be a strike, along with its duration should one occur. For now, we need consider only (1) through (4), as we focus initially on understanding free collective bargaining—bargaining between employers and unions in the absence of any outside intervention. Once this is understood, we proceed to consider third-party involvement in the form of binding arbitration.

Conceptualizing the free collective bargaining process. It is reasonable to view a union as an organization made up of two groups with somewhat conflicting preferences, the union leadership and the union rank and file.[1] Union leaders typically place a high value on political survival within the union. This objective requires them to try to satisfy the rank and file's expectations with respect to wage agreements. Sometimes, though, a union's membership wants a wage settlement that union leaders know greatly exceeds what management will readily accept. In this case the union leadership has three choices: (1) convince workers that a smaller wage increase is desirable, (2) sign a wage agreement that is less than what workers expect, or (3) begin a strike. Should the first of these fail, union leaders will typically prefer a strike, because an agreement that the rank and file dislikes is likely to lessen the political power and appeal of union leaders. More important, a strike will move members' wage demands toward what employers will actually accept by making workers aware of the "economic facts of life."

Ashenfelter and Johnson believe that, during the course of a strike, a union's desired wage package will follow the pattern illustrated in Figure 7-2. The pattern of union wage demands during the course of a strike has *three* key aspects, each one represented by a different property of the curve in Figure 7-2. The intersection of the curve with the vertical axis indicates the union's **most preferred wage (ŵ).** Based on the tastes and preferences of the workers in the union, there is some wage rate they would most like to have as the result of the collective bargaining process. There is also some wage rate that will be their **minimum acceptable wage (w̄).** Given workers' tastes and preferences, their job opportunities in the nonunion sector, and

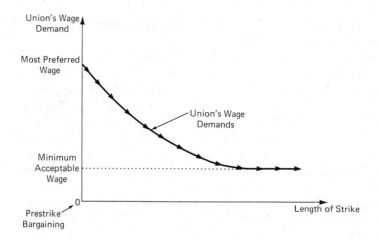

FIGURE 7-2. The pattern of union wage demands during the course of a strike

[1] Orley Ashenfelter and George E. Johnson, "Bargaining Theory, Trade Unions, and Industrial Strike Activity," *American Economic Review,* 59:1 (March 1969), 35–49.

the unemployment compensation and income support programs available to strikers, they will hold out indefinitely for $\bar{w}$. This is indicated by the flattening of the curve in Figure 7-2 to horizontal at $\bar{w}$. The third key aspect of union wage demands relates to the slope of the curve. In particular, it is **the speed with which union workers give in (γ)**—that is, reduce their wage demands during the strike.

There is really nothing very complicated about the ideas presented in Figure 7-2. We are simply saying that union workers know what they would most like to have in terms of wages, have a lower-bound wage in mind, and are willing to moderate their demands if they do not get what they want. The curve in Figure 7-2 is drawn to reflect these ideas in as simple a way as possible. How would the curve look if union workers were *totally* unwilling to give in during the course of the negotiations? How would it look if their demand was not met in the prestrike bargaining session and they *immediately* offered to work for their minimum acceptable wage?

A subtle point about the economics of strikes is worth noting. One or both parties must have some degree of ignorance concerning the other's behavior during the course of the negotiation process. If the union knew exactly what the firm would be offering and the firm knew exactly what the union would be asking, then there would be no strike. The reason is that when each side knows what the other will do, they also know the *particular* wage settlement that will eventually occur. They would obviously both be willing to settle for that wage *without any strike at all!* Union workers would be happy to avoid the wages lost during the strike, and the firm would be more than willing to avoid the sales foregone and profits lost during the strike. So, when a strike occurs, one or both parties is ignorant of how the other one will act during the course of the negotiations. It should also be obvious that for economists to have anything meaningful to say about strikes, we cannot have the situation where both the firm and the union are *totally ignorant* of how the other will act during the course of the negotiation process. The Ashenfelter and Johnson model of strikes treats the firm as anticipating the union's wage demands in Figure 7-2. They characterize the union, however, as simply submitting these wage demands to the firm. When the firm refuses to accept the wage demanded in a bargaining session, the union submits a lower wage demand in the next session. The process stops and the strike ends when the firm agrees to a union wage demand.[2] How does the firm determine *when* to agree to a wage contract?

The decision facing the firm at the beginning of wage negotiations is whether to agree immediately to the union's most preferred wage or, by refusing, to generate a strike. Although a strike will eventually lead to a lower wage settlement, this benefit is purchased at the expense of foregone

---

[2] An interesting alternative representation of the bargaining process is developed in John Kennan, "Pareto Optimality and the Economics of Strike Duration," *Journal of Labor Research,* 1:1 (Spring 1980), 77–94.

sales revenues and profits. If the value to the firm of lower wages exceeds the foregone sales revenues, it will reject the union's initial wage demand and a strike will ensue.

How long will the strike last? Because the firm is assumed to know the eventual pattern of union wage demands, it holds out until the union drops its wage demand to the point where the firm's profit is greatest, given the length of the contract period. The curve in Figure 7-3 illustrates how a typical firm's total future profit is related to the wage rate being demanded by the union at various points in the strike. If the firm were to accept the union's initial wage demand for the contract period, typically the next three years, it would lose money over the course of the contract period. Notice, however, that profit rises during the early part of the strike as the firm waits out the union. It is cutting its future labor costs by refusing to agree to the union's wage demands, and these cost cuts exceed the foregone sales revenue during the strike. At some point, though, foregone sales revenues begin to exceed labor cost savings. It is at this bargaining session that the firm agrees to the union's wage demand, signs a contract, and the strike is over.

The strike length and wage settlement associated with the union and the firm under consideration are depicted in Figure 7-4. Notice that the union got neither the wage agreement it would most like to have nor the worst possible one. The same holds true for the firm. Although it is maximizing its profit, it is doing so *conditional* on the pattern of union wage demands in Figure 7-2. The firm would certainly prefer a wage of zero, but cannot get it. Of course, not every wage negotiation results in a strike, and sometimes the firm agrees to the union's initial wage demand. How would Figure 7-3 look if the firm agreed to settle without a strike?

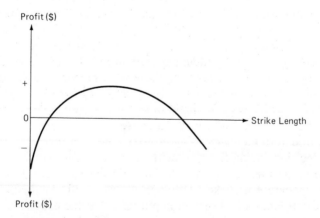

FIGURE 7-3. The firm's future profits if the union's wage demand were accepted at various points in the strike

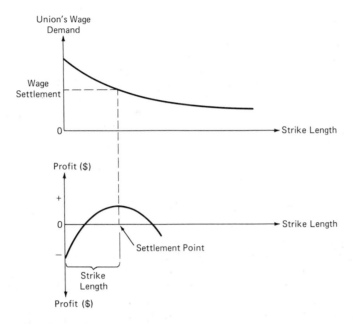

FIGURE 7-4. Strike length and wage settlement

At this point in our discussion it seems reasonable to summarize the key aspects of the Ashenfelter-Johnson model of the bargaining process. At the start of negotiations, the union has a most preferred wage, which it presents to the employer. Should the firm refuse to sign a contract at that wage, a strike ensues. During the course of the strike the union moderates its wage demands. The rate at which workers' demands become more moderate reflect, among other things, the hardships imposed upon them by the strike. The firm, assumed to have a reasonably complete advance knowledge of the pattern these demands will take, signs an agreement at the point that maximizes its total profit during the new contract period. This process determines both strike length and wage settlement, with immediate wage settlement preventing a strike. That firms in a sense may "purchase" lower wage agreements by submitting to strikes is underscored by the following statement, appearing in the *Ford Motor Company Report to Stockholders,* November 1967:

> We are convinced that, in this situation, the UAW leadership concluded that no realistic settlement could be reached and ratified without a strike. . . . Given these difficult conditions, we believe the settlement we reached is a realistic one, even though it is higher than desirable. . . . A longer strike would have raised strike costs out of proportion to any resulting improvement in the outcome. In short, we believe the settlement represents the lowest

possible combination of strike costs and settlement costs to the Company and the country.[3]

Does this mean, then, that firms are responsible for strikes? Yes and no. Does it mean that unions are responsible for strikes? Yes and no. Although firms contribute to strikes by refusing to agree to unions' wage demands, unions contribute to strikes by demanding wages that firms find too costly. We cannot assign blame for a strike to only *one* of the two parties, because a strike is the result of an interaction between them. Socrates said it best—It takes two to make a quarrel.[4]

This completes our development of the basic economics of wage negotiations, strikes, and contract settlements. We now present some evidence concerning the length of strikes in the United States and the three variables that define a union's wage demands during the course of a strike: $\hat{w}$, their most preferred wage; $\bar{w}$, their minimum acceptable wage; and γ, the rate at which their wage demands are reduced in the face of employer opposition.

Free collective bargaining and strikes: Evidence.   Henry S. Farber utilizes the conceptualization of the collective bargaining process presented in the previous section to examine 80 contract negotiations for 10 large manufacturing firms in various industries during 1954–70.[5] Twenty-one of the negotiations resulted in strikes. The dependent variable in Farber's analysis is the negotiated average annual percentage change in the base wage of janitors during the new contract period. This is the conventional base wage over which many negotiations take place. Farber uses data on certain economic aspects of the firm and the union, information on previous contract negotiations, and data on the state of the economy to infer the values of the three key parameters underlying the bargaining process: $\hat{w}$, $\bar{w}$, and γ. The key results from his research are summarized in Table 7-1.

The unions in Farber's sample sought to achieve wage increases of about 5 percent per year on average. They would, however, have settled for wage *reductions* of almost 7 percent on average had firms endured extremely long strikes. Finally, the average length of time it took unions to reduce their wage demands from their most preferred levels halfway to their minimum acceptable levels was approximately 5 months.

A number of the results presented in Table 7-1 are rather interesting. First, the actual wage settlements are quite close to the union's most preferred wage outcomes. In every case the difference is less than 2 percentage points. This means that strikes happen relatively infrequently, and those that do are generally of rather short duration. This is consistent with aggregate

---

[3] Ashenfelter and Johnson, "Bargaining Theory," p. 38.

[4] *Diogenes Laertius,* Bk. ii, sec. 36.

[5] Henry S. Farber, "Bargaining Theory, Wage Outcomes, and the Occurrence of Strikes: An Econometric Analysis," *American Economic Review,* 68:3 (June 1978), 262–71.

TABLE 7-1 Economic Aspects of Wage Negotiations in Ten Large Manufacturing Firms, 1954–1970

Firm	Union	$\hat{w}^a$	$\bar{w}^b$	γ^c	Wage Settlement[d]
American Cyanamid	International Chemical Workers Union	+5.8%	−4.7%	4.2 mos.	+5.2%
Ewing Oil Co.	Dallas Derrick Designers and Drillers, Local 13	+5.3	−6.7	5	+4.5
Firestone Tire & Rubber Co.	United Rubber, Cork, Linoleum, and Plastic Workers of America	+6.2	−4.8	3.9	+5.0
General Electric	International Union of Electrical, Radio, and Machine Workers	+6.8	−8.7	8.7	+5.1
General Motors	United Automobile, Aircraft, and Agricultural Implement Workers of America	+5.1	−4.1	3.8	+4.6
International Paper	International Brotherhood of Pulp, Sulphite, and Paper Mill Workers, United Papermakers and Paper Workers	+4.7	−4.0	3.6	+4.6
PPG Industries	United Glass and Ceramic Workers of North America	+4.7	−5.3	5.5	+3.6
Simmons	United Furniture Workers of America	+5.9	−6.1	5.3	+5.2
Sinclair Oil Corp.	Oil, Chemical and Atomic Workers International Union	+5.0	−13.7	2.5	+3.9
U.S. Steel	United Steelworkers of America	+4.7	−10.5	11.7	+3.9
Weyerhaeuser Timber Co.	International Woodworkers of America	+4.4	−5.8	4.4	+3.9
	AVERAGE:	+5.3%	−6.7%	5.0 mos.	+4.5%

[a] Estimated value of the union's most preferred wage expressed as the *annual percent change* in the base wage of janitors during the new contract period.

[b] Estimated value of the union's minimum acceptable wage expressed as the *annual percent change* in the base wage of janitors during the new contract period. A negative number means that a union is willing to accept that percentage wage *reduction* from year to year.

[c] Estimated speed at which the union is willing to reduce its wage demand. The estimated value of γ is expressed as the *number of months of* strike necessary for the union to reduce its wage demand from its most preferred level to *halfway* between its most and its least preferred levels, or from $\hat{w}$ to $(\hat{w} - \bar{w})/2$.

[d] Actual wage settlement expressed as the *annual percent change* in the base wage of janitors during the new contract period.

Source: Henry S. Farber, "Bargaining Theory, Wage Outcomes, and the Occurrence of Strikes," *American Economic Review*, 68:3 (June 1978), Tables 1 and 2.

data for the United States. Since 1960 less than 2 percent of all employed workers have been involved in a work stoppage each year, and the average duration of a work stoppage has been approximately one month. In conclusion, unions seem to get nearly what they want and get it rather quickly.

Arbitration.   There are numerous ways in which third parties become involved in labor disputes in the United States. Arbitration refers to the situation where a third party, upon hearing arguments presented by management and labor justifying their respective desired settlements, is empowered to resolve the contract dispute.[6] When might binding arbitration occur? One possibility is that the two parties directly involved in the dispute agree to permit settlement by an arbitrator. This is still relatively rare in the United States, because labor and management both generally prefer to avoid outside intervention in the collective bargaining process. A number of states provide for arbitrated settlements to contract disputes by public employees.[7] In light of the recent growth of unionization and strikes by public employees, it seems reasonable to spend some time attempting to understand the forces that determine an arbitrated wage settlement.

Several factors lie at the root of the arbitration process. They include the way in which the arbitrator evaluates the arguments by the two parties involved in the contract dispute and the ways in which the union's and the firm's strategies for arguing the relative merits of their positions are influenced by their perceptions of how the arbitrator will evaluate these arguments.[8] For the purpose of trying to understand the arbitration process, let us assume that both parties have a reasonably accurate idea of how the arbitrator will respond to their arguments. Figure 7-5 collects information of this sort in what is known as a **payoff matrix.** We have assumed here for the purposes of example that the firm will select one of four possible strategies or ways to justify its position to the arbitrator, and that the union will also select one of four possible ways to justify its position. These are indicated by F_1, F_2, F_3, and F_4 and U_1, U_2, U_3, and U_4, respectively. The elements of the payoff matrix, w_{11} to w_{44}, indicate the arbitrator's decision as to the wage rate for the next contract period, given how the firm and the union have chosen to justify their respective positions. We realize that the concept of a payoff matrix may be somewhat confusing, so before we go any farther let us consider a specific example of a payoff matrix for binding arbitration.

In Figure 7-6, the entries indicate the particular hourly wage rates the arbitrator will choose in light of how the firm and the union justify their

---

[6] For a list and discussion of other forms of outside intervention in labor disputes see Herbert Northrup, *Economics of Labor Relations* (Homewood, Ill.: Richard D. Irwin, Inc., 1981), p. 742.

[7] For details see Northrup, *Economics of Labor Relations,* pp. 785–87.

[8] The idea that the union and the firm base their behavior on their anticipations of how the arbitrator will respond is developed in Henry S. Farber, "Splitting-the-Difference in Interest Arbitration," *Industrial and Labor Relations Review,* 35:1 (October 1981), 70–77.

The Firm's Possible Strategies

	F_1	F_2	F_3	F_4
U_1	w_{11}	w_{12}	w_{13}	w_{14}
U_2	w_{21}	w_{22}	w_{23}	w_{24}
U_3	w_{31}	w_{32}	w_{33}	w_{34}
U_4	w_{41}	w_{42}	w_{43}	w_{44}

The Union's Possible Strategies

FIGURE 7-5. A payoff matrix for arbitration

desires for low and high wages, respectively. The possible strategies which the union and the firm may use are assumed to include a legalistic approach to arguing their cases, an agreeable approach, an aggressive approach, and a reasoning approach. In our example in Figure 7-6, if the union were to choose to be aggressive in arguing its position before the arbitrator while the firm were to reason that on the basis of costs and market position only a small wage increase should be granted, the arbitrator would decide upon a $6.40 wage rate for the next contract period. If, though, the union argued aggressively that the firm could well afford a substantial wage increase and the firm chose to employ a labor lawyer to justify its desire for low wages on legalistic grounds, the arbitrator would decide upon a $22 wage rate. In summary, the numbers in a payoff matrix indicate the hourly wage rate that

The Firm's Possible Strategies

	Legalistic	Agreeable	Aggressive	Reasoning
Legalistic	$13	$11	$8.45	$20
Agreeable	$15	$9.90	$6.65	$7.45
Aggressive	$22	$5.50	$7.45	$6.40
Reasoning	$4.50	$6.35	$8.10	$5

The Union's Possible Strategies

FIGURE 7-6. Possible wage settlements in a contract arbitration: Numerical example of a payoff matrix

the arbitrator will choose when confronting a *set* of arguments by the two parties directly involved in the dispute. These numbers reflect the arbitrator's evaluation of the merits of one party's argument coupled with how the other party has chosen to argue its position. Of course, there are more than four possible ways of justifying low or high wages, and the firm or the union could also blend strategies. The information in a payoff matrix summarizes the possible outcomes of the arbitration process based on the behavior of the three parties involved. In light of the uncertainty over what the other side will do, how does a union or a firm go about selecting a strategy for use before the arbitrator?

As you might expect, there are numerous rules that might be used for selecting a strategy. If the firm, for example, already happened to have a top-notch labor lawyer in its employ, it might want to take a legalistic approach in the arbitration proceedings. If it turned out that the union had chosen to be reasoning, then the outcome would be extremely favorable to the firm; the arbitrated wage settlement of $4.50 is the best possible outcome for the firm in the payoff matrix in Figure 7-6. Notice, though, that if the firm's legalistic arguments were met by an aggressive set of justifications by the union, then the outcome of the arbitration proceeding would be a wage rate of $22, the best possible outcome for the *union*. So, even though the firm may possess excellent legal talent, it may not want to take the risk of a $22 wage rate by choosing a legalistic argument for its position. Similarly, the union may not wish to risk being aggressive. Even though it may obtain a $22 wage settlement, it could also obtain as little as $5.50 if confronted with a firm arguing in an agreeable fashion.

Of course, things can get even more complicated. Parties may try to *trick* one another in the arbitration process. A firm could hire a famous labor lawyer to represent it in the arbitration proceedings with the hope that the union would assume the firm would argue its case on legalistic grounds. Given the data in Figure 7-6, if the union expected legalistic arguments by the firm, it would take an aggressive approach. The firm, anticipating that the union would respond to its employment of a legal expert by being aggressive in its arguments, would choose to be reasoning. The result is a relatively low wage settlement, $6.40. Given the amount of complications potentially involved, how do firms and unions ever decide upon the strategies they will use?

Hopefully it is clear by now that an arbitration proceeding is similar to a baseball or a football game in the sense that the parties involved each attempt to obtain a desirable outcome, that what is a good outcome for one is a bad one for the other, and that the outcome is determined by the participants' *joint* behavior. This similarity is convenient because we can draw upon the branch of mathematics known as **game theory** in discussing the selection of a strategy. It is probably reasonable to assume that the two parties involved in the arbitration process each wish to avoid disaster. In the language of game theory, this means that they will select their strategy based on a decision rule known as **minimax.** Let us see how the use of the minimax decision rule leads to the selection of a strategy that ensures disaster will be avoided.[9] From the perspective of the firm a disaster would be a relatively high wage rate such as $20 or $22, and from the viewpoint of the union a disaster would be an especially low rate such as $4.50 or $5.

In seeking to avoid disaster, the firm will *assume* that no matter what strategy it may select, the union's response will always be optimal from the perspective of the union. This means that the firm will assume that (1) if it were to be legalistic, it would be confronted with an aggressive union, (2) if it were to be agreeable, it would be confronted with a legalistic union, (3) if it were to be aggressive, it would be confronted with a legalistic union, and (4) if it were to be reasoning, it would also be confronted with a legalistic union. The firm will then select a strategy that gives it *the best of the worst!* This means the firm will choose to be *aggressive* in arguing its case. Even if the union were to choose its optimum response to an aggressive firm, the firm would *never* have a wage settlement that exceeded $8.45. Of course, by being aggressive in order to avoid wage rates greater than $8.45, the firm is also eliminating the possibility of a settlement less than $6.65, the minimum value in the column associated with aggressive behavior by the firm in Figure 7-6.

The union makes similar calculations. It assumes that the firm will choose to argue in a way leading to the *lowest* wage settlement for any given way the union might choose to argue. This means that the union will assume that (1) if it were to be legalistic, the firm would be aggressive, (2) if it were to be agreeable, the firm would be aggressive, (3) if it were to be aggressive, the firm would be agreeable, and (4) if it were to be reasoning, the firm would be legalistic. Based on the information in Figure 7-6, the union then minimizes disaster by choosing to argue its case in a legalistic fashion. No matter what the firm might do, the union is ensuring that the wage for the next contract period will be *at least* $8.45 per hour. What, then, is the outcome of the arbitration process?

The minimax strategy selection rule means that during the arbitration proceedings in our example, the arbitrator listens to aggressive arguments by the firm and legalistic arguments by the union. As a result, the arbitrator will decide upon a wage rate of $8.45 for the new contract period. It is interesting that the minimax strategy selection rule means that once a party selects a strategy, it does not matter if the other party finds out in advance what it is. In our example, if the union were to discover that the firm planned to be aggressive, the union would *still* be legalistic. Similarly, if the firm were to

---

[9] For those readers interested in learning more about game theory, two excellent, relatively nontechnical references are Morton D. Davis, *Game Theory, A Nontechnical Introduction* (New York: Basic Books, Inc., 1970), and J. D. Williams, *The Complete Strategist* (New York: McGraw-Hill Book Company, 1966).

find out that the union planned to be legalistic, it would still be aggressive.

What, then, are the *basic* forces that determine an arbitrated wage settlement? At the heart of the arbitration process is the arbitrator's set of values or sense of fairness of outcomes and how the participants deal with the uncertainties involved in the process. Estimates of the arbitrator's sense of fair play and equitable outcomes determine the information contained in the payoff matrix used by the firm and the union to determine their strategies. Other key forces involved are the strength of the preferences of the union and the firm for a relatively unspectacular, but safe, outcome as opposed to a relatively successful, but risky, outcome. Finally, there is the ability of the respective parties to use trickery in the arbitration process.

Before we leave the topic of arbitration, a few odds and ends are worth discussing. The arbitration process we have been analyzing is known as **splitting-the-difference,** in the sense that the arbitrator's decision will lie somewhere between the desired outcomes of the firm and the union. There is a feeling among observers of industrial relations in the United States that splitting-the-difference arbitration has a narcotic effect on government employees' contract negotiations. Specifically, once arbitration is used to solve a contract dispute, the parties involved may tend to become increasingly dependent upon arbitration to the point of never again reaching an agreement on their own. As a result, some states have instituted an alternative form of arbitration, known as **final-offer arbitration,** in an attempt to encourage bargaining by the firm and the union. In this type of process, the firm and the union each submit their interpretation of a fair contract settlement. The arbitrator is required to pick one of these two offers as the new contract settlement. Two recent papers by Farber examine (1) whether final-offer arbitration encourages bargaining and (2) the key forces underlying the outcomes of final-offer arbitration as opposed to splitting-the-difference arbitration.[10] Farber shows theoretically that final-offer arbitration is *not necessarily* more likely to encourage bargaining than conventional arbitration. However, *in practice,* final-offer arbitration might still be more effective. In addition, Farber shows that the outcome of final-offer arbitration is highly reflective of the party less inclined to take chances. Specifically, the party with a greater dislike for the risk of an unfavorable outcome will submit a more "reasonable" offer in the sense of being closer to the arbitrator's personal opinion concerning an equitable settlement. This is important because a majority of final-offer arbitration proceedings have led to acceptance of the *union's* position. Farber's research indicates that this does not necessarily mean that arbitrators are more inclined to select a union's position, but

---

[10] Henry S. Farber, "Does Final-Offer Arbitration Encourage Bargaining?" *Proceedings of the 33rd Winter Meeting of the Industrial Relations Research Association, 1980,* pp. 219–26; and "An Analysis of Final-Offer Arbitration," *Journal of Conflict Resolution,* 24:4 (December 1980), 683–705.

rather that unions may be less willing than firms to take chances in the arbitration process.

Postscript: Union givebacks.   It is sometimes said that unions can be described very simply as wanting MORE, NOW. Sometimes, though, unions attempt to preserve employment opportunities in the face of severe reductions in the demand for labor. This was the case in the early 1980s when certain unions agreed to so-called givebacks in order to preserve jobs. This situation is described graphically in Figure 7-7. Initially, the firm has demand curve d. Workers receive $w(0)$ and have employment $L(0)$. Suppose now that the firm experiences a reduction in the demand for its product and therefore wants to reduce its work force. This is demonstrated by a shift in the demand for labor to d'. If the union were to attempt to maintain wage $w(0)$, or perhaps achieve one higher through collective bargaining, workers would suffer a substantial loss of employment. It is even possible that wage $w(0)$ lies above the shutdown point on the new demand for labor. Thus, a way to maintain job opportunities is for workers to agree to *lower* wages. In 1981, workers agreed to wage cuts in five major industries: airlines, automobiles, rubber, steel, and trucking.[11]

The point to remember is that although workers generally form unions to achieve higher wages, the wages they seek are determined with regard to the effect they will have on employment opportunities. Put differently, workers' desire for higher wages is tempered by a desire for a minimal

---

[11] For details of the wage reductions see "Labor Seeks Less," *Business Week,* December 21, 1981, pp. 82–88.

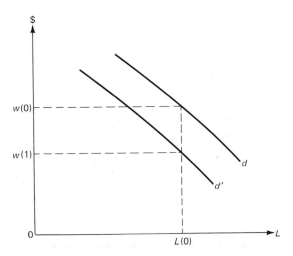

FIGURE 7-7. Reducing wages to maintain employment

employment loss. In the case where employment may decline severely owing to structural or business-cycle changes in the economy, workers may
prefer to maintain jobs at their current level in exchange for a wage reduction.

This completes our discussion of collective bargaining as the primary
way unions seek their basic objectives of higher wages and better conditions
for workers. Of course, bargaining is supplemented by other activities. In
general, unions also attempt to achieve their goals by affecting the supply or
demand for labor or the way in which supply and demand lead to a particular
outcome in the labor market.

Activities that Reduce the Supply of Labor

American unions have historically supported legislation restricting the
supply of labor. There is an interesting parallel between the labor market
effects of collective bargaining and a reduction in the market supply of labor.
Strikes are a *temporary reduction* in the supply of labor designed to impose a
cost on the employer that is large enough to make him or her agree contractually to a higher wage rate. We saw this in Figure 7-1. A higher wage can
also be achieved by a *long-term reduction* in the available labor force. The
firms in Figure 7-8 also pay higher wages to union workers, but here it is the
forces of supply and demand that lead to the higher wage. Thus, a short-term
elimination of labor supply (a strike) can bring about contractually what a
long-term reduction in the available work force can do through market
forces. For this reason the ability of a union to control the supply of labor is

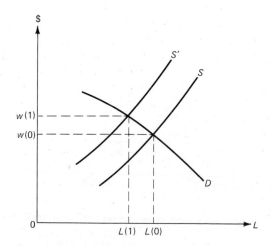

FIGURE 7-8. The labor market effect of
a reduction in the supply
of labor

often the key to its ability to raise wage rates, just as OPEC's ability to control the supply of oil has been the key to its ability to raise oil prices.

One way that unions in the United States have attempted to reduce the supply of labor is through support of legislation restricting foreign immigration. Limitations on worker mobility of this sort decrease the supply of labor to United States labor markets and lead to higher wages for United States workers, both union and nonunion. In 1866, a group of union leaders held a conference in Baltimore that has been called the first national labor congress ever convened in the United States.[12] Its primary purpose was to unify organized labor. One of the objectives set forth at the Baltimore conference was the restriction of immigration, particularly that of Chinese coolies in the West. Behind this was a desire to safeguard the living standards of native workers. This goal is powerfully illustrated by the following stanzas from an anti-Chinese song sung by members of Denis Kearney's Working Men's Party in California during the 1870s.[13]

TWELVE HUNDRED MORE

O workingmen dear, and did you hear
The news that's goin' round?
Another China steamer
Has been landed here in town.
Today I read the papers,
And it grieved my heart full sore
To see upon the title page,
O, just "Twelve Hundred More!"

O, California's coming down,
As you can plainly see.
They are hiring all the Chinamen
And discharging you and me;
But strife will be in every town
Throughout the Pacific shore,
And the cry of old and young shall be,
"O, damn, 'Twelve Hundred More'."

They run their steamer in at night
Upon our lovely bay;
If 'twas a free and honest trade,
They'd land it in the day.
They come here by the hundreds—
The country is overrun—
And go to work at any price—
By them the labor's done.

This state of things can never last
In, this our golden land,

---

[12] Foster Rhea Dulles, *Labor in America: A History,* 3d ed. (New York: Crowell, 1966).
[13] Philip S. Foner, *American Labor Songs of the Nineteenth Century* (Urbana, Ill.: University of Illinois, 1975), p. 135.

For soon you'll hear the avenging cry,
"Drive out the China man!"
And then we'll have the stirring times
We had in days of yore,
And the devil take those dirty words
They call "Twelve Hundred More!"

The Working Men's Party helped bring about legislation in California excluding the Chinese. However, it was not until 1921 that specific numerical restrictions on immigration were established by federal legislation.[14] Although the formal (legal) movement of foreign labor into the United States has been severely curtailed, illegal aliens are still viewed by American unions as a threat to their members' economic welfare. For example, a resolution adopted at a recent AFL-CIO national convention urged that "Illegal immigration . . . be stopped. Employers who hire illegal aliens and those who traffic in transporting and placing illegal immigrants should be subject to stiff penalties."[15]

Union workers are not unique in their desire to avoid competition from immigrants. Native workers in general have never been in favor of immigration when the result is low wages in their particular labor market. As evidence, remember the statements made by individuals directly affected by the Vietnamese immigration of the middle to late 1970s or the immigration of Cubans and Haitians into Florida in the early 1980s. Moreover, during 1982 Congress considered the Immigration Reform and Control Act, which sought to impose civil and criminal penalties on employers who knowingly hire illegal aliens.[16] Thus, unions speak for many nonunion workers when they back laws to restrict entry of foreign workers into the U.S. labor markets.

We have just seen that political support of immigration restrictions will help both union and nonunion workers. Other restrictions on the supply of labor, however, have a positive effect primarily on the wage rate of union workers alone. In addition, they are more subtle than immigration restrictions. What we have in mind is that certain occupations require licenses in order to practice in a state. Data on the extent of occupational licensing in the United States are rather difficult to obtain; however, it has been estimated that there are over 1,500 state licensing boards.[17] By raising the cost

---

[14] For a concise history of federal restrictions on immigration, see the section "Immigration and Naturalization" in a recent edition of the *Statistical Abstract of the United States*.

[15] *The National Economy 1977*, a pamphlet reprinted from the National Economy section of the *Report of the Executive Council of the AFL-CIO to the Twelfth Convention* (Los Angeles, December 1977).

[16] "Employers as Cops," *Wall Street Journal*, August 12, 1982, p. 18.

[17] "State Licensed Occupations Get More Criticism, But the System is Defended As Insuring Quality," *The Wall Street Journal*, June 14, 1977, p. 48. A not-so-recent, but important reference on licensing in the United States is Benjamin Shimberg et al., *Occupational Licensing: Practices and Policies* (Washington, D.C.: Public Affairs Press, 1973).

of entry, licensing serves to reduce the flow of labor into an occupation. The additional cost generally takes the form of fees, formal training in an approved institution, an apprenticeship, and a passing score on a licensing examination. Alex Maurizi points out a number of reasons why a passing score may be more difficult to obtain than you might think.[18] The exam may be held infrequently and in only one location. Applicants may be required to provide their own materials or tools; this can be quite difficult or expensive if you are a cosmetologist who needs a live human head or a truck driver who needs a semi rig. Finally, information concerning the exact types of knowledge and skills to be examined may be withheld from examinees so that the first time they take the test they probably fail it.

The licensing of occupations has been justified to state legislators on the grounds that it protects the public interest. Often, however, it is the *sellers* of a particular service, through their unions or quasi-unions, such as bar or medical associations, who present the consumer-protection argument to state legislators. One result has been that those individuals who have the most to gain from entry restrictions, the existing practitioners, have frequently been given the power to determine licensing requirements.

There are two primary ways in which licensing requirements affect the flow of individuals into an occupation. In the long term, there are adjustments, sometimes fairly dramatic, in the amount of formal (in-school) training necessary to become a licensed practitioner. For example, a good term-paper topic would be to compare what it takes to become a licensed attorney or physician today to what was required a century ago. In the short term, there are changes from year to year in the pass rate—the proportion of applicants who are designated as passing the licensing examination.

Maurizi examines the hypothesis that the pass rate (p) has been used by licensing bodies to fine-tune entry into licensed occupations from year to year. This is clearly *possible,* because p has typically been under the control of the licensing board, and decisions regarding the pass rate have normally been made *after* all applications have been received. This means that licensing boards have usually known the potential number of new entrants, and thus the potential long-term effect on wages, *before* they had to define the passing performance on a licensing examination. Moreover, in many cases the licensing agency has not even been required to cite its reason for failing applicants.[19] Thus, the opportunity has clearly existed for licensing boards to use the licensing examination to restrict entry.

How do we know that changes in the pass rate from year to year do not simply reflect changes in the quality of applicants? The key lies in examining the relationship between the relative number of applicants and p. If a licensing examination is simply used to eliminate unqualified individuals

[18] Alex Maurizi, "Occupational Licensing and the Public Interest," *Journal of Political Economy,* 82:2, part I (March–April 1974), 399–413.
[19] Maurizi, "Occupational Licensing," pp. 404–405.

from professional practice, then there is no obvious relationship between the relative number of applicants and the pass rate from one year to the next. Put differently, there is no particular reason to suspect that when the size of the group taking the test is relatively large in one year, the quality of the group taking the test is *relatively* low. However, if the test is being used to eliminate potential supply so as to keep wages of existing licensees high, we would expect that when the number of applicants taking the test is relatively large, the pass rate on the licensing exam is relatively low. Evidence of an inverse relationship between p and the relative number of applicants, then, suggests that licensing boards have used licensing examinations to limit entry into professions.

Maurizi estimates simple linear regressions of the form

$$p = \alpha + \beta a \tag{7-1}$$

where $p \equiv$ a state's pass rate on a licensing exam for a particular occupation in a particular year
     $a \equiv$ the ratio of the number of applicants in a state to the number of practitioners already licensed at the time of the exam in a particular year
  $\alpha,\beta \equiv$ parameters

and he tests whether β is significantly less than zero. His data cover 18 occupations[20] in each of two years, 1940 and 1950. A separate regression was run for each occupation within a given year. The total number of observations employed in a pass-rate regression are the number of states for which values of p and a are available. Although most of the 18 occupations used by Maurizi were licensed in nearly every state, his data typically permitted regression samples of less than 24 states.

The estimated value of β is negative in 27 of Maurizi's 36 regressions; it is *significantly* negative in 18 of these regressions. For simple bivariate cross-section regressions, Maurizi generally obtains rather high degrees of explanatory power. R^2 adjusted for degrees of freedom exceeds 0.1 in 16 of the 17 cases where β is significantly negative, exceeds 0.2 in 12 of the cases, and exceeds 0.3 in 9 cases. Finally, Maurizi uses the estimated values of the βs to calculate elasticities of p with respect to a. He finds that these elasticities generally lie in the interval -0.5 to -1.0, or that a 10 percent increase in a generates, on average, a 5 to 10 percent lower pass rate. Thus, Maurizi's regression results are consistent with the notion that state licensing boards have used the pass rate on licensing examinations to fine-tune the flow of entrants into an occupation.

---

[20] Accountant, architect, attorney, barber, beautician, chiropodist, chiropractor, dentist, embalmer, professional engineer, funeral director, registered nurse, optometrist, osteopath, pharmacist, physician, real estate broker and salesman, and veterinarian.

Activities that Increase the Demand for Labor

Figure 7-9 reminds us that anything that increases the demand for union labor is especially good for the welfare of union workers, because it ultimately leads to more employment opportunities as well as upward pressure on wages. We are all familiar with attempts by unions to convince consumers to boycott products produced with nonunion labor and purchase instead union-made goods and services. Where successful, such campaigns increase the demand for union labor at the expense of nonunion labor. Unions also politically support high tariffs and stringent quotas on imports. One example of such restrictions strongly supported by the United Auto Workers' Union is the so-called domestic content legislation introduced in Congress during 1982 as the Fair Practices in Automotive Products Act.[21] The provisions of this bill required companies selling more than 500,000 autos in the United States to manufacture them with 90 percent American parts and labor. Laws of this sort raise the relative price of foreign-produced items, leading to an increase in the consumption of American-produced goods and services. The result is an implicit substitution of American for foreign workers in the manufacturing process. A resolution adopted unanimously by the twelfth AFL-CIO convention is indicative of unions' position on international trade:

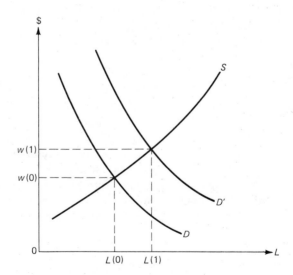

FIGURE 7-9. The labor market effect of an increase in the demand for labor

---

[21] See "The Made-in-America Trap," *New York Times,* August 2, 1982, p. A14.

. . . We oppose the continued export of American jobs and industry, which has undermined the economy. We shall pursue . . . new legislation to halt the drain on this nation's economy. . . . will use all departments, legislative, education, research, public relations, publications, organization, and field services—to assure protection for American workers' jobs and living standards.[22]

Unions have also historically supported federal minimum wage legislation, and there is a reasonable amount of evidence that this political support has been effective.[23] Many economists feel that one of the reasons for this support is that minimum wage laws are likely to increase the demand for union labor. Because union workers are generally skilled and receive wage rates above the legal minimum, the law will have no direct effect on them. (Remember our discussion in Chapter 5, where we saw that the federal minimum wage in the United States tends to be one-half the average wage in manufacturing.) The increased relative price of unskilled, typically nonunion, labor leads, however, to a relative increase (substitution) in the use of skilled, typically union, labor in the production process. Of course, because the cost of production is also increased by the minimum wage, there is also a negative effect on output. If the substitution effect of the wage increase predominates, then the demand for skilled, union labor shifts upward, bringing with it the increased employment and wage depicted in Figure 7-9. The point is that because unions are in general composed of relatively skilled workers, it is in their economic interests to support minimum wage legislation in industries where the output (scale) effect is relatively small. This is over and above any genuine desire to try to help the poor through support of policies that establish a floor on wages.

Finally, the Fair Labor Standards Act is not the only federal legislation establishing a floor on wages. The Davis-Bacon Act, passed in 1931 and later amended, mandates employers engaged in federally funded construction projects valued at $2,000 or more to pay so-called prevailing wages. Under the Davis-Bacon procedures, the Secretary of Labor determines the prevailing wages for the various crafts; since 1931 the Secretaries have usually defined *prevailing* as *union*, even if the nearest union labor market is some miles away. A similar wage minimum was applied to government-contract on-site services other than construction in 1965 as a result of the O'Hara-McNamara Services Act. These two pieces of legislation, along with the Fair

---

[22] *The National Economy.*

[23] See Jonathan I. Silberman and Garey C. Durden, "Determining Legislative Preferences on the Minimum Wage: An Economic Approach," *The Journal of Political Economy*, 84:2 (April 1976), 317–29; James B. Kau and Paul H. Rubin, "Voting on Minimum Wages: A Time-Series Analysis," *Journal of Political Economy*, 86:2, Part I (April 1978), 337–42; and Noel D. Uri and J. Wilson Mixon, Jr., "An Economic Analysis of the Determinants of Minimum Wage Voting Behavior," *Journal of Law and Economics*, 23:1 (April 1980), 167–78.

Labor Standards Act, have tended to increase the relative price of nonunion labor, thus leading to an increase in the demand for union labor.[24]

Activities that Make the Demand for Labor Less Elastic

It is in the best interests of union members to reduce the elasticity of demand for their services, thus reducing the employment losses from any union-induced wage gains. This is illustrated in Figure 7-10, where a wage increase from $w(0)$ to $w(1)$ has almost no disemployment effect if the demand curve is D' as opposed to D, where the employment loss is rather substantial. As we noted earlier in this chapter, one of the things unions can do to reduce the elasticity of demand for labor is to increase the proportion of firms subject to the union wage increase. Moreover, in Chapter 3 we saw that four factors influence the elasticity of demand for labor by an industry: (1) the ease of substituting other inputs for labor in the production process, (2) the elasticity of demand for final output, (3) the importance of labor in total production costs, and (4) the elasticity of supply of other inputs. The greater is each of these factors, the greater is the elasticity of demand for

---

[24] For more discussion, see Robert S. Goldfarb and John F. Morrall III, "The Davis-Bacon Act: An Appraisal of Recent Studies," *Industrial and Labor Relations Review*, 34:2 (January 1981), 191–206, and Robert S. Goldfarb and John S. Heywood, "An Economic Evaluation of the Service Contract Act," Working Paper, George Washington University, Washington, D.C., February 1982.

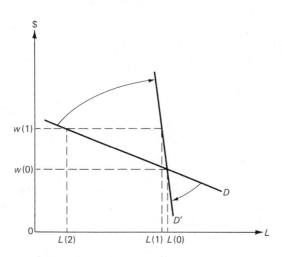

FIGURE 7-10. A union-induced wage increase produces a smaller employment loss when labor demand becomes less elastic

labor by an industry, and the more severe the disemployment effect of a union-induced wage gain.

Remember that because they were developed by the famous nineteenth-century economist Alfred Marshall, the relationships between the elasticity of demand for labor and the four factors mentioned above are known as **Marshall's rules.** The next time the weather is bad and you are stuck inside with nothing to do, see if your friends would like to play a great game, *Understanding Unions.* It is played as follows. All players first discuss the concept of labor demand elasticity and its link to Marshall's rules. Next, they take turns identifying and explaining some union activities in the real world that work through Marshall's rules to make the demand for union members' services less elastic. Here are some examples.

> *Hold the Phone.* Fearing a loss of 100,000 jobs, the communications workers' union asks Congress to review the new FCC policy allowing Americans to buy telephones, instead of renting them from the phone company. The union also wants a law curbing the growing imports of foreign-made telephone equipment designed to supply the new market.[25]
>
> *Sizzling Cinema?* A local projectionists union in Milwaukee claims new multiple-movie houses using only one operator to run several projectors risk fire from bursting bulbs, which can melt film, releasing poison gas. It may seek state laws to require theaters to hire more of its members.[26]
>
> *Food Faddists* are costing bakery workers jobs, unions complain. The AFL-CIO food and beverage trades department blames food and diet "faddists" for encouraging less bread consumption. The group endorses legislation to promote "the use of wheat and wheat products as human foods."[27]

Consider *Hold the Phone.* If union lobbying is successful in prohibiting Americans from buying or installing their own telephones, this will reduce the substitutability of the labor of telephone *users* for that of professional telephone *installers*. One of Marshall's rules tells us that this should reduce the elasticity of demand for the services of unionized telephone installers. Moreover, because curbing imports of telephones should reduce the number of substitutes for domestically produced telephones available to consumers, this should also reduce the elasticity of demand for telephone equipment produced by unionized American workers. Now try your hand at interpreting *Sizzling Cinema?* and *Food Faddists.* One point is awarded for each correct example, and the player with the most points at the end of the game is declared the winner. The game ends when all players get bored, which is sure to happen in five minutes. The winning player is declared an honorary

---

[25] *The Wall Street Journal,* November 29, 1977, p. 1. Reprinted by permission of *The Wall Street Journal,* © Dow Jones & Company, Inc., 1977. All rights reserved.

[26] *The Wall Street Journal,* October 28, 1975, p. 1. Reprinted by permission of *The Wall Street Journal,* © Dow Jones & Company, Inc., 1975. All rights reserved.

[27] *The Wall Street Journal,* February 22, 1977, p. 1. Reprinted by permission of *The Wall Street Journal,* © Dow Jones & Company, Inc., 1977. All rights reserved.

labor economist, and the losers must buy pizza and beer for everyone. In the case of ties, duplicate pizzas must be purchased.

Featherbedding

There is something similar about all of the situations we have been discussing up to now. It is that an employer has been able to respond to what the union has done by moving to a new point *on* the labor demand curve, thus continuing to maximize profit at a given wage. Of course, the *total level* of profit is smaller when wages are raised through collective bargaining. **Featherbedding,** also known as **restrictive working practices,** is the situation where a firm hires *more* than the profit-maximizing amount of labor at a given wage. Point A in Figure 7-11(a), which lies to the *right* of the labor demand curve, shows us what is meant by featherbedding. One reason for featherbedding might be a desire on the part of workers to maintain employment level L(0) in the face of automation that shifts the demand curve for labor from a position through A in Figure 7-11 to a position to the left of A, say B. See if you can think of some other situations that might cause workers, through their unions, to want to featherbed. Now that we understand what is meant by featherbedding, let us turn our attention to the forms featherbedding takes, how unions achieve featherbedding, and the natural economic limitations on featherbedding.

In general, featherbedding will take the form of pay for little or no work or pay for work that is not used. Here are some examples. It has often been the case among unionized musicians in large cities that if a visiting group gives a concert or works a gig, the musicians union will receive money equal to the union scale wages of an equivalent number of local musicians. Back

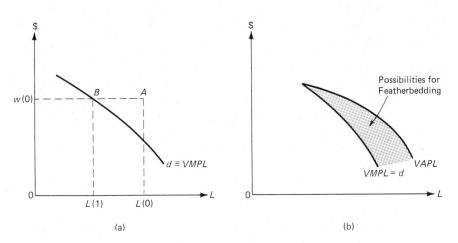

FIGURE 7-11. Featherbedding

when newspaper type was set largely by hand, advertising type often had to be set by the newspaper's workers, even though advertising copy would sometimes be received by the newspaper in a form *already* useable for printing. The second set of type, done by the newspaper's workers, was called bogus and was discarded. A third example of featherbedding occurred where railroads switched from steam to diesel locomotives. As the result of union activity, firemen continued to be used on diesel trains even though their duties and skills related largely to steam locomotives. In recent years the practice of using firemen on diesel trains has been basically eliminated by an agreement between railroads and the unions not to replace firemen who leave.[28]

Unions achieve featherbedding by threatening the firm with enough revenue loss to make it worthwhile to accept featherbedding. In short, unions will attempt to achieve featherbedding by making the firm a deal it can't refuse. One example might be to tell the firm it will have a total loss of labor or a loss of enough key labor so that it will have to close down if it does not agree to a wage-employment combination such as that denoted by A in Figure 7-11(a). When the need arises, how do unions justify this to the public? In the case of firemen for diesel locomotives, it was claimed that safety necessitated an extra worker who could take over for an engineer in the event of a heart attack or illness. In other situations featherbedding has been justified on the grounds that workers have property rights in their jobs and that they should not be forced to suffer because of changes in business conditions, the structure of the economy, or the production process that reduce the demand for labor.

Do not get the impression, however, that featherbedding has no limit. There are natural economic restrictions on the degree of featherbedding a union can achieve, and some are easily analyzed with the tools we learned in Chapter 3. Suppose that a union can offer an all-or-nothing bargain of the form that the firm will be forced to close if it does not accept more than the profit-maximizing labor at the current wage rate, $w(0)$. Suppose further that the period of time involved is too short for the firm to adjust its nonlabor inputs. In this case, the firm will agree to featherbedding as long as it can cover its variable labor costs. Thus, the limit on the amount of featherbedding the union can achieve, assuming it can effectively shut off the flow of labor to the firm, is whether or not the amount of labor the union requests leaves the firm in the position where total revenue exceeds the wage bill.

In Chapter 3 we saw that a profit-maximizing competitive firm with fixed nonlabor inputs has a labor demand schedule that is the value-of-marginal-product curve where it lies below the value-of-average-product curve. We also saw that the *VAPL* schedule identifies the firm's total reve-

---

[28] For elaboration on these and other forms of featherbedding that have occurred throughout United States history see *Featherbedding and Technical Change,* ed. Paul A. Weinstein (Boston: D. C. Heath & Co., 1965).

nue and the *VMPL* schedule identifies its wage bill for a given amount of labor. The importance of these two tidbits is that so long as the union featherbeds to a point that lies inside the value-of-average-product of labor schedule, the firm will find it desirable to accept this rather than close down completely. The shaded region in Figure 7-11(b), therefore, defines the union's featherbedding possibilities. If a union attempts to achieve a wage-employment combination to the right of *VAPL*, it will lose everything. Don't get us wrong. We do not imply that unions go about drawing the curves in Figure 7-11, but simply that their experience leads them to find out how far they can go in effectively featherbedding.

One of the most interesting aspects of featherbedding is that it has been declared an unfair labor practice in Section 8(b)(6) of the Taft-Hartley Act, but that little effort has been made to impose any real restrictions on featherbedding in the United States. One reason is that according to the Taft-Hartley Act, it is an unfair labor practice for a union "to cause or attempt to cause an employer to pay or deliver or agree to pay or deliver any money or other thing of value in the nature of an extraction, for services which are not performed or not to be performed." This is an extremely narrow definition of featherbedding. As such, it has resulted in restrictions by the National Labor Relations Board against payment where *no* work is done, but not if *some* work has been performed, no matter how "unnecessary" the work would seem to be. For example, the Supreme Court has ruled that requirements to pay for setting so-called bogus type or for musicians to stand by when a visiting group comes to town are not considered unfair labor practices under the provisions of the Taft-Hartley Act.[29] Second, there has been a reluctance on the part of firms to seek enforcement of antifeatherbedding legislation because of a desire to avoid increased government involvement in the workplace. This lack of desire by employers for more stringent restrictions on featherbedding probably also indicates that featherbedding is relatively rare in the United States. This is important, because it contradicts the popular belief that featherbedding is widespread.

UNION MEMBERSHIP

Workers' decisions to form or join unions, and thus the proportion of the labor force that is unionized at any moment in time, depend upon the benefits from union membership. The story does not end here, because the tastes and attitudes of workers toward union membership as such, the costs of organizing and maintaining worker participation in unions, and the costs of collective bargaining with employers must also be considered. This suggests that we can study the development of modern unionism in the United States

---

[29] Northrup, *Labor Relations*, p. 701.

within the context of the economist's favorite tool, supply and demand analysis.

A Supply and Demand Model for Union Services

There are many services that an individual might buy, including the services of a union. In return for negotiating members' wages and working conditions, processing their grievances, and helping them search for jobs, unions are typically paid one-time initiation fees plus monthly dues. The schedule labeled $D(U)$ in Figure 7-12 is a demand curve for union services, U. It indicates the amount of union services workers desire to purchase at any given price. It reflects workers' willingness to pay for unionism—which, of course, is positively related to the benefits they receive from being in a union. D is negatively sloped just as any other demand curve. Given the benefits of being in a union, a lower price induces the desire for a greater amount of unionism.

Of course, the price of U is not the only factor determining the quantity of union services workers desire. We know from principles of economics that income, tastes and preferences, and the prices of complementary and substitute services also matter. So, when we draw the demand schedule in Figure 7-12, it is for a *given* set of these other factors. Should any of them change, the demand schedule would have to be redrawn. For example, instead of using a union to bargain for you with your employer, or doing it

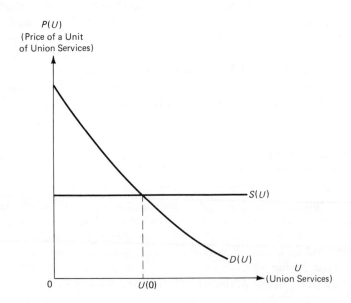

FIGURE 7-12. Demand curve for union services

yourself, you could be represented by a famous agent or lawyer. Should the price of the services of an agent or an attorney fall dramatically, then the demand curve for unionism will shift to the left, and less union services will be demanded at any given price. Alternatively, should your current boss quit and be replaced by someone who is much more antagonistic to your point of view, face-to-face bargaining becomes much more unpleasant and costly than it was before. This means that the cost (price) of bargaining for yourself has increased, and you will increase the demand for the services of a substitute such as unionism. In addition to the factors just mentioned, the *quality* of a service determines the amount of the service individuals want at a given price per unit. One important dimension of the quality of unionism is the potential employment loss workers will suffer due to union activities. The employment loss will be greater, the more elastic is the demand curve for union labor. Thus, the elasticity of demand for workers' services is one aspect of union quality. In particular, the more elastic is the demand for labor, the lower is the quality of unionism, and the lower is the demand for union services.

Before we go on to discuss the supply of union services, we would like you to do two things. First, make sure you understand what the demand curve for unionism in Figure 7-12 represents. If it is not clear in your mind, then review the last two paragraphs. Second, make sure you are clear on the factors that position the demand curve, especially the tastes and preferences of workers and the quality of unionism as measured by the elasticity of demand for labor. If the latter items are still somewhat unclear, then read the next section, which is a more detailed explanation of how workers' tastes and preferences and the elasticity of demand for labor determine the demand for unionism. If you feel comfortable with your understanding of how tastes and preferences of workers and the elasticity of demand for labor position $D(U)$, then skip the next section and proceed to our discussion of the supply of union services on page 253.

Aside: The elasticity of demand for labor, tastes and preferences, and the individual's decision to join a union.   Figure 7-13 illustrates the utility function of a potential unionist. You are familiar with a similar diagram in our analysis of labor supply in Chapter 4. Remember that the horizontal axis measures hours not worked, and that $h(\text{max})$ is the total number of nonwork hours available during the period under consideration. Thus, measuring from $h(\text{max})$ to the left denotes the number of hours worked. Remember also that income is measured along the dashed vertical axis. We will ignore for simplicity any nonlabor income, so that earnings equals total income.

Suppose that, in the absence of any union, employers purchase $h(\text{max}) - h(1)$ hours from each worker, yielding each total earnings of C. Now suppose that a union is to be formed that will include all workers and will be successful in raising the

---

* This section contains more technical material that may be skipped without loss of continuity. If you skip, go to p. 253.

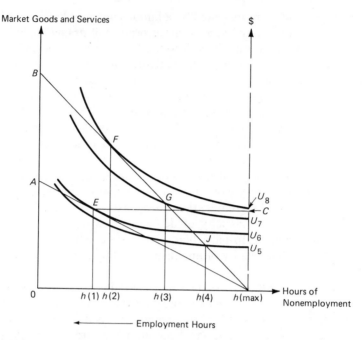

FIGURE 7-13. The roles of tastes and preferences and the elasticity of demand for labor in the individual's decision whether or not to join a union

wage rate to a level represented by the slope of the budget line $h(\max)B$ in Figure 7-13. It is not clear whether union members will want to work more or less at the higher wage rate. Let us presume that the income effect of a wage increase outweighs the substitution effect, so that each potential unionist will desire F, a point associated with increases in (a) earnings, (b) consumption of market goods, and (c) leisure. So, it is clear that were each individual permitted to choose any point along $h(\max)B$, the new wage rate would definitely be preferable to the old one. Everyone could be better off than before. However, we know that in response to the wage increase, firms will reduce employment from $h(\max) - h(1)$ per worker to some lower level, say $h(\max) - h(3)$ represented by point G.

If F lies to the southeast of G, overtime work or an increase in the number of workers would be required. But should F lie to the northwest of G, as in Figure 7-13, rationing of work among union members will be required. In this case, the indifference curve passing through G indicates each potential union member's level of well-being. Because U_7 is higher than U_6, the indifference curve through E, each worker will still be better off with the higher wage rate. However, if J [*any* point on $h(\max)B$ *below* U_6] were the best attainable point on $h(\max)B$, workers would be better off with the lower wage rate.

The change in workers' welfare that results from a union-induced wage increase depends upon two factors: (1) the elasticity of demand for labor and (2) workers' preferences for leisure versus market goods. The greater the elasticity of demand for labor, the greater the horizontal distance between F and G or J, and the greater the likelihood that an increase in the wage rate makes a worker worse off. Moreover, remember from Chapter 4 that one aspect of a worker's tastes and preferences for leisure versus market goods is the marginal rate of substitution between leisure and market goods, which is measured by the curvature of the indifference curves. The flatter are the indifference curves, indicating that a relatively large amount of leisure is required to compensate for a given loss of goods and services, the more likely it is that a worker's best attainable point will lie below U_6. A key thing to remember here is that if workers are to form or join a union, it must lead to an increase in their welfare, because unionism is not free.

In summary, we have just shown how workers' tastes and preferences for leisure versus consumption affect their decisions whether or not to join unions. We have also demonstrated the role of the elasticity of demand for labor in determining the desirability of unionization. You can think of the elasticity of demand for labor as measuring one dimension of union *quality,* because unions that avoid substantial employment losses for their workers provide a higher-quality service than unions that raise wages but lose many jobs in the process. It should be noted that we have not dealt with the issue of tastes and preferences for unionism per se. Of course, the demand for unionism will be greater among workers who are more prone to collective action and will be less among workers who are more individualistic. This will become clearer in the course of our discussions of union membership over time and the relationship between interstate differences in unionism and right-to-work laws.[30]

The supply of union services.   The curve labeled $S(U)$ in Figure 7-12 is the supply of union services by unions to workers. It reflects unions' costs of producing their services. The supply curve of unionism drawn in Figure 7-12 is horizontal. This amounts to assuming that unions have a constant marginal cost of producing their services. This is nothing more than an assumption to simplify our analysis, and you should satisfy yourself that none of the implications we will develop are altered if the supply curve is drawn with an upward slope.

$S(U)$ is drawn for (1) a fixed set of input prices and (2) a given technology for transforming those inputs into union services. A change in either of these two factors will cause a shift in $S(U)$. For example, an increase in the rental price of office space used by the union will lead to an upward shift in $S(U)$. Were union leaders and business agents to take salary cuts, the cost of producing unionism would be reduced, and the supply curve would shift downward. Perhaps the most interesting factor underlying the cost of producing unionism is the technology available for producing unionism. This is critically related to society's labor laws. If there are very severe restrictions on the types of things unions can do to attract members, then forming and maintaining a union will be very costly. However, if virtually nothing a union does is considered an unfair labor practice, then it will be comparatively

---

[30] For more discussion and empirical analysis of the roles played by the elasticity of demand for labor and other factors in determining the demand for unionism see Henry S. Farber and Daniel H. Saks, "Why Workers Want Unions: The Role of Relative Wages and Job Characteristics," *Journal of Political Economy,* 88:2 (April 1980), 349–69, and John H. Pencavel, "The Demand for Union Services: An Exercise," *Industrial and Labor Relations Review,* 22:2 (January 1971), 180–91.

cheap to form and maintain a union. The point here is that the regulations governing the formation and maintainance of unions are crucially important in positioning the supply curve of unionism. Changes in these restrictions over time, by affecting $S(U)$, will be seen to have an important impact on the amount of unionism in the United States.

The equilibrium amount of union services. The intersection of $S(U)$ and $D(U)$ determines the equilibrium amount of union services, $U(0)$. This is where the amount of unionism buyers wish to buy exactly matches the amount sellers wish to sell at a given price. It should come as no surprise that we will use the supply and demand model developed in Figure 7-12 to discuss how changes in the factors that underlie the supply and demand schedules affect the equilibrium amount of union services or unionism in society. But before we can perform such comparative statics analyses, we must first discuss how we will measure U, the quantity of union services.

We will view each union member as consuming one unit of union services of a given quality. In this case, U is equal to the total number of union members, and the per capita consumption of U is simply the percentage of the labor force that is unionized. The latter will serve as the variable of interest in our discussions to follow. You may be troubled by our empirical representation of the theoretical variable U. Truthfully, we know of no acceptable alternative; data on unions in the United States are just too scarce. In any event, if we understand differences in the incidence of union membership over time or among groups at a point in time, we will have gone a long way toward understanding the institution of unionism in the United States.

Before proceeding, it might be a good idea for you to construct a list of all the factors that shift the supply schedule and all the factors that shift the demand schedule in Figure 7-12. In the process, think about Marshall's rules, and how they are related to the demand for unionism. This should help you in understanding and using the model of supply and demand for union services to analyze the forces affecting union membership.

Union Membership Over Time

The year 1900 is a convenient place to begin examining union membership in the United States, because it marks roughly the beginning of modern American unionism. In particular, the American Federation of Labor (AFL) was formed about then. Two distinct trends appear in the data on union membership presented in Table 7-2. First, union membership grew from near zero to a high of approximately 26 percent of the labor force in the mid 1950s. Second, union membership has declined by about 4 percentage points since 1950. How do these two historical trends fit into the supply and demand model just developed?

TABLE 7-2   Union Membership as a Percentage of the Civilian Labor Force, 1900–1978

Year	(1) Union Membership—NBER Data* (percent of the total civilian labor force)	(2) Union Membership—BLS Data† (percent of the total civilian labor force)
1900	3%	—
1910	6	—
1920	12	—
1930	6	7%
1933	5	5
1940	13	16
1945	22	22
1950	22	22
1953	26	26
1960	22	24
1970	—	23
1978	—	20

* The series summarized in column 1 are from Leo Troy, *Trade Union Membership, 1897–1962*, National Bureau of Economic Research, Occasional Paper 92 (New York, 1965), p. 2. These data represent individuals paying dues to a union or individuals for whom dues were paid to a federation such as the AFL, the CIO, or the AFL-CIO. In general, these data were created by dividing unions' receipts by dues per full-time worker.
† The data summarized in column 2 are from *Historical Statistics of the United States, Colonial Times to 1970*, U.S. Department of Commerce, Bureau of the Census, Series D-949 and the *Statistical Abstract of the United States, 1980*, p. 429. These data have been collected by the Bureau of Labor Statistics largely from questionnaires requesting information on unions' average annual dues-paying membership. When the BLS and NBER figures are compared, the former are generally larger. For more discussion of the differences between the two sets of data, see *Historical Statistics*, pp. 157–58.

1900–1953.   Since 1900, Americans have generally been more accepting or tolerant of unions.[31] This was not the only factor at work, however. The growth of the industrial sectors in the economy and the decline in the importance of foreign labor are probably the principal reasons for the shifts in the supply and demand schedules that underlie the increase in union membership during 1900–1953. Let us elaborate on the three factors just mentioned.

World War I and federal legislation severely curtailed migration to the United States after about 1915. We noted earlier that this reduction in labor supply works to raise the wages of union labor. This raises the benefits of unionism and leads workers to demand more of it. Moreover, making it more difficult for foreign workers to enter the United States reduces the elasticity

---

[31] Of course, there are some exceptions to this, and we will be sure to point out the important ones.

of supply of immigrant labor. Marshall's fourth rule tells us that this, in turn, reduces the elasticity of demand for union labor, thus mitigating some of the employment losses union workers suffer because of union activities. The result is a rightward shift in the demand for unionism. Moreover, to the extent that immigrant labor was more costly to unionize, the reduction in immigration should also have lowered the cost of unionizing the United States work force.

We have also noted that there was a major change in the structure of the United States economy during this century. In particular, the proportion of the labor force employed in agriculture fell from about 36 percent in 1900 to about 12 percent in the early 1950s.[32] The demand for labor is probably more elastic in agricultural than in industrial production. Workers are also more dispersed and, therefore, costly to unionize when employed in agricultural production. Both of these facts mean that the shift in the structure of the work force from agricultural to industrial production should have reinforced the rightward movement in the demand for unionism and the downward movement in the supply (cost) of unionism illustrated in Figure 7-14.

The third key event contributing to the increase of unionization during 1900–1953 was the increased willingness of workers to join unions. This was mirrored in the changes in labor legislation occurring during this period. In particular, the **Norris-LaGuardia Act of 1932** greatly restricted employers'

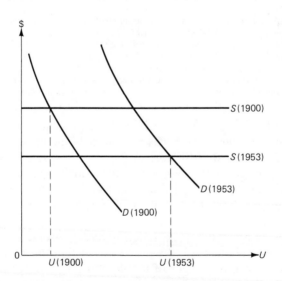

FIGURE 7-14. Union membership in the United States, 1900–1953

---

[32] *Historical Statistics of the United States, Colonial Times to 1970*, p. 27.

use of court injunctions as a weapon against union organization and collective bargaining. It also made legally unenforceable the so-called **yellow dog contract,** an agreement between employers and employees in which the latter consented not to join unions as a condition of employment. The **Wagner Act of 1935** ushered in the current era of labor legislation, establishing the **National Labor Relations Board** and defining unfair labor practices. The rights of workers to organize, bargain, and strike were given clear legal sanction, and the NLRB was established as a court for the settlement of many labor-management disputes. So there seems to be reasonably straightforward evidence that (1) the changes in the social environment surrounding unions and (2) the labor legislation of 1900–1953 served to increase unionization of the work force. The former led to an increased desire by workers to participate in or demand union activities and the latter lowered the cost of forming and maintaining unions.

Having identified the three key factors that seem to be responsible for the trend in union membership during the first half of this century, we now turn our attention to the trend in union membership since then.

1953–1978.   The 1950s saw the peak in union affiliation in the United States—26 percent in 1953. Since then, union membership as a fraction of the civilian labor force has fallen below its 1945 level. What caused the shifts in the supply and demand depicted in Figure 7-15?

Although the relatively high unemployment rates during much of the time since 1950 have probably played a role, other factors were also at work

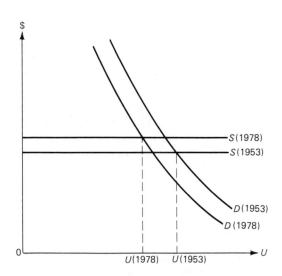

FIGURE 7-15. Union membership in the United States, 1953–1978

that were probably more important in increasing the cost of unionization and decreasing the demand for unionism. Included are changes in the occupational, industrial, and sex mix of the labor force.

White collar workers—defined as professional and technical workers, managers and administrators, sales workers, and clerical workers—tend to consider themselves more independent and more like self-employed workers than the more team-oriented **blue collar workers,** defined as craft workers, operatives, and nonfarm laborers. This means that white collar workers will also tend to want fewer collective activities in general and demand less unionism in particular. So, as the labor force becomes more white collar and less blue collar, the aggregate demand for unionism will shift to the left as depicted in Figure 7-15, because the demand for union services among white collar workers is lower than among blue collar workers. To try to get an idea of the importance of this shift in the occupational distribution, consider that between 1960 and 1970, blue collar workers decreased from about 41 percent of the labor force to about 33 percent.[33] Also note that during the late 1970s approximately 42 percent of all blue collar workers were union members and approximately 9 percent of all white collar workers were union members.[34] These two sets of facts imply that the 8-percentage-point decline in the proportion of blue collar workers in the labor force noted above would bring with it a 2.6-percentage-point decline in union affiliation for the labor force at large. This is approximately 65 percent of the *actual* percentage-point decline in union membership in the United States since 1960.

Recent estimates indicate that the percentage of the labor force unionized in **goods-related industries,** defined as mining, construction, and manufacturing, is almost three times greater (37.1 percent) than the percentage unionized in all other industries (13.4 percent), which are largely comprised of **service-related industries.**[35] One reason is probably that the demand for output by service-related industries is generally more elastic than that of goods-related industries. (Can you offer some reasons why?) Marshall's rules tell us that this should lead to a more elastic demand for the workers employed in service industries. Marshall's rules also tell us that the relative labor intensity of service industries further works to make the elasticity of demand for labor relatively greater there. All of this means that the demand for unionism will be less by service workers than by workers in goods-related industries. The result is that the shift in industrial composition of the United States labor force away from goods-related industries and toward service-related industries during 1960–80 also contributed to the reduction in

---

[33] *Statistical Abstract of the United States, 1980,* p. 418.
[34] Richard B. Freeman and James L. Medoff, "New Estimates of Private Sector Unionism in the United States," *Industrial and Labor Relations Review,* 32:2 (January 1979), 143–74.
[35] *Ibid.*

the aggregate demand for unionism depicted in Figure 7-15.[36] An additional subtlety is that there has also been a reduction in the fraction of the labor force unionized *within* the goods-producing industries. This has reinforced the impact of the shift in industrial composition we have been discussing. The reasons for the reduction in unionization within the goods-related industries remain an interesting unsolved research question.[37]

The relative growth of female employment since World War II is a third factor that may have contributed to the decline in union membership as a fraction of the labor force in the United States. Women comprised approximately 42 percent of the labor force in 1980 compared to only about 28 percent in 1947.[38] Over their lifetimes women have a smaller amount of full-time labor force participation than men because of child-rearing activities. Thus, they may be less inclined to join unions because of the relatively smaller benefit of *any* work-related activities, including unionism. This implies that the demand for unionism may be lower for women than for men. Moreover, unionism in the United States is a male-dominated institution; only about 24 percent of all union members are women.[39] It may also be true that union membership is relatively more "expensive" for women because men make it relatively more difficult for them to gain entry into the unions. This may take the form of subtle or overt sexual harassment or relatively strict requirements for women who try to join union-sponsored apprenticeship programs. The factors just mentioned will lead women to have a relatively lower demand for unionism and a relatively higher supply (cost) of unionism compared to men. In particular, recent estimates show that approximately 29 percent of males versus 14 percent of females belong to unions.[40]

In summary, as the labor force becomes more female over time, the aggregate supply and demand curves for unionism will exhibit the shifts depicted in Figure 7-15. It should be noted that the most important channels of influence seem to be through occupation and industry. That is, women are more likely than men to hold the types of jobs where workers, regardless of sex, are less likely to be union members.[41]

This completes our analysis of unionism in the United States over time. In addition to the substantial growth in union membership during 1900–1953

---

[36] In 1960 about 38 percent of all workers were employed in goods-related industries, in 1980 only 29 percent. See the *Statistical Abstract of the United States, 1980,* p. 411.

[37] Freeman and Medoff, "Private Sector Unionism," p. 174.

[38] *Statistical Abstract of the United States, 1980,* p. 394.

[39] *Ibid.,* pp. 429.

[40] Joseph R. Antos, Mark Chandler, and Wesley Mellow, "Sex Differences in Union Membership," *Industrial and Labor Relations Review,* 33:2 (January 1980), pp. 162–69.

[41] *Ibid.,* see also Farber and Saks, "Why Workers Want Unions," and Henry S. Farber, "The Determination of Union Status of Workers," Working Paper No. 299, Department of Economics, Massachusetts Institute of Technology, July 1982.

and the decline in union membership since 1953, two other dimensions of union membership in the United States are quite interesting. They are (1) the relationship between right-to-work laws and differences in unionism among the states and (2) the recent rapid growth of unionism among government employees. To these two topics we now turn our attention.[42]

Right-To-Work Laws and Differences in Unionism Among States

Section 14B of the **Taft-Hartley Act**, passed in 1947, permits states to pass what are known as **right-to-work laws.** Such laws typically prohibit any requirement that a person become a union member or refrain from becoming a union member in order to obtain or retain employment. If you look at the current *Statistical Abstract of the United States* or the article by Richard Freeman and James Medoff mentioned above (see footnote 34), you will see that in virtually all states with right-to-work laws, union membership as a fraction of the nonagricultural labor force is below the national average. Are we justified in concluding from this observation that right-to-work laws deter union affiliation? Our supply and demand analysis of union membership provides some interesting insights into this question.

There are two key things to have in mind when examining the behavioral impact of right-to-work laws, or any legislation such as minimum schooling requirements. They are: (1) whether or not the law is enforced and (2) who is responsible for the law's existence. In states where right-to-work laws are enforced, they raise the cost of providing union services because unions must allocate resources to *persuading* employees to join. In contrast, union membership is frequently a condition for continued employment in states without right-to-work laws, and such expenses are absent. So, a right-to-work law may shift upward the supply curve in our model of union membership. Of course, no shift will occur if the laws are not enforced. If this were all to the story, states where right-to-work laws are enforced would be characterized by an upward shift in the supply of unionism from $S(U)$ to $S(U)'$ in Figure 7-16, and unionism would be decreased from $U(0)$ to $U(1)$. However, right-to-work laws are enacted by popular vote or by a vote of a state legislature, which should reflect the popular will, at least to some extent. This means that right-to-work laws may also reflect anti-union senti-

---

[42] Readers interested in a formal econometric analysis of trade union membership over time in the United States using the supply and demand model presented in this section should consult Orley Ashenfelter and John H. Pencavel, "American Trade Union Growth: 1900–1960," *Quarterly Journal of Economics,* 83:3 (August 1969), 435–48. Those readers interested in more detailed descriptions of the history of trade unionism in the United States should consult Joseph G. Rayback, *A History of American Labor,* 2d ed. (New York: Free Press, 1966), and Foner, *American Labor Songs.* The last reading is especially recommended because much insight into the American trade union movement can be gained by examining the songs sung by union members at various times in our history.

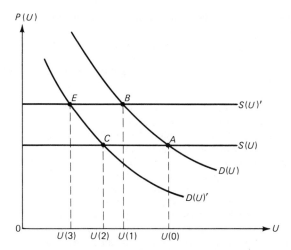

FIGURE 7-16. A right-to-work law and the supply and demand for union services

ment.[43] In other words, people who politically support right-to-work laws may also be unlikely to join unions, so in states where right-to-work laws are in effect, the demand for union services may also be lower. In terms of Figure 7-16, states with right-to-work laws are characterized by $D(U)'$ whereas states without the laws are characterized by $D(U)$.

The key point here is that when we observe states with right-to-work laws having relatively little unionism, we cannot infer from this information *alone* that the lower unionism is caused by extra costs of union services (the law itself). Notice that in Figure 7-16 points B, C, and E *all* lie to the left of A. Point C tells us that the law itself may have absolutely nothing to do with lower unionism in right-to-work states. Why? Before proceeding, make sure you understand how points A, B, C, and E correspond to the various situations where (1) the law is or is not enforced and (2) the law does or does not reflect the tastes and preferences of the state's workers toward unions.

An empirical analysis of right-to-work laws and union membership. Lumsden and Petersen attempt to separate empirically the demand (taste) effect from the supply (cost) effect of right-to-work laws. Specifically, they run regressions for 1939, 1953, and 1968 of the form

$$U = \alpha(0) + \alpha(1)R + \alpha(1)Z \tag{7-2}$$

[43] Keith Lumsden and Craig Petersen, "The Effect of Right-to-Work Laws on Unionization in the United States," *Journal of Political Economy,* 83:6 (December 1975), 1237–48.
* This section contains more technical material. If you skip, go to p. 263.

where $U \equiv$ percentage of a state's nonagricultural civilian labor force holding union membership

$R \equiv$ dummy variable capturing the eventual or actual presence of a right-to-work law in a state (yes = 1; no = 0)

$Z \equiv$ set of variables to control for exogenous shifts in the supply and demand for union services.[44]

In their regression for 1939, R represents whether a state would get a right-to-work law by 1968. Because no right-to-work laws were actually in existence in 1939, $\hat{\alpha}(1)$, the estimated value of $\alpha(1)$, should reflect *only* the relative demand (taste and preferences) for union membership. In the regressions for 1953 and 1968, $\hat{\alpha}(1)$ captures not only tastes and preferences concerning unions, but also any cost effect of right-to-work laws. If the relative tastes and preferences of workers for unionism changed little from 1939 to 1968, then the *difference* between the $\hat{\alpha}(1)$s for 1939 and 1953 and the *difference* between the $\hat{\alpha}(1)$s for 1939 and 1968 measure the cost effect of right-to-work laws during 1939–53 and 1939–68, respectively. Put differently, if the states comprised of workers who were relatively prone to join unions are the same in 1953 and 1968 as in 1939, so that the horizontal distance between $D(U)$ and $D(U)'$ is the same in 1939, 1953, and 1968, then the values of $\hat{\alpha}(1)$ for 1953 and 1968 estimate the horizontal distance AE in Figure 7-16. This means that [$\hat{\alpha}(1)$ for 1953 $-$ $\hat{\alpha}(1)$ for 1939] and [$\hat{\alpha}(1)$ for 1968 $-$ $\hat{\alpha}(1)$ for 1939] are estimates of the horizontal distance CE, which is the effect of the laws themselves, the so-called cost effect. Finally, because 1953 is fairly close to when states initially adopted right-to-work laws, comparing the two *differences* in the $\hat{\alpha}(1)$s tells us whether it took some time for the laws to have an effect.

Lumsden and Petersen find the estimated value of $\alpha(1)$ to be statistically less than zero in all three years. In the regression for 1939, $\hat{\alpha}(1)$ is -4.6. This means that in 1939, states that *would eventually* have right-to-work laws had 4.6 percentage points less union membership than states that would not adopt the laws, all other things being equal. Remember that because the laws did not actually exist in 1939, $\hat{\alpha}(1)$ for 1939 can be interpreted as reflecting only interstate differences in tastes and preferences for union services. The estimated value of $\alpha(1)$ from the regression for 1953 is about the same, -4.5. A comparison of the coefficients for 1953 and 1939 indicates no effect of the laws themselves.

What we are saying is that the data imply that $S(U)$ shifts little, owing to lax enforcement of the laws. This conclusion is reinforced by a comparison of $\hat{\alpha}(1)$ for 1968 (which takes on a value of -3.4) with $\hat{\alpha}(1)$ for 1939. Again the hypothesis that, on average, right-to-work laws themselves have little or no effect on union membership cannot be rejected. So, if the variables in Z adequately control for exogenous shifts in the supply and demand for union services, and the relative tastes and preferences for union membership among the states have not changed greatly over time, as seems reasonable, right-to-work laws themselves have little to do with interstate differences in unionism. States with such laws appear to be largely composed of people who are relatively less prone to join unions. This factor seems to underlie the difference in unionism among the states with and without the laws, *not the laws themselves.*

Before we leave the topic of right-to-work laws, we must make two additional

---

[44] Included are the percentage of the state's labor force that is nonwhite, female, engaged in manufacturing and mining, engaged in construction, and engaged in transportation-public utilities. Also included as an independent variable is the state's median wage and salary income. For a discussion of the magnitude and interpretation of the coefficients of these variables, see Lumsden and Petersen, "Right-to-Work Laws," pp. 1239–48.

points. First, because right-to-work laws have loosely coincided with the downward trend in unionism that began in the early 1950s, they have sometimes been blamed for this trend. The statistical analysis of Lumsden and Petersen seems to indicate that the laws have little to do with interstate differences in unionism and are, therefore, unlikely to have had any effect on the overall amount of unionism in the United States. Second, even though right-to-work laws seem to have little effect on union membership, they still represent an interesting *political* issue: whether or not someone should be compelled to affiliate with and to support economically an association desired by a majority of his peers.

Public Employee Unionism

In contrast to unions overall, public employee unions have grown quite rapidly in recent years. From 1956 to 1978, the number of government employees holding membership in unions or employee associations grew from 915,000 to 3,626,000.[45] The American Federation of State, County and Municipal Employees (AFSCME) in 1968 was the fourteenth largest labor union and in 1980 was the sixth largest union overall and the third largest union in the AFL-CIO. With these facts in mind, let us use our supply and demand analysis of union membership to examine (1) the cause of the recent rapid growth in government employee unionism, and (2) the reasons why government employees will tend to be highly unionized relative to employees in the private sector.

These issues are of social concern for a variety of reasons. As government employee unionism grows, so will the number of strikes by government workers, especially among municipal employees. The cessation of services that goes with those strikes can impose severe hardships on citizens, especially in the case of strikes by police, firefighters, or hospital workers. Some social scientists have even begun to worry about strikes by government workers in outer space, such as on space stations.[46] Second, as government employee unions gain membership, it is likely that they will also gain economic strength in achieving higher wages for their members. A number of localities, New York City and Cleveland in particular, have experienced severe financial difficulties during the 1970s. In some cases, unions were blamed for sharply rising operating costs, and proposals made for curbing their bargaining power. So the growth of government employee unionism may bring with it a spread of financial difficulties among municipalities.

The reasons behind the substantial growth in both the number and proportion of government employees holding union membership are fairly straightforward and need only be noted. One is that the proportion of the total nonagricultural labor force that works in state and local governments

---

[45] Albert Rees, *The Economics of Trade Unions*, rev. ed. (Chicago: The University of Chicago Press, 1977), p. 182, and *Statistical Abstract of the United States, 1982*, p. 409.

[46] Mark M. Hopkins, "The Economics of Strikes and Revolts During Early Space Colonization: A Preliminary Analysis," The Rand Corporation, Report P-6324, April 1979.

almost doubled between 1945 and 1980.[47] Moreover, recent legislation at both the federal and state levels has legitimized unionization of government employees.[48] Although strikes are still generally prohibited, other changes in the labor laws make government employees more similar to private employees in their ability to form and maintain unions. This has reduced the cost of unionization for government employees. In terms of our supply and demand analysis, this leads to a downward shift in the supply curve of government employees' unionism, resulting in an increase in the fraction of public employees unionized.

More subtle, and perhaps more interesting, is the issue of why in many cases public employees will be more highly unionized than their private sector counterparts. Our discussions in Chapter 3 lead us to expect a relatively low elasticity of demand for labor of government employees. One reason is that much of the output of government is services such as police and fire protection, education, garbage collection, and public health. Although not impossible, the substitution of capital for labor is relatively difficult in many services. For example, except for some increased use of visual aids and computers, the process of classroom teaching is not all that different now than it was in the days of the one-room schoolhouse. In general, we still have a teacher lecturing and writing on a chalkboard observed by a group of note-taking students. It is difficult to believe that ignorance on the part of administrators, featherbedding by teachers, or prohibitively high prices of capital have kept the educational process so labor-intensive for so long. Instead, it is more likely that substitutions of other inputs for teacher services have generally been unsuccessful. Anyone who has taken a "tube course" at a large state university knows what we mean. The point is that when the substitution of other inputs for labor is relatively difficult, elasticity of demand for labor is relatively low; this in turn leads to a relatively high demand for *unionism*. The demand for the labor of government employees is also relatively inelastic because many things that governments supply are, by nature, inelastically demanded. Although taxpayer revolts do occur, it takes a rather drastic tax increase before the public is willing to reduce by very much its consumption of, say, police protection. This is another reason to expect a relatively inelastic demand for labor by governments and a relatively large demand for union services by government workers.

Figure 7-17 presents what we think is a reasonable general picture of supply and demand differences for unionism in the government versus the private sector. Because of a generally greater elasticity of demand for labor, the demand for unionism in the private sector is less than in the public sector. Because public sector unions do not have all the rights and privileges of private sector unions, particularly the right to strike, the cost of providing union services of a given quality will be somewhat higher in the public sector. This is reflected by the supply curve differences in Figure 7-17. So

---

[47] Northrup, *Labor Relations*, p. 762.
[48] For details see *ibid.*, pp. 776–787.

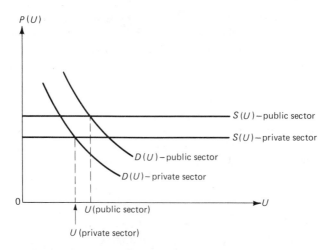

FIGURE 7-17. The supply and demand for unionism in the public and private sectors

the configuration of supply and demand curves in Figure 7-17 is for the situation where, despite the higher cost of unionism, the public sector has greater union membership as a proportion of total employment than the private sector.

In closing, two other points are worth noting. First, as public sector workers get more and more of the collective bargaining rights and privileges of private sector workers, as seems likely in the future, the relative benefits of membership in a government employees' union will grow. The result should be an increase in the demand for unionism in the government sector that further widens the public-private sector gap in unionism. Second, while Figure 7-17 is *generally* correct, it does not characterize *every* individual situation. A prime example is that of PATCO, the air-traffic controllers' union that became defunct in the early 1980s. Because it was relatively easy to substitute nonunion air-traffic controllers for PATCO members, and because there was a plentiful supply of trainees at the going wage rate, the demand for the labor of the air-traffic controllers was relatively elastic. So the PATCO strike of 1981 was a complete failure from the perspective of workers, in the sense that the federal government was able to make a wholesale substitution of nonunion controllers for union controllers and put the union out of business.

MEASURING THE ECONOMIC EFFECTS OF UNIONS

We now seek to quantify some of the economic benefits of union membership in the United States. Moreover, we will attempt to identify some of the effects unions have on the economic well-being of nonunion workers in particular and society in general. To be a knowledgeable citizen who can make sensible decisions concerning the public regulation of union activities, you need to know how the benefits and the costs of unionism are distributed among the various groups in society.

Wages

Our theoretical analysis of the formation of unions is built on the premise that workers join unions to improve their wages and working conditions. Is it really true, though, that union workers get higher wages than they would otherwise? This is probably the basic economic issue concerning the institution of unionism. Unfortunately, it is also probably the one about which labor economists have the least empirical knowledge. The presence of a significant number of union workers in the labor force alters the structure of wages in a way that eliminates the benchmark necessary to address this issue simply and straightforwardly. That is to say, in order to conclude that unionism has changed the wage rate of union members, we really need to know what their wages would have been were there no unions. However, because unions also influence the wage rates of *nonunion* workers, the wages of nonunion workers cannot serve as a measure of union workers' wages in the absence of unions.[49]

Economists do, however, have rather extensive and reasonably reliable information on the wage rates of union workers *relative to* the wage rates of similar nonunion workers. This is an important issue for two reasons. First, differential wage rates for similar workers means that society is foregoing some GNP because too little labor is being used in the relatively high-wage sectors of the economy and too much labor in the relatively low-wage sectors. Second, from the standpoint of social policy it is important that we know whether the institution of unionism causes some groups of individuals to gain income relative to others. We will return to these issues in the course of this section.

Studies of relative wage effects prior to 1960 compare the wage rates of workers in industries or occupations differing in extent of unionism, adjusting for the influence of factors other than unionism. Typical measures of unionism include the proportion of the occupation or industry belonging to unions or the share of the industry's or occupation's total wages that is paid to union members. Most of these early studies of relative wage effects have been collected, made comparable, and summarized by H. Gregg Lewis in his

---

[49] Of course, it is possible to examine *theoretically* the issue of whether workers are better off after unionizing. For an eloquent, albeit complex, analytical treatment of this topic see W. E. Diewert, "The Effects of Unionization on Wages and Employment: A General Equilibrium Analysis," *Economic Inquiry,* 12:3 (September 1974), 319–39. As you should expect, the effect of unions on wages of union versus nonunion workers depends on the properties of the production functions in the union and nonunion sectors and the properties of the utility functions of union and nonunion workers.

classic work, *Unionism and Relative Wages in the United States.*[50] It is beyond the scope of this book to examine in any detail the wealth of information presented by Lewis. We encourage you to do that on your own.[51] Instead, we discuss at some length three recent studies of relative wage effects.

*The union-nonunion wage gap in recent years.   In his paper, "Union Relative Wage Effects: New Evidence and a Survey of Their Implications for Wage Inflation,"[52] Orley Ashenfelter utilizes cross-sectional data for individual workers from the Survey of Economic Opportunity (SEO) and the Current Population Surveys (CPS) to examine wage differentials between union and nonunion workers during 1967, 1973, and 1975. There are a number of benefits to using these disaggregated data. One is that they contain detailed, accurate measure of workers' personal attributes and job characteristics. Thus, Ashenfelter is able to purge his estimates of some omitted variable biases present in studies where this information is not available. For example, labor market experience helps to determine an individual's earning capacity and is also typically correlated with union status. If, in statistically examining the difference between the wages of union and nonunion workers, a researcher ignores differences in labor market experience, part of the union-nonunion wage gap will be incorrectly attributed to union activity rather than to the fact that the two groups of workers differ in labor market experience. (Based on what you learned in Chapter 2, will the wage gap be overestimated or underestimated if the role of experience is ignored?) Moreover, the SEO and CPS contain enough data to permit rather precise estimates of how the union's relative effect varies by race, sex, industry, and occupation.

Ashenfelter's empirical results come from separate linear regressions for black males, white males, black females, and white females for each of the three years mentioned above. The form of his regression equation permits estimated union relative wage effects to vary across occupations for white collar workers and to vary across both occupations and industries for blue collar workers. To see how this is done, let us suppose that there were only two industries, call them 1 and 2, and two occupations, blue collar and white collar. In addition, suppose all workers were of the same race and sex and there were only one personal trait influencing wages, called X. Finally, suppose that the particular mathematical equation describing how a labor market translates an individual's amount of X, union status, industry of employment, and occupation into earning capacity were

$$W_t = \tilde{\alpha}(0)e^{[\alpha(1)X_t + \alpha(2)U_t \cdot O_{wt}) + \alpha(3)(U_t \cdot O_{Bt} \cdot I_{1t}) + \alpha(4)(U_t \cdot O_{Bt} \cdot I_{2t})]} \qquad (7\text{-}3)$$

where $W_t \equiv$ average hourly earnings of individual t
$e \equiv$ base of natural logarithms
$X_t \equiv$ personal characteristic of individual t
$U_t \equiv$ dummy variable (= 1 if individual t is a union member)
$O_{wt} \equiv$ dummy variable (= 1 if individual t is a white collar worker)

[50] Chicago: University of Chicago Press, 1963.
[51] A useful summary of the Lewis volume is "Unionism and Relative Wages in the United States," in John F. Burton, Jr., et al., eds., *Readings in Labor Market Analysis* (New York: Holt, Rinehart and Winston, 1971), pp. 438–76.
[52] In Richard Stone and William Peterson, eds., *Econometric Contributions to Public Policy* (London: Macmillan; New York: St. Martin's Press, 1978).

* This section contains more technical material. If you skip, go to p. 269.

$O_{Bt} \equiv$ dummy variable (= 1 if individual t is a blue collar worker)

$I_{1t} \equiv$ dummy variable (= 1 if individual t is employed in industry 1)

$I_{2t} \equiv$ dummy variable (= 1 if individual t is employed in industry 2)

$\tilde{\alpha}(0)$, $\alpha(1)$, $\alpha(2)$, $\alpha(3)$, $\alpha(4) \equiv$ constants (parameters).[53]

Fortunately, we can make equation (7-3) much less formidable by taking its natural logarithm, yielding

$$\ln W_t = \alpha(0) + \alpha(1)X_t + \alpha(2)(U_t \cdot O_{wt}) + \alpha(3)(U_t \cdot O_{Bt} \cdot I_{1t}) + \alpha(4)(U_t \cdot O_{Bt} \cdot I_{2t}) \tag{7-4}$$

where ln $W_t \equiv$ natural logarithm of average hourly earnings of individual t and $\alpha(0) \equiv$ ln $\tilde{\alpha}(0)$.

Equation (7-4) simply says that the natural logarithm of an individual's average hourly earnings is linearly related to his or her union status, personal traits (X), industry of employment, and occupation. To understand the meaning of this expression, let us consider two individuals. Both are white collar workers. Both are identical, except that one belongs to a union and the other does not. If we denote the logarithm of average hourly earnings for the first person by ln W_1 and for the second person by ln W_2, equation (7-4) tells us that

$$\ln W_1 - \ln W_2 = \alpha(2) \tag{7-5}$$

It is not difficult to show that when (W_1/W_2) is between about 1.0 and 1.15, $(\ln W_1 - \ln W_2)$ is *approximately* equal to $[(W_1 - W_2)/W_2]$. Thus, $\alpha(2)$ is approximately the proportionate difference between the wages of union and nonunion white collar workers. (For an exact method, see Chapter 2, pp. 41–44.) By similar reasoning, $\alpha(3)$ is approximately the proportionate difference in wages for blue collar workers employed in industry 1 and $\alpha(4)$ the difference for blue collar workers employed in industry 2.

The regression equation actually utilized by Ashenfelter to estimate values for the αs is much more complex than (7-4). Numerous personal characteristics such as education and marital status are included, along with six industrial classifications, five white collar occupational classifications, and three blue collar occupational classifications. The point to remember, though, is that with regression equations *in the spirit of* (7-4), Ashenfelter estimates union/nonunion wage gaps by occupation for those workers classified as white collar (professional, managerial, sales, clerical, service) and by occupation and industry for those workers classified as blue collar (craft, operative, laborer). Finally, his analysis looks at the four possible race-sex pairings *separately* for 1967, 1973, and 1975.

Because Ashenfelter presents over 260 estimates of wage differentials, it would be useful if we could capture the essence of his findings in fewer than 260 sentences. Probably the best way to do this is to examine the average wage gap for each of the four race-sex groups and for society as a whole. To see how such figures are created, return to equation (7-4), which is a simplified version of Ashenfelter's wage-generating equation for a particular race-sex group. The weighted sum of the estimated values of $\alpha(2)$, $\alpha(3)$, and $\alpha(4)$, where the weights are the fraction of white collar workers, the fraction of blue collar workers in industry 1, and the fraction of

---

[53] The reasoning behind this particular mathematical expression is developed in Chapter 8. At this point it may also prove useful to review the discussions in Chapter 2 on parameters, functions, and logarithms.

blue collar workers in industry 2, respectively, is the estimated average proportionate union/nonunion wage differential for that race-sex group. Remember that there can be *different* values of $\alpha(1)$, $\alpha(2)$, and $\alpha(3)$ for white males, black males, white females, and black females. The weighted sum of the estimated values of the 12 αs, where the weights are the fractions of the total labor force falling into the particular race-sex-occupation-industry categories, is the economywide average proportionate union/nonunion wage differential. Figures calculated this way by Ashenfelter are in Table 7-3. A number of interesting situations emerge. First, females seem to obtain about the same relative benefit from unionism as white males. Second, the relative benefits of unionism appear to be relatively large for black men. Third, the relative benefits of union membership are reasonably stable in recent years for black men and white women, while they appear to be increasing somewhat for white men and substantially for black women. This leads to an upward trend in the overall average union/nonunion wage gap.[54] It should be mentioned, however, that this last result may be due to the set of general economic conditions in the United States from 1967 to 1975. Ashenfelter notes that during this period the unemployment rate rose rather steadily from 3.8 percent to 8.5 percent. If, as we suspect, union contracts make wages in the unionized sectors of the economy less responsive to aggregate demand conditions than in the nonunion sectors, then the proportionate union/nonunion wage differential will increase or decrease as the overall unemployment rate rises or falls.

Estimated union/nonunion wage differentials: Three recent refinements. The estimates of wage differences between union and nonunion workers presented in Table 7-3 were constructed by calculating the proportionate wage differential between the two groups of workers at a point in

TABLE 7-3 Proportionate Union/Nonunion Wage Differentials by Race and Sex, 1967, 1973, 1975*

		Males		Females	
Year	All Workers	White	Black	White	Black
1967	0.116	0.096	0.215	0.144	0.056
1973	0.148	0.155	0.225	0.127	0.132
1975	0.168	0.163	0.225	0.166	0.171

* All entries are more than twice their estimated standard errors.

Source: Orley Ashenfelter, "Union Relative Wage Effects: New Evidence and a Survey of Their Implications for Wage Inflation," in Richard Stone and William Petersen, eds., *Econometric Contributions to Public Policy* (London: Macmillan; New York: St. Martin's Press, 1978). Reprinted by permission of The International Economic Association and Macmillan, London and Basingstoke.

---

[54] For a survey of the empirical literature on the type of union/nonunion wage differentials estimated by Ashenfelter see C. J. Parsley, "Labor Unions and Wages: A Survey," *Journal of Economic Literature,* 18:1 (March 1980), 1–31.

time, controlling for many of the labor market factors related to wages *other than unionism*. Recent research by Greg Duncan and Frank Stafford[55] attempts to shed further light on the exact nature of these earnings differences. In particular, they wish to decompose the earnings differences into two sources: (1) that portion due to the monopoly power of unions which enables them to raise wages above their competitive level and (2) that portion due possibly to the fact that union workers tend to have worse jobs in terms of working conditions. To the extent that union jobs are on average more dirty, unpleasant, or unsafe, part of the union/nonunion wage differential may be the compensation workers receive for these undesirable aspects of employment. In other words, unionism may also function much like a competitive labor market that establishes higher wages to offset unpleasant aspects of the workplace. On the other hand, our discussions in Chapter 5 showed us the undesirable aspects of the inefficiency that occurs when equally qualified workers with equally pleasant or unpleasant jobs receive *unequal* rates of pay. So, the research of Duncan and Stafford can basically be characterized as an attempt to "parcel out" the wage impact of unionism into its monopoly versus competitive elements.

Stafford and Duncan utilize data for 149 blue collar workers, both male and female, from the 1975–76 Time Use Survey done by the University of Michigan's Survey Research Center. This survey consists of four interviews designed to gather detailed data on how adults allocate their time. The particular information they use comes from the second interview, taken during May and June of 1976.

Duncan and Stafford run two general sets of regressions. First, they look at the impact of unionism, ceteris paribus, with a regression equation similar to the one discussed in the last section. They then rerun this regression with variables that control for working conditions. Included are variables measuring the amount of break time, effort, and tedium involved in the work. When working conditions are ignored, so that the results are analogous to those presented in Table 7-3, Duncan and Stafford find a union/nonunion wage differential of 24 to 28 percent. When characteristics of the workplace are included, so that the estimated union/nonunion wage effect has its "competitive aspects" netted out, they find a 17 percent wage differential that is *not* statistically significant. Because of the rather small sample size in their analysis, the results of Stafford and Duncan should probably best be considered as suggestive. However, they certainly seem to indicate that more research is needed to determine whether the so-called monopoly impact of unionism is indeed as large as the estimates presented in Table 7-3.

Whereas Duncan and Stafford suggest that the difference in wages among union versus nonunion workers may be overstated by the numbers in

---

[55] "Do Union Members Receive Compensating Wage Differentials?" *American Economic Review*, 70:3 (June 1980), 355–71.

Table 7-3, Richard Freeman[56] offers us a reason why unions' impact on wages may be *understated* by these figures. Freeman reminds us that the wage differentials in Table 7-3 do not include an impact of unions on fringe benefits. If, in fact, unions raise fringe benefits for their workers relative to nonunion workers, then the simple difference in gross hourly wages understates the impact of unionism on the *full* wage rate. By combining data from the Current Population Survey with data from the Expenditures for Employee Compensation Survey of the Bureau of Labor Statistics, Freeman is able to examine the effect of unions on fringes and total hourly compensation.

During the period covered by Freeman's data, 1967–72, fringe benefits averaged about 50 cents per hour. This was approximately one-seventh of total compensation per hour. He finds that, *ceteris paribus*, unionism raises fringe benefits—especially life, accident, and health insurance, pensions, and vacation and holiday pay. In particular, unions increased fringes by about 10 cents per hour. This means that union workers were found to receive, on average, approximately 21 percent higher fringe benefits per hour than similar nonunion workers. Freeman finds that when he examines *total compensation* per hour, the union/nonunion difference is 17.3 percent.[57] So, while Stafford and Duncan raise the possibility that the figures in Table 7-3 may overstate unionism's impact, Freeman illustrates another potential bias, one that works in the *opposite* direction.

Finally, it is possible that the set of individual characteristics contained in Ashenfelter's regressions underlying the results in Table 7-3 do not adequately control for ability or quality of worker. This means that there may be a systematic unmeasured difference in worker productivity that contaminates the estimate of the union/nonunion wage differential. Let us elaborate in some detail. If a union is successful in raising the wage rate above its competitive level, an employer then has the incentive to try to offset the increased labor cost somewhat by hiring relatively high-quality workers. Suppose that in using regression analysis to examine union/nonunion wage differences, productivity differences between union and nonunion workers are not adequately measured by the independent variables. In this case part of the estimated union/nonunion wage differential is really a worker quality difference rather than collective bargaining effect of unionism. This is known as **selectivity bias,** in the sense that workers who are union members have been systematically selected into those jobs because of their relatively high quality but this factor is not accounted for in the statistical analysis. The result is a bias in the estimates of the union/nonunion wage difference.

---

[56] "The Effect of Unionism on Fringe Benefits," *Industrial and Labor Relations Review,* 34:4 (July 1981), 489–509.

[57] When differences in simple straight-time pay per hour are calculated, Freeman finds a proportionate difference of 14.8 percent for 1967–72. This is exactly the figure in the first column of Table 7-3 for 1973.

If all of this seems somewhat complicated, there is perhaps a simpler way to think about it. The results presented in Table 7-3 compare the wage rate of union to nonunion workers in a given year, holding constant personal characteristics that economists think (1) are related to productivity and earnings and (2) can be measured by data sets currently available. This is much different than performing a controlled experiment where a nonunion worker suddenly becomes a union worker, all other things are held constant, and the resulting wage difference is measured. This latter wage differential would be the true effect of unionism on wages. In the regressions underlying Table 7-3 the wage change a worker receives from joining a union is inferred from wages of *different* individuals, some who belong to unions and others who do not. However, workers who become unionized may have systematic differences in traits that cannot be measured, such as good luck, ability, or labor market "connections." This means we can never be *sure* that the measured wage differences between union and nonunion workers are not partly, or perhaps totally, the result of things that have little to do with the collective bargaining process. In the absence of a controlled experiment, what can be done to improve the likelihood that the estimated union relative wage effects are the result of unionism and not of systematic, but unmeasured, differences in workers?

Jacob Mincer[58] uses regression analysis in a clever way to refine our estimates of what unions do to wages. Mincer utilizes two of the micro data sets described in Chapter 2, the Panel Study of Income Dynamics (PSID) of the University of Michigan and the National Longitudinal Survey (NLS) of The Ohio State University. These are detailed surveys of individuals in the United States over time. The PSID is sufficiently extensive to allow examination of wages and unionization over a ten-year period, 1968–78. The NLS permits similar study, although over a much shorter period, 1969–71. Mincer limits his analysis to white men, so as to avoid issues of labor market discrimination, and divides them into two groups, young (less than 30) and old (over 30 years of age). By looking at the *change* in wages for workers, Mincer statistically eliminates the influence of unmeasured personal characteristics that do not change over time. These are known as **fixed effects.** For example, if someone is relatively intelligent, this will be reflected in his or her wage level at a point in time. Intelligence typically is not accurately measured and is excluded from regression analyses of union/nonunion wages. As a result, the statistical effect of intelligence is "distributed" to other variables. Because intelligence does not change that much over time, its effect is "netted out" if wage *changes* are considered, however. Mincer's results for the young men from the NLS show that those workers who joined unions during 1969 to 1971 experienced approximately an 18 percent in-

---

[58] "Union Effects: Wages, Turnover, and Job Training," Working Paper, Columbia University and National Bureau of Economic Research, August 1981.

crease in their wage rate (net of inflation) over and above similar workers who remained nonunion during that period. The wage gain was only about 7 percent for older men during this period.

Are these figures the relative wage effect of unions? Not exactly. Remember that the primary way individuals join unions is to change employers. Mincer recognizes the need to distinguish between the wage growth that comes from moving to a *better* job and that which comes from moving to a *unionized* job. How can this be done? The simplest way is first to measure the wage growth of nonunion workers who switched jobs during this period, but remained *nonunion* throughout. These workers experienced a wage growth of about 4 percent. This means that workers who switched jobs, other factors the same, experienced about a 4 percent wage growth, while workers who both switched jobs *and* switched from nonunion to union status experienced a wage growth of about 18 percent. The *difference* (14 percent) is an estimate of the net effect of becoming a union member. Mincer's estimates for older workers from the NLS for 1969–71 show a net wage growth from joining a union equal to about 10 percent. These figures are not much different from the ones in Table 7-3.

As an additional check on the wage effects of unionism, Mincer examines the "flip side" of the issue, whether or not individuals who *leave* unions suffer wage *reductions*. He finds that among younger workers, those who left unions during 1969–71 suffered a real wage reduction of about 26 percent compared to similar workers who remained nonunion throughout. To obtain an estimate of the effect of leaving the union, net of switching jobs, this figure should be compared to what happened to those individuals who were nonunion throughout but switched jobs during this period. Workers who remained nonunion but switched jobs, remember, had a wage *growth* of about 4 percent. Thus, young workers who left the union during 1969–71 suffered about a 30 percent wage loss due to the switch in union status. Mincer's estimates show a net real wage loss of about 5 percent for older workers who left unions.

Because the Panel Survey of Income Dynamics covers a ten-year period, Mincer is able to examine whether the results discussed in the preceding paragraph hold over a longer period. The union wage effects estimated from the PSID are generally smaller than those from the NLS reported above. Among younger workers, Mincer found a net annual wage gain from joining a union of only about 5 percent. Older workers seemed to gain only about 3 percent per year. The net real wage loss of those younger workers who left unions is about 7 percent on average per year during 1968–78. The wage loss is approximately zero for older workers.

We have just discussed three pieces of recent research that attempt to refine our knowledge of the union/nonunion wage differential. Owing to data limitations, the biases suggested by Stafford and Duncan, Freeman, and Mincer cannot all be eliminated in a single statistical analysis. In the next section we need estimates of the union/nonunion wage gap to discuss some of the economywide effects of unions. We will use the results in Table 7-3. However, you should keep in mind the possible biases in these estimates of unions' relative wage effects that we have identified in this section.

The effect of unions on earnings over the life cycle. To this point our discussions of unions' impact on wages have been limited to a comparison of union/nonunion wage differentials at a point in time or to how wages change after individuals join unions. If you think of someone's lifetime earning power as a motion picture of labor market experiences, the two measures of a union's impact we have just discussed come from freezing a frame of this motion picture. Although evidence is far from plentiful, there have been some recent attempts to examine how unions affect earning power over the lifetime of a representative individual.

In this case the crucial question is whether unions change the shape of an individual's age-earning power profile or merely shift it up parallel to where it would have been. Cross-sectional analyses seem to indicate a flattening. This is implicit in Mincer's results just cited. There, the measured union impact was far smaller for the older workers than for younger workers, so as to imply a convergence of the profiles. At first glance, this convergence would seem to indicate that unions flatten the age-earning profile.

Remember, though, that union and nonunion workers may comprise quite heterogeneous groups. If this is the case, then it may not be unions that flatten the profiles, but rather unmeasured characteristics that cause individuals to join unions in the first place. However, if a researcher has enough data, *given* individuals can be followed over a period of time long enough to observe their age-earnings profile before and after they shift from nonunion to union status. In this way, the lifetime wage effects of unionism can be discerned somewhat more accurately.

Hutchins and Polachek[59] adopt this approach to measure the impact of unions on the shape of the earnings profile. They use a regression analysis where individuals are followed over time. Their dependent variable is the logarithm of earnings. Among their independent variables is an interaction term, which is the product of union membership and chronological time. This interaction term indicates whether union membership steepens or flattens the profile, *ceteris paribus,* for individuals who change union status. (Age, education, experience, and job tenure are held constant.) Unlike findings from cross-sectional data, those of Hutchins and Polachek indicate no ascertainable flattening of the age-earnings profile. Instead, an insignificant, though positive, effect of unionism is found on the slope of the age-earnings profile among both union joiners and union leavers. In short, unions may

---

[59] Michael T. Hutchins and Solomon W. Polachek, "Do Unions Really Flatten the Age-Earnings Profile? New Estimates Using Panel Data," paper presented at the Eastern Economic Association Meetings, Washington, D.C., May 1982.

actually steepen age-earnings profiles. Try to think of some reasons why this might be the case.

National Income

In Chapter 5 we saw that whenever the wages received by similar workers are not equal, society would obtain increased production (national income) from its limited set of resources if more labor were to flow into the high-wage sectors of the economy and less into the low-wage sectors. We have just seen that unionism is one force producing such wage differentials, although they are not outrageously large. There has been little analysis of the severity of the aggregate income loss in the United States due to the union/ nonunion wage gap except for that by Albert Rees.[60] With data on union/ nonunion wage differentials for 1957, Rees estimates that society lost at least $1.3 billion (0.3 percent) of GNP through the effects of unions on the intra-industry and the interindustry wage structures. In addition, he feels that the loss due to unions' restrictive working practices was at least that large. The result was a total social cost stemming from the resource misallocation effects of unions in 1957 of approximately $2.6 billion, or 0.6 percent of GNP.[61]

Because it is rather difficult to interpret this figure in isolation, consider that in 1957 there were approximately 67 million workers in the United States labor force. This means that the social cost of unionism stemming from resource misallocation was approximately $39 per worker. This is equivalent to $114 per worker in 1980 dollars. So, on a per worker basis the loss is quite small. However, it is important to point out that the loss we have just been discussing is what economists call a **deadweight loss.** By this we mean everyone in society could be better off if it were eliminated.

In terms of the pie analogy of Chapter 5, we are saying that if the resource misallocation effects of unionism were eliminated, the pie representing society's total income would increase in size. More importantly, this increase would be sufficient to increase the slices received by *everyone*, union and nonunion workers alike. Thus, the $2.6 billion GNP loss could have been used to fight poverty. For example, it would have been enough to bring 520,000 poor families out of poverty by giving them $5,000 apiece, quite a large sum in 1957. This could have been done with no loss to *anyone*, including union members.

Why, then, don't we eliminate the union/nonunion wage differentials through public policy and in the process make everyone better off? Or why

---

[60] Albert Rees, "The Effects of Unions on Resource Allocation," *The Journal of Law and Economics*, 6:2 (October 1962), 69–78.
[61] As an exercise, read Rees' article and make similar calculations of the economic loss with more recent data. All the figures you will need are contained in the *Statistical Abstract of the United States* and the first column of Table 7-3.

don't we fight poverty without cost to the nonpoor, including union members? First, from a technical standpoint the set of taxes and subsidies to accomplish these outcomes are probably quite difficult to design and implement. Second, put yourself in the shoes of a typical union member. Would you find it easy to believe a policymaker who told you that everyone, yourself included, could be made better off if the union-nonunion wage gap were eliminated? It is these rather substantial practical and political difficulties that most surely have prevented the implementation of such a seemingly desirable economic policy.[62]

*FRONTIERS OF LABOR ECONOMICS: THE SECOND FACE OF UNIONISM

Our focus in the main body of this chapter has been on unions' effects on wages and the implications of these effects for wage equality and economic efficiency. Another dimension of unionism has been referred to as **unions' second face**—their impact on the nonwage aspects of the workplace. An article by Richard Freeman and James Medoff[63] presents an especially clear statement of these more subtle impacts of unions on the workplace. We close this chapter by discussing some aspects of the second face of unionism. Because it generally refers to activities of unions that can be thought of as socially desirable, the second face of unionism is an especially interesting area of research.

Unions as a Collective Voice

Our discussion of the "first face" of unionism in the main body of this chapter can best be thought of as an examination of the monopoly effects of unions that stem from their ability to limit access to employment, raising wages in the process. The second face of unionism has to do with the fact that unions are also a *collective voice* for workers. By this we mean that when workers form and participate in a union, they tend to reach a consensus over their desired wages, working conditions, and hopes for future relations with their employer. The subtle implications of unionism for resource allocation, the second face of unionism, stem from the more intimate involvement workers may have in the management of their jobs when they speak as one rather than as separate individuals.

In a competitive labor market, workers tend to indicate dissatisfaction with their jobs by quitting. Because of severance pay and the cost of hiring and training a replacement, it can be very costly for a firm to learn that it has unsatisfactory wages or working conditions through workers quitting. Freeman and Medoff point out that a union establishes a *long-term* relationship with the firm where union workers speak as a group, rather than as individuals who may be singled out for retribution. As a result, union workers are more inclined to voice a complaint or grievance over their working conditions before they take the relatively drastic step of quitting. Thus, a unionized firm may find out quite easily that it needs to improve its wages or working

---

[62] For more discussion of the optimal public regulation of trade union activities, see H. Gregg Lewis, "The Labor-Monopoly Problem: A Positive Program," *Journal of Political Economy,* 59:4 (August 1951), 277–87.

[63] "The Two Faces of Unionism," *The Public Interest,* 57 (Fall 1979), 69–93.

* This section contains more technical material. If you skip go to p. 280.

conditions in order to retain workers. It is much more costly to obtain such information by deducing it from statistics on worker turnover, as is typically the case in nonunion firms. Freeman and Medoff also cite the possible productive effects of a unionized workforce being more stable owing to reduced employee quits.

Other dimensions of the second face of unionism stemming from collective-voice effects are enumerated in the lower portion of Table 7-4. This table also describes the dimensions of unionism's so-called first face, its monopoly effects.

Let us make sure we understand the point being made above and in Table 7-4. It is that in order to really understand unions we need to understand *both* its faces. In the main body of the chapter we have examined unionism's first, or monopoly, face. We have just seen the second face of unionism in that union workers speak collectively rather than individually in their relationships with employers. We now turn our attention to some of the most recent research on the second face of unionism. We focus on some effects of unions that are readily quantifiable and tend to increase economic efficiency.

The Impact of Unions on Employment Stability

We know that union-induced wage differentials and featherbedding lead to resource misallocation and reduced output for society. One possible offset to this is that unionism reduces worker quits because, rather than exiting the firm, workers voice complaints through a formal grievance process. This in turn reduces hiring and training costs and disruptions due to employee turnover.

In two recent articles, Richard Freeman[64] assembles an impressive amount of econometric evidence that, ceteris paribus, unions reduce the probability of a worker's quitting and increase job tenure as measured by years on the job with the current employer. One impressive aspect of Freeman's research is that this result appears in four different micro data sets, even after the impact of unionism on wages is held constant. It is important to control statistically for the higher wages due to unionism, because they may also induce workers to quit less and stay on their jobs longer. Freeman's research indicates that the probability of a union worker's quitting is approximately 33 to 100 percent below that for a nonunion worker with similar characteristics. Job tenure is approximately 15 to 40 percent higher among union than nonunion workers, other factors held constant. To help interpret these effects you should realize that the average probability of a union worker's quitting is approximately 5.8 percent compared to 9 percent for other workers. Job tenure among union workers is approximately 9 to 10 years, compared to 6 to 7 years for other workers.[65]

Two important, related issues are (1) whether unions, while reducing quits and increasing job tenure, perhaps prevent employers from discharging relatively unproductive employees or (2) whether union workers are absent more frequently from their jobs. Steven Allen presents evidence that absenteeism differs little between union and nonunion workers, ceteris paribus.[66] Freeman examines the impact of unions, ceteris paribus, on what are called other separations. These include discharges and permanent layoffs.[67] His results indicate *no* negative effect of unions on

---

[64] "The Exit-Voice Tradeoff in the Labor Market: Unionism, Job Tenure, Quits and Separations," *Quarterly Journal of Economics,* 94:4 (June 1980), 643–74, and "The Effect of Unionism on Worker Attachment to Firms," *Journal of Labor Research,* 1:1 (Spring 1980), 29–62.
[65] Freeman, "The Exit-Voice Tradeoff," p. 658.
[66] "An Empirical Model of Work Attendance," *Review of Economics and Statistics,* 63:1 (February 1981), 77–87.
[67] Freeman, "Worker Attachment."

TABLE 7-4 The Two Faces of Unionism

	Union Effects on Economic Efficiency	Union Effects on Distribution of Income (Equity)	Social Nature of Union Organization
The First Face: Monopoly Effects	Unions raise wages above competitive wage levels, which leads to too little labor relative to capital in unionized firms. Union work rules decrease productivity. Unions lower society's output through frequent strikes.	Unions increase income inequality by raising the wages of highly skilled workers. Unions create horizontal inequities by creating differentials among comparable workers.	Unions discriminate in rationing positions. Unions (individually or collectively) fight for their own interests in the political arena. Union monopoly power breeds corrupt and non-democratic elements.
The Second Face: Collective-Voice Effects	Unions have some positive effects on productivity—by reducing quit rates, by inducing management to alter methods of production and adopt more efficient policies, and by improving morale and cooperation among workers. Unions collect information about the preferences of all workers, which leads the firm to choose a "better" mix of employee compensation and a "better" set of personnel policies. Unions improve the communication between workers and management, leading to better decision making.	Unions' standard-rate policies reduce inequality among organized workers in a given company or a given industry. Union rules limit the scope for arbitrary actions concerning the promotion, layoff, recall, etc., of individuals. Unionism fundamentally alters the distribution of power between marginal (typically junior) and inframarginal (generally senior) employees, causing union firms to select different compensation packages and personnel practices than nonunion firms.	Unions are political institutions that represent the will of their members. Unions represent the political interests of lower-income and disadvantaged persons.

Source: Adapted from Richard B. Freeman and James L. Medoff, "The Two Faces of Unionism," *The Public Interest*, 57 (Fall 1979), 75.

these forms of separations. In short, unionism's impact on tenure seems to operate through workers' decisions rather than through employers' decisions.

Finally, Freeman takes extra care to be reasonably sure that unionism, and not some unmeasured variable correlated with unionism, underlies the statistical associations between unionism and (1) quits and (2) job tenure. We noted earlier that he controls for union wage effects when looking at the impact of unionism on employment stability. In addition, he employs sophisticated statistical techniques to control for the possibility that workers who are less prone on average to quit their jobs may also happen to join unions somewhat more frequently. Put differently, Freeman takes care to show that unions probably change worker behavior rather than simply including workers who are less likely to quit in the first place. Freeman presents interesting evidence, for example, that existence of a grievance processing system increases job tenure.

To summarize, unionism seems to increase employment stability by reducing quits and increasing workers' willingness to stay with a given employer. In addition, the positive effect of unionism on job tenure seems to be the result of worker behavior rather than of reduced layoffs by the firm.[68]

Why Are Managers Opposed to Unions, Then?

This section has focused on subtle economic benefits that unionism may bring to the workplace. An issue that seems natural to raise, then, is why managers are generally not more favorable toward unionism.

One possibility is that unionization makes managers' jobs more difficult because they must share their decision-making power with workers. Because the benefits of any subtle effects of unionism go to others, the stockholders, while the costs of unionization go directly to the managers, this may be one reason for management's opposition to unions. A second possibility raised by Freeman and Medoff is that managers are short-sighted, looking only at the present or set-up costs of unionism that occur today and ignoring the benefits of unionism that may accrue in the future. The argument we like best is that unionism must be considered as a *package,* which sometimes includes restrictive working practices and wage increases along with any positive effects on productivity and worker tenure. What this means is that unionization entails both costs and benefits to the firm and that the cost to the firm may outweigh the benefit.

One of the most interesting aspects of recent research on the two faces of unionism, as typified by the work of Freeman and Medoff, is the attempt to create an economic balance sheet for the institution of unionism. Although not all the entries have yet been made in the assets and liabilities columns, management opposition to unions suggests that unions probably bring greater costs than benefits to the firms. An important, related issue is the optimal public regulation of trade union activity. If one were to design the perfect policy toward trade unions, it would be a set of laws and regulations that provided the incentives for unions to minimize their inefficiency-producing relative wage effects and maximize their efficiency-enhancing effects discussed in this section.[69]

---

[68] See also James L. Medoff, "Layoffs and Alternatives Under Trade Unions in U.S. Manufacturing," *American Economic Review,* 69:3 (June 1969), 380–95.

[69] An interesting treatment of the optimal public regulation of unions is contained in H. Gregg Lewis, "The Labor Monopoly Problem: A Positive Program," *Journal of Political Economy,* 59:4 (August 1951), 277–87.

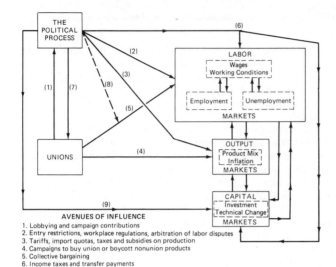

AVENUES OF INFLUENCE
1. Lobbying and campaign contributions
2. Entry restrictions, workplace regulations, arbitration of labor disputes
3. Tariffs, import quotas, taxes and subsidies on production
4. Campaigns to buy union or boycott nonunion products
5. Collective bargaining
6. Income taxes and transfer payments
7. Laws which regulate union organizing
8. Programs which affect union bargaining power
9. Investment tax incentives

FIGURE 7-18.
The interaction
between unions
and the economy

CONCLUSIONS

In this chapter we have examined the determination of wages and employment when workers have their mutual interests represented by labor unions. Our goal has been to identify the avenues through which unions affect the economy and, in the process, affect the economic well-being of society and the distribution of well-being among groups within society. Figure 7-18 summarizes our general findings.

To understand the role played by unions in the United States economy, we examined the variety of techniques they use to try to improve wages and working conditions. First and foremost is bargaining, backed by the possibility of a strike. We devoted considerable effort to describing the wage and negotiation process, paying special attention to the divergent preferences of the three parties involved—union leaders, the union rank and file, and employers. We saw that most strikes are of relatively short duration and yield a settlement rather close to the union's desired outcome. We also examined the role for outside intervention in the form of binding arbitration, including the way in which such arbitration may or may not encourage bargaining by the parties directly involved in the labor dispute. Also interesting are the subtle methods used by unions to reduce the supply of labor or increase the demand for workers' services. These include political support of particular kinds of legislation, licensing, and campaigns to buy products made by union workers or boycott products made by nonunion workers.

Our knowledge of the economic and political activities of unions gave us insight into the trends in union membership in the United States over time and across states and industries. We saw that a union will be more successful in increasing the economic welfare of its members the more inelastic is the labor demand schedule. As a result, unions will tend to form where the elasticity of demand for labor is relatively low and engage in activities aimed at diminishing the elasticity of demand for union labor. More generally, the

280

fraction of the labor force affiliated with unions depends on the relative benefits of union activities enjoyed by members, the relative tastes and attitudes of workers toward union membership as such, and the relative costs of union activities. These notions proved useful in interpreting the effect of right-to-work laws on union affiliation across states, interdecade movements in overall union membership in the United States, sex differences in union membership, and the recent growth of government employees' unions.

The effect of unions on wage rates is one of the first topics given serious empirical attention by labor economists. Recent data on the earnings and personal attributes of large numbers of workers have facilitated reasonably precise estimates of the earning power of union workers relative to their nonunion counterparts. Depending upon race and sex, econometric estimates place the wages of union workers approximately 6 to 22 percent higher than those of nonunion workers. To go with these benefits of union membership to union workers are some costs to the rest of society. Crude calculations indicate a GNP loss due to union-induced resource misallocation of about 0.6 percent, or approximately $4 billion based on current GNP calculations.

In the final section of this chapter we examined some very recent research on the nonwage effects of unions. We saw that unions seem to have a positive impact on employment stability through reducing worker quits and increasing the amount of time the average worker spends with a given employer. It is interesting that this research also seems to indicate that the increase in employment stability is not the result of a reduction in employers' ability to fire or lay off workers. Rather, it appears to stem from an increased willingness on the part of workers to stay with an employer because of the ties to the job established by the collective activities of unions.

The real importance of the research on unions' second face is to point out some activities of unions that are socially desirable, serving to offset the resource misallocation effects stemming from unions' so-called first or monopoly face. If one could devise the perfect public policy toward unions, it would be to reduce their adverse economic effects while preserving their activities that have the potential of increasing the economic well-being of union and nonunion workers alike.

REFERENCES AND SELECTED READINGS

ALLEN, STEVEN, "An Empirical Model of Work Attendance," *Review of Economics and Statistics,* 63:1 (February 1981), 77–87.

ANTOS, JOSEPH R., MARK CHANDLER, AND WESLEY MELLOW, "Sex Differences in Union Membership," *Industrial and Labor Relations Review,* 33:2 (January 1980), 162–69.

ASHENFELTER, ORLEY, AND JOHN H. PENCAVEL, "American Trade Union Growth: 1900–1960," *Quarterly Journal of Economics,* 83:3 (August 1969), 435–48.

———, AND GEORGE E. JOHNSON, "Bargaining Theory, Trade Unions, and Industrial Strike Activity," *American Economic Review,* 59:1 (March 1969), 35–49.

———, "Racial Discrimination and Trade Unionism," *Journal of Political Economy,* 80:3, Pt. I (May/June 1972), 435–64.

———, "Union Relative Wage Effects: New Evidence and a Survey of Their Implications For Wage Inflation," in Richard Stone and William Peterson, eds., *Econometric Contributions to Public Policy.* London: Macmillan; New York: St. Martin's Press, 1978.

ATHERTON, WALLACE N., *Theory of Union Bargaining Roles.* Princeton, N.J.: Princeton University Press, 1973.

BARTOS, OTOMAR J., *Process and Outcome of Negotiations.* New York: Columbia University Press, 1974.

BLOOM, GORDON F., AND HERBERT R. NORTHRUP, *Economics of Labor Relations.* Homewood, Ill.: Richard D. Irwin, Inc., 1981.

BURTON, JOHN F., JR., et al., *Readings in Labor Market Analysis.* New York: Holt, Rinehart and Winston, 1971.

BUTLER, RICHARD J., AND RONALD G. EHRENBERG, "Estimating the Narcotic Effect of Public Sector Impasse Procedures," *Industrial and Labor Relations Review,* 35:1 (October 1981), 3–20.

CLARK, KIM B., "The Impact of Unionization on Productivity: A Case Study," *Industrial and Labor Relations Review,* 33:4 (July 1980), 451–69.

CROSS, JOHN G., *The Economics of Bargaining.* New York: Basic Books, 1969.

DAVIS, MORTON D., *Game Theory, A Nontechnical Introduction.* New York: Basic Books, Inc., 1970.

DERTOUZOS, JAMES N., AND JOHN H. PENCAVEL, "Wage and Employment Determination Under Trade Unionism: The International Typographical Union," *Journal of Political Economy,* 89:6 (December 1981), 1162–80.

DIEWERT, W. E., "The Effects of Unionization on Wages and Employment: A General Equilibrium Analysis," *Economic Inquiry,* 12:3 (September 1974), 319–39.

DULLES, FOSTER RHEA, *Labor in America: A History,* 3d ed. New York: Crowell, 1966.

DUNCAN, GREG, AND FRANK STAFFORD, "Do Union Members Receive Compensating Wage Differentials?" *American Economic Review,* 70:3 (June 1980), 355–71.

FARBER, HENRY S., "An Analysis of Final-Offer Arbitration," *Journal of Conflict Resolution,* 24:4 (December 1980), 683–705.

———, "Bargaining Theory, Wage Outcomes, and the Occurrence of Strikes: An Econometric Analysis," *American Economic Review,* 68:3 (June 1978), 262–71.

———, "Does Final-Offer Arbitration Encourage Bargaining?" *Proceedings of the 33rd Winter Meeting of the Industrial Relations Research Association, 1980,* 219–26.

―――――, "Splitting-the-Difference in Interest Arbitration," *Industrial and Labor Relations Review,* 35:1 (October 1981), 70–77.

―――――, "The Determination of Union Status of Workers," Working Paper no. 299, Department of Economics, Massachusetts Institute of Technology, July 1982.

―――――, AND DANIEL H. SAKS, "Why Workers Want Unions: The Role of Relative Wages and Job Characteristics," *Journal of Political Economy,* 88, no. 2 (April 1980), 349–69.

Featherbedding and Technical Change. ed. Paul A. Weinstein, Boston: D.C. Heath and Co., 1965.

FONER, PHILIP S., *American Labor Songs of the Nineteenth Century.* Urbana, Ill.: University of Illinois, 1975.

"Food Faddists," *The Wall Street Journal,* February 22, 1977, p. 1.

FREEMAN, RICHARD B., AND JAMES L. MEDOFF, "New Estimates of Private Sector Unionism in the United States," *Industrial and Labor Relations Review,* 32, no. 2 (January 1979), 143–74.

―――――, "The Effect of Unionism on Fringe Benefits," *Industrial and Labor Relations Review,* 34, no. 4 (July 1981), 489–509.

―――――, "The Effect of Unionism on Worker Attachment to Firms," *Journal of Labor Research,* 1:1 (Spring 1980), 29–62.

―――――, "The Exit-Voice Tradeoff in the Labor Market: Unionism, Job Tenure, Quits and Separations," *Quarterly Journal of Economics,* 94:4 (June 1980), 643–74.

―――――, AND JAMES L. MEDOFF, "The Impact of the Percentage Organized on Union and Nonunion Wages," *Review of Economics and Statistics,* 63:4 (November 1981), 561–72.

―――――, AND ―――――, "The Two Faces of Unionism," *The Public Interest,* 57 (Fall 1979), 69–93.

―――――, AND ―――――, "The Impact of Collective Bargaining: Illusion or Reality?" in Jack Stieber, et al., eds., *U.S. Industrial Relations 1950–1980: A Critical Assessment.* Madison, Wisconsin: The Industrial Relations Research Association, 1981.

―――――, "Unionism and the Dispersion of Wages," *Industrial and Labor Relations Review,* 34:1 (October 1980), 3–23.

GOLDFARB, ROBERT S., AND JOHN F. MORRALL III, "The Davis-Bacon Act: An Appraisal of Recent Studies," *Industrial and Labor Relations Review,* 34:2 (January 1981), 191–206.

"Hold the Phone," *The Wall Street Journal,* November 29, 1977, p. 1.

HOPKINS, MARK M., "The Economics of Strikes and Revolts During Early Space Colonization: A Preliminary Analysis," The Rand Corporation, Report P-6324, April 1979.

HUTCHINS, MICHAEL T., AND SOLOMON W. POLACHEK, "Do Unions Really Flatten the Age-Earnings Profile?'' Working Paper, University of North Carolina, Department of Economics, June 1981.

KAU, JAMES B., AND PAUL H. RUBIN, "Voting on Minimum Wages: A Time-Series Analysis," *Journal of Political Economy,* 86:2, part 1 (April 1978), 337–42.

KENNAN, JOHN, "Pareto Optimality and the Economics of Strike Duration," *Journal of Labor Research,* 1:1 (Spring 1980), 77–94.

KILLINGSWORTH, MARK R., "Union-Nonunion Wage Gaps and Wage Gains: New Estimates from an Industry Cross-Section," forthcoming in *Review of Economics and Statistics.*

"Labor Seeks Less," *Business Week,* December 21, 1981, pp. 82–88.

LAZEAR, EDWARD P., "A Competitive Theory of Monopoly Unionism," Working Paper No. 672. Cambridge, Mass.: National Bureau of Economic Research, May 1981.

LEWIS, GREGG H., "The Labor-Monopoly Problem: A Positive Program," *Journal of Political Economy,* 59:4 (August 1951).

———, *Unionism and Relative Wages in the United States.* Chicago: University of Chicago Press, 1963.

LUMSDEN, KEITH, AND CRAIG PETERSEN, "The Effects of Right-to-Work Laws on Unionization in the United States," *Journal of Political Economy,* 83:6 (December 1975), 1237–48.

MAURIZI, ALEX, "Occupational Licensing and the Public Interest," *Journal of Political Economy,* 82:2, part 1 (March–April 1974), 399–413.

MEDOFF, JAMES L., "Layoffs and Alternatives Under Trade Unions in U.S. Manufacturing," *American Economic Review,* 69:3 (June 1979), 380–95.

MINCER, JACOB, "Union Effects: Wages, Turnover, and Job Training," Working Paper, Columbia University and National Bureau of Economic Research, August 1981.

PARSLEY, C. J., "Labor Unions and Wages: A Survey," *Journal of Economic Literature,* 18:1 (March 1980), 1–31.

PENCAVEL, JOHN H., "The Demand for Union Services: An Exercise," *Industrial and Labor Relations Review,* 22:2 (January 1971), 180–91.

RAYBACK, JOSEPH G., *A History of American Labor,* 2d ed. New York: The Free Press, 1966.

REES, ALBERT, *The Economics of Trade Unions,* rev. ed. Chicago: The University of Chicago Press, 1977.

———, "The Effects of Unions on Resource Allocation," *Journal of Law and Economics,* 6:2 (October 1962), 69–78.

SHIMBERG, BENJAMIN, et al., *Occupational Licensing: Practices and Policies.* Washington, D.C.: Public Affairs Press, 1973.

SILBERMAN, JONATHAN I., AND GAREY C. DURDEN, "Determining Legislative Preferences on the Minimum Wage: An Economic Approach," *Journal of Political Economy,* 86:2, part 1 (April 1978), 337–42.

"Sizzling Cinema?" *The Wall Street Journal,* October 28, 1975, p. 1.

"State Licensed Occupations Get More Criticism, But the System is Defended As Insuring Quality," *The Wall Street Journal,* June 14, 1977, p. 48.

The National Economy 1977, a pamphlet reprinted from the National Economy section of the *Report of the Executive Council of the AFL-CIO to the Twelfth Convention.* Los Angeles, December 1977.

TROY, LEO, *Trade Union Membership, 1897–1962,* Occasional Paper 92. New York: National Bureau of Economic Research, 1965.

U.S. DEPARTMENT OF COMMERCE, BUREAU OF THE CENSUS, Series D-949, *Historical Statistics of the United States, Colonial Times to 1970.*

————, *Statistical Abstract of the United States,* 1980.

URI, NOEL D., AND J. WILSON MIXON, JR., "An Economic Analysis of the Determinants of Minimum Wage Voting Behavior," *Journal of Law and Economics,* 23:1 (April 1980), 167–78.

WILLIAMS, J. D., *The Complete Strategist.* New York: McGraw-Hill Book Company, 1966.

EXERCISES

Choose whether statements 1, 2, and 3 are *True, False,* or *Uncertain* (whether true or false depends on unspecified circumstances). Justify your answer. Your justification is the most important part of your answer.

1. "Right-to-work" laws have probably not been an important factor contributing to the decline of union membership (as a fraction of the labor force) since the 1950s.

2. On average, United States labor unions have raised the wage rates of their members about 15 percent.

3. It is possible for unions to raise the relative wage rates of their members while lowering their real wage rates.

4. In discussing the collective bargaining process we learned the main ideas behind *free* collective bargaining and strikes. Explain and show graphically why strikes occur.

5. Data for the United States indicate that states with right-to-work laws also have below-average unionism. Suppose that the Supreme Court were suddenly and unexpectedly to declare right-to-work laws unconstitutional. What effect would this have on union membership? Support your answer with the appropriate graph(s).

*6. The following statement was overheard at a meeting of a women's group: "We should support the institution of unionism because it helps women achieve earning power parity with men." Use the data below to comment on this statement.

Fraction of Race/Sex Group in Unions				Proportionate Union/Nonunion Wage Differential			
White		Black		White		Black	
Male	Female	Male	Female	Male	Female	Male	Female
0.30	0.10	0.40	0.20	0.20	0.10	0.25	0.15

* Indicates a more difficult exercise.

8

LONG-RUN LABOR SUPPLY:
Human Capital
and the Household

---

* Indicates more technical material that can be skipped without loss of continuity.

In Chapter 4 we considered short-run labor supply decisions: whether or not to participate in the labor force, and if so, how many hours to work. In Chapter 5 we developed a concept of competitive labor market equilibrium in which all workers tend to earn the same wage, once working conditions are accounted for. More realistically, even if we do not take into consideration noncompetitive influences such as product market monopoly, labor market monopsony, or labor unions, wage rates vary. Individual workers earn different amounts because they have acquired different skills and different amounts of training, have completed different amounts of schooling, have made decisions to move from one labor market to another, have different endowments of ability, and vary in health and strength. All these variables affect labor *quality*. In the long run, the appropriate measure of the quantity of labor supplied must reflect the *quality* of labor as well as hours of work.

In this and the next chapter we focus on long-run labor supply decisions. Some of the most important ones are how much schooling to obtain, whether to take a low-paying job that offers training opportunities and the promise of future wage increases, and whether to change place of residence to obtain higher earning potential. Clearly, such long-run labor supply decisions are extremely important determinants of individual and family economic welfare. In order to obtain maximum economic well-being, individuals choose whether to incur direct costs such as tuition as well as indirect costs of lower current earnings, moving expenses, and the inconvenience of looking for a new job in order to reap future benefits. Since long-run labor supply adjustments involve *current* costs, but *future* returns, they are **investments,** and the theory of long-run labor supply is therefore the theory of decisions to invest in **human capital.**

Investments in human beings may take many forms, but it is useful to divide our discussion between those that take place on the job, as part of market work activity, and those acquired elsewhere. Job-associated investments in human capital consist mainly of formal and informal training programs that take place within firms. Alternatively, schooling, health care, and job search primarily involve activities with which one's employer has much less direct involvement. Changing one's place of residence to obtain a better job sometimes means advancement within a given firm but often goes with a change of employer; migration, therefore, is sometimes an on-the-job investment activity and sometimes not. Schooling and health care, too, sometimes take place on the job. This chapter deals with investments in human capital that are usually made by households away from the workplace. Chapter 9 treats investments occurring within firms.

A moment's thought should reveal that anyone who is interested in the fundamental determinants of wealth, its distribution, and government efforts to improve the lot of the poor must understand the process of investment in human capital. One can then better understand the answers to important economic and social questions: Why do some individuals earn more than others? Who has access to the most desirable jobs? Why do some children finish college while others drop out of high school? Why do blacks earn less than whites and women less than men?

More than 70 percent of national income in the United States consists of wages and salaries.[1] Similar magnitudes prevail in other industrialized nations. For example, in 1979, the share of salaries and wages in domestic national income was 0.67 in Japan and 0.80 in the United Kingdom.[2] Thus, the distribution of economic benefits among individuals can largely be analyzed in terms of the distribution of returns to investments in human capital. Government policies on unemployment, health, and schooling are much less likely to achieve their desired goals if they are not designed with consideration of their impact on human investments and returns. The theory of investment in human capital not only helps us to understand individual long-run labor supply decisions, but it can also serve as a useful guide for governmental decisions concerning society's allocation of scarce resources to develop human productive capacity.

THE HOUSEHOLD INVESTMENT FRAMEWORK

Labor supply decisions that have consequences over several years can best be understood by means of the theory of human capital. At first it may seem morally wrong or factually incorrect to speak of human beings as though they were merely machines, but nothing (im)moral or (un)ethical is implied in discussing human capital. The subject matter is quite appropriate for situations in which workers have complete freedom of choice in their labor market decisions. In fact, the law that human capital can only be "owned" by the person in whom it is embodied is an important factor making the theory of human capital distinct from conventional capital theory—and more interesting. Whether the theory is considered correct can be decided only on the basis of whether it is useful in helping us to understand labor markets and related topics.

Utility and Wealth

The theory of human capital requires, first of all, an assumption about the individual's, or family's, goals in deciding whether to choose more or less human investment and in selecting among alternative types. As noted before, human capital investment includes health, schooling, and geographical mobility, as well as choices among occupations such as becoming a

---

[1] See the *Statistical Abstract of the United States,* 1980, Table 737.
[2] United Nations *Yearbook of National Account Statistics,* 1979, Vol. II, Table 5.

doctor or a dentist or a lawyer. Fundamentally, the behavioral goal we assume in human capital theory is identical to that postulated for the short-run theory of labor supply in Chapter 4—*utility maximization*. Frequently, maximizing utility in human capital decisions boils down to the simpler concept of deciding which choice will produce the greatest *wealth*.

Suppose, for example, that someone were deciding whether to attend school for one additional year and that attending school itself were neither bad nor good in itself. Moreover, suppose that the jobs one could expect to obtain with one more year of schooling were no more or less pleasant than those obtainable without the additional education. Then, it would certainly seem reasonable to choose more schooling if, and only if, the monetary benefits were expected to exceed the monetary costs. Under these circumstances, utility maximization implies wealth maximization. Wealth maximization provides a much simpler basis upon which to analyze human capital investment decisions than utility maximization.

Of course, every job has many characteristics in addition to its rate of pay. The nonmonetary qualities of jobs do have pecuniary equivalents, however, insofar as individuals are prepared to accept wage premiums in the case of unpleasant job characteristics or lower rates of pay in the case of pleasant ones. For example, construction workers who helped build the Alaska oil pipeline were willing to put up with extreme cold, long work weeks, and a poor social life in return for extraordinarily high pay and good meals provided by their employer. However, some job attributes that make a line of work unattractive for one worker, such as frequent travel, may be just what appeals to another, so that, on average, many nonpecuniary aspects of human capital investments cancel out. Thus, for the population at large wealth maximization is likely to be a fairly good starting point in developing a useful theory of human capital.

Another reason for using wealth maximization as a good approximation to utility maximization is that many applications of human capital theory deal with responses to *changes* in *monetary aspects* of labor market alternatives. For example, consider the effects of reducing government funding of low-interest loans to medical school students. This would raise the *costs* of becoming a physician. Individual *tastes* for being a medical doctor would not be affected, nor would such nonmonetary aspects of physicians' work such as the pleasure or displeasure of treating sick people, dealing with individuals in need of assistance, and so on. However, the prospective gains in wealth to anyone planning to enter medical school would be smaller, and wealth maximization would be a sufficient assumption for predicting a decline in decisions to choose medicine as a career. Because it is much simpler, without requiring that we sacrifice a lot of realism, throughout most of this chapter and the next we will treat wealth maximization as a good approximation to utility maximization in the theory of human capital.

Present Value

Wealth maximization means obtaining one's largest net money return in the labor market over the long run. What does this imply? Often, discussions of the total amount of earnings in alternative occupations take the form of urging young people to continue their education because high school degrees may add, say, $100,000 to total lifetime earnings. Yet maximization of total lifetime earnings may not lead to wealth maximization, because the $100,000 is not gained without cost. One reason why someone may hesitate to acquire additional schooling is that even if the tuition is "free," the *opportunity cost* of more education is by no means zero. Market earnings must be sacrificed while attending school, and unless a sizable scholarship is available, these foregone earnings must be subtracted from future income gains. Even at Ivy League schools with tuition of, say, $10,000 per year, a student's full cost of a year of college will consist more than half of foregone earnings. Suppose you had entered the job market right out of high school. You would probably be earning considerably more than $10,000 per year now. These are earnings that most high school graduates must forego while attending college. But even if the net gain is positive, this would not necessarily mean that acquiring more schooling would increase wealth, because a dollar received in the future does not have the same weight in calculating the net returns to a long-run labor market choice as a dollar's cost paid in the present. One of the essential features of the theory of investment and capital, both human and physical, is the role of time—the comparison of *future* and *present* dollars.

Suppose you are interested in maximizing your monetary wealth and you face two alternatives: (1) to repay a $10,000 debt immediately, or (2) to repay the same debt one year from now. Which alternative do you choose? If you think about it carefully, you will choose the second. If you already have the $10,000, you can place it in a savings account or invest it for a year and earn interest—say, 10 percent. Thus, one year from now you can pay the $10,000 debt and have $1,000 left over. Alternatively, you could put a little over $9,000 in the bank now and spend the remainder; a year from now you would have $10,000 in your account that could be used to satisfy your creditors. The same considerations apply to the choice between being paid $10,000 today versus one year hence. If you receive the money now, you can earn a year's interest on it that you would not receive if the payment of $10,000 occurred a year from now. To summarize, your wealth will be larger to the extent you can *postpone* expenditures and *accelerate* receipts, other things equal.

As long as there is a positive interest rate, decisions among economic alternatives must consider the timing of costs and returns. A dollar today is worth more than a dollar tomorrow. A simple technique for evaluating costs and returns occurring through time is invaluable in deciding among investment alternatives so as to maximize wealth. This technique expresses the value of a future expenditure or receipt in terms of an equivalent amount paid out or received today. The value today of a future receipt or expenditure is called its **present value.** By expressing monetary amounts that occur in the future in terms of their present values, we have a valid means of comparing costs and returns that accrue over a period of years. In terms of the example we started with, if the rate of interest were 10 percent, it would be necessary to put only $9,090.91 in a savings account today in order to make a $10,000 payment one year hence. In other words, if interest is paid once each year, the *present value* of $10,000 to be paid (or received) one year from today is $9,090.91 or $10,000 $(1 + r)^{-1}$, where r, the rate of interest, is 0.10.

Consider the alternative of repaying the $10,000 debt two years from now. What is the present value of $10,000 two years hence? We follow the same procedure as above. If you have $10,000 now, you can save it, earning $1,000 the first year, if the interest rate is 10 percent. The second year, if you let the interest accumulate, you will earn $1,000 plus $100 (10 percent on the first year's $1,000 interest), or $1,100. Thus, you could repay the debt at the end of two years and have $2,100 left. The longer you can delay repaying the debt, the better off you are; the present value of the $10,000 debt is smaller, the further away the date of repayment. This is because the longer you can wait before paying out the $10,000, the smaller the sum of money you have to set aside today in order to have $10,000 when the debt is due. In our example, in order to have $10,000 two years from now, you have to set aside today only $10,000 $(1 + 0.10)^{-2}$ or $8,264.46. In general, the present value of $10,000 to be paid or received in two years is $10,000$(1 + r)^{-2}$. Suppose more than one payment or receipt is involved. The present value of $10,000 next year *plus* $10,000 the following year is the *sum* of their individual present values, or $10,000$[(1 + r)^{-1} + (1 + r)^{-2}]$.

The present-value concept is easily applied to long-run labor market choices. Consider an individual faced with deciding between two occupations. One of them, which we will call Y, requires two additional years of schooling but promises a greater future income than the other occupation, which we will call X. Assume that the individual is *already* capable of doing X without further education or training and that the occupations are equally "pleasant." Thus, the only choice here is to choose the occupation that yields the greatest present value. Suppose the direct cost of additional schooling required to gain access to occupation Y (tuition, books, and so on) is zero and that part-time work is available that yields $1,000 income in each year while attending school. The net income in each year for the two occupations is shown in Table 8-1, which for illustrative purposes is limited to six years.

Which occupation will provide the greatest present value—that is, maximize the individual's wealth? In Table 8-1 it is obvious that the available

TABLE 8-1 Income Received and Present Values in Occupations X and Y at Various Interest Rates

| | Net Income | | Present Value | | | | | | | |
| | | | $X_j(1+r)^{-i}$ | | | | $Y_j(1+r)^{-i}$ | | | |
Year (j)	(1) X	(2) Y	(3) r = 0	(4) r = 0.05	(5) r = 0.20	(6) r = 0.25	(7) r = 0	(8) r = 0.05	(9) r = 0.20	(10) r = 0.25
0	$10,000	$ 1,000	$10,000	$10,000	$10,000	$10,000	$ 1,000	$ 1,000	$ 1,000	$ 1,000
1	10,000	1,000	10,000	9,524	8,333	8,000	1,000	952	833	800
2	10,000	18,000	10,000	9,070	6,944	6,400	18,000	16,327	12,499	11,520
3	10,000	18,000	10,000	8,638	5,787	5,120	18,000	15,549	10,417	9,216
4	10,000	18,000	10,000	8,227	4,822	4,096	18,000	14,809	8,680	7,373
5	10,000	18,000	10,000	7,835	4,018	3,277	18,000	14,103	7,232	5,899
Sum	$60,000	$74,000	$60,000	$53,294	$39,904	$36,893	$74,000	$62,740	$40,661	$35,809

income in occupation X exceeds that in Y during years 0 and 1, but that the reverse holds during years 2 through 5. Moreover, the simple sum of the annual incomes in Y exceeds that in X by $14,000. If the interest rate (r) were zero, these simple sums would in fact also be the present values of the earnings yielded by each occupation, as a comparison of columns (3) and (7) with columns (1) and (2) shows. Columns (4) and (8) show how to determine the present value of the earnings in X and Y when the interest rate $r = 5$ percent. Column (4), for example, shows that the present value of X's $10,000 earnings during the initial year is $10,000.[3] However, the present value of the second payment of $10,000 (as of the date when the occupational choice is made) is $10,000(1.05)^{-1} = $9,524$. The present value of the third payment is $10,000(1.05)^{-2} = $9,070$, and so on. The *sum* of the present value of X's earnings through year 5, if $r = 0.05$, is the present value of alternative X at a 5 percent rate of interest and equals $53,294. This is shown at the bottom of column (4).

To generalize, we calculate present value of occupation X's earnings $PV(X)$ by computing the present value of each year's income and summing. Denoting each year's earnings as X_j, where the index j represents the year during which income is received (starting from the present, $j = 0$),

$$PV(X) = \sum_{j=0}^{5} X_j(1 + r)^{-j} \qquad \text{(8-1)}$$

Similarly, the present value of future earnings in occupation Y is

$$PV(Y) = \sum_{j=0}^{5} Y_j(1 + r)^{-j} \qquad \text{(8-2)}$$

As Table 8-1 shows, whether X or Y is the most advantageous occupation (whether X or Y offers the earnings stream with the greatest present value) depends not only on the net earnings in each year, but also on the rate of interest. The wealth-maximizing decision is to choose occupation Y at relatively low rates of interest. But when the rate of interest equals 25 percent, the present value of future earnings in occupation Y is less than that of occupation X, and the net economic advantage belongs to occupation X.

In this example, the only cost of choosing occupation Y is the earnings foregone during the two years of schooling required. Foregone earnings constitute an *indirect cost* of choosing occupation Y. *Direct costs* include outlays for tuition, books, and the like, which we assumed were nonexistent in order to keep the example simple. Direct costs are easy to treat, however.

---

[3] To be precise, we must specify whether income is received at the beginning or end of each year. We assume that income is received at the beginning of each year.

They are simply subtracted from any earnings received in the year during which the costs are incurred. If, say, there were tuition payments of $500 to attend school during years 0 and 1, then Y_0 and Y_1 would each equal $500 ($1,000 less tuition), and $PV(Y)$ would be correspondingly smaller. The *returns* from choosing Y consist of the excess of income in Y over income in X after the two years of schooling have been completed.

Whether $PV(X)$ exceeds $PV(Y)$ depends on the rate of interest, the direct and indirect costs of investing in occupation Y, the excess of earnings in Y over those in X after the schooling (or other investment) necessary to enter occupation Y occurs, and the number of years during which the returns to investing in Y are received. By carefully studying the present-value formulas, you should be able to see that $PV(Y) - PV(X)$ is more likely to be positive the smaller the costs of choosing Y, the greater the returns and the sooner they start to roll in, the greater the number of time periods during which net positive returns to Y are received, and the lower the rate of interest.

Rate of Return

At this point it should be clear that the alternative course of action that yields a stream of income with the greatest present value will maximize wealth. Despite the conceptual simplicity of viewing wealth maximization in terms of present value, it is frequently more convenient to use another, related concept in studying investment in human capital. This concept is called the **internal rate of return** or simply the **rate of return on investment.** It will soon become clear that using the rate of return as a guide to wealth maximization will generally lead a wealth-maximizing investor to select the alternative that has the highest present value. Thus, the two approaches to investment theory are for practical purposes equivalent.[4]

Before showing how the rate of return can be used to choose between alternative occupations X and Y in the preceding example, it will be helpful to go back to the simple numerical illustration presented earlier. Suppose you owe $10,000 and your creditor offers you two choices: (1) repay the $10,000 when it is due, one year from today; or (2) pay $9,009 immediately, whereupon your creditor will tear up the promissory note, and you will owe

---

[4] This statement is not *universally* true, however. For example, while the difference between the present values of two income streams is *unique*, in some cases there may be *more than one* rate of return. We shall ignore those complex cases in which present value and rate of return do not necessarily lead to the same choices. In general, choosing among alternative investments on the basis of which yields the greatest present value is always wealth-maximizing. When the rate-of-return approach is wealth-maximizing, it does not conflict with the present-value approach. If you would like to pursue this topic further, consult Chapter 3 of J. Hirshleifer, *Investment, Interest, and Capital* (Englewood Cliffs, N.J.: Prentice-Hall, Inc., 1970).

nothing more. A way to decide between these alternatives in order to maximize your wealth is to view the $9,009 that you would have to pay now as the *cost* of an investment. The *return* to the investment is $10,000, the amount of your promissory note, which you are forgiven. Since this return should be viewed as accruing to you one year from now, when you have to repay your note, it is analogous to a future payment of interest ($991) plus principal ($9,009) on an investment expenditure of $9,009 today. Thus, there is an *implicit interest rate* on this expenditure of $991/$9,009 = 0.11, or 11 percent. *This implicit interest rate is the rate of return.* If the rate of return is greater than the market rate of interest, it will increase your wealth to choose alternative 2. For example, if you can borrow $9,009 from a bank at a rate of interest of 10 percent, you will have to pay only $900.90 interest next year to the bank instead of $991 to your creditor. If you do not have to borrow the $9,009, but can place it in a money market fund yielding 10 percent, you will receive $900.90 in interest next year, while if you repay your creditor now, you save $991 as of next year. Either way, you are better off by $90.10.

The rate of return when a payoff of $10,000 to an investment of $9,009 occurs one year from the date the investment must be paid for is defined implicitly by the equation

$$\$9,009 = \$10,000(1 + \rho)^{-1} \tag{8-3}$$

where ρ is the rate of return. Equation (8-3) shows that the rate of return is equivalent to the rate of interest that makes the present value of the return to an investment exactly equal to its cost. The similarity between the formulas for calculating present value and the rate of return is not accidental. Each approach to making a choice among alternative investments requires the decision maker to solve an equation for an unknown quantity. When using the present-value approach, the decision maker uses knowledge of the *rate of interest* and *future returns* to solve for present value. In the rate-of-return approach, the decision maker uses knowledge of an investment's *cost* and *returns* to solve for the *rate of return*.

When returns occur more than one year in the future, the similarity with the formula for calculating present value still holds. Suppose you know of an investment opportunity that you expect to yield two net payments of $10,000, one a year from now and the other two years from now. If you can purchase this investment (for example, a building, machine, or a year of schooling) for $C today, the rate of return to investing $C now is defined by the equation

$$C = \$10,000(1 + \rho)^{-1} + \$10,000(1 + \rho)^{-2} \tag{8-4}$$

where, once again, it is necessary to solve for ρ given C and two payments of $10,000.

To see how the rate-of-return approach leads to the same choice between occupations X and Y in the example given earlier, go back and look at Table 8-1 once again. You should recognize that as r increases from zero up through 5 percent to 25 percent, $PV(Y) - PV(X)$ becomes smaller and smaller, and that at some value of r between 20 and 25 percent, $PV(Y) - PV(X) = 0$. This rate of interest, at which the present value of choosing Y and attending two more years of school exactly equals the present value of X, is by definition the rate of return on Y. In Table 8-2 you can see that the rate of return implicit in the data on X and Y presented in Table 8-1 is approximately 0.22.

The factors affecting the rate of return are the same as those determining whether $PV(Y)$ exceeds $PV(X)$. The rate of return is higher, the smaller the opportunity costs of choosing occupation Y, the greater the earnings in Y, and the greater the length of time during which net positive returns to Y are received. If you understand how ρ is defined, it should not be difficult to see how it can be used to describe wealth-maximizing investment choices. In the present-value approach, choosing Y is wealth-maximizing so long as r, the rate of interest, is low enough that $PV(Y)$ exceeds $PV(X)$. This will be the case for values of r less than approximately 22 percent. Thus, as Table 8-1 shows, when $r = 0.20$, $PV(Y) > PV(X)$. However, when $r = 0.25$, $PV(X) > PV(Y)$. Therefore, choosing Y is wealth-maximizing so long as $r < \rho$. *Whenever the rate of return on a possible investment exceeds the rate of interest, the present value of the investment exceeds its cost; thus, undertaking such an investment leads to wealth maximization.* You should now have a good grasp of the definition of the rate of return and how it can be used to choose among alternative investments in human capital.

TABLE 8-2 Calculation of Rate of Return to Investing in Occupation Y

Year (j)	Net Income Occupation X	Net Income Occupation Y	$Y_j - X_j$	$(Y_j - X_j)(1 + \rho)^{-j}$
0	$10,000	$ 1,000	$-9,000	$-9,000
1	10,000	1,000	-9,000	-7,377
2	10,000	18,000	8,000	5,375
3	10,000	18,000	8,000	4,406
4	10,000	18,000	8,000	3,611
5	10,000	18,000	8,000	2,960
Sum	$60,000	$74,000	$ 14,000	$ -25
				$(\rho = 0.22)$

The Demand Curve for Investment in Human Capital

To recap the preceding discussion, the rate of return on investment can be defined as the interest rate that makes the present value of a possible investment choice just equal to its cost. A nice feature of the rate-of-return approach is that it fits conveniently into the demand and supply framework we have become accustomed to using in understanding economic behavior of all kinds. The demand curve for investment in human capital is easy to construct, once the rate of return is defined.

To simplify things, imagine that a wealth-maximizing individual (or the individual's parents) can foresee all the possible human capital investments that could be undertaken during the individual's lifetime—schooling, training, health care, moving to a location where wages are higher, and so on. Two further assumptions will also make our analysis easier. The first is to postulate that investments in human capital can be made in small enough incremental amounts so that the cost of each additional unit of investment always occurs in a period equal to or less than one year. Thus the *cost* of each investment is the current value of the direct and indirect expenditures required.

The second assumption is that the return to each investment in human capital is a constant flow of market earning power (that is, an equal amount each year) that persists forever. *Note:* We are not saying that the returns to all investments are equal. Each investment may yield a different return. It is simply that each investment's return does not rise or fall over time. This assumption is not as drastic as it may first appear. Of course, no one lives forever. However, most investment in human capital occurs relatively early in life. Consider an individual who expects to work until age 65. What error do we commit if we ignore that the returns to schooling undertaken at age 20 will accrue over only 45 years rather than forever? The magnitude of the error is usually quite small, and in return for bearing the cost of this minor inaccuracy, we gain much in simplicity. [For example, the present value of $10,000 50 years from now for $r = 0.10$ is only $10,000(1.10)^{-50} = \$85.19$.]

Now we can proceed to reap the returns from the assumptions we have just made. When the payoff to an investment never ceases and is a constant amount per time period, the following simple formula holds:

$$C\rho = R \qquad (8\text{-}5)$$

where C is the sum of the investment's direct and indirect costs, ρ is the rate of return, and R is the annual payoff, or return, in monetary terms. Compare equation (8-5) with (8-4), and you will see it is much simpler and easier to use.[5] For example, if a dollar is invested at a rate of return equal to 10 percent, equation (8-5) states that the additional earning power yielded by this investment is $0.10 per year forever.

Remember that we are assuming all of an individual's possible investments in human capital are known, along with their costs and effect on future potential income. It is therefore possible to calculate the real rate of return (the return after adjusting for inflation) on each dollar's worth of investment and place them in rank order, starting with the investment dollar promising the highest rate of return. Such a hypothetical list, in abbreviated form, would contain information such as that shown in Table 8-3.

In Table 8-3, the first dollar invested in human capital yields an extraordinary high rate of return, increasing market earning power by $2 per year—a rate of return of 200 percent. Why is this rate of return so high? The returns on the earliest investments in human capital are large, since much in later years depends on them. Can you imagine how little benefit you would obtain from schooling if you had not first learned to speak, to spell your name, or to count? The cost of some human capital investments to investors (although not necessarily to society) are very small, since child labor laws and compulsory school attendance greatly reduce foregone earnings while children are enrolled in the early years of (subsidized public) schooling. Given returns R, low private opportunity cost C raises the rate of return ρ.

---

[5] Here is the proof that equation (8-5) holds. By extending (8-4) to the constant-R, infinite-lifetime case, and ignoring any return during the initial period, we have

$$C = \frac{R}{1 + \rho} + \frac{R}{(1 + \rho)^2} + \frac{R}{(1 + \rho)^3} + \cdots + \frac{R}{(1 + \rho)^n} \qquad \text{(a)}$$

multiplying both sides of equation (a) by $1/(1 + \rho)$, we obtain:

$$C \left(\frac{1}{1 + \rho} \right) = \frac{R}{(1 + \rho)^2} + \cdots + \frac{R}{(1 + \rho)^{n+1}} \qquad \text{(b)}$$

Subtracting equation (b) from equation (a) yields

$$C \left(\frac{\rho}{1 + \rho} \right) = \frac{R}{1 + \rho} - \frac{R}{(1 + \rho)^{n+1}} \qquad \text{(c)}$$

Dividing by $\rho/(1 + \rho)$ and combining terms,

$$C = R \left[\frac{1}{\rho} - \frac{1}{\rho(1 + \rho)^n} \right] \qquad \text{(d)}$$

Taking limits, for the infinite time horizon, shows us that

$$\lim_{n \to \infty} C = \frac{R}{\rho} \qquad \text{Q.E.D.} \qquad \text{(e)}$$

Note that when returns are received and compounded once a year, it matters whether we consider the initial period's return, which is omitted from equation (a). When returns accrue continuously, instead of once a year, and are compounded every instant, advanced algebra or calculus will show that equation (e) holds *exactly* at all times. Footnote 14 contains an illustration of this point.

TABLE 8-3 Possible Human Capital Investments Ranked by Their Rates of Return

Rank	Cost	Rate of Return (%)	Annual Earning Power Generated by This Investment
1st dollar invested	$1.00	200	$2.00
1000th dollar invested	1.00	100	1.00
2000th dollar invested	1.00	50	0.50
3000th dollar invested	1.00	40	0.40
4000th dollar invested	1.00	30	0.30
5000th dollar invested	1.00	20	0.20
6000th dollar invested	1.00	15	0.15
7000th dollar invested	1.00	10	0.10
8000th dollar invested	1.00	5	0.05
9000th dollar invested	1.00	1	0.01

In Table 8-3, successive dollars invested, up to $1,000, yield rates of return that are still high, but declining to 100 percent. After $1,999 have been invested, the two-thousandth dollar yields a 50 percent rate of return. After $8,999 is invested in human capital, the nine-thousandth dollar invested raises market earning power by only an additional $0.01 per year—a rate of return of one percent.

Table 8-3 describes the *marginal* rate of return to investment in human capital, because the annual earning power payoffs are the returns on *increments* to an individual's stock of human capital. The marginal rate of return to human capital investment is assumed to decline as the quantity of human capital acquired by an individual grows. The main reason is that each individual has a fixed capacity (e.g., number of brain cells) to benefit from human capital, so that as the ratio of human capital to capacity grows, the principle of *diminishing marginal productivity* applies.

In the last section we showed that wealth maximization requires undertaking all investments that yield a rate of return in excess of the interest rate. *Therefore information on the marginal rate of return allows us to construct the demand curve for human capital.* The individual (or parent) would undertake each investment in Table 8-3 on which the rate of return exceeds the rate of interest. Given diminishing returns to investment in human capital, an individual's demand will look like the curve $d(\rho)$ graphed in Figure 8-1. It describes the relationship between the rate of interest at which an individual can borrow (or lend)[6] money and the amount of desired investment in human capital.

The Supply of Funds for Investment in Human Capital and the Amount Invested

The demand curve for human capital reflects the marginal benefits to investment. As we have seen, given these marginal benefits, the total amount invested depends on the interest rate. It would be possible to construct a table similar to Table 8-3, showing the interest rate foregone or paid on each successive dollar used to purchase a human capital investment. This would provide us with a rank-ordering of the marginal opportunity cost of each dollar invested. It should come as no surprise that the wealth-maximizing amount of investment in human capital is determined by equating marginal benefit with the marginal cost of the funds required.

The schedule of interest rates on incremental funds used to finance investments in human capital provides the information needed to graph the *supply of funds for investment* in human capital. If human beings could be used as collateral against loans made to finance human capital (if indentured servitude or slavery were currently legal), then the supply curve of funds for investment would be like that for investment in physical capital. If you want to buy an apartment house for investment purposes, or if an established business firm wishes to purchase new equipment, there is a well-defined market for loanable funds in which it is possible to borrow at a market-determined rate of interest. The apartment house or equipment can be repossessed if there is a default in loan repayment. This is not to say that lenders are indifferent to the risk associated with lending very large amounts to a single investor. Rather, the collateral provided by the physical asset(s) financed with borrowed funds reduces risk sufficiently to make the supply of funds relatively elastic, in contrast to the supply of funds to finance human capital.

In Figure 8-2, $s(r)$ represents the supply curve of funds for investment in human capital. It shows the relationship between the marginal rate of interest on funds borrowed (or not lent) to finance human capital investments. Some families can finance further investments in human capital, say

---

[6] We must emphasize that this analysis applies equally when it is not necessary to borrow money to invest in human capital. The opportunity cost of investment in this case is the foregone interest on funds that could have been used elsewhere. For example, if you don't go to college, you could invest your earnings in a savings account.

The discussion of the demand and supply curves for investment in human capital draws heavily on Gary S. Becker, *Human Capital,* 2d ed. (New York: National Bureau of Economic Research, 1975), pp. 94*ff.*

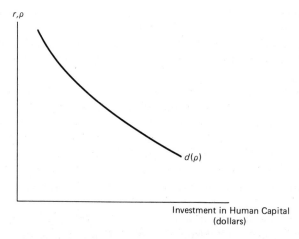

FIGURE 8-1. Marginal rate of return schedule and individual demand for human capital

up to $I(1)$, by selling stocks or bonds or by using them as collateral for borrowed funds to finance college tuition. For such families, the supply of loanable funds for additional investment in human capital will coincide with the cost of funds for investment in physical capital. Eventually (sooner for less wealthy families), as more human capital investment is undertaken, financing becomes increasingly difficult as assets that may be sold or used to provide collateral for borrowed funds are exhausted. It becomes necessary

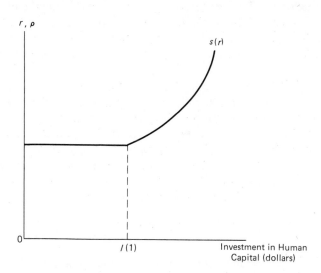

FIGURE 8-2. Supply of funds for investment in human capital

to rely on increasingly costly sources of funds. For example, a young family may desire to invest in human capital by accepting low-paying jobs that promise increased earnings in later years. The family may be able to maintain current consumption of goods and services by borrowing on credit cards—using "plastic money." However, once they reach their credit limit, additional sources of funds will be more costly. If an emergency should arise, the only source of borrowed funds may be a pawn shop or even a loan shark, charging very high interest rates. As more investment is undertaken, funds may be available, but only at higher rates of interest, as shown by the upward-sloping portion of $s(r)$ after $I(1)$.

Equilibrium Investment in Human Capital and Earnings

Figure 8-3 depicts the interaction of the supply and demand curves for investment in human capital from the point of view of an individual investor. Since wealth maximization requires undertaking all investments for which the rate of return exceeds the rate of interest, it is easy to see that $I(0)$ represents the amount invested, while $r(0)$ and $\rho(0)$ represent the equilibrium interest rate and marginal rate of return, respectively. Factors making it easier to finance human capital investments, such as greater family wealth, will shift the supply curve to the right, increasing the amount invested and lowering the equilibrium rate of return to human capital. Similarly, equilibrium investment and rate of return are influenced by the position of the demand curve.

An important condition underlying the demand curve is the ability, talent, or intellectual capacity of the individual. The influence of these factors on investment in human capital is discussed in detail later on.

The simple model of human capital developed here is also a theory of market earning power, since wages constitute a major return to investing in human capital. (Investing in human capital raises efficiency in household production as well. For example, relatively well-educated parents may be better able to rear children.) Recall that in developing the demand curve $d(\rho)$ we made simplifying assumptions that lead to equation (8-5). Equation (8-5) states that the *increase* in market earning power that constitutes the return to *each* human capital investment is *proportional* to the amount invested. The constant of proportionality is the rate of return. To remind you of this, equation (8-5) can be rewritten as

$$\frac{R}{C} = \rho \qquad\qquad \textbf{(8-6)}$$

where R is the increase in earning power, C is the amount invested, and ρ is the marginal rate of return. Now, if we make the further simplifying assumption that hours of work are constant (that is, they do not change as the

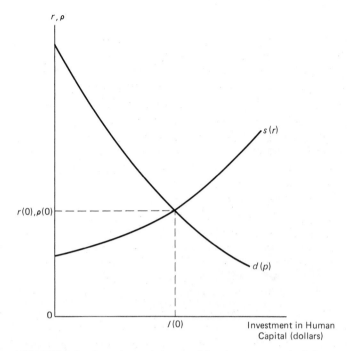

FIGURE 8-3. Supply and demand for investment in human capital

amount invested in human capital changes), equation (8-6) also implies that investing one more dollar in human capital raises labor income by a fraction equal to ρ.

The relationship between earnings and investment in human capital is illustrated in Figure 8-4. Suppose a typical individual is endowed at birth with an initial stock of human capital (which could be a very small amount) that provides annual earnings equal to $\bar{Y}$. In Figure 8-4 the quantity $I(1)$ represents $I(1)$ dollars invested in human capital at a rate of return equal to $\rho(1)$. From equations (8-5) and (8-6) it is clear that the increased earnings resulting from investing $I(1)$ dollars equals $\rho(1) \times I(1)$ dollars, which is approximately the area under $d(\rho)$ between its intercept with the ρ axis and $I(1)$. [The match between the rectangle whose area is $\rho(1) \times I(1)$ becomes exact as we let $I(1)$ become very small.]

This calculation can be carried out for each successive investment in human capital. The height of each rectangle is approximately the height of $d(\rho)$ corresponding to the cumulative amount of investment. For example, $\rho(2)$ is the marginal rate of return to a further investment in human capital after $I(1)$ dollars have been invested. The increase in earnings from the additional investment is the *increment* in investment multiplied by the mar-

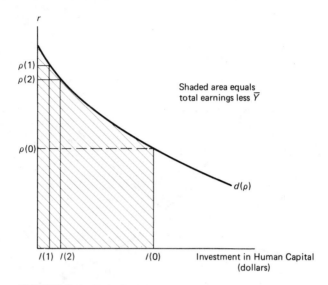

FIGURE 8-4. Relationship between human capital and market earnings

ginal rate of return, or $[I(2) - I(1)] \times \rho(2)]$. Total earnings equal $\bar{Y}$ plus the sum of the marginal returns on each dollar invested in human capital. Therefore, if $I(0)$ is the *total* amount invested, the *total* earnings attributable to investment in human capital is depicted by the shaded area to the left of $I(0)$ in Figure 8-4.

The Supply and Demand for Human Capital: Application to Occupational Choice

Figure 8-4 describes a very simple analytical framework, or model, of human capital investment decisions. To show how this supply and demand approach is helpful in understanding human capital investment decisions, we apply it to the choice among alternative occupations.[7] Figure 8-5 depicts the situation of a typical high school graduate who is considering attending college, which would require an expenditure of $\$I(1)$ involving foregone earnings and direct expenditures. A graduate degree in business administration would cost more, bringing total investment to $\$I(2)$. Finally, the high school graduate contemplates that obtaining an M.D. degree, including the

---

[7] Occupational choice is the subject matter of several pioneering studies in which the concept of human capital was significantly advanced. These early studies include J. R. Walsh, "Capital Concept Applied to Man," *Quarterly Journal of Economics,* February 1935, pp. 255–85 (which contains numerous references to still earlier work); G. Stigler and D. Blank, *The Demand and Supply of Scientific Personnel* (New York: NBER, 1957); and M. Friedman and S. Kuznets, *Income from Independent Professional Practice* (New York: NBER, 1945).

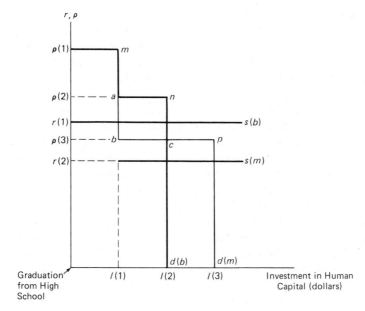

FIGURE 8-5. The demand and supply of human capital
applied to occupational choice

residency required before one can begin private practice of medicine, would
involve a total investment of $I(3)$. Since pre-business and pre-medical-
school undergraduate curriculums are different, it is important for the high
school graduate to answer the following two questions: (1) should I attend
college at all; and (2) if I do, should I plan to attend graduate school in either
medicine or business administration?

These questions can be answered on the basis of the rate of return and
interest rate on funds required to finance schooling. The marginal rate of
return schedules $d(b)$ and $d(m)$ are drawn as downward-sloping step functions, rather than as continuous demand curves, like $d(\rho)$ in Figure 8-4,
because it is not realistic to plan in advance to obtain, say, only $\frac{5}{16}$ rather than
$\frac{3}{8}$ of a bachelor's degree, or to attend medical school for only 21 instead of 22
months. It is more reasonable to plan a lumpy investment of four years as an
undergraduate and to recognize that a graduate degree in business will require, say, three additional years (the same as medical school), while medical residence after obtaining the M.D. degree will require two more years
still. Curve $d(b)$ represents the business school alternative. It starts at $\rho(1)$
on the vertical axis, reaches a step at point m (the end of four years of
college), and passes through a and n (three years of graduate school) on its
way down to $I(2)$ on the horizontal axis. Curve $d(m)$, representing the medicine alternative, also starts at $\rho(1)$, but it steps all the way down to b and

over to p before reaching $I(3)$ on the horizontal axis. Curve $s(b)$ represents the rate of interest $[r(1)]$ that must be paid on borrowed funds or foregone on funds invested elsewhere if *either* the business or medical alternatives are chosen. We have assumed that the supply of funds for investment in human capital is not upward-sloping simply to keep Figure 8-5 as easy to read as possible.

Curves $d(b)$ and $d(m)$ tell us that, regardless of undergraduate curriculum, a prospective college student can expect a rate of return equal to $\rho(1)$ for obtaining a bachelor's degree after four years of college. This will yield annual earnings of $\$[\rho(1) \times I(1)]$ *in excess of* the earnings that a typical high school graduate could expect. Since $\$I(1)$ measures the *additional* investment required to attend college, over and above all previous investments in human capital, the area under $d(b)$ up to $I(1)$ represents the increase in income a high school graduate would anticipate from completing college. Since $\rho(1)$ exceeds $r(1)$, attending four years of college will increase wealth. If the choice to attend college were rejected, $\$I(1)$ could be invested, say, in a certificate of deposit yielding an annual income of $\$[I(1) \times r(1)]$, which shows that the *net* income *gain* (or "profit") accruing to an undergraduate college degree is $\$I(1) \times [\rho(1) - r(1)]$ per year.

Attending graduate business school is also wealth-increasing, since the rate of return to this additional schooling is $\rho(2)$, still in excess of $r(1)$. A decision to attend medical school, however, will reduce wealth, since $\rho(3)$, the rate of return to the additional schooling involved, is less than the interest rate $r(1)$. Note that this is so even though, in Figure 8-5, a doctor will earn more per year than someone with a graduate business degree. [The *difference* between a doctor's annual earnings and the annual earnings of the business administrator is the excess of the area of rectangle $I(2)cpI(3)$ over the area *banc*.] However, a doctor will not earn enough to compensate for all the costs that must be borne, which include the foregone earnings during three years of medical school *plus* two more years as a resident. In Figure 8-5 the labor market is signaling that choosing a medical career will not increase wealth, while choosing a business career will do so. (Remember: This is an example; we are not telling our readers to switch to pre-business in order to increase their wealth.)

Eventually, if the number of physicians falls because fewer doctors graduate from medical school, higher fees for their services will result in increased earnings, and the rate of return to choosing medicine as a career will rise. The rate of return schedule $d(m)$ will shift upward. A sufficient increase will induce some high school graduates to choose medicine as a career, eventually increasing the supply of physicians and halting the increase in doctors' fees. Alternatively, the government may decide that it would be politically advisable to "do something" about rising physicians' fees. One policy it might choose would be to offer low-interest loans to medical school students. If it became possible to finance medical training by borrowing at interest rate $r(2)$, then the supply of funds would be $s(b)$ up to $\$I(1)$ of investment and would fall to $s(m)$ for amounts medical students invest in excess of $\$I(1)$. Wealth could then be increased by attending medical school, and there would eventually be an increase in the number of physicians. (Strictly speaking, for the individual depicted in Figure 8-5 to choose medical school over business school, the rate of interest along $s(m)$ would have to be low enough to make the area $[\rho(3) - r(2)] \times [I(3) - I(1)]$ greater than the area $[\rho(2) - r(1)] \times [I(2) - I(1)]$. Why?)

Evidence on Occupational Choice

The supply and demand model of human capital implies that the rate of return is an important variable determining occupational choice and educational decisions. Other things equal, an increase in an occupation's earnings will raise the rate of return, and this should induce entry into the occupation.

There have been a number of applications of the human capital approach to the study of occupational earnings and occupational choice. Richard Freeman has examined the market for lawyers and estimated the responsiveness of choices to enter the legal profession to relative salaries. As part of his study, he estimated the following regression equation for the United States over the years 1947–71:

$$\log LENT = 5.18 + 1.92 \log LSAL + -1.21 \log ASAL \qquad \textbf{(8-7)}$$
$$\qquad\qquad\quad (0.79) \qquad\qquad\quad (0.87)$$

where $LENT \equiv$ first-year law school enrollees
$\quad LSAL =$ salaries of young attorneys
$\quad ASAL =$ salaries of alternative occupations as measured by
$\qquad\qquad$ the income of all salaried professionals.

Both salary variables are deflated by the consumer price index. (The numbers in parentheses are standard errors.) Since all the variables are in logarithmic form, equation (8-7) tells us that every 1 percent increase in the salaries of young attorneys (relative to the salaries of other professionals) results in nearly a 2 percent increase in the number of first-year law students. Similarly, an increase in the relative salaries of other professional occupations *reduces* law school enrollments. Freeman uses more complex equations to overcome statistical problems in estimating equation (8-7). These estimates lead him to conclude that the supply of new law students is very responsive to relative salaries, with an elasticity of approximately 4.0. This large elasticity, along with variation in the relative salary position of lawyers, resulted in wide swings in the number of first-year law students. Over the period 1960–71, the ratio of young attorneys' salaries ($LSAL$) to the earnings of salaried professionals ($ASAL$) ranged from 1.08 to 1.27, a variation of about 20 percent. The proportion of male B.A.'s enrolling in first-year law school varied by about one-third over the same period. Moreover, Freeman finds that the number of first-year students who complete their course of study also responds positively to annual salaries, although the elasticity is considerably smaller.

The Rate of Return and Investment in Schooling

One of the most important applications of human capital theory is in helping us to understand the distribution of income among individuals in our society. A very important component of human capital is investment in schooling, and differences in level of education are associated with interpersonal differences in income. In this section we first extend the supply and demand model of human capital theory to explore some difficulties in interpreting the strong correlation between schooling and earning power and deriving policy applications for educational policy. Then we go on to examine evidence of the effect of schooling on earnings.

The principal goals of most studies of investment in schooling have been to estimate the rate of return to schooling, to relate the marginal rate-of-return schedule to the demand for schooling, and to draw inferences for educational policy. For example, has there been underinvestment or overinvestment in education from a social perspective? What would happen to the earning power of a typical individual if he or she received more schooling? A successful study, one that provides reliable answers to these questions, must address the following question: Is schooling the only systematic force causing the incomes of, say, college graduates to be higher than the incomes of others who have received less schooling—high school graduates, for instance? Economists and others who study the effect of schooling on market earning power are not in general agreement as to the answer. Some reasons for this uncertainty are that college graduates come from wealthier families (thereby making it easier for them to finance higher education), that they may have greater ability to benefit from college (intelligence), and that they may have better contacts for jobs due to their family backgrounds. To what extent does the neglect of these conditions bias estimates of the return to schooling?

Let us examine the possible biases listed above in terms of the supply and demand framework.[8] Insofar as the only influence of family wealth is to lower the effective rate of interest in financing human capital investment, we have a situation like that depicted in Figure 8-6. If everyone benefited equally from a given amount of schooling, observed schooling levels would correspond to investments $I(1)$, $I(2)$, $I(3)$, and $I(4)$, depending on the

[8] Once again our discussion draws heavily on Becker's *Human Capital,* pp. 94*ff.* See also Gary S. Becker and Barry R. Chiswick, "Education and the Distribution of Earnings," *American Economic Review,* 56 (May 1966), 358–69.

family's supply of funds. The corresponding marginal rates of return would be $\rho(1)$, $\rho(2)$, $\rho(3)$, and $\rho(4)$, respectively.[9] A bit of review will help you to see how Figure 8-6 might be constructed from available data. For illustrative purposes, suppose that all costs of schooling are *indirect* costs consisting of foregone earnings while in school. Let $I(1)$ equal the earnings foregone during the first three years of high school. The area under $d(\rho)$ between the vertical axis and the vertical line connecting $I(1)$ and $d(\rho)$ is the earnings of a typical individual who has finished only three years of high school and then dropped out, over and above the earnings of someone with only an eighth-grade education. Thus, $\rho(1)$ approximately equals the ratio of this area to $I(1)$. It is the marginal rate of return to completing three years of high school. The fourth year of high school would cost $I(2) - I(1)$ in foregone earnings and yield additional annual earnings after graduation equal to the area under $d(\rho)$ between $I(1)$ and $I(2)$. The ratio of this area to $I(2) - I(1)$ equals $\rho(2)$, the rate of return to completing high school. The rates of return $\rho(3)$ and $\rho(4)$ are calculated similarly for, say, the first two years of college.

In the world depicted by Figure 8-6, the effect of encouraging more schooling would be relatively easy to predict. The reason is that everyone would have the same capacity to benefit from further investment. Therefore the earnings of those who have, say, graduated from college would be received by any high school graduate if only he or she were to complete a college education. Technically speaking, with only one demand curve, variation in family wealth does not bias estimates of the rate of return. Quite the

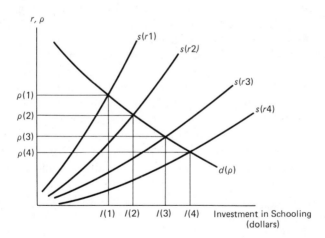

FIGURE 8-6. Possible influence of family wealth on investments in schooling

---

[9] Note that the horizontal axes of Figures 8-6 to 8-8 measure human capital in *dollars* corresponding to each year of schooling. The dollar amount corresponding to each year of schooling is the sum of foregone earnings plus direct costs incurred during that year.

contrary, it is necessary to *identify* the relationship between the rate of return and the amount invested along the demand curve.

Individual differences in talent or in intelligence may affect the demand curve for investment in human capital—and the supply curve as well. However, the direction of the effect of talent or ability on the demand for investment in human capital is uncertain.[10] More able persons may have access to higher-paying jobs, independent of the amount of schooling acquired, thus raising indirect schooling costs and lowering the amount of schooling chosen. This is obviously the case when a superstar athlete such as John McEnroe quits college after the freshman year to turn pro.

Alternatively, ability may increase the net benefits derived from schooling, partly by enabling students to succeed in school with relatively little effort. Whether through reducing indirect schooling costs or by increasing the relative earning power resulting from higher levels of education, such ability would raise the demand for investment by relatively able persons. In Figure 8-7 we describe the case in which ability *increases* the *demand* for schooling but has *no effect* on *supply*. The observed relationship between schooling and earnings would then consist of the shaded areas under $d(\rho1)$, $d(\rho2)$, and $d(\rho3)$ corresponding to amounts invested of $\$I(1)$, $\$I(2)$, and $\$I(3)$, respectively. This would yield rates of return $\rho(1)$, $\rho(2)$, and $\rho(3)$ corresponding to investment levels $I(1)$, $I(2)$, and $I(3)$. We can infer nothing from this relationship observed in the general population about what would happen to a typical individual on, say, curve $d(\rho1)$ if expenditures on his or her schooling were increased from $\$I(1)$ to $\$I(2)$. This individual's marginal rate of return on $\$I(2) - \$I(1)$ additional investment would be less than $\rho(1)$, not $\rho(2)$, which the *observed* pattern of schooling and earnings would imply.

A strong possibility is that ability will influence not only the demand for human capital, but also the supply of funds. Insofar as selective admission policies and scholarship and fellowship aid based on ability make it easier for able persons to attend school, the supply of funds for able persons is increased. If the effect of ability is also to increase demand, then a positive correlation between demand and supply results, as depicted in Figure 8-8, where $s(r_1)$ goes with $d(\rho_1)$ and so on. The observed rate of return is $\rho(3)$ for everyone, and the relationship between income and schooling observed in the general population yields no direct information about supply or demand. Connecting up the observed points that correspond to the intersection of $s(r_1)$ with $d(\rho_1)$, $s(r_2)$ with $d(\rho_2)$, and $s(r_3)$ with $d(\rho_3)$ might lead one to infer that the rate of return declines very little, if at all, as a given individual acquires more schooling. In fact, if a typical individual who attends school long enough to invest $\$I(1)$ in schooling were to attend school longer, investing $\$I(2)$, this individual's marginal rate of return on incremental investment

---

[10] See, for example, Zvi Griliches, "Estimating the Returns to Schooling: Some Economic Problems," *Econometrica*, 45:1 (January 1977), 1–22.

would fall to $\rho(2)$ along schedule $d(\rho_1)$. It would not remain at $\rho(3)$, as the *observed* pattern of earnings and schooling would suggest. To test your understanding of Figures 8-6 through 8-8, use a diagram like those in Figures 8-7 and 8-8 to show the difference in the effects on earnings of college scholarships based only on ability and those based only on family income.

Another potential problem in attributing observed differences in earnings or earning power only to differences in schooling is that persons who acquire additional schooling are likely to acquire other forms of human capital, such as on-the-job training, as well. So it would be wrong to attribute their entire additional income to schooling alone. Surprisingly, however, investment in different kinds of human capital will not necessarily result in a misleading estimate of the rate of return to schooling if two conditions hold: (1) all the costs of the other investments are indirect—foregone earnings—rather than direct expenditures, and (2) the rate of return to the other investments is equal to the rate of return to schooling. These conditions are not as restrictive as they may at first appear. It is widely believed that on-the-job training is the most important investment in human capital other than schooling made by those who acquire relatively large amounts of schooling

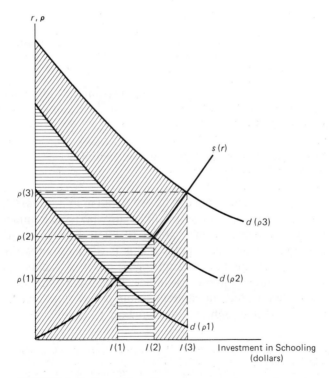

FIGURE 8-7. Possible effect of ability on investment in schooling

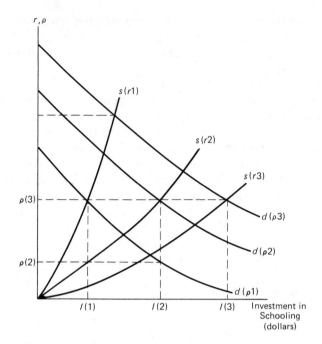

FIGURE 8-8. Effects of ability on supply and demand of investment in schooling

and that the principal cost of on-the-job training from the individual worker's point of view is foregone earnings. A detailed analysis of on-the-job training is presented in Chapter 9.

Estimating Rates of Return: The Human Capital Earning-Power Function

Rates of return to schooling can be estimated in two ways. One method is simply to compare the earnings of individuals who have completed different amounts of schooling, being careful to allow for factors other than schooling that may influence earnings. (This is the method we used as an illustration of how you might construct Figure 8-6.)[11] A second method has been used more frequently in recent studies. It involves estimating a regression equation called a "human capital earning-power function."

A human capital earning-power function is usually specified as an

---

[11] For examples of this technique, see Giora Hanoch, "Personal Earnings and Investment in Schooling" (unpublished Ph.D. dissertation, University of Chicago, 1965); and "An Economic Analysis of Earnings and Schooling," *Journal of Human Resources,* Summer 1967, 310–29. See also Richard B. Freeman, "Overinvestment in College Training," *Journal of Human Resources,* 10, Summer 1975, 287–311.

equation with the *natural logarithm* of earnings on the left-hand side and the *arithmetic* value of schooling and other variables on the right-hand side, such as

$$\ln Y = \alpha(0) + \alpha(1)S + \alpha(2)Z \tag{8-7}$$

where Y is the wage rate or earnings and S is schooling in years. A brief review of Table 2-3 will remind you that $\alpha(1)$ measures the proportionate or percentage effect of one year's additional schooling on Y. In the more technical section that follows, we show that $\alpha(1)$ can be interpreted as ρ, the rate of return to schooling. The term $\alpha(0)$ represents the log of earnings when there is no investment in human capital. The variable Z represents one or more additional factors influencing earnings, which may be included in an equation like (8-7). The additional variables included depend on what it is considered necessary to hold constant in order to answer the question: How would one more year of schooling affect the earning power of a typical individual? Equation (8-7) can be easily modified to estimate whether the proportionate effect of additional schooling on earning power is constant, increasing, or declining as an individual's schooling increases. This is done, for example by adding the term S^2, obtaining

$$\ln Y(S) = \alpha(0) + \alpha(1)S + \alpha(2)S^2 + \alpha(3)Z \tag{8-8}$$

Those readers who have learned calculus will see that in equation (8-8) the effect of an additional year of schooling is not simply the coefficient of S, $\alpha(1)$. It is now a function of the level of schooling, namely $\alpha(1) + 2\alpha(2)S$. Thus, the rate of return to additional schooling in equation (8-8) is $\rho(S) = \alpha(1) + 2\alpha(2)S$. If the estimated value of $\alpha(1)$ is positive, while that of $\alpha(2)$ is negative, the rate of return will decline as schooling increases, as in Figure 8-6.

   A difficulty in applying equations (8-7) and (8-8) is that they imply that earning power never changes after schooling is completed. As we will see in Chapter 9, most individuals experience *increasing* earnings after leaving school (even after allowing for the influence of inflation). The principal reason for this discrepancy is that equations (8-7) and (8-8) do not allow for postschooling investments in human capital through on-the-job training (OJT). In Chapter 9 we will explore this at length. For now, we will simply note the following. After leaving school, most graduates find jobs that offer the opportunity to increase their value to an employer through further training. In most cases employees must pay for part of this training by accepting earnings that fall short of the amount implied by the rate of return to schooling. They are rewarded with higher earnings later on.

*A Deeper Look at the Earning-Power Function[12]

Derivation of the human capital earning-power function can be illustrated graphically. In Figure 8-9, a high school graduate contemplates attending college. For simplicity, suppose this prospective college student knows the rate of return ρ that attending college will yield and that ρ is a constant, $\bar{\rho}$, no matter whether the student drops out after 1, 2, or 3 years of college or graduates after 4 years. The only cost of attending college is foregone earnings, and part-time work is not available.

If the prospective college student attends no college, but enters the full-time labor force immediately, annual earnings will be $X paid at the beginning of year 0, the first year after leaving high school. If no further investment in human capital occurs, earnings of $X per year will continue forever, as indicated by the **age-earnings profile**, X_t. On the other hand, if the decision is made to attend college for one year, $X is invested in schooling, which yields a rate of return $\bar{\rho}$. Therefore, if the student enters the labor force after completing one year of college, earnings (received at the beginning of the year 1) will be greater than $X—$X(1 + \bar{\rho})$ to be exact. This increment is shown as the shaded area of the bar representing annual earnings at the beginning of year 1, the second year after leaving high school. That is to say, one year of schooling will result in *increased* earning power equal to the amount invested ($X) multiplied by the rate of return $\bar{\rho}$.

If, instead of dropping out after one year of college, the student attends school for one more year, the $X(1 + \bar{\rho})$ second year's earnings are also invested in human capital. Thus, earning power at the beginning of year 2 (the third year after leaving school) is $X(1 + \bar{\rho})(1 + \bar{\rho}) = $X(1 + \bar{\rho})^2$. Each year the student remains in school, earning power is increased by $\bar{\rho}$ *times* the amount invested. Since the amount invested grows every year, because earning power is increasing, earning power after four years of college will be

$$Y = X(1 + \bar{\rho})^4 \qquad (8\text{-}9)$$

and if there is no further investment, it will continue forever (or until retirement) as indicated by the age-earnings profile Y_t in Figure 8-9.

---

* This section contains more technical material. If you skip, go to p. 318.

[12] The intellectual origins of this useful and important tool of theoretical and empirical analysis can be traced back at least to Friedman and Kuznets' *Income from Independent Professional Practice*. An important advance in the development of the relationship is found in Jacob Mincer's Ph.D. dissertation, "A Study of Personal Income Distributions," (Columbia University, 1957). See also his "Investment in Human Capital and Personal Income Distribution," *Journal of Political Economy*, August 1958. The equation of the form "log Earnings = $\alpha(0)$ + $\alpha(1)$ Schooling" was first published in Becker and Chiswick's "Education and the Distribution of Earnings." Thomas Johnson and Jacob Mincer showed that the capacity of the equation to explain earnings is substantially enhanced by the inclusion of variables in representing labor market experience and on-the-job training. See "Returns from Investment in Human Capital," *American Economic Review* (September 1970) and *Schooling, Experience and Earnings* (New York: National Bureau of Economic Research, 1974). We are indebted to Barry Chiswick, Gary Becker, and Jacob Mincer for helping us to sort out the intellectual history of this important development in human capital theory.

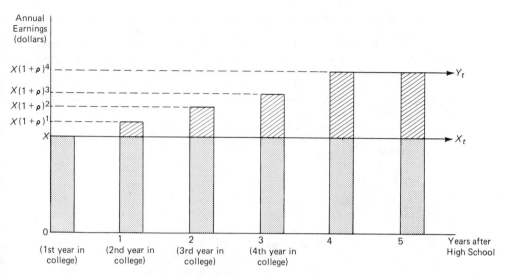

FIGURE 8-9. Earning power and schooling

Equation (8-9) can be generalized. When schooling costs exactly equal the earnings that are foregone by attending school,[13] the earning power of the individual who has acquired S years of schooling can be expressed by the equation

$$Y(S) = \bar{Y}(1 + \rho)^S \tag{8-10}$$

where $Y(S)$ is earning power (or annual earnings of full-time workers after S years of schooling), $\bar{Y}$ is the earning power of someone with no schooling, and ρ is the rate of return. Taking *natural* logarithms, equation (8-10) becomes

$$\ln Y = \ln \bar{Y} + S \ln (1 + \rho) \tag{8-11}$$

We now use an approximation. Since ρ, the rate of return, is a decimal number taking on values in the range 0.05–0.20, $\ln (1 + \rho)$ is approximately equal to ρ. (For example, $\ln 1.10 = 0.0953$.) Thus we can write the *human capital earning-power function* as

$$\ln Y(S) = \ln \bar{Y} + \rho S \tag{8-12}$$

For those of you who know calculus, you should see that in equation (8-12),

---

[13] This is not a terribly restrictive assumption. It requires only that tuition, books, and other direct expenditures are about equal to the earnings on any jobs maintained while attending school.

the marginal rate of return is the partial derivative of the natural log of earning power with respect to schooling.[14]

The effect of OJT on observed earnings is shown in Figure 8-10. The curve labeled $Y_t Y_t$ represents what a typical worker's age-earnings profile would look like after leaving school if there were no OJT. (Profile Y_t is the same as Y_t in Figure 8-9.) It is a horizontal line implying constant earnings per year from the first year after leaving school through year t^*, when retirement occurs. Profile $Y_t^\prime Y_t^*$ reflects OJT, which involves earning less than Y_t for several years and then earning more in later years. To be more precise, during the earlier years on the job, part of an employees' earnings are paid implicitly in the form of OJT. The returns to this OJT are reflected in higher earnings of later years. As an individual grows older, productivity may decline, resulting in diminished earnings. This possibility is reflected in the downward-sloping portion of Y_t^* after maximum earnings is reached. Figure 8-10 shows that there is a potentially serious problem in estimating the rate of return to schooling using an equation like (8-7) or (8-8).

If earnings profiles were flat, like $Y_t Y_t$, then it would be fairly easy to estimate the rate of return to different levels of schooling. The earnings observed any year after leaving school could be used to estimate ρ in equation (8-10) or one of its variations. However, since earnings profiles more closely approximate $Y_t^\prime Y_t^*$, it can make a big difference whether earnings are measured as of the first, fifth, tenth, or twentieth year after leaving school. One point in Figure 8-10 is of particular interest to us because it provides a way out of this problem. This is the point where $Y_t^\prime Y_t^*$ crosses $Y_t Y_t$, t^0 years after the end of schooling. The year t^0 is called the "overtaking year of experience."[15] The significance of the overtaking year is that earnings during this year equal the amount that exactly reflects the rate of return to schooling without taking into consideration the effect of OJT.

If we knew how many years of experience after leaving school were required before individuals with different amounts of schooling earned an amount just equal to

---

[14] If you know differential calculus, then another interpretation should be clear. Since

$$\frac{d \ln Y}{dx} = \frac{dY}{dx} \frac{1}{Y}$$

the rate of return is measured by the proportionate change in earning power due to an additional increment of schooling.

Equations (8-10) and (8-11) implicitly assume that "interest" on prior investments is paid and compounded annually. If we assume that interest is paid and compounded every instant, then equation (8-12) holds exactly. The proof is as follows. If we were to divide each year into n equal periods, with interest paid and compounded each period, (8-10) would become

$$Y(S) = \bar{Y} \left(1 + \frac{\rho}{n} \right)^{nS} \tag{8-10$'$}$$

Instantaneous payments and compounding of interest requires n to become infinitely large. From a well-known algebraic formula,

$$\lim_{n \to \infty} \bar{Y} \left(1 + \frac{\rho}{n} \right)^{nS} = \bar{Y} e^{\rho S} \tag{8-10$''$}$$

where e is the base of natural logarithms. Therefore, taking the natural log of (8-10$'''$)

$$\ln Y(S) = \ln \bar{Y} + \rho S \quad \text{Q.E.D.} \tag{8-10$''$}$$

[15] Mincer, *Schooling, Experience and Earnings*, p. 17.

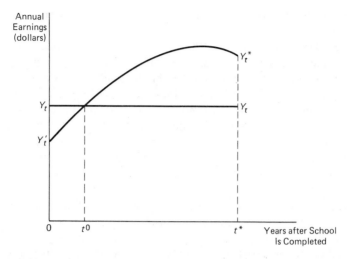

FIGURE 8-10. Age-earnings profile reflecting on-the-job
training

the return on their investments in schooling, then we could compare their observed earnings in these overtaking years and thus estimate the rate of return to schooling. Fortunately, it turns out that a rough approximation of t^0 is possible. Mincer has shown that t^0 is approximately equal to $1/\rho$. Earlier studies of schooling, OJT, and earnings suggest that ρ takes on values in the neighborhood of 0.10 or more for high school and college graduates. Therefore, if an earning power equation is estimated using information on earnings of individuals who have been out of school a little less than 10 years, it should be possible to obtain estimates of ρ that are not seriously biased by failure to consider the effects of OJT.

Mincer has estimated equation (8-8) using earnings data gathered in the 1960 United States Census of Population.[16] His sample consisted of white males in non-farm jobs who had been out of school between seven and nine years. Estimating the rate of return to schooling using the overtaking-year concept, he obtained

$$\ln Y(S) = 4.78 + 0.424S - 0.0105S^2, \qquad R^2 = 0.35 \qquad \textbf{(8-13)}$$
$$(10.0) \qquad (6.1)$$

where the numbers in parentheses are t ratios. Equation (8-13) implies that the marginal rate of return to graduating from high school (12 years of school) is 0.242 − $(2 \times 0.0105 \times 12) = 0.172$, while the rate of return to finishing the fourth year of college is $0.424 - (2 \times 0.0105 \times 16) = 0.088$. Since Mincer's data consist of individual earnings all measured in the same year, his estimates are of *real* rates of return to schooling. They are not affected by inflation. In Chapters 9 and 10 we will discuss the rate of return to schooling derived from equations that take into consideration a number of other variables that also influence annual earnings, including experience, and that are based on more recent data.

---

[16] *Schooling, Experience and Earnings,* p. 53. See also p. 55.

Screening: An Alternative View of the Role of Schooling

The role of schooling as a "filter" or "screen" versus its role in creating labor market productivity has been the subject of a number of recent studies. In the screening hypothesis, schooling and worker productivity are positively correlated, but schooling does not produce or create increases in worker efficiency on the job. A simple way of viewing this complex problem is that individuals differ in their value to employers who, because of imperfect knowledge, cannot differentiate among the workers prior to hiring. Completion of a certain level of schooling is a signal to employers that a worker has certain desirable characteristics for which employers are willing to pay a particular wage. Thus, there is some incentive for workers to acquire schooling, even though providing additional schooling for disadvantaged workers would not bring their market earning power up to the level of those who have obtained good jobs. Paradoxically, not only would increasing the schooling of low-income workers such as teenage dropouts through public policy schooling be a waste of resources if schooling provided primarily a screening function, but a further waste of resources would also be created if individuals who had previously been able to obtain good jobs by acquiring a given level of schooling then had to acquire further schooling to create an effective signal to potential employers.

We will not dwell here on the complex issue dealing with whether there would be too little or too much schooling from the point of view of social welfare if its only purpose were to differentiate workers on the basis of characteristics schooling itself did nothing to create. Schooling could well be socially useful under such circumstances, even if it were not effective in raising the market earning power of low-income workers by raising their labor market productivity. The question that concerns us here is whether there is evidence that the main function of schooling has been to serve as a screening device rather than as a means of generating human capital in the traditional sense. Unfortunately, we have to rely on rather indirect evidence. In order to discover whether schooling increases labor market skills, we would need knowledge of worker productivity before and after obtaining schooling. However, if such direct information on worker skills were available to social scientists, it would presumably also be available to employers, and the problem of schooling as a screen would not arise. It is primarily because there is no general agreement on just how skills are enhanced by education that the screening question is a live issue. (The main concern here is with "general" education as opposed to "professional" education, where the labor market skills imparted are more apparent.)

Most economists do not deny the potential importance of screening in labor markets, although many tend to be skeptical of the view that screening is a significant function of schooling. The reason for this skepticism is simply that schooling is so expensive that business firms and workers have a strong incentive to develop lower-cost methods of obtaining and providing information about worker productivity.

Kenneth Wolpin has proposed a test of the importance of the screening function of schooling. In his test, the individual supposedly knows his or her skill potential in alternative employments much better than does a prospective employer. Therefore, schooling as a screen is assumed to be much less important among self-employed persons than among salaried workers. There are problems with this test of the screening hypothesis, particularly that those who ultimately become self-employed may not have decided to do so before completing their schooling. Moreover, customers may demand the screening function in the case of the self-employed. This might be true, for example, in the case of physicians, whose patients would be happier if there were diplomas from prestigious medical schools on the office wall. In order to minimize the first problem, Wolpin examined only workers who were either self-employed or salaried throughout their observable working lives (which cover a twenty-year period in the data he uses). To deal with the second problem, he limited his sample to nonprofessional workers. Wolpin found that the average level of schooling for self-employed workers in his sample was 13.95 years, while that of salaried employees was 14.55 years. Wolpin concluded that while the direction of the difference in average years of schooling between these two groups is that implied by the screening hypothesis, it is small and is not statistically significant by conventional standards. However, in another study, Eliakin Katz and Adrian Ziderman conclude that evidence supports the hypothesis that schooling acts as a screening device as well as a contributor to worker skills.

*FRONTIERS OF LABOR ECONOMICS:
A MORE DETAILED LOOK AT CHOICE OF OCCUPATION
AND LEVEL OF SCHOOLING

Earlier in this chapter we took a brief look at how relative starting salaries have influenced the choices of college graduates to enter law school, indicating the choice of law as an occupation. Occupational choice and educational decisions are closely intertwined, even at lower levels of education. If a high school graduate wishes to choose a professional or managerial job, the chances of success in carrying out this occupational choice will be greatly enhanced if he or she successfully completes four years of college. For example, among 30- to 34-year-old men and women in 1974, the probability of being employed in a professional or managerial job was 0.61 *greater* for college graduates than for high school graduates.

Throughout the first two and one-half decades following the end of World War II, high school graduates were increasingly likely to choose an occupation for which a college degree, if not a prerequisite, greatly increased the probability of success. The proportion of 18- to 24-year old males enrolled in college grew from approxi-

---

* This section contains more technical material. If you skip, go to p. 322.

mately 15 percent in 1950 to nearly 45 percent in 1969.[17] Was this growth in college enrollment consistent with the theory of human capital? A growing proportion of high school graduates enrolling in college would be consistent with the simple supply-demand model of human capital as represented in Figure 8-3 if either or both of the following events occurred: (1) there was a rightward shift in the supply of funds for investment in human capital; (2) there was a rightward shift in the marginal rate of return schedule, which would tend to raise the rate of return to acquiring a college education, given the existing ratio of college graduates to less well-educated members of the workforce.

Evidently *both* changes affected the market for college-trained workers in the period following World War II. The supply of funds for higher education was substantially increased through growth in public funding. Between 1940 and 1968, enrollment in public institutions grew sixfold, from 46 percent of total enrollment to 62 percent. Net instruction expenditures in public institutions grew from $230 million to $6.71 billion, a thirtyfold increase, while that in private institutions grew to 16.6 times the 1940 level.[18] Income of institutions of higher education from federal, state, and local governments per member of the United States population age 15–24 grew from $237 in 1940 to $1,321 in 1964 (in 1958 dollars).[19]

If the demand function (marginal rate of return schedule) for investment in college education had been steady throughout this period, the massive increase in the availability of nonprivate funds would have shifted the supply function relative to the demand function, causing the rate of return to college education to decline. The demand curve was also shifting to the right, however. Freeman has estimated an index of demand for college graduates based on the proportion of college graduates in the total employment of 46 industries. Industries that typically hire a large proportion of college graduates were growing relatively more rapidly than others. Freeman's index of relative demand grew by 40 percent between 1950 and 1964.[20] As a result of these simultaneous increases in demand and supply, the rate of return to college evidently did not immediately fall, even though the number of college graduates was increasing much more rapidly than total employment.

Mincer has calculated the rate of return to college for 1939, 1949, and 1958 using the overtaking-year method. He used 33–34 years of age as the overtaking point for college graduates. (The calculations for 1939 and 1949 are based on all college graduates, while for 1958 only the earnings of those with exactly four years of college are used.) With the overtaking-year method and equation (8-10), Mincer calculated the marginal rate of return to college as 12.8 percent in 1939, 10.6 percent in 1949, and 10.2 percent in 1958. Equation (8-10) is used as follows. $Y(16)$ is the average earnings of college graduates and $Y(12)$ that of high school graduates who are 33–34 years old. Thus, $Y(16)/Y(12) = \bar{Y}(1 + \rho)^{16}/\bar{Y}(1 + \rho)^{12} = (1 + \rho)^4$, and the fourth root of $Y(16)/Y(12)$ is an estimate of the rate of return to completing all four years of college. With a more exact method that uses income data for all ages, he estimated the rate of return to be 10.0 percent in 1939, 10.6 percent in 1949, and 11.5 percent in 1958.[21] The regression equation that Mincer estimated, using data on 1959 earnings of men in their overtaking years of experience [see equation (8-13) above], can also be

---

[17] Richard B. Freeman, "Overinvestment in College Training?" *Journal of Human Resources,* 10:3 (Summer 1975), 287–311.

[18] Theodore W. Schultz, "Optimal Investment in College Instruction: Equity and Efficiency," *Journal of Political Economy,* 80:3, Part 2 (May/June 1972), S1–S30.

[19] Source of data is *Historical Statistics of the United States, Colonial Times to 1970,* series A32, E13, and H720-22.

[20] "Overinvestment in College Training?" p. 306.

[21] *Schooling, Experience and Earnings,* p. 50.

used to estimate the rate of return to completing college compared to completing high school. It is only necessary to substitute the values 12 and 16 for the terms in S to obtain an estimate of the natural logarithm of annual earnings of high school graduates and college graduates, respectively. These estimated mean values of the log of earnings are used, as above to calculate $[Y(16)/Y(12)]^{1/4}$. This procedure yields an estimated marginal rate of return equal to 0.139 in 1959. It seems safe to conclude on the basis of these three sets of estimates that the rate of return to college did not decline appreciably during the first one and one-half decades after World War II; on the contrary, it may have risen.

Although the rate of return to college remained near or above its prewar level through at least the first half of the 1960s, it evidently began to decline soon thereafter. Freeman estimated regression equations to obtain estimates of the rate of return to schooling at various years in the 1960s and 1970s. His regressions are of the general form

$$\ln Y(i, j) = \ln \bar{Y} + \sum_{i=1}^{8} \sum_{j=1}^{4} \alpha(i, j) S(i) E(j) \tag{8-14}$$

where the Ys are weekly earnings and

$S_i \equiv$ dummy variables $= 1$ for eight categories of schooling completed:

0–7 ($i = 1$), 8 ($i = 2$), 9–11 ($i = 3$), 12 ($i = 4$), 13–15 ($i = 5$), 16 ($i = 6$), 17 ($i = 7$), and 18+ ($i = 8$)

$E_j \equiv$ dummy variables $= 1$ for four categories of "experience" after leaving school:
0–5 ($j = 1$), 6–10 ($j = 2$), 11–30 ($j = 3$), and 31+ ($j = 4$).

Freeman estimated this regression for over 20,000 white, wage and salary, nonagricultural workers with data from the *Current Population Survey*. There are 32 schooling-experience combinations in all. The constant term $\bar{Y}$ represents the natural logarithm of earnings for an individual with whichever schooling/experience combination is dropped from equation (8-14) for estimation purposes. (See Chapter 2, pp. 41–43.) The regression coefficients $\alpha(i, j)$ have the following interpretation. Each coefficient is an estimate of the logarithm of earnings of a typical individual with i years of schooling and j years of postschooling labor market experience minus $\ln \bar{Y}$. Thus $\alpha(6, 2)$ corresponds to a worker who graduated from college between 6 and 10 years earlier. Similarly $\alpha(4, 2)$ corresponds to a high school graduate with the same exposure to the postschooling labor market. These two coefficients permit us to estimate the marginal rate of return to completing four years of college, using the overtaking-year approach.

Since Freeman's data set is similar conceptually to that used by Mincer in estimating the equation reported in equation (8-13), his results can be compared to Mincer's 1959 estimates. In terms of the procedure outlined above, $\alpha(6, 2) - \alpha(4, 2)$ is an estimate of $\ln \bar{Y}(16) - \ln \bar{Y}(12)$ for individuals with 6–10 years experience. This allows us to calculate $[Y(16)/Y(12)]^{1/4}$. When this calculation is performed, using Freeman's results based on yearly earnings in 1968,[22] the marginal rate of return to completing four years of college appears to have been 10.5 percent. The same calculation based on *weekly* earnings yields an estimate of only 9.4 percent. The larger figure is more closely comparable with Mincer's 1959 regression, which was estimated using annual earnings.

---

[22] Richard B. Freeman, "The Decline in the Economic Rewards to College Education," *Review of Economics and Statistics*, 54 (February 1977), 18–29 (Table 2).

Subsequently, the rate of return to completing four years of college declined abruptly, reaching a low of 6.4 percent in 1975 (based on weekly earnings).[23] The lion's share of the decline in the relative earnings of college graduates was borne by those just entering the labor force. Freeman makes a forceful case that *both* demand and supply shifts were responsible for the economic misfortune of college graduates that started in the late 1960s. He also shows that in response to declining rate of return, high school graduates were less likely to enter college.

POSTSCRIPT: DO WE HAVE OVER- OR UNDERINVESTMENT IN SCHOOLING?

Entire books can be (and have been) devoted to answering this question, and we will only sketch an answer here, concentrating on the investment decision from the private individual's point of view. We have assumed that the individual investor is interested in maximizing wealth. If schooling's only effect were to increase market earning power, then wealth maximization would require that schooling be undertaken up to the point where the rate of return to the last dollar spent on schooling equaled that obtainable to other forms of investment, physical capital included. To the extent that schooling is an enjoyable experience yielding consumption value in addition to increased future earnings, and to the extent that efficiency in home production is increased, the rates of return as usually estimated are too small. On the other hand, most studies ignore the effect of progressive income taxation on private rates of return, and thereby may present estimates that are too large.[24] Note that the bias from ignoring income taxes when estimating the rate of return may not be as large as it at first seems, since income taxation reduces the *cost* as well as *returns* to schooling. Why?

Many studies of schooling and the educational system focus on the *social* return to schooling as opposed to the private return we have discussed thus far.[25] The social rate of return to schooling is less than the private rate of return to the extent that public contributions supplement private expenditures on the direct cost of schooling. The social rate of return is greater than the private rate of return to the extent that individuals with more schooling (say, a college degree) increase not only their own earning power, but that of others. For example, workers whose supervisors are well educated may be more productive than other workers and thereby earn more. Income taxes, which probably should be subtracted from calculations of private rates of return (because taxpayers may not value government expenditures as highly as an equal amount they would spend themselves), should not be subtracted from calculations of social rates of return.

---

[23] Richard B. Freeman, "The Facts About the Economic Decline of College," *Journal of Human Resources,* 15 (Winter 1980), 124–42.

[24] If taxes are viewed as payment for "value received," then it would not be appropriate to reduce private rate-of-return calculations to correct for income taxes paid.

[25] For a more detailed discussion, see Becker, *Human Capital,* chap. 5.

What then do estimated private rates of return suggest about wealth-maximizing behavior? Until the mid-1960s, the private marginal rate of return for white male college graduates was probably 10 percent or more. It would not be correct to compare this figure with the return obtainable on a highly liquid, low-risk investment such as a government bond, because investments in human capital have a relatively uncertain outcome. The cost of investment in human capital, then, includes not only the interest that must be given up by not placing funds in a safe, liquid investment, but also a premium that most investors require if they are to invest in less secure projects, such as common stocks or business firms.

A widely used benchmark against which to measure the rate of return to investment in schooling has been the real rate of return to corporate manufacturing investments. Stigler has estimated this to be approximately 7 percent, which is lower than all but the lowest rate of return estimated by Freeman during the most depressed period for college graduates in the mid-1970s. Taken at face value, a comparison of the rate of return to college education with that on physical capital in manufacturing suggests that over most of the last 45 to 50 years, wealth could have been increased if additional white males had invested in college education—even acquiring some graduate school experience. In drawing this conclusion, however, it is essential to bear in mind all the possible biases inherent in estimating the rate of return to investment in human capital. Economists are not in agreement as to whether the rate of return to schooling has been correctly estimated or, if so, whether the rate of return to acquiring a college degree for a typical college graduate is that which would accrue to a typical high school graduate were a degree to be obtained.[26]

Whether the decline in the economic rewards to a college degree that Freeman observes after the mid-1960s are the result of temporary or permanent forces remains to be seen. The demographic reasons for the cause of this decline discussed in Chapter 3 suggest that the rate of return will rebound from the low levels of the 1970s. It has probably started to do so already.

From the point of view of the private individual, investment in schooling does not appear to have frequently exceeded the amount implied by the assumption of wealth maximization. Even with the possible decline in the rate of return to a college degree in recent years, it is likely that the rate of return to investment in human capital for most persons is not now below that

---

[26] Another interpretation of the excess of the rate of return to schooling over that to physical capital is possible. Acquiring schooling may be distasteful (a "bad" instead of a "good") to the average individual. If so, then pecuniary wealth maximization and utility maximization do not amount to the same thing, because the displeasure of attending school must be taken into account. Edward Lazear reaches the conclusion that schooling affects utility negatively and that is why rates of return to schooling exceed those to physical capital ["Education: Consumption or Production," *Journal of Political Economy*, 85:3 (June 1977)].

to physical capital. The rate of return to graduation from high school is almost surely considerably higher.[27]

CONCLUSION

We have introduced the analysis of long-run labor supply decisions by focusing on human capital from the household point of view. Investment in human capital involves long-run labor supply decisions in that the forces affecting the allocation of time between market and nonmarket activities that were assumed to be outside the control of the household in Chapter 4 are now seen to be the subject of economic decision making. Although short-run labor supply decisions and long-run decisions involving investments in schooling, health, job search, movement from one labor market to another, and the like (for oneself and for one's children) affect the constraints under which time-allocation decisions are made, it is also true that work-leisure choices feed back to human capital investment decisions as well. For example, the rate of return to investment in schooling will be greater, the larger the amount of time one expects to supply to the labor market and thereby reap the benefits of higher wage rates. These interdependencies between short-run and long-run labor supply decisions constitute the framework within which some of the most recent and advanced studies of labor supply and human capital behavior have been conducted.

We began this chapter by introducing the concept of wealth maximization and connecting to the more basic motivation of maximizing utility. The concepts of present value and the rate of return are the analytical tools used in understanding how wealth maximization determines behavior in the human capital framework. Investment in human capital was linked to the determination of learning capacity, and these tools were then applied to occupational choice and decisions on the amount of schooling individuals attain. One of the important concepts used in the discussion of schooling and earnings is the human capital earning-power function.

Finally we used the theory of human capital and the earnings function to analyze trends in schooling, the rate of return to college, and the supply

---

[27] Because of its complexity, we do not discuss the problem of the socially optimum amount of schooling and that of justifying publicly subsidized education. These issues involve questions of both economic efficiency (Do individual borrowing difficulties make private opportunity costs of schooling greater than the social opportunity cost? Do external benefits of education warrant the encouragement of more schooling than individuals would normally choose for themselves?) and equity (Should government support education through grants to individuals or through loans? Should the rich receive these forms of aid as well as the poor?). The interested reader may wish to consult one or more of several books and monographs on these topics. Some suggested sources are: Gary S. Becker, *Human Capital*, 2d ed. (New York: Columbia University Press, 1975), Chap. 5; *Journal of Political Economy*, 80:3, part 2 (May–June 1978), particularly the paper by T. W. Schultz; Byron W. Brown and Daniel H. Saks, "The Production and Distribution of Cognitive Skills within Schools," *Journal of Political Economy*, 83:3 (June 1975), 571–94.

and demand for college enrollment in the United States over the past thirty-five years. In the next chapter the model will be extended to cover on-the-job training and other job-related investments in human capital.

REFERENCES AND SELECTED READINGS

ARROW, KENNETH, "Higher Education as a Filter," *Journal of Public Economics,* 2:3 (July 1973), 193–216.

BECKER, GARY S., AND BARRY R. CHISWICK, "Education and the Distribution of Earnings," *American Economic Review,* 56:2 (May 1966), 358–69.

———, *Human Capital,* 2d ed. New York: National Bureau of Economic Research, 1975.

BLINDER, ALAN, AND YORAM WEISS, "Human Capital and Labor Supply: A Synthesis," *Journal of Political Economy,* 84:3 (June 1976), 449–472.

BROWN, BYRON W., AND DANIEL H. SAKS, "The Production and Distribution of Cognitive Skills within Schools," *Journal of Political Economy,* 88:3 (June 1975), 571–94.

FREEMAN, RICHARD, "Legal 'Cobwebs': A Recursive Model of the Market for New Lawyers," *Review of Economics and Statistics,* 57:2 (May 1975), 171–79.

———, "Overinvestment in College Training?" *Journal of Human Resources,* 10:3 (Summer 1975), 287–311.

———, "The Decline in the Economic Rewards to College Education," *Review of Economics and Statistics,* 54:1 (February 1977), 18–29.

———, "The Facts About the Economic Decline of College," *Journal of Human Resources,* 15:1 (Winter 1980), 124–42.

FRIEDMAN, MILTON, AND SIMON KUZNETS, *Income from Independent Professional Practice.* New York: National Bureau of Economic Research, 1945.

GRILICHES, ZVI, "Estimating the Returns to Schooling: Some Econometric Problems," *Econometrica,* 45:1 (January 1977), 1–22.

HECKMAN, JAMES J., "A Life-Cycle Model of Earnings, Learning, and Consumption," *Journal of Political Economy,* 84:4, part 2 (August 1976), S11–S44.

HIRSHLEIFER, J., *Investment, Interest and Capital.* Englewood Cliffs, N.J.: Prentice-Hall, Inc., 1970.

JOHNSON, THOMAS, "Returns from Investment in Human Capital," *American Economic Review,* LX:4 (September 1970), 546–60.

KATZ, ELIAKIM, AND ADRIAN ZIDERMAN, "On Education, Screening and Human Capital," *Economics Letters,* 6 (1980), 81–88.

MINCER, JACOB, "A Study of Personal Income Distributions," Ph.D. dissertation, Columbia University, 1957.

———, "Investment in Human Capital and Personal Income Distribution," *Journal of Political Economy,* 66:4 (August 1958), 281–302.

———, *Schooling, Experience and Earnings.* New York: National Bureau of Economic research, 1974.

ROSEN, SHERWIN, "A Theory of Life Earnings," *Journal of Political Economy*, 84:4, part 2 (August 1976), S45–S68.

SCHULTZ, THEODORE W., "Optimal Investment in College Instruction: Equity and Efficiency," *Journal of Political Economy*, 80:3 (May/June 1972), S1–S30.

SPENCE, MICHAEL, "Job Market Signaling," *Quarterly Journal of Economics*, 87:3 (August 1973), 355–79.

STIGLER, GEORGE J., *Capital and Rates of Return in Manufacturing Industries*. Princeton, N.J.: Princeton University Press, for the National Bureau of Economic Research, 1963.

————, and D. BLANK, *The Demand and Supply of Scientific Personnel*. New York: National Bureau of Economic Research, 1957.

STIGLITZ, JOSEPH, "The Theory of 'Screening,' Education, and the Distribution of Income," *American Economic Review*, 45:3 (June 1975), 283–300.

UNITED NATIONS, *Yearbook of National Account Statistics*, Vol. 2, 1979.

U.S. DEPARTMENT OF COMMERCE, BUREAU OF THE CENSUS, *Historical Statistics of the United States, Colonial Times to 1970*. Washington, D.C.: Government Printing Office, 1975.

————, *Statistical Abstract of the United States*, 1980.

WALSH, J. R., "Capital Concept Applied to Man," *Quarterly Journal of Economics*, 49:2 (February 1935), 255–85.

WELCH, FINIS, "Education in Production," *Journal of Political Economy*, 78:1 (January/February 1970), 35–51.

WOLPIN, KENNETH I., "Education and Screening," *American Economic Review*, 67:5 (December 1977), 949–58.

EXERCISES

Choose whether statements 1, 2, and 3 are *True, False,* or *Uncertain* (whether true or false depends on unspecified circumstances). Justify your answer. Your justification is the most important part of your answer.

1. Strictly speaking, in the equation

$$\log \text{Wage} = \alpha(0) + \alpha(1) \text{ Schooling}$$

   the coefficient $\alpha(1)$ equals the rate of return to schooling only if all costs of schooling consist of foregone earnings.

2. The effect of an increase in the minimum wage on school attendance is indeterminate a priori.

3. Providing scholarships according to students' ability will promote income equality.

4. Joe Oxx has just graduated from high school. Joe desires to maximize his human wealth (present value of his income stream), but unfortunately for him, he can't plan any further in advance than two years. As a result of a recent program to aid college athletes, Joe may borrow or lend as much money as he desires at a

constant market interest rate of 10 percent. Finally, he has available only three occupational possibilities:

Occupation	Pays Income This Year of	Pays Income Next Year of
Professional football player	$ 21,000	0 (body wears out)
Secretary	$ 9,000	$13,000
Tennis instructor	$-10,000 (training costs)	$33,000

Which occupation gives Joe the highest present value of income? In formulating your answer, assume that income is received or costs paid at the *beginning* of a year. Show your calculations.

5. At a recent meeting of the Rocky Mountain Economic Association, Professor Berry Bush, chairman of the department of economics at Aspen State Teacher's College, was heard to remark: "Human capital theory says that individuals with identical amounts of investment in human capital will have equal labor market incomes." Is he right? Explain your answer carefully and support it graphically.

9

INVESTMENT
IN HUMAN CAPITAL:
Firms

A. Educational objectives

1. To extend the theory of human capital to cover investments via on-the-job training (OJT)
2. To present quantitative estimates of the importance of OJT
3. To apply the concept of OJT investments to several forms of labor market behavior

B. On-the-job training (OJT) as investment in human capital (p. 329)

1. Overview—difficulties in measuring OJT costs and returns (p. 330)
2. Theoretical analysis (p. 332)
   a. The effect of OJT on VMP
   b. General and specific training
   c. Calculating investment in OJT and the rate of return
   d. The earning-power-function approach
3. Extension of OJT theory: life-cycle work and consumption (p. 348)
4. Applications of OJT theory: geographic mobility and the family (p. 350)
5. Implicit labor contracts and internal labor markets (p. 353)
   a. Wage flexibility
   b. Internal labor markets

*C. Frontiers of labor economics: Fixed costs, training costs, and the employment-hours mix (p. 361)

---

* Indicates more technical material that may be skipped without loss of continuity.

In Chapter 8 we focused on human capital investment that takes place for the most part outside of firms. The most important form of human capital examined was investment in schooling. An important investment activity we mentioned only briefly in Chapter 8 is generation of human capital by job-related activities. Schooling increases labor market productivity in a multitude of ways—communication skills, mathematical and logical facility, occupation-specific instruction in business administration, data processing, medicine, and so on—but few individuals enter the labor market with sufficient knowledge to perform a job as efficiently as an experienced worker. It is necessary to gain occupation-specific knowledge that is either taught in school or requires additional practice to develop proficiency—how to sell a pair of shoes, take a blood sample, write a will, prepare an income tax statement. Moreover, each firm has its own special way of doing business that requires *firm-specific* knowledge to perform properly.

Workers' value to employers increases with the accumulation of such productivity-enhancing *training*. Training is an intrinsic component of most jobs, leading to improved performance on given tasks and, in many cases, to advancement toward supervisory roles in the firm. The labor market provides incentives to acquire training. *Job training* is a much broader concept than formal training programs. It is probable that the great bulk of investment in job training is informal—learning by doing—rather than well-defined formal programs. For example, a mechanic newly employed by an auto repair shop needs to learn where the tools are kept; someone beginning work for a large corporation may not learn all "the ropes," such as who to see for what problems, for several months; young trial lawyers need to know the characteristics and attitudes of local judges and the other attorneys in town. The relatively small amount of data on firms' training activities supports this assumption. For example, Mincer[1] reported results of a survey of New Jersey industries made by the New Jersey Bureau of Apprenticeship and Training which indicated that about 5 percent of workers were participating in formal training programs. Only 16.2 percent of New Jersey firms had formal training programs. Such programs—especially apprenticeship training—seem to have declined historically, having been supplanted to some extent by increased schooling.[2] Thus, in order to capture the full dimension and impact of on-the-job training (OJT), indirect measures that focus mainly on informal training must be used.

---

[1] Jacob Mincer, "On-the-Job Training: Costs, Returns, and Some Implications," *Journal of Political Economy*, 70:5, part 2 (October 1962).

[2] Paul G. Keat, "Long-Run Changes in Occupational Wage Structure 1900–56," *Journal of Political Economy*, 68:6 (December 1960).

AN OVERVIEW OF MEASUREMENT PROBLEMS

Indirect measurements of OJT are needed because firms do not typically keep track of such training costs as they do of, say, raw material costs. This is not to say that firms are unaware of the informal training process. Profit-maximizing firms could hardly remain unaware of the growth in worker productivity that goes with experience and of the costs that go with losing experienced workers and hiring replacements. Mincer[3] quotes the following passage from a New York Merchants and Manufacturers Association study:

> [On-the-job training costs include] the expense brought about by substandard production of new employees while learning their job assignments and becoming adjusted to their work environment; the dollar value of time spent by supervisors and other employees who assist in breaking in new employees on their job assignment, and costs of organized training programs.

Calculations by the R. G. Barry Corporation presented in Table 9-1 indicate that training new workers can be extremely expensive.[4] These costs, incurred during the early years of experience, yield returns throughout the term of employment and hence represent an investment in human capital. To them should be added the costs of a personnel department whose function is to search for, recruit, and process new employees. In evaluating the magnitude of the costs reported in Table 9-1, remember that today, inflation since 1969 alone would probably make them at least $2\frac{1}{2}$ times larger.

It is quite difficult for a firm to assess accurately OJT costs. The effort involved in apportioning supervisory time between overseeing new and experienced employees, in evaluating the expenses due to substandard produc-

TABLE 9-1   Amount of Money Invested per Employee, R. G. Barry Corporation, 1969

Skill Level	Investment by Firm
Least skilled (i.e., materials handler)	$ 273
Semi-skilled (i.e., maintenance mechanic)	1,712
First-line supervisor	4,000
Middle manager	16,000
Top-level manager	34,500

Sources: "The Roving Kind, Penchant of Americans for Job Hopping Vexes Companies Increasingly," *The Wall Street Journal*, March 25, 1970, p. 1; and "R. G. Barry Includes Its Employees' Value on Its Balance Sheet," *The Wall Street Journal*, April 3, 1970, p. 14.

---

[3] Mincer, "On-the-Job Training," p. 62.
[4] For older (1951), but more disaggregated, data concerning the cost of a new employee, see Walter W. Oi, "Labor as a Quasi-Fixed Factor," *Journal of Political Economy*, 70:6 (December 1962), 546.

tion, and so on, will in many cases be so great compared to the benefits to the firm that relatively casual information is used to guide the firm's employment policies. Even if such cost data were readily available, it would not tell us who—the firm or the employee—actually bears the costs and reaps the returns of investment in OJT human capital. It is the answer to this question, as well as knowledge of the magnitude of OJT capital, that is of interest to us in examining how OJT affects earnings and other important aspects of the labor market.

Whether the firm or the employee actually bears the cost and reaps the return of OJT has no relationship to who makes the nominal payment—writes the check, so to speak. Just as with a tax or subsidy on the sale of a good or service, who bears the cost depends on the interaction of market supply and demand forces and not on whom the tax is levied upon or to whom the subsidy is paid by law. (Recall the example of the social security tax in Chapter 5.) Some firms may have the reputation of providing excellent training programs on which they spend substantial sums. They may be very selective in their hiring policies and offer employees fine opportunities for advancement as their tenure with the firm grows. Nevertheless, employees may actually be paying for these OJT investments by accepting relatively low rates of pay during the early years of employment. Other firms, who pay higher starting salaries, may not increase wage rates as rapidly as job tenure grows. In the former case, the worker, through accepting a relatively low rate of pay to begin with, is actually bearing a substantial portion of the cost of investing in OJT. The return to this human capital investment occurs in later years in the form of a higher rate of pay. In the latter case, assuming the growth in workers' productivity is the same, the firm is actually bearing OJT costs by paying workers more than their value when they are first hired, and it is the firm that reaps the returns as worker productivity grows along with job tenure, while wage rates rise less rapidly.

Investment in OJT is extensive and an important component of total human capital in the United States. Mincer, in a pathbreaking empirical study of OJT, estimated annual aggregate investment in OJT actually paid for by workers in 1958 as $13.5 billion, and investment in schooling as $21.6 billion. Since 1958 was near the peak of the postwar "baby boom," the proportion of school-age persons in the population was relatively large, and the proportion of investment via schooling was larger than usual. Mincer estimated that in 1949, the amount of annual human capital investment via OJT was approximately equal to that taking place via schooling. It is unfortunate that more recent estimates of the magnitude of OJT and schooling investments have not been published. As we develop the theoretical analysis of OJT in the next section, it will become clearer to you how Mincer arrived at his estimates. The analysis of OJT builds on the study of investment in schooling presented in Chapter 8.

The estimates of the amount of investment and rate of return to OJT apply only to investment by workers, not to those actually paid for by firms. In order to obtain information on the amount of OJT investment actually paid for by firms, data on the value of workers' marginal product comparable in detail to wage or earnings data would be needed. Since such information is not generally available, studies of the cost and returns to OJT have usually been limited to the worker's point of view.

THEORETICAL ANALYSIS

The theoretical analysis of OJT is an extension of the framework developed to study investment in schooling. Complications arise, however, because, as suggested above, OJT investment may be undertaken by either firms or workers. In order to understand this problem, recall that if schooling were the only form of investment in human capital, typical worker value to an employer—the value of the worker's marginal product—would depend only on schooling (ignoring interpersonal differences in luck and ability). Therefore, ignoring depreciation of human capital attributable to aging, obsolescence of knowledge, and environment changes such as increases in the quantity or quality of physical capital, worker's marginal product would not change after schooling was completed. It would be constant throughout one's working life. A typical worker's age-VMP profile both with and without OJT is shown in Figure 9-1 for a worker who has acquired $S(2)$ years of schooling. Along the horizontal axis of Figure 9-1, age is measured in years. The origin represents the age at leaving school with $S(1)$ years of school obtained—say, age $S(1) + 5$ years if children typically enter school when they are 5 years old. The vertical axis measures VMP in dollars. It will make Figure 9-1 easier to read, without loss of information, if we assume that a

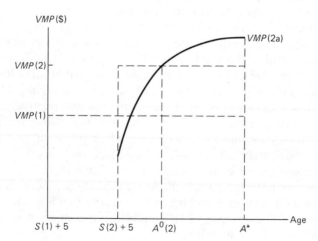

FIGURE 9-1. Age-VMP relationship with OJT

worker who acquires $S(1)$ years of schooling acquires no OJT and has a constant VMP equal to $VMP(1)$ dollars until the age of retirement, which we assume to be age A^* years. Another worker, identical to the worker with $S(1)$ years of schooling in all respects except that $S(2)$ years of schooling are acquired, would have a VMP equal to $VMP(2)$ starting at age $S(2) + 5$ and continuing until retirement.

With competitive labor market conditions, market wage rates would equal VMP for each worker, and a worker's return to acquiring $S(2) - S(1)$ additional years of schooling would be $VMP(2) - VMP(1)$ dollars per year. When OJT occurs, a worker will no longer have an age-VMP profile exactly equal to $VMP(2)$ after age $S(2) + 5$. Rather, as training occurs, a worker's VMP grows as a result. Thus, the relationship between VMP and age has an upward tilt, leveling off as training ceases. If we assume no depreciation of skills with age, VMP eventually stops growing and then remains constant until retirement, as shown in Figure 9-1. In Figure 9-1, $VMP(2a)$ is the age-VMP profile corresponding to $S(2)$ years of schooling when OJT occurs. Initially $VMP(2a)$ is less than $VMP(2)$ because OJT is costly, and these costs reduce net VMP. At age $A^0(2)$, $VMP(2a)$ equals $VMP(2)$, and this is therefore similar to the "overtaking" age of Figure 8-10, except that Figure 9-1 refers to VMP, not earnings.

With OJT, VMP grows over time as training occurs, eventually attaining a level higher than without OJT. Note that because of OJT costs, the *net* VMP of a worker with $S(2)$ years of schooling may initially be less than that of a worker who attended school for fewer years. Many of you may have had some experience as interns in business firms or worked summers in a plant where the experienced employees, many of whom did not attend college, made fun of the neophyte workers. While the teasing may hurt, it may reflect in part the "old-timers'" perception that you really didn't contribute much to output, as well as their envy of your future VMP and earning power.

The existence of OJT introduces an important new problem in labor market analysis. While, under competitive conditions, we have so far seen that wage rates equal VMP, OJT introduces the likelihood that this equality will not hold at each moment in time. To explore this relationship further, we will take a closer look at the worker who acquires $S(2)$ years of schooling. In Figure 9-2, $S(2)$ represents graduating from college (16 years of schooling); $S(2) + 5$ corresponds to 21 years of age $(16 + 5)$. The curve $VMP(2a)$ represents the age-VMP profile of a typical college graduate. $VMP(2)$ measures the value of marginal product of a college graduate if there were no OJT. $VMP(2a)$ equals $VMP(2)$ less all the costs of OJT, plus all the returns. These costs may include direct costs such as salaries of instructors, materials used, and indirect costs such as wasted production, time taken by other employees who are not instructors as such but who help new workers "learn the ropes," and so on. Another item that must be subtracted from $VMP(2)$ is the expense associated with hiring a new worker, such as giving aptitude

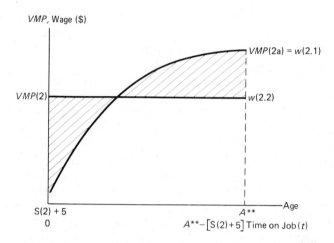

FIGURE 9-2. Wage rates and *VMP* over time with OJT

tests, filling out forms, and so on. After these costs are subtracted, it is possible that *VMP*(2a) is zero or even negative during the early years of a worker's tenure on a job, although in Figure 9-2 *VMP*(2a) is always positive.

Given the age-*VMP* profile (2a), what age-wage profiles might be adopted by a competitive, profit-maximizing employer? One possibility would be to set $w = VMP(2a)$ at all times. The resulting wage profile, $w(2.1)$, would coincide exactly with *VMP*(2a) and satisfy the competitive condition, established in Chapter 3, that the wage rate always equals the value of marginal product. With $w = VMP(2a)$, the firm would have no incentive to hire additional workers, and each worker would be unable to earn a higher wage anywhere else, because no other employer would be willing to pay a higher wage rate. (Why?) Suppose now that the employer is sure that a typical employee will stay on the job for $A_t - S(2) - 5$ years. A_t is an age equal to or less than the worker's expected retirement age A^*. (This knowledge need not be held with certainty for each employee but may be an expectation based on experience with a large number of employees or on evidence gathered by observing the experience of other firms.) Under these circumstances, the employer would be willing to pay workers an amount greater than *VMP*(2a) during the early years of tenure with the firm, provided that this "loan" would be repaid, with interest, later on. To keep Figure 9-2 simple, suppose this wage profile is $w(2.2)$, which just happens to coincide with *VMP*(2). (This means we don't have to draw still another line in Figure 9-2.) Workers might prefer this wage profile, because it would be one way of maintaining spending capacity without borrowing money formally while *VMP*(2a) is relatively low. Each year that *VMP* fell short of w the employer would be "lending" an amount $w(2.2) - VMP(2a)$ to the employee. After *VMP*(2a) rises above $w(2.2)$, the employer's "loan" is eventually repaid.

To show how we apply the theory of human capital to OJT, we turn to Figure 9-3, where investment in OJT takes place only during the first year on the job, between ages $S(2) + 5$ and $S(2) + 6$. Suppose that during the first year an employee works for a firm (which happens to be the first year after the employee leaves school), $VMP(2a)$ falls short of the wage paid by x dollars. The area between $w(2.2)$ and $VMP(2a)$ going from age $S(2) + 5$ to age $S(2) + 6$ is equal to x. The firm is said to invest x dollars in the OJT of this worker. Since this is the only year during which training takes place, and subsequently $VMP(2a)$ increases sufficiently to exceed the wage rate, the rate of return on the employers' investment is ρ, such that the *sum* over t of $[VMP(2a)_t - w_t]/(1 + \rho)^t$ equals x, where $t = 1$ during the first year *after* the firm invests in OJT, 2 the next year, 3 the following year, and so on up to the last year of the worker's tenure with the firm. (You may wish to review the sections on the rate of return in Chapter 8 before going on.)

The rate of return to OJT can also be determined in situations in which the firm invests in training for a period longer than one year, even if the investment period is not known with certainty. (This corresponds to the case shown in Figure 9-2.) To see why it is not necessary to know the number of years during which investment occurs, we will reexamine the expression for the rate of return to OJT where the investment period is only one year. This expression is an implicit definition of ρ, the rate of return to OJT. It is based on setting the sum over t of $[VMP(2a)_t - w_t]/(1 + \rho)^t$ equal to x, and solving for the value of ρ that makes the equation true. In Figure 9-3, x is exactly the same as $[w_1 - VMP(2a)_1]/(1 + \rho)^0$, since $t = 0$ during the first year on the job and $(1 + \rho)^0 = 1$. Therefore, the method for calculating ρ would work just as well if we *subtracted* $x \equiv [w_1 - VMP(2a)_1]/(1 + \rho)^0$ from both sides of the equality. Since $(-x) \equiv [VMP(2a)_1 - w_1]/(1 + \rho)^0$, ρ would then be defined by

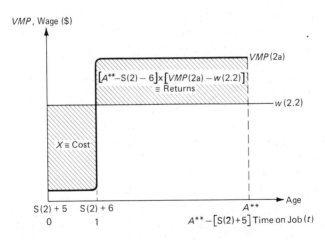

FIGURE 9-3. Wage profile showing firm investing in OJT during first year of job, with returns occurring after the first year

setting the *sum* over t of $[VMP(2a)_t - w_t]/(1 + \rho)^t$ equal to 0. This procedure requires knowledge only of $VMP(2a)_t$ and w_t. Thus, it is unnecessary to specify over how many years the firm invests in OJT. This method allows us to calculate ρ whenever w exceeds VMP for at least one year and VMP exceeds w for at least one year.

To make sure that you understand the discussion in the last two paragraphs, go back to Figure 9-2 and examine wage profile $w(2.1)$. You should see that in the case of wage profile $w(2.1)$, since $VMP - w$ is always 0, there is no investment by the firm in OJT. The OJT equation developed above holds trivially, as $0 = 0$, with ρ undefined.

The "loans" in the form of $w_t - VMP_t$ represent *investment* by the firm in the OJT human capital of its employees. Under the assumption that firms want to maximize profits, we have the same rule for investing in human capital as we derived for the household in Chapter 8: The firm will maximize its profit, or wealth, by undertaking all investments for which the rate of return ρ exceeds the market rate of interest (r). In equilibrium, therefore, the rate of return on the firm's last investment will equal the market rate of interest. If ρ exceeded r, it would pay the firm to take advantage of this opportunity to earn more profits by hiring additional workers and investing in their training, and additional firms would enter the industry, increasing the demand for workers. Given increasing costs for each firm and a downward-sloping demand curve for the industry's output (and possibly an upward-sloping supply curve of labor), VMP must eventually fall (and wage rates rise) so that equality of r and ρ on each firm's last, or marginal, investment in human capital is achieved. (Why?)

An important implication of the preceding paragraphs is that once the possibility of the firm's investing in OJT is considered, wage profile $w(2.1)$ in Figure 9-2 need not hold: VMP need not equal w at every moment in time, even under conditions of competitive equilibrium. All that need hold is that the *present value* of a typical worker's VMP over the period of expected job tenure with the firm equal the *present value* of the wages paid. The insight that, under competitive conditions, wage-marginal product equality need hold only in the present-value sense is one of the most important in labor market analysis and bears implications for numerous forms of economic behavior including migration, quits, layoffs, and unemployment rates.

General and Specific Training

Under what circumstances will the rate of return be sufficiently high to induce an employer to invest in OJT? The answer depends in part on the effect of OJT on the length of time a typical employee is expected to remain with the firm. The employer's decision whether to invest in OJT depends crucially on *expected* returns. Obviously, if an employee is likely to quit as soon as training is completed and take a job elsewhere, it will not pay an employer to invest in training. Other things being equal, an employee will quit to take a new job if it pays more than the current job. Suppose a worker receives OJT that raises his or her *VMP* in other jobs by the same amount as in the firm providing the training. In this case, if the firm adopts wage profile $w(2.2)$ in Figure 9-3, thus paying for the full amount of OJT investment, a typical worker will soon be able to earn more than $w(2.2)$ in alternative jobs. The employee will quit, and the employer's investment in OJT will be lost. When OJT increases *VMP* in a large number of jobs by the same amount, we say that the worker receives **general training.** Clearly, a profit-maximizing firm will not invest in general OJT. Employers will not adopt wage profile $w(2.2)$ when training is general; rather, they will adopt wage profile $w(2.1)$, which implies that the *employees,* not employers, must bear the cost (and reap the returns) of general OJT.

The analysis of general OJT is formally similar to schooling. Schooling increases an individual's earning power equally in a large number of alternative jobs, and it is normally paid for by the individual or the family, frequently with public aid. Thus, the analysis of investment in schooling readily meshes with that of investment in OJT paid for by the individual. Postschooling OJT investment paid for by the individual is reflected in earnings that remain below the amounts that would be observed if no such training occurred and the returns to schooling were immediately reflected in money wages. There are numerous examples of general OJT. Perhaps the most obvious is apprenticeship training in various crafts, where apprentices receive considerably lower rates of pay than journeymen or master craftsmen. Young lawyers typically work for experienced practitioners at relatively low rates of pay before going out on their own. Physicians seeking to become specialists earn much less as residents in hospitals than they could receive in private practice without specializing. An "exception that proves the rule" regarding the employer's willingness to pay for general training is found in the armed services. One of the enticements used to induce voluntary enlistment by the military is the provision of vocational training. A major cost of military personnel is the loss of trained enlisted men who seek civilian employment at the end of their first or second terms in order to receive higher rates of pay than can be obtained in the military. The armed services may attract enlistments by paying for general training, but unless the enlistment terms are sufficiently long, these investments will not yield returns to military employers because enlisted men tend to quit after their *VMP* rises above their military rates of pay.

There is another instructive example of an exception to the rule that a firm will not invest in its workers' general OJT. This exception, which occurred during the early days of the nuclear power industry, represented a serious business error on the part of a company that should have known better. One of the largest and oldest companies in the steam-generating business, Babcock and Wilcox Co., contracted to build nuclear pressure vessels in southern Indiana for delivery to nuclear electric power generating plants elsewhere in the United States. Babcock and Wilcox engaged in an immense program to train farmers and farm workers to become skilled welders and machinists, thus providing general training. They hoped to create their own cheap labor force. By September 30, 1968, over 1,100 workers—two-thirds of those hired over the preceding three years—had quit, many to take jobs with competitors. B. and W. suffered large losses because of the defected trainees and because they could not meet their contractual obligations to deliver the nuclear pressure vessels.[5]

There are circumstances under which a profit-maximizing firm might invest in the general training of its workers. Any condition that reduces the probability of a worker's quitting and thereby increasing an employer's returns to OJT investment will increase the willingness of an employer to pay for OJT. Thus, when there are significant money and psychic costs to a worker of leaving one job to take another (moving expenses, leaving friendly neighbors and co-workers), it would not necessarily be inconsistent with the theory of OJT to observe employers investing in the general training of workers. Such a situation might come about owing to the geographic isolation of the place of employment. A likely example due to legal barriers to interfirm movement until a few years ago was in professional baseball (recall our discussion in Chapter 6), where the reserve clause may have protected the employer's interest in the general training of young players. Employers claimed the reserve clause was necessary because of the expense of running farm teams in which young players could be brought up to major league quality. From the players' point of view, however, the reserve clause was simply a tool with which management was able to retain players at lower salaries than would otherwise have been possible, since a disgruntled athlete's only option was to quit baseball or move to a different country to play.

Not all OJT is general training. Work experience with a firm may also raise an employee's *VMP* to the current employer, but not to others. For example, work practices differ among firms, and employees become more valuable to their employers as they learn the firm's characteristic ways of doing things, adjust to the personalities of supervisors and co-workers, and perhaps learn trade secrets. Such increases in *VMP* are firm-specific, because if an employee were to quit and take a job with another firm (even if the job were similar), all of these OJT investments would be lost; hence they are called **specific OJT.** Human capital investments in specific OJT raise workers' *VMP* where they are currently employed, but not elsewhere; consequently, specific OJT does not increase the wage rates workers can obtain in alternative employment. This means it is possible for an employer to reap returns from investing in specific OJT. If a typical worker accumulates only

---

[5] "The Great Nuclear Fizzle at Old B. and W.," *Fortune,* 80:6 (November 1969). We are grateful to Gary Margeson for suggesting this example.

specific OJT human capital as job tenure lengthens, so that *VMP* rises over time as in Figure 9-2, the employer will not automatically lose by adopting wage profile $w(2.2)$, thus investing in all of the worker's specific OJT and reaping all the returns. Other employers will not be willing to pay more than $w(2.2)$, so the worker will have no incentive to leave and thereby destroy the employer's investment in OJT.

Specific OJT raises the *VMP* of workers in the firm in which they are employed, but not elsewhere. Consequently, employers may invest in specific OJT. As we have seen, they may also invest in general OJT if conditions inhibit worker mobility to other jobs. It would be easy to assume that whenever opportunities to invest in specific OJT arise such that p exceeds r, the firm will always undertake the investment. However, the problem is not so simple. If the rate of return to specific OJT exceeds the rate of interest, it pays the wealth-maximizing worker as well as the employer to undertake the investment. Who, then, pays for and receives the returns to firm-specific OJT? A little reflection on this problem suggests that employees and employers will share specific OJT investments, whereas employees are more likely to pay for investments in general training. The reason is that the expected rate of return to OJT investments is greater if both employer and employee share costs and returns. Suppose, to the contrary, that an employee paid for all training investments and received all returns. The employee's wage rate would then always equal *VMP*. Under these circumstances, any unforeseen decline in the worker's value to the employer due, say, to adverse business conditions, would cause *VMP* to fall below w. The profit-maximizing employer would then lay off the worker, and the worker would lose all or part of his OJT investment. The worker's loss would depend on the probability of being recalled, the length of time it takes to find a new job, and the proportion of specific training in total OJT.

On the other hand, if the firm pays for all specific OJT investments, the worker's wage will never exceed the amount warranted by general training, and *VMP* will exceed w after the firm begins to reap the returns to its investment. Under these circumstances, the worker is much less likely to be laid off if *VMP* declines unexpectedly, because a "cushion" exists representing the employer's returns on investment—the excess of *VMP* over w. In fact, the employer may not lay off the worker even if *VMP* falls below w, because to do so increases the probability that the employee will not be available when recalled, and the employer will then have the expense of hiring and training new workers when business conditions improve. Unfortunately for the employer, however, if the worker's wage rate is based only on general training, an unanticipated increase in the worker's *VMP* in *other* firms will cause the worker's alternative opportunities to improve, and he or she may therefore quit to take another job. The employer's OJT investment would thus be lost.

Suppose for simplicity that all OJT is firm-specific and that firm and worker *share* specific OJT costs and returns. This situation is described in Figure 9-4. The horizontal line $g(s)$ in Figure 9-4 represents the marginal productivity of the worker with S years of schooling and no OJT. Assuming that the skills acquired through schooling do not depreciate, *VMP* due to schooling is constant over the working life. The worker's *VMP* to an employer may be less than g, however, during the initial time on the job if OJT occurs, because OJT requires supervisory and training personnel, materials, and so on. Thus, Figure 9-4 shows *VMP* to lie below $g(s)$ at first, rising above it later on. The worker's actual *VMP* overtakes the *VMP* that would exist without OJT at age $A^0(g)$. If the employer paid for all firm-specific OJT, w would always coincide with $g(s)$, while if the worker paid, w and *VMP* would always be equal. In Figure 9-4, firm and worker share the firm-specific OJT costs and returns as indicated by the fact that w crosses both the $g(s)$ and *VMP* profiles. During the early years of tenure with the firm, the worker receives more than *VMP*, but less than $g(s)$, which is what would be earned if no firm-specific OJT were undertaken. During later years, the worker earns more than would be earned elsewhere, since w exceeds $g(s)$; the wage overtakes $g(s)$ at age $A^0(w)$. This is the overtaking age at which we measured the rate of return to schooling in Chapter 8. The firm also benefits from its investment in OJT as shown by the fact that *VMP* crosses w at age $A^0(V)$.

The firm's investment in OJT starts when the employee is hired and continues beyond age $A^0(V)$. It is easy to make the mistake of concluding that $A^0(V)$ is the age at which the firm stops investing in OJT and starts to reap the returns. A moment's reflection will show why this is incorrect. If the returns

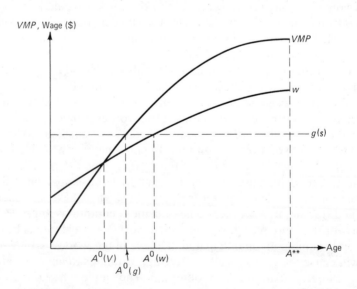

FIGURE 9-4. The firm and worker share specific OJT costs and returns

to each investment in human capital are constant over time, once the firm's investment ceases, *VMP* will remain constant until the worker leaves the firm. This is also the case in the schooling-only *VMP*s reflected in the profiles *VMP*(1) and *VMP*(2) in Figure 9-1 and in the one-year investment in OJT depicted in Figure 9-3. In Figure 9-4, although *VMP* exceeds *w* after age $A^0(V)$, it does not exceed *w* by a magnitude as large as the full return on prior OJT investment. The firm is still investing after $A^0(V)$, as reflected in the continuing increase in *VMP* for some years. Eventually *VMP* levels off, reflecting the end of the firm's investment period. Similarly, the worker's investment in OJT continues beyond the overtaking age $A^0(w)$, and the end of the investment period is reflected in the eventual leveling off of the age-wage profile *w*.

In the next section we present some calculations of worker investments in OJT for the United States, based on 1958 data. These calculations should help clarify the point that the investment period continues to the age at which *w* (or *VMP*, in the case of the firm's investment) levels off. Unfortunately, there are no data on *VMP* comparable to wage or earnings data that permit similar calculations to be carried out for firms' OJT investments.

Before going on to discuss applications and empirical studies of OJT, we need to deal with a common objection to the approach developed above. It has been argued that earning power in some jobs just "grows with experience," without any training taking place at all. This objection, while possibly accurate, does not invalidate the human capital approach. In a competitive economy, suppose that the wages obtainable in a given job are represented by a curve like *w* in Figure 9-4. Suppose that an alternative job pays wages equal to *g(s)*. If *w* always exceeded *g(s)*, workers would leave the low-paying occupation and seek jobs in the high-paying occupation. This would cause the *w* curve to fall and the *g(s)* curve to rise until they crossed, as in Figure 9-4. In other words, competition for jobs would force workers who desire to obtain the excess of *w* over *g(s)* in later years to pay for it by investing in the job that pays less than *g(s)* during the early years on the job. This payment is a human capital investment, and the analysis of OJT helps us to understand the relationship between investment cost and later returns.

Calculating Investment in OJT and the Rate of Return

In Chapter 8 we mentioned that two methods may be used to calculate the rate of return to investment in human capital. One involves the direct comparison of earnings profiles, while the other, which we developed fully in Chapter 8, involves the human capital earning-power function. In this chapter we will use both methods. The comparison of earnings streams is particularly useful when analyzing investment in OJT, because it shows the amount invested at each age and the age at which investment ceases.

The earnings-stream comparison method. Calculating OJT invest-ments and the rate of return by examining earning streams involves building up the amount invested stepwise, by comparing the age-earnings, or age-wage rate profiles of persons who have acquired a given amount of schooling and OJT with those of other individuals who have acquired a somewhat lower level of schooling and training. Theoretically, by starting with workers who never attended school, we could work our way up, comparing the earnings of individuals with adjacent schooling amounts, to the earnings of those who have graduate degrees, calculating the incremental dollar values and rates of return to investment in schooling and OJT for individuals at each level of schooling. The procedure requires solving for the rate of return by finding the interest rate that equates the present values of the earnings streams being compared. Our example is taken from the work of Jacob Mincer, who pioneered research in estimating the quantitative significance of OJT investments.

Mincer employed the earnings-stream comparison approach in his 1962 paper, "On-the-Job Training: Costs, Returns, and Some Implications." Ta-ble 9-2 shows some of Mincer's earnings-stream calculations. Although Mincer carried out his analysis for all schooling levels, we will show only how he calculated the *marginal* rate of return and the *additional* investments made by college graduates compared to high school graduates. (Mincer did not assume that direct schooling costs exactly equal earnings while in school. In fact, he estimated that direct costs exceeded the earnings of those attending college, hence the negative earnings for 18- to 21-year-old persons who were attending college.) The figures in Table 9-2 are age-earnings pro-files based on **synthetic cohorts.** A synthetic cohort is based on the assump-tion that the earnings *next* year of an individual who is now *t* years of age and who has acquired *S* years of schooling will be equal to the *current* earnings of someone else who also has attended school for *S* years, but who is now *t* + 1 years old. Similarly, earnings two years hence are estimated with data for someone with *S* years of schooling who is now *t* + 2 years old.

Mincer assumed that the marginal rate of return to schooling equals the marginal rate of return to OJT. While he assumed that both rates of return may change as schooling level increases, at each level of schooling individ-uals are assumed to add to their OJT until its rate of return equals the rate of return to schooling. This makes sense because, at least through college, the option presumably remains to continue schooling if its rate of return lies above the rate of return to training on a job. It would not be wealth-maximiz-ing to invest in OJT at a rate of return equal to, say, 10 percent, if going on for another year of school would yield 12 percent.

Mincer proceeded as follows. Calculating the earnings differentials shown in Table 9-2, column (3), he computed the interest rate that makes the present value of the sum of these earnings differentials equal to zero. This is the estimated *marginal* rate of return to college education *and* to OJT for

TABLE 9-2   Net Earnings Streams for United States
Male High School and College Graduates, 1958

Age	(1) 16+	(2) 12	(3) Differential in Earnings, (1) − (2)
	Years of Schooling		
18–21	$ −682	$2,800	$−3,482
22–24	3,663	3,537	126
25–29	5,723	4,381	1,342
30–34	7,889	5,182	2,707
35–44	10,106	6,007	4,099
45–54	11,214	6,295	4,919
55–64	10,966	6,110	4,856

Source: Jacob Mincer, "On-the-Job Training: Costs, Returns, and Some Implications," *Journal of Political Economy*, 70:5, part 2 (October 1962), Table A3. Reprinted by
permission of The University of Chicago Press. © by the
University of Chicago, 1962.

college-educated males, compared to acquiring both a high school education
and the OJT that a typical high school graduate acquires. Mincer estimated
this marginal rate of return to be 11.5 percent in 1958. Having computed this
rate of return, Mincer was then able to go back to the earnings streams and
calculate the incremental OJT investments of college graduates year by year.
In showing how this was done, we can also demonstrate why the point at
which the earnings streams cross—that is, where the earnings differentials of
Table 9-2, column 3, equal zero—does *not* show where OJT ceases to occur.

The procedure for using comparative earnings streams to calculate the
quality of OJT for college students (compared to high school graduates) is
shown in detail in Table 9-2A. Column (1) shows the earnings differentials
between college and high school graduates for single years for ages 18 to 44.
Direct schooling costs are subtracted to obtain net earnings of college students. The earnings of high school graduates are affected by the opportunity
cost of the OJT they are undertaking. Therefore, the earnings differential
(Table 9-2A, column 1) for age 18 represents the indirect plus direct costs
(times −1) of attending the first year of college, over and above the OJT cost
born by a typical high school graduate during the first year after graduation.
This differential, $3,246, is entered in the age 18 row of column 4. Following
this logic, it would be easy to assume that the additional cost of attending the
second year of college is therefore $3,403, the negative of the earnings
differential at age 19. This would be incorrect, however, because the earnings differential at age 19 is an understatement of the cost of attending the
second year of college! Since $\rho = 11.5$ percent, the student who attends

TABLE 9-2A   OJT Calculations Based on Data Supporting Table 9-2

Age	(1) Earnings Differential[a]	(2) Return on Last Year's Cost[b]	(3) Return on All Previous Cost	(4) Cost at Age Shown [−(1) + (3)]
18	$−3,246	$ −	$ −	$3,246
19	−3,403	373	373	3,776
20	−3,561	434	807	4,368
21	−3,719	502	1,308	5,027
22	− 203	578	1,887	2,090
23	126	240	2,127	2,001
24	455	230	2,357	1,902
25	685	219	2,576	1,891
26	913	217	2,793	1,880
27	1,349	216	3,009	1,660
28	1,672	191	3,200	1,528
29	2,009	176	3,376	1,367
30	2,336	157	3,533	1,197
31	2,522	138	3,671	1,149
32	2,707	132	3,803	1,096
33	2,892	126	3,929	1,037
34	3,077	119	4,048	971
35	3,260	112	4,160	898
36	3,448	103	4,263	815
37	3,638	94	4,357	719
38	3,824	83	4,440	616
39	4,010	71	4,511	501
40	4,145	58	4,568	423
41	4,278	49	4,617	339
42	4,411	39	4,656	245
43	4,540	28	4,684	144
44	4,674	17	4,701	27

[a] Difference between earnings of high school and college graduates from Table 9-2.
[b] Based on $\rho = 0.115$. See text.

the second year of college is giving up not only the earning power of a high school graduate and direct costs, but also the return on the first year of college attendance, which is $3,246 \times 0.115 = \$373$ [column (3)]. Assuming, as we have, that human capital does not depreciate, this return of $373 remains part of the student's earning power until the age of retirement. Thus, the cost of attending the second year of college is shown in column 4 to be $3,776. Similarly, the additional cost of attending the third year of college is the sum of foregone earnings at age 20 ($3,561) plus $0.115 \times \$3,776$

= \$434, the return on the second year's cost, plus \$373, the return on the first year's cost. \$434 + \$373 = \$807, shown in column (3), and the total additional cost of the third year of college is consequently \$4,368. The same calculations, adding 0.115 × \$4,368 = \$502, the return to the third year of college, yield \$5,027, the additional cost of the last year of college.

Age 22 is assumed to be the first year on the job. By now you should see that the earnings differential of \$203 between high school graduates and college students who are performing their first postschool year of market work is a gross understatement of the cost of whatever OJT they undertake during that year. According to the human capital model, if the typical college graduate undertook no OJT during the first or any subsequent year of post-school employment, his or her market earnings would be equal to full earning power, or the earning power of a high school graduate plus the returns to all previous training. In other words, the earnings of the college graduate would exceed those of a high school graduate by \$1,887, not fall short by \$203. The sum of \$1,887 and \$203, \$2,090, is therefore an estimate of the dollar amount of OJT incurred by a typical college graduate during the first year of employment in excess of that incurred by a high school graduate during the fifth year of employment. Now you should be able to see why the point at which the earnings differential becomes zero (between ages 22 and 23) does not reveal the age at which OJT ceases. Investment in OJT vanishes when no additional investment cost is implicit in the earnings-stream differential—that is, when the excess of the earning power of a typical college graduate over that of a typical high school graduate is sufficient to cover the returns on all prior investments. This does not occur in the 1958 data used to develop Table 9-2A until age 44.

The procedure described above compares the earnings of college graduates with those of high school graduates. Since high school graduates also invest in OJT, which affects their earning power and observed earnings, the investment costs from age 22 on tell us only the OJT investments made by college graduates in addition to those made by high school graduates of the same age. Mincer also developed OJT estimates for high school graduates and elementary school graduates. By assuming that persons with only one to four years of schooling received no OJT,[6] he was able to cumulate the OJT investment of calculations across schooling groups to obtain the total OJT investment costs for college graduates. To illustrate, while the *additional* OJT investment at age 30 is shown in column (4) of Table 9-2A to be \$1,197, *total* investment at that age was estimated by Mincer to be \$1,547. This is the sum of the additional investments made by college, high school, and elementary school graduates: \$1,197 + \$189 + \$161. In general, the amount invested in OJT is considerably greater, the higher the level of formal school-

---

[6] This assumption is undoubtedly false, and Mincer relaxed it, obtaining new estimates of the amount of OJT, in his later work, *Schooling, Experience and Earnings.* The OJT estimates for college graduates were not changed much, however.

ing. Evidently schooling and OJT are complementary factors of production. Mincer calculated the total lifetime OJT investment of a typical college graduate to be $30,700, based on 1958 data, while he estimated total schooling costs to be $26,000. In order to put these dollar amounts in perspective, remember that they are based on earnings data for 25 years ago. Considering the inflation and economic growth that have occurred over the years since, the investments measured in terms of today's wage levels would be four or five times as large.

Although the OJT investments of persons with less schooling were calculated to be considerably smaller, the age at which investment ceased was always around 40, the annual amount declining with age. It makes sense that human capital investments tend to occur relatively early in life, rates of return decline as one grows older. (Why?)

The earning power function approach.   The trick in adapting an earning-power function such as equation (8-7) or (8-8) to analyze OJT was developed by Jacob Mincer. A crucial assumption underlying these equations is that all the cost of an additional year of schooling consists of foregone earnings. Therefore, since 100 percent of potential work time is devoted to schooling, earning power after schooling is completed has grown to the point where it exceeds the earning power that would exist without any schooling ($\bar{Y}$) by the rate of return during each year of schooling. To see how this approach can be used to analyze investments in OJT, go back and look at Figure 9-3. Suppose that Figure 9-3 now represents an individual *worker's* investment in OJT rather than the *firm's* investment. Thus, imagine that curve $VMP(2a)$ represents the worker's *earnings* during the year OJT occurs and thereafter, while the curve $w(2.2)$ represents the worker's earnings if no OJT occurred. Figure 9-3 shows that, in general, foregone earnings when investment in OJT occurs does not amount to 100 percent of earning power. The shaded area between age $S(2) + 5$ and $S(2) + 6$ below the wage line represents these foregone earnings. Define k to be the ratio of this shaded area to the entire area between $S(2) + 5$ and $S(2) + 6$ below $w(2.2)$. Thus k is the ratio of foregone earnings, the cost of OJT, to earning power. As investment in OJT gradually approaches zero, so does k. The fraction k is also a measure of the *proportion of worktime* devoted to OJT. The returns to OJT will be smaller than if all worktime had been devoted to OJT by the fraction $(1 - k)$.

A reasonable procedure to allow for the likelihood that k and the rate of return to OJT are not constant is to use a human capital earning-power function that is similar in form to equation (8-8). Equation (8-8) reflects the possibility that the rate of return to schooling $\rho(1)$ changes as schooling changes. A comparable expression incorporating the effect of OJT is to add variables to equation (8-8) reflecting years of job experience after leaving school. The result is a human capital earning-power function

$$\ln Y = \ln \bar{Y} + \alpha(1)S + \alpha(2)S^2 + \alpha(3)X + \alpha(4)X^2 \qquad \textbf{(9-1)}$$

where $X \equiv$ years of experience on the job and, as in equation (8-8), the marginal rate of return to schooling $[\rho(1)]$ is $\alpha(1) + 2\alpha(2)S$. The coefficients $\alpha(3)$ and $\alpha(4)$ reflect not only the rate of return to OJT $[\rho(2)]$ but also k, the (changing) fraction of time allocated to OJT. With declining $\rho(1)$, $\rho(2)$, and k, we would expect both $\alpha(2)$ and $\alpha(4)$ to be negative. Mincer estimated the following equation (which does not include the variable S^2) with 1959 data for approximately 31,000 white, nonfarm, nonstudent men up to age 65. He obtained[7]

$$\ln Y = 6.20 + 0.107S + 0.081X - 0.0012X^2, \qquad R^2 = 0.29$$
$$\quad\quad\quad (72.3) \quad\ (75.5) \quad\ (-55.8) \qquad\qquad\qquad \textbf{(9-2)}$$

(The numbers in parentheses are t values.) The variable X measures experience as age minus S minus 5. The results show that a substantial proportion of annual earnings can be attributed to two variables—schooling and experience.

A major advantage of the human capital earning-power equation is its flexibility and the richness of the information it can yield. For example, it is not necessary, as in the earnings-streams comparison approach, to assume that the rate of return to schooling, $\rho(1)$, equals the rate of return to OJT, $\rho(2)$. Through a chain of mathematical manipulation (which we will not repeat here) Mincer shows that if an assumption is made regarding the period over which some OJT occurs (T), then $\rho(2)$ and k can be identified. Mincer shows that if T is assumed to equal 20 years, then $\rho(2) = 6.3$ percent, and k during the first year of OJT (k_0) is 0.58 (that is, over half of a typical worker's time is devoted to OJT); for $T = 30$ years, $\rho(2) = 11.9$ percent, and $k_0 = 0.42$.[8] Since the earnings comparison approach suggested that for high school and college graduates T is closer to 20 than to 30 years, it may be inferred from these results that the rate of return to OJT is somewhat lower than that to schooling. If that were true, society (and individuals) would be investing too little in schooling relative to OJT if it is desired to maximize wealth. Too little is known about the correct form of the human capital earning-power function, however, to be sure that this comparison between $\rho(1)$ and $\rho(2)$ is correct.

---

[7] Mincer, *Schooling, Experience and Earnings,* Table 5-1.
[8] *Ibid.,* p. 94.

EXTENSION OF OJT THEORY:
LIFE-CYCLE WORK AND CONSUMPTION PATTERNS

OJT causes earning power to rise with labor market experience. We have seen that in the case of persons with continuous labor force experience between the age of leaving school until the age of retirement, OJT occurs until about age 40, causing a continual increase in market earning power. After the age when OJT ceases, market earning power would remain constant if nothing else changed. However, two additional forces affect worker productivity, resulting in a tendency for wage rates to rise or fall after OJT investment ceases. One of these is depreciation of human capital. As we become older, we may suffer from failing physical strength and, perhaps, from declining mental capacity, causing market earning power to fall with age. Synthetic age-earning power profiles constructed from cross-section data typically look like curve Y_t^* in Figure 8-10 (p. 317). This reflects depreciation of human capital in later years.

A second force affecting worker productivity is general productivity growth in the economy. This productivity growth raises wage rates. Productivity growth affects market earning power in an opposite direction to human capital depreciation. Therefore, a typical individual's earning power is more likely to vary with age in a manner described by curve w in Figure 9-4 than by curve Y_t^* in Figure 8-10. That is, after the age at which OJT investment ceases, earning power may remain constant or even continue to grow slightly until quite late in life because of economywide increases in labor productivity.

For most persons, then, it would be reasonable to expect earning power to grow over a major portion of one's working life, with a decline in earning power occurring not at all or relatively late. This predictable life-cycle variation in the *price of time* bears implications for several forms of behavior: (1) the allocation of time between market work and the household; (2) the timing of investment in human capital; and (3) the estimation of labor supply functions. The key to these insights is based on labor supply analysis. Given the present value of lifetime earnings, it pays to allocate market work more intensively toward years when the price of "leisure" time is highest.

It may at first seem unreasonable to assume that individuals correctly anticipate the future course of their earning power. To be sure, many people will have good luck and underestimate the degree of economic success they eventually experience, while others suffer unanticipated misfortune. These random events tend to cancel out in large groups of people, however, so it is not really so hard to believe that, on the average, age-earning power profiles are correctly anticipated at the beginning of a typical worker's labor market years.

In this life-cycle framework, *anticipated* year-to-year changes in wage rates do not change an individual's wealth. Full lifetime wealth is the *present value* of total time available evaluated at each year's respective wage rate. When wage rates are correctly anticipated, *wealth* does not change from year to year; on the other hand, the relative price of goods and time *does* change, and this affects the optimal allocation of time between market work and the household. The individual is also concerned with the production of human capital, and the cost of investment which is also affected by the time path of market earning power.

The tendency of market earning power to rise as an individual grows older and perhaps to reach a peak before retirement creates a matching pattern of work and schooling incentives. It is cheaper to attend school early in life when earning power is low than to return to school after work experience has increased it. One implication is that the life-cycle correlation between wage rates and hours of work may tell us very little about the size of the income and substitution effects on labor supply, as discussed in Chapter 4. When life-cycle full wealth is known in advance, anticipated year-to-year variation in the wage rate has no income (wealth) effect. This means that a wage rate difference between two years will have only a relative price effect, affecting the allocation of market work time between the years. Thus, in studying labor supply, it is important to be sure that variation in the wage variable is not due to a life-cycle (anticipated) effect if it is desired to estimate what happens to labor supply when there is an *unanticipated* upward or downward shift in the age-wage profile.

Empirical investigations of the implications of OJT for labor supply behavior over the life cycle have been carried out in the studies referred to in the references at the end of this chapter. Some investigators have tackled the even more complex problem of the feedback from life-cycle labor supply to optimal investment in human capital. Since the returns to investment in schooling are affected by the amount of market work eventually supplied, simultaneous determination of lifetime labor supply, consumption, and human capital investment must be dealt with. So far, attempts to estimate labor supply, schooling, and OJT equations simultaneously have not yielded very reliable empirical results. The main reason for the difficulties encountered in these frontier studies is lack of information. In the more traditional approaches to estimating returns to investment in human capital, labor supply is taken as determined exogenously, while in analysis of labor supply, schooling has been taken as given. Unfortunately, existing data sources do not provide much information on individual characteristics that are not determined by the interaction of labor supply and human capital investment. More information on such variables as individual resources to finance human capital investments and abilities to benefit from them is needed.

APPLICATION OF OJT THEORY:
GEOGRAPHIC MOBILITY AND THE FAMILY

Wealth maximization requires that individuals accept jobs in those geographic areas (labor markets) where the present value of their real earnings will be highest, all other things being equal. Since moving from one place to another is costly, the gain in earning power obtained by leaving one labor market and moving to another must exceed the cost of doing so. In its simplest form, wealth maximization implies that workers will quickly move from one labor market to another whenever persistent wage differentials exist that are sufficiently large to cover the costs of moving. Nevertheless, although considerable migration does occur in the United States, many individuals who apparently could gain from moving do not do so. Research by economists into the reasons for individual differences in the propensity to move from one labor market to another has dealt with improving the accuracy with which the returns and costs of moving are measured. Understanding of labor mobility is important not only because of the insights gained into individual human capital investment decisions, but also because the outcome of mobility decisions has important implications for the efficiency of labor markets. As we saw in Chapter 5, movement of workers to jobs where their marginal productivity is highest generally promotes the efficient allocation of labor in the economy. Geographic mobility is a crucial component of this allocative process.

Observed wage differentials are not what they seem.   Job tenure and age have long been recognized as deterrents to all kinds of labor market mobility—between employers within a labor market as well as between employers in geographically separate locations. Is this negative correlation between the probability of job change and tenure, given observed wage differentials due to "noneconomic" behavior, inconsistent with wealth maximization? An understanding of human capital theory and OJT suggests it is not. The difference between the average level of wage rates in two labor markets reflects not only returns to the general human capital investments of workers in those markets, but also returns to job-specific investments. Worker investments in job-specific OJT will eventually result in the worker's earning a wage higher than he or she could obtain elsewhere. Therefore, observed wage differentials among labor markets tend to overstate the gain that would be obtained by a typical worker who moved from the low-wage market to the high-wage market. This overstatement is greater, the longer a given worker has remained on his or her current job.

Individual and family gains are not necessarily the same.   Even after observed wage differentials have been corrected for specific OJT investments, an individual worker may not respond to a potential wage gain because of family considerations. Following Jacob Mincer,[9] we can state the condition for geographic mobility as

$$G_f \equiv R_f - C_f > 0 \qquad (9\text{-}3)$$

where G_f is the net real income gain from migration *to the family*, R_f the returns (in present value), and C_f the costs. G_f is the *sum* of individual family member gains, or

$$G_f \equiv \sum_i G_i \qquad (9\text{-}4)$$

where i denotes the individual family members. Clearly, if we denote the principal earner of the family (usually the husband) as 1, it is possible that $G_1 > 0$ while $G_f < 0$. Some obvious reasons for such an intrafamily conflict of interest include (1) the pressure of school-age children, and (2) the labor force participation of the wife. It is costly to search for satisfactory new school arrangements for children; although the husband may be able to improve *his* labor market position by moving, the wife may be forced to relinquish a job in which she has acquired a specific OJT investment without an equally satisfactory job prospect in the new destination. These sources of conflict do not eliminate geographic mobility, but will tend to reduce it. If the gains from the marriage itself (marriage-specific human capital) are great enough, the wife will be willing to sacrifice her job prospects to facilitate the husband's labor market advancement. (A similar argument applies to the husband, of course. But since the husband's labor market attachment is generally stronger than the wife's, the sacrifice is usually that of the wife.)

Table 9-3 shows the negative influence of husband's age (a proxy for job tenure) and of wife's employment status on family migration.[10] The proportion of married men who moved from one state to another between 1965 and 1970 declines steadily with age and is smaller for husbands with working wives. The right-hand column of Table 9-3 suggests the negative impact on the wife's labor market opportunities of the husband's mobility. Of the employed wives of movers, 40 percent or more were not working in 1970. Some of these women would have left the labor force in any event, but much of the reduction in labor force participation can be attributed to the loss of specific human capital resulting from migration.[11] Table 9-4 shows that not only does wife's employment inhibit family migration, but the family

---

[9] "Family Migration Decisions," *Journal of Political Economy*, 86:5 (October 1978), 749–74.
[10] Jovanovic and Mincer confirm that geographic mobility declines with job *tenure*, holding age constant [Boyan Jovanovic and Jacob Mincer, "Labor Mobility and Wages," in *Studies in Labor Markets*, ed. Sherwin Rosen (Chicago: University of Chicago Press, 1981), Table 1.2].
[11] Data from National Longitudinal Surveys shows that between 1966 and 1969, only 24 percent of wives (husband's age 45–59) who worked at least one week in 1966 did not work in 1969.

TABLE 9-3   Percentage of Married Men 30 to 59 in 1965 with Nonfarm
Occupations in 1970 Who Moved between States between 1965 and 1970,
by Age and Wife's Employment Status in 1965

Husband's Age in 1965 and Wife's Employment Status in 1965		Percentage of Wives Employed in 1970
30–39		
Wife employed	7.7%	54.7%
Wife not employed	9.0	23.9
40–49		
Wife employed	4.1	61.7
Wife not employed	5.4	22.8
50–59		
Wife employed	2.5	57.4
Wife not employed	3.1	16.8

Source: Jacob Mincer, "Family Migration Decisions," *Journal of Political Economy,*
86:5 (October 1978), Table 5. Reprinted by permission of The University of Chicago
Press. © by the University of Chicago, 1978.

is less likely to move the longer the wife has been employed at her current
job. This is what the theory of human capital would lead us to expect. Table
9-4 also shows the negative association between the presence of school-age
children and migration.

Since the labor force participation of both wife and husband creates a
potential strain on family ties when one family member expects to gain from
geographic mobility while the other does not, it is tempting to attribute the
upward trend in divorce rates over the past thirty years to the rising labor
force participation of married women. Of course, causation may also run in
the opposite direction. Women may expect their marriages to be less stable

TABLE 9-4   Probability of Family
Migration, 1967–1972

	Children 6–18	
Wife's Job Tenure	None	Some
0	0.132	0.107
5	0.079	0.063
10	0.055	0.044

Source: S. H. Sandell, "The Economics of
Family Migration," *NLS Report on Dual Careers,* Vol. 4 (Columbus: Center for Human Resource Research, Ohio State University, 1975). Reported by Jacob Mincer in
"Family Migration Decisions."

than they did before World War II and thus engage in labor force activity as a hedge against future disruption. In an exploratory study of this fascinating question, Robert Michael concludes: ". . . the labor force participation rate of married women (with spouse and young children present) is causally prior to the divorce rate and fertility."[12] The application of the theory of human capital to socioeconomic behavior promises to be a rewarding area of future research.

IMPLICIT LABOR CONTRACTS AND INTERNAL LABOR MARKETS

Human capital theory draws our attention to the importance of the future in economic decisions. When individuals invest in human capital in the form of schooling, they must do so on the basis of *expectations* about the course of the future incomes they will be able to earn if they acquire different levels of schooling. Planning for the future is intrinsically risky. Changes in economic conditions brought on by birth rate fluctuations or changes in the industrial composition of labor demand can, for example, cause significant changes in the payoff to acquiring a higher level of education. If these changes are not correctly anticipated, plans may not be realized. The problems faced by individual workers and their employers in anticipating the future returns to investments in OJT are even more severe, because additional elements of uncertainty are present. Investment in schooling, at least through high school, and through college for most persons, is largely general in the sense that the returns are not tied to one employer or, in many cases, even to one industry or occupation. On the other hand, the payoff to specific OJT is by definition tied to one employer. From the employer's point of view, the investment in each worker is at risk whenever an employee contemplates quitting to take another job or to leave the labor force.

Risk cannot always be avoided, but it can be shifted to others, and the insurance industry exists to provide the benefits of specialization in the bearing of certain kinds of risk. Thus, firms can, and do, purchase life insurance to protect them against the risk of loss that would occur if important employees or partners were to die. Other kinds of risk are not subject to such shifting to specialist firms, however, because the existence of insurance might induce a firm or worker to engage in a specific act in order to collect the insurance; this situation is called **moral hazard.** Thus, it would be much more difficult for the insurance industry to underwrite the risk that an employer or employee would act in bad faith and renege on an implicit or explicit agreement not to discharge, to grant a raise, or not to quit. Risks of lack of good faith are substantially reduced in transactions involving physi-

---

[12] "Causation among Socioeconomic Time Series," Working Paper No. 246 (Stanford, Calif.: National Bureau of Economic Research, 1978).

cal assets through mortgages, leases, promissory notes, and similar con-tracts. However, *explicit* contracts in which human capital is collateral are by and large illegal documents in most societies today. Consequently, em-ployer-employee relations often involve *implicit* agreements that cannot be enforced legally. Collective bargaining agreements between employers and unions representing workers are legally enforceable contracts which fre-quently specify *some* actions that workers or employers may take when unforeseen events change the economic environment in which a firm or industry operates.

We have seen that there exist strong economic incentives on both sides of the labor market to minimize the costs and threat of losses due to uncer-tain future events. Economists have found it increasingly useful to analyze the way in which investors in human capital deal with risk by means of an **implicit contract theory.** The concept of implicit labor market contracts has contributed much to our understanding, not only of investment in human capital, but also of behavior that had long been difficult to understand in the areas of wage "stickiness," unemployment, job quits, and firms' layoff poli-cies. In a separately developing line of thought, the possibility that some individuals find it more difficult than others to find secure jobs paying better wages has led some economists to develop the concept of **segmented** or **dual labor markets.** In the next few pages we will devote attention to both of these topics.

Implicit contracts and wage flexibility.[13]   The concept of an implicit labor market contract ties in with a firm's reputation for fairness to its employees. It would make no sense for a worker to bear some costs of investing in firm-specific OJT if the firm had a reputation for discharging workers before they reaped returns in the form of higher pay. Neither would workers willingly enter into a long-term commitment to a firm that was likely to want to renegotiate the rate of pay when it came time for expected, and deserved, raises. Thus, employers have an interest in gaining a reputation for fairness for the same reason that they can profit from adapting the length of the workweek and other working conditions to worker preferences—by doing so they can attract employees at lower wage rates. On the other side of the market, the employee is expected to be loyal to the firm and not quit opportunistically after the firm has invested resources in firm-specific OJT but before the firm has received its share of the returns. This is an important reason why employers are concerned with the job history of applicants for work and frown upon prospective workers with a history of frequent job turnover. By establishing reputations as reliable employees, workers gain more access to higher-paying jobs and opportunities for investing in OJT than would otherwise be available to them.

---

[13] References to important research on implicit contracts are provided at the end of this chapter and also in Chapters 11 and 12.

An implicit contract, if it were explicitly written out, would specify the circumstances under which the firm is permitted to lay off or discharge a worker and the manner in which raises in pay are to be granted. The conditions justifying reductions in pay would also be spelled out. An implicit contract also restrains the worker from taking actions harmful to the employer's interest in receiving returns on its investment. Implicit contracts may exist for a variety of reasons, of which three are particularly important. (1) One reason, as we have discussed at great length, is to protect workers' and employers' interests in their OJT investments. (2) Some economists have suggested an additional motive, namely the desire of workers to shift the risk of a decline in the demand for their services to employers.[14] If employers wish to specialize in bearing such risks and employees do not, implicit contracts may well be so motivated, and we consider the ramifications of this aspect of implicit contract theory in Chapter 12, dealing with unemployment. (3) A third possible reason for implicit contracts is that employers—particularly large ones—find it difficult to monitor the work effort of their employees. Consequently they offer their workers the chance to participate in a lottery, or "tournament," in which the winners are determined on the basis of output or profitability to the firm.[15] Their reward is to be paid a large premium—more than their *VMP*—after they have been deemed "productive," or winners. The employees pay for the right to participate in the game by accepting jobs that initially pay less than their *VMP*. This leads to a view of the age-earnings profile different from the one depicted in Figure 9-4. The *VMP* and *w* curves are interchanged, with *w* rising above *VMP* for winners, who are kept on as "permanent" employees. Still, the present value of wages paid by the firm to its workers equals the present value of *VMP*.

The three possible reasons for implicit labor market contracts are not mutually exclusive. It is possible that all three motives are satisfied to some degree in worker-employer relationships. Their relative importance has yet to be evaluated in theoretical and empirical analysis of labor markets. An important line of thought, however, implies that the motivation to shift the risk of fluctuating incomes from employees to employers because employees are less willing to bear risk is not likely to be important. One reason is that a floor under posttraining wages enables the worker to avoid fluctuating income only so long as the employer does not temporarily or permanently

---

[14] See, in particular, Costas Azariadis, "Implicit Contracts and Underemployment Disequilibria," *Journal of Political Economy*, 83 (December 1975), 1182–1202; Martin N. Baily, "Wages and Employment Under Uncertain Demand," *Review of Economic Studies*, 41 (January 1974), 37–50; and Donald F. Gordon, "A Neo-Classical Theory of Unemployment," *Economic Inquiry*, 12 (December 1974), 431–59.

[15] See Edward P. Lazear, "Why Is There Mandatory Retirement?" *Journal of Political Economy*, 87 (December 1979), 1261–84, and Edward P. Lazear and Sherwin Rosen, "Rank-Order Tournaments as Optimum Labor Contracts," *Journal of Political Economy*, 89 (October 1981), 841–64.

terminate the job. When the demand for labor declines, employer-initiated job termination is more likely if wages are fixed than if they can be adjusted downward. Once job termination occurs, both workers and employers risk losing their entire specific OJT investments. Since both sides have incentives to avoid such losses, it seems unlikely that they would unnecessarily expose themselves to this risk. Second, workers can avoid risk in other ways—by purchasing physical capital such as their own homes or savings accounts, for example. Third, it is argued that empirical evidence on downward wage rigidity—that wage rates are not lowered when demand falls—is statistically suspect.[16] To summarize, it appears that the most fruitful area in which to look for the attributes and effects of implicit labor market contracts is ways in which they enhance the value of OJT investments. This view of the role and nature of implicit contracts implies that wage flexibility is allowed when it is possible for both sides to feel confident that downward or upward wage adjustments are warranted by economic events and will provide for increased protection to their OJT investments.[17]

No contract, explicit or implicit, can prescribe mutually agreeable responses to all future events. Life is too uncertain for that. Thus, when events occur that are outside the range of previous experience, one side may find it necessary to request renegotiation of an implicit or explicit agreement. This can create considerable ill will, because the other party to the agreement is likely to feel that a request for renegotiation—a change in seniority provisions, a wage reduction, a postponement of a wage increase, or the like, is no more than a claim to an unjustified benefit. Of course, it will not generally be in either party's interest to insist on enforcing an agreement that would ruin the other party financially, so that it could no longer perform its tasks. Examples of disagreements over explicit contractual agreements are often newsmakers. For example, the owners of professional athletic teams constantly emphasize their investments in player development, while superstar and even ordinary star athletes claim that the team owners exploit their talents (after the talents are recognized as star quality). A theatrical or television producer bears great risk in developing a new play or TV series and hopes occasionally to reap large returns to compensate for frequent losses. Nevertheless, when a once-in-five years super-success play, TV series, or star occurs, some actors may feel justified in requesting upward adjustment of their contracted pay. If the producer does not agree, a disgruntled actor may be so unhappy that future performances will be less

---

[16] Masanori Hashimoto and Ben T. Yu, "Specific Capital, Employment Contracts, and Wage Rigidity," *Bell Journal of Economics,* Autumn 1981, 536–49; and "Firm-Specific Human Capital, Transaction Costs, and Employment Contracts," Unpublished paper, University of Washington, 1981.

[17] See also M. Hashimoto, "Firm Specific Capital As a Shared Investment," *American Economic Review,* 71:3 (June 1981), 475–82.

effective than otherwise. Thus, costly legal suits and countersuits are a distinct possibility.[18]

The employer and employee interests in wage flexibility are illustrated in Figure 9-5. The vertical axis of Figure 9-5 measures a worker's *VMP*. The horizontal axis measures the worker's tenure on a particular job, starting at year 0 and ending at year T_t. The profiles *VMP*(1), *VMP*(2), and *VMP*(3) represent the worker's *VMP* in the current job as influenced by OJT and demand for the firm's output. The profile $g(s)$ represents the worker's *VMP* in the best alternative job as influenced by schooling and prior training on any other jobs. The *w* profile is the worker's wage. Consider the situation after the worker has been on the job for T_1 years. If the firm should experience a decline in the demand for its output so that *VMP* falls, there will be no incentive for the employer to lay off or discharge the worker until *VMP* falls below *w*. On the other hand, if *VMP* should permanently fall below $g(s)$, to *VMP*(3), the worker is more productive in an alternative job. The firm cannot remain in business and pay the worker $g(s)$ or more. Therefore, it maximizes the worker's wealth to separate from the firm and take the job paying $g(s)$. Both the firm's and worker's OJT investments have been wiped out by unforeseen economic circumstances.

Consider the firm and worker's position if the *VMP* profile should fall to *VMP*(2), below the *w* profile but above $g(s)$. The worker is still more productive on this job than anywhere else. An implicit (or explicit) contract might require the firm to continue to pay the worker a wage of *w*(1) even though *VMP* has fallen to *VMP*(2). This is a temporary possibility, but it

---

[18] See, for example, "Gary Coleman Set Back in Pay Fight," *New York Times*, October 6, 1981.

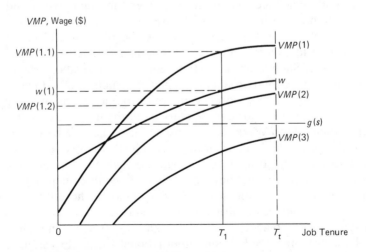

FIGURE 9-5. Wage rate, *VMP*, and job tenure

cannot continue if *VMP* is never expected to return to its original level. If the decline is expected to persist, it becomes in the employer's interest to lay off or discharge the worker unless the wage can be reduced so that it no longer exceeds *VMP*. If the employee knew for sure that *VMP* was lower than *w*, it would be in his or her best interest to negotiate a new wage rather than demand strict adherence to the contractual *w* and risk losing the entire OJT investment. If a worker is discharged or laid off while *VMP* remains above $g(s)$ or if the employer goes bankrupt, both the worker and employer lose an OJT investment that could still be salvaged if only a reallocation of the gains could be negotiated. [Recall that in Chapter 5, we showed that from society's point of view, maximum labor productivity occurs when the *VMP* of each type of labor is equal in all alternative employments. With specific OJT, *VMP* for each worker should be no lower in a worker's current job than in alternative jobs. This condition is violated when *VMP* falls below $g(s)$.]

The problem is one of information. How is the employee to know, when *VMP* is not directly observable, that the employer is not simply lying in order to increase profits at the employee's expense? A similar problem arises if $g(s)$ should rise above *w* owing to an increase in the demand for labor in other firms. An employer under these circumstances may find that the employees begin demanding wage increases exceeding implicit contract terms. The employer will find it profitable to grant a wage increase so long as $g(s)$ does not rise above $VMP(1)$, and it will be socially efficient for workers to remain with the current employer. (Why?) Once again, given information difficulties, the employer may be worried that an employee who threatens to quit is lying in order to obtain an "unjustified" wage increase.

Studies of labor markets in Japan and to a lesser extent in the United States provide evidence that when employers and employees find it relatively easy to monitor fluctuations in *VMP*, wage adjustments do occur, and socially wasteful layoffs are less likely. A socially wasteful layoff occurs when a worker loses a job in which *VMP* is higher than in the next best job for that worker. Such a job separation reduces overall labor productivity in the economy. Since total production is higher if such layoffs do not occur, it is in both employers' and workers' interests to find means of renegotiating implicit (and explicit) labor contracts to avoid them. For example, in early 1982 the United Auto Workers renegotiated its collective bargaining agreements with Ford and GM in order to prevent further employment reductions in the auto industry. Both sides recognized that by reducing labor costs relative to those in Japan they could enhance auto firm profitability and preserve employee investments in OJT specific to the auto industry. In recent years, employees of firms in other industries have been asked—and they have agreed—to accept pay cuts as an "investment" in their job security. These firms included Braniff International Corp., Firestone Tire and Rubber Co., and Weirton Steel, Wheeling-Pittsburgh Steel Corp. Do you think calling a wage cut an "investment" is accurate? Why?

Labor contracts and wage flexibility in Japanese industry.   Another example of the role of contracts and wage flexibility when OJT human capital is an important determinant of wages is the system of bonus payments and "lifetime" employment in Japanese industry.[19] Rather than being an implicit and poorly documented component of pay practices as in the United States, the payment of semiannual bonuses is regularly reported in official Japanese labor statistics. These payments are made both to blue collar and white collar workers and in 1975 constituted 20 to 25 percent of total cash earnings. Bonuses depend in part on firm profitability; as such, they are a reward to a firm's employees (as a group) for industriousness and a means of profit-sharing and wage flexibility. The practice of profit-sharing is not widespread and is relatively controversial in the United States.

Economists and Japanese specialists offer a variety of explanations for the development of the bonus and *nenko* (seniority) systems in Japan.[20] One thing is clear, however—they are associated with a much lower job separation rate and longer job tenure for individual workers (particularly males) in Japan than in the United States. Hashimoto shows that the ratio of bonus payments to cash earnings is highest in those industries in which the workers have attributes likely to be associated with large investments in specific OJT—high years of experience on their current job and high levels of education in particular. He also finds evidence that *fluctuations* in the bonus-earnings ratio are correlated with the cyclical variability of industry output. Thus, the bonus system behaves in a manner consistent with the theory of implicit contracts and wage flexibility outlined above. The Japanese wage system appears to foster the preservation of OJT human capital investments by reducing layoffs and quits and probably is one reason Japanese productivity has reached such high levels compared with other economies. (Recall our discussion of international productivity levels and trends in Chapter 3.)

One explanation of the Japanese bonus system is in terms of cultural differences between Japan and the United States. Japan emerged from a feudal system much later than other industrial nations and proceeded rather quickly to become the modern society we know today. To the extent that Japanese workers and employers have greater trust in each other not to abuse wage flexibility for personal or firm profitability, the problems associated with assessing when worker productivity has declined or increased may be considerably smaller than in the United States. This is a fascinating and important area for future research.

---

[19] This discussion is based on research of Masanori Hashimoto. In particular, see "Bonus Payments, On-the-Job Training, and Lifetime Employment in Japan," *Journal of Political Economy,* 87 (October 1979), 1086–1104. See also, "Year-End Bonuses Aid Japanese Economy," *New York Times,* November 30, 1981.

[20] For references to several studies, see Hashimoto, "Bonus Payments."

Internal labor markets.   The distinction between **internal** and **external labor markets** has a long history in the labor economics literature.[21] Despite a wide diversity in emphasis and implications, many authors—going back at least to Karl Marx—have drawn attention to the concept that not all workers appear to be able to compete for all jobs. The concepts of **noncompeting groups** and **segmented labor markets** (SLM) have long been recognized as important features of industrial economies. While most economists recognize the relationship between these concepts and observed labor market behavior, there is disagreement on their quantitative importance and significance for policy. Here we present a brief description of the SLM, or internal-external labor market, concept and show how it is linked to the theory of human capital developed in this chapter and in Chapter 8.

The idea of an internal labor market is inherent in the relationship between specific OJT, wage growth, and job tenure. To the extent OJT pays off for employers and employees, it will be reflected not only in wage and productivity growth for workers with given job titles but also, and perhaps largely, in the form of promotion to higher job levels. Moreover, promotion from within the firm as the principal means of filling higher-level jobs assures workers that they will reap the returns to their OJT investments. Thus, competitions for entry-level jobs will occur in the *external* labor market open to workers who have just left school or who have quit their jobs with other firms, while competition for jobs at higher skill levels or for supervisory positions will largely occur in the *internal* labor market consisting of the firm's employees.

The concept of the internal labor market can help us to understand how firms determine their optimal strategies when faced by the need to reduce or increase their use of labor in the face of falling or rising demand for output. Consider the situation of a firm that experiences a decline in output demand. Its labor force will consist of workers in whom it has invested varying amounts of hiring costs and OJT. Since a worker who is laid off has an incentive to find another job, the firm will reduce the risk of loss of its OJT investments by reassigning workers with longer job tenure to perform tasks of less-skilled junior employees rather than reduce its work force uniformly at all levels. Thus, job seniority is a natural outgrowth of the impact of OJT on firm costs and profitability. It would, and does, occur in the absence of collective bargaining agreements. Similarly, a firm experiencing an increase in the demand for labor will find it easier to adjust by accelerat-

---

[21] See the excellent survey by Glen G. Cain, "The Challenge of Segmented Labor Market Theories to Orthodox Theory: A Survey," *The Journal of Economic Literature,* 14 (December 1976), 1215–57. Contemporary interest was stimulated greatly by Peter B. Doeringer and Michael J. Piore, *Internal Labor Markets and Manpower Analysis* (Lexington, Mass.: D. C. Heath & Co., 1971).

ing job promotions, adding to its workforce more at junior than at higher levels.[22]

Where economists differ on the importance of internal labor markets is in their assessment of the access that some groups have to the internal track toward preferred jobs. If women, blacks, and other minority groups do not or cannot compete on an equal footing for entry-level jobs in the external labor market, then they are thereby consigned to inferior labor market, economic, and social status. Some of the issues associated with the debate over equal access to the inside job tracks of the internal labor market are dealt with in Chapter 10.

*FRONTIERS OF LABOR ECONOMICS: FIXED LABOR COSTS, TRAINING COSTS, AND THE EMPLOYMENT-HOURS MIX

One of the important insights of OJT analysis is that firms *invest* in their workers. Employers' investments in their employees take two basic forms: (1) hiring costs that occur prior to and at the beginning of each worker's tenure on the job, and (2) training costs that are incurred while the employee is working. The characteristic of these costs that we want to focus on now is that *training and hiring expenditures vary with the number of workers hired by the firm, but not with hours worked by each employee.* It is clearly to an employer's advantage, other things equal, to economize on these fixed hiring and training costs by obtaining a given quantity of labor input from fewer employees working longer hours.

Three forces prevent the employer from economizing on fixed labor force to the physical limit of requiring each employee to work, say, an 80-hour workweek. The first is that after the workweek reaches some length, worker productivity will begin to decline owing to exhaustion or boredom. The second is that employee preferences for leisure time would require the payment of a much higher wage rate to work, say, 80 hours weekly rather than, say 40 hours. The third reason is that, quite apart from worker preferences, the federal Fair Labor Standards Act (FLSA), as well as a number of state laws, establishes a legal premium (1.5 times the normal wage) for all hours in excess of 40 per week for the vast majority of employees. Most union contracts also contain overtime pay provisions.

Given the above considerations, we now proceed to a formal analysis of a competitive firm's optimal mix of employees and hours of work per employee. To simplify the problem, we will examine how a competitive firm minimizes the cost of a given level of output when its capital input is fixed and one skilled class of labor is used in production. If output is predetermined, cost minimization is also profit maximization. Remember that cost minimization is necessary for profit maximization in any event.

---

[22] The implications of the internal labor market for wage structure, layoffs, promotions, and unemployment are cogently stated in several papers by M. W. Reder. See, in particular, "The Theory of Occupational Wage Differentials," *American Economic Review,* 45:5 (December 1955), 833–52; "Wage Differentials: Theory and Measurement," in H. G. Lewis, et al., *Aspects of Labor Economics* (Princeton, N.J.: Princeton University Press, 1962): and "Wage Structure and Structural Unemployment," *Review of Economic Studies,* 21:3 (October 1964), 309–21.

* This section contains more technical material. If you skip, go to page 367.

The existence of a premium rate for overtime means that if a competitive firm purchases an hour of work in excess of the standard workweek ($\bar{H}$), it must pay a wage that is αw, where w is the constant straight-time hourly wage rate and α is a number greater than 1 (typically 1.5).[23] Finally, let the firm's given capital input be denoted by $\bar{K}$, and its fixed cost of hiring an additional employee be denoted by f. Expressed algebraically, the firm's expenditures on inputs are

$$wHN + fN + r\bar{K}, \quad \text{if } H \leq \bar{H} \tag{9-5}$$

and

$$w\bar{H}N + \alpha wN(H - \bar{H}) + fN + r\bar{K}, \quad \text{if } H > \bar{H} \tag{9-6}$$

where r is the price of capital inputs and N is the number of employees.

With a little manipulation, we can create an isoexpenditure curve from equations (9-5) and (9-6). This will permit a graphical analysis of the firm's cost-minimizing (H, N) combination. Consider a particular amount of spending on resources, $\bar{C}$. An isoexpenditure curve indicates combinations of H and N that can be purchased for $\bar{C}$ dollars (given $w, \alpha, r, \bar{K}, \bar{H}$, and f). To obtain the expression for an isoexpenditure curve when the workweek is at or below the standard workweek, we set equation (9-5) equal to $\bar{C}$ and solve it for N, yielding

$$\text{(isoexpenditure curve when } H \leq \bar{H}) \quad N = \frac{\bar{C} - r\bar{K}}{f + wH} \tag{9-7}$$

Since all variables but N and H are given to the firm, equation (9-7) indicates how many employees it can hire working H hours per week when it spends $\bar{C}$. Analogously, combinations of N and H that the firm may purchase for $\bar{C}$ when hours of work per employee exceed the standard workweek are given by the expression

$$\text{(isoexpenditure curve when } H > \bar{H}) \quad N = \frac{\bar{C} - r\bar{K}}{f + wH + \alpha w(H - \bar{H})} \tag{9-8}$$

Unlike the examples in Chapter 3, neither segment of the firm's isoexpenditure curve is linear. The isoexpenditure curve expressed in equations (9-7) and (9-8) is illustrated in Figure 9-6. Notice that there is a kink at $\bar{H}$.[24] The steeper slope immediately to the right of $\bar{H}$ is due to the overtime wage premium. Specifically, the premium wage rate that must be paid when the workweek is increased from $\bar{H}$ to $(\bar{H} + 1)$ means that if expenditures are to be held constant at $\bar{C}$, the firm must give up more employees than when it increases the workweek from $(\bar{H} - 1)$ to $\bar{H}$.

Before we can determine the cost-minimizing hours-employment mix, however, we must examine the firm's production possibilities, with special reference to L, the total labor input. Since output depends on the utilization of labor and capital, and K is fixed at $\bar{K}$ in the problem at hand, the firm's level of L is dictated by its production function (technology) and the predetermined level of output, which we

---

[23] The fact that workers are assumed to be homogeneous means that they will each work the same number of hours per period. For convenience, we assume that the period under consideration is a week.

[24] As an exercise, select values for $\alpha, w, r, \bar{K}, \bar{C}, f$, and $\bar{H}$, and plot the associated isoxpenditure curve. It should have the same basic shape as the one in Figure 9-6. Can you explain the economics of the nonlinearity of equations (9-7) and (9-8)?

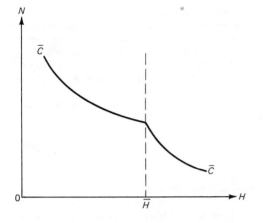

FIGURE 9-6. An isoexpenditure curve for combinations of employees and hours of work per employee

will denote by $\bar{Q}$. To see this, we write the firm's production function in its general form

$$Q = F(K, L) \tag{9-9}$$

Since Q and K are fixed at $\bar{Q}$ and $\bar{K}$, respectively, the production function tells the firm what particular level of L it must choose.[25] What is L, though?

Our first inclination might be to say that the answer is obvious: the labor input is simply the product of number of employees and hours of work per employee ($N \cdot H$). Consider the figures in Table 9-5, where the number of employees is held at 100. Compare what happens to total employee hours as the average workweek is increased from 0 to 1 hours, from 30 to 31 hours, and from 167 to 168 hours. In each of the three cases, total employee-hours increases by 100. If we measure the labor input in the production function by ($H \cdot N$), then we are implicitly saying that the firm will obtain the *same* increment in L when the average workweek is increased by 1 hour *no matter what the average workweek is to begin with*. There are various reasons why this is probably not reasonable. Suppose it takes a worker one hour each day to set up. This includes time necessary to reach the work station, prepare

TABLE 9-5   Employees, Hours of Work per Employee, and Total Employee-Hours

N	H	$(N \cdot H)$	$\Delta(N \cdot H)$
100	0	0	
100	1	100	100
100	31	3,100	
100	32	3,200	100
100	167	16,700	
100	168	16,800	100

---

[25] Consider the case where the firm has a Cobb-Douglas type production function, $Q = \alpha K^\beta L^\gamma$. If Q is fixed at $\bar{Q}$, and K is fixed at $\bar{K}$, then Q and K are treated as parameters (constants) and the production function solved for the level of L that satisfies the firm's technology, given preselected values of output and capital. In this case, $L = [(\bar{Q}/\alpha)(1/\bar{K}^\beta)]^{1/\gamma}$.

tools and equipment, and receive supervision. Were the firm to have a workweek of 1 hour, its effective labor input would be zero! Moreover, it is unreasonable to expect that workers never become fatigued. To take an extreme example, if the workweek really were 167 hours, the marginal effect on L of an increase in the workweek to 168 hours would probably be zero or even negative. Workers might become so fatigued that an increase in the workweek would cause them to make so many mistakes, for example, that output would decrease.

What we are saying is that the firm's labor input, L, may be thought of as a function of hours of work per employee and number of employees:

$$L = G(H, N) \tag{9-10}$$

and that this transformation of H and N into L *does not* have the specific form, $L = N \cdot H$.[26] In what follows we shall assume that the labor services function (9-10) has the property that the marginal contributions of H and N to the firm's labor input are usually positive, but that after a certain level of H, an additional hour of work per worker decreases L.

Since the properties of the labor services function are similar to those of a production function (Figure 3-4, p. 52), we can easily express equation (9-10) geometrically. Figure 9-7 illustrates an iso-L curve, labeled $\bar{L}\bar{L}$. It is a locus of combinations of H and N that are associated with the level of labor services ($\bar{L}$) necessary to produce the firm's given amount of output ($\bar{Q}$).[27] It is convex and downward-sloping (over most of its range), indicating that the firm is able to trade off N for H (at a decreasing rate) while maintaining a fixed labor input. Notice that the iso-L curve begins to turn upward at $H(0)$. At this point enough fatigue has set in that an additional hour of work per employee lowers the firm's labor input, so that more employees are necessary to hold L constant.

Also included in Figure 9-7 are two isoexpenditure curves. Each represents a given amount of total spending on inputs, and $\bar{C}_2\bar{C}_2$ depicts more total spending than $\bar{C}_1\bar{C}_1$. The firm's optimal (cost-minimizing) combination of employees and hours of work per employee occurs at point P, where $\bar{L}\bar{L}$ is tangent to $\bar{C}_2\bar{C}_2$. Combinations of H and N along $\bar{C}_1\bar{C}_1$ are cheaper than $[H(1), N(1)]$ but do not yield the necessary labor input. Other combinations of H and N along $\bar{L}\bar{L}$ also provides the required labor input, but are more expensive (lie on a higher isoexpenditure curve) than the combination of employees and hours of work per employee at point P. Notice that the firm in Figure 9-7 has a cost-minimizing workweek that exceeds the standard workweek. The economic interpretation of the tangency point in Figure 9-7 is analogous to the cost-minimizing combination of capital and labor discussed in Chapter 3. When the firm has found the mix of N and H that is the cheapest way to achieve its required labor input, the last dollar spent on N must increase labor services by the same amount as the last dollar spent on H. Were this not true, the firm could spend one less dollar on $N(H)$, and have to spend less than an additional dollar on $H(N)$ to obtain the required labor input, $\bar{L}$. It would continue to reallocate its spending until it found the H-N combination at point P.

[26] For a technical discussion of the specific mathematical forms the labor services function can take, see Ronald G. Ehrenberg, *Fringe Benefits and Overtime Behavior* (Lexington, Mass.: D. C. Heath & Co., 1971), p. 9; Martin Feldstein, "Specification of the Labor Input in the Aggregate Production," *Review of Economic Studies*, 34:4 (October 1968), 337; and Sherwin Rosen, "Short-Run Employment Variation on Class-I Railroads in the U.S., 1947–1963," *Econometrica*, 36:3–4 (July–August 1968), 515.

[27] Remember that the production function (9-9) tell us $\bar{L}$, and that the labor services function (9-10) tells us possible N-H combinations associated with any L.

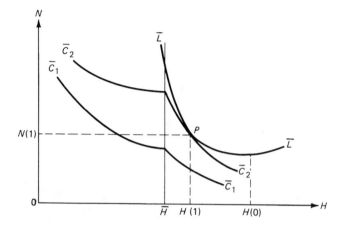

FIGURE 9-7. The firm's cost-minimizing H-N mix

Although we have attempted to simplify whenever possible, it is obvious that the theory of the demand for labor by a competitive firm becomes complex when the labor input is specified more completely and fixed costs of employment and a premium wage rate for hours in excess of a standard work week are introduced. What benefits make this greater complexity worthwhile? In general, the answer is that we can examine important new issues.

Application: The effects of an increase in the penalty rate. The competitive firm in Figure 9-8 is initially in equilibrium at point R where iso-L curve $\bar{L}\bar{L}$ is tangent to isoexpenditure curve $\bar{C}_2\bar{C}_2$. If federal or state laws were amended to increase the premium rate (α) for hours of work in excess of $\bar{H}$, what would happen to the number of employees and the average workweek? An increase in α means that for any workweek in excess of the standard, the firm can purchase less N for a given amount of total spending on factors of production. This can be seen from equation (9-8), where the denominator of the expression for the isoexpenditure curve is made larger with an increase in α. Expressed graphically, the increase in α generates a downward rotation in the portion of the isoexpenditure curves to the right of $\bar{H}$. Combinations of H and N that the firm can purchase for $\bar{C}_2$ dollars are now denoted by $\bar{C}_2 A \bar{C}_2'$. Since the increase in α makes it more expensive to purchase hours of work, the firm in Figure 9-8 must increase its total expenditures on labor (to C_3 dollars) in order to maintain its output at the required level (remain on iso-L curve $\bar{L}\bar{L}$). (Put differently, the increase in α means that $[H(1), N(1)]$ can no longer be purchased for C_2 dollars.) As before, cost is minimized at a point of tangency (R') and, owing to the convexity of the iso-L curve, the firm now hires more employees $[N(2)]$ and reduces the workweek to $H(2)$. By raising the cost of hours of work relative to number of workers, the increase in the penalty rate for overtime leads the firm to substitute N for H in production.

CAUTION! Does it follow from the preceding analysis that an increase in the overtime premium rate will automatically increase employment? The principal reason given for legislation of such increases is that employment will be shared more

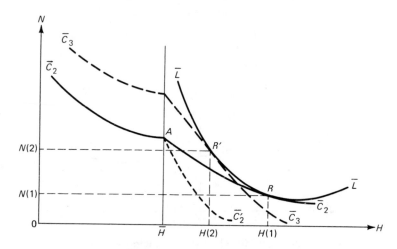

FIGURE 9-8. The effects on an increase in the overtime penalty rate on H and N

equally among workers.[28] It is clear that an increase in the overtime premium will cause firms to increase the ratio N/H. But there is also an increase in labor cost, which reduces the quantity of labor services, L, demanded.[29] Thus, the increased proportion of N used in "producing" L will be offset by a reduction in L. In addition, workers who had sought overtime but can no longer obtain as much as they like will tend to "moonlight" in order to maintain their incomes. Other family members—spouses or children—may seek work more frequently than they had in the past. This induced increase in labor supply will tend to force down wages, offsetting the gains to workers from any increase in the number of employees demanded. Ehrenberg has concluded on the basis of his empirical studies that, when all these factors are considered, an increase in the FLSA overtime premium to doubletime would not be likely to improve worker well-being.[30]

There are many further applications of the concept of fixed employment costs. One of them is to the effects of an increase in the minimum wage on employment versus hours worked. Another application is to a firm's decision on adjusting the size of its labor force when its sales change. If the change in sales is expected to be temporary, it may be better to adjust weekly hours per employee rather than add or lay off workers. Can you carry out these extensions of the application developed above?

---

[28] For example, legislation was introduced in 1979 (HR1784) to increase the FLSA overtime premium from time and a half to double time. The AFL-CIO supported this legislation as a means of increasing employment. See Subcommittee on Labor Standards Hearings on HR1784, October 23, 1979.

[29] See M. I. Nadiri and Sherwin Rosen, *A Disequilibrium Model of Demand for Factors of Production*, NBER General Series 99 (New York: Columbia University Press, 1973), chap. 2.

[30] See Ronald Ehrenberg and Robert S. Smith, *Modern Labor Economics* (Glenview, Ill.: Scott Foresman and Co., 1982), pp. 124–25.

CONCLUSION

In this chapter we extended the theory of human capital developed in Chapter 8 to cover investment in the context of the firm through on-the-job training. The analysis of general and specific human capital investments provides important insights into the determination of wage rates after the period of formal schooling and explains why age-earning power profiles are rising, rather than flat, over much of the working life for those individuals with continuous labor force experience. One of the most important insights provided by OJT theory is that the value of a worker's marginal product need not equal his or her wage rate at any moment in time under competitive conditions. The $w = VMPL$ equality derived in Chapter 3 is replaced by a comparable equality between the *present value* of wage costs and returns from the employer's point of view, and important implications are derived for the behavior of labor turnover (quits and layoffs).

The OJT concept has many extensions and applications. Some of the topics discussed in this chapter include the life-cycle implications of age-earnings profiles for the timing of work and investment in human capital, implicit and explicit labor contracts, wage flexibility over the business cycle, internal labor markets, the hours-employment tradeoff facing the firm, and the impact of OJT and wage differentials on geographic mobility.

Many of the topics treated in this chapter are the subject of on-going research on the frontiers of labor economics, and unsettled issues remain. One interesting avenue of research brings the theory of human capital full circle by applying the analysis of firm-oriented investments to the behavior of the family as an entity. In the study of the economics of divorce, for example, years of marriage, the growth of common interests, and the accumulation of property and children are treated as investments in specific human capital that reduce the probability of "quits" in the form of divorce or separation. This is not just topical; it bears potentially important implications for understanding other aspects of the labor market—the supply of labor, for example, which we have analyzed in previous chapters as resulting from intrafamily decisions on the allocation of time between home and market. Time allocated to home activities is often devoted to child care—investment in children. It should now be apparent that the theory of human capital is a powerful economic tool, one which provides insights into a broader spectrum of social behavior than almost any other body of economic analysis.

REFERENCES AND SELECTED READINGS

AZARIADIS, COSTAS, "Implicit Contracts and Underemployment Disequilibria," *Journal of Political Economy,* 83:6 (December 1975), 1183–1202.

BAILY, MARTIN N., "Wages and Employment Under Uncertain Demand," *Review of Economic Studies*, 41:1 (January 1974), 37–50.

BECKER, GARY S., *Human Capital*. New York: National Bureau of Economic Research, 1975.

BEN-PORATH, Y., "The Production of Human Capital Over Time," in *Education, Income and Human Capital*, ed. W. Lee Hansen. New York: National Bureau of Economic Research, 1970.

BLINDER, ALAN, AND YORAM WEISS, "Human Capital and Labor Supply: A Synthesis," *Journal of Political Economy*, 84:3 (June 1976), 449–72.

CAIN, GLEN G., "The Challenge of Segmented Labor Market Theories to Orthodox Theory: A Survey," *The Journal of Economic Literature*, 14:4 (December 1976), 1215–57.

DOERINGER, PETER B., AND MICHAEL J. PIORE, *Internal Labor Markets and Manpower Analysis*. Lexington, Mass.: D. C. Heath & Company, 1971.

EHRENBERG, RONALD G., *Fringe Benefits and Overtime Behavior*. Lexington, Mass.: D. C. Heath & Company, 1971.

———, AND ROBERT S. SMITH, *Modern Labor Economics*. Glenview, Ill.: Scott, Foresman & Company, 1982.

FELDSTEIN, MARTIN, "Specification of the Labor Input in the Aggregate Production Function," *Review of Economic Studies*, 34:4 (October 1967), 375–86.

FLEISHER, BELTON M., *Minimum Wage Regulation in the United States*. Washington, D.C.: National Chamber Foundation, 1982.

"Gary Coleman Set Back in Pay Fight," *The New York Times*, October 6, 1981.

GHEZ, G., AND G. BECKER, *The Allocation of Time and Goods Over the Life Cycle*. New York: National Bureau of Economic Research, 1975.

GORDON, DONALD F., "A Neo-Classical Theory of Unemployment," *Economic Inquiry*, 12:4 (December 1974), 431–59.

HASHIMOTO, MASANORI, "Bonus Payments, On-the-Job Training and Lifetime Employment in Japan," *Journal of Political Economy*, 87:5 (October 1979), 1086–1104.

———, "Firm-Specific Human Capital as a Shared Investment," *American Economic Review*, 71:3 (June 1981), 475–82.

———, "Firm-Specific Human Capital, Transaction Costs, and Employment Contracts," Unpublished paper, University of Washington, 1981.

———, AND BEN T. YU, "Specific Capital, Employment Contracts, and Wage Rigidity," *The Bell Journal of Economics*, 11:2 (Autumn 1980), 536–49.

———, "Wage Reduction, Unemployment, and Specific Human Capital," *Economic Inquiry*, 13:4 (December 1975), 485–504.

HECKMAN, JAMES J., "A Life-Cycle Model of Earnings, Learning, and Consumption," *Journal of Political Economy*, 84:4, part 2 (August 1976), S11–S44.

JOVANOVIC, BOYAN, AND JACOB MINCER, "Labor Mobility and Wages," in *Studies in Labor Markets*, ed. Sherwin Rosen. Chicago: University of Chicago Press, 1981.

KEAT, PAUL G., "Long-Run Changes in Occupational Wage Structure 1900–56," *Journal of Political Economy,* 68:6 (December 1960), 584–600.

KNIESNER, THOMAS, AND JOHN V. MCINTOSH, "Predicting Presidential Performance: A Human Capital Approach," *Social Science Research,* 9 (1980), 178–92.

LAZEAR, EDWARD P., AND SHERWIN ROSEN, "Rank-Order Tournaments as Optimum Labor Contracts," *Journal of Political Economy,* 89:5 (October 1981), 841–64.

————, "Why Is There Mandatory Retirement?" *Journal of Political Economy,* 87:6 (December 1979), 1261–84.

MCCURDY, THOMAS E., "An Empirical Model of Labor Supply in a Life-Cycle Setting," *Journal of Political Economy,* 89:6 (December 1981), 1059–85.

MICHAEL, ROBERT, "Causation Among Socioeconomic Time Series," Working Paper No. 246. Stanford, Calif.: National Bureau of Economic Research, 1978.

MINCER, JACOB, "Family Migration Decisions," *Journal of Political Economy,* 86:5 (October 1978), 749–74.

————, "On-the-Job Training: Costs, Returns, and Some Implications," *Journal of Political Economy,* 70:5, part 2 (October 1962), 50–79.

————, *Schooling, Experience and Earnings.* New York: Columbia University Press, for the National Bureau of Economic Research, 1974.

NADIRI, M. I., AND SHERWIN ROSEN, *A Disequilibrium Model of Demand for Factors of Production,* National Bureau of Economic Research General Series 99. New York: Columbia University Press, 1973.

OI, WALTER W., "Labor as a Quasi-Fixed Factor," *Journal of Political Economy,* 70:6 (December 1962), 538–555.

REDER, MELVIN W., "The Theory of Occupational Wage Differentials," *American Economic Review,* 45:5 (December 1955), 833–52.

————, "Wage Differentials: Theory and Measurement," in *Aspects of Labor Economics.* Princeton, N.J.: Princeton University Press, 1962.

————, "Wage Structure and Structural Unemployment," *Review of Economic Studies,* 21:3 (October 1964), 309–21.

"R. G. Barry Includes Its Employees' Value on Its Balance Sheet," *The Wall Street Journal,* April 3, 1970, p. 14.

ROSEN, SHERWIN, "Short-Run Employment Variation on Class I Railroads in the U.S., 1947–1963," *Econometrica,* 36:3–4 (July–October 1968), 511–29.

"The Roving Kind, Penchant of Americans for Job Hopping Vexes Companies Increasingly," *The Wall Street Journal,* March 25, 1970, p. 1.

SANDELL, STEVEN H., "The Economics of Family Migration," *NLS Report on Dual Careers,* Vol. 4 (December 1975).

"Year-End Bonuses Aid Japanese Economy," *The New York Times,* November 30, 1981.

EXERCISES

Choose whether statements 1–4 are *True, False* or *Uncertain* (whether true or false depends on unspecified circumstances). Justify your answer. Your justification is the most important part of your answer.

1. Only a nonprofit firm can benefit from paying for its workers' general OJT.
2. Because of firm-specific OJT, the profit-maximizing condition $w = VMPL$ need not hold at all times.
3. The theories of implicit contracts and firm-specific OJT provide alternative explanations of firms' layoff policies.
4. Monopsony in labor markets promotes the formation of specific human capital, so we should find that the age-earnings profiles of workers in monopsonistic markets are steeper than the age-earnings profiles of other workers.
5. **(a)** Explain carefully and depict graphically the concepts of *general* and *specific* on-the-job training (OJT). Be sure to explain who absorbs the costs and who reaps the benefits in each case.
   (b) What are the advantages of specific OJT in terms of long-term employment opportunities for workers? Explain briefly.
   (c) What are the advantages to the firm of specific OJT in terms of stability of its work force (employee turnover)? Explain briefly.
6. Consider a *cost-minimizing* firm. Suppose that antidiscrimination legislation is passed that requires the firm to keep much more accurate (expensive) payroll records. What will this do to its number of employees and hours of work per employee? Explain carefully and support your answer with the appropriate graphs.
*7. Consider a competitive labor market in which only *specific* training is available, and where training occurs only during the first period of a worker's job tenure (period 0). Let

$$w(t) \equiv \text{wage rate in period } t \; (t = 0, 1, \ldots , T)$$
$$VMP(t) \equiv \text{value of marginal product in period } t \; (t = 0, 1, \ldots , T)$$
$$C(t) \equiv \text{cost of training in period } t \; (t = 0).$$

[Assume that $w(t)$, $VMP(t)$, and $C(t)$ occur at the *beginning* of a period.] In the Beltom Corporation (BC), a profit-maximizing organization, the VMP of an untrained worker is a constant $200 per period, and $C(0)$ is equal to $130. After training, VMP rises to a constant $400 per period.
   (a) Beltom needs a new worker. Mr. Y walks into the personnel office and makes Beltom the following offer: He will work for a wage of $200 during his initial employment period (period 0), BC will absorb the cost of specific training, and after he is trained, he will work for two periods (periods 1 and 2) at a wage of $325 in each period. What is Beltom's rate of return on this investment in specific training?
   (b) While they are thinking about Mr. Y's offer, an equally productive potential employee, Ms. X, walks into the personnel office and makes Beltom the following offer: She will work for $200 during her first period of employment (period 0), BC will pay for her specific training, and after completing training she will work for one period (period 1) for a wage of $244. What is the rate of

---

* Indicates a more difficult exercise.

return to investment in the specific training of Ms. X? Why might Ms. X desire to work less after training than Mr. Y?

(c) If Beltom can hire only one of the two, which will it hire? Why?

(d) Suppose that society has an equal-opportunity law saying that Ms. X must be paid the same in each period as Mr. Y, since they are equally productive workers; in particular, after training, Ms. X must receive a wage of $325 for the one period she desires to work. If Beltom can hire only one of the two individuals, which one will it hire? Support your answer mathematically. Has the equal-opportunity law provided Ms. X with equal opportunity for employment?

10

WAGES
AND WAGE STRUCTURE

A. Educational objectives
  1. To utilize the theoretical structure developed in previous chapters to identify factors underlying the general growth of real wages in the United States over time
  2. To see the reasons for income inequality among individuals and how it is influenced by public policy
  3. To delve more deeply into the determinants of how people are paid

* Indicates more technical material that may be skipped without loss of continuity.

In this chapter we extend our analysis of labor markets developed in previous chapters to try to identify the reasons for the general growth of real wages in the United States over time and the structure of wages in the United States in recent years. Knowledge of this sort provides insight into a variety of important social issues, including poverty and discrimination.

Understanding real wages and the wage structure is an extremely difficult task. Moreover, this is an area of considerable disagreement among economists when interpreting the data. We will often have to admit that the behavior of wages, although consistent with the competitive framework, is also consistent with other interpretations. It is reasonable to say that comprehending wage structures and trends and how they are influenced by public policy currently constitutes *the* major challenge to researchers in labor economics.

THE HISTORICAL BEHAVIOR OF REAL WAGE RATES IN THE UNITED STATES

Real wage rates are measured in terms of the goods and services they can buy. Theoretically, the real wage rate is the slope of the budget constraint describing the individual's tradeoff between hours of leisure and market goods. If this seems somewhat unfamiliar, please review pages 117–118. In practice, real wage rates are usually estimated by dividing a measure of the individual's nominal or paycheck wage rate by an index of the cost of living, usually the Consumer Price Index. So, while real wage rates are measured in terms of dollars, those dollars refer to the purchasing power of the wage relative to some base period.

A numerical example is quite helpful. In 1981, the average hourly wage rate in the United States was $7.25, and the consumer price index (base 1967) was 272. The value for the consumer price index tells us that goods and services that cost $1 in 1967 cost approximately $2.72 in 1981. In general, a real wage rate is calculated by dividing the nominal wage rate in a given year by the value of the consumer price index for that year and multiplying the result by 100. This means that the average real wage rate in the United States for 1981 was $2.67 in 1967 dollars. Because 1967 is the base year for the consumer price index we are using, it has the value 100. So, the real wage rate (base 1967) for the United States in 1967 is also the nominal wage for that year, $2.68. From this we can see that the real wage was about 1 cent lower in 1981 than in 1967. To make sure you understand the concept of a real wage rate, note that the average hourly wage rate in the United States for 1975 was $4.53 and the consumer price index (base 1967) was 161. What was the real wage rate (in terms of 1967 purchasing power) for 1975, then?

Before we go on to discuss the data available for real wage rates in the United States, it is important to reiterate briefly the forces we identified in

TABLE 10-1   Some Indicators of Real Wage Rates in the United States: 1832–1890

	Nominal Wages		
	---	---	---
	(1)	(2)	(3)
Year	Nominal Average Annual Earnings of Full-Time Workers in Iron and Steel Manufacturing	Nominal Average Daily Earnings of Common Laborers (with board)	Nominal Average Daily Earnings of Common Laborers (without board)
1830			
1832	$313	$0.62	
1840			
1849	292		
1850		0.61	$0.87
1859	346		
1860			1.06
1869	524		1.55
1870			
1879	349		
1880			1.23
1889	522		
1890			1.46

previous chapters as determining wage rates. Chapters 3, 4, and 5 showed us that, in a competitive environment, nominal wage rates tend to equal labor's value of marginal product, $VMPL$. When investment in on-the-job training is considered, the equality between nominal wage rates and $VMPL$ still holds, but in a lifetime context—that is, the *present value* of workers' marginal contribution to output will tend to equal the *present value* of their lifetime earnings. Even if the economy were permeated with monopolies and monopsonies, our analysis of Chapter 6 showed us that wage rates should rise with productivity. So, in order to understand the general growth of real wages in the United States, we must identify the factors that have influenced the physical productivity of labor. In particular, we will take note of increases in physical capital per worker and human capital per worker.

Data on Real Wages Since 1800

Data concerning real wages prior to 1890 are difficult to find. Prior to 1860 they are unreliable. Available information suggests a moderate and

Price Indexes		Real Wages		
(4)	(5)	(6)	(7)	(8)
Price Index^a (Base 1830)	Consumer Price Index (Base 1830)	Real Average Annual Earnings of Full-Time Workers in Iron and Steel Manufacturing^b	Real Average Daily Earnings of Common Laborers^c (with board)	Real Average Daily Earnings of Common Laborers^d (without board)
100				
		$313	$0.62	
91				
		400		
73			0.84	$1.19
		444		
78	78			1.35
		430		1.27
	122			
		410		
	96			1.28
	95^e	549		
	95^e			1.54

[a] Weighted index of retail prices of textiles, shoes, rum, whiskey, coffee, and tea.
[b] (1) ÷ (4) × 100 for 1830–60 and (1) ÷ (5) × 100 for 1860–90.
[c] (2) ÷ (4) × 100.
[d] (3) ÷ (4) × 100 for 1830–60 and (3) ÷ (5) × 100 for 1860–90.
[e] Author's estimates.

Source: Stanley Lebergott, *Manpower in Economic Growth* (New York: McGraw-Hill, 1964), pp. 541, 545, 548–49.

unsteady secular (long-term) increase prior to 1860 and a rather steady increase from about 1880 to 1920.[1] Except for the period of 1930 to 1938, the secular increase in real wage rates continued through 1972. Between 1972 and 1981, however, real wages fell by about 7 percent.[2]

Table 10-1 shows us some indicators of real wage rates prior to 1890. Until 1860, relatively many workers (slaves and the self-employed) were not represented in these average wages, and a large portion of wages was paid in

[1] Stanley Lebergott, *Manpower in Economic Growth* (New York: McGraw-Hill, 1964), pp. 137–64.
[2] *Economic Report of the President, 1982*, pp. 276, 278, and 291. Remember that these data ignore fringe benefits. In Chapter 11 we see that the real value of fringe benefits has increased greatly during 1972–81.

kind, so these data must be interpreted with appropriate caution. Real wages prior to 1860 seem to grow at an annual rate in the neighborhood of 1 percent. Although real wage rate growth seems to have halted between 1860 and 1880, it resumed at an annual rate of about 1 percent during the 1880s.[3]

Wage rate data for manufacturing since 1890 are presented in Table 10-2. These data are considerably more reliable than those of Table 10-1, and they show that the growth of real wage rates continued at about 1 percent per year through 1915. Since 1915, real wage rates have been increasing by approximately 1.8 percent per year.[4] If we consider the period 1890–1980, over which the best data are available, we see that real wage rates in manufacturing were about four times higher in 1980 than in 1890, and that the average annual rate of growth was about 1.6 percent.

Reasons for the Wage Growth: Relative Increases in Physical and Human Capital per Worker

Background. Is the historical growth of real wages consistent with the theory of labor supply, demand, and investment in human capital under competitive conditions? In particular, can this theory provide insight into the rather sharp increase in annual wage growth after 1915? If so, then we should be able to find evidence of concomitant growth in the marginal physical product of labor. We will focus on two possible sources of growth in *MPPL*: (1) an increase in the ratio of physical to human capital in the economy and (2) an increase in the amount of human capital embodied in each worker. The first source of *MPPL* growth is an implication of the principle of variable proportions that we learned in Chapter 3—the marginal physical product of labor rises as the production process becomes relatively more capital intensive. Concerning the second source of growth, *MPPL* refers to the extra output generated by a small increment in labor of a given quality. A greater amount of human capital per worker increases labor quality and thus raises the marginal physical productivity of labor. Not only, then, is a marginal unit of labor more productive when used with a greater amount of capital, but it is also more productive when of higher quality because more human capital is embodied in it.

---

[3] Clarence Long's figures in *Wages and Earnings in the United States, 1860–90* (Princeton, N.J.: Princeton University Press, 1960), Tables A-11 and A-12, suggest that real wage rates rose between 1870 and 1880 as well as from 1880 to 1890. Thus, we are unsure of the behavior of real wage rates, by decade, between 1860 and 1890.

[4] Long reports average real wage increases of about 1.5 percent annually from 1860 to 1890 and about 2.8 percent from 1914 to 1953. Although these figures are higher than those derived from Tables 10-1 and 10-2, the change in the annual rate of growth of wages that seems to occur around 1915 is similar. See *ibid.*, p. 109.

TABLE 10-2 Real Wage Rates in Manufacturing in the United States: 1890–1980

Year	Nominal Wages		Price Index	Real Wages	
	(1) Nominal Average Hourly Earnings	(2) Nominal Average Hourly Earning of Production Workers	(3) Consumer Price Index (Base 1914)	(4) Real Average Hourly Earnings[a]	(5) Real Average Hourly Earnings of Production Workers[b]
1890	$0.199		91	$0.219	
1895	0.200		84	0.238	
1900	0.216		84	0.257	
1905	0.239		89	0.269	
1910	0.260		95	0.274	
1915	0.287		101	0.284	
1920	0.663	$0.55	200	0.331	$0.28
1925	0.645	0.54	175	0.368	0.31
1930		0.55	166		0.33
1935		0.54	137		0.40
1940		0.66	140		0.47
1945		1.02	179		0.57
1950		1.44	240		0.61
1955		1.86	267		0.70
1960		2.26	294		0.77
1965		2.61	314		0.83
1970		3.35	386		0.87
1975		4.83	536		0.90
1980		7.27	821		0.89

[a] (Nominal average hourly earnings ÷ consumer price index) × 100.
[b] (Nominal average hourly earnings of production workers ÷ consumer price index) × 100.

Sources: Column (1) *Historical Statistics of the United States, Colonial Times to 1970*, Series D766; (2) *Ibid.*, Series D802, and *Economic Report of the President, 1982*, p. 276; (3) *Historical Statistics of the United States*, Rees index through 1914, Series E186; Consumer Price Index, all items 1915–75, Series E135 (1975 and 1980) from *Economic Report of the President, 1982*, p. 291. The indexes were adjusted to 1914 = 100.

*[To firm up our understanding of how these two factors positively influence *MPPL*, consider a simple production function, the Cobb-Douglas production function, that we encountered in Chapter 3:

$$Q = \gamma K^{\beta}(aL)^{1-\beta} \tag{10-1}$$

This function says that output (Q) depends on the use of physical capital (K) and labor, where labor is the product of the quantity of labor services (L) and the quality of labor measured by the amount of human capital per unit of labor (a). γ and β are the parameters of this production function which translate the firm's use of capital and quality-adjusted labor into its output. Because γ and β are positive constants, it is easily seen that the Cobb-Douglas production function expresses output as a positive function of the services of physical capital (K) and of human capital (aL). To see the relationship between marginal physical productivity of labor and human capital per worker, remember that the marginal physical product of labor, *MPPL*, is the effect of a small change in L on the firm's output, ceteris paribus. For this production function

$$MPPL = (1 - \beta)a\gamma K^{\beta}(aL)^{-\beta} \tag{10-2}$$

which can be rewritten as

$$MPPL = (1 - \beta)\gamma \left(\frac{K}{L}\right)^{\beta} a^{1-\beta} \tag{10-3}$$

Because γ, β, and $1 - \beta$ are all positive, the marginal physical product of labor is a positive function of K/L and a. Thus, we will look for changes in physical capital per worker and human capital per worker when we attempt to understand the pattern of growth rates of real wages presented in Tables 10-1 and 10-2 and discussed above.]

The growth of the physical capital per worker.   Data on the value of the stock of nonfarm, nonresidential structures and equipment adjusted for inflation provide an indicator of the amount of physical capital in the United States for the period 1850–1978.[5] This stock increased at an average annual rate of about 3 percent from 1850 to 1912. From 1912 to 1978 the average annual rate of growth was about 2 percent. During similar periods, the labor force grew at rates of approximately 2.5 percent (1850–1910) and 1.5 percent (1920–78).[6] Clearly, the capital-to-labor ratio was increasing at the same time wages were rising. However, we are concerned with whether the growth of the capital-to-labor ratio *accelerated* about 1915, the year in which the growth wages increased from about 1 percent to 2 percent per year. The annual growth rate of K/L is approximately the rate of growth of K minus the rate of growth of L. So, before 1915 the rate of growth of K/L was approximately 0.5 percent per year, while afterward the rate slowed slightly to about 0.4 percent per year. The point here is that the acceleration in the rate of

---

* Represents more technical material, which can be skipped without loss of continuity. If you skip it go to the next section.
[5] *Historical Statistics of the United States,* p. 255, and *Statistical Abstract of the United States,* 1980, p. 474.
[6] *Historical Statistics,* pp. 126–139, and *Statistical Abstract,* p. 394.

growth of real wages does not seem to be readily attributable to the behavior of the ratio of capital to labor. What else may be responsible for the rather remarkable increase in the rate of growth of real wages around 1915?

The growth of human capital per worker.   Between 1870 and 1910 the proportion of the 17-year-old population graduating from high school rose from 2 percent to 8.6 percent, or by about 1.7 percentage points per decade. From 1910 to 1930 the proportion rose to 28.8 percent, or by slightly more than 10 percentage points per decade. In addition, the trends in the school-age population and educational expenditures combined to increase the growth of the resources devoted to the average student since 1915. Finally, declining immigration probably also contributed to rising labor force quality, because immigrants tended to have less schooling than the native-born population. For example, the illiteracy rate among native-born whites in 1900 (age 10 and over) was 4.6 percent, while among foreign-born whites it was 12.9 percent.[7] Thus, there is circumstantial evidence that a significant increase in labor force quality, as measured by human capital per worker, underlies the historical wage trends we seek to understand.

Although data on the trends in human capital per worker match up better with data on real wages in the United States over time than do the data on the growth of physical capital per worker, these data are of only limited accuracy. This and our inability to control for the possible intervening factors prohibit us from creating a more thorough explanation of the historical trend of real wage growth during the last 200 years. In later sections we analyze recent data on earnings in much more detail. We formulate more precise hypotheses from the theory of supply, demand, and investment in human capital, and use more and better data on earning capacity. The result is that our understanding of the level and distribution of economic well-being in recent years greatly exceeds our understanding of the historical trends of wages.

Unions and minimum wage laws.   Before turning our attention to the distribution of earned income during the last few decades, we must consider the roles played by unionism and minimum wage legislation in the historical trends of real wages. It would be difficult to attribute the wage growth before 1915, as well as the increased wage growth beginning around 1915, to unions or minimum wage legislation. The proportion of the labor force consisting of union members was too small and unstable for unions to have exerted an important influence on wages during this period. Nationwide minimum wage legislation was not enacted until the 1930s. Data presented in Chapters 5 and Chapter 7 showed us that minimum wages in the United States have averaged about 50 percent of the average hourly wage in manufacturing and that

---

[7] *Historical Statistics of the United States,* Series H666-667.

unions establish approximately a 15 percent wage differential between union and nonunion workers. Both of these effects have been fairly *constant* over time, however. Thus, recent data for the economic impacts of minimum wages and unions support the conclusion that these institutions have not had much effect on the *growth* of real wages in recent years.

THE DISTRIBUTION OF EARNING CAPACITY AMONG INDIVIDUALS

Examine the data in Figures 10-1 and 10-2. A number of conclusions leap out at you. Not everyone has the same hourly wage rate. Men tend to earn more than women. Blacks earn less than whites. Many families had incomes below $7,500 in 1978. In this section we examine the structure of individuals' earning capacities in detail. The topic has occupied the attention of economists for two reasons: (1) a concern with the determinants of income inequality, (2) a concern over how quickly and smoothly labor markets allocate labor among alternative employments and, in the process, determine wages. These two topics are clearly related. If policymakers wish to alter the income distribution, a knowledge of how it is generated is essential. In addition, an evaluation of the desirability of a particular wage structure may depend on whether workers seem to be paid according to their productivities.

The importance of understanding the determinants of income inequality when formulating economic policy may become clearer if we consider a simple example. Suppose that society decides the earnings of corporate executives are too high relative to the earnings of production workers. It imposes a progressive income tax to reduce this inequality. If the earnings of executives are relatively high because they are paid for specialized skills acquired through education and training and for a willingness to assume risk and responsibility, the tax may eventually reduce the willingness of individuals to supply these qualities. In this case, the pretax pay of executives will increase and, after a period of adjustment, the pretax income distribution may become *more* unequal than before the income tax. Suppose, though, executives receive large **economic rents**—wages far in excess of those in their next best job opportunity. This might be because they possess special talents that are inborn traits whose only use is in business management. In this case, an income tax would reduce such rents along with the salaries of executives but probably would not reduce the amount of executive talent supplied to the economy in the long run. Thus, as noted in Chapter 1, positive or scientific knowledge of the income distribution is necessary before policy dealing with the normative or ethical aspects of income distribution is formulated. We will return to this issue in depth later in this chapter when we discuss discrimination and wage differences between blacks and whites and men and women.

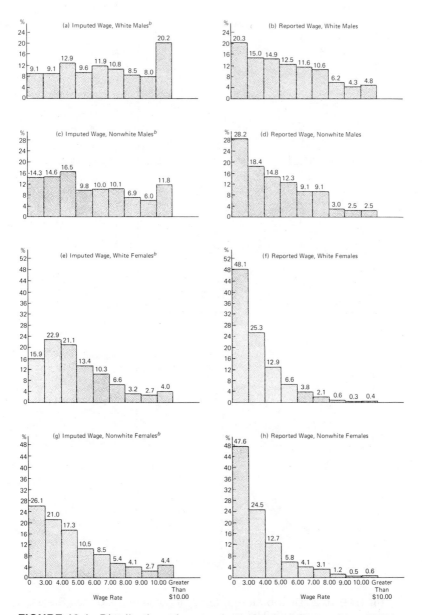

FIGURE 10-1. Distribution of wages in the United States, May 1978[a]

[a] Height of each bar denotes percentage of designated population receiving wage in range indicated.

[b] Imputed wage is equal to earnings divided by hours of work for those persons not paid by the hour.

Source: Julie Lotspeich, "An Empirical Analysis of the Linkage Between Low Wages and Poverty in the U.S.," Undergraduate Honors Thesis, University of North Carolina, Chapel Hill, May 1982. Data are from Current Population Survey.

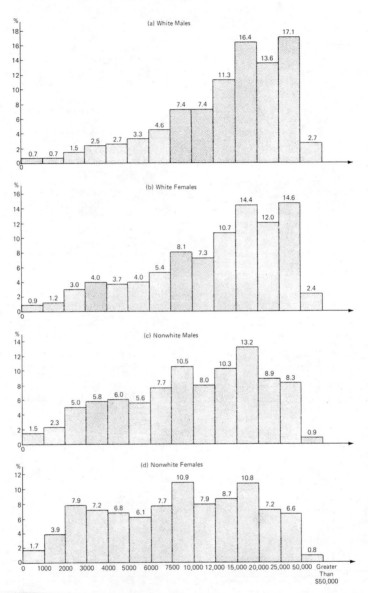

FIGURE 10-2. Distribution of family income in the United States, May 1978[a]

[a] Height of each bar denotes percentage of designated population receiving income in range indicated.

[b] Imputed wage is equal to earnings divided by hours of work for those persons not paid by the hour.

Source: Julie Lotspeich, "An Empirical Analysis of the Linkage Between Low Wages and Poverty in the U.S.," Undergraduate Honors Thesis, University of North Carolina, Chapel Hill, May 1982. Data are from Current Population Survey.

Some Theoretical Considerations

There are many ways to define wage structure. The appropriate definition depends upon the particular economic or public policy question under consideration. The basis for understanding the wage structure is the theory of supply, demand, and human capital developed in previous chapters and used in the last section to help interpret the historical pattern of real wage rates. This analytical framework was summarized in Chapter 8 in terms of the individual's supply and demand curves for human capital investment. It is repeated in Figure 10-3. Remember that a particular individual could be characterized, for example, by a demand curve such as $d(\rho)$ or $d(\rho)'$ and a supply curve such as $s(r)$ or $s(r)'$. Individual differences in aptitude, ability, or family wealth, among other things, determine the relative positions of the supply and demand curves. Because wealth maximization requires investing up to the point where the relevant supply and demand curves intersect, the correlation between demand and supply has an important influence on the distribution of wage rates and earning power.

Suppose, for example, that persons who enjoy relatively large benefits from investment in human capital also have relatively easy access to investable funds. This might be due to scholarships given out on the basis of ability, for example. The result is that $s(r)'$ is paired with $d(\rho)'$ and $s(r)$ with $d(\rho)$. Earning power is determined by the area under the demand curve up to the amount invested. Thus, the difference between the earning power of the two individuals with demand curves $d(\rho)$ and $d(\rho)'$ will be greater if their supply curves are $s(r)$ and $s(r)'$, respectively, than if the supply curves were reversed. *That is, a positive correlation between the demand and supply of human capital investment will work toward increasing the dispersion of labor market earning power among individuals.*

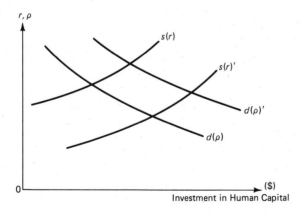

FIGURE 10-3. Human capital supply and demand schedules and earning-power differences

If everyone had the same demand curve but different availability of funds for investment in human capital, only supply curves would vary among individuals. In this case, the intersections of supply and demand would constitute a locus of points describing the demand curve for human capital. Earnings would increase, and the rate of return would decline, with rising investment per person in schooling, training, and other forms of human capital. Alternatively, if everyone had the same supply curve but different demand curves, the rate-of-return and earning-power differences would rise with human capital investment. Finally, if everyone had the same demand and supply curve, there would be equality in the amount of human capital investment. Everyone would have similar amounts of schooling and training, and real earning power would be equal across individuals. The only reason for observed wage inequality would then be nonwage differences in job characteristics. Persons who worked at relatively unpleasant or hazardous jobs would receive compensatory wage premiums—a topic we examine in the next chapter.

Some Statistical Considerations

Let us reflect a moment on the nature of the statistical tools we will employ in the investigation of wage structure, most of which were covered in Chapter 2. In the remainder of this chapter, we will apply these methods to observed behavior, guided by the competitive theory of wage determination. In utilizing competitive theory to help us understand the observed wage structure, limited information forces us to test simple hypotheses. Specifically, we must assume that many variables omitted froms our regressions are uncorrelated with the independent variables under consideration. Also, the contrasts we have drawn between the behavioral implications of the theory of competition and those of theories with noncompetitive postulates (monopoly or monopsony) are mainly *qualitative* and not quantitative. Thus, it is difficult to judge with a high degree of certainty whether empirical studies confirm or refute competitive theory. Nevertheless, we will see that testing simple hypotheses derived from competitive theory provides important insights into the determinants of wage behavior.

Income Inequality among Individuals in General: Empirical Analysis

To gain insight into the distribution of earning power in general, we rely on the model of human capital investment depicted in Figure 10-3 and summarized in the human capital earning-power function developed in Chapters 8 and 9. Remember that its simplest form is

$$\ln w = \ln w(0) + \rho(1)S + \rho(2)kX \qquad (10\text{-}4)$$

where $\rho(1)$ and $\rho(2)$ are the rates of return to schooling and OJT, respectively, k is the proportion of the workers' time devoted to OJT investment, and X is years of labor market experience. [What is ln $w(0)$?] Inequality of market earning power among individuals is captured by variation in the left-hand side of equation (10-4). In the human capital framework, this inequality is explained by the variables on the right-hand side representing human capital investments. Although schooling and OJT are not the only forms of human capital investment economists use to explain income inequality, the practical matter of data availability limits the extent to which they incorporate other variables into empirical work on the distribution of earning power. We will examine this issue in greater deatil in a little while.

The human capital approach emphasizes the importance of *life-cycle* considerations in determining the distribution of wages in the economy, and it points out the importance of a theoretical framework when interpreting economic data. The natural measure of economic well-being emerging from human capital analysis is the present value of lifetime earnings, rather than wages received in a particular year. Equation (10-4) makes it clear why this is so. Market earning power is not completely determined once schooling is over. It rises over the life cycle as experience is acquired. This is illustrated in Chapter 9, where we saw that the annual earnings of someone who completes five years of schooling initially fall short of the earnings of a worker who receives slightly less schooling, then later overtake and fully surpass them. Moreover, in a population with persons of the *same age* but different amounts of schooling we would obtain quite different pictures of the degree of income inequality, depending upon the year of age at which we measured earning power. Why?

Unfortunately, data on individuals' complete lifetime earnings streams are not generally available. This makes it quite difficult to study the distribution of present values of lifetime earnings. However, interpersonal differences in current earning power often represent a concomitant disparity of lifetime earnings prospects. So there seems to be some merit, as well as necessity, in analyzing earning-power dispersion with data on current wage rates or earnings or on earning power over short segments of individuals' lives. The point is that economists would like to have a complete motion picture of earnings over a large number of individuals' lives. Instead we must settle for either a snapshot taken at one point in time or a short motion picture which captures a few years out of people's lives. The hope is that the snapshot or the short movie gives us correct information as to the wage dispersion that we would see if we had the entire lifetime picture in front of us.

When the human capital earning-power equation is used to estimate the returns to schooling and experience with data for individuals, it also provides some evidence on how investments in human capital affect the personal distribution of income. Consider the following estimate of the relationship between earning power and investments in human capital:

$$\ln w = 4.92 + 0.075S + 0.0070X(1) + 0.0014X(2), \qquad R^2 = 0.28 \quad \textbf{(10-5)}$$
$$(163.0) \quad (34.6) \qquad (10.3) \qquad\quad (16.2)$$

where w is the actual hourly wage rate in 1976, S is years of schooling completed, $X(1)$ is the number of years worked since age 18, and $X(2)$ is number of months worked for the present employer.[8] The numbers in parentheses are t-values, and the data used for this equation come from the University of Michigan's Panel Study of Income Dynamics. What is interesting about this equation is that experience has been divided into two components, so that we may see how the impact of experience-in-general may differ from that of experience specific to the current job. Before reading any further you should make sure you understand what each of the coefficients in equation (10-5) represents.

Our interest here is in studying the personal distribution of earning power, so we will focus more sharply on the R^2 statistic than we did when our major interest was the rate of return to schooling or experience. The coefficient of determination (R^2) equals 0.28, which tells us that the variables representing the above three dimensions of investment in human capital can account for about 28 percent of the variation in the wage rate of a representative sample of the out-of-school population of the United States. When you think of the host of additional factors that must also influence earnings—such as individual differences in ability, health, luck, the pleasantness or unpleasantness of particular jobs, and unemployment experience, to name only a few—the amount of variation in earning power explained by just schooling and experience seems rather impressive.

A word of caution: Some of the variables omitted from the human capital earning-power function given above may be correlated with schooling and experience. In this case, their influence on earning power may be represented indirectly. Can you name some possible omitted variables that may be affecting the coefficients of schooling and experience? Two obvious ones that come to our minds are ability and time unemployed.

Let us discuss these possible biases in some detail. There is some evidence that the estimated rate of return to schooling does *not* increase markedly with ability.[9] In this case, the estimated coefficients of (10-5) are generally unaffected by the omission of ability as an explanatory variable. Recall from Chapter 9 that firm-specific OJT reduces the probability that the

---

[8] Richard F. Kamalich and Solomon W. Polachek, "Discrimination: Fact or Fiction? An Examination Using an Alternative Approach," *Southern Economic Journal*, 49:2 (October 1982), 450–61.

[9] Zvi Griliches, "Estimating the Returns to Schooling: Some Econometric Problems," *Econometrica*, 45:1 (January 1977), 1–22.

firm will lay off a worker when there is a decline in the demand for final output. Ashenfelter and Ham[10] find that schooling has a negative impact on spells of unemployment, ceteris paribus. However, to the extent that schooling and other investments in human capital increase economic welfare by reducing the risk of unemployment, it may be fair to omit unemployment experience from the human capital earning-power function in (10-5) when attempting to explain the income distribution. What this says is that the influence of schooling and experience work in many different ways, and the coefficients in equation (10-5) are capturing all the different avenues through which these variables affect earning power.

In summary, interpersonal differences in human capital investment appear to be capable of accounting for a significant amount of income inequality. In discussing the dispersion of labor market success among individuals, we have taken a somewhat casual approach. Specifically, we have not gone beyond the level of theoretical and statistical analysis of earning capacity developed thus far to introduce more complex measures of the disparity in wages.[11] We feel that Figures 10-1 and 10-2 provide easily understood pictures of the degree of wage and income inequality in the United States and that our efforts are better used in developing a more complete analysis of the earning-power differences between the races and the sexes.

Earning-Power Differences Between the Races and the Sexes

Background. Figures 10-1 and 10-2 show us that, on average, blacks earn less per hour than whites and women less per hour than men. Note also that the earnings gap is more substantial between the sexes than between the races. Social concern over these facts manifested itself in the Civil Rights Act of 1964 and in the drive for an Equal Rights Amendment during the 1970s and 1980s. One of the main themes of our text is that no matter what type of labor market we consider—competitive, monopolistic, or monopsonistic—earnings are positively related to productive capabilities. Many institutions within society influence an individual's collection of personal attributes determining labor market productivity. First and foremost is the family. What role does the family play in determining race and sex wage differences in the United States?

Genetic makeup will determine an individual's success as a worker as well the capacity to benefit from investments in schooling or on-the-job

---

[10] "Education, Unemployment, and Earnings," *Journal of Political Economy,* 87:5, part 2 (October 1979), S99–S116.

[11] On this issue see Jacob Mincer, *Schooling, Experience, and Earnings* (New York: Columbia University Press, for the National Bureau of Economic Research, 1974), chap. 2, and Lloyd G. Reynolds, *Labor Economics and Labor Relations,* 8th ed. (Englewood Cliffs, N.J.: Prentice-Hall, 1982), pp. 271–74.

training. Time spent out of the labor force by mothers during their children's preschool years may contribute to the intellectual development of their children and, through this, the success of their children in school. Transfers of wealth from parents play an important role in whether or not someone can finance investments in human capital. Moreover, parents, brothers, and sisters can be valuable sources of job contacts and help in developing the social skills necessary to obtain and maintain a good job. What we have just described are the avenues through which the **family of orientation** (parents and siblings) influences an individual's productive traits. A person's **family of procreation** (spouse and children) also influences his or her earning capacity. Health and wealth of your spouse and the number, spacing, and health of your children all affect the amount and type of human capital investment you will undertake over your lifetime.

Other institutions within society that influence an individual's productive traits over the life cycle include *firms, unions,* and *governments.* Among other things, each of these affects the availability and net out-of-pocket costs of postschool training. How? As an exercise, construct a table listing additional ways that these three institutions affect the personal traits that determine a person's lifetime job productivity. Be specific.

The economics of discrimination. To the extent that personal traits affecting job productivity—such as intelligence, ability, strength, schooling, occupational training, and health—differ *systematically* among age-race-sex groups in the population, so will earning capacity. What about the situation, though, where labor market minority groups such as women or blacks have low earning power relative to white males even if we account for productivity differences? We will term this situation **labor market discrimination.** Figure 10-4 illustrates what we mean by labor market discrimination. At any given amount of investment in human capital, the majority group has a greater payoff. Its demand curve for investment in human capital lies above that of the minority group. At a particular amount of investment, say $I(0)$, the shaded area measures the lifetime earning-power difference we are calling labor market discrimination. Remember, demand curves for human capital may vary because of interpersonal differences in characteristics that determine productivity, such as strength, intelligence, or ability. Market discrimination, however, refers to race or sex differences in the payoff from human capital investment that are *unrelated* to the personal traits determining labor market productivity. What forms does such discrimination take, and what institutions within society are responsible?

One possibility is that women and blacks have the same types of jobs as white males, but firms simply pay them less. More subtle is the situation where firms regularly exclude minorities from what are thought to be better jobs by differential criteria applied to hiring, layoff, firing, promotion, and retirement decisions.

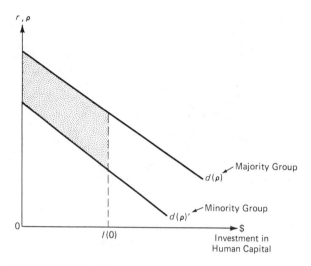

FIGURE 10-4. Labor market discrimination

Why is it that firms might discriminate? One reason may be that owners and managers have a distaste for associating with minorities. Another reason is that they collude in order to increase their wealth at the expense of certain groups of workers. This latter situation is known as **exploitation.** It is also possible either that managers have incorrect information concerning the true productive capabilities of minorities or that accurate information is relatively costly to obtain. This can also result in systematically low wages for blacks and women compared to white males. It is important to note that even though firms are the "place" in the economy where labor market discrimination occurs, owners and managers may not be at fault. For example, if white males dislike working alongside women, or customers dislike being waited on by blacks, this can produce wage differentials between the sexes and the races even if managers and owners of firms are totally unprejudiced. Moreover, if local governments establish separate, lower-quality schools for minorities, this will also result in a lower payoff for minorities with a given amount of investment in human capital.

Our story would be reasonably simple if things ended here. They do not, of course. Some of the reasons productive traits differ between majority and minority workers can also be viewed as the result of what we will term **societal discrimination.** In this case we are speaking of situations where opportunities to accumulate skills that enhance job success or to obtain funds for investment are rationed on the basis of race or sex. Figure 10-5 illustrates what we mean by societal discrimination. We have isolated societal discrimination by ignoring any labor market discrimination and attributing identical human capital demand curves to both the majority and minority

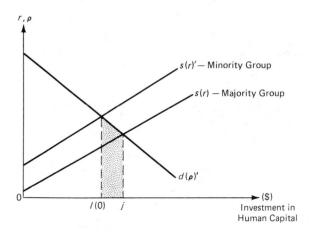

FIGURE 10-5. Societal discrimination

groups. What differ in the figure are the supply curves for investment in human capital. The majority group has a lower rate of interest to pay for any given dollar of investment in human capital. As a result, the majority group invests more, j instead of $I(0)$, and has a lifetime annual earning power that exceeds the minority group's by the shaded area. Although the institutions doing the discriminating and the motives behind it include those mentioned above, we must expand the list when discussing societal discrimination.

The *family of orientation* can be a source of discrimination. For example, parents may have preset notions concerning acceptable occupations for their children, such as that little girls can become secretaries or nurses but not physicians. The family of orientation is also where discrimination is spread from generation to generation. Past discrimination will lower parental income, which in turn leads to lower income transfers and less human capital investment among children. Moreover, relatively low incomes may contribute to bad health, which is passed on from generation to generation. Similarly, the *family of procreation* can contribute to discriminatory wage differences. Suppose, for example, that wives are expected (forced?) to stay home with children, thus suffering depreciation of their labor market skills. *Lending institutions* may restrict credit for reasons independent of the ability to repay. Finally, *unions, firms,* and *institutions of higher education* may consistently restrict minority admission into training programs. The relative exclusion of blacks and women from major medical schools until rather recently is one example. Can you cite some others?

The final source of discrimination we will discuss is what can be called **secondary discrimination.** To the extent that minorities *expect* to suffer labor market discrimination and therefore receive lower payoffs from investment in human capital, they will rationally invest in less human capital than majority workers. This is shown in Figure 10-6, where we have given both groups the same supply curve and shaded the earnings differences that will occur because the higher payoff makes the majority worker invest more. The shaded area is what we mean by secondary discrimination. The point to remember here is that some of the wage differences between workers caused by differences in productive traits due to differential investments in human capital should also be included in any attempt to measure discrimination.

Now let us make sure we understand discrimination and its components by collecting all the knowledge learned thus far in one diagram, Figure 10-7. We will focus on *only* those differences in supply and demand curves for investment in human capital that are due to discrimination of one form or another. We have illustrated the possibilities that because of discrimination the labor market minority group has less funds for investment at any given interest rate and a lower rate of return for any given amount of investment. These are reflected in a supply curve for the minority group that lies to the left of that for the majority group and a demand curve for the minority group that lies to the left of the demand curve for investment by the majority group. The total earnings difference in Figure 10-7 is the shaded area $abkI(1)I(0)e$. The earnings difference illustrated in Figure 10-7 can be decomposed into the three forms of discrimination we have been discussing. The area $abce$ illustrates labor market discrimination—the fact that even if the majority group invested no more than the minority group, $I(0)$, they would nonetheless earn more from that investment. The area $I(0)efj$ is societal discrimination. It illustrates the difference in earning power that would result from the majority group's greater access to funds even if the minority and majority group both had the same rate-of-return schedule, $d(\rho)'$. The remaining difference in earning power, $jfeckI(1)$ includes the most subtle component of total discrim-

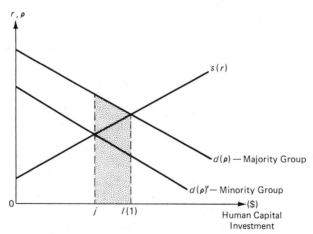

FIGURE 10-6. Secondary discrimination

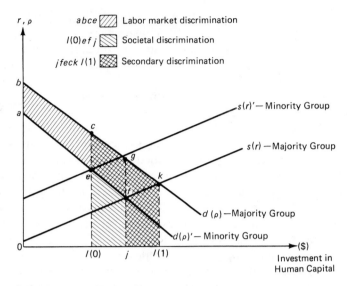

FIGURE 10-7. Total discrimination and its components

ination: secondary discrimination. It meters the gain in income accruing to the majority group because they have greater returns from investment in human capital, which leads them to invest more and earn more than the minority group. The area *gfec*, which was not shaded in figures 10-4 through 10-6, reflects the combined effects of market and societal discrimination on the difference in earning power between the majority group and the minority group.

To summarize, secondary discrimination stems from the *interaction* between investment, the rate of return, and the interest rate at which funds for investment can be obtained. It is most important to realize that in reality there will be differences between the races and sexes in demand and supply curves that are *not* due to discrimination. These differences will also lead to race and sex differences in earning power. What we are illustrating in Figure 10-7 are differences in the supply and demand curves stemming from the various forms of discrimination discussed above.

It should be clear by now that race and sex differences in earning power can be extremely difficult to measure accurately. The economic literature is extensive and the result of the work of some of the best economists. The most we can accomplish here is to develop the flavor of the subject in a few ways. In what follows we will examine some of the details of labor market discrimination, because this is what most people have in mind when they think of discrimination. Moreover, it is important to identify more clearly some of the winners and losers as well as the social costs involved in market discrimination. We will also consider in some detail the appropriate public policy to reduce wage differences between the races and sexes. We conclude this section with an empirical analysis of race and sex differences in earning power in the United States. In the process we examine recent attempts to measure both discrimination and the effectiveness of equal-pay and fair-employment legislation.

Additional Theoretical Analysis of Discrimination. To repeat, labor market discrimination is the result of one or a combination of two or three factors underlying the behavior of managers, majority-group workers, or majority-group customers: (1) incorrect information concerning the productivity of minority workers, (2) a desire to try to make themselves better off at the expense of labor market minorities, or (3) a dislike for associating with minority workers.

The details of statistically distinguishing race or sex differences in productivity are somewhat complex and will not be considered here.[12] The basic implications of such distinctions are not all that complicated and can be understood quite quickly. In short, managers, majority workers, and majority customers will have personal estimates of the productivity of minority workers *as a group*. They will have the tendency to attribute this estimate to *every* minority worker. The image having these attributes is known as a **stereotype.** As a result, even if they encounter someone who seems to be an especially talented minority worker, they may discount this experience somewhat because of what they perceive are the general group productivity characteristics. Elimination of this source of race or sex differences in earning power requires managers, majority workers, or customers to change their perceptions of the productivity of minority workers. This could come about from a more accurate assessment of the true productivity of individual minority workers or from an increase in the general skill levels of minority workers or both. We would not expect race or sex wage differences from this source to persist over long periods of time. Managers have an economic incentive to find out the true productivity of their employees. Moreover, there has been much effort by government and religious groups to eradicate race and sex stereotypes.

When incorrect perceptions of productivity seem to persist despite efforts to eliminate them, this may be due to prejudice or a dislike for associating with minority workers. To see how prejudice affects race and sex wage differences, consider a given occupation that already contains two groups of equally productive workers. The two groups are readily distinguishable by employers according to some personal trait such as race or sex, which is assumed in our example to be unrelated to job skills. Finally,

---

[12] See Dennis J. Aigner and Glen G. Cain, "Statistical Theories of Discrimination in Labor Markets," *Industrial and Labor Relations Review,* 30:2 (January 1977), pp. 175–87, and Thomas Johnson, "Selection Without (Unfair) Discrimination," *Communications in Statistics—Theory and Methods,* A7:11 (1978), pp. 1079–1098

assume that some managers prefer not to employ members of one of the groups, the minority group. Gary Becker labels an employer a discriminator if he or she hires minority workers only if they are paid less than majority workers.[13]

Now let us develop the demand curve for minority labor, given a particular amount of majority employment. The curve labeled D-minority in Figure 10-8 expresses the number of minority workers that employers desire to hire at various majority/minority wage ratios. The schedule is flat at 1.0 because some employers do not discriminate. Eventually, additional minority employment will be demanded only if the wage ratio falls below unity, inducing additional (discriminating) firms to hire minority workers. The actual amount of minority employment, as well as the equilibrium wage ratio, results from the intersection of supply and demand, of course.

The curve labeled S-minority in Figure 10-8 illustrates the number of minority workers seeking employment at various wage ratios. In the situation depicted below, the equilibrium wage ratio is less than unity, although this need not be the case. Should nondiscriminating employers be relatively large or plentiful, supply and demand will intersect in the horizontal portion of the demand curve. In this case, majority and minority wages will be equal, despite the fact that some employers have a distaste for minority workers. In

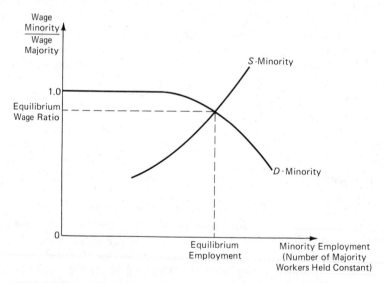

FIGURE 10-8. Employer prejudice and majority/minority wage differentials

---

[13] See Gary S. Becker, The *Economics of Discrimination,* 2d ed. (Chicago: University of Chicago Press, 1971), for more detailed discussion of discrimination resulting from consumer, employer, worker, or government prejudice.

this case, all minorities will have been hired before discriminating employers "come into play."

As in the situation of minimum wages with incomplete coverage and union/nonunion wage differences discussed in previous chapters, society suffers a loss in total output from a wage differential for equally productive workers. It should also be noted that unless all firms are discriminators or there is widespread monopoly or monopsony power, labor market discrimination due to employer distaste for minority workers should disappear in the long run. Let us elaborate.

In Chapter 6 we analyzed the theory of monopsony. We saw that workers will be exploited if there is only one buyer of labor, because of a "company town," or if buyers collude, as in the case of professional baseball. In particular, waiters will be paid less than the marginal value of their services. Employment will also be smaller than in competition. If, in reality, firms are generally owned by white males who form monopsonies when hiring minority workers, then minorities will be the victims of monopsonistic exploitation. This will lead to wage differences between the races and sexes. Put differently, if white male employers decide they want to exploit workers for purposes of increasing their own incomes, they may do it at the expense of minority workers through collective monopsony power.

Even if we ignore the costs and other difficulties associated with such collusion on any widespread scale, two questions naturally arise: (1) Why don't owners of firms attempt to exploit *all* workers? (2) Will such exploitation *necessarily* lead to race and sex differences in wages? Concerning the second issue, suppose majority and minority workers have identical supply curves. In this case, while both groups may be exploited, there should be no majority/minority wage differences. Wage differences between the races and sexes in the face of monopsony require different supply curves. You should show for yourself, by using the geometric analysis of monopsony developed in Chapter 6, that exploitation is more severe, the more inelastic (vertical) the supply curve of labor. So, if minority workers have a more inelastic supply of labor, this will produce the race and sex wage differences we observe.

It should be obvious such explanation of race and sex wage differences based on monopsony power entails a number of problems. First, we have seen in Chapter 6 that the best available evidence indicates a lack of severe employer concentration at the local labor market level. Because collusion is difficult and costly when a large number of firms are involved, we suspect that the monopsony argument may not go very far in helping us to understand race and sex wage differences in the United States. Second, labor supply evidence tends to indicate a *more* elastic supply of the labor of minority workers. Although these estimates are for aggregate behavior, and it is the supply of labor to individual or small sets of buyers of labor that we are interested in here, the theory of labor supply still suggests a *more* elastic supply curve for minority workers. To the extent that they have lower incomes to begin with, minority workers will be more sensitive to wage changes because of government income-support programs. Specifically, we expect teenagers, the elderly, and poor blacks and women to make larger proportionate adjustments in their labor supply as wages change because of the link between their income support payments and their earnings.[14] Prime-aged white males, who are generally ineligible for programs such as AFDC and social security, will therefore have less labor market sensitivity to wage changes. Thus, it seems that we must look elsewhere if we are to find a possible reason for persistent discrimination.

Occupational segregation refers to the situation in which minority workers are systematically overrepresented in low-paying occupations owing to activities on the part of majority workers to reserve the high-wage, high-prestige occupations for themselves. To see this, draw demand curves for labor in two separate occupations, one where the value of workers' services is high and another where it is low. In the absence of any discrimination or productivity differences between the two groups, there will be a blend of minority and majority workers in each of the two occupations, roughly in proportion to their representation in the labor force at large. What we are saying in the rarified example just mentioned is that if the labor force is approximately 60 percent majority workers and 40 percent minority workers, and both are equally talented, there will be a 60/40 distribution of majority and minority workers in both occupations.

Occupational segregation exists where the majority workers, through control of the licensing or educational process, through control of apprenticeship or training programs, or through an old-buddy network, are able to claim the good occupations for themselves and relegate the low-paying jobs to the minority workers. In an extreme case, the high-wage sector of the economy will be populated totally by the 60 percent of the labor force that belongs to the majority group and the low-wage sector of the labor force will be populated totally by the 40 percent of the labor force that belongs to the minority group. The notion of occupational segregation is what people have in the back of their minds when they cite the facts that historically most physicians have been men while most nurses have been women, or that managers are currently mostly male and secretaries currently mostly female, or that railroad engineers and conductors have mostly been whites and porters and waiters on trains mostly blacks.

The situation is much more complicated, of course, because one of the reasons that minority groups may not obtain high-paying high-prestige jobs

---

[14] See Donald O. Parsons, "The Decline in Male Labor Force Participation," *Journal of Political Economy*, 88 (February 1980), 117–34, and "The Male Labor Force Participation Decision: Health, Reported Health, and Economic Incentives," *Economica*, 49 (February 1982), 81–91, for elaboration.

is that their parents have not provided them with much wealth with which to invest in human capital. This could be the result of parental choice or of past discrimination that has caused parents not to have much wealth to transfer. Similarly, intergenerational considerations come into play when factors that mitigate against labor market success, such as bad health, are passed on from parents to children. These, too, may be the result either of parental choice or of past discrimination that made medical care prohibitively expensive.

The key point to remember here, though, is that occupational segregation can be pervasive and persistent if there are barriers to mobility and training. Unlike the other reasons for discrimination we have been discussing, there is much less natural tendency for occupational segregation to disappear over time. In light of our analysis thus far, we now consider the problem of formulating efficient and effective public policy to reduce individual differences in earning power.

Public policy to reduce earnings differences: Theoretical analysis. We have just examined why lifetime earning power may differ among individuals. Suppose that society wishes to close earning power gaps. What public policy will be effective? One possibility is a progressive income tax. Here is something else to consider: anything that increases the rate of return on investments in human capital or the availability of resources for investment in human capital by the poor will tend to narrow the gap in earnings. However, just as there are many reasons why individuals differ in their supply and demand curves for investment in human capital, there are many possible government actions that will close the gaps between the supply and demand curves of high and low earners. Different policies are appropriate depending upon whether low earners have been the victims of discrimination, are characterized by poor health, have low ability, or have parents with little or no wealth with which to help them invest in human capital.

The human capital model we have been developing in the past few chapters implies that earning power can be increased by extra doses of schooling, training, and other forms of human capital. Should interpersonal differences in human capital investments be due primarily to differences among families in the availability of funds to finance these investments, subsidies to the poor for schooling and training ought to improve their market earning power. A belief that extra schooling is an effective way to raise labor market productivity is one of the traditional reasons for government subsidies to education in the United States.

Discrimination against workers on the basis of race, sex, or other personal characteristics also influences wage rates. On top of this, an individual may lack certain forms of human capital or ability that enhance the effectiveness of schooling in creating labor market productivity. For example, if someone comes from a disadvantaged background in which good work habits, knowledge of how to get the most out of school, and so on, were not developed, this can lower the effectiveness of schooling in providing access to higher-paying jobs. Because family background may influence manner of speech, social behavior, and the like, and these individual characteristics may alter the effectiveness of schooling and training in generating labor market success, the effect of family background versus discrimination in determining earning power becomes rather hazy. The point here is that much more than simply schooling and OJT is involved in determining someone's labor market success. From the point of view of public policy, the debate over how best to improve the earning power of the poor centers on (1) the degree to which family background variables interact with, and perhaps even dominate, schooling and OJT in determining labor market success and (2) the most effective and ethically proper way to offset adverse background differences.

In terms of the human capital model, it is reasonable to characterize the policy debate as emphasizing the importance of individual differences in demand and supply for human capital investment. Some economists feel that the differences in supply and demand for investment in human capital are quite dramatic between advantaged and disadvantaged individuals. This latter view is depicted in Figure 10-9, where family background, pessimistic expectations about the future, and discrimination interact to cause the demand for human capital investment of the disadvantaged to lie *far* to the left of that for advantaged workers. Because families of disadvantaged workers tend also to have relatively low incomes, their supply curves of investable funds are felt to lie *far* to the left of those for advantaged workers. The result is much less human capital investment and much lower earnings for some workers. In this case, social policy that provides free tuition, low-cost loans,

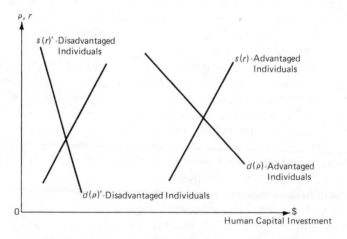

FIGURE 10-9.   Public policy and severe differences in human capital supply and demand curves

subsidized training, and so on to make it easier for disadvantaged workers to invest in human capital will not increase their incomes as much as might be expected on the basis of advantaged workers' experience. The reason is that the two human capital demand curves reflect the relative effectiveness of these forms of investment in generating labor productivity. So, it may be that disadvantaged workers are doomed to holding bad jobs with little opportunity for advancement, while advantaged workers get what are thought to be good jobs with higher incomes and plentiful opportunities for OJT. In this interpretation of income differences, low-income workers not only acquire relatively little schooling, but they also have little incentive to do so. Moreover, efforts to increase their schooling will in this case fail to provide them with the more favorable labor market opportunities of advantaged workers.

To summarize: From the perspective of public policy designed to increase the relative earning power of the disadvantaged, it is crucial to know whether interpersonal differences in earning power stem largely from differences in ability to finance or obtain investments in human capital or from substantially different payoffs from such investments due to discrimination, poor health, or family background. Because both factors are generally present among the poor, the real policy issue concerns the most effective *blend* of policy to subsidize schooling and eliminate differences in the payoff from schooling.

Race differences in wages, discrimination, and public policy in the United States.   Richard Freeman notes that the relative labor market success of black Americans has improved noticeably in recent years, with most of the improvement coming since the middle 1960s.[15] Aggregate statistics on the ratio of black to white earnings show a noticeable increase across age, sex, and occupation subgroups. Among full-time male workers, for example, the black/white earnings ratio rose from 0.64 in 1955 to 0.66 in 1964 and to 0.75 in 1976.[16] The data for female full-time workers indicate increases in the black/white earnings ratio from 0.57 in 1955 to 0.66 in 1964 to 0.94 in 1976. In light of the noticeable increase in the relative earning power of blacks since the middle 1960s, it is reasonable to ask two questions: (1) How much of the black/white wage inequality in the recent data is due to discrimination? (2) To what extent can we conclude that the dramatic increase in the black/white earnings ratio is due to government antidiscrimination activities stemming from the Civil Rights Act of 1964?

Freeman uses data from 1966 and 1969 for men, taken from the National Longitudinal Survey, to address the first question. (These data have

---

[15] "The New Job Market For Black Americans," *Industrial and Labor Relations Review,* 30:2 (January 1977), 161–74, and "Black Economic Progress After 1960: Who Has Gained and Why?" in Sherwin Rosen, ed., *Studies in Labor Markets* (Chicago: University of Chicago Press for the National Bureau of Economic Research, 1981).

[16] Freeman, "Black Economic Progress," p. 251.

been described in Chapter 2.) He employs regression analysis to calculate how an individual's family background and personal traits affect earning capacity.[17] Freeman's regressions permit black/white wage differentials to be decomposed into the portion stemming from racial differences in personal traits and family background that contribute to job productivity versus the portion due to labor market discrimination. When separate regressions for the two races are run, the results can be used to calculate, for example, what whites would earn if they faced blacks' wage structure. These predicted earnings can then be used to separate the gross wage rate differential between the races into the part that is due to differences in group characteristics and the part that remains, which is typically considered to be a measure of labor market discrimination.[18]

Before we elaborate on this procedure, however, it is important to point out several facts that sometimes escape even professional economists. First, the portion of racial wage differences stemming from family background differences cannot be further disentangled. Without a more complex analysis we do not know, for example, what part reflects societal discrimination as opposed to parental generosity with funds for investment in human capital. For the same reasons we cannot estimate what we denoted earlier as secondary discrimination. Third, there are potential biases in the measure of labor market discrimination. To the extent that the regression equations employed by Freeman fail to incorporate important individual characteristics determining productivity and therefore wages, part of racial wage differences may be incorrectly attributed to labor market discrimination. For example, should whites have more ability than blacks, and we omit ability from the regressions, part of the relatively higher wage rate of whites will be attributed to discrimination instead of to race differences in ability. To the extent, however, that blacks have relatively *more* of a productive trait, such as intelligence, and intelligence is omitted from the regressions, then the estimate of labor market discrimination will be too small. In reality, regressions of the type utilized by Freeman and other economists to explain earnings differences probably omit productive characteristics of both types just mentioned. Thus, we hope that the positive and negative biases cancel out on average and that the measure of labor market discrimination he estimates is reasonably accurate. Finally, it must be noted that even if we have precise

---

[17] The variables Freeman uses to capture the influence of family background include years of schooling of the head of the family of orientation, whether or not the mother and father were present when the individual was age 14, occupational attainment of the head of the household when the individual was 14, region and type of residence at age 14, and indicators of household reading resources when the individual was 14.

[18] For more discussion of the technical details of this technique see Ronald Oaxaca, "Sex Discrimination in Wages," in Orley Ashenfelter and Albert Rees, eds., *Discrimination in Labor Markets* (Princeton, N.J.: Princeton University Press, 1973), and David E. Bloom and Mark R. Killingsworth, "Pay Discrimination Research and Litigation: The Use of Regression Analysis," *Industrial Relations,* 21:3 (Fall 1982), 318–39.

knowledge of the size of labor market discrimination, this tells us nothing about the institutions producing such discrimination, including who they are and the motives involved.

A simple example will help us understand the way in which Freeman decomposes the total racial wage difference into labor market discrimination versus productivity differences. This involves determining statistically what blacks' earning capacity would be if they face whites' earning structure. That is, Freeman's results can be used to answer the question: How much would blacks earn if they had whites' set of regression coefficients? An estimate of this wage is obtained by predicting blacks' earning power from the averages of their personal characteristics multiplied by *whites'* regression coefficients. The *difference* between this predicted wage and the *actual* average wage for blacks is an estimate of labor market discrimination. A point made a few sentences ago bears repeating: To the extent that we, the analysts of labor market discrimination, are ignorant of the true determinants of productivity and wages, we will be misestimating discrimination. If we are largely ignorant of factors that make whites more productive than blacks, then we will overestimate discrimination with this method. If we are largely ignorant of factors that make blacks more productive than whites, then we will underestimate primary labor market discrimination with this method.

Alternatively, Freeman's results may be used to calculate what whites' earnings would be if they faced *blacks'* earning structure. The difference in the predicted white average earning level and the actual average white earning level is an alternative estimate of labor market discrimination against blacks. Of course, the same warnings concerning under- or overestimation of discrimination apply here. Also, estimates of labor market discrimination from the two methods we have mentioned will not generally be the same. They can best be thought of as determining the *interval* in which the true value of labor market discrimination falls. By using data from 1966 for older (48 to 62 years of age) men and from 1969 for younger (17 to 27 years of age) men, Freeman is able to see how estimates of labor market discrimination vary between two generations of males.

The data utilized by Freeman indicate substantial racial differences in background and personal characteristics. Among the younger men, for example, parents of blacks average 7.9 years of schooling versus 10.5 for whites. The difference in schooling between the younger men themselves was somewhat smaller, 13.2 years versus 11.5 years. Using weekly earnings as his measure of earning capacity, and the coefficients from the regressions for blacks, Freeman finds that only about 3 percent of the average earnings difference between black and white younger workers seems to be attributable to labor market discrimination, as opposed to 32 percent of that between black and white older men. When the alternative way of measuring labor market discrimination is adopted (using blacks' regression coefficients with the average values of whites' independent variables to predict what whites would have earned had they been black and comparing the result to whites' actual earnings), the results are quite similar. Labor market discrimination estimated this way is 3 percent of the earnings difference of young workers and 22 percent of the earnings difference of the older workers. One reason for the age difference in the estimates of race discrimination is that the older blacks probably received schooling that was significantly below the quality of that received by older whites. Alternatively, race differences in quality of schooling should have been relatively smaller among the younger workers. Be sure that you can explain how such differences in school quality lead to larger estimates of primary labor market discrimination for older workers.[19] What are some other reasons why estimates of labor market discrimination should be larger for older workers?

Finally, Freeman examines the role played by civil rights legislation in the growth of black/white earnings ratio since the middle 1960s. The Civil Rights Act of 1964 caused significant changes in how firms recruit and promote workers. Before the Act there was really no federal law against labor market discrimination and no serious effort to increase minority or female employment in sectors where they were severely underrepresented. Title VII of the Civil Rights Act created the Equal Employment Opportunities Commission (EEOC) in March 1965, giving it the power to mediate complaints and, recently, to bring lawsuits itself against employers who are believed to have violated the law.[20] Title VII has led to court cases that established the legal definition of discrimination by employers. For example, employment tests must be related to job performance activities. Other restrictions have been placed on how employers can recruit and the standards they can use for promotion.

Supplementing Title VII is Executive Order 11246, which established the Office of Federal Contract Compliance (OFCC). Its stated purpose is to increase the hiring and promotion of women and blacks by firms that supply goods and services to the federal government. These firms must detail their plans to recruit and promote labor market minorities or face possible current and future loss of federal contracts. Freeman also notes that there was significant growth during 1964–75 of similar activities by states' Fair Employment Practices Commissions.[21]

To summarize, following the Civil Rights Act of 1964 there were substantial anti-bias activities at the state and federal level. The effect of these activities on firms' personnel practices are documented in Table 10-3. It

---

[19] For more discussion of the history of race differences in school quality see Finis Welch, "Education and Racial Discrimination," in Orley Ashenfelter and Albert Rees, eds. *Discrimination in Labor Markets* (Princeton, N.J.: Princeton University Press, 1973).
[20] See Charles O. Gregory and Harold A. Katz, *Labor and the Law,* 3d ed. (New York: W. W. Norton and Company, 1979), chap. 17.
[21] "Black Economic Progress," p. 269.

TABLE 10-3   Evidence of Changes in Personnel Practices Due to EEO

	Percent of Companies
1. That have a *formal* EEO program including an affirmative action plan (of those subject to OFCC regulations)	86 / 96
2. That have had an investigation or other action under Title VII	63
3. Experiencing changes in selection procedures for EEO reasons:	60
Testing procedures	39
Revised job qualifications	31
Application forms	20
Recruiting techniques	19
4. That have special recruiting programs:	
For all minority workers	69
For minorities in professional/managerial positions	58
5. With programs to ensure EEO policies are implemented:	
Communications on EEO policy	95
Follow-up personnel or EEO office	85
Training sessions on EEO	67
Periodic publications of EEO results	48
EEO achievements including in performance appraisals	33
6. With special training programs:	
For entry-level jobs	16
For upgrading	24
For management positions	16

Source: Bureau of National Affairs, "Equal Employment Opportunity: Programs and Results," Personnel Policies Forum Survey 112, March 1976, lines 1, 2, table 9, p. 15; line 3, table 3, p. 4; line 4, table 1, p. 2; line 5, table 6, p. 9; line 6, table 5, p. 8.

seems likely that these government activities, by increasing the relative demand for black labor and reducing labor market discrimination against blacks, increased the relative earning power of blacks. This leads us to two questions: What was the quantitative impact of these activities? How effective were they relative to policies that, at the same time, were working to reduce the gap in schooling between the races?

To examine the issue of whether government anti-bias activity played a major role in increasing the earning power of blacks relative to whites during the last two decades, Freeman uses aggregate data to estimate separate regressions for males and females. His primary dependent variable is the median wage and salary earnings of nonwhites relative to whites (annual data 1948–75). Freeman's independent variables capture general trends in racial wage differences, the business cycle, trends in racial differences in schooling, civil rights legislation, and government programs such as AFDC and unemployment compensation that, by changing the relative supply of labor for blacks versus whites, may also affect racial differences in earnings. To capture the effect of government actions designed to reduce labor market discrimination, Freeman uses the logarithm of real cumulated expenditures by the Federal Equal Employment Opportunity Agency per nonwhite worker. For purposes of calculation, he uses an expenditure of $1 per year for the period prior to 1965. (Can you explain why?) Freeman's EEOC expenditures variable is essentially a post-1964 trend with the value of zero through 1964. It is best viewed as reflecting shifts in the relative black/white demand for labor during 1948–75, *not* as a measure of the effectiveness of the EEOC or any specific government agency.[22]

Freeman's results indicate that expenditures on equal employment opportunity programs increased the ratio of black to white earning power by a statistically significant amount. It should be noted that because the EEOC expenditures follow a post-1964 trend, they may also be signaling a decline in tastes for discrimination that began with passage of the Civil Rights Act of 1964. However, the interpretation that government activity has tended to increase the relative earning power of blacks is generally supported by studies of the impact of federal contract compliance on *individual companies* during the same period.[23]

At the same time that the government anti-bias activities discussed above were taking place, there was a dramatic increase in the relative schooling of blacks due, also in part, to government policy. In 1948 the median level of schooling for black males was 6.8 years versus 10.4 years for white males. Schooling differences had been nearly eliminated by 1975. In particular, black males had a median schooling of 12.1 and white males a median schooling of 12.6 years in 1975. Most of this relative gain in schooling came *after* 1964. A similar trend appears in the data for females. Median schooling for black females was 7.7 years in 1948 versus 12 years for white females. By 1975, black females had achieved a median level of schooling of 12.4 years versus 12.6 years for white females.

The question naturally arises, then, whether the movement toward racial equality in schooling, due partly to government policy, was more effective in increasing the relative earning power of blacks than were the EEOC activities noted above. Freeman's results indicate no statistically noticeable effect of relative schooling on the aggregate trend in black/white earnings differences during 1948–75. The coefficient of relative education is statistically insignificant in all his regressions. The coefficient of schooling is

---

[22] Freeman, "Black Economic Progress," p. 271.
[23] See, for example, Orley Ashenfelter and James J. Heckman, "Measuring the Effect of an Antidiscrimination Program," in Orley Ashenfelter and James Blum, eds., *Evaluating the Labor Market Effects of Social Programs* (Princeton, N.J.: Industrial Relations Section, Princeton University, 1976) and "Evaluating the Impact of Affirmative Action: A Look at the Federal Contract Compliance Program (A Symposium)," *Industrial and Labor Relations Review*, 29:1 (July 1976).

also erratic in the sense that sometimes it is a small positive number, sometimes a large positive number, and sometimes even negative, depending upon the other independent variables in Freeman's regression. Freeman acknowledges, though, that the relative schooling variable is so highly correlated with the postwar trend variable that an impact of schooling really cannot be ruled out. It is more accurate to conclude, perhaps, that the regression cannot completely distinguish between the effects of schooling and the underlying general trend in earnings differences.

From a policy perspective Freeman's research results can be termed optimistic in that they indicate a noticeable narrowing in the average wages of blacks versus whites. This result is especially true for individuals at younger ages.[24] Freeman's results also imply an important role for civil rights activity designed to increase the relative demand for black labor. Finally, Freeman's research suggests that government activities designed to provide blacks with equal employment opportunities are more effective at reducing racial earnings differences than are policies aimed at narrowing the gap in schooling between the races.

Not everyone agrees with Freeman's conclusion that things are getting better for blacks. Edward Lazear[25] presents evidence that employers have responded to government antidiscrimination activities by equalizing the starting salaries of blacks and whites while reducing the training opportunities for young blacks. This means that blacks who may be earning at a parity with whites during the early parts of their careers will experience less wage growth and lower lifetime earnings. Put differently, civil rights activity may cause blacks to have relatively lower wages twenty years from now. Lazear's work indicates that policy must be examined in a *lifetime* context to be sure it is having the intended effect. Only time will tell whether Freeman's observed narrowing of black/white wage differences is meaningful in this sense.

Sex differences in wages, discrimination, and public policy in the United States.

> And the Lord spake unto Moses saying, and thy estimation shall be of the male from twenty years old even unto sixty years old, . . . fifty shekels of silver. . . . And if it be a female, then thy estimation shall be thirty shekels.
>
> Leviticus 27:3–4

---

[24] For additional discussion see Finis Welch, "Black-White Differences in Returns to Schooling," *American Economic Review*, 63:6 (December 1973), 893–907; Thomas J. Kniesner, Arthur H. Padilla, and Solomon W. Polachek, "The Rate of Return to Schooling and the Business Cycle," *Journal of Human Resources*, 13:2 (Spring 1978), 264–77; and James P. Smith and Finis Welch, "Black-White Male Wage Ratios: 1960–70," *American Economic Review*, 67:3 (June 1977), 323–38.

[25] "The Narrowing of Black-White Wage Differentials is Illusory," *American Economic Review*, 69:4 (September 1979), 553–64.

Things really haven't changed that much since biblical times. In 1970, the average hourly earnings of males was $4.46 versus $2.70 for females.[26] If you use these numbers to calculate a female/male earnings ratio, you will see it is almost identical to the one mentioned in the above passage from Leviticus. Things also have not improved much for women in general since 1970. Have you ever wondered why some women wear buttons that say "59¢"? It is because recent data indicate that, among full-time workers, the median earnings of women are still only about 59 percent of the median earnings of men.[27] The fact that for every dollar earned by the average man, the average women earns only about 59 cents is especially disturbing to women because there is very little difference in the level of schooling between men and women. Remember, however, that the figures we have just noted are simply group averages, and some very interesting information underlies them.

If you look at the ratio of average hourly earnings of females who were *never married* to the average hourly earnings of males who were *never married,* you discover it to be approximately 0.85.[28] Because the data show a far less dramatic sex gap in earnings between singles than between marrieds, this suggests that the institution of marriage is crucially involved in the determination of relative male/female earnings. Recent economic research has shown that we really cannot understand sex differences in earnings without understanding how marriage and children are involved.

We have already discussed at great length some of the reasons, including discrimination, why earning power may differ between groups of individuals. We will attempt now to sort out empirically how much of the crude average difference in earning power of men versus women is due to women with similar productive traits being paid less than men and how much to differences in productive traits between the sexes. Remember that even if we find no sex differences in the payoff from investment in human capital, this does not mean that discrimination is absent. Differences in quality, quantity, or type of investment may be due to past or current discrimination as well as choice. Moreover, sex differences in the payoff to productive traits may be due to factors *other than* discrimination, such as differences in type of schooling (college major or professional degree) or in type of job (career path chosen).

Our primary goal in this section is to get an idea of the degree of labor market discrimination against women in the United States. This requires us to separate the differences in earning power into two categories. One includes earnings differences that stem from differences in personal characteristics related to job productivity. The other is earnings differences that stem from sex differences in the payoff to a given set of productive traits. Sex

---

[26] Victor R. Fuchs, "Recent Trends and Long-Run Prospects for Female Earnings," *American Economic Review,* 64:2 (May 1974), 238.
[27] *Statistical Abstract of the United States,* 1980, p. 422.
[28] *Statistical Abstract.*

differences in return to a *given* set of productive traits are the measure of labor market discrimination typically employed by economists. We emphasize again that this measure suffers from many potential biases due to omitted variables in the regression equations used to predict the structure of earnings. Keep this in mind, and we will do our best to point out such biases in the course of our discussions.

As noted a few paragraphs ago, there seems to be a link between marital status and sex differences in earnings. What is it about marriage that may cause a difference in earning power between men and women? It is the difference in job experience due to the fact that most women eventually have children. In the process, they frequently spend a substantial amount of time out of the labor force. Men and women who never marry or have children tend to have more continuous labor force participation over their lifetimes. For example, among women who were ages 30–44 in 1966, white women with children who had married once and were currently living with their husbands had worked only about six years since leaving school and had been out of the labor force over ten years. In contrast, white women who never married had spent only 1.5 years out of the labor force.[29] Thus, there is a large amount of labor market *nonparticipation* among married women compared to men and single women. While out of the labor force in order to bear and raise children, a married woman loses earning power for two reasons: (1) atrophy of skills and (2) foregone job-oriented human capital investments.[30]

The effect of discontinuous labor force participation on lifetime earnings can be seen in the simple diagram adapted from a recent article by Jacob Mincer and Haim Ofek.[31] In Figure 10-10, line *abkoh* indicates a woman's lifetime age-earning power profile if she were a continuous labor force participant. If, however, she interrupts her career between ages *c* and *d*, her earnings fall to zero for this period. Moreover, her earning power upon reentry in the labor force is not the same as if she had not left the labor force (*k*). Rather, it is lower by the amount *ke*. The difference *ke* can be divided into two parts, *ki* and *ie*. Part *ki* is the opportunity cost of nonparticipation in the form of foregone earnings *growth* as job experience accumulates. Part *ie* stems from the atrophy of skills due to nonuse when out of the labor force. Another implication of Figure 10-10 is that a woman may undergo a so-called catch-up in wages upon reentry into the labor force. (This is illustrated by the relatively steep slope of *ef*.) Specifically, when job experience is reaccu-

---

[29] Jacob Mincer and Solomon Polachek, "Family Investments in Human Capital: Earnings of Women," *Journal of Political Economy*, 82:2, part II (March 1974), S82.

[30] For a discussion and evidence concerning the link between labor force participation of women and lifetime earning power see Solomon W. Polachek, "Discontinuous Labor Force Participation and Its Effect on Women's Market Earnings," in Cynthia B. Lloyd, ed., *Sex Discrimination, and the Division of Labor* (New York: Columbia University Press, 1975).

[31] "Interrupted Work Careers: Depreciation and Restoration of Human Capital," *Journal of Human Resources*, 27:1 (Winter 1982), 3–24.

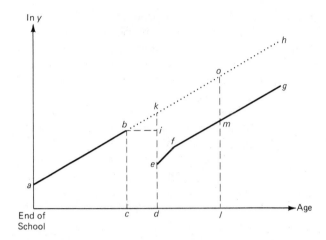

FIGURE 10-10. Interrupted careers and lifetime earning power

mulated, earnings may grow at a somewhat faster rate than for someone who has worked continuously.[32] Try thinking of some reasons why this might occur.

Figure 10-10 tells us that we must account for the effect of time out of the labor force if we want to disentangle sex differences in earning power into (1) the component due to sex differences in the payoff to human capital and (2) the component representing sex differences in the amount of human capital investment. To make this point clear, let us assume for the time being that females and males have *identical* earnings structures. In this case, both have the age-earnings profile *ah* in Figure 10-10 when no time is spent out of the labor force, or they both have *abcdefg* if there is nonparticipation during ages *cd*. Now consider the situation where women drop out of the labor force during ages *c* to *d*, while men do not.

The sex difference in earnings at age *l* is equal to the vertical distance *mo*. Based on standard practices, economists would try to decompose this earnings difference into (1) sex differences in the coefficients describing the

---

[32] A similar phenomenon is observed in immigrants to the United States who interrupt their careers by leaving their homelands. Upon entering the United States labor force their earnings are lower but the growth more rapid than before immigration. Some interesting theoretical and empirical analyses of this phenomenon, along with the ability of immigrants to the United States to overcome discrimination and earn salaries commensurate with native-born Americans, are Mincer and Ofek, "Interrupted Work Careers," pp. 16–21; Barry R. Chiswick, "The Effect of Americanization on the Earnings of Foreign Born Men," *Journal of Political Economy*, 86:5 (October 1978), 897–921; and Barry R. Chiswick, "The Economic Progress of Immigrants: Some Apparently Universal Trends," in William Fellner, ed., *Contemporary Economic Problems 1979* (Washington, D.C.: American Enterprise Institute for Public Policy Research, 1979). This is a very interesting and important topic, and we urge you to consult these references on your own.

earnings structures of men versus women and (2) sex differences in productive characteristics. If data are used for earnings in a range of ages reasonably close to age *l,* males will have estimated earnings functions *kh* and females will have lower, but identically sloped, estimated earnings functions *fg.* Suppose, now, that time out of the labor force is ignored. This was frequently the case in the early research on sex differences in earnings. Instead of looking at actual measures of job experience, researchers looked at potential job experience, equal to age minus years of schooling minus six. Thus, when the sex difference in labor market experience is ignored, *all* the earnings difference, *mo,* could be incorrectly attributed to market discrimination. By contrast, in the example we are developing in Figure 10-10, all the difference in earnings is due to a difference in job-related experience and none is due to labor market discrimination. The general point here is that if we had failed to adjust for sex differences in earning power due to women's intermittent labor force participation, we would have overestimated the severity of labor market discrimination.

As you might expect, much of the debate over the importance of labor market discrimination against women has centered around the accuracy of econometric estimates of female earning-power functions that incorporate skill atrophy.[33] Because they are able to employ both retrospective and panel data on experience and earnings of women, Mincer and Ofek have probably the most statistically accurate estimates of depreciation in earnings due to career interruptions. It is interesting that their estimates are remarkably close to those from previous research. Mincer and Ofek find that the long-run effect of nonparticipation is to reduce wages by approximately 1.5 to 2.0 percent per year of nonparticipation, with about two-thirds of this percentage loss per year due to atrophy and one-third due to foregone experience.[34] What does this imply about the severity of labor market discrimination against women in the United States?

Mincer and Ofek use their estimates of the male/female earning structure to decompose the total (40 percent) differential in wages between males and females. The results indicate that approximately one-fifth to one-half of the overall 40-percentage-point gap is due to sex differences in actual experience in the labor market and other productive traits, leaving approximately one-half to four-fifths of the gap unexplained by sex differences in these factors. What we are saying is that, if we adjust for career interruptions and other differences in personal characteristics believed to be related to job productivity, the male/female earnings gap would shrink to something like 20 to 32 percent rather than 40 percent. But what about this 20 to 32 percent

---

[33] See, for example, Steven H. Sandell and David Shapiro, "The Theory of Human Capital and the Earnings of Women: A Reexamination of the Evidence," *Journal of Human Resources,* 13:1 (Winter 1978), 103–17, and Jacob Mincer and Solomon W. Polachek, "Women's Earnings Reexamined," *Journal of Human Resources,* 13:1 (Winter 1978), 118–34.
[34] "Interrupted Work Careers."

earnings difference? Mathematically, it is due to differences in the coefficients of the earnings regressions for men versus women.

Mincer and Ofek's results imply that the male age-earnings profile is in reality steeper than *ah* in Figure 10-10. To see the importance of this, draw a line in Figure 10-10 that begins at *a* but is steeper than *ah*. Make it steep enough so that earnings at age *l* would be approximately 20 to 32 percent greater than the vertical distance *lo*. Now, continue the dashed vertical line from *l* up to your newly drawn age-earnings profile and label the intersection point *n*. The vertical distance *mn* will be a 40 percent gap in earnings, and the vertical distance *no* will be the remaining earnings gap due to the sex difference in the parameters of the two earnings structures. To what can we attribute this remaining 20 to 32 percent gap? Many things are involved, including sex differences in schooling, sex differences in career paths, and discrimination.

Look in a recent *Statistical Abstract of the United States* for data on the occupational distribution in the United States. You will see that a large percentage of women (54 percent in 1981) are employed as clerical and service workers—relatively poorly paid occupations. In contrast, a large percentage of men (51 percent in 1981) are employed as professionals, managers, and craft workers—relatively highly paid occupations. Because the average schooling differs little between men and women, we must look for differences in type of schooling or discrimination to explain the noticeable differences in occupational attainment. Some recent research indicates that sex differences in college major and occupation are consistent with the notion that women foresee career interruptions and thus have a tendency to choose careers with relatively low rates of depreciation. The cost of this lower depreciation rate is a lower average level of lifetime earnings.[35] Moreover, even within a given career, say executive, women may take a path of lower wages, less travel, and so forth in exchange for opportunities to leave the labor force with as little atrophy in skills as possible. The point is that *one* of the things causing a relatively flatter and lower age-earnings profile for women compared to men may be differences in *type* of education and career chosen rather than sex discrimination. *This means that we must be extremely careful how we interpret sex differences in the coefficients of regression equations for age-earnings profiles.*[36]

This brings us to the issue of how much of the difference in earnings structure between the sexes is due to rational choice by women versus occupational segregation that stems from societal or secondary discrimina-

---

[35] Solomon W. Polachek, "Sex Differences in College Major," *Industrial and Labor Relations Review*, 31:4 (July 1978), 498–508, and Solomon W. Polachek, "Occupational Self-Selection: A Human Capital Approach to Sex Differences in Occupational Structure," *Review of Economics and Statistics*, 63:1 (February 1981), 60–69.

[36] Solomon W. Polachek, "Potential Biases in Measuring Male-Female Discrimination," *Journal of Human Resources*, 10:2 (Spring 1975), 205–29.

tion. Solomon Polachek shows that the estimated male-female earnings gap is dramatically reduced if we control for sex differences in the amount of human capital people *plan* to accumulate over their lives.[37] Moreover, recent research has been unable to find what could be called a major role for empirical measures of occupational segregation in explaining sex differences in earnings. For example, there was a 33 percent wage gap between white men, ages 24 to 34, and white women, ages 24 to 34, in the late 1970s. When this difference in hourly rate of pay is decomposed with the regression techniques we have been discussing, approximately 15 percentage points can be attributed to sex differences in human capital investment and other productive traits. Only 7 percentage points of the gap seem to be attributable to occupational segregation.[38] (To what can one attribute the remaining 11 percentage point difference?) The indication seems to be, then, that occupational segregation is less important in determining male-female earnings differentials than commonly believed.

Summary.   This has been a long and rather complicated section. At this point it seems reasonable to summarize the key issues we have been discussing. There are two general reasons for the fact that women, on average, earn a wage that is roughly 60 percent that of men. (1) Within a given occupation women are paid less than men. (2) Women are overrepresented in the relatively low-paid occupations in the United States. So far, this is nothing but simple arithmetic. The complications set in when we try to decompose this information into discrimination versus sex differences in career choices.

The relatively lower pay women receive within a given occupation is arithmetically more important in determining the total sex gap in earning power than the difference in occupational structure between the sexes.[39] In addition, we have seen that women's earnings would rise to approximately 68 to 80 percent those of men if women had comparable lifetime work histories. This leaves a 20 to 32 percent difference in earnings due to differences in the earnings structure of males versus females. This remaining difference occurs because different types of careers characterize males versus females in the United States.

A second key question, then, is how much of the difference in careers between men and women is due to occupational segregation (societal and

---

[37] "Differences in Expected Post-School Investment as a Determinant of Market Wage Differentials," *International Economic Review*, 16:2 (June 1975), 451–70.

[38] June O'Neill, *The Determinants and Wage Effects of Occupational Segregation*, Project Report (Washington, D.C.: The Urban Institute), March 29, 1983. For additional discussion see Solomon W. Polachek, "Occupational Segregation: A Defense of Human Capital Predictions," *Journal of Human Resources*, forthcoming.

[39] Barry R. Chiswick, James Fackler, June O'Neill, and Solomon Polachek, "The Effects of Occupation on Race and Sex Differences in Hourly Earnings," *Review of Public Data Use*, 3:2 (April 1975), 2–9, and O'Neill, *Occupational Segregation*.

secondary discrimination) and how much to differences in the economic choices made by women in light of their complicated requirements for balancing family versus career? This section showed us that a good portion of the male-female earnings gap seems to be explained by women's foreseeing career interruptions and therefore investing in less and in different types of human capital than men. Also, measures of occupational segregation seemed to explain relatively little of the sex gap in earning power. The key issue is that *many* forces underlie the crude 40 percent gap in wages between the sexes. Thus, we must address numerous complex issues if we desire to decompose this gap into what seems to be fair (based on economic considerations) versus unfair (based on discrimination).

It would be nice to leave this section with a clear message. The message is this: quantitatively, discrimination against women is probably much smaller than the crude 40 percent wage gap. It seems reasonable to say that about 5 to 15 percent of the total wage gap between men and women can be attributed to discrimination, *as commonly measured by economists*. This is by no means a trivial difference in earning power, and any discrimination is unpleasant and unfair to the individuals affected. Again, however, we must emphasize that sex discrimination is probably not the primary reason for the earnings gap between the sexes in the United States. With this in mind, we turn our attention to public policy toward sex differences in earnings in the United States.

Public policy and sex differences in earnings in the United States.   In keeping with the two general factors underlying earnings differences between the sexes, public policy has attempted to (1) ensure equal pay for men and women with equal labor market productivities and (2) provide equal access to education and professional training for men and women. Prior to the early 1960s, laws in approximately 22 states required equal pay in certain private-sector jobs. The Equal Pay Act of 1963 was the first federal legislation covering sex differentials in income and employment. Its provisions are intended to create equal pay for men and women in the same establishments who "do equal work on jobs, the performance of which requires equal skill, effort and responsibility, and which are performed under similar working conditions, except where such payment is made pursuant to (i) a seniority system, (ii) a merit system, (iii) a system which measures earnings by quantity or quality of production; or (iv) a differential based on any other factor than sex."[40] The EPA initially covered only those workers also covered by federal minimum wages. In 1972 it was extended to include small firms and educational institutions. Lloyd and Niemi are careful to point out that the EPA does not prohibit sex segregation in jobs and any resulting pay differentials.

---

[40] See Cynthia B. Lloyd and Beth T. Niemi, *The Economics of Sex Differentials* (New York: Columbia University Press, 1979), p. 288.

We have already discussed Title VII of the Civil Rights Act of 1964 (see pp. 402–405). One of its provisions attempts to limit job segregation by sex or race. In particular, the Office of Federal Contract Compliance seeks to establish affirmative-action hiring programs for blacks and women in firms holding federal contracts.

Finally, Title IX of the Educational Amendments of 1972 is intended to provide both sexes with equal access to the facilities and benefits of educational institutions requiring federal financial assistance. To the extent that sex differences in occupation stem partly from unequal access to training, this law helps to eliminate them. Backers of this legislation expect that the prohibitions on using sex as a sole criterion for admission to graduate and professional programs will have a noticeable impact on the occupational distribution in the future.[41]

How have these regulations we have just mentioned affected male-female differences in wages or occupation? Much less research examining the impact of public policy has focused on male-female earnings differences than on black-white earnings differences. Lloyd and Niemi give us one reason. Not until 1972 were conflicts between state laws regulating the labor market activities of women and federal regulations, especially those of the EEOC, sorted out to give precedence to the activities of EEOC. Studies from the early 1970s of the Federal Contract Compliance Program show them yielding a gain in employment for black men *at the expense of women.*[42] This perhaps surprising finding may be due to the fact that blacks were really the only group protected during this period. Andrea Beller finds a small positive effect of EEOC activities on female-male wage differentials, although her results must be interpreted with caution because of some underlying assumptions and a lack of control for the state of economy in her cross-section results.[43] Finally, Edward Lazear examines whether any narrowing of current starting salaries between the sexes seems to be offset by reduced training opportunities for women resulting in increased male-female differences in *lifetime* earning power.[44] Interestingly, his findings indicate that the narrowing of starting salaries *understates* the narrowing of sex gaps

---

[41] For an interesting discussion of the ways in which the courts have interpreted the sex discrimination statutes being discussed in this section, see Lloyd and Niemi, *Sex Differentials,* pp. 292–300.

[42] Morris Goldstein and Robert S. Smith, "The Estimated Impact of the Antidiscrimination Program Aimed at Federal Contractors," *Industrial and Labor Relations Review,* 29:4 (July 1976), 523–43, and James J. Heckman and Kenneth I. Wolpin, "An Economic Analysis of the Contract Compliance Program," in Orley C. Ashenfelter and Wallace Oates, eds., *Essays in Labor Market Analysis* (New York: John Wiley, 1977).

[43] "The Impact of Equal Employment Opportunity Laws on the Male/Female Earnings Differential," in Cynthia B. Lloyd, Emily Andrews, and Curtis L. Gilroy, eds., *Women in the Labor Market* (New York: Columbia University Press, 1979).

[44] "Male-Female Wage Differentials: Has the Government Had Any Effect?" in Cynthia B. Lloyd, Emily Andrews, and Curtis L. Gilroy, eds., *Women in the Labor Market* (New York: Columbia University Press, 1979).

in earnings; training opportunities seem to have *increased* for women so as to narrow sex differences in lifetime earnings. This is in stark contrast to his findings on the impact of public policy on racial wage differences that we discussed earlier.

Recent public policy debate: The comparable-worth issue.   Figure 10-11 shows two occupations that have equivalent *VMPL* schedules within a particular firm. In this case we say the two occupations are of **comparable worth** to the firm. Wages can still differ for the two types of workers, however, if the market supply of labor for one is relatively plentiful and that for the other relatively scarce. Earlier in this chapter we noted that one reason for a relative scarcity of women in high-paid occupations could be barriers to entry and training placed there by men to keep men's wages high. These are the cause and effect of occupational segregation.

Earlier we mentioned that a straightforward policy to deal with occupational segregation is to eliminate the barriers that may prevent women from entering certain occupations. The Educational Amendments of 1972 discussed on p. 413 are an example of such policy. Recently, a new alternative has been suggested—regulations that would require equal pay for jobs with comparable worth.

Remember that we said the jobs in Figure 10-11 have comparable worth because they are in the same firm and have the same value-of-marginal-product schedules. Comparable-worth regulations would require that firms pay such employees identical wages. Although the details of proposed comparable-worth regulations have not been carefully worked out, the basic idea is for the federal government to require firms to pay identical salaries to workers with jobs of comparable worth.[45] Two key questions surrounding any comparable-worth laws are (1) How is comparable worth to be determined? and (2) Who checks this calculation and sets what the pay level will be? Think about these as we look at some problems entailed by even a quite simple law requiring equal pay for comparable worth.

Consider a comparable-worth law that requires firms to hire job analysts to examine the activities of workers. Each activity is assigned a point value based on its importance to the firm. (Let us conveniently ignore for now the problem of defining "importance.") The points given to each activity are then added together for a worker to get an index of the firm's value of his or her work. Our hypothetical comparable-worth regulations require that these calculations be checked by some government agency to make sure they have been calculated correctly. The firm is then required to pay equal

---

[45] See *The Comparable Worth Issue,* the Bureau of National Affairs, Inc., Washington, D.C., October 28, 1981, DLR No. 208; Donald J. Treiman and Heidi I. Hartmann, eds., *Women, Work, and Wages: Equal Pay for Jobs of Equal Value* (Washington, D.C.: National Academy of Sciences Press, 1981); and Graef S. Crystal, "Comparable Worth?" *The Wall Street Journal,* November 5, 1979, p. 30.

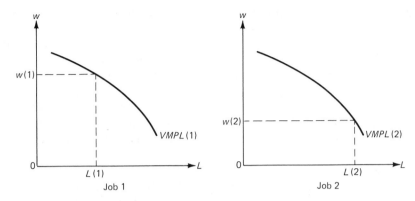

FIGURE 10-11. Pay differentials may exist even when there is comparable worth for two jobs within a firm

salaries to its employees with equal point values. Finally, assume that the firm gets to pick what those salaries are. (A more complex possibility is that the government agency also establishes the wages for jobs with equal point values within a firm.)

The labor market effects of comparable-worth laws such as those described in the paragraph above depend crucially upon whether job analysts accurately identify *VMPL* schedules. To see this more clearly, let us consider two cases: (1) job analysis correctly identifies *VMPL* schedules and (2) job analysis incorrectly identifies *VMPL* schedules.

Figure 10-12 illustrates the situation where two jobs have comparable worth but unequal wage rates to begin with. Before comparable-worth regulations are introduced, job 1 has wage $w(1)$ and job 2 has wage $w(2)$. Let us assume that the lower wage on job 2 is caused by barriers to entry that create occupational segregation. Now let us consider how comparable-worth regu-

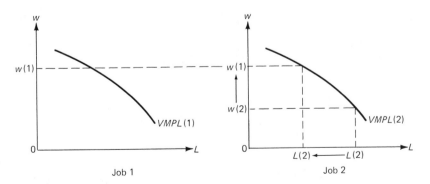

FIGURE 10-12. The effect of requiring equal pay for comparable worth when job analysis correctly identifies *VMPL*

lations would differ in their outcome from policies to remove the barriers to entering the high-wage occupation.

In the absence of any labor supply differences between men and women, the removal of barriers to entry would lead to equal wages in the two jobs in the long term. Now let us consider the effect of possible comparable-worth regulations.

It seems likely that comparable-worth regulations will require the firm to raise the wage rate of workers on job 2 to $w(1)$ so that both jobs are paid the higher wage. In this case, requiring equal pay for jobs with comparable worth is similar to a minimum wage law on job 2. Wages are increased but employment opportunities are reduced in job 2. In the situation where the two jobs have comparable worth and job analysis accurately identifies *VMPL* schedules, some workers are made better off and others worse off by comparable-worth laws. Those who keep their jobs at the higher wage are made better off, and those who lose their jobs and seek alternative employment are made worse off.

Now consider the possibility that job analysis says that two jobs have the same *VMPL* schedules when in fact they do not. Figure 10-13 illustrates the situation where the *VMPL* of the low-paid occupation is *overstated* if job analysis mistakenly says that $VMPL(1) = VMPL(2)$. An example will help to clarify why such overstatement may be likely.

If you think about it casually, the coaches in the men's and women's basketball programs at major universities such as Indiana University, UCLA, or the University of North Carolina perform similar activities. They recruit players, they instruct players in practice, and they provide directions during game situations. Based on this, it would be easy to conclude that both sets of coaches have identical *VMPL*s. But it seems likely that in reality the coaches in the men's programs will be described by $VMPL(1)$ in Figure 10-13 and the coaches in the women's programs by $VMPL(2)$. Why the higher *VMPL* for the coaches of the men's teams?

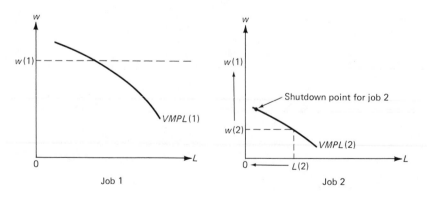

FIGURE 10-13. The effect of requiring equal pay when job analysis mistakenly attributes comparable worth to two jobs

Remember that *VMPL* is physical productivity monetized by the price of output being produced. The price is higher for the output of the men's basketball coaches because the basketball programs they produce generate more revenue. Men's basketball teams have more attendance, higher ticket prices, and more national TV revenue dollars than women's teams. In this case, it is reasonable to expect that the labor markets for the two sets of coaches will establish a higher wage rate for the coaches of the men's programs.

Suppose, now, that job analysis mistakenly determines that the two *VMPL* schedules in Figure 10-13 are the same because the two sets of coaches do similar things. Suppose further that comparable-worth regulations require the salaries of the women's coaches to be increased to the level of the men's coaches. In the case described in Figure 10-13, this would put the salaries of the women's coaches above the shutdown point and lead to the elimination of the women's basketball programs. In light of this possibility, why don't job analysts take into account the different products that the two sets of coaches produce? The answer is simple. If they did, they would be doing what labor markets do! The point behind laws to require equal pay for jobs of comparable worth is that market forces are deemed to cause discrimination and must therefore be "taken out of the game." If market forces are totally ignored, however, we have just seen that this could have quite detrimental effects on the very group comparable-worth laws are designed to help. If you were a policymaker, what would you do to solve this dilemma?

The objective of this section has been to introduce you to a new and controversial policy proposal—equal pay for jobs with comparable worth. Because they deal with the *outcomes* rather than with the *causes* of occupational segregation, comparable-worth regulations will have a different labor market impact on policies that seek to eliminate barriers to entry. There is much to think about here. We hope we have stimulated you to do some thinking on your own.

FRONTIERS OF LABOR ECONOMICS: A DEEPER LOOK AT THE ECONOMICS OF WAGE PAYMENT SYSTEMS

There are probably three dimensions of wages that economists and other students of industrial relations have found most interesting: (1) the timing of wages over the life cycle, (2) the mix of money wages and fringe benefits in the pay package, and (3) the way in which wages are calculated. We have already examined the timing of wages over the life cycle in Chapter 9. The question of how total payments to workers are divided between dollar incomes and fringe benefits is saved for Chapter 11, where we examine the nonwage dimensions of the employment relationship. In this section we turn our attention to the economics of wage payment methods.

In general, workers receive wage payments calculated in one of three ways. Some are paid by the hour, so that earnings equal an hourly rate multiplied by the amount of time spent on the job during the pay period. Other workers receive incentive-based pay. In this case, earnings reflect their output multiplied by some rate of pay per unit of output. Workers paid this way are sometimes referred to as **piece-rate workers.** Sometimes the pay per unit of output can be highly variable, as in the case of those who work largely for tips. Finally, some workers are paid according to a mixture of both systems. An example would be sales personnel who receive a monthly salary plus a commission on sales. Another example would be a tour guide who is paid an hourly wage plus tips. In what follows we will focus our attention on the relative economic advantages of time-based versus incentive-based pay structures.

Data are not all that plentiful, but a paper by John Pencavel presents some figures on the incidence of incentive versus time-based pay in manufacturing in the United States and Great Britain.[46] A number of interesting patterns emerge from the data he presents. First, there is wide variation among industries in the incidence of incentive-based pay. For example, in 1958, 63 percent of production workers in leather manufacturing were paid on an incentive basis, whereas less than 4 percent of production workers in the printing industry were paid in this way. Second, incentive-based pay systems are much less prevalent in the United States than in Great Britain and other European countries. Third, although incentive-based pay tends to be more prevalent in Great Britain, the rankings of industries by percentage of workers paid on a piece-rate basis are similar. Put differently, those industries in Great Britain where there are relatively many workers paid on an incentive basis are also those industries in the United States with the highest proportions of workers paid in such a fashion. Finally, there seems to be little change over time, at least in manufacturing, in the proportion of workers who receive payment by results, both in the United States and in Great Britain.[47]

There are some straightforward economic reasons why some workers receive incentive-based pay while others receive time-based pay. Much less obvious are the reasons for the greater reliance on the former type of wage payment system in Great Britain. Let us look at these two questions in more detail.

A key issue underlying the determination of wage payment systems, is that, ceteris paribus, a given output level seems to be more costly when produced under a piece-rate system than under an hourly wage rate. To see this, assume that an individual worker is equally productive under both types of payment systems. Now let us have some fun with a four-sector diagram.[48] The straight line AB in quadrant I of Figure 10-14 indicates the individual's (constant) hourly wage rate. Notice that the axes are the reverse of what they were in our discussions of the individual's labor supply in Chapter 4. This will make the whole diagram easier to understand. At the wage depicted in Figure 10-14, the individual worker maximizes utility along indifference curve U_0 by working AC hours. The other three quadrants in Figure 10-14 are necessary to demonstrate the shape of the budget constraint when the worker is paid under a piece-rate system.

Quadrant II shows how output varies with the individual's work hours. The concavity of line AF indicates the diminishing marginal physical productivity of work

---

[46] "Work Effort, On-the-Job Screening, And Alternative Methods of Remuneration," in Ronald G. Ehrenberg, ed., *Research in Labor Economics* (Greenwich, Conn.: JAI Press, 1977), 225–58.

[47] See also Eric Seiler, "Piece Rate Vs. Time Rate: The Effect of Incentives on Earnings," Working Paper No. 879 (Cambridge, Mass.: National Bureau of Economic Research, April 1982).

[48] This is the approach taken by Koon-Lam Shea in his paper, "The Economic Effect of Alternative Wage Payment Systems," Department of Economics, United College, Chinese University of Hong-Kong, 1976.

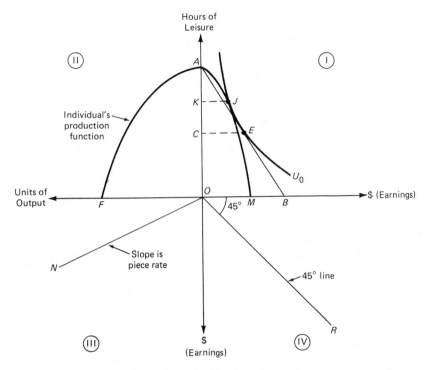

FIGURE 10-14. Labor supply and output under a piece-rate payment system versus an hourly wage rate

hours. Line *ON* indicates the piece rate, or how the worker's income varies with the level of physical production. The line *OR* in quadrant IV is simply a device for transferring information displayed in quadrants II and III back to quadrant I. It is a 45-degree line that takes the individuals' dollars of income under the piece-rate system and transfers it geometrically back to quadrant I, so that we can draw a *curve* relating hours of work to the amount of income received when the individual is paid a fixed number of dollars per unit of *output*. Because the piece rate in quadrant III is a constant per unit of output, the individual's budget constraint under the piece rate simply mirrors the shape of the production function in quadrant II.

For purposes of analysis, we have conveniently chosen the particular piece rate (slope of *ON*) that gives the same level of utility to the worker as he or she would receive under the wage payment system illustrated in quadrant I. Notice, though, that owing to diminishing marginal physical productivity the tangency point *J* lies to the left of that under the wage payment structure (*E*). This means that the utility-maximizing worker would want to work more (*AC*) under the wage payment system than under the piece-rate system (*AK*). The reason is that the hourly wage system provides a higher marginal wage for hours of work in excess of *AK*. The key point here, however, is that when the two wage payment systems produce the same level of utility for the worker, they do not produce the same level of output for the firm. Thus, we must also consider the employer's side of the issue.

If the firm is competitive, we know this means that it can sell as much output as it wants to at a constant price. So, from its perspective the preferred payment system is the one that produces a given level of output with a lower labor cost. In Figure 10-15 we reconstruct quadrant I of Figure 10-14. For the purpose of discussion let us consider the situation where the worker responds to a higher hourly wage or a higher piece rate with a desire to work more hours. This means that in order to induce a worker to offer the same number of hours under a piece-rate system as under a wage payment system (AC), the employer has to increase the piece rate to the point where the individual's earning opportunities become AM'. Notice, though, that this produces a tangency at point E', where the individual has a higher level of utility than under the wage rate system and is earning more money. What Figure 10-15 tells us is that, ceteris paribus, in order to obtain a given level of output from a worker, the employer may have to pay more (both totally and per hour) under the piece-rate system of wages. Of course, this would also make the worker better off, generating a higher level of utility in the process.

How, then, would an employer ever be willing to accept the piece-rate system of pay? The answer lies in all the ceteris paribuses that we have been adding. In particular, the employer would be willing to adopt a piece-rate system of wage payments if workers became more productive as the result, so that AC hours of work produced *more* output when workers were paid by the piece rather than by the hour. Put differently, there would have to be two different production possibility curves in quadrant II of Figure 10-14, where the production possibility curve for a worker who is paid by the piece lies *outside of* the production possibility curve for the same worker when he or she is paid by the hour. This could come about because workers are induced to put more effort into their activities when they observe a direct link between their productivity and pay, rather than the indirect link that occurs through an hourly payment system. In the next chapter we examine the issue of monitoring worker productivity. For now, the point is that we have two interesting empirical implications. First, we might expect to observe piece-rate workers being paid more

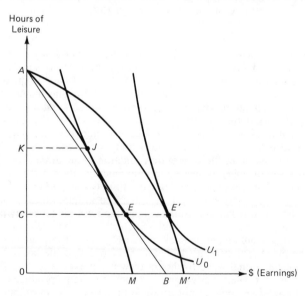

FIGURE 10-15. A piece-rate system is more expensive for employers, ceteris paribus

per hour of work than workers paid under an hourly payment system. As a result, we would also expect piece-rate workers to be more productive in terms of physical output produced.[49]

Pencavel examines these issues with data for male and female punch-press operators in the Chicago area labor market. He presents some evidence, at least among males, that piece-rate workers are paid 7 to 9 percent more per hour than time-rate workers.[50] Moreover, there is also some indication that piece-rate punch-press operators are more productive. Schooling differs little between workers paid under the two systems, but years on present job and occupational experience prior to present job are substantially greater for piece-rate workers.

CONCLUSION

In this chapter we have attempted to understand the forces underlying real wages and the wage structure. We saw that wages, adjusted for inflation, grew at approximately 10 percent per decade during the nineteenth century and somewhat faster, approximately 15 percent per decade, during the present century in the United States. Owing to severe limitations on data, we were unable to examine these trends in any detailed statistical sense. We did see, though, that they are consistent with the hypothesis that the growth of human capital per worker is the major force underlying the historical behavior of real wages in the United States.

Individual differences in earning power are an important policy issue. In this chapter we used the supply and demand model of investment in human capital to identify much more clearly why earning power may differ among individuals. In the process, we identified the key institutions involved, including governments and the family. We then attempted to present measures of the degree of income equality and saw that there is substantial variation among individuals in their wages. On average, women earn less per hour than men, and blacks less than whites.

There are many reasons why earning power may differ between the races and sexes. Productivity will underlie wages in both competitive and noncompetitive labor markets. To the extent that there are differences in job productivity between individuals, wages will reflect this. However, when we observe differences in earning power that appear to be unrelated to productivity, but rather to gender or skin color, this is one form of labor market discrimination. Other forms include an inability to obtain access to training and that if a labor market minority will receive a lower return on training there will be less incentive to invest in human capital. Differential pay for seemingly equal levels of productivity is the dimension of discrimination that has received most attention by economists and policymakers.

---

[49] For more analysis of wage payment systems and their relationship to job and worker characteristics see James R. Markusen, "Personal and Job Characteristics as Determinants of Employee-Firm Contract Structure," *Quarterly Journal of Economics*, 93:2 (May 1979), 255–79.
[50] "Work Effort," p. 243.

Our empirical analyses of race and sex differences in earning power could be termed especially interesting and encouraging. We found virtually no gap in earning power between young whites and young blacks at a given level of schooling, although this result will have to be watched carefully to see if it endures in a life-cycle context. The rather substantial (40 percent) gap in the gross hourly wage rate of married men and married women is substantially reduced when allowances are made for sex differences in the quantity and type of human capital investment over the life cycle. Nonetheless, there seems to be a significant (5 to 15 percent) wage gap remaining after such adjustments are made. Empirically, civil rights laws, or the changes in attitudes that produced them, seem to have played a major role in narrowing the wage differences between the races. Government activities, though, seem to have had very little effect on sex differences in earnings, because public policy has only recently attempted to affect sex differences in wages. Our discussions of proposals to require equal pay for jobs of comparable worth pointed out that their administrative details and full economic implications must be carefully evaluated.

Some workers are paid according to the amount of time they supply and others according to the amount of output they produce. Recent research into the economics of wage-payment systems links the answer to the amount of effort induced by the wage-payment system. We saw that labor would tend to cost more per hour under the piece-rate system. This meant that for the employer to prefer a piece-rate system of pay, productivity (output per hour) would have to be greater when workers are paid by the piece. Research tends to support the hypothesis that piece-rate workers are paid more per hour and offset this by being more productive.

REFERENCES AND SELECTED READINGS

AIGNER, DENNIS J., AND GLEN G. CAIN, "Statistical Theories of Discrimination in Labor Markets," *Industrial and Labor Relations Review,* 30:2 (January 1977), 175–87.

ASHENFELTER, ORLEY, AND JAMES J. HECKMAN, "Measuring the Effect of an Anti-discrimination Program," in *Evaluating the Labor Market Effects of Social Programs,* eds. Orley Ashenfelter and James Blum. Princeton, N.J.: Industrial Relations Section, Princeton University, 1976.

————, AND JOHN C. HAM, "Education, Unemployment, and Earnings," *Journal of Political Economy,* 87:5, part 2 (October 1979), S99–S116.

BECKER, GARY S., *The Economics of Discrimination,* 2d ed. Chicago: University of Chicago Press, 1971.

BELLER, ANDREA H., "Occupational Segregation by Sex: Determinants and Changes," *Journal of Human Resources,* 17:3 (Summer 1982), 371–92.

————, "The Impact of Equal Employment Opportunity Laws on the Male/Female Earnings Differential," in *Women in the Labor Market*, ed. Cynthia B. Lloyd, Emily Andrews, and Curtis L. Gilroy. New York: Columbia University Press, 1979.

BLOOM, DAVID E., AND MARK R. KILLINGSWORTH, "Pay Discrimination Research and Litigation: The Use of Regression," *Industrial Relations*, 21:3 (Fall 1982), 318–39.

CHISWICK, BARRY R., "The Economic Progress of Immigrants: Some Apparently Universal Trends," in *Contemporary Economic Problems 1979*, ed. William Fellner. Washington, D.C.: American Enterprise Institute for Public Policy Research, 1979.

————, "The Effect of Americanization on the Earnings of Foreign Born Men," *Journal of Political Economy*, 86:5 (October 1978), 897–921.

————, JAMES FACKLER, JUNE O'NEILL, AND SOLOMON POLACHEK, "The Effects of Occupation on Race and Sex Differences in Hourly Earnings," *Review of Public Data Use*, 3:2 (April 1975), 2–9.

The Comparable Worth Issue, DLR No. 208. Washington, D.C.: The Bureau of National Affairs, Inc., October 28, 1981.

CRYSTAL, GRAEF S., "Comparable Worth?" *The Wall Street Journal*, November 5, 1979, p. 30.

ENGLAND, PAULA, "The Failure of Human Capital Theory to Explain Occupational Sex Segregation," *Journal of Human Resources*, 17:3 (Summer 1982), 358–70.

"Evaluating the Impact of Affirmative Action: A Look at the Federal Contract Compliance Program (A Symposium)," *Industrial and Labor Relations Review*, 29:1 (July 1976).

FREEMAN, RICHARD, "Black Economic Progress After 1960: Who Has Gained and Why?" in *Studies in Labor Markets*, ed. Sherwin Rosen. Chicago: University of Chicago Press for the National Bureau of Economic Research, 1981.

————, "The New Job Market for Black Americans," *Industrial and Labor Relations Review*, 30:2 (January 1977), 161–74.

FUCHS, VICTOR R., "Recent Trends and Long-Run Prospects for Female Earnings," *American Economic Review*, 64:2 (May 1974), 236–42.

GOLDSTEIN, MORRIS, AND ROBERT S. SMITH, "The Estimated Impact of the Antidiscrimination Program Aimed at Federal Contractors," *Industrial and Labor Relations Review*, 29:4 (July 1976), 523–43.

GREGORY, CHARLES O., AND HAROLD A. KATZ, *Labor and the Law*, 3d ed. New York: W. W. Norton and Company, 1979.

GRILICHES, ZVI, "Estimating the Returns to Schooling: Some Econometric Problems," *Econometrica*, 45:1 (January 1977), 1–22.

HECKMAN, JAMES J., AND KENNETH I. WOLPIN, "An Economic Analysis of the Contract-Compliance Program," in *Essays in Labor Market Analysis*, eds. Orley C. Ashenfelter and Wallace Oates. New York: John Wiley, 1977.

JOHNSON, THOMAS, "Selection Without (Unfair) Discrimination," *Communications in Statistics—Theory and Methods*, A7:11 (1978), 1079–98.

KAMALICH, RICHARD F., AND SOLOMON W. POLACHEK, "Discrimination: Fact or Fiction; An Examination Using an Alternative Approach," *Southern Economic Journal,* 49:2 (October 1982), 450–61.

KNIESNER, THOMAS J., ARTHUR H. PADILLA, AND SOLOMON W. POLACHEK, "The Rate of Return to Schooling and the Business Cycle," *Journal of Human Resources,* 13:2 (Spring 1978), 264–77.

LAZEAR, EDWARD, "Male-Female Wage Differentials: Has the Government Had Any Effect?" in *Women in the Labor Market,* eds. Cynthia B. Lloyd, Emily Andrews, and Curtis L. Gilroy. New York: Columbia University Press, 1979.

————, AND ROBERT MICHAEL, "Real Income Equivalence Among One-Earner and Two-Earner Families," *American Economic Review,* 70:2 (May 1980), 203–208.

————, "The Narrowing of Black-White Wage Differentials is Illusory," *American Economic Review,* 69:4 (September 1979), 553–64.

LEBERGOTT, STANLEY, *Manpower in Economic Growth.* New York: McGraw-Hill, 1964.

LLOYD, CYNTHIA B., AND BETH T. NIEMI, *The Economics of Sex Differentials.* New York: Columbia University Press, 1979.

LONG, CLARENCE, *Wages and Earnings in the United States, 1860–90.* Princeton, N.J.: Princeton University Press, 1960.

LOTSPEICH, JULIE, "An Empirical Analysis of the Linkage Between Low Wages and Poverty in the U.S." Undergraduate Honors Thesis, University of North Carolina, May 1982.

MARKUSEN, JAMES R., "Personal and Job Characteristics as Determinants of Employee-Firm Contract Structure," *Quarterly Journal of Economics,* 93:2 (May 1979), 255–79.

MINCER, JACOB, AND SOLOMON POLACHEK, "Family Investments in Human Capital: Earnings of Women," *Journal of Political Economy,* 82, no. 2, pt. 2 (March 1974), S76–S108.

————, AND HAIM OFEK, "Interrupted Work Careers: Depreciation and Restoration of Human Capital," *Journal of Human Resources,* 17:1 (Winter 1982), 3–24.

————, *Schooling, Experience and Earnings.* New York: Columbia University Press, for National Bureau of Economic Research, 1974.

————, AND SOLOMON POLACHEK, "Women's Earnings Reexamined," *Journal of Human Resources,* 13:1 (Winter 1978), 118–34.

O'NEILL, JUNE, *The Determinants and Wage Effects of Occupational Segregation,* Project Report, Washington, D.C.: the Urban Institute, March 29, 1983.

PENCAVEL, JOHN, "Work Effort, On-the-Job-Screening, and Alternative Methods of Remuneration," in *Research in Labor Economics,* ed. Ronald G. Ehrenberg. Greenwich, Conn.: JAI Press, 1977.

POLACHEK, SOLOMON W., "Differences in Expected Post-School Investment as a Determinant of Market Wage Differentials," *International Economic Review,* 16:2 (June 1975), 451–70.

————, "Discontinuous Labor Force Participation and Its Effect on Women's Market Earnings," in *Sex Discrimination, and the Division of Labor,* ed. Cynthia B. Lloyd. New York: Columbia University Press, 1975.

————, "Occupational Segregation: A Defense of Human Capital Predictions," *Journal of Human Resources,* forthcoming.

————, "Occupational Self-Selection: A Human Capital Approach to Sex Differences in Occupational Structure," *Review of Economics and Statistics,* 63:1 (February 1981), 60–69.

————, "Potential Biases in Measuring Male-Female Discrimination," *Journal of Human Resources,* 10:2 (Spring 1975), 205–29.

————, "Sex Differences in College Major," *Industrial and Labor Relations Review,* 31:4 (July 1978), 498–508.

REYNOLDS, LLOYD G., *Labor Economics and Labor Relations,* 8th ed. Englewood Cliffs, N.J.: Prentice-Hall, 1982.

SANDELL, STEVEN H., AND DAVID SHAPIRO, "The Theory of Human Capital and the Earnings of Women: A Reexamination of the Evidence," *Journal of Human Resources,* 13:1 (Winter 1978), 103–17.

SEILER, ERIC, "Piece Rate Vs. Time Rate: The Effect of Incentives on Earnings," Working Paper No. 879. Cambridge, Mass.: National Bureau of Economic Research, April 1982.

SHEA, KOON-LAM, "The Economic Effect of Alternative Wage Payment Systems," Department of Economics, United College, Chinese University of Hong-Kong, 1976.

SMITH, JAMES P., AND FINIS WELCH, "Black-White Wage Ratios: 1960–70," *American Economic Review,* 67:3 (June 1977), 323–38.

U.S. DEPARTMENT OF COMMERCE, BUREAU OF THE CENSUS, *Historical Statistics of the United States, Colonial Times to 1970.* Washington, D.C.: Government Printing Office, 1975.

————, *Statistical Abstract of the United States.* Washington, D.C.: Government Printing Office, 1980.

WELCH, FINIS, "Education and Racial Discrimination," in *Discrimination in Labor Markets,* eds. Orley Ashenfelter and Albert Rees. Princeton, N.J.: Princeton University Press, 1973.

————, "Black-White Differences in Returns to Schooling," *American Economic Review,* 63:6 (December 1973), 893–907.

Women, Work, and Wages: Equal Pay for Jobs of Equal Value. Washington, D.C.: National Academy of Sciences Press, 1981.

EXERCISES

Choose whether statements 1, 2, and 3 are *True, False,* or *Uncertain* (whether true or false depends on unspecified circumstances). Justify your answer. Your justification is the most important part of your answer.

1. Data on wage growth in the United States support the argument that immigration depresses wages by increasing the ratio L/K.
2. If there were no labor market discrimination against women, they would be likely to earn lower wage rates than men do.
3. The increase in the ratio of black workers' to white workers' wages proves that discrimination against blacks has diminished.
4. Here is an exercise to test your knowledge of real wage rate calculations. Suppose you are interested in expressing real wages in terms of base *1975*—that is, the ability of wages to purchase goods and services expressed in 1975 prices. Use the data on p. 373 to calculate the real wage rate (base 1975) for the years 1967, 1975, and 1978. You should find that they are $4.31, $4.53, and $4.23. The point here is that there is nothing sacred about the particular year upon which you base your real wage rate calculations. Some year has to be selected for purposes of comparison, and you should become accustomed to making calculations for real wages using any year as the base of your calculations.
5. Why does earning power differ among individuals? Be as complete as possible and support your answer with specific references to the supply and demand for investment in human capital.
6. Will an *exogenously imposed, effectively enforced* minimum schooling law increase, decrease, or leave unchanged individual differences in earning power? Explain carefully and support your answer graphically. Which individuals are helped and which are hurt by such a law?
*7. Appearing below is a regression equation that describes the relationship between *female* earning power and investment in human capital (the number in parentheses below a regression coefficient is its *standard error*):

$$\ln Y = 1.15 + 0.39S - 0.01S^2 + 0.008X_1 + 0.016X_2 - 0.006h, \qquad R^2 = 0.29$$
$$\quad\ (2.30)\ \ (0.13)\ \ (0.001)\ \ \ (0.002)\ \ \ \ (0.004)\ \ \ \ \ (0.001)$$

where $\ln Y \equiv$ natural logarithm of hourly earnings
$S \equiv$ years of schooling; $S^2 \equiv$ years of schooling squared
$X_1 \equiv$ years of labor market experience since leaving school
$X_2 \equiv$ years worked on current or last job
$h \equiv$ number of years since leaving high school in which at least six months were spent out of the labor force

(a) Interpret the constant term in the above regression.
(b) What is the rate of return to an additional year of schooling for a woman who is currently a high school graduate? Show your work.
(c) Suppose the rate of return on investment in physical capital is 7 percent. Based on the above results, what is a woman's *economically* optimal investment in schooling? Show your work.
(d) "The rate of return to *on-the-job training* for a woman is 0.024." True, false, or uncertain? Explain your answer. Be brief.
(e) Interpret the coefficient of h. What phenomenon is it reflecting?
(f) Based on the above results, if a woman drops out of the labor force for 10 years, what is the percentage *difference* in lifetime earning power between her and an otherwise identical woman who does not drop out at all but rather works at the same job for all ten years? Show your calculations.

---

* Indicates a more difficult exercise.

11

NONWAGE
ASPECTS
OF EMPLOYMENT

A. Educational objectives
 1. To identify and explain the economic forces that determine some important aspects of jobs *other than* wages
 2. To examine the historical trends in these nonwage aspects of employment
 3. To see the role played by public policy in shaping the nonwage characteristics of jobs in the United States

B. The economics of industrial safety (p. 428)
 1. Background (p. 428)
 2. The determinants of industrial safety (p. 430)
   a. A firm's safety production function
  *b. An in-depth look at equalizing wage differences and the value of saving a human life
   c. The marginal cost of safety and the marginal benefit of safety
 3. The effect of Workers' Compensation Insurance on industrial safety (p. 437)
   a. The social issues involved
   b. Theoretical analysis
   c. Empirical analysis
 4. The effect of the Occupational Safety and Health Act on industrial safety (p. 441)
   a. Theoretical analysis
   b. The policy issues surrounding OSHA
   c. Empirical analysis

C. The economics of fringe benefits (p. 445)
 1. Background (p. 445)
 2. Employers' willingness to offer cash wages versus fringe benefits (p. 448)
 3. Workers' preferences and the equilibrium wage-fringe benefit mix (p. 450)
 4. Evidence on wage-fringe benefit tradeoffs (p. 453)

*D. Frontiers of labor economics: Hours-to-work restrictions, fixed employment costs, and pensions (p. 453)
 1. Background (453)

---

* Indicates more technical material that may be skipped without loss of continuity.

2. Implicit contracts, explicit contracts, and shirking (p. 454)
3. Deferred benefits, bonuses, pensions, and mandatory retirement (p. 455)
   a. Theoretical analysis
   *b. Evidence

E. **Conclusions (p. 457)**

Our discussions in the last chapter focused on wages. It is hardly a secret that workers also receive other forms of remuneration from their employers, such as fringe benefits. Another important dimension of workers' jobs is their degree of exposure to risks of injury or disease. A third is restrictions on how much and when individuals may work. In this chapter we examine these three key nonwage aspects of employment, which we feel are the most socially important ones and which have been the object of much government policy.

Our primary goal in this chapter is to identify and understand the economic forces determining the nonwage aspects of employment. The recent study by economists of nonwage aspects of employment has been labeled the **new industrial relations.** Some of the things we are about to discover are fairly obvious, while others are subtle.

To begin, the government frequently plays a crucial role in determining the nonwage aspects of employment. For example, the proportion of the pay package comprised of fringe benefits has increased dramatically in the last twenty years in the United States, owing in no small part to the relatively low (sometimes zero) tax rates on fringe benefits. Other important pieces of labor market legislation are the Workers' Compensation law and the Occupational Safety and Health Act of 1970 (OSHA). Both are designed to influence workplace safety and affect the welfare of workers by creating economic incentives for a safer work environment. Social security, the Employees' Retirement Income Security Act (ERISA), and antidiscrimination legislation all affect when workers retire and whether mandatory retirement can be part of the employment relationship between a worker and the firm. Because of the crucial role public policy plays, it is one of the focal points of this chapter.

THE ECONOMICS OF INDUSTRIAL SAFETY

Background

Whenever someone becomes ill or injured at work, especially if a permanent physical impairment results, the costs of medical treatment, rehabilitation, and foregone earnings can be substantial. Enormous psychic

---

* Indicates more technical material that may be skipped without loss of continuity.

costs can result from disfigurement. Historically, these costs have largely been borne by injured workers. Based on a program begun in Germany, New York in 1908 passed the first workers' compensation law for the purpose of shifting the legal burden of work-related disability toward the owners of firms and away from workers; other states in the United States enacted similar statutes by 1948.

Workers' compensation laws provide covered employees and their families with two general types of benefits: (1) direct cash payments for death or loss of income and (2) medical services or cash payments for medical services, including rehabilitation.[1] Workers' compensation benefits stem from insurance carried by employers. In general, the direct cash payments made to injured workers are a proportion of the affected workers' earnings up to a statutory maximum. Because reductions in the frequency or severity of injuries will tend to reduce firms' insurance premiums, workers' compensation laws provide somewhat of an economic incentive to improve workplace health and safety. Most states permit firms to self-insure, and a similar economic incentive to reduce injuries and diseases is present for these firms. Despite these economic incentives, in 1981 there were approximately 12,300 people killed on the job in the United States, and about 2.1 million workers disabled on the job. As a point of reference, traffic accidents killed over 52,000 people during 1979.[2]

Political pressure to increase workplace safety led to the passage of the **Occupational Safety and Health Act of 1970 (OSHA).** Designed to "assure insofar as possible every working man and woman in the nation safe and healthful working conditions," OSHA applies to almost all employees not covered by special statutes such as the Coal Mine Safety and Health Act. Employers are required to maintain safe and healthful places of work and to comply with the safety and health standards of the Act. Although workers are also expected to adhere to OSHA's rules, there are no provisions in the law for penalizing them if they do not. All responsibility for compliance is placed on employers, who are subject to fines or shutdowns for violations.[3]

Only recently have economists systematically examined the topic of workplace safety. We now present some of their ideas concerning the determination of job safety in general and the effect of workers' compensation and OSHA in particular on workplace health and safety.

---

[1] For a detailed discussion of the provisions of workers' compensation laws, see Linda Darling-Hammond and Thomas J. Kniesner, *The Law and Economics of Workers' Compensation* (Santa Monica, Calif.: The Rand Corporation, The Institute for Civil Justice, 1980).

[2] U.S. Bureau of the Census, *Statistical Abstract of the United States, 1982–83*, Tables 119 and 687.

[3] For a detailed description of the provisions of the Occupational Safety and Health Act of 1970, see *ABCs of the Job Safety and Health Act* (Washington, D.C.: The Bureau of National Affairs, Inc., 1971).

The Determination of Industrial Safety[4]

Work-related injuries and diseases are undesirable spinoffs from the production of goods and services. In this respect they are similar to noise, smoke, and other forms of pollution. Moreover, both the abatement of pollution and the limitation of industrial diseases and injuries can be costly. A formal safety awareness program requires hiring instructors to lecture workers on ways to reduce accidents, giving employees time off from work to attend this instruction, and employing plant safety inspectors. Up-to-date machinery and additional equipment, such as rubber gloves and goggles, will decrease accidents or their severity. Installation of a better ventilation system may eliminate lung ailments. More liberal sick leave benefits will reduce accidents due to workers being fatigued or not fully recovered from illness. Finally, there are implicit expenditures a firm may make to improve the health and safety of its workers. Examples are reducing the temperature of a chemical process below its most efficient level in order to reduce the severity of burns and slowing the pace of an assembly line. Such actions reduce output.

The firm's safety production function.   Figure 11-1 depicts the relationship between a representative firm's total explicit and implicit expenditures on the prevention of worker injury and disease (J) and the fraction of its work force that will be injured or become ill during a given period (n), holding constant its total number of employees. Notice that many different levels of safety (disease or injury) are possible. A firm can drastically reduce the level of injury or disease by spending much for prevention. Alternatively, few employees may escape harm if little is spent. The relationship between a firm's expenditures on safety and the proportionate number of injuries may be thought of as a **safety production function.**

What are the key properties of the safety production function as we have drawn it in Figure 11-1? The value of the slope tells us how much money the firm must spend in order to reduce n by 0.01. The curve is convex to the origin, becoming relatively steep as it approaches an injury rate of zero and relatively flat as it approaches injury rate n(max). This says that there is a minimum and a maximum degree of job safety. Why might a firm's injury rate never *exactly* reach zero, no matter how much it spent? Why would its injury rate probably not be 1.0 even if it spent nothing in safety? The safety production function in Figure 11-1 also says that decreasing the injury rate from 0.69 to 0.68, say, is much easier (cheaper) than decreasing it from 0.12 to 0.11. Can you explain why this is reasonable? Finally, it is important to note that the position and shape of the safety production func-

---

[4] The basic theoretical structure developed in this section is that of Walter Oi, "An Essay on Workmen's Compensation and Industrial Safety," in *Supplemental Studies for the National Commission on State Workmen's Compensation Laws,* Vol. I, 1974, pp. 41–106.

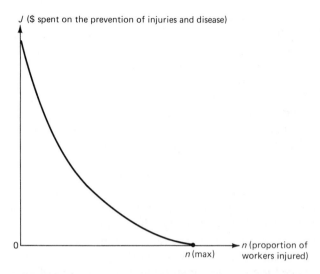

FIGURE 11-1. A firm's safety production function

tion may differ across firms. What would the curve look like for a firm in an intrinsically hazardous industry such as underground mining as opposed to one in a basically safe industry such as aboveground banking?

Thus far we have noted the economic similarity between pollution and injuries—namely, that they are socially undesirable offshoots of production, and they are costly to eliminate. There is a crucial economic difference between the two, however. Firms typically have little or no financial incentive to reduce effluents because they find it difficult to charge the other firms or individuals who benefit from the reduction of pollution. In contrast, there is an economic incentive for employers to improve workplace safety, because production costs decline when jobs are made less hazardous. A lower injury rate reduces labor costs in two ways. First, employee turnover is decreased, as fewer new workers must be hired to replace those unable to work. Think back to our discussion in Chapter 9 and the data of Table 9-1, which points out the rather substantial expenses a firm may have whenever it hires a worker. Second, firms that offer relatively safe working conditions can attract employees at relatively lower wage rates, because workers generally require financial compensation for exposure to job-related health hazards. Consider this passage from a column by Jack Anderson:[5]

> We sent our associate Vicki Warren to work undercover at the Washington Regional Bulk Mail Center, and when she saw the appalling conditions the facility's employees must work in, she asked them why they didn't quit. The universal response was that the pay was too good to pass up. The postal workers are, in effect, being paid to risk life and limb.

---

[5] *The Washington Post,* March 7, 1979, p. B16.

The idea that workers must be compensated for unpleasant or dangerous aspects of their jobs through higher money wages is one of the oldest in economics, dating back to Adam Smith. It is depicted graphically in Figure 11-2. Economists use the term **equalizing wage differences** to define the premium wage required by workers to accept job-related health hazards and other dangers of employment. The schedule depicted in Figure 11-2 is known as a **hedonic wage function** because it presents a picture of how the labor market "packages" jobs to have both desirable and undesirable characteristics. The hedonic wage function in Figure 11-2 illustrates the relatively high or "equalizing" wages a firm must pay if it has a relatively unsafe workplace. Alternatively, a firm does not have to have as high a wage if it has a very safe workplace. The hedonic wage function in Figure 11-2 can best be thought of as the wage-injury rate combinations available to a firm that competes for workers with many other firms. The firm will take information on equalizing wage differences into account when it decides how much to spend on workplace safety. We will develop more of the technical details of hedonic wage functions in our subsequent discussions of the economics of fringe benefits.

If you are interested in some of the quantitative details of how workers are compensated for increased injury risk, the next section presents estimates from a regression analysis of the relationship between wages and job-related mortality. The estimates are especially interesting because they tell us something about how individuals value their own lives.

An in-depth deeper look at equalizing wage differences and the value of saving a life.   One of the most interesting and controversial applications of the economic theory of equalizing wage differences has been to attempt to determine the economic value of saving a human life. The answer also implies how individuals

---

* This section contains more technical material. If you skip, go to p. 435.

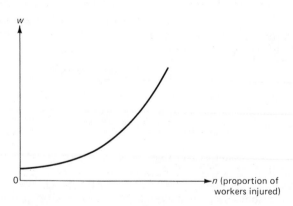

FIGURE 11-2. Job-related health hazards and equalizing wage differences

value their own lives. We noted above that in a labor market where a large number of firms and workers buy and sell labor, workers are compensated for increased exposure to health hazards on the job. This characteristic of a competitive labor market has an important additional interpretation: workers who choose relatively safe employment implicitly pay for this safety by receiving lower wage rates. By examining empirically the difference in wages between workers with relatively safe versus relatively hazardous jobs, ceteris paribus, Richard Thaler and Sherwin Rosen obtain an estimate of the economic value of reducing work-related deaths.[6]

Thaler and Rosen utilize data from a sample of insurance company records for 1955–64 to calculate the relative riskiness of various occupations. Specifically, they first compute an expected number of deaths for men in a particular occupation in a particular industry from the age distribution of individuals in that industry based on sample records and standard life tables. They then subtract the expected number of deaths in an industry-occupation category from actual deaths in that category to produce an estimate of the *extra* risk of death due to the job-related hazards in the particular occupation under consideration.

Calculations for selected occupations are presented in Table 11-1. Consider the figure for boilermakers. Compared to a set of men with the same age distribution in the population at large, boilermakers endure approximately 230 *additional* deaths per 100,000. As a point of reference, standard life tables for 1967 indicate that the expected number of deaths for white males 35 years old was 200 in 100,000. This means that if some one worked as a boilermaker, the likelihood of mortality was more than twice as large as the likelihood of mortality in general. Remember that the figures in Table 11-1 reflect more than just fatal accidents; deaths from every aspect of an occupation, such as tension-induced heart attacks, are represented. Moreover, it is possible for an occupation to have a negative additional mortality risk, so that the value for it in Table 11-1 would be less than zero. How can this be the case?

Thaler and Rosen estimate a regression equation where the dependent variable is a man's weekly earnings and the independent variables are his personal characteristics, job characteristics, residence location, and the *additional* mortality risk associated with his occupation. By including squared values of the independent variables in some of their regressions and by using the semilogarithmic form discussed in Chapters 2, 8, and 9, Thaler and Rosen permit their estimated hedonic wage function to have the shape depicted in Figure 11-2.

The regressions they estimate are for 907 adult male heads of households in 37 occupations. Their data on occupational risks described in Table 11-1 were paired with information from the 1967 Survey of Economic Opportunity to obtain values for all other independent variables. The estimated coefficient of additional mortality risk indicates the average weekly wage premium associated with *one* additional death per 100,000 workers, ceteris paribus.

Let us examine one of the values of the coefficient for additional mortality risk reported by Thaler and Rosen: 0.0352. This coefficient means that for each additional death per 100,000 workers, an individual's wage is increased on average by approximately 3.5 cents per week. To put this in perspective, consider the average workyear as containing 50 weeks. The coefficient 0.0352 implies that jobs having about 100 additional deaths per 100,000 (the sample average) pay about $176 more per year $(0.0352 \cdot 50 \cdot 100)$ than jobs with *no* mortality risk. What does this tell us about the value of safety?

Consider the following conceptual experiment. Suppose that 1,000 men are

[6] "The Value of Saving a Life: Evidence from the Labor Market," in *Household Production and Consumption,* ed. Nestor E. Terleckyj (New York: Columbia University Press, 1975), pp. 265–98.

TABLE 11-1   Additional Mortality Risk in Selected Occupations, Males, 1966

Occupation	Additional Mortality Risk per 100,000 Workers*
Actors	73
Bartenders	176
Boilermakers	230
Cooks	132
Electricians	93
Elevator operators	188
Firemen	44
Fishermen	19
Guards, watchmen, and doorkeepers	267
Hucksters and peddlers	76
Longshoremen and stevedores	101
Lumbermen	256
Mine operatives	176
Power plant operatives	6
Railroad conductors	203
Sailors and deckhands	163
Taxicab drivers	182
Waiters	134

* Actuarial data were used to calculate the expected number of deaths per 100,000 male workers in each occupation based on standard life tables and the age distribution of workers in that occupation. Expected deaths per 100,000 were then subtracted from actual deaths to yield the data for additional risk.

Source: Richard Thaler and Sherwin Rosen, "The Value of Saving a Life: Evidence from the Labor Market," in Nestor E. Terleckyj, ed., *Household Production and Consumption* (New York: Columbia University Press for the National Bureau of Economic Research, 1975), p. 288.

employed in a work setting with the likelihood that one of them will be killed during the coming year. The above value for the labor market effect of additional mortality risk means that *each man* would be willing to work for $176 less if the one work-related death were eliminated. Because *together* they would pay $176,000 to prevent the one anticipated death, the value of saving a life is *at least* this much. To the extent that their families and friends would also be willing to pay to reduce industrial mortality, this must be added to the $176,000.

Although the estimated value for the wage premium associated with additional mortality risk varies with the particular set of independent variables and the mathematical form of the regression equation estimated by Thaler and Rosen, the minimum value of saving a life still seems to lie within a fairly narrow range: $140,000 to $260,000. Remember, however, that these values are for the late 1960s; they would be at least two and one-half times as large today. Moreover, because Thaler and Rosen utilize workers in relatively hazardous occupations, their data probably over-represent the "gamblers." Men who work in risky occupations are also likely to have less aversion to risk than the average worker. This means that the wage premium they will receive in order to accept work hazards will be less than that required by the average worker to accept similar hazards. A more recent analysis by W. Kip Viscusi[7] supports this conclusion. He finds substantial variation in risk premiums and the value of life across workers. His estimates for the value of life range from about $3 million to over $8 million, with workers who have the safest jobs placing the highest values on their lives.

Marginal cost, marginal benefit, and equilibrium safety. Except, perhaps, for government agencies, firms will typically seek to minimize their production costs. The total cost of production for a firm is composed of purchases of labor services, purchases of nonlabor (capital) services, and expenditures on workplace health and safety. Efforts to minimize the total cost of production will result in a particular level of injury risk. The **marginal cost of safety (MCS)** is defined as the increase in production costs stemming from an increase in expenditures (J) to improve safety.

MCS slopes upward in Figure 11-3, indicating that it is relatively cheap to make a small improvement in safety when jobs are quite dangerous, and it is relatively expensive to reduce injury and disease when safety is nearly perfect to begin with. The marginal cost of safety is the slope of the safety production function as we look from right to left in Figure 11-1. Although extra safety is costly, it also leads to reductions in some of the firm's expenditures. In particular, expenditures associated with (1) the replacement of disabled workers, (2) the benefits paid to disabled workers, and (3) wages and fringe benefits necessary to attract workers to jobs with health hazards are all reduced. The reductions in costs due to additional safety are the firm's **marginal benefit of safety (MBS).**

MBS slopes downward in Figure 11-3 because the wage required by workers to accept a risk of injury or disease and the firm's nonwage cost per worker are both assumed to grow with n, the injury rate. The first of these is represented by the increasing slope of the hedonic wage function in Figure 11-2. The second stems from the experience-rating aspect of workers' compensation insurance premiums: the per worker premiums are greater, on average, the higher is the risk of injury. Finally, it is important to remember that *injury risk* is increasing as you look from *right to left* in Figure 11-3, and *safety* is increasing as you look from *left to right* in Figure 11-3. If you remember this, you will see more clearly why there is increasing marginal cost and decreasing marginal benefit of safety, and how they are related to the safety production function and the firm's costs of labor, respectively.

More important for our purposes here is the fact that an increase in industrial safety (a reduction in the injury rate, n) reduces the firm's total

[7] "Labor Market Valuations of Life and Limb: Empirical Estimates and Policy Implications," *Public Policy,* 26 (1978), 359–86, and "Occupational Safety and Health Regulation: Its Impact and Policy Alternatives," in John P. Crecine, ed., *Research in Public Policy Analysis and Management,* Vol. 2 (Greenwich, Conn.: JAI Press Inc., 1981).

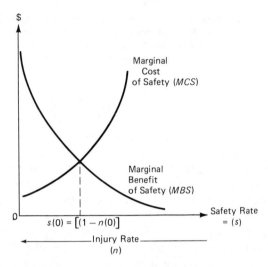

FIGURE 11-3. The determination of the injury
rate in a cost-minimizing firm

production cost whenever *MBS* exceeds *MCS* and increases it whenever the
reverse is true. So, to minimize its total cost, the firm must find the level of
total expenditures on safety and disease prevention that equates the marginal benefit of safety to the marginal cost of safety. This occurs at safety
rate $s(0) = 1 - n(0)$ in Figure 11-3. At a safety rate lower than $s(0)$, extra
safety is a good buy; safety in excess of this level costs more than it is worth
to the employer. Note that we have a general result: there *will* be work-
related injuries and illnesses. Perfect safety is generally too costly even
though technologically feasible.

It should also be pointed out that workers will not be better off with
safety in excess of $s(0)$. How can this possibly be? Remember that workers
have a choice of jobs across firms that vary by safety levels and wages. In
light of their assumed knowledge of safety and wages (jobs) available, the
workers in this firm chose it because of its particular safety level, $s(0)$, and
associated wage. A safety level higher than $s(0)$, and a lower wage to go with
it, is not what they wanted. The point is that they could have had more
safety at another firm but did not take a job there. We will deal in a later
section with the case where workers have poor knowledge of job hazards
and their alternatives for employment.

This completes our discussion of the basic economics of industrial
safety. Before we proceed to discuss policies designed to augment industrial
safety, such as workers' compensation and OSHA, you should have clearly
in mind a list of the factors that underlie *MBS* and *MCS*, because they are the
source of differences in industrial safety across industries or over time

within an industry. First, the firm's marginal cost of safety is determined by the technology available to it for producing safety and the prices of the inputs it purchases to produce safety. These determine the shape of the safety production function in Figure 11-1 and, therefore, the *MCS* schedule in Figure 11-3. Should safety technology or any input price change, the *MCS* schedule will shift, leading to a new level of safety. *MBS* reflects the number of employees, the fringes and wages they must be paid to be willing to accept health hazards on the job, and the cost of replacing ill or injured workers. Should any of these change, *MBS* will shift in a predictable way, leading to a predictable change in the level of safety. You should think through how each of the factors just mentioned affects *MBS* or *MCS* and thus the level of industrial safety. For example, how is the marginal benefit of safety changed if the firm's labor force becomes larger? We will do comparative statics analysis of this type in the next two sections when we try to understand the impact of OSHA and workers' compensation on job-related injuries and diseases.

The Effect of Workers' Compensation on Industrial Safety[8]

Theoretical analysis. Workers' compensation (WC) places a lower boundary on one dimension of the total compensation package received by workers: injury insurance protection.[9] Oi notes that the impact of workers' compensation on industrial safety depends upon how aware workers are of job-related hazards before and after WC coverage is introduced.[10]

Workers' compensation insurance will have little or no effect on workplace safety if workers were previously well informed of the likelihood and severity of industrial hazards. In this case, WC insurance simply substitutes for direct wage payments, and workers purchase less injury insurance on their own. Put differently, workers' willingness to accept risks is unaffected by the introduction of mandatory insurance when they had accurate knowledge of the health hazards of their jobs to begin with. The end result is that WC does not affect the marginal benefit of safety, and the level of industrial safety is unchanged by the imposition of WC.

Let us elaborate. When workers are well informed, the total pay pack-

---

[8] This section draws heavily on the analysis of Darling-Hammond and Kniesner, *Workers' Compensation,* chap. III.

[9] One of labor economists' favorite pastimes is swapping stories of the "comprehensiveness" of WC insurance coverage. Here is our favorite. A Michigan man's wife and family were awarded WC survivor benefits after he was asphyxiated by a faulty space heater while making love to "another woman" during a business trip. The authorities ruled that this was a work-related death. The logic was that boredom leads business travelers to leave their hotels in search of "entertainment." (Reported to the *Cleveland Press,* June 27, 1981, Religion Section.)

[10] Oi, "An Essay on Workmen's Compensation," pp. 69–71.

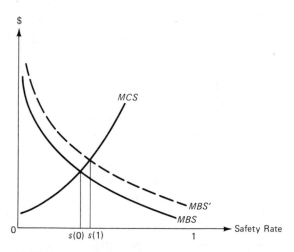

FIGURE 11-4. Possible effects of workers' compensation on industrial safety

age should be unaffected by the introduction of workers' compensation insurance. Before the implementation of WC, employers paid workers a salary that reflected their expected earnings losses due to injuries. After implementation of WC, employers pay for insurance to protect workers against those losses. If WC insurance is **actuarially fair,** in the sense that benefits collected by the injured roughly equal premiums paid, then the total cost to employers of hiring a worker should be the *same* with and without WC insurance.[11] In terms of Figure 11-4, this means that *MBS* is the marginal benefit of safety before *and* after workers' compensation insurance is instituted, and the equilibrium safety rate remains at $s(0)$. *Workers' compensation insurance has no impact on industrial safety in the case where workers are reasonably well informed of the degree of job-related health hazards before the introduction of WC.*

Suppose, however, that workers underestimate the true risk of industrial injury or disease. This will mean that the pay premium they receive for exposure to job-related hazards is too low in the sense that the hedonic wage schedule in Figure 11-2 would be higher and steeper if workers knew how

---

[11] For additional discussion of the role played by the premium-benefit structure of WC insurance, see Peter Diamond, "Insurance Theoretic Aspects of Workers' Compensation," in Alan S. Blinder and Philip Friedman, eds., *National Resources, Uncertainty, and General Equilibrium Systems* (New York: Academic Press, 1977); W. Kip Viscusi, "Imperfect Job Risk Information and Optimal Workmen's Compensation Benefits," *Journal of Public Economics*, 14:3 (1980), 319–37; Louise B. Russell, "Safety Incentives in Workmen's Compensation Insurance," *Journal of Human Resources*, 9:3 (Summer 1974), pp. 361–75; and James R. Chelius and Robert S. Smith, "The Responsiveness of Injury Rates to Experience-Rating of Workers' Compensation Insurance," Working Paper, Center for the Study of American Political Economy, Cornell University, January 1982.

dangerous their jobs really were. This leads to a marginal benefit of safety, *MBS*, in Figure 11-4, that is also "too low." In particular, it lies below MBS', the marginal-benefit-of-safety schedule that goes with the wage premium where workers *accurately* assess injury risks.

All this means that the safety rate is *s(0) rather than s(1)*, which would occur if workers correctly gauged risk. The point is that it is possible for the forced consumption of WC insurance to awaken workers to the true degree of hazard associated with their jobs. This awareness can then increase equalizing wage rate differentials in Figure 11-2, resulting in a shift of the marginal-benefit-of-safety schedule to *MBS'*. So, if workers underestimate job-related health hazards, and WC makes them aware of those hazards, workers' compensation insurance will increase industrial safety and health.

Finally, it is also possible for WC to *reduce* industrial safety. Suppose that before the passage of WC, workers systematically *overestimate* the health risks of their jobs, and *MBS'* in Figure 11-4 represents their marginal benefit of safety in this situation. *The introduction of WC will reduce the level of safety if the associated mandatory consumption of insurance leads workers to assess risks more accurately when workers overestimate health risks to begin with.* We will not go into the details behind the downward shift in the marginal benefit of safety from *MBS'* to *MBS* and the resulting reduction in safety from *s(1)* to *s(0)*. They are exactly the reverse of those described in the previous paragraph. You should practice thinking things through in reverse on your own.

In summary, the effect of WC on workplace health and safety is theoretically indeterminate even when we look only at the bare bones of the workers' compensation system. Thus, we need to look at some empirical research on the effect of WC on industrial safety in the United States.

Empirical analysis. We have just seen that the accuracy with which individuals estimate the severity of work-related hazards plays a key role in determining the labor market effect of workers' compensation. In fact, the question of how accurately individuals estimate the likelihood of uncertain events in general underlies many public policy debates. For example, one justification often used for government support of victims of natural disasters is that they did not know the true risks they were taking. As a result, they took few precautions or purchased very little insurance. Occupational licensing has been justified on the grounds that clients underestimate the likelihood that they will be injured by "quacks." One might say it is conventional wisdom that individuals systematically underestimate the likelihood of occurrence of *anything* bad. In line with this, the typical worker is often characterized as having the philosophy, "It will never happen to me."

In his analysis of WC, James Chelius argues, though, that this interpretation need be no more accurate than one characterizing the average worker as unjustifiably fearful of his environment.[12] Moreover, laboratory experiments indicate that individuals generally form what are known as **conservative probability estimates.** Specifically, they tend to think that probabilities near zero or one are instead about 0.5; probabilities near one-half are correctly estimated. In nonlaboratory settings, however, people appear to evaluate risks less conservatively.[13] W. Kip Viscusi presents evidence that when a worker discovers employment conditions that are more hazardous than initially believed, the primary adjustment to this information is to quit and take another job.[14]

All of these facts seem to argue that workers inaccurately assess the risk of work-related injury or disease, but that the direction of any systematic bias is not completely clear. Even if we should accept the notion that workers systematically *underestimate* job hazards, this still does not tell us whether the introduction of WC has reduced that underestimate, left it unchanged, or perhaps even increased it. This means that econometric studies are needed to establish the impact of WC on industrial safety in the United States.

There are really very few statistical studies of the safety impact of WC. The best known research is that of Chelius.[15] As an admittedly crude approximation to the overall risk of industrial injury or disease in a state, Chelius utilizes the number of deaths due to machinery accidents (other than motor vehicle) in the state relative to its labor force. His data cover the period 1900–1945. In terms of our simple model developed in Figures 11-3 and 11-4, Chelius sought to isolate shifts in *MBS* caused by the introduction of WC.

Chelius' results indicate that imposition of a workers' compensation insurance system reduced the rate of machine-related industrial deaths. In particular, his findings suggest that if a state's injury rate was about 32 percent higher than the national average 5 years before WC was introduced, the rate dropped to equality with the national level 5 years after WC was introduced.

Chelius also examines the variation of industrial injuries among states according to their generosity of WC benefits. His multiple regression controls for factors that may cause *MBS* and *MCS* to differ across states so as to isolate the effect of WC benefit generosity to job safety. Somewhat surprisingly, he finds that more generous WC benefits are associated with *higher* levels of industrial injuries, ceteris paribus. There is no obvious reason why higher benefit levels should lead to more injuries. It is possible, though, that higher benefit levels result in increased reporting of injuries rather than an

[12] James Robert Chelius, *Workplace Health and Safety, The Role of Workers' Compensation* (Washington, D.C.: The American Enterprise Institute for Public Policy Research, 1977), p. 7.
[13] David M. Grether, "Recent Psychological Studies of Behavior Under Uncertainty," *American Economic Review,* 68:2 (May 1978), p. 71.
[14] "Job Hazards and Worker Quit Rates: An Analysis of Adaptive Worker Behavior," *International Economic Review,* 20:1 (February 1979), 28–58.
[15] *Workplace Safety,* chaps. 4 and 5.

actual increase in the number of injuries. Other literature on the economics of disability provides some support for this interpretation.[16]

To summarize, available evidence seems to indicate that WC significantly reduces industrial accidents, but that greater dollar benefits are associated with more reported accidents. Little, if anything, is known about how WC affects the other dimension of industrial safety: work-related diseases.

The Impact of OSHA on Industrial Safety

Theoretical analysis. OSHA, or any other job safety standard for that matter, attempts to influence work-related injuries or diseases by requiring employers to spend more than they normally would on safety equipment and health-preserving activities. Figure 11-5 illustrates a firm's cost-minimizing injury rate, $n(0)$. It reproduces the firm's safety production function, introduced in Figure 11-1, which indicates the total spending on injury and disease prevention associated with $n(0)$. What OSHA does is to require the firm to spend a particular amount on safety, in this case $J(1)$, which exceeds the amount the firm is currently spending, $J(0)$. Although the *intended* effect of OSHA is to reduce injuries, a requirement of this sort will adversely affect firms when the extra safety costs outweigh their financial benefits. Remember, point *a* is determined by the intersection of *MBS* and *MCS* and is the firm's cost-minimizing amount of expenditures on workplace health and safety. One reason why OSHA has received a less than totally favorable evaluation from the business community has been that, in the eyes of the firms involved, the mandated extra safety costs more than it is worth.

---

[16] See Donald O. Parsons, "The Male Labor Force Participation Decision: Health, Declared Health, and Economic Incentives," *Economica*, 49:193 (February 1982), 81–92.

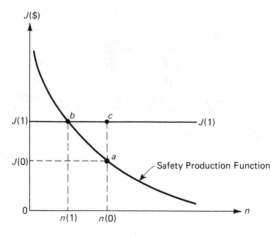

FIGURE 11-5. The intended effect of OSHA on industrial injuries

Because OSHA seeks to force firms to provide more safety than they have in the past found most cost effective, financial punishment for noncompliance must be imposed. An employer who has not satisfied OSHA's standards will compare the cost of immediate compliance [$J(1) - J(0)$ in Figure 11-5] net of benefits with the costs of being discovered in violation of the safety standards. Remember that, once detected, violators must pay the cost of compliance *plus* a fine. Of course, not every firm out of compliance will be caught and punished, so that a cost-minimizing firm will weight the costs just mentioned by the likelihood of detection and punishment.[17] In particular, let $\bar{O} \equiv$ net cost of complying with OSHA's safety standards; $F \equiv$ fine if discovered out of compliance with OSHA's safety standards; and $c \equiv$ probability of being caught out of compliance and fined. Firms will choose to comply with OSHA if

$$\bar{O} < c(\bar{O} + F) \tag{11-1}$$

and choose not to comply if the inequality is reversed. You should prove to yourself that if the probability of being caught and fined is, say, 0.1, then F must be at least 9 times greater than $\bar{O}$ in order to induce firms to comply with the provisions of OSHA.

Thus far we have seen that one of the issues determining the effectiveness of OSHA in increasing workplace safety is whether the frequency of inspection and the fines for noncompliance are substantial enough to induce firms to adhere to OSHA's safety standards. A second issue lurking in the background is whether or not the particular expenditures required by OSHA have any impact on the causes of industrial accidents and diseases. Specifically, OSHA has historically not only mandated increased spending on workplace safety in general but also designated the particular items firms must purchase. The intended impact of OSHA, which is to move from point a to point b on firm's safety production function in Figure 11-5, will not actually take place if the OSHA requirements have little or no effect on those factors that produce workplace injuries and diseases. Another reason that firms have objected to OSHA is that they feel OSHA has tended to move them to a point such as c in Figure 11-5. In short, many firms have felt that the extra spending, $J(1) - J(0)$, leads to little or no reduction in injuries. Evidence on whether or not this has been the case is presented in the next section.

It should also be noted that from an economist's perspective, it would be preferable for OSHA to establish performance standards or target injury rates and let the firms spend whatever it takes to achieve these target injury

[17] Robert S. Smith, *The Occupational Safety and Health Act: Its Goals and Its Achievements* (Washington, D.C.: The American Enterprise Institute for Public Policy Research, 1976), and W. Kip Viscusi, "The Impact of Occupational Safety and Health Regulation," *The Bell Journal of Economics*, 10:1 (1979), 111–40.

rates. The government could still meter performance and levy fines for non-compliance, but firms would be able to take advantage of the more precise knowledge they have concerning what actually causes workplace safety.[18] In this way they would minimize the cost of whatever level of safety the government seeks to establish. There has recently been movement within the Occupational Safety and Health Administration toward performance standards and away from dictating exactly how firms must organize their workplaces.

The social policy issues surrounding OSHA.   If the extra expenditures required of firms by OSHA possibly have little to do with industrial safety, and typically are not cost-effective from the perspective of firms, what is the justification for OSHA as economic policy? The answer comes back to the issue of whether workers are reasonably well informed of the hazards associated with their jobs. Many substances, such as benzene, cotton dust, or lead, may pose long-term health hazards to workers who are exposed to them on a daily basis. Workers are unlikely to be aware of the health problems from lead exposure that will occur ten to twenty years from now. In terms of our analysis of industrial safety developed in this section, we are saying that if workers knew the true health hazards involved when their jobs have long-term health hazards, then they would demand higher wages. This would make the hedonic wage function in Figure 11-2 higher and steeper. This would also mean that *MBS* in Figure 11-3 would be higher, as there would be greater benefits to the firm from improved safety. The end result would be that firms would have greater degrees of injury protection for their workers.

The logic behind OSHA is that none of this occurs because workers cannot possibly know how dangerous certain substances can be to their health in the long term. In light of this, there are a number of policies the government might try. One is to overwhelm workers with the accurate information, so that they reflect it in their behavior. Another is to try to regulate worker behavior. OSHA, by its nature, is the latter approach to the perceived shortage of information on the part of workers concerning the health hazards of their jobs.

This concludes our discussion of how OSHA attempts to alter workplace safety and of what the justifications are for OSHA.[19] We have also attempted to point out why firms may strongly object to OSHA. In the next section we summarize the evidence on OSHA's *actual* impact on industrial safety in the United States.

---

[18] For more analysis of such a proposal see Robert S. Smith, "The Feasibility of An 'Injury Tax' Approach to Occupational Safety," *Law and Contemporary Problems,* 37:4 (Summer 1974), 730–44.

[19] Another extremely important, but little-researched, policy issue is the interface between OSHA and WC. See John Leeth, "Regulation Versus Mandatory Insurance: The Interface Between OSHA and Workers' Compensation," Ph.D. dissertation, University of North Carolina, Chapel Hill, 1983, for some preliminary findings.

Empirical analysis. Our theoretical discussion of how OSHA operates led us to the two key requirements for OSHA to have an impact on
workplace safety. First, the structure of fines and likelihood of inspection
must be such that firms are induced to comply with safety standards. Second, the standards must limit hazards or exposure to substances that are in
fact related to industrial injuries and diseases. If either of these requirements
is violated, OSHA will have little impact on workplace safety.

Robert S. Smith reports estimates that the financial outlays necessary
to meet OSHA's early requirements [$J(1) - J(0)$ in Figure 11-5] were substantial. In the early 1970s they were about $35,000 for firms with 1 to 100
employees, about $74,000 for firms with 101 to 500 employees, and about
$350,000 for firms with 501 to 1,000 employees.[20] (How high would these
numbers be if they were expressed in terms of today's dollars?) Even if
Smith's data greatly overstate the true cost of initial compliance with
OSHA, though, there still seemed to be little economic incentive for cost-
conscious firms to comply. The reason was that the probability of inspection
was quite low. Smith finds that during fiscal 1973, the early days of OSHA,
only 1.3 percent of all covered plants were inspected. At this rate, the
average plant would be inspected only once every 77 years. Smith adds that
even workplaces receiving special attention, manufacturing plants with over
1,000 employees, had an inspection rate of only about 10 percent. Moreover,
when violations were uncovered, fines tended to be rather small. The average noncomplying firm was fined only about $170 ($25 per violation).

Although the incentive to comply with OSHA's early standards was
somewhat greater after a violation was found, it was still far from strong.
Smith notes that while fines for willful and repeated violations averaged
$1,104, less than one-fourth of the plants with violations received follow-up
inspections. Finally, remember that even if firms *totally* complied with
OSHA's provisions, industrial injuries would not have decreased greatly if
the safety standards did not remove the hazards that led to accidents. Smith
cites studies of accidents in Wisconsin and New York indicating that compliance with safety standards could eliminate only about a quarter to a third of
hazards leading to industrial injuries. The majority of injuries seemed to
stem from either transitory hazards or worker carelessness.

All of this leads us to expect a very small effect of OSHA's early safety
standards on industrial injuries in the United States. It is probably fair to say
that this is what econometric evidence shows. In a regression analysis of the
safety effects of OSHA's early standards, Smith cannot reject the hypothesis that the injury rate in heavily inspected industries was the *same* as it
would have been *without* any OSHA safety inspections. Further evidence on
this issue is presented by W. Kip Viscusi in an extremely well done and

---

[20] *The Occupational Safety and Health Act: Its Goals and Its Achievements* (Washington,
D.C.: The American Enterprise Institute for Public Policy Research, 1976), p. 62.

complete statistical analysis of the safety impact of OSHA during 1972–75.[21] He finds no noticeable effect of OSHA on industrial injury rates. Viscusi attributes this result primarily to the weak incentives firms have had to comply with OSHA's standards. Viscusi's results are especially important because his data encompass approximately 84 percent of workers under OSHA's jurisdication at a period in time during which economists expect OSHA to have had its biggest impact. Finally, Smith presents some evidence that OSHA inspections reduced manufacturing injury rates by about 16 percent during 1973 but had no noticeable impact on manufacturing injury rates in 1974.[22] Based on the best evidence currently available, then, OSHA seems to have had little effect on industrial injuries in the United States.

It is important to note that, in light of the difficulties workers may have in identifying the risks of industrial *diseases,* standards of the type advocated by the Occupational Safety and Health Administration may be useful and effective ways to influence this type of job hazard. The desirability and effectiveness of OSHA-type standards in reducing industrial disease is an important topic for future research.

THE ECONOMICS OF FRINGE BENEFITS

One of the main points of this chapter, and perhaps one of the major hypotheses held by labor economists, is that the cash component of pay should be positively related to undesirable characteristics of jobs and negatively related to desirable characteristics of jobs, other factors held constant. If you remember only *one* thing from the hedonic theory of wages developed earlier in this chapter, it should be that when a desirable aspect of employment is on the horizontal axis, the hedonic wage function slopes downward, and when an undesirable aspect of employment is on the horizontal axis, the function slopes upward. An obvious nonwage characteristic that we have yet to discuss is fringe benefits, which comprise a desirable aspect of employment.

The data in Table 11-2 indicate two interesting things: (1) fringe benefits are quite diverse in the United States and (2) they are a quantitatively important component of average total compensation. The data in Table 11-2 are for the entire private nonfarm economy. A recent survey by the U.S. Chamber of Commerce indicates that fringe benefits were about 30 percent of total compensation in *larger* firms during 1980.[23] The Chamber of Commerce survey also found that fringe benefits were greatest in petroleum manufacturing and lowest in textile manufacturing. Probably the most important and interesting fact to come out of the survey, however, relates to the relative

---

[21] "Occupational Safety and Health Regulation."

[22] "The Impact of OSHA Inspections on Manufacturing Injury Rates," *Journal of Human Resources,* 14:2 (Spring 1979), 145–70.

[23] "The Growing Value of Those Fringe Benefits," *U.S. News & World Report,* December 21, 1981, p. 69.

TABLE 11-2 Employee Compensation per Hour, by Compensation Item: 1977 (Private nonfarm economy. Covers establishments employing 1 or more workers)

COMPENSATION ITEM	ALL EMPLOYEES			OFFICE EMPLOYEES			NONOFFICE EMPLOYEES		
	Percent of Compensation	Compensation per Hour		Percent of Compensation	Compensation per Hour		Percent of Compensation	Compensation per Hour	
		All Paid Hours	Work Hours		All Paid Hours	Work Hours		All Paid Hours	Work Hours
Total compensation	**100.0**	**$7.43**	**$8.04**	**100.0**	**$9.04**	**$9.96**	**100.0**	**$6.49**	**$6.96**
Wages and salaries (gross payroll)[a]	84.6	6.28	6.80	85.6	7.74	8.52	83.7	5.44	5.82
Supplements to wages and salaries[b]	15.5	1.15	1.24	14.4	1.30	1.43	16.3	1.06	1.13
Pay for time worked	76.7	5.70	6.17	75.8	6.85	7.54	77.5	5.03	5.39
Straight-time pay	74.8	5.56	6.02	75.0	6.78	7.47	74.6	4.85	5.19
Premium pay	1.9	0.14	0.15	0.8	0.07	0.08	2.9	0.19	0.20
Paid leave (exc. sick leave)	6.1	0.45	0.49	6.7	0.61	0.67	5.6	0.36	0.39
Vacations	3.4	0.25	0.27	3.8	0.35	0.38	3.0	0.20	0.21
Holidays	2.3	0.17	0.19	2.6	0.24	0.26	2.1	0.13	0.14
Other	0.4	0.02	0.03	0.2	0.02	0.02	0.4	0.03	0.03

Employer expenditures for									
Social security retirement	4.4	0.33	0.36	4.1	0.37	0.41	4.7	0.31	0.33
Private retirement plans	4.1	0.30	0.33	4.8	0.43	0.48	3.5	0.23	0.25
Life, accident, health insurance									
ance	4.0	0.30	0.32	3.6	0.32	0.36	4.3	0.28	0.30
Sick leave	0.8	0.06	0.07	1.2	0.11	0.12	0.6	0.04	0.04
Workers' compensation	1.2	0.09	0.10	0.5	0.04	0.05	1.8	0.12	0.13
Unemployment insurance	1.2	0.09	0.10	0.9	0.08	0.09	1.4	0.09	0.10
Severance pay[c]	0.1	0.01	0.01	0.1	0.01	0.01	0.1	0.01	0.01
Nonproduction bonuses	1.1	0.08	0.08	1.9	0.17	0.19	0.4	0.02	0.03
Savings and thrift plans	0.2	0.02	0.02	0.4	0.04	0.04	0.1	0.01	0.01

[a] Pay for time worked, vacations, holidays, sick leave, and civic and personal leave; severance pay; and nonproduction bonuses.

[b] Retirement programs (including direct pay to pensioners under pay-as-you-go private pension plans), life insurance and health benefit programs (except sick leave), unemployment benefit programs (except severance pay), and payments to vacation and holiday funds and to savings and thrift plans.

[c] Severance pay and severance pay funds and supplemental benefit funds.

Source: U.S. Bureau of the Census, *Statistical Abstract of the United States,* 1980, Table No. 710.

growth of fringe benefits versus cash wages since 1969. Adjusting for inflation, the survey found that fringe benefits had grown almost 10 times faster
than paycheck wages. In particular, *real* wages grew only about 4 percent
between 1969 and 1980 while real fringe benefits increased by over 37 percent. In this section we seek first to understand the economic reasons for the
particular wage-fringe benefit mix for a job. Second, we seek to identify the
reasons behind the substantial growth in fringe benefits in the United States
in recent years.

Employers' Preferences for Fringe Benefits Versus Cash Wages

Other factors held constant, the total value of compensation matters
most to employers when the pay package is considered. It is the dollar cost
of fringe benefits plus cash wages they care about. What, then, describes
employers' willingness to offer various combinations of wages and fringe
benefits? Suppose, for the purposes of example, there were no government
and, therefore, no taxes or regulation of the workplace or pay package. Even
in such a world, it is unlikely that employers would be indifferent to one
dollar spent on wages versus one dollar spent on fringe benefits. For example,,to the extent that workers are happier when paid in cash as opposed to
being given a life insurance policy, an employer may be better off in terms of
worker productivity by offering cash versus an equivalent amount in a fringe
benefit such as life insurance. This also means that a given amount of labor
would be less costly to obtain if workers were paid in cash as opposed to
fringe benefits. There are other reasons why a fringe benefit may be more
costly to an employer than cash wages. Sick leave benefits, by their very
nature, increase worker absenteeism.

The government and its tax system also influence employers' willingness to offer fringe benefits versus cash wages. For example, social security
taxes and workers' compensation premiums are each calculated as a fraction
of the payroll paid in wages. Thus, these expenses are reduced if an employer pays $1 in the form of fringes as opposed to $1 in cash wages. The
general inability of government agencies to keep track of and evaluate certain fringe benefits has important economic implications for the mix of total
compensation between cash wages and fringes. There have been periods in
United States history—World War II, for example—where wages have been
regulated by a government agency. One of the ways in which employers
attempted to retain good workers and attract new ones in light of fixed cash
payments was to introduce and increase fringe benefits. The mother of one
of your authors worked as a secretary during World War II and was
given a paid vacation instead of a cash raise. In fact, if you look at the data
on paid holidays and vacations for the United States, you will find that they

begin to be a noticeable part of the total compensation package during World War II.

Based on our discussion thus far, what can we say *in general* about employers' willingness to offer fringe benefits versus cash wages to their workers? First, there will be a tradeoff between cash wages and fringe benefits. Because total compensation for labor services is what concerns employers, they will be willing to provide relatively high fringe benefits if they are coupled with relatively low wages, and relatively high wages if they are coupled with relatively low fringe benefits. This says that the curve describing the combinations of wages and fringe benefits they will offer slopes downward. Second, we have very little to say in general about the steepness of this curve. We have just seen above that employers may be willing to trade more than, less than, or perhaps exactly $1 in wages for $1 of fringe benefits in the total pay package. The willingness of employers to offer the tradeoffs depends on the particular fringe benefit and how it affects worker diligence, effort supplied, and absenteeism.

The downward-sloping straight line in Figure 11-6 indicates an example of combinations of cash wages and fringe benefits that might be offered by employers. Because of the tax savings discussed above, the employer is willing to offer *more* than a dollar of this particular fringe benefit if cash wages are to be reduced by $1. In particular, the line in Figure 11-6 shows that employers are willing to implicitly trade $1 of wages for $1.15 of fringe benefits.

The line in Figure 11-6 is a locus of wage-fringe benefit combinations that produce a constant level of profit for firms from workers on a given job. You can think of it as an **isoprofit locus.** This means that there are many possible (parallel) lines such as the one displayed in Figure 11-6, each one associated with a different level of profitability. The particular one we have picked to show you in Figure 11-6 is also the *equilibrium* wage-fringe benefit combination. It is the one associated with *zero* economic profits. In a labor

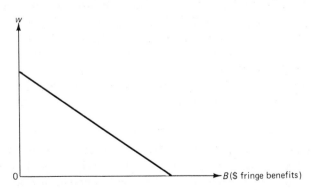

FIGURE 11-6. Wage-fringe benefit combinations offered by employers

market with many buyers and sellers, competition will lead to the pay packages depicted in Figure 11-6. Because firms' profits are equal at every point
on an isoprofit line, firms are indifferent to the various combinations of
wages and fringe benefits in Figure 11-6. Remember, there are other lines of
this sort with flatter and steeper slopes for the other fringe benefits. Each
describes firms' willingness to offer cash versus a *particular* fringe benefit to
workers on a given job. It is important to recognize that Figure 11-6 is also a
hedonic wage function because it shows how the labor market offers workers jobs that differ in their mix of wages and nonwage characteristics. In this
way, Figure 11-6 is similar to Figure 11-2, which deals with another nonwage
characteristic of jobs—the health hazards involved.

   With all this in mind, what determines an employer's particular wage-
fringe benefit package? This is where workers' preferences come in.

Workers' Preferences and the
Equilibrium Wage-Fringe Benefit Mix

   The line in Figure 11-6 that represents employers' willingness to offer
various combinations of wages and fringes is also the locus of pay opportunities for workers. Which package a worker selects depends on how he evaluates the various ones available.

   Employees care about *after-tax* consumption power. To the extent that
most of the fringe benefits listed in Table 11-2 are not taxable, whereas cash
wages are, workers will need more than a dollar of cash wages to have the
same real income per hour as with one dollar's worth of fringe benefits,
ceteris paribus. The exact economic tradeoff between after-tax wages and
fringes from the perspective of workers is not a simple as you might think,
though. At first glance, we might be tempted to conclude that for a worker in
the 25 percent tax bracket, a fringe benefit of a lunch worth $5 is equivalent
to $4 of cash wages. This is only true, however, if the worker would (1) buy
lunch rather than skip lunch, (2) spend exactly $4 on lunch, and (3) buy
exactly the lunch that is provided by the employer. The point is that while
fringe benefits are not taxed, cash provides more flexibility than income in-
kind. In the extreme, a fringe benefit that a worker does not use at all is of
virtually no value to him. An example might be on-the-job day care services
provided to someone whose children are already grown or who plans not to
have any children.

   Because wages and fringe benefits are generally both desirable items to
a worker, we can draw indifference curves that describe the fringe benefit-
wage combinations that produce equal levels of satisfaction. In Chapter 4 we
saw that the indifference curves for market goods and leisure are downward-
sloping and convex to the origin. The indifference curves describing a worker's preferences for wages versus fringe benefits have similar properties.

A set of typical wage-fringe benefit indifference curves is pictured in Figure 11-7. Because, as we have just seen, an individual's willingness to trade cash wages for a fringe benefit will vary with the type of fringe benefit, there will be a different set of indifference curves for each fringe benefit. Moreover, the indifference curves become steeper for higher levels of total compensation. Why? A number of factors come into play. (1) It is *after-tax* consumption that matters to a utility-maximizing individual. (2) We have a progressive personal income tax in the United States. (3) Fringe benefits are generally not taxed as part of total income in the United States. As total compensation rises over time, a worker will not only move to higher levels of utility and desire more of *both* cash wages and fringe benefits but also desire a larger proportion of total compensation to be paid in the form of nontaxable fringes. This makes the indifference curves associated with higher levels of utility have progressively steeper slopes. Keep this in mind when we discuss the equilibrium combination of fringes and cash wages chosen by workers.

In a labor market where many buyers and sellers interact, we have seen that firms will offer jobs with different combinations of wages and fringes. Depending upon a worker's tastes and preferences for the two dimensions of remuneration, a job will be taken with a firm that offers relatively high wages but few fringes or one with a somewhat lower wage and more fringes. For example, positions on the staff of certain high-prestige institutions such as a university, hospital, or law firm typically pay relatively low wages. One of the reasons is that such places offer excellent professional contacts that are absent in less prestigious organizations. Thus, new Ph.D.s and M.D.s may be confronted with the opportunity to work at Harvard for relatively low pay

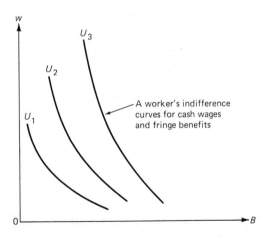

FIGURE 11-7. Worker preferences for cash wages versus fringe benefits

or at a lesser-known place where wages are relatively high but prestige and fringe benefits in the form of contacts lower.

Figure 11-8 illustrates the equilibrium wage-fringe benefit combination for a utility-maximizing worker. The combination $w(0)$, $B(0)$ is the best one for that individual in light of his personal preferences and available opportunities. Of course, people differ in their desire for wages versus fringe benefits. This leads to a diversity of jobs. It is important to realize that we are not saying that *every* firm offers a choice of fringe benefits. (Some firms do; this is known as a **cafeteria plan**.) What we are saying is that even if *individual* firms do not offer choices, the labor market does, and workers will ultimately match up with firms that give them their utility-maximizing wage-fringe benefit combination.

Think about two other aspects of the worker's choice of a cash wage-fringe benefit mix: (1) What would the indifference curves in Figure 11-8 look like in terms of their tangency point if the individual had a higher nonlabor income? When formulating your answer, remember that we have a progressive income tax in the United States. (2) Draw wage-fringe benefit combinations offered by employers for some higher levels of total compensation. (Be sure to use a felt-tip marking pen so that you can't sell the book when you're done.) Now draw higher levels of indifference curves reflecting the pattern described in Figure 11-7. Finally, connect the tangency points with a line. Your line will be upward-sloping, nonlinear, and become flatter as you move to higher levels of total compensation. Be sure you can explain the economics of this geometric result.[24]

---

[24] For more detailed discussion of hedonic equilibrium see Sherwin Rosen, "Hedonic Prices and Implicit Markets: Product Differentiation in Pure Competition," *Journal of Political Economy*, 82:1 (January 1974), 34–55.

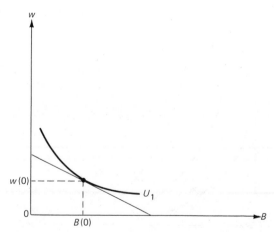

FIGURE 11-8. The equilibrium wage-fringe benefit combination for a util-ity-maximizing worker

Evidence on Wage-Fringe Benefit Tradeoffs

Our basic result from the last section is that, ceteris paribus, equally talented and productive workers should have available to them a tradeoff between wages and fringe benefits. The observed combinations of wages and fringes offered in a labor market with many buyers and sellers may not exactly be dollar for dollar, but a tradeoff should exist. Econometric research *fails* to provide general support for a cash wage-fringe benefit tradeoff, however. Regression analyses with the wage or earnings as the dependent variable and personal characteristics and fringe benefits as independent variables generally show insignificant coefficients for fringe benefits.[25] Taken literally, this would mean that employers can provide fringe benefits at no cost, which is certainly not true.

Of course, it is always possible that the hedonic theory of wages is an incorrect description of how labor markets work. Still, it is so loaded with common sense as to be strongly believed by most economists. Thus, as you read this, at least one economist is sitting at a blinking glass-eyed computer terminal typing in commands in an attempt to verify the hypothesis that, ceteris paribus, there is a tradeoff between wages and fringe benefits on a given type of job.

* FRONTIERS OF LABOR ECONOMICS: HOURS OF WORK RESTRICTIONS, FIXED EMPLOYMENT COSTS, AND PENSIONS

Background

General or firm-specific OJT gives the age-earning power profile an upward tilt over much of a worker's career. This affects the optimal timing of work hours. In particular, OJT causes the supply of work hours to increase as a worker's job tenure with a firm grows.

The firm's fixed hiring and training costs can also affect the demand and supply of work hours. Although the firm typically "writes the check" for fixed hiring costs, the worker often shares these costs by receiving lower wages during the initial years on the job (and a higher rate of pay later on). In this way, the effect of fixed costs on work hours is similar to worker investments in firm-specific OJT. To the extent that the firm pays some or all fixed costs, *VMPL* must exceed the wage rate for enough years to make the *present value* of the excess *VMPL* at least as large as the firm's share of fixed costs. As we will soon see, however, it is difficult to *monitor* work effort. Thus, we have an additional reason why workers must pay a major part of firm-specific training and fixed employment costs.

Given *VMPL* and the total labor-hours demanded by the firm, fixed labor costs mean that the firm will pay a higher wage rate if its employees are willing to work longer hours. Why? The reason is that fewer employees will be needed and total

[25] For examples of econometrically sophisticated studies that fail to find a wage-fringe benefit tradeoff see Robert Smith and Ronald G. Ehrenberg, "Estimating Wage-Fringe Benefit Tradeoffs: Some Data Problems," Working Paper No. 827, National Bureau of Economic Research, Cambridge, Mass., December 1981; and Charles Brown, "Equalizing Differences in the Labor Market," *Quarterly Journal of Economics,* 94:1 (February 1980), 113–34.
* Indicates more technical material that can be skipped without loss of continuity.

expenditures on fixed labor costs will be lower. All of this suggests that a relatively long workweek is in the best interests of both workers and firms.

When there are fixed hiring costs, employees may have the following choices. One firm, which has low fixed costs, may offer employees a job with a relatively low wage rate but the ideal workweek, from the perspective of employees. Another firm may find that through an elaborate, but costly, search procedure it can find especially talented workers. This raises *VMPL* and permits the firm to offer higher wages. At these higher wage rates, however, employees may prefer to work fewer hours than employers find necessary to ensure that the present value of *VMPL* per worker equals the present value of wages paid. Under these circumstances, the second firm may be able to attract workers by offering them the higher rate of pay *provided* that they agree to work longer hours than they would like. Workers may still be able to attain higher utility than they would by working for the first firm at a lower wage. To refresh your memory that this is possible, go back to Chapter 7 and review Figure 7-13. It shows how union members can benefit from accepting work-hours restrictions in order to obtain higher wage rates.

Implicit Contracts, Explicit Contracts, and Shirking

When employees agree to work relatively long hours in return for a relatively higher wage, there will usually be only an *implicit contract* with the employer requiring the relatively long work hours. This means that employers will have a strong incentive to try to keep workers from shirking their obligations by arriving for work late, leaving early, taking unauthorized vacations or unnecessary sick leaves, and so on. Workers, too, have an interest in providing employers with assurances they will not shirk and in helping to reduce shirking by other workers, because this will ensure their high rates of pay. One way to reduce shirking is to withhold a substantial portion of pay until workers have proven that they are nonshirkers. Indeed, pay schemes may provide that only when a worker retires or leaves the employer will he or she receive the excess pay that made working the extra hours worthwhile. Such bonuses for good performance may take the form of a pension plan that increases significantly in value only after the employee has spent a minimum number of years on the job. When a collective bargaining agreement with a labor union exists, there may be an *explicit* contractual agreement enforced by the union leadership calling for a specified workweek or overtime hours. Thus, part of the observed effect of unions on wage rates may be simply a substitution of current wages for a future "good performance bonus." Recall that in Chapter 7 we noted that union workers may have flatter age-wage profiles than nonunion workers.

In Chapter 9 we mentioned that employee-employer relationships may be described in terms of a theory of implicit contracts because of the mutual interest of firms and workers in ensuring that their commitments to each other are carried out. These commitments arise for several reasons. One is that both workers and firms can increase their wealth by investing in firm-specific OJT. A second reason is the one we have just mentioned: Both parties can be better off if a means can be found to reduce shirking.[26] A substitute for a bonus to reduce shirking would be increased supervi-

---

[26] The theory of implicit contracts as a means of ensuring worker performance (apart from OJT considerations) has only recently been developed. Pioneering articles in this area include the following: Edward P. Lazear, "Why Is There Mandatory Retirement?" *Journal of Political Economy,* 87:6 (December 1979), 1261–84; "Agency, Earnings Profiles, Productivity, and Hours Restrictions," *American Economic Review,* 71:3 (September 1981), 606–20; "Severance Pay, Pensions, and Efficient Mobility," Working Paper No. 854, National Bureau of Economic Research; and Edward Lazear and Sherwin Rosen, "Rank-Order Tournaments as Optimal Labor Contracts," *Journal of Political Economy,* 89:5 (October 1981), 841–54.

sion, but this may be very costly or impractical. It is difficult to imagine how, in a free society, employers could follow their employees from work to home and back, making sure that they went to bed on time, did not drink too much alcohol, woke up early in the morning, and so forth. Not only would this be morally and politically unacceptable in the United States, it would also probably be much too costly and counterproductive in terms of worker attitudes and effort on the job. The experience of totalitarian societies suggests the latter.

Not all employee incentives to shirk take the form of not working the agreed-upon hours. Work efforts may be even more difficult for the firm—especially a large firm—to monitor frequently and economically.[27] Moreover, because many jobs, particularly white collar jobs, involve producing an output that is difficult to evaluate on a daily or even a monthly basis, it is often impossible to form a reliable assessment of worker ability or quality until an employee has been on the job for a relatively long time. Again, firms are often best able to monitor these aspects of worker performance after the fact. They will be able to reward good workers more if employees agree to accept a deferred bonus for effort or quality work. This means that employees may be *paid less* than their *VMPL* early in their relationship with an employer and more after they have been on the job for some time. Their inducement to accept these terms of employment is that the firm can offer a wage package with a higher *present value* than if the wage equaled *VMPL* at every moment. The increased real wage payments stem from increased returns to OJT and investments in fixed hiring costs, reduced costs of monitoring workers' performance, and increased employee incentives to supply work effort.

Deferred Benefits: Bonuses, Pensions, and Mandatory Retirement

The employee incentive schemes described above may take several forms. The reason is that employees have borrowing constraints, which limit their ability to finance human capital investments, and a progressive income tax structure that affects the tradeoffs between cash bonus payments, accumulated pension rights, and wages paid during the initial years on a job. Notice that a common element in all these is a *deferred benefit*. Deferral of wage payments may mean that wages fall short of *VMPL* during a worker's initial years on a job. If they do, labor market competition assures that wages must exceed *VMPL* later on, since employers cannot earn economic profits over the long term. Specifically, there may be an initial period during which wages fall short of *VMPL* followed by a period when wages exceed *VMPL*.

Another possible scenario is that the relationship between wages and *VMPL* corresponds to the one described in Chapter 9, Figure 9-5. There we see the firm financing specific OJT investment and reaping returns up to a particular worker age [$A(t)$]. After this age, a typical worker's *VMP* may fall below his or her wage because of deterioration in physical or mental capacity. The employee's bonus for good performance after $A(t)$ would take the form of a wage that continued at its preexist-level, or even was raised, despite declining productivity. Such an excess of wage payments over *VMPL* would be consistent with commonly heard "gripes" by younger workers about "overpaid" older workers. It would also mean that workers receiving such bonuses will have an incentive to work more than their employers want them to.

[27] See John Edward Garen, "The Effect of Firm Size on Wage Rates," Ph.D. dissertation, The Ohio State University, Columbus, Ohio, 1982.

At this point it seems useful to summarize what we have learned. Fixed hiring costs may lead to implicit or explicit contracts in which workers agree to work more hours than they "want" in return for higher wages. A bonus-typed reward for not shirking provides the firm with increased effort but may lead to another restriction on work hours—a *lid* instead of a floor. This means that in return for a higher present value of wage payments, workers may agree to curtail their work hours during their later years on the job. The ultimate limitation of this type would be mandatory retirement at a prespecified age. Of course, a worker approaching retirement age would like to continue to work at (what we have seen will be) a high rate of pay. Nevertheless, when viewed from the perspective of an entire lifetime, a worker is better off accepting mandatory retirement as part of a deal for higher wages overall. What does this say about recent proposals by the federal government to ban mandatory retirement?

In addition to mandatory retirement, pension plans can be used to ensure that workers do not remain on the payroll too long during the period in which their earnings exceed their value to employers. Specifically, pension plans can be arranged in such a way that the total expected present value of an employee's wage plus pension payments begin to *fall* after age $A(t)$. This provides an incentive to retire at the appropriate time. Indeed, a bonus structure can be built into the pension scheme with devices that limit the employee's pension rights (vesting) until a certain number of years on the job have passed, arranging the pattern of increments in pension value so that the value of future pension payments peaks when "good" employees are to receive their bonuses, and so on.

*Evidence.   Edward Lazear has compiled an extensive data set containing the important financial features of 244 of the largest pension plans in the United States, covering about 8 million workers in 1974.[28] He finds evidence that pension plans frequently contain provisions amounting to severance pay in return for retirement at an earlier date than an employee would normally prefer. As part of his research, Lazear creates twelve hypothetical employees for each of the 244 pension plans in his data set. Each employee is assumed to have job tenure of either 10, 20, or 30 years and a salary on retirement of $9,000, $15,000, $25,000, or $30,000. Thus 3 (tenure categories) × 4 (salary categories) × 244 (pension plans) = 2,928 "observations." Using data from the Current Population Survey described in Chapter 2, Lazear projected what typical 55- to 63-year-olds in 1974 would earn in 1976 when they were 57 to 65 years old. He then calculated the present value of retirement benefits. He found that in the majority of cases, present value rises to a peak near "normal" retirement age and then declines. This is consistent with the hypothesis that pensions serve an important role in providing bonus and severance-pay incentives in employer-employee relationships.

Lazear used the following regression equation to summarize the features of the pension plans he analyzed:

$$PV(-10, N, +10) = \alpha(0) + \alpha(1)\text{Tenure} + \alpha(2)AS$$
$$+ \alpha(3)E + \alpha(4)N + \alpha(5)M + \alpha(6)D(1) + \alpha(7)D(2) \qquad \textbf{(11-2)}$$

where $PV(-10, N, +10) \equiv$ the expected present value of pension on retirement at
(a) 10 years early, (b) at normal age, and (c) 10 years late
Tenure $\equiv$ years on job at normal retirement
$AS \equiv$ annual salary at normal retirement

---

* This section contains more technical material. If you skip, go to p. 457.
[28] "Severance Pay, Pensions, and Efficient Mobility."

$N \equiv$ number of employees enrolled in the particular pension plan

$M \equiv$ number of plans in the firm

$D(1), D(2) \equiv$ dummy variables defining plan types

Equation (11-2) was estimated for the three separate dependent variables, $PV(-10)$, $PV(N)$, and $PV(+10)$. Of particular interest are the coefficients $\alpha(1)$ and $\alpha(2)$, which tell us how the present value of pension benefits grows with job tenure and salary. The estimates of $\alpha(1)$ are all highly significant. They imply that an additional year on the job adds either \$5,244, \$2,616, or \$435 to the present value of pension benefits, depending on whether early, normal, or late retirement is taken. Thus, for a 2,000-hour workyear, the pension component of fringe benefits amounts to over \$2.50 per hour for a typical worker ten years before normal retirement age and declines to about \$0.50 an hour by ten years after normal retirement. The estimated values of $\alpha(2)$ are also highly significant. They indicate that for each additional dollar of salary, pension benefits grow by \$3.17, \$2.87, and \$0.62, respectively, for early, normal, and late retirement. The lower values of $\alpha(1)$ and $\alpha(2)$ that go with later retirement are consistent with the hypothesis that pension plans are used to encourage retirement after employees reach a certain age.

To summarize, restrictions on hours of work, age of retirement, and pension vesting may appear to harm workers when viewed superficially. They are best understood within the context of a theory of labor markets that recognizes the importance of fixed hiring costs, investment in firm-specific human capital, and the need to monitor work effort and reward ability in employees. In a competitive labor market, restrictions of the type we have been discussing probably serve to *increase* employee wealth, rather than reduce worker welfare. Consequently, legislation that limits freedom of workers and their employers to enter into either explicit or implicit contracts is likely to harm the very people it is designed to help. Examples of such legislation are provisions in the Employee Retirement Income Security Act of 1974 (ERISA) and the Age Discrimination in Employment Act of 1978.

The issues we have been discussing will probably take on greater importance in the next decade, as the problem of maintaining the financial integrity of the social security system becomes more severe. In order to reduce the financial obligations of the social security system, Congress will be under pressure to further restrict the ability of employers and employees to negotiate agreements calling for mandatory retirement. As we have seen, such legislation is likely to induce offsetting financial incentives through the private pension systems. Thus, it is uncertain what effect the banning of mandatory retirement will have on social security benefit obligations of the federal government.

CONCLUSIONS

In this chapter we have explored important components of job "packages" other than money wages. We first analyzed the economics of job safety. This is an important and interesting topic in its own right. However, job safety is only one of many job attributes that lead to the payment of compensating wage differentials. So, by developing a thorough understanding of workers' demands for job safety and employers' supply of safety, we better understand the process through which other job characteristics, such as the need for punctuality, required work effort, number of rest breaks, and so on, are determined. Subsequently, the analysis of job safety was applied to the effects of workers' compensation legislation and OSHA on industrial safety.

Next, we explored the tradeoffs between fringe benefits and cash wages. The effects of taxes and worker preferences on the equilibrium wage-fringe benefit mix were analyzed and evidence on wage-fringe benefit tradeoffs discussed.

Finally, we looked at some of the reasons why jobs often contain restrictions on hours worked per employee (both maximums and minimums). We saw the roles played by fixed employment costs, bonuses, pensions, mandatory retirement, and the need for incentives to assure worker effort and reduce shirking. The general lesson to be learned from the three major topic areas discussed in this chapter is that job attributes do not arise in a vacuum. By and large they represent the interaction of workers' preferences with competition among employers for labor services at the lowest possible cost. An important implication of these interactions is that legislation designed to "protect" workers by mandating minimum safety levels, by limiting the forms fringe benefits can take, and by prohibiting "mandatory" retirement may not improve employees' well-being. On the contrary, it can easily harm both firms and their workers.

REFERENCES AND SELECTED READINGS

ABCs of the Job Safety and Health Act. Washington, D.C.: The Bureau of National Affairs, Inc., 1971.

ANDERSON, JACK, "Doors of Death," *The Washington Post,* March 7, 1979, p. B16.

BROWN, CHARLES, "Equalizing Differences in the Labor Market," *Quarterly Journal of Economics,* 94:1 (1980), 113–34.

CHELIUS, JAMES ROBERT, *Workplace Health and Safety, The Role of Workers' Compensation.* Washington, D.C.: The American Enterprise Institute for Public Policy Research, 1977.

————, AND ROBERT S. SMITH, "The Responsiveness of Injury Rates to Experience Rating of Workers' Compensation Insurance," Working Paper, Center for the Study of American Political Economy, Cornell University, January 1982.

DARLING-HAMMOND, LINDA, AND THOMAS J. KNIESNER, *The Law and Economics of Workers' Compensation.* Santa Monica, Calif.: The Rand Corporation, The Institute for Civil Justice, 1980.

DIAMOND, PETER, "Insurance Theoretic Aspects of Workers' Compensation," in *Natural Resources, Uncertainty, and General Equilibrium Systems,* eds. Alan S. Blinder and Philip Friedman. New York: Academic Press, 1977.

GAREN, JOHN E., "The Effect of Firm Size on Wage Rates," Ph.D. dissertation, The Ohio State University, 1982.

GRETHER, DAVID M., "Recent Psychological Studies of Behavior Under Uncertainty," *American Economic Review,* 68:2 (1978).

"The Growing Value of Those Fringe Benefits," *U.S. News & World Report,* December 21, 1981, p. 69.

LAZEAR, EDWARD P., "Agency, Earnings Profiles, Productivity, and Hours Restrictions," *American Economic Review,* 71:3 (September 1981), 606–20.

————, "Severance Pay, Pensions, and Efficient Mobility," Working Paper No. 854, National Bureau of Economic Research.

————, "Why Is There Mandatory Retirement?" *Journal of Political Economy,* 87:6 (December 1979), 1261–84.

————, AND SHERWIN ROSEN. "Rank-Order Tournaments as Optimum Labor Contracts," *Journal of Political Economy,* 89:5 (October 1981), 841–54.

LEETH, JOHN, "Regulation versus Mandatory Insurance: The Interface Between OSHA and Workers' Compensation," Ph.D. dissertation, University of North Carolina, Chapel Hill, 1983.

OI, WALTER, "An Essay on Workmen's Compensation and Industrial Safety," *Supplemental Studies for the National Commission on State Workmen's Compensation Laws,* 1 (1974), 41–106.

PARSONS, DONALD O., "The Male Labor Force Participation Decision: Health, Declared Health, and Economic Incentives," *Economica,* 49:193 (February 1982), 81–92.

REA, SAMUEL A., JR., "Workmen's Compensation and Occupational Safety Under Imperfect Information," *American Economic Review,* 71:1 (1981), 80–93.

ROSEN, SHERWIN, AND RICHARD THALER, "Hedonic Prices and Implicit Markets: Product Differentiation in Pure Competition," *Journal of Political Economy,* 82:1 (January 1974), 34–55.

————, "The Value of Saving a Life: Evidence from the Labor Market," in *Household Production and Consumption,* ed. Nestor E. Terleckyj. New York: Columbia University Press, 1975.

RUSSELL, LOUISE B., "Safety Incentives in Workmen's Compensation Insurance," *Journal of Human Resources,* 9:3 (1974), 361–75.

SMITH, ROBERT S., "Compensating Wage Differentials and Public Policy: A Review," *Industrial and Labor Relations Review,* 32:3 (1979).

————, "The Impact of OSHA Inspections on Manufacturing Injury Rates," *Journal of Human Resources,* 14:2 (1979), 145–70.

————, *The Occupational Safety and Health Act: Its Goals and Its Achievements.* Washington, D.C.: The American Enterprise Institute for Public Policy Research, 1976, 62.

————, AND RONALD G. EHRENBERG, "Estimating Wage-Fringe Benefit Tradeoffs: Some Data Problems," Working Paper No. 827. Cambridge, Mass.: National Bureau of Economic Research, 1981.

U.S. BUREAU OF THE CENSUS, *Statistical Abstract of the United States.* Washington, D.C.: Government Printing Office, 1980, Tables 121, 195, and 710.

VISCUSI, W. KIP, *Employment Hazards.* Cambridge, Mass.: Harvard University, 1979.

————, "The Impact of Occupational Safety and Health Regulation," *The Bell Journal of Economics*, 10:1 (1979), 117–40.

————, "Imperfect Job Risk Information and Optional Workmen's Compensation Benefits," *Journal of Public Economics*, 14:3 (1980), 319–37.

————, "Job Hazards and Worker Quit Rates: An Analysis of Adaptive Worker Behavior," *International Economic Review*, 20:1 (1979), 28–58.

————, "Labor Market Valuations of Life and Limb: Empirical Estimates and Policy Implications," *Public Policy*, 26 (1978), 359–86.

————, "Occupational Safety and Health Regulation: Its Impact and Policy Alternatives," in *Research in Public Policy Analysis and Management,* ed. John P. Crecine. Greenwich, Conn.: JAI Press, Inc., 1981.

EXERCISES

Choose whether statements 1 and 2 are *True, False,* and *Uncertain* (whether true or false depends on unspecified circumstances). Justify your answer. Your justification is the most important part of your answer.

1. The observed correlation between real wages and an index of pleasantness of working conditions implies that compensating wage differentials do not exist. (Assume the observation is correct.)

2. A law requiring that employers purchase workers' compensation insurance for their employees will generate an offsetting change in wages or other benefits.

3. One aspect of employment is *hours flexibility*—the ability of workers to vary their hours of work so as to be at the job when it is most convenient for them.
   (a) Draw a hedonic wage function that describes the combinations of cash wages and hours flexibility that will confront a worker in a competitive labor market.
   (b) Suppose that married women tend to choose jobs with more hours flexibility than those typically chosen by married men. Depict this situation graphically. Explain why this difference in choice of jobs might occur.
   (c) Suppose that the government now effectively outlaws all sex differences in cash wages. What will such a law do to the hedonic wage function under consideration? How will it affect male-female differences in hours flexibility? Who is made better off by such a law and who is hurt by it? Support your answer with reference to your hedonic wage function diagram. Be careful.

4. Suppose that for a particular large cost-minimizing firm

   $\bar{O} \equiv$ net cost of complying with OSHA's safety standards $= \$500,000$

   $c \equiv$ probability of being caught out of compliance and fined $= 0.10$

   $F \equiv$ fine if caught out of compliance $= \$200$.

   (a) Demonstrate that this firm will *not* have an incentive to voluntarily comply with OSHA's safety standards.

(b) *Given* the above value of F ($200), how high would c have to go so as to induce the firm to voluntarily comply with OSHA?

(c) *Given* the above value of c (0.10), how high would F have to go so as to induce the firm to voluntarily comply with OSHA?

(d) Suppose you are a policymaker with the goal of getting firms to voluntarily comply with OSHA *at minimum cost to society*. What policy would you suggest? Justify your answer.

12

UNEMPLOYMENT AND WAGE INFLATION

Unemployment, along with wage rates and the other variables examined in Chapter 10 and Chapter 11, is one of the most important determinants of economic welfare. However, the association between unemployment and economic well-being is not always negative. Whereas it is difficult to conceive of a situation in which an increase in the real rate of pay would make a worker worse off, all other things being equal, it is easy to demonstrate a situation in which a reduction in unemployment would also reduce a worker's economic welfare. In this chapter we explore why this seemingly paradoxical statement is true, and in the process we investigate in some detail the behavior of unemployment in the United States over time and its incidence across geographic areas and demographic groups. We will pay special attention to the fact that much unemployment is "normal" and to the efficacy and practicability of certain public policies designed to reduce unemployment.

UNEMPLOYMENT IN LABOR MARKETS

What is Unemployment?

We saw in Chapter 2 that the data gathered in the Current Population Survey are used to classify an individual as out of the labor force, employed, or unemployed. Figure 12-1 illustrates how the population breaks down into the various official categories of labor force attachment. Remember that a worker is considered to be unemployed if during the week preceding the survey he or she is (1) on temporary layoff, (2) waiting to report to a new job that is to begin within 30 days, or (3) without a job *and* has not worked, wants to work, is able to work, and has actively sought work in the recent past. It is also important to note that the official definition of unemployment makes no reference to the wage rate at which an unemployed worker would accept a job offer. Although an ideal definition of unemployment would

---

* Represents more technical material that may be skipped without loss of continuity.

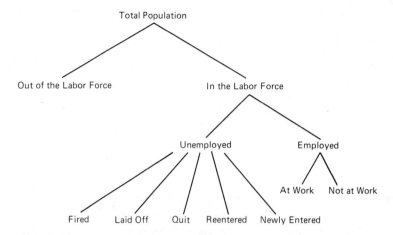

FIGURE 12-1. Labor force attachment

probably incorporate the concept of an **acceptance wage,** our discussions will take the official definition of unemployment as given.[1]

Unemployment is probably the economic concept most misunderstood by noneconomists. It is common to view unemployment in the manner portrayed in Figure 12-2. Labor is thought to be elastically supplied at some constant wage rate $w(0)$ up to some "full-employment" level $N(F)$, beyond which the labor supply curve becomes perfectly inelastic. The labor demand curve is viewed as having the typical negative slope with respect to the wage rate, but intersecting the supply curve to the left of $N(F)$. Thus, the actual level of employment, $N(0)$, is determined by demand, as is the level of unemployment $N(F) - N(0)$. According to this naive view, unemployment is simply an excess supply of labor, and any reduction in the gap between $N(F)$ and $N(0)$ would be socially beneficial because more individuals who desire jobs at wage $w(0)$ would be able to obtain them.

One problem with this naive view of unemployment is that it ignores the question of why the labor supply curve is a horizontal line at $w(0)$. The theory of labor supply developed in Chapters 3, 8, and 9 rests on the notion that time has economically valuable uses in activities other than market work. Individuals who cannot find work at a given wage can use their time to search for work in another labor market, return to school, or engage in non-

---

[1] Melvin Reder has suggested a way of introducing acceptance wages into the official definition of unemployment. He proposes that a public employment program be implemented that offers a job at a socially acceptable (politically determined) wage to anyone registering with his or her state employment service. Individuals who refuse these jobs and opt instead for welfare or unemployment compensation benefits would, in Reder's plan, no longer be included in the official unemployment rate. For an elaboration of the details of his plan see Melvin Reder, "The Coming Demise of Unemployment," *Proceedings of the American Philosophical Society,* 122:3 (June 1978), 139–44.

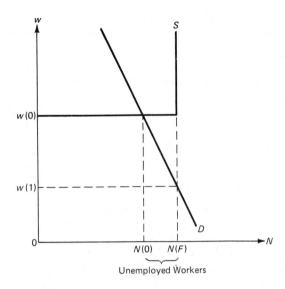

FIGURE 12-2. A naive view of unemployment

labor-market activities. Moreover, some individuals who cannot find work will surely adjust downward the wage they are willing to accept. Modern economic analysis recognizes that the causes of unemployment are to be found in the forces impinging upon labor supply (and demand) and that unemployment cannot in general be interpreted as a simple form of excess labor supply.

Economists have moved away from the stereotype of the helpless worker who is victimized by unemployment and have begun to consider the role played by the individual in determining job opportunities. According to the official definition of unemployment, unemployed workers who are not temporarily laid off and waiting to be recalled to their jobs are supposed to be looking for work (searching). There are, of course, alternatives to unemployment (search), including accepting the best job available at the moment or quitting active search and withdrawing from the labor force. *Job search* is, then, a means of finding a better job and, like schooling, is a form of investment in human capital.

This does not imply that all workers would be better off if they were unemployed; nor does it imply that individual labor force members enjoy being unemployed. To say that a worker is actively involved in determining his or her job opportunities through job search while unemployed means only that he or she is attempting to do what is best *given a set of constraints* which include wealth, labor market knowledge, unemployment compensation benefits, number of children, and more. These constraints may be more severe than anticipated or quite unfavorable compared to those faced by other workers. The fact that economists recognize the close relationship between unemployment and job search yields no more information concerning worker happiness than does, say, the economic theory of labor supply. In our analysis of labor supply in Chapter 4, an individual was seen as choosing to work a certain number of hours, given the market wage rate and nonemployment income. A worker would, of course, be better off if the wage or nonemployment income were higher or if it were possible to obtain the same income with less work. Similarly, someone searching for a job would prefer to find a given quality job with less time spent unemployed. Our analysis of unemployment focuses on how individuals determine their optimal job search strategies subject to constraints imposed upon them by the operation of labor markets.

In a world of scarce information it would be undesirable to reduce the measured unemployment rate to zero, even if it were possible to do so. Severe restrictions on workers' choices among alternative job opportunities would be required, as in the Soviet Union or China. After all, who wants to be forced to take a particular job or prevented from quitting a "lousy" one? A certain amount of unemployment is a normal occurrence in a society where job information is a scarce commodity and where workers are permitted to quit undesirable jobs or where they are free to seek their own jobs upon leaving school, coming out of retirement, or returning to the labor force after bearing and raising children. An important issue is *how much* unemployment is normal, given the population's demographic composition and government policies concerning unemployed workers.

Why Worry about Unemployment?

In few markets are buyers and sellers readily matched to one another. If this is not obvious, visit a used car lot or read the listing of houses for sale in your local newspaper. In the course of this chapter we will see that much of the unemployment in labor markets in the United States since World War II has been what we have referred to above as "normal." Why, then, is unemployment in labor markets singled out for so much attention? The answer lies in the fact that human capital accounts for the lion's share of wealth for most families and individuals. Therefore, failure of buyer and seller of labor to meet can result in considerable hardship. If unemployment were mainly an activity of the wealthy, it would probably not be of much social concern.

In the United States, however, unemployment is more common among low-wage workers than among high-wage workers. In 1979, 3.3 percent of white collar workers in the experienced civilian labor force were unemployed, compared to 6.9 percent of blue collar workers; within the latter group, 10.8 percent of laborers (the lowest-paid) experienced some unemployment.[2] Although nonfarm laborers accounted for only 4.8 percent of the labor force in 1979, they accounted for approximately 9 percent of workers who were unemployed 27 weeks or more.[3] As additional evidence of the linkage between unemployment and low incomes, consider the fact that in 1978 roughly half of the males (who were not ill or disabled) heading families with incomes below the poverty level did not have year-round full-time jobs.

Although unemployment is a phenomenon that disproportionately affects the poor, this need not be so. Why unemployment and low income happen to be linked is a question to which we will return. Let us look now at the varieties of unemployment and what we know about their causes.

THE VARIETIES OF UNEMPLOYMENT AND THEIR CAUSES

In order to understand how the flow of individuals into and out of unemployment affects economic welfare and how much unemployment is normal as opposed to "excessive," it is useful to develop an unemployment taxonomy. That is, we would like to categorize different types of unemployment experience according to their underlying economic causes. What proportion of unemployment is due to relatively low aggregate demand for output? How much is due to shifts in the structure of supply and demand for output of a particular industry or region? How important are labor market "frictions?" Our attempts to answer these questions should help us to understand the causes of unemployment and to develop appropriate policies to deal with it.

Frictional Unemployment

Even if there were no business cycles or structural changes in the economy, there would still be unemployment. People leaving school, women returning to the labor force after bearing children, or workers coming out of retirement must seek information concerning their job opportunities. During this process they are unemployed. In addition, experienced workers who feel that their present or previous jobs do not represent the best they can obtain will be searching for better opportunities. Scarcity of information concerning alternatives ensures that many labor force participants will actively seek better jobs while unemployed. So, the 22-year-old who spends the summer after graduating from college looking for her first job or the 40-year-old assembly line worker who tells his boss to "Take this job and shove it" are two examples of the frictionally unemployed. Finally, employers seek to improve the quality of their work forces by screening new employees carefully, laying off certain workers, and searching for others. To summa-

---

[2] *Employment and Training Report of the President,* 1980, Table A-23.
[3] *Ibid.,* Tables A-16 and A-31.

rize, labor market "frictions" due to less than perfect knowledge by workers (firms) of job opportunities (available employees) constantly replenish the pool of unemployed workers.

The preceding discussion treats **frictional unemployment** as arising from the difficulties involved in matching workers and jobs in an environment that is always changing. Change affects labor markets if for no other reasons than the entrance of new workers into the labor force and the aging and retirement of existing workers. As such, frictional unemployment is a natural situation in a modern economy. Frictional unemployment is one component of what we have been referring to as *normal unemployment*. This is not to say, though, that our economy tends to generate a socially acceptable amount of frictional unemployment or that economic policy cannot or should not be undertaken to reduce the typical period of job search. We will return later in this chapter to the issue of policies designed to reduce frictional unemployment.

Structural Unemployment

The line between frictional and structural unemployment is by no means clear and distinct. The basic difference is that difficulties in matching workers to jobs arise not only because information depreciates (on both sides of the labor market) because of the constant entry and exit of employers and workers, but also because of sharp changes in the industrial and regional structure of labor markets or the demographic composition of the labor force. Suppose, for example, that there is an important and perhaps unanticipated change in the demand for workers by a firm or industry whose production activities constitute an important component of employment in a particular labor market or among a particular skill group of workers. Then previous information reflected in workers' view of the labor market will need to be revised. The crucial issue here is the *speed* with which such revisions occur. When a substantial number of the workers in a market are slow to perceive a deterioration in the wage offers they can obtain, or when firms are slow to realize that they can attract workers of a given quality with conditions more favorable to themselves than previously, there will be a reduction in the speed with which unemployed workers find jobs or decide to leave the labor force. **Structural unemployment** is the result of *slow* adjustment to major changes in labor market circumstances.

Structural unemployment derives its name from the idea that it is caused by changes in the industrial, occupational, demographic, or regional structure of the economy, such as when many of the steel mills in the Ohio River Valley close, or when automatic elevators replace elevator operators, or when the federal government deemphasizes the space program. Structural unemployment does not *always* result when demand falls relative to the supply of labor. Most economists agree that the economy adjusts reasonably well, even to rather major changes in labor market conditions; sluggish responses are the exception rather than the rule. Nevertheless, such situations warrant careful discussion. Let us explore why the adjustment of labor markets to changing conditions may occur too slowly to keep structural unemployment from reaching undesirably high levels.

First of all, adjustments to a changing economic structure are costly. They often require relocation or reeducation of workers, new plant and equipment, production slowdowns until new methods are effectively incorporated into the production process, and so on. As a result, neither firms nor workers will necessarily take steps to adjust to a changing economic environment unless the changes are thought to be sufficiently permanent to justify the cost. With imperfect information, it takes time to decide whether or not gathering more information, relocation, and so on will pay. In addition to monetary costs, there are the psychological costs of adjustment, especially when worker migration is required.[4] Still another cause of structural unemployment is the interdependence of the supply of and the demand for labor. That is, adjustment of the labor force to changing demand conditions—for instance, moving out of a declining community—often further reduces the demand for labor. Finally, wage rigidity due to minimum wage rates, union contracts, or firms' fear of social disapproval may hinder or prevent adjustment of the wage structure that would quickly lead to a balance between the amounts of labor supplied and demanded.

A hypothetical example should further clarify the possible causes of structural unemployment. Suppose that technological changes make the introduction of labor-saving mining machinery economical at existing wage rates. In a typical small agricultural and mining community in the Appalachian region, if miners were willing to quickly accept substantial reductions in wages, a decline in employment would be offset. Wages are *not* immediately reduced, however, and people are thrown out of work. The ensuing decline in the price of coal does not bring about a sufficient increase in the amount of coal demanded to restore mining employment to its previous level. There will, of course, be some smaller mines in which the introduction of the new machinery is not feasible, and any decline in wage rates that does occur may make previously marginal mines economical to operate. It is likely, though, that substantial unemployment remains. Some of the unemployed may find work in agriculture, but the elasticity of demand for labor in

---

[4] Many university and public libraries have collections of videotapes of television documentaries. If such an archive is available to you, take the time to view the NBC White Paper, *America Works When America Works,* which appeared on national television on June 25, 1981, 9:30–11:00 P.M. Eastern Daylight Time. The main theme of this program is structural unemployment, and it contains some quite interesting interviews with steel workers who refuse to move from their lifelong homes in Youngstown, Ohio, despite the severe reductions in job opportunities in the steel industry in their area. These interviews underscore the substantial emotional upheaval that accompanies the thought of leaving one's home for a job in another part of the country.

local agriculture is not large enough to absorb substantial numbers of such workers.

As some of the unemployed emigrate from the area, repercussions are felt in industries that have supplied local needs (services, construction, and so on) as the demand for their output falls. So, a decline in demand for labor in mines has the effect of reducing the demand for labor in other industries in the area. Prime-aged workers, workers with few or no children, and workers with favorable attitudes toward moving will leave the area and find jobs in more prosperous locations. As a result, the remaining population will tend to be made up disproportionately of those who, for reasons having to do with their age, the likelihood of their finding work elsewhere, the size of their families, or their attitudes toward moving per se, remain in the declining area despite the increasing difficulty of earning a living.

Now, if this area happens to be marginally attractive to some industry (for example, textiles or apparel) that had not yet located there, the declining wage rates and the increasing availability of workers might induce a change in the local industrial structure and restore the demand for labor sufficiently to keep unemployment reasonably low. This is most likely to happen if the unemployed workers have relatively high skill levels or are readily adaptable to new jobs. Workers are more likely to have such characteristics if they are relatively well educated and have been employed in jobs where the work contributes to adaptability. Alternatively, high unemployment may persist, with no new industries being attracted; able workers will continue to leave the community until it is indeed depressed, with few readily employable workers among the unemployed. Gradually, some workers become discouraged and leave the labor force, lowering both the labor force participation and unemployment rates of the community.

We have just seen that structural unemployment stems from the fact that jobs and workers are in different parts of the country or in different sectors of the economy. As such, structural unemployment can also be thought of as a part of normal unemployment. This is not to say that the structurally unemployed do not suffer severe hardships, or that such hardships are not perhaps more severe than those endured by the frictionally unemployed. The point to remember is that we live in a changing world, and adaptation to change is costly and does not occur instantaneously. This leads to the phenomenon known as structural unemployment.

Cyclical Unemployment

Much of our concern with unemployment stems from The Great Depression of the 1930s. Much unemployment is associated with the economy's periodic reductions in the rate of growth of aggregate demand for output and the derived demand for labor. These "business cycles" result in parallel movements in the nation's unemployment rate. The relationship

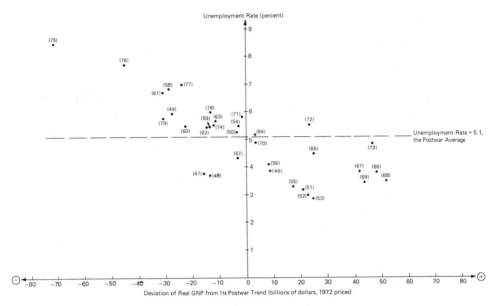

FIGURE 12-3. Unemployment and deviations in real GNP from its trend value, 1947–1979

between the business cycle and unemployment is illustrated in Figure 12-3, which is a plot of the unemployment rate against deviations in real GNP from its postwar trend value.[5] The average unemployment rate during the postwar period was approximately 5.1 percent. Notice that when GNP is below normal, unemployment is almost always above average. For every 27-billion-dollar deviation of real GNP above (below) its postwar trend value there was, on average, a 1-percentage-point lower (higher) than average unemployment rate.[6]

The single most important source of unemployment during recessions is the increased number of workers who have been laid off from their jobs.

---

[5] The formula for the (estimated) postwar trend of real GNP (billions of dollars, 1972 prices) is GNP* $= 468e^{0.0345t}$, where t takes on the values 0 in 1946, 1 in 1947, and so on through 34 in 1979. The trend equation indicates the value that real GNP would have obtained in each year, had it grown at a constant annual rate. You should be able to demonstrate that this equation says real GNP has grown at an average rate of 3.45 percent per year since World War II. [*Hint:* Take the logarithm of the above expression for annual real GNP.]

[6] This result was obtained from a regression with the annual unemployment rate (u) as the dependent variable and the *deviation* of real GNP from its postwar trend value (GNP − GNP*) as the independent variable. [The data for the annual unemployment rate appear in Table 12-7 and (GNP − GNP*) is calculated using the equation in footnote 5.] This estimation yielded $u =$ 5.1 − 0.037 (GNP − GNP*). The slope coefficient (−0.037) indicates the impact of a 1-billion-dollar deviation in real GNP from its trend value on the unemployment rate. From this you should be able to verify the conclusion presented in the text. Notice that the intercept in this regression equation (5.1) is equal to the average unemployment rate during the postwar era. Can you explain why?

During 1971–79, for example, an average of 45.2 percent of unemployed workers in each year had lost their last job, as opposed to those who had quit their last job (13.3 percent), had reentered the labor force and were seeking employment (28.4 percent), or had never worked before and were seeking employment (13.2 percent).[7] We ask now why employers choose to lay off workers when aggregate demand declines rather than temporarily reduce wage rates.

Why are there layoffs during recessions? If firms could predict the course of demand for their output and if goods could be stored for future sale at low cost, a temporary downturn in aggregate demand would not necessarily result in a concomitant decline in labor demand. Firms would find it profitable to maintain production and employment and would store output for future sale. Unfortunately, firms do not know how long a given recession will last or how it will affect their particular product line; output cannot be stored at low cost; and buyers' behavior will change in unknown ways. Thus, the demand for labor shifts in the same direction as the demand for output. So, during recessions, profit-maximizing firms will want to reduce wage rates or the number of employees.

To help us understand the interrelation between the firm's demand for output, the derived demand for labor, wage rates, and layoff behavior, it will be useful to recall the theory of human capital and OJT developed in Chapter 9. Figure 12-4 is a recapitulation of Figure 9-6 and shows that investment in firm-specific OJT creates a wedge between *VMPL* and the wage. Thus, when there is a downturn in economic activity that reduces the value of marginal product of labor to $VMP(2)$, the value to the firm of the worker with, say, $\mathfrak{X}_0$ years of experience will not necessarily fall below w. So, the firm may wish to retain a worker even though the value of marginal product of labor has been reduced. Even if *VMPL* falls below w, a profit-maximizing firm may still not lay off workers if it believes that there is a sufficiently high risk of workers finding other jobs and therefore being unavailable for recall when *VMPL* once again exceeds w. Studies by Oi, Rosen, and Parsons have shown the importance of the firm-specific OJT in explaining patterns of layoffs in the presence of depressed demand for labor. As we saw in Chapter 9, however, these studies do not explain why, when *VMPL* falls far enough below w to make layoffs profitable, firms and workers do not agree to reduce wage rates rather than discharge workers. Moreover, when aggregate demand is temporarily low, making it difficult or impossible for workers to switch jobs, why do employers not take advantage of the situation by lowering wages *regardless* of the level of *VMPL*?

One possible answer is that collective bargaining agreements preclude wage reductions and force layoffs as the alternative adjustment on the part

---

[7] For more detailed data, see *Employment and Training Report of the President, 1980,* Table A-27.

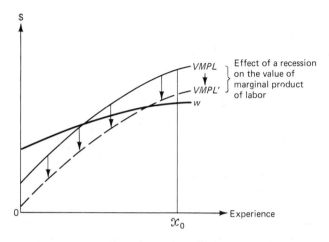

FIGURE 12-4. The impact of a recession on the relationship between *VMPL* and wages when there is firm-specific OJT

of firms. This cannot be the entire story, or even most of it, because downward wage flexibility does occur in extreme circumstances in the United States, even under collective bargaining. Moreover, layoffs, rather than wage reductions, also occur in firms, industries, and occupations that are not covered by collective bargaining agreements. Also, the negative relationship between unemployment and aggregate economic activity is not limited to the past 40 years, the period of history in which unions have been most powerful in the United States. Finally, remember that today 70 to 75 percent of workers are *not* covered by collective bargaining agreements. Although unionism may play a role, forces more fundamental to labor markets must be responsible for the basic nature and behavior of cyclical unemployment.

Two reasons are generally given for employers' apparent unwillingness to lower wage rates. These reasons are also consistent with the downward inflexibility of wage rates associated with collective bargaining agreements. (After all, collective bargaining agreements are not imposed upon employers unilaterally, but rather result from an agreement by both parties involved.) The first reason bears on the credibility of the employer and the firm's long-term ability to attract new employees. The theory of OJT and implicit contracts covered in Chapter 9 implies an unwritten contract between employer and employee regarding the terms of employment over time. Lowering wage rates to take advantage of depressed labor market conditions might be profitable in the short run but would negatively affect long-run profits as workers discovered that an employer could not be trusted to honor an implicit job contract. The second reason for wage stability is related to employees' apparent preferences for avoiding the risks of fluctuating incomes and employers' interests in long-term cost minimization and profit maximization. Specifically, economists see the firm as providing its employees not only the opportunity for OJT but also insurance against fluctuating income.[8] In the process, employees agree to accept a stream of wage payments lower than it might otherwise be (in present-value terms) in return for freedom from the risk of a reduced wage rate when the demand for their services declines. The terms on which employees can "purchase" income insurance are governed by the expected course of future fluctuations in *VMPL*. Because income insurance is not free, employees do not typically demand complete freedom from the risk of fluctuating incomes. So, during periods of particularly low demand for output, the implicit contract for "income insurance" permits the firm to lay off employees.

But why do implicit income insurance contracts not provide for wage reductions rather than layoffs when *VMPL* falls below a critical level? After all, when workers are laid off, income is reduced. It is not reduced to zero, of course, because unemployment compensation and transfer payments provide income support for most families experiencing unemployment or low incomes. (The impact of unemployment compensation on layoffs is discussed later on in this chapter.) One appealing explanation is that if the wage rate were cut by enough to make the firm willing to maintain employment, workers would find it preferable to use their time in nonmarket activities— that is, the home wage rate would exceed the market wage rate and workers would withdraw from the labor force temporarily. The home wage rate is increased, of course, by government income-maintenance programs and unemployment compensation. Thus, firms lay workers off because they know that if they offered the workers the lower wage rates they would be willing to pay, workers would choose to quit until wages rose again.[9]

Downward wage inflexibility in the face of declining labor demand is evidently considerably greater in the United States than in other nations. In a recent paper, Robert J. Gordon shows that wage rate variation over time is considerably larger in both the United Kingdom and in Japan than in the United States, and that employment variation is considerably less. He attributes these differences in wage and employment fluctuations to differences in collective bargaining institutions and customs. This explanation must be viewed with caution in view of the small proportion of the United States labor force covered by collective bargaining agreements and of the relative

---

[8] A basic, quite readable reference on this topic is Donald F. Gordon, "A Neoclassical Theory of Keynesian Unemployment," *Economic Inquiry*, 12:4 (December 1974), 431–59. For more technical elaboration the interested reader should consult Costas Azariadas, "Implicit Contracts and Underemployment Equilibria," *Journal of Political Economy*, 83:6 (December 1975), 1183–1202, and Martin Neil Baily, "Wages and Employment Under Uncertain Demand," *Review of Economic Studies*, 41:1 (January 1974), 37–50.

[9] The reasonableness of thinking of layoffs as a kind of vacation is suggested by the adoption of "inverse seniority" in some industries. Senior workers have a type of first option on being laid off when the firm wishes to reduce employment temporarily. See Sheldon Friedman, Dennis C. Bernstead, and Robert T. Lund, "Inverse Seniority as an Aid to Disadvantaged Groups," *Monthly Labor Review*, 99:4 (April 1976), 36–37.

wage inflexibility in the United States before unions became a significant force in labor markets.

Having established that there are valid economic reasons for cyclical unemployment, we turn our attention to two important issues: (1) Is cyclical unemployment part of what we are referring to as normal unemployment? (2) How significant is the role played by workers' job search in determining cyclical unemployment?

Is cyclical unemployment part of normal unemployment?   Normal unemployment, as we have noted, is that portion of unemployment due to the regular entry of workers into the labor force and the relocation of workers from firm to firm and from industry to industry as the structure of the demand for final output changes or as workers seek to improve their employment situations. As such, it is the rate of unemployment to which the economy tends in the *absence* of macroeconomic shocks. Thus, cyclical unemployment, which is the result of the macroeconomic business cycle, is *not* part of the economy's normal unemployment. In the course of this chapter we will discuss many aspects of normal versus total unemployment, including the size of normal unemployment in the United States today, whether or not there is a particular unemployment rate that should be viewed as a policy goal, and the relationship between the rate of inflation and total and normal unemployment. For now, it is important to remember the following distribution of total unemployment into its component parts:

$$u(\text{total}) = [u(\text{frictional}) + u(\text{structural}) + u(\text{cyclical})]$$

Job search and cyclical unemployment.   We know that cyclical unemployment results from workers being laid off or discharged from their jobs during economic recessions. Those workers who are laid off have some expectation of being recalled when the recession is over. Those who have been discharged also have some hope of being rehired, although they are probably more pessimistic than those who have been laid off.

Before presenting our model of job search, we want to discuss what we believe is an unhelpful distinction that is sometimes made between *search* unemployment and *other* unemployment. When those who are concerned with unemployment make this distinction, it seems that they believe only frictional and, perhaps, some structural unemployment is adequately described by the search paradigm. We believe that the search model is an essential aid in understanding unemployment, *regardless* of the proximate cause for an individual's being out of work and *regardless* of whether an individual is an active job searcher. A worker who has been laid off or discharged for whatever reason must decide whether to search for another job, to drop out of the labor force, or simply to await recall (which amounts to temporarily dropping out). The search model shows the circumstances under which the gains from search will be so small relative to cost that search (or continued search) is not worthwhile; the potential searcher then drops out of the labor force. The search model is as relevant to an unemployed individual who waits or drops out as to one who actively searches for a job. It also is useful in understanding the behavior of someone who elects not to enter the labor force, having been engaged in household activities exclusively or in attending school.

Of course, the reemployment of the cyclically unemployed is partly determined by firms' recalling or rehiring laid-off or fired workers. Thus, a full understanding of unemployment requires an analysis of the recall process. At this point we will investigate the degree of job search undertaken by the cyclically unemployed. At various points throughout this chapter we also analyze the firm's layoff and rehiring strategy as it affects cyclical unemployment.

Those who end their cyclical unemployment by taking a job with a different employer most likely have had to search for that job. Thus, it is reasonable to conclude that people who were laid off or fired and ultimately switched jobs in order to become reemployed engaged in some job search. Those individuals who were cyclically unemployed and ultimately regained employment with their old employer may or may not have searched while unemployed. If they searched, they probably searched less than those workers who switched employers. So, one way to get a crude indication of how important active job search is in determining the length of time someone is cyclically unemployed is to determine the proportion of cyclically unemployed workers who ultimately switch employers versus those who are recalled by their previous employers. David Lilien examines the relative importance of these two groups in manufacturing during 1974–75, a period in which unemployment in the United States rose rather sharply, with virtually all the increase being due to cyclical unemployment. In particular, the overall unemployment rate rose from 5.6 to 8.6 percent, and the unemployment rate of experienced workers in manufacturing rose from 5.7 to 10.9 percent.

We will not go into the details of Lilien's somewhat statistically technical analysis but simply report his findings. Although the results vary by detailed industry class, *temporary layoffs with rehire* accounted for only about 35 percent of the increase in cyclical unemployment in manufacturing during 1974–75. Lilien feels that this rather small contribution of temporary layoffs to total unemployment in manufacturing suggests that most of cyclical unemployment is due to the longer unemployment spells of job losers who change jobs (search).

Lilien's research is important, because it indicates that cyclical unemployment is closely related to the issue of active job search. Active search is not confined only to frictionally and structurally unemployed workers. This reinforces our argument that if we really want to understand the variation in unemployment over time or across industry or population groups, or if we wish to understand the role of government policy in influencing unemployment, we have to take a careful look at the job search process. To this topic we now turn.

A DEEPER LOOK AT JOB SEARCH AND UNEMPLOYMENT

The essence of the link between search and unemployment is the notion that the unemployed individual seeks work while refraining from working at a job. Although not all individuals classified in the government's statistics as unemployed are really looking for a new job and not all job search is carried on while the worker is unemployed, the assumption that unemployment and job search go hand in hand permits us to capture the key behavioral and policy issues without too much violence to reality. We will treat the unemployed job searcher as desiring the greatest possible economic benefit from search activity. Thus, the decision to *remain* unemployed is based on the benefits and costs of *continued* search. These costs and benefits are determined by the economic environment in which the individual exists.

In particular, the cost of unemployed job search is the greater of foregone earnings on the best immediately available job or the value of commodities ("leisure" as well as various forms of investment in human capital) that could be produced if the worker devoted all search time to nonmarket activities. The benefit to search is the expected improvement in job offers over immediately available alternatives. More specifically, the benefit of remaining unemployed derives from the expectation that a higher market wage will be obtained through further search. Insofar as an unemployed individual typically expects to hold a job for several years, the *present value* of increased future earnings is the appropriate measure of the gain to remaining unemployed. Job search activity is a form of investment in human capital. Because not everyone is unemployed at the same time or, if unemployed, remains unemployed for the same length of time, the scenario we are sketching suggests that costs or benefits of search vary across individuals.

The search model encompasses not only the length of a given period of unemployment but also the frequency of unemployment. As Figure 12-4 illustrates, the higher is a worker's minimum acceptable wage, the greater is the probability that an unexpected downward shift in $VMPL$ will result in a layoff. Thus, by establishing a lower acceptance wage, a job seeker can reduce the risk of future unemployment. This is not to say that all unemployment is "voluntary" in the sense that workers prefer unemployment to employment, given their acceptance wage rates; rather, the search model focuses attention on the various *constraints* determining individual workers' $VMPL$s and acceptance wage rates. For some persons these constraints may be unfavorable indeed. To find oneself "between a rock and a hard place" is to be forced to choose among unpleasant alternatives; the fact that a choice is made under difficult conditions does not mean that the result is a happy one.

To the extent an individual can rely on the earnings of other family members, unemployment compensation, or transfer payments, there is less incentive to lower the acceptance wage in order to reduce future unemployment risk. An acceptance wage low enough to substantially reduce the frequency of layoffs might be less than an individual's reservation wage. (The **acceptance wage** is the minimum required by the worker to accept a given job; the **reservation wage** is the minimum required to work at all.) Moreover, minimum wage legislation makes it fruitless to lower the acceptance wage for many individuals with limited skills. Thus, rather than accept a job in which steady employment is assured in return for a relatively low rate of pay, many low-wage workers may well choose, or be forced to accept, more frequent unemployment. Other individuals facing the same constraints may choose not to work at all.

A Model of the Job Search Process

Time costs vary among individuals in accordance with their immediately available labor market and household opportunities. The variation in benefits of job search is related to different values placed on a given worker's services by alternative prospective employers. Remember that information about labor market alternatives is a valuable asset that can be *produced* with the input of one's own time and market goods (for example, advertisements and transportation). Clearly, an important source of gain is the expected wage increase resulting from further search, which depends on the degree of information imperfection in the labor market and on job heterogeneity. Given the increase in wage rate that one can obtain by searching, the expected gain will be greater, the greater the proportion of time to be devoted to market work and the length of the period one expects to remain on a new job. If accurate information were widely available about all alternative jobs, no search would be necessary. A person could immediately decide whether, and where, to work. Similarly, if all jobs were identical, there would be very little search. An individual would take the first job offered, as further search would provide no improvement in employment opportunities. In the world as we know it, however, workers do not know all the details of their employment opportunities, and different employers pay different wage rates to similar workers doing similar work. Of course, the spread among these wage rates is limited by workers' search behavior, as well as being a partial determinant of search behavior and of unemployment itself.

In order to see how costly information and imperfect knowledge about alternative jobs interact to determine unemployment, we will develop a simple model of search behavior. In the process, we will show that wealth-maximizing search behavior requires that the individual choose a wage rate, called the **acceptance wage,** such that if a job offering the acceptance wage or more is received, it will be accepted; otherwise the job will be rejected and search continued. This search procedure is called **sequential search**, because it involves rejecting each job offered until the first offer equal to or exceeding the acceptance wage is received. But how does the goal of wealth maximization coupled with the costs and benefits of search lead to a particular acceptance wage for an unemployed worker?

The answer involves a comparison of marginal benefit with marginal cost. Wealth-maximizing search requires the formulation of a search strategy such that the marginal benefit of further search is equal to its marginal cost. As illustrated in Figure 12-5, the searcher who wants to maximize the net benefit from search will choose an acceptance wage, labeled $\tilde{w}$, such that the marginal benefit of additional search equals the marginal cost of additional search. It is not immediately obvious, though, how marginal benefit and marginal cost of search are determined. We must elaborate on their determination in order to reach our ultimate goal of being able to analyze the impact of various economic policies on the incidence and duration of unemployment.

The marginal benefit of search.   We have already noted that the benefits of search are related to the diversity of jobs available and the amount of knowledge that the searcher has about job opportunities. Both job diversity and imperfect knowledge of opportunities are prerequisites for search to occur at all. In what follows we assume that the job searcher knows *in general* what types of jobs are available along with the *likelihood* that a particular type of offer will be forthcoming. The unemployed worker does not know, however, when the best or any other available job will be offered.

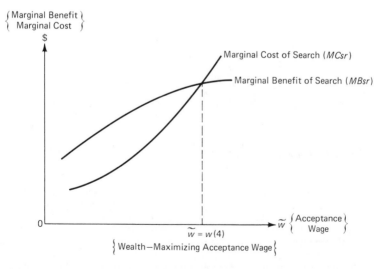

FIGURE 12-5. Marginal benefit of search, marginal cost of search, and the acceptance wage

If jobs are indexed by the present value of earnings expected over the course of the employment relation, then the information available to the unemployed job searcher can be described geometrically as in Figure 12-6. The vertical distance between each of the crosses and the horizontal axis in Figure 12-6 indicates the proportion of job opportunities that pay a particular (expected) value of earnings over the course of the employment relationship. The horizontal axis measures the present (dollar) value of the prospective job offers. Jobs can also be indexed by the starting hourly wage rate associated with the expected present value of earnings over the course of the employment relationship.[10] For convenience we shall measure the benefit of search by the dollar value of the starting wage on a job, bearing in mind that this is just a shorthand way of indexing the full benefit—the job's expected present value.

Figure 12-6 shows only eleven possible job opportunities for an individual worker. In a large economy there are numerous job offers an individual might receive, and Figure 12-7 is a more realistic description of the possibilities faced by an unemployed job searcher. Two key properties of the frequency distribution of starting hourly wages are the average wage and the dispersion of wages. The average wage is related to the position of the frequency distribution of wages (farther to the right represents a higher average), and the dispersion relates to its width.[11] In Figure 12-7 the average

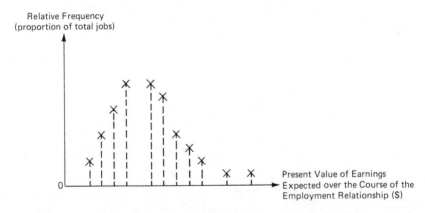

FIGURE 12-6. A frequency distribution of the present value of possible job offers

---

[10] The linkage between the present value of earnings expected over the course of a job and the starting hourly wage rate is obvious in a case where the rate of discount is zero and wages are constant over the work life. In this case, the present value of earnings is simply the number of years of expected employment times the starting hourly wage.

[11] Notice that the frequency distributions in Figures 12-6 and 12-7 do not touch the vertical axis. What information does this convey concerning the searcher's job opportunities? Suppose the frequency distribution in Figure 12-7 did touch the vertical axis. What information would the point where it touched the vertical axis provide?

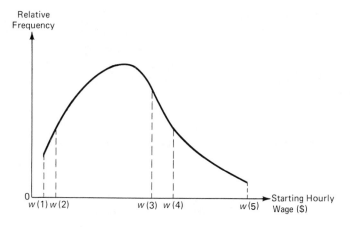

FIGURE 12-7. A frequency distribution of starting hourly wages when there are many different jobs available

wage is $w(3)$, and the dispersion can be measured by the range of wages $w(5) - w(1)$.

Suppose we consider a worker who, given the information in Figure 12-7, has decided to accept any available job with a starting wage of $w(1)$ or more. Thus $w(1)$ is the worker's acceptance wage, and the *expected* total benefit of job search is simply the average wage rate, $w(3)$. Suppose, though, that our unemployed worker considers the possibility of accepting only jobs that pay a starting wage somewhat higher than the minimum available, say $w(2)$. This decision would make the expected total benefit of search the average wage of those jobs that pay *at least* $w(2)$. The **marginal benefit of search (*MBsr*)** is the *increase* in the total benefit of search as the unemployed worker considers progressively higher and higher acceptance wage rates. With a little thought you should see that the marginal benefit of search is going to be positive. For example, if the average wage of jobs paying at least $w(2)$ is $w(4)$, then the *MBsr* of increasing the acceptance wage from $w(1)$ to $w(2)$ is $w(4) - w(3)$. Figure 12-5 depicts the general result that *MBsr* increases as the acceptance wage, $\tilde{w}$, increases. Although this may seem a complicated phenomenon, it means only that in general the extra benefit from setting a somewhat higher acceptance wage is larger, the larger is the acceptance wage in the first place.

The marginal cost of search.   The total cost of searching for a job that pays at least $w(1)$, say, is simply the number of periods (weeks, months, or whatever) it takes on average to find such a job multiplied by the average opportunity cost of search per period. It should be noted that the cost of search includes direct and indirect opportunity costs. Included among direct costs are those for travel, postage, telephone, clothes, and other goods and services used to help find employment. (Can you name some others?) Indirect costs include the value of leisure (home production) or foregone earnings, net of any subsidies paid through public or private unemployment compensation benefits. Because higher-paying jobs take more time to find, the total cost of search rises with the acceptance wage. The **marginal cost of search ($MCsr$)** is the increase in total search costs as the searcher demands a more and more lucrative starting salary. Figure 12-5 depicts the general result that $MCsr$ is positive and increases with the searcher's minimum acceptable wage.

Maximizing the net gain from search.   The net gain from search is maximized by setting w so that the difference between the total benefit from search and the total cost of search is greatest. In particular, the searcher establishes the acceptance wage that equates the marginal cost of search to the marginal benefit of search and continues seeking jobs until receiving an offer that pays at least $\tilde{w}$. For a searcher confronting the benefit and cost structure illustrated by the curves in Figure 12-5, $\tilde{w} = w(4)$. For acceptance wages less than this particular value of $\tilde{w}$, the marginal benefit of raising the acceptance wage, and searching longer, outweighs the marginal cost, and the searcher would be better off economically if the acceptance wage were higher. Acceptance wages in excess of $w(4)$, however, would lead one to search *too long*, in the sense that although there are extra benefits from searching for a wage higher than $w(4)$, those extra benefits are exceeded by the extra costs of achieving such a job offer. There is really nothing too complicated about the wealth-maximization goal we are attributing to unemployed job searchers. It merely means that they are doing the best they can to obtain new jobs in light of the costs of doing so.[12]

---

[12] The sequential search strategy just described is neither the most simple nor the most complex possible method to use in seeking employment. If, for example, a searcher could always decide to accept a job offered in the past without fear of its being filled by someone else, then it would be almost as desirable economically to decide in advance the number of searches, as opposed to a minimum acceptable wage rate, and then take the best job offered in that set of searches. Such behavior has been termed a *lump-search strategy*. Alternatively, a more complex search strategy than that in our example would allow for uncertain knowledge of the frequency distribution of wage offers. In this case, the searcher would adjust the acceptance wage as more and more information was gathered through the search process, as opposed to having the constant acceptance wage we have seen above. Such a situation might result from a relative ignorance on the part of the searcher concerning available wage offers. Readers interested in the basic details of these alternative job search strategies should consult Donald O. Parsons, "Models of Labor Market Turnover: A Theoretical and Empirical Survey," *Research in Labor Economics,* Ronald G. Ehrenberg, ed. (Greenwich, Conn.: JAI Press), Vol. 1, 1977, pp. 185–224. An *extensive, mathematically technical* treatment of optimal job search behavior is available in Steven A. Lippman and John J. McCall, "The Economics of Job Search: A Survey, Part I," *Economic Inquiry,* 14:2 (June 1976), 155–89.

Search and unemployment rates.   Having seen how the wealth-maximizing searcher goes about seeking employment, we now turn our attention to the linkage between searchers' acceptance wages and measured unemployment rates. This relationship provides the key to understanding demographic differences in unemployment rates and the impact of various government policies on unemployment rates. Although you may not yet have thought of it in exactly these terms, the annual average unemployment rate for a demographic group, or for the economy as a whole for that matter, is described by the following relation:

$$u = \frac{\left(\begin{array}{c}\text{number of individuals who}\\ \text{begin to search during a year}\end{array}\right) \times \left(\begin{array}{c}\text{average fraction of year}\\ \text{spent searching}\end{array}\right)}{\text{civilian labor force}}$$
$$+ \frac{\left(\begin{array}{c}\text{number of workers entering temporary}\\ \text{layoff and not searching during a year}\end{array}\right) \times \left(\begin{array}{c}\text{average fraction of}\\ \text{year spent on layoff}\end{array}\right)}{\text{civilian labor force}}$$

This means that increases in either the relative number of workers seeking jobs in a year or the average duration of search increase the measured unemployment rate, other things equal. As we stated above, the decision whether or not to begin to search depends on whether or not there exists an acceptance wage rate at which the marginal benefit of search exceeds the marginal cost of search. If the marginal cost of search exceeds the marginal benefit of search at all feasible acceptance wages, then there is no point in searching. Put differently, search is just not worth it. The marginal benefit of search exceeds the marginal cost for the individual described by the curves in Figure 12-5, who is therefore an unemployed job searcher.

The link between the average duration of search and a searcher's acceptance wage is somewhat more difficult to see than the link between *MBsr*, *MCsr*, and the decision whether or not to search at all. In Figure 12-7 the height of the curve above a particular wage indicates the likelihood that an unemployed job searcher will receive that wage offer. The wealth-maximizing searcher we have been discussing has an acceptance wage of $w(4)$. If you draw a vertical line from $w(4)$ to the point directly above it in Figure 12-7, the height of the line, by definition of a frequency distribution, is the probability of finding a job that pays *exactly* $w(4)$. Consider now the likelihood that our searcher receives a wage a little bit higher than $w(4)$. In Figure 12-7 select a wage a little higher than $w(4)$, take a pencil, and connect the point on the horizontal axis associated with this wage to the point directly above it on the curve representing the relative frequency distribution of wage rates. The length of this vertical line is the probability that our searcher receives exactly the wage rate you have selected.

What, though, is the likelihood that our searcher receives *any* wage greater than or equal to the acceptance wage of $w(4)$? To arrive at this information you would add up the probabilities of receiving a wage of exactly $w(4)$, a wage a little higher than $w(4)$, a wage a little higher yet, and so forth, until you accounted for *all* wage offers above $w(4)$. If you were to keep track of all of these probabilities by drawing pencil lines of the type we just described—that is, from the particular wage rates on the horizontal axis to the relative-frequency curve directly above them—and did this for all wages that are greater than or equal to the searcher's acceptance wage $w(4)$ in Figure 12-7, you would have totally blackened the area under the curve to the right of a vertical line through the searcher's acceptance wage $w(4)$.

The point to be remembered is that the area under a frequency distribution to the right of a vertical line through the acceptance wage illustrates the fraction of total jobs paying the acceptance wage or more and is, therefore, the probability that a searcher will receive an acceptable job offer. If we denote as l this probability of an acceptable job being offered, then $1/l$ is the number of periods it will take, on average, for an unemployed worker to find a satisfactory job. For example, suppose that a period of search is one month, because this is the time necessary to process a job application, interview for a job, and so forth. If one-half of all jobs are acceptable to the searcher, then an unemployed worker will spend, *on average*, two months looking for work and will be unemployed for that period. How long will a searcher be unemployed, on average, if one-fourth of all jobs are acceptable?

We now have some general results to cite. First, factors that lead to a relatively high marginal cost of search lead one to search for a relatively short time or not to search at all. Factors producing a relatively low $MCsr$ contribute to a relatively lengthy search effort. Thus, demographic groups with relatively high marginal costs of search will have relatively low unemployment rates. Second, factors that lead to a relatively high marginal benefit of search cause relatively high acceptance wages, relatively long periods of search, and, therefore, relatively high incidences of unemployment. Thus, a demographic group with a high marginal benefit from job search will have a relatively high measured unemployment rate, because a relatively large fraction of the group is engaged in job search and the search lasts relatively long. Similarly, factors, including public policy, that raise the marginal benefits of search to various groups or individuals also raise unemployment rates.

An increase in unemployment corresponding to an *improvement* in a group's economic environment is not just a remote theoretical possibility. J. Peter Mattila notes that the increase in teenage unemployment rates since the early 1960s can be explained in terms of improved job opportunities, not a deteriorating labor market. This appears to be particularly the case for 16- and 17-year-old males. In 1961 the proportion of 16- and 17-year-old males who were employed equaled 32 percent. By 1979 this ratio had risen to 40 percent. Despite this one-fourth increase in the employment ratio, *unemployment* as a fraction of the population of 16- and 17-year-old males *in-*

creased from 8.3 percent to 10.3 percent.[13] Mattila resolves this paradox with evidence that growing job opportunities in the retail and service industries were particularly suited to teenagers. Because of the availability of numerous part-time jobs requiring little previous experience in retail trade and services, teenagers not only found it easier to obtain employment but were encouraged to seek jobs in greater numbers.

Search and labor force participation.   We noted above that if the marginal cost of search exceeds the marginal benefit, there is no point in searching. Conditions that lower *MBsr*, such as recessions, can increase the likelihood that some individuals will find it is not worthwhile to engage in, or continue, job search. People in this situation have been called **discouraged workers.** At the same time, when one earner in a family is laid off, other family members may find that the value of their time in household activities is reduced sufficiently to push their *MCsr* below their *MBsr*. If these individuals begin to seek jobs, they are called **added workers.** Thus, the net impact of cyclical or structural declines in labor market opportunities on labor force participation is uncertain. If the discouraged-worker effect dominates the added-worker effect, labor force participation will decline when labor demand falls—apart from the effect of any decline in wage rates. Moreover, the increase in the unemployment rate will understate the number of disemployed individuals who would be prepared to work at jobs for the wages they previously earned. Thus, for policy purposes, the change in the *employment rate* (the number of employed persons relative to the population) is probably a better indicator of a change in the demand for labor than is the change in the unemployment rate.

Empirical studies tend to confirm that the discouraged-worker effect dominates the added-worker effect. This is borne out in studies of the labor supply of married women and is probably typical of fringe or marginal labor force groups, such as youth and the elderly. (Can you explain why labor market discouragement is more common among these groups in terms of their *MBsr* or *MCsr*?) There is considerable disagreement, however, regarding the magnitude of "net discouragement" when labor demand declines.[14]

---

[13] *Employment and Training Report of the President,* 1981, Tables A-3 and A-30. See also Table 12-5 of this chapter.

[14] In general, when the effect of unemployment on labor force participation is estimated with aggregate time-series data (data that vary over time for the entire economy), the net negative effect of a decline in demand on unemployment is much smaller than when cross-section data (such as data on local labor markets at a given point in time) are used. See, for instance, Jacob Mincer, "Labor Force Participation and Unemployment: A Review of Recent Evidence," in R. A. and M. S. Gordon, eds., *Prosperity and Unemployment* (New York: Wiley, 1966), pp. 91–98; and Belton M. Fleisher and George F. Rhodes, Jr., "Labor Force Participation of Married Men and Women: A Simultaneous Model," *Review of Economics and Statistics,* 58 (November 1976), 398–406.

We are now almost ready to delve deeper into demographic differences in unemployment. First, however, it will be a useful exercise for you to create a table listing the various factors that you feel affect the marginal benefits of search and the marginal costs of search. Put a star by the factors that you feel are under the control of government policy—that is, can be altered through legislation or executive action at some governmental level. Such a table should prove helpful when we discuss particular demographic factors and public policies affecting *MBsr* and *MCsr* and their ultimate impact on unemployment rates.

Before we do this, however, perhaps you are still a bit hazy about the key concepts that we have been developing in this section. The next section is a numerical example that utilizes all the concepts of this section. If you wish more discussion of the concepts of marginal benefit of search, marginal cost of search, acceptance wage, probability, relative frequency distribution of wages, and wealth-maximizing amount of search, then you should read the next section and work through the calculations contained within it. If you feel quite comfortable with the concepts just mentioned, skip the next section and go directly to the following one, where we begin to apply our search model to understanding demographic differences in unemployment rates and public policies designed to influence unemployment rates.

*A Numerical Example of Job Search Activity

In order to develop our example, let us assume that a job, if accepted, is expected to last for two years, that it will involve 2,000 hours of work per year, and that the interest rate for calculating the present value of prospective wage offers is zero. The jobs offered to the individual are assumed to differ only in the rate of pay; other working conditions are the same. In Figure 12-8 we depict the situation in which 20 percent of the job offers an unemployed worker might receive would have a present value of $20,000 ($5 per hour × 2,000 hours per year × 2 years), 30 percent at present value of $24,000, 30 percent $28,000, 15 percent $32,000, and 5 percent $36,000. Although search is required to find out just *which* employers offer the highest wage, the searcher does have knowledge of the information contained in Figure 12-8. That is, he or she knows that the probability of receiving a job offer with a present value less than $20,000 or greater than $36,000 is zero, the probability of being offered a job worth as much as $36,000 is only 5 percent, and so on. On the basis of these assumptions, we can analyze how the wealth-maximizing searcher arrives at an acceptance wage $(\tilde{w})$.

If we knew nothing about the economics of search, we might conclude from the information in Figure 12-8 that the acceptance wage will be $9 per hour, because if the searcher has sufficient patience, a job with a present value of $36,000 will eventually be offered. Why would a searcher ever settle for less? We already know the answer; it would be all right to wait for the best possible job offer to come along if there were no opportunity costs of doing so. Unfortunately, search uses scarce time and other resources so that the searcher must weigh the expected gains from future search, should the $36,000 job not be immediately offered, against the cost of that

---

* This section contains more technical material. If you skip, go to p. 492.

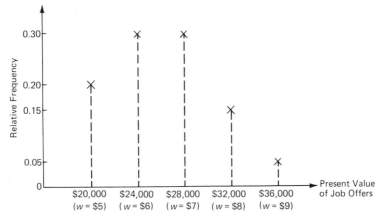

FIGURE 12-8. Frequency distribution of present value of job offers

search. Therefore, in order to complete our numerical example, we must provide information about search costs. We will assume that each job offer received requires two months of searching, that time is valued at $600 per month, and that other costs such as transportation and telephone calls amount to $100 per month. So, the cost of generating one job offer (C) is $1,400.

The information in Table 12-1 permits us to calculate the expected returns to search, and we know the cost per period of search. How does this information determine the optimal search strategy for a wealth-maximizing individual? The optimal strategy, remember, involves establishing an acceptance wage ($\tilde{w}$) that maximizes the difference between the expected present value of the search process and the expected cost.

The expected present value of job search.   By establishing the wage at which a job offer will be accepted (the acceptance wage), the searcher establishes the expected present value (total benefit) of job search. Given an acceptance wage, the expected present value of search associated with that acceptance wage is *greater* than the present value of a job offering exactly the acceptance wage. This is an important point; let us try to understand exactly why it is true.

Remember that by setting an acceptance wage $\tilde{w}$, the job searcher is assured of ultimately being offered a rate of pay of *at least* $\tilde{w}$. For example, if $\tilde{w}$ is set at $6, the present value of a job with exactly this wage rate is $24,000, as shown in Figure 12-8 and Table 12-1. To calculate the present value of search associated with a $6 acceptance wage, we must take into consideration the chance that a job paying more than $6 per hour will be offered to the searcher (and accepted). When $\tilde{w} = $6, this means that the searcher in our example will accept jobs paying $6, $7, $8, or $9. It is necessary to calculate the probability that the worker will be offered one of these jobs, given that the decision has been made to accept only jobs paying at least $6.

The likelihood of receiving a job offer of *exactly* $6 is somewhat tricky to calculate. To see how it is done, consider once more the information contained in Figure 12-8. It tells us that the probability a job offer will equal or exceed $6 is the sum of the probabilities attached to each offer of $6 or more—namely, 0.3 + 0.3 + 0.15 + 0.05 = 0.8. If we divide 0.3, the *unconditional* (simple) probability that a job

TABLE 12-1 The Relative Frequency of Wages, the Present Values of Jobs, and the Expected Total Benefit of Search

(1) Hourly Wage	(2) Present Value of a Job Paying the Wage in Col. (1)[a,b]	(3) Probability of Receiving the Wage in Col. (1)	(4) Probability of Receiving at Least the Wage in Column (1)	(5) Probability of Obtaining a Job with the Wage in Col. (1) If the Acceptance Wage Is $5	(6) Probability of Obtaining a Job with the Wage in Col. (1) If the Acceptance Wage Is $6	(7) Probability of Obtaining a Job with the Wage in Col. (1) If the Acceptance Wage Is $7
$5	$20,000	0.2	1.0	0.2	0	0
$6	$24,000	0.3	0.8	0.3	$\frac{0.3}{0.8} = 0.375$	0
$7	$28,000	0.3	0.5	0.3	$\frac{0.3}{0.8} = 0.375$	$\frac{0.3}{0.5} = 0.60$
$8	$32,000	0.15	0.2	0.15	$\frac{0.15}{0.8} = 0.1875$	$\frac{0.15}{0.5} = 0.30$
$9	$36,000	0.05	0.05	0.05	$\frac{0.05}{0.8} = 0.0625$	$\frac{0.05}{0.5} = 0.10$

[a] These data are taken from Figure 12-8.
[b] Jobs are assumed to last two years and involve 2,000 hours of work per year. A zero rate of interest is used to compute the present values in this table.

(8) Probability of Obtaining a Job with the Wage in Col. (1) If the Acceptance Wage Is $8	(9) Probability of Obtaining a Job with the Wage in Col. (1) If the Acceptance Wage Is $9	(10) Expected Present Value (Total Benefit) of Search If the Wage in Col. (1) Is the Acceptance Wage
0	0	$26,200 = (0.2)($20,000) + (0.3)($24,000) + (0.3)($28,000) + (0.15)($32,000) + (0.05)($36,000)
0	0	$27,750 = (0.375)($24,000) + (0.375)($28,000) + (0.1875)($32,000) + (0.0625)($36,000)
0	0	$30,000 = (0.6)($28,000) + (0.3)($32,000) + (0.1)($36,000)
$\frac{0.15}{0.20} = 0.75$	0	$33,000 = (0.75)($32,000) + (0.25)($36,000)
$\frac{0.05}{0.20} = 0.25$	1.0	$36,000 = (1)($36,000)

offer will equal $6, by the sum 0.8, we obtain 0.375, the probability of *accepting* an offer of $6, *conditional on* $\tilde{w}$ = $6. Similarly, we divide 0.3 by 0.8 to obtain 0.375, the conditional probability of accepting an offer of $7; 0.15 ÷ 0.8 = 0.1875, the conditional probability of accepting an offer of $8; and 0.05 ÷ 0.8 = 0.0625, the conditional probability that a job offering $9 per hour will be accepted. Note that the sum of these conditional probabilities 0.375 + 0.375 + 0.1875 + 0.0625 = 1, the probability that the job *accepted* will offer a wage equal to or exceeding $6, conditional on $\tilde{w}$ = $6. These calculations are shown in column (6) of Table 12-1. The conditional probabilities of obtaining jobs given the possible acceptance wages of $5, $7, $8, and $9 are shown in columns (5) and (7)–(9) of this table.

To calculate the expected present value of job search associated with an acceptance wage of $6, we simply multiply each of the values in column (2) corresponding to wage offers of $6 or more by their respective conditional probabilities and take the sum of the products. Thus, the expected present value of search for $\tilde{w}$ = $6 is calculated as $24,000 × 0.375 + $28,000 × 0.375 + $32,000 × 0.1875 + $36,000 × 0.0625 = $27,750, which is shown in the second line of column (10) of Table 12-1. By a similar procedure, you should be able to calculate that the expected present value of search corresponding to an acceptance wage of $7 is $30,000, and so on. Although this calculation is done for you in Table 12-1, we suggest that you verify *all* the calculations in columns (6)–(10) as a way of testing your understanding of the expected present value of search versus the present value of a job.

The expected cost of search.   Just as the expected present value of search increases with $\tilde{w}$, so does the cost. Because the unconditional probability of receiving an offer equal to or exceeding $\tilde{w}$ falls as $\tilde{w}$ rises, the *expected number of periods of search* rises with $\tilde{w}$. As shown in Table 12-2, the expected number of periods of search equals the *reciprocal* of the probability that an offer equal to or exceeding the acceptance wage will be received. Calculating the expected number of periods of search is analogous to calculating the expected number of times a six-sided die must be thrown before coming up with a number equal to, say, four or more. Because there are six possibilities (1, 2, 3, 4, 5, or 6), the probability of any throw's yielding a four or more is $\frac{3}{6} = \frac{1}{2}$; thus one must expect to throw the die (1/$\frac{1}{2}$) = 2 times on average to be "sure" of obtaining a number of four or more.

If we assume it is possible to search for a fraction of a period (for example, an offer might be received closer to the beginning of the period than to the end), then the expected number of periods of search can be multiplied by the cost per period of search to derive the *expected cost* associated with each possible acceptance wage. This calculation appears in column (5) of Table 12-2. Notice that the expected cost of search rises with the acceptance wage because of the rise in the amount of time necessary to receive an acceptable job offer.

Maximizing the net gain from search.   The net gain from search is maximized by setting $\tilde{w}$ so that the difference between the expected present value of search and the expected total cost of search is greatest. As shown in Table 12-3, this occurs when the reservation wage is $7 per hour. Note that for an acceptance wage less than $7, the marginal benefit of raising $\tilde{w}$ and increasing the expected duration of unemployment exceeds the marginal cost of doing so. For an acceptance wage greater than $7, the marginal cost exceeds the marginal benefit. (Remember that the marginal benefit and marginal cost columns in Table 12-3 are simply the changes in the expected present value of search and the expected total cost of search, respectively, as $\tilde{w}$ increases.) Notice also that when the expected total gain from search is maximized, by setting an acceptance wage of $7, marginal benefit of search is not *exactly*

TABLE 12-2 Calculating Expected Search Costs

(1) Hourly Wage	(2) Probability of Receiving at Least the Wage in Col. (1)[a]	(3) Expected Number of Search Periods If the Wage in Col. (1) Is the Acceptance Wage[b]	(4) Expected Number of Months Unemployed If the Wage in Col. (1) Is the Acceptance Wage[c]	(5) Expected Total Cost of Search If the Wage in Col. (1) Is the Acceptance Wage[d]
$5	1	1	1	$ 1,400
$6	0.8	1.25	2.5	$ 1,750
$7	0.5	2	4	$ 2,800
$8	0.2	5	10	$ 7,000
$9	0.05	20	40	$28,000

[a] These data are from Table 12-1, Col. (4).

[b] Expected number of search periods = $\dfrac{1}{\text{probability of receiving at least the wage in Col. (1)}}$.

[c] Each job offer is assumed to take, on average, two months of searching.

[d] The direct and indirect (opportunity) costs of search are assumed to be $700 per month.

TABLE 12-3 The Net Gains from Search

(1) Hourly Wage	(2) Expected Present Value of Search If the Wage in Col. (1) Is the Acceptance Wage[a]	(3) Marginal Benefits of Search (MBsr)	(4) Expected Total Cost of Search If the Wage in Col. (1) Is the Acceptance Wage[b]	(5) Marginal Cost of Search (MCsr)	(6) Expected Total (Net) Gain from Search If the Wage in Col. (1) Is the Acceptance Wage[c]
$5	$26,200	$26,200	$ 1,400	$ 1,400	$24,800
$6	$27,750	$ 1,550	$ 1,750	$ 350	$26,000
$7	$30,000	$ 2,250	$ 2,800	$ 1,050	$27,200
$8	$33,000	$ 3,000	$ 7,000	$ 4,200	$26,000
$9	$36,000	$ 3,000	$28,000	$21,000	$ 8,000

[a] From Table 12-1, Col. (10).

[b] From Table 12-2, Col. (5).

[c] Col. (2) − Col. (4).

equal to marginal cost of search. The reason is that the searcher described by the information in Table 12-3 cannot "fine-tune" his or her acceptance wage to the exact point of a quality of $MBsr$ and $MCsr$, as in the general case described in Figure 12-5.

It is important to realize that the outcome of the job search process is uncertain, even though our individual searcher is assumed to have perfect knowledge of the relative frequency distribution of wage offers. Individuals with the search costs and frequency distribution of wage offers equal to those in our example would receive, *on average*, a net gain from search of $27,200 by setting $\tilde{w} = \$7$. They would experience an *average duration of unemployment* of two search periods (four months). Some would be lucky and receive an offer exceeding $7 the first search period, while others might be so unfortunate as to remain unemployed a long time, receiving no offers greater than $6. Nevertheless, regardless of what an individual searcher's experience may be under the sequential search strategy, the beginning of each search period is a "new ballgame." Past bad luck does not alter the fact that the expected net gain from setting $\tilde{w} = \$7$ is still the maximum net gain. Past search costs are gone and do not affect present wealth-maximizing search strategy.

The wealth-maximizing searcher in the numerical example we are discussing searches for a job (is *not* a discouraged worker) because the marginal benefit of search exceeds the marginal cost of search for at least one acceptance wage. In our example, the marginal benefit curve rises as $\tilde{w}$ rises, because the expected present value of the job accepted rises at an increasing rate as the minimum acceptable wage rate rises. The marginal cost curve (and the expected duration of unemployment) rises even faster, however, so that in general it pays to stop short of "going for broke" (the maximum conceivable wage offer). Thus, we have the general results described in Figure 12-5 also appearing in our numerical example.

Job Search and Unemployment: Applications

Probably the most obvious application we might make of the theory of job search as it pertains to unemployment experience is to attempt to understand demographic differences in unemployment rates in the United States. Table 12-4 reports unemployment rates by age, race, and sex for 1955–80. Three aspects of the data displayed in this table are quite interesting. First, the major demographic difference in unemployment rates is between teenagers and adults. In 1980, for example, the teenage unemployment rate was three to four times higher than that of adults ages 25–54. Second, the data indicate a somewhat smaller, yet substantial, difference in unemployment rates between the races: in 1980 the unemployment rate of blacks was approximately 1.5 to 2.5 times that of whites for the two age groups under consideration. Finally, the data seem to show little difference between the unemployment rates of males and females. In 1980 the unemployment rate for adult white females was only 0.8 percentage points higher than that of adult white males. Among whites, the teenage unemployment rate was actually lower for white females. The same comparison holds true for black women and black men ages 25–54. Let us now see how much insight our analysis of job search and unemployment provides concerning the observed race and age differences in unemployment rates in the United States.

TABLE 12-4   Unemployment Rates by Age, Race, and Sex, 1955–1980

Race, Sex, and Age	Unemployment Rate (%)					
	1955	1960	1965	1970	1975	1980
White males						
16–19	11.3	14.0	13.1	13.9	18.4	16.2
25–54	2.7	3.7	2.4	2.6	5.4	4.5
White females						
16–19	9.6	12.9	14.1	13.5	17.5	14.8
25–54	3.9	4.7	4.0	4.4	7.3	5.3
Black and other males						
16–19	13.8	24.1	23.7	25.2	35.6	34.9
25–54	8.0	9.3	5.5	4.9	10.3	9.6
Black and other females						
16–19	19.7	24.9	32.3	34.5	36.5	36.9
25–54	7.9	8.1	7.3	6.2	10.6	9.5

Source: *Employment and Training Report of the President,* 1980, Tables A-20 and A-21, and *Employment and Earnings,* January 1981, Table 3.

Age differences in unemployment.   We have seen that the unemployment rate of teenagers has been three to four times that of adults in recent years. When we examine the distribution of the unemployed by prior labor force status in Table 12-5, we see that about two-thirds of the unemployed youth in 1979 were experiencing unemployment in connection with labor force entry or reentry. Among teenagers who were working prior to their unemployment, the incidence of unemployment was not much higher than that of adult men, as shown in columns (3) and (4).

The point here is that much unemployment among youth is associated with job search, almost necessarily accompanying mobility from outside the market labor force to jobs in the market sector. Of course, individuals seeking work would be better off if they could find jobs of given characteristics with less search and unemployment experience. However, a substantial amount of unemployment is attributable to the process of learning which jobs are available and what the labor market has to offer to those who have relatively little work knowledge and experience—an inherently costly process. To understand more fully the phenomenon that inexperienced searchers have longer spells of unemployment, let us view the issue within the context of our model of the job search process developed above.

In general, experienced or "mature" workers have formed a rather firm picture of their labor market opportunities, as depicted by the rather compact relative frequency distribution of wage offers for experienced workers in Figure 12-9. New workers, of course, have less experience upon which to base their assessments and will generally view their alternatives as

TABLE 12-5   Distribution of Unemployed by Prior Labor Force Status and Reason for Leaving Last Job, 1979

	Percent Distribution of Unemployed		Percent of the Total Civilian Labor Force in the Respective Unemployment Groups[a]	
	(1) *Both Sexes* *16–19* *Years Old*	*(2)* *Male* *20+ Years*	*(3)* *Both Sexes* *16–19* *Years Old*	*(4)* *Male* *20+ Years*
Total	100.0%	100.0%	17.7%	5.9%
Working	32.3	82.2	5.8	4.8
Lost last job	23.3	71.6	4.1	4.2
Left last job	9.4	10.6	1.7	0.6
Out of labor force	67.3	17.9	11.9	1.1
Reentered labor force	28.8	15.3	5.1	0.9
Never worked before	38.5	2.6	6.8	0.2

[a] The sum of the unemployment rates by prior activity equals the *total* unemployment rate at the head of the column.

Source: *Employment and Training Report of the President,* 1981, Table A-36.

relatively more diverse than older workers, as depicted by the rather diffuse curve on the left in Figure 12-9. Holding the mean wage offer constant, increase the "spread" of the wage offer curve increases the probability of receiving a relatively high wage offer. Given the *cost* of search, therefore, increasing the spread of the wage offer curve increases the net payoff to setting a higher acceptance wage. Finally, notice that Figure 12-9 is drawn to depict, as we expect, a higher average wage available to more experienced workers.

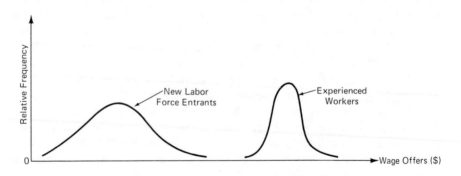

FIGURE 12-9. Relative frequency distribution of wage offers for new labor force entrants and experienced workers

These considerations suggest that although experienced workers will most likely have higher absolute acceptance wages, the acceptance wage for new entrants is closer to the maximum possible wage offer than in the case of experienced workers. These conclusions are depicted graphically in Figures 12-10 and 12-11.

Figure 12-10 shows us a higher acceptance wage for experienced workers, owing largely to the fact that the wages they can expect are noticeably higher than the wages new labor force entrants can expect. However, because of the relatively greater benefits of search for new labor force entrants due to the more diffused pattern of possible wage offers, the acceptance wage for new workers is *relatively* higher than that of experienced workers. Figure 12-11 illustrates this. The unshaded area to the right of $\tilde{w}$ for new workers, indicating the probability of an acceptable wage offer, is much smaller than the analogous area indicating the probability of an acceptable offer for experienced workers. Thus, although experienced workers can expect higher wages, new workers will be unemployed on average for longer periods. (Remember that the number of periods one can expect to be unemployed is the inverse of the probability of an acceptable wage offer.)

Our analysis of the job search process has suggested that anything that reduces the dispersion in wage rates expected by new workers will tend to lower the acceptance wage and in the process reduce the search time (unemployment rates) of new workers. Government programs that provide training for the least skilled teenagers is an example of public policy that can reduce the relatively high unemployment rates of teenagers. Can you name some others?

Can you suggest anything besides the *dispersion* of the wage offer curve that might lead to higher teenage unemployment? What about the opportunity cost of job search for teenagers—how does it compare to search benefits?

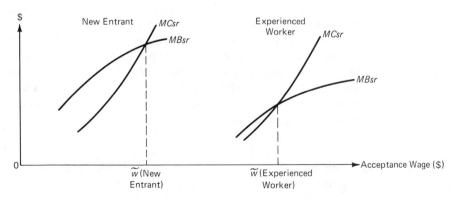

FIGURE 12-10. The wealth-maximizing acceptance wages of new and experienced workers

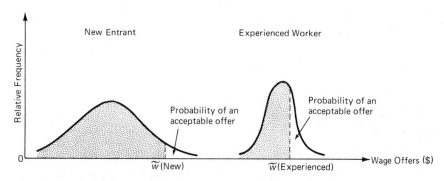

FIGURE 12-11. The probability of an acceptable wage offer for a new versus an experienced worker

Race differences in unemployment rates. We know that the unemployment rate for blacks, or any other demographic group for that matter, depends on both the proportion of the group experiencing unemployment during a year and the average duration of unemployment for those experiencing it. The almost double unemployment rate for blacks seems to be more the result of greater quits and layoffs for blacks than of a longer duration of unemployment. For example, in 1979, 23.2 percent of all unemployed workers were black. Among individuals unemployed 15 weeks or more in 1979, 27.1 percent were black; of those unemployed 27 weeks or more in 1979, 30.7 percent were black.[15] In his study of turnover in the United States labor force, Robert Hall finds that blacks have spells of unemployment that are about one-third to one-half longer than whites. These differences in duration of unemployment, however, are far less severe than the race differences in incidence of unemployment experience in a year; Hall finds that blacks experience approximately *twice* as many unemployment spells per year as whites. Thus, the key to understanding racial differences in unemployment rates in the United States seems to lie in understanding why blacks have a higher probability of being laid off from or quitting a job.

The theory of on-the-job training (OJT) developed in Chapter 9 showed us that workers with relatively large amounts of specific OJT are less likely to be laid off by their employers or to quit their jobs. Historically, blacks have, on average, fewer years of schooling than whites. To the extent that individuals with more general training (education) will receive greater benefits from specific OJT, employers will provide blacks with proportionately fewer opportunities for specific OJT. Moreover, should employers discriminate against blacks or feel that blacks have systematically higher probabilities of quitting their jobs in the future, these are additional reasons why relatively few opportunities for firm-specific training may be offered to

---

[15] *Employment and Training Report of the President,* 1980, Table A-30.

blacks. In closing, it should be noted that the unemployment rates in Table 12-5 indicate a reduction (although small) over time of race differences in adult unemployment rates for the United States. This is consistent with the relative increase over time in the quantity and quality of schooling for blacks and the secular reduction in racial discrimination noted in Chapter 10.

The impact of unemployment insurance on unemployment: Theory, evidence, and an appraisal.   Unemployment compensation benefits in the United States affect the economy's unemployment rate through two channels. First, payments to the unemployed raise the level of household expenditures that can be maintained when one or more family members are not working. These payments reduce the economic pressure to find work immediately, encouraging a longer period of job search during which the unemployed worker hopes to find a more attractive job than might otherwise be found. Such benefits may also reduce the intensity of search, encouraging those without work to use more of their time between jobs as "leisure" or to perform more household tasks (for example, home repairs and improvements) than would be the case without unemployment insurance payments. The impact of unemployment insurance on an individual's decision to search for or to accept a job is significantly magnified by the fact that unemployment benefits are not taxed as heavily as wage income and are not subject to the social security tax.[16]

Second, although unemployment insurance payments are financed through a system of taxes levied on firms' payrolls and adjusted upward for firms that contribute more to unemployment through relatively high layoffs, the method of "experience rating" is incomplete. Firms that have the highest frequency of layoffs are not taxed as much per additional dollar of unemployment insurance paid to their laid-off workers as firms with more stable employment. In this way, our present system of government unemployment insurance (UI) subsidizes layoffs. Thus, UI contributes to higher unemployment than would otherwise exist.

The avenues through which the unemployment insurance system raises the unemployment rate for the United States can be seen more clearly within the context of our analysis of job search developed earlier in this chapter. Consider first the impact of unemployment compensation on length of search by an unemployed worker. In analyzing the impact of unemployment insurance on a worker's decision to accept a job or continue searching, it is crucial to recognize that UI payments are primarily available to individuals who have had recent work experience. As we have seen in Table 12-6, two-thirds of unemployed teenagers in 1979 were entering the labor force—over half of them for the first time. Over 46 percent of unemployed females over

---

[16] Payments to unemployed workers by firms negotiated as part of a union contract, such as the Supplementary Unemployment Benefits (SUB) received by auto workers, *are* subject to such taxes, though.

19 in 1979 fell into this category, as did slightly over one-fifth of the men in this age group. Altogether, labor force entrance and reentrance was associated with approximately 43 percent of total unemployment in 1979.[17] The job search model clearly applies to the labor force entrants. However, because unemployment compensation is generally not available to them, it cannot affect their search behavior. Unemployment compensation is generally available to the remainder of unemployed workers who were laid off from or quit their previous jobs; an exception is that workers who were laid off for "misconduct" or who quit without "good cause" may be disqualified, depending upon state laws.

The degree to which unemployment compensation raises unemployment rates overall through increased length of search is limited by the proportion of the unemployed who qualify for benefits. Of course, not all those who qualify for benefits should be classified as *genuine* job seekers. Some who are laid off because of cyclical, seasonal, or other factors have such strong reason to believe they will be recalled soon that it does not pay them to search for a new job. In terms of our search model, the expected returns from any search fall short of the costs; such workers may even view time on layoff as a substitute for vacation time. The unemployment compensation system may, then, have a significant impact on the willingness of firms and workers to use temporary layoffs as a means of allocating time between work and nonwork activities of employees and in this way affect the unemployment rate. For now, though, we will concentrate on discussing the impact of unemployment compensation on the unemployment rate stemming from UI's affect on length of time spent searching for a job.[18] Later in this section we return to the issue of the way in which unemployment insurance influences the number of job searchers in the economy (quits and layoffs).

One of the most likely channels through which UI alters search behavior appears to be through lowering the cost of search. For purposes of our discussion, we will follow the most common assumption in empirical studies of search behavior and assume that the main cost of job search consists of foregoing the best alternative use of time while searching. Although it might be tempting to assume that the value of search time to a laid-off worker is zero, this is unlikely to be the case. The theory of labor supply implies that the market wage rate is the value of an additional hour of leisure for an employed worker. Moreover, it is reasonable to believe that many unemployed job searchers know of jobs and implicitly reject them because of unsatisfactory wages or working conditions. Such jobs set a floor on the opportunity cost of search time. In the absence of UI, a worker would

---

[17] *Employment and Training Report of the President,* 1980, Table A-27.
[18] Remember that individuals who are on layoff from their job may be classified as unemployed even though they are not actively seeking work. Moreover, a worker may satisfy the criterion of actively seeking work while engaging in only desultory search and establishing very stringent personal criteria for accepting a new job.

formulate a search strategy based on equating the marginal benefit and marginal cost and behave accordingly. *When UI is available, the attractiveness of longer search increases, because UI payments cease when a new job is begun. This lowers the implicit opportunity cost of remaining unemployed.*

The effect of UI benefits on the relative attractiveness of continued search depends upon the dollar amount of weekly benefits and the number of weeks an unemployed worker is eligible to receive them. Both weekly benefits and the period of eligibility vary according to state law, with weekly benefits generally depending on prior earnings of the unemployed worker and the period of eligibility normally equal to 26 weeks.[19] During periods of prolonged high unemployment, however, benefit periods are sometimes extended. There are also significant differences among states in the stringency with which eligibility criteria are applied and the requirements that the recipient be actively seeking and available for work enforced. These differences in enforcement criteria also influence the impact of UI on the unemployment rate, as we will see below.

How large are unemployment benefits relative to earnings for a typical worker? It would be too complicated to provide all the data necessary to answer this question in detail. However, it has been estimated that unemployment compensation replaces approximately 70 percent of lost after-tax earnings (unadjusted for fringe benefits) for male family heads with relatively low incomes, and 40 percent for those with higher earnings.[20] Martin Feldstein[21] provides an example for a worker in Massachusetts in 1975 whose before-tax earnings are $120 per week or $6,240 per year if he experiences no unemployment, and whose wife earns $80 per week or $4,160 per year for full-time work. They have two children. Suppose the husband is unemployed for ten weeks. After one week of waiting, he is eligible to receive a weekly benefit equal to one-half of his wage plus $6 weekly for each child. These nontaxable benefits amount of $648 after ten weeks of unemployment (9 × $72). At the same time, his after-tax wages (ignoring fringe benefits) fall by only $875, because had he been working he would have paid $194 in federal income tax, $71 in social security tax, and $60 in state tax. Thus, unemployment compensation in our example replaces 648/875 = 0.74 of his net wage loss. That is, the UI **replacement rate** is 74 percent. Moreover, part of this income difference is offset by reduced expenses of transportation to work.

More relevant for the search decision, though, is the marginal cost of an additional week of unemployment. This is quite low in the preceding example, primarily because the one-week waiting period before becoming eligible to receive benefits typically does not have to be repeated, regardless of the number of unemployment *periods* per year. In Feldstein's example, an

---

[19] See U.S. Department of Labor, *Comparison of State Unemployment Laws,* 1971.

[20] Council of Economic Advisors, *Economic Report of the President,* 1975.

[21] "The Unemployment Caused by Unemployment Insurance," *Proceedings of the Industrial Relations Research Association 28th Annual Winter Meetings,* 1975, pp. 225–33.

additional week of unemployment would cost $120 in gross earnings, but only $15.50 after being offset by tax reductions and UI benefits. Put differently, by accepting a job in the eleventh week that is identical to his former job, the husband would raise his family's net income by less than 40 cents per hour of work. It would not be surprising in view of these figures to learn that the frequency and length of unemployment periods are increased by UI availability.

Probably the most careful analysis of job search in general and of the impact of unemployment compensation payments on duration of unemployment in particular appears in a set of papers by Nicholas M. Kiefer and George R. Neumann. Their research permits a careful analysis of the behavioral implications of UI just developed: that by lowering the marginal cost of search, UI (1) increases an individual's reservation wage rate and (2) as a result leads to both a longer duration of search (unemployment) and higher wages upon reemployment. Through advanced statistical techniques we will not discuss here, Kiefer and Neumann avoid potential biases present in other work on job search that uses only data for completed spells of unemployment. Specifically, the econometric analysis they employ permits them to include even people who are still unemployed and thus have neither a postunemployment wage to report nor exact data on how long they will ultimately have been unemployed.

The analysis of Kiefer and Neumann utilizes a sample of *low-wage* United States workers who were displaced from their jobs by shifts in international trade patterns.[22] These workers were permanently separated from employment—in most cases because an entire plant shut down. One implication is that Kiefer and Neumann's sample consists entirely of job searchers who are not waiting to be recalled from *temporary* layoffs. Another important implication is that their empirical research concentrates on those types of workers likely to be the financially most severely affected by unemployment.

One of the more important hypotheses examined by Kiefer and Neumann in the course of their research is whether or not the acceptance wage rate remains constant during the course of search. Their findings indicate that it does not; for the sample in question the acceptance wage falls by about 1 percent for each month unemployed. This means that the likelihood of leaving unemployment rises with duration of unemployment; the probability that a worker will find an acceptable job during any given week of search is greater, the greater the number of weeks the worker has already searched for a job. (What are some possible reasons why the acceptance wage rate

---

[22] These data were gathered by the Institute for Research on Human Resources of Pennsylvania State University. A complete description of these data is contained in George R. Neumann, "The Labor Market Adjustments of Trade Displaced Workers: The Evidence from the Trade Adjustment Assistance Program," in Ronald Ehrenberg, ed., *Research in Labor Economics*, Vol. 2 (Greenwich, Conn.: JAI Press, 1978), pp. 353–81.

might change in the course of job search?) Interestingly, Kiefer and Neumann find only a small impact of the magnitude of UI benefits on the duration of job search. For example, they find that raising the average replacement rate of UI by about 8 percentage points (from 42.1 percent to 50.5 percent) leads to an increase in unemployment by about one-half week for the workers in their sample. Although this additional waiting does result in better job offers on average, as you might expect, the rather small increase in duration of unemployment due to a change in UI leads to only a small (0.5 percent) increase in reemployment earnings. This is not sufficient to offset the overall decline in real earnings experienced by the average unemployed worker. The average worker in the sample who had ended his search experienced a decline in real weekly earnings of 26.7 percent from his preunemployment wage and spent 39.1 weeks unemployed.[23]

Another way in which unemployment insurance can increase the economy's rate of unemployment is by increasing the proportion of the population who are searching because they have been laid off from their jobs. This second avenue through which UI may raise unemployment rates comes about because firms with a high frequency of layoffs typically do not pay an unemployment insurance payroll tax sufficient to cover the payments received by their laid-off workers. Consequently, the UI system tends to subsidize the use of temporary layoffs rather than other devices by means of which firms might allocate labor between times of high and low production.[24] Put differently, from *firms'* point of view, UI can provide an extremely low-cost way to compensate workers who are laid off, thus reducing firms' incentives to smooth out employment fluctuations as an alternative to layoffs.

The effect of UI on wage rates and employment in industries prone to fluctuating labor demand is depicted in Figure 12-12, where D represents firms' demand for labor during periods of peak demand and S represents the supply curve of labor to firms when there is no UI subsidy to layoffs. In an extreme situation, where there is *no* cost to firms of UI benefits, introduction of UI has no effect on the *demand* for labor, because UI does nothing to change the cost of employing workers. The *supply* curve of labor is shifted to the right, however. Some workers are willing to accept lower wages, given the probability of layoff, because they are assured of UI benefits whenever

---

[23] Because our topic here is the impact of UI on duration of unemployment, we will not discuss the other results presented by Kiefer and Neumann. We encourage those of you with a strong background in mathematical statistics to examine them for yourselves, as they provide many interesting conclusions concerning the economic factors influencing the wages available to job searchers as well as the factors influencing job searchers' reservation wage rates.

[24] For a detailed theoretical study of the influence of UI taxes on layoffs, see Frank Brechling, "The Incentive Effects of the U.S. Unemployment Insurance Tax," in Ronald G. Ehrenberg, ed., *Research in Labor Economics* (Greenwich, Conn.: JAI Press, 1977), pp. 41–102, and "Unemployment Insurance Taxes and Labor Turnover: Summary of Theoretical Findings," *Industrial Labor Relations Review*, 30 (July 1977), pp. 483–92.

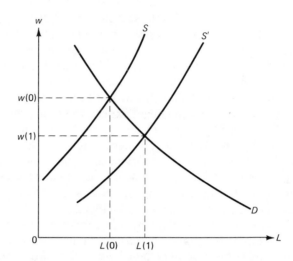

FIGURE 12-12. Effect of subsidized UI on wage rates and employment in industries with fluctuating employment

they become unemployed.[25] Put differently, competition for jobs by workers will lower the equilibrium wage rate and increase employment during periods of peak labor demand, because part of the total payments to workers (those which used to be paid by firms as extra wages to accept the risk of unemployment) are now provided through UI. Because lower wages mean lower production costs, the output of goods in industries characterized by volatile employment is increased relative to what it would be in the absence of subsidized UI.

Moreover, because the gains to workers from steady employment have been reduced, firms have less incentive to reduce employment fluctuations through such means as adding to their product line goods and services with offsetting seasonal or cyclical demand fluctuations. These changed incentives tend to increase the number of workers who are laid off during periods of low demand. Because such layoffs will typically be perceived by both workers and employers as temporary, these employees probably have little to gain by seeking new jobs, although they may give the appearance of doing so to satisfy UI eligibility requirements. The important point is that they would be counted as unemployed for census purposes even without active search, because they would be classified as on temporary layoff.

---

[25] The positive impact of UI on labor supply due to the fact that by working today, individuals become eligible for unemployment compensation benefits in the future, has been termed the "entitlement effect." For evidence of its magnitude, see two articles by Daniel S. Hamermesh, "Entitlement Effects, Unemployment Insurance, and Employment Decisions," *Economic Inquiry,* 17:3 (July 1979), pp. 317–32; and "Unemployment Insurance and Labor Supply," *International Economic Review,* 21:3 (October 1980), pp. 517–27.

We have just seen that because not all firms are fully taxed for the unemployment insurance recipients they produce, UI tends to increase the number of worker layoffs in the United States and, therefore, the unemployment rate. The exact quantitative impact of UI on the unemployment rate through this channel is not known. We do know that a substantial number— probably over half—of firms do not increase the UI payroll taxes they pay by increasing the number of workers they lay off.[26] Moreover, a study by Barry Chiswick of the effect of Special Unemployment Assistance (SUA) in agriculture during 1975 provides evidence of a significant impact of unemployment insurance on unemployment (and employment) in that industry.

Chiswick's study explored the effect of SUA on agricultural employment and unemployment using the simple analytical framework summarized in Figure 12-12. Agricultural wage and salary workers are typically not covered by UI legislation and, therefore, do not receive UI benefits. The logic behind this is that, because of the pronounced seasonal nature of agricultural production, agricultural unemployment is highly predictable. However, the Emergency Jobs and Unemployment Assistance Act, which was signed into law on December 31, 1974, provided such coverage. This legislation provided for complete federal funding; there was no direct cost to the firms involved. More than any previous UI legislation, then, SUA subsidized firms' use of temporary layoffs as part of their overall employment strategy.

In particular, Chiswick hypothesized that SUA would result in an increase in the agricultural labor force, with a concomitant increase in on-season employment and off-season unemployment. To test these hypotheses Chiswick first set up *prediction equations* in which quarterly agricultural unemployment rates and employment for a period preceding the SUA legislation, 1948 through 1974 (unemployment) and 1950 through 1974 (employment), were each expressed as a function of a set of exogenous variables. The exogenous variables in his agricultural unemployment equation are the unemployment rate of males aged 20 and over, the unemployment rate of all males aged 16–19, and time-trend variables; the exogenous variables in his agricultural employment equation are an index of prices received by farmers, the wholesale price index for all industrial commodities, the unemployment rate of all males 16–19, and time-trend variables. These two equations were estimated by regression analysis, and the resulting regression coefficients then used to predict what the unemployment rate and employment in agriculture *would have been* during the nine months following the date of the passage of the SUA legislation had the legislation *not* been put into effect. Deviations of the actual values of employment and the unemployment rate in agriculture from their predicted values are taken as measures of the influence of SUA on employment and the unemployment rate in agriculture, respectively.

---

[26] See Joseph Becker, *Experience Rating in Unemployment Insurance* (Baltimore: Johns Hopkins University Press, 1972).

Chiswick's test covers both the first on-season and the first off-season following the SUA legislation. Specifically, data for 1975 provide the test of the labor market impact of this program. The data indicate that on-season employment was about 2 percent higher than it would have been in the absence of SUA, while off-season unemployment was increased by approximately 1.6 percentage points or about one-sixth of its expected value in the absence of SUA.[27]

It seems proper to end our discussion of the effect of UI on employment in the United States with a "score card." The economic analysis and evidence presented in this section suggests that overall unemployment is increased by current unemployment insurance programs. The magnitude of the impact is much less certain than the direction, however. Feldstein "guesstimates" that the normal unemployment rate in the United States may be 1.25 percentage points higher than it would be in the absence of UI.[28] Hamermesh disagrees with this figure and offers his own "guesstimate" of 0.7 percentage points.[29] If we round off both of their "guesstimates," we may conclude that the normal unemployment rate in the United States is increased by about 1 percentage point due to UI. Does this mean that UI causes "too much" unemployment?

We have just presented evidence that UI raises the supply of workers to jobs with a high risk of layoff, in the process raising the size of the high-unemployment sector of the economy. In this way, UI probably causes a socially undesirable increase in unemployment. It is more difficult to evaluate the impact of UI on unemployment attributable to the increase in the length of time taken by genuine job searchers to look for new jobs. From the perspective of human capital theory, UI may enable those individuals who face difficulties in financing human capital investment to invest search up to a point more closely approximating the social optimum—that is, to invest up to the point where the social cost of the last week spent searching equals the gain in expected labor market productivity that results from a better allocation of labor. Indeed, if this latter effect were sufficiently great, the economy's unemployment rate might in the long term be *reduced* as a result of a better matching of workers and jobs. To the extent that UI subsidizes unproductive search or leisure, though, the unemployment rate is raised undesirably.

In conclusion, unintended effects of UI legislation have emerged because, as with other government programs initially intended to alleviate

[27] "The Effect of Unemployment Compensation on a Seasonal Industry: Agriculture," *Journal of Political Economy*, 84 (June 1976), 591–602.

[28] "The Unemployment Caused by Unemployment Insurance," p. 232.

[29] Daniel S. Hamermesh, "Transfers, Taxes, and the NAIRU," in *The Supply-Side Effects of Economic Policy*, Proceedings of the 1980 Economic Policy Conference (St. Louis: The Center for the Study of American Business, Washington University in St. Louis and the Federal Reserve Bank of St. Louis, 1981).

economic hardship, the receipt of UI payments depends not upon being poor but rather upon being "unemployed." Whether the socially undesirable properties of UI outweigh the benefits of supporting those who suffer from genuinely low incomes because of unemployment or whether an alternative program would be able to furnish income maintenance as rapidly and as efficiently to intended recipients is unclear.[30] A number of interesting refinements or alternatives to UI have been suggested. Steven Shavell and Lawrence Weiss examine theoretically the socially optimal payment stream of UI benefits over the course of an individual's unemployment experience. They find that in certain (not unreasonable) circumstances it would be cheaper for society and perhaps also better for unemployed workers if UC benefits *declined* with duration of unemployment as opposed to the current scheme of a waiting period followed by a constant stream of UI benefits to the unemployed. Kiefer and Neumann use their empirical results to simulate the impact on unemployed job search of a subsidy program to employers that raises the average wage. They find that, although the increase in the average wage leads to an increase in the acceptance wage, the increase in the acceptance wage is somewhat smaller. Thus, the impact of a wage subsidy program would be to *reduce* duration of unemployment in contrast to their findings concerning UI. Moreover, in contrast to UI, a direct wage subsidy would seem to impact *noticeably* on the job search process. Their results imply that a 20 percent wage subsidy should *increase* reemployment earnings by about 19 percent and *reduce* duration of unemployment by from one to six weeks.

The equilibrium wage distribution. The search view of unemployment implies that the acquisition of information by workers and employers should narrow the dispersion of rates of pay for workers of given quality. One implication is that as means of communication have improved, reducing search costs in the United States, the variation of wages among regions of the United States should have declined over time. In his classic article, "Information in the Labor Market," George Stigler found that between 1904–1909 and 1947–1954 the coefficient of variation[31] of earnings in selected

---

[30] For elaboration on this point see George A. Akerloff, "The Economics of 'Tagging' as Applied to the Optimal Income Tax, Welfare Programs, and Manpower Planning," *American Economic Review,* 68:1 (March 1978), 8–19.

[31] The **coefficient of variation** of a set of numbers is the standard deviation of those numbers divided by their mean (average) value. The **standard deviation** of a set of numbers is a measure of their dispersion. Let X_i, $i = 1, \ldots, n$, represent one of a set of numbers. The standard deviation is defined as

$$\sigma \equiv \left[\sum_{i=1}^{n} \frac{(X_i - \bar{X})^2}{n} \right]^{1/2}$$

where $\bar{X}$ is the arithmetic mean of the set of n numbers. The coefficient of variation, then, is $\sigma/\bar{X}$. Thus, the standard deviation of the set of numbers 1, 2, 3, 4, 5 is $[(4 + 1 + 1 + 4)/5]^{1/2}$, which equals $(2)^{1/2} = 1.414$. The coefficient of variation, then, would be $1.414/3 = 0.47$.

manufacturing industries among a set of identical states declined by about one-third. These findings are consistent with the notion that it is necessary to understand search theory and the acquisition of information if we are to understand the distribution of market prices, including wage rates.

One of the ultimate goals of search theorists is to be able to say something about how the final form of wage offers for identical jobs differs from the distribution of wage offers that would exist if no search took place. Such an analysis requires a detailed depiction of search on both sides of the market—employer as well as employee search. In this section we have largely ignored employer search, although the basic decision rules and goals are basically identical to those that guide search by employees. Specifically, employers set reservation characteristics for their workers such that the marginal cost of continued search equals the marginal benefit to employers of continued search. When both employer and employee search are considered in conjunction, it seems reasonable that wages, when corrected for differences in nonpecuniary aspects of employment, should be brought to equality for similar jobs for similar workers.

Although the data are consistent with a narrowing over time in wage rates, it is unlikely that anyone examining current wage rate data for the United States would be led to conclude that search has, indeed, produced wage equality. This has led search theorists to some elaborate theoretical examinations of the so-called equilibrium wage distribution after search. In the process, they have considered numerous reasons why search would not lead to a unique wage rate for identical workers. Included in their list of possibilities are that: (1) searchers do not know as much about the distribution of potential offers at the beginning of the search process as we have been assuming; (2) the distribution of wage offers fluctuates more quickly than searchers learn about their alternatives; (3) search in *more than one* labor market is required for employers and employees to match up. In the last case, the requirement that one determine not only how many labor markets to search in, but also how much to search in any one market, is sufficient to generate the inequality of wage offers we know exists in reality even after search takes place.[32]

Concluding remarks.   In this section we have attempted to gain some special insights into the job search process and, in the course of our discussions, increase our understanding of a number of important topics. In particular, we sought to see how knowledge of the way the marginal cost and marginal benefit of search determine an acceptance wage rate provides us with important information concerning demographic differences in unemployment rates. Knowledge of the economist's analysis of the job search

---

[32] Readers interested in more of the *technical* details of equilibrium wage distributions should consult Lippman and McCall, "The Economics of Job Search," pp. 185–87.

process also enabled us to link unemployment insurance to the magnitude of unemployment in the United States. We also saw that job search was expected to lead to a reduction in the dispersion of wages for workers of a given type. All the examples of this section have been microeconomic in nature, dealing with subsets of individuals within United States society. In the next section we use our knowledge of the search process to disentangle quantitatively the contributions of frictional, structural, and cyclical unemployment to the total unemployment rate in the United States.

FRONTIERS OF LABOR ECONOMICS (1): DISTINGUISHING AMONG FRICTIONAL, STRUCTURAL, AND CYCLICAL UNEMPLOYMENT

There is no obvious way to discern from the answers provided to current labor force surveys whether unemployed workers owe their circumstances to frictional, structural, or cyclical causes. Not only is the required information difficult to obtain, but also the ways in which labor market frictions and structural changes affect unemployment are interrelated and depend on the state of the entire economy (the business cycle) as well.

For example, a young person entering the labor market will face different job prospects and search costs during a period characterized by depressed demand as opposed to a period of labor market "boom." A downturn in economic activity will affect the costs and returns of search for experienced workers differently than those for inexperienced members of the labor force. During an especially prosperous time, an experienced worker who would like to change jobs may decide that the probability of regaining his or her old job is fairly high even if a period of job search proves unrewarding. The *frictional* unemployment of mature workers might therefore rise when labor market conditions are improving. On the other hand, during an economic upswing a new labor force entrant might find the job offers available without search so attractive that frictional unemployment among younger workers could decline. Moreover, structural unemployment and frictional unemployment become progressively more difficult to distinguish from one another as we take a more aggregated view of the labor market. In the aggregate economy, changes in the structure of labor markets are part of the ongoing process determining normal unemployment.

It is probably impossible to separate unemployment due to labor market frictions from cyclical and structural forces in such a way that they add up to total unemployment. Too many important interrelationships are involved. Nevertheless, it is important from the viewpoint of policymakers to know, to the extent possible, whether a *change* in unemployment experienced by the economy's labor force is attributable to cyclical forces as opposed to changes in labor market frictions or structure, because the appropriate policy actions differ. Cyclical unemployment may be offset by macro monetary and fiscal policies, while changing structural and frictional unemployment may be offset by altering the flow of information, workers, and firms within and among labor markets. Much important information for the purposes of formulating sound economic policy can be obtained if we are able to determine empirically to what extent changes in the unemployment rate are attributable to changes in *normal* unemployment compared to *cyclical* unemployment. As we have said, increases in *normal* unemployment may respond to appropriate policies aimed at information and worker flows. Moreover, policymakers are constantly searching for a value of the unemployment rate to serve as a trigger for initiating antirecessionary monetary and fiscal policies. In the next section we present data on the historical trend of the normal unemployment rate in the United States and compare it to the total unemployment rate.

The Historical Trend of the Normal Unemployment Rate in the United States

We know that normal unemployment stems from job search activity necessarily arising in a labor force with a changing demographic, industrial, and occupational structure. But how do we actually go about estimating the normal unemployment rate? Economists have utilized a number of different techniques to calculate the normal unemployment rate for the United States.

Probably the simplest way to calculate the normal unemployment rate is to designate years in which we believe the economy is operating with near-zero cyclical unemployment. In these years the total unemployment rate is an estimate of the normal unemployment rate. Because the normal unemployment rate reflects forces that tend to change rather slowly over time, one can then interpolate between the years for which we have estimated values of the normal unemployment rate. For example, if one has two figures for the normal unemployment rate that are ten years apart and that differ by one percentage point, one could simply assume that the normal unemployment rate changed by 0.1 points per year. This is known as linear interpolation. The normal unemployment rates for 1900–55 presented in the third column of Table 12-6 have been constructed by Robert Gordon primarily by interpolation of the type we have just discussed.[33] Gordon's normal unemployment rate data for 1900–55 are important because we know of no other data that cover the first half of the twentieth century. We urge you to look carefully at these data in Table 12-6. In which years was the economy operating with little or no cyclical unemployment? How severe was cyclical unemployment during the Great Depression?

Finally, when comparing the total unemployment rate series for 1900–55 with Gordon's normal unemployment rate series, you will notice that in some years the total unemployment rate is *less than* the normal unemployment rate. Should this be surprising? Think about some reasons why it might be "reasonable." In the next section we offer a careful explanation as to why and how the macroeconomy may produce a total unemployment rate that is lower than its normal unemployment rate.

Because the unemployment arising from labor force entry and job search varies among demographic groups, changes in the relative size of these groups in the population will influence the normal unemployment rate for the economy as a whole. A second way of calculating the normal unemployment rate is to take account statistically of the way in which unemployment varies as the demographic composition of the United States varies over time. This is the technique Michael Wachter uses to calculate his normal unemployment rate series presented in Table 12-6. This technique is probably preferable to the simple interpolation technique Gordon uses for 1900–55, because Wachter attempts to formally capture the role played by the demo-

---

[33] *Macroeconomics,* 2d ed. (Boston: Little, Brown & Company, 1981), Appendixes B and C. In particular, Gordon assumes that the economy was operating with little frictional unemployment in the mid to late 1950s, such that the normal unemployment rate in 1955 was approximately 5 percent. He uses this figure, along with data for total unemployment rates that have been adjusted for the proportion of the labor force that is self-employed, to calculate normal unemployment rates for 1902, 1907, 1913, 1929, and 1950. Linear interpolation is then utilized to produce a *complete* series of normal unemployment rates for 1900–55 from the values for the six years just mentioned. For more details see Gordon's Appendix C.

graphic composition of the labor force. Wachter's unemployment series reflects the substantial influence on normal unemployment that resulted from the increased proportion of young workers in the labor force after the late 1960s. It also reflects the smaller effect of the rising labor force participation of married women. Unfortunately, the requisite data are not available to calculate the normal unemployment rate with Wachter's method for 1900–47.

The differences between the total and normal unemployment rates provide us with an indication of cyclical unemployment in recent years. This is important; it illuminates, for example, proposals hotly debated during the 1970s concerning the use of macroeconomic policy, including the designation of the federal government as "employer of last resort," to force the unemployment rate down to a level of 4 percent, a national economic goal established in the "Full Employment and Balanced Growth Act of 1977," the so-called Humphrey-Hawkins Act. The values of normal unemployment in Table 12-6 clearly indicate that such a target for the total unemployment rate would be *extremely low* in view of the normal (job search) behavior of the labor force and its demographic (age) distribution.

Having seen that the data seem to indicate an increase in recent years in the normal unemployment rate in the United States, let us examine what economists know about the forces responsible for this trend.

Factors Underlying the Recent Trend of the Normal Unemployment Rate

The factors underlying the fairly substantial increase in the normal unemployment rate since the Korean War are numerous and complex. The secular change in the age-sex composition of the labor force is only one factor at work. Herbert Stein, a former chairman of the President's Council of Economic Advisors, has speculated that several additional changes in the economy are potentially important: (1) increases in the marginal tax rate faced by the average worker; (2) increases in the proportion of the labor force covered by the minimum wage; (3) growth in the level and availability of welfare benefits and unemployment compensation; (4) new requirements that welfare recipients register for work; and (5) increases in general affluence. Very little "hard" evidence is available concerning the influence of these factors. In a recent article, Hamermesh discusses how our knowledge of the labor market effects of taxes and transfer programs provides important insights into the impact of Stein's factors (1), (3), and (4). Let us summarize briefly his conclusions.

Hamermesh notes a tendency by economists, when evaluating the impact of a social program or tax, to conclude that the particular program or tax in question increased the normal unemployment rate by 1 percentage point. Table 12.6 suggests that the normal unemployment rate has increased by about 1.5 to 2 percentage points since 1955, the same period in which most of the tax and transfer programs analyzed became economically important. There are at least eight important tax and transfer programs in the United States.[34] If each added 1 percentage point to normal unemployment, the normal unemployment rate should have grown by at least 8 percentage points since 1955, even ignoring the other factors noted by Stein. As a result, Hamermesh feels that the major tax and transfer programs have to be analyzed somewhat more carefully.

Of the eight major transfer and tax programs in the United States, UI most

---

[34] These include old age and survivors' insurance, unemployment insurance, workers' compensation, general assistance (AFDC), food stamps, disability insurance (under OASDHI), supplemental security income, and the personal income tax.

TABLE 12-6 Total and Normal Unemployment Rates for the United States, 1900–1982, and Projections to 1990

Year	Total Unemployment Rate[a]	Normal Unemployment Rate — Gordon Series[b]	Normal Unemployment Rate — Wachter Series	Year	Total Unemployment Rate	Normal Unemployment Rate — Gordon Series	Normal Unemployment Rate — Wachter Series	Year	Total Unemployment Rate	Normal Unemployment Rate — Gordon Series	Normal Unemployment Rate — Wachter Series
1900	5.0%	3.4%		1928	4.2%	3.7%		1956	4.1%	4.3%	3.9%
1901	4.0	3.4		1929	3.2	3.7		1957	4.3	4.3	3.9
1902	3.7	3.4		1930	8.9	3.7		1958	6.8	4.3	3.9
1903	3.9	3.4		1931	16.3	3.7		1959	5.5	4.3	4.1
1904	5.4	3.4		1932	24.1	3.8		1960	5.5	4.4	4.2
1905	4.3	3.5		1933	25.2	3.8		1961	6.7	4.4	4.2
1906	1.7	3.5		1934	22.0	3.8		1962	5.5	4.4	4.2
1907	2.8	3.5		1935	20.3	3.8		1963	5.7	4.5	4.4
1908	8.0	3.5		1936	17.0	3.8		1964	5.2	4.6	4.6
1909	5.1	3.5		1937	14.3	3.9		1965	4.5	4.7	4.8
1910	5.9	3.5		1938	19.1	3.9		1966	3.8	4.8	4.9
1911	6.7	3.5		1939	17.2	3.9		1967	3.8	4.9	5.0
1912	4.6	3.5		1940	14.6	3.9		1968	3.6	4.9	5.0
1913	4.3	3.5		1941	9.9	3.9		1969	3.5	5.0	5.2
1914	7.9	3.5		1942	4.7	3.9		1970	4.9	5.1	5.3
1915	8.5	3.5		1943	1.9	4.0		1971	5.9	5.2	5.5
1916	5.1	3.5		1944	1.2	4.0		1972	5.6	5.3	5.7
1917	4.6	3.5		1945	1.9	4.0		1973	4.9	5.4	5.8

Year				Year				Year			
1918	1.4	3.6		1946	3.9	4.0		1974	5.6	5.4	5.8
1919	1.4	3.6		1947	3.9	4.0		1975	8.5	5.4	5.8
1920	5.2	3.6		1948	3.8	4.1	4.6%	1976	7.7	5.5	5.9
1921	11.7	3.6		1949	5.9	4.1	4.5	1977	7.0	5.5	5.9
1922	6.7	3.6		1950	5.3	4.1	4.4	1978	6.0	5.5	5.9
1923	2.4	3.6		1951	3.3	4.1	4.1	1979	5.8	5.6	5.8
1924	5.0	3.6		1952	3.0	4.2	4.0	1980	7.1	—	5.7
1925	3.2	3.6		1953	2.9	4.2	3.8	1981	7.6	—	—
1926	1.8	3.7		1954	5.5	4.2	3.8	1982	9.5	—	5.6
1927	3.3	3.7		1955	4.4	4.3	3.8	1983			5.3
								1984			5.1
								1985			5.0
								1986			4.8
								1987			4.6
								1988			4.5
								1989			4.4
								1990			

[a] Sources for the total unemployment rate are (1) 1900–39: Long-Term Economic Growth, 1860–1970 (Washington, D.C.: U.S. Department of Commerce, 1973), Series B1; (2) 1940–70: ibid., Series B2; (3) 1971–81: Statistical Abstract of the United States, 1982 (Washington, D.C.: U.S. Department of Commerce, 1983), p. 375. 1982 unemployment is for June.
[b] Robert J. Gordon, Macroeconomics, 2d ed. (Boston: Little, Brown & Company, 1981), Appendix B.
[c] Michael L. Wachter, "The Changing Cyclical Responsiveness of Wage Inflation Over the Postwar Period," and personal communication.

clearly increases the normal unemployment rate, by 0.7 to 1.2 percentage points, as we have already shown (see pp. 497–505). In an interesting discussion of the impact of the other (six) transfer programs and the personal income tax, Hamermesh concludes that *together* they have *reduced* the normal unemployment rate by about 1 percentage point. In particular, he feels that social security has probably reduced the normal unemployment rate by causing the least productive–highest unemployed groups to leave the labor force. This is also likely to be true for Special Disability Benefits, as we saw in Chapter 4. In addition, Hamermesh notes that the primary effect of requiring food stamp recipients to register for jobs at state employment agencies has been a "one-shot" increase in unemployment but little contribution to the *growth* of normal unemployment reported in Table 12-6. If anything, the worker disincentive effects of food stamps have, as disability benefits, moved the least productive–most likely to be unemployed workers out of the labor force *entirely*, thus reducing the normal unemployment rate. The impact of welfare (AFDC) on the normal unemployment rate should be similar.

Finally, Hamermesh feels that the progressive income tax probably reinforces the negative effects on the normal unemployment rate noted above by also changing the composition of the labor force. Although its impact on the labor supply of high-wage workers is likely to have been a reduction in their hours of work, they have probably not been induced to withdraw from the labor force to any great extent. The largest labor supply impact of the personal income tax has probably been on secondary workers, who have relatively low wages but the marginal tax rate of the high-wage primary worker owing to the progressivity in the income tax. So, one of the labor market impacts of the personal tax on earned income has probably been to discourage labor force participation entirely by those workers who suffer the highest unemployment rates. In this way the personal income tax in the United States also probably contributes to a reduced normal unemployment rate.

If we accept Hamermesh's interpretation of economists' empirical knowledge concerning the labor market impact of the seven main transfer programs and the personal income tax in the United States, we are led to conclude that *as a group* they have had basically no effect on the normal unemployment rate. Which of the remaining possible factors cited by Stein, then, have been responsible for the portion of the secular increase in the normal unemployment rate as yet unexplained? Put differently, which of the other factors have added to the increase in normal unemployment due to the change in the age-sex composition of the labor force?

There is no real way to evaluate the empirical importance of Stein's factor (5), increases in general affluence. If our interpretation of job search as human capital investment is correct, then wealth increases should increase investments in human capital of all sorts, on average, including job search (unemployment). Because economists have only recently begun to analyze job search empirically, there is no time-series evidence that we can cite concerning the secular trend in job search in the United States. This leaves us with Stein's factor (2), the increase in the proportion of the labor force covered by the minimum wage laws, a factor emphasized by Gordon.[35] Overall, however, evidence of the impact of minimum wages on unemployment is mixed, and we cannot conclude that minimum wages have increased unemployment rates on balance. (This is not to say that minimum wage rates have not reduced employment).[36]

To summarize, estimates of the normal unemployment rate in the United States seem to indicate an increase of about 1.3 to 2 percentage points since 1955.

---

[35] Robert J. Gordon, "Structural Unemployment," pp. 206–10.
[36] For an extensive survey, see Belton M. Fleisher, *Minimum Wage Regulation in the United States* (Washington: National Chamber Foundation, 1983).

Although the analysis we have presented is more casual than we would like, there seems to be reasonable agreement among economists that the primary force at work is the change in the demographic structure of the United States labor force over time. Second, although it is common to cite the growth of the personal income tax, minimum wages, and transfer programs as also contributing to normal unemployment rate growth, *when taken as a group*, these programs have probably had little effect on the normal unemployment rate in recent years. Although UI has probably increased the normal unemployment rate by about 1 percentage point, this has probably been offset by the other social programs we have mentioned that work to reduce unemployment. Of course, this is not to say that adjustments in the properties any individual program would leave the normal unemployment rate unchanged, but rather to point out that the *net* effect of the currently existing *package* of programs probably is small. What is probably most interesting about all of this is that so much of the increase in the normal unemployment rate has been due to a factor generally outside the control of government economic policy in the United States—the change in the age-sex composition of the labor force.

International differences in unemployment.   A topic of considerable interest that may be analyzed with the framework we have used for evaluating frictional, structural, and cyclical unemployment is international differences in unemployment rates. Some economies have unemployment rates that have traditionally been lower than those in the United States, while others experience unemployment about equal to ours. The U.S. Department of Labor occasionally publishes international comparisons of unemployment rates adjusted to be comparable in definition with those in our country. See, for example, the article by Joanna Moy listed at the end of this chapter. In the years 1976–78, Japan, France, Italy, and Sweden had unemployment considerably lower than in the United States, while unemployment in Australia, Canada, and Great Britain approached or exceeded the levels experienced in this country.

FRONTIERS OF LABOR ECONOMICS (2): UNEMPLOYMENT, MONEY WAGES, AND INFLATION

We propose now to connect the theories of job search and the firm's wage-employment strategy with the behavior of the general level of money wages and prices. Thus, we focus on the relationship between unemployment and inflation.

Up to this point we have considered only the determinants of real and relative wage rates. But important questions of economic policy also deal with the rate at which money wages and prices are growing and how these growth rates are related to the level of unemployment. The average growth rate of prices is, of course, the rate of inflation in the economy. This is closely connected with the rate of growth of the general level of wages both through firms' profit-maximizing behavior and through workers' attempts to achieve the highest real wages obtainable subject to the constraint of the demand for labor.

Search Behavior and Inflation

One important means by which inflationary pressures are transmitted to changes in labor market variables is through job search behavior. We now use the theory of search to show how inflation and search unemployment are intertwined. Figure 12-13 depicts the relative frequency distribution of expected money wage

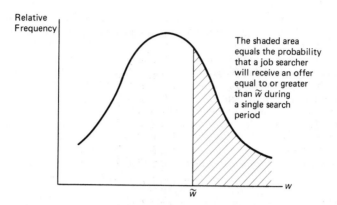

FIGURE 12-13. The distribution of expected wage offers
and the acceptance wage

offers for a typical job searcher during a period of general wage and price stability. Since the price level of goods and services is assumed constant, Figure 12-13 also represents the distribution of *real* wage rates. This is so, because we can derive the real wage rate from the money wage W simply by dividing by the Consumer Price Index, P.

Suppose now that expansionary monetary policy generates inflationary pressure in the economy, and the rates of change of both money wages and prices increase by the same amount. In a world of perfect knowledge about the future, a typical job searcher would have no difficulty forecasting the change in the real wage rates that would be offered: it would be zero, the increase in prices offsetting the increase in money wage rates. A searcher would know that the whole relative frequency curve was about to shift to the right and would adjust search strategy accordingly by adopting a new, proportionately higher acceptance wage rate.

In a world of scarce information, however, searchers will not be able to forecast the future with perfect accuracy. Thus, there may be *unanticipated* inflation. When inflation is not fully anticipated, the distribution of wage offers will shift to the right before individual searchers recognize there has been a change in the rate at which wages and prices are rising. Job searchers will be temporarily deceived into thinking real wage offers have improved, and they may accept jobs that they would have rejected if they had correctly anticipated the rate of inflation.

The effect of unanticipated inflation on search behavior is depicted in Figure 12-14. The unforeseen increase in the rate of inflation has caused the true distribution of money wage offers to shift to the right, as indicated by the broken line. Because job seekers continue to formulate their search strategy on the assumption that the solid line is the true distribution, the acceptance wage remains unchanged at $\tilde{w}$. It is easy to see in Figure 12-14 that this ignorance results in a greater proportion of job offers exceeding $\tilde{w}$. The duration of unemployment for the typical job seeker will decline, since the area to the right of w on the new relative frequency distribution is greater than on the old one.

As workers and job seekers gradually perceive that the rate of inflation has increased, they will adapt their labor market behavior accordingly. To continue our example, suppose that the rightward shift in Figure 12-14 is due to an increase in the rate of inflation from zero to 10 percent per year. That is, in one year, the relative

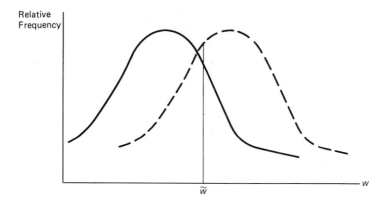

FIGURE 12-14. When there is unanticipated inflation, the perceived wage offer distribution lies to the left of the true distribution

frequency distribution moves 10 percent to the right and *continues to do so each year thereafter*. Wage rates and prices continue to rise 10 percent. By observing the rate at which wage offers (one's own and those of other workers) are rising and noticing that prices are now rising as well, job searchers gradually become aware that $\tilde{w}$ is no longer the wealth-maximizing acceptance wage. It, too, has shifted to the right. With no other change in the economy besides the increase in the rate of inflation from zero to 10 percent *annually,* the acceptance wage will also rise by 10 percent per year when searchers have learned of the new rate of inflation. Although the acceptance wage rises 10 percent in *nominal,* or dollar, terms, it does not change in *real* terms, since the numerator and denominator of W/P both rise by the same proportion. Thus, the acceptance wage will ultimately assume the relationship to the actual distribution of wage offers that it held when the rate of inflation was zero.

Figure 12-15 depicts the 10 percent rightward shift of the acceptance wage that eventually follows the increase in the rate of inflation from zero to 10 percent. As you can see, the area to the right of $\tilde{w}'$, under the broken curve, is the same as the area to the right of $\tilde{w}$ under the solid curve. Once searchers have learned that the rate of inflation is now 10 percent, the expected duration of unemployment for the typical worker returns to the level that existed when the rate of inflation was zero. The amount of search unemployment in the economy, which fell when the rate of inflation initially shifted upward, rises once workers adapt to the new rate.

Job searchers' lagging perception of the true rate of inflation generates the relationship between search unemployment and the *percentage rate of change of money wage rates* ($\dot{W}/W$) shown in Figure 12-16. When the rate of inflation was zero, the amount of search unemployment in the economy was represented by the "normal" unemployment rate u^* (point A). During the period before the labor market adapted to the new 10 percent rate of inflation per year, the amount of unemployment declined, so that the unemployment rate fell to a lower level, u' (point B). However, when searchers increased their acceptance wages to match the new rate of inflation, the unemployment rate rose, regaining its old value of u^* (point C).

A similar scenario would characterize the labor market response to a *reduction* in the rate of inflation. If a restrictive monetary policy reduced the rate of inflation to zero, search unemployment would initially rise to an abnormally high level such as

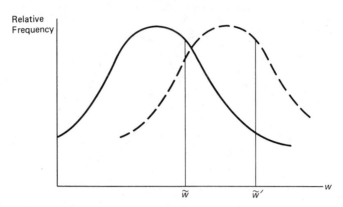

FIGURE 12-15. When the relative frequency curve shifts, $\tilde{w}$ eventually shifts to $\tilde{w}'$

u'', but as workers became convinced that the distribution of wage offers had permanently shifted to the left, unemployment would gradually approach its normal rate u^{*}.[37] Unfortunately, in an economy that has become accustomed to long-term inflation, the length of time it takes for unemployment to fall from a "temporarily" high level such as u'' to its normal level u^{*} may be discouragingly long. Twice since 1974 the United States economy has gone through cycles of inflation and unemployment that closely match the scenario we have just described. Following the removal of the price controls imposed by the Nixon administration in 1972, the annual rate of

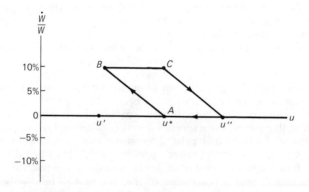

FIGURE 12-16. The short-run and long-run relationship between wage inflation and search unemployment

---

[37] The position that real economic magnitudes, such as the unemployment rate and the real value of the acceptance wage, are ultimately determined by *correct* perceptions of prices and wages has been most rigorously propounded by supporters of the **rational expectations** view of the way individuals make decisions. See, for example, Robert E. Lucas, Jr., "Econometric Testing of the Natural Rate Hypothesis," in Otto Eckstein, ed., *Econometrics of Price Determination*. Papers from a conference held October 30–31, 1970, in Washington, D.C., by the Federal Reserve Board of Governors and the Social Science Research Council.

change of the Consumer Price Index (CPI) rose to 11.0 percent in 1974.[38] Restrictive monetary policy brought the rate of inflation down to 5.8 percent by 1976, but as Table 12-6 shows, the unemployment rate rose from approximately its normal value in 1974 to three percentage points above it in 1975 and gradually declined thereafter.

Under the Carter administration, monetary and fiscal expansionary policies resulted in a renewed acceleration of inflation, so that the annual rate of change of the CPI reached 13.5 percent in 1980. This time, inflationary anticipations had become part of the public's way of thinking (inflationary psychology), and the unemployment rate did not fall below its normal value as it did during the early phase of the preceding inflationary episode. Moreover, when restrictive monetary policies were once again imposed during the early 1980s, the unemployment rate soared to a higher level than during the earlier "cure" and remained high for a longer period.

Inflation, the Firm's Employment Strategy, and "Waiting"[39]

Not all unemployed workers are actively seeking new jobs. As we have seen, the firm's decisions to lay off and hire workers can best be understood if we recognize the importance of anticipated future events in current wage and employment decisions. As outlined in Chapter 9, firm-specific OJT and implicit contract considerations mean that *VMPL* may fall considerably before even a short-sighted firm would lay off its trained workers.

Firms and workers both have an incentive to honor their implicit long-term commitments to each other. Under these circumstances, a worker who is laid off will have an incentive to remain available for recall, since the wage rate on the old job will be higher than that which could be obtained elsewhere. Moreover, knowledge of the former employer's reputation makes the old job more attractive than an alternative job offering an equal wage. That is, laid-off workers have a much smaller incentive to search for new jobs than individuals who are unemployed because they are entering or reentering the labor force permanently, who were discharged from their last job, or who quit because of job dissatisfaction. We will define laid-off workers who are awaiting recall as **waiters,** in contrast to other unemployed workers (searchers) who find it rewarding to engage in an active job search.[40]

How does waiting unemployment relate to the rate of inflation? Should we expect to observe, as with search unemployment, a negative short-term correlation between waiting unemployment and inflation that disappears when employers and workers fully anticipate the future course of inflation in the economy?

Suppose, as in our description of the relationship between inflation and search unemployment, that the government has engaged in expansionary monetary and fiscal policies that raise the economy's long-term rate of inflation from zero to 10 percent. Individual firms will notice that sales are rising faster than expected, but it will be some time before they realize that a period of economywide inflation has begun. Even though we hypothesized an initial state in which there is no inflation and what might be called full employment, some firms and industries at any moment in time have recently experienced slack demand for their product, while others have experienced unusually prosperous times. Firms in the former category will find it

---

[38] *Statistical Abstract of the United States,* 1981, p. 459.

[39] The discussion in this section draws heavily on Donald F. Gordon, "A Neoclassical Theory of Keynesian Unemployment," *Economic Inquiry,* 12 (December 1974).

[40] Once again, it should be emphasized that this theory of the firm's (and worker's) employment strategy is consistent with, but by no means requires, the existence of collective bargaining agreements that deal with wage and layoff policies.

relatively easy to expand output as demand increases by simply recalling laid-off workers who have been waiting to return to their old jobs. These workers have already been trained, and output can be increased relatively easily without increasing unit production costs. Other firms that have been experiencing relatively strong demand for their products will not find it quite so easy to expand output. They will probably initially ask their existing labor force to work overtime at premium wage rates, raising production costs. The increase in unit production costs coupled with strong sales will tempt these relatively more prosperous firms to raise prices.

As the number of experienced unemployed workers falls, firms face only three options if they wish to continue to increase their labor forces: (1) Hire the experienced unemployed whose prior employment was with another firm. Such workers will require some training, raising production costs. (2) Hire new employees from the pool of relatively inexperienced individuals who are searching for employment. This also will force the firm to invest in considerable training expense. (3) A third option is to hire employed workers away from other firms by offering them higher wage rates. In a world where firms offer implicit long-term contracts to workers, none of these three options will be undertaken until the firm has become convinced that the increase in demand is going to persist for a considerable length of time. Option 3 is particularly costly, because it would be difficult to maintain employee belief in the employer's fairness if wages paid to newcomers rose above the pay of a firm's older employees. Thus, firms will be forced to raise the wages of old employees as well. This should not be viewed as simply a charitable act on the part of an employer. During a period of tight labor markets, employers will wish to reduce quits in order to maintain and expand employment. Raising wage rates of existing employees is an obvious means of accomplishing this goal. Clearly, all the options open to the firm that wishes to expand employment when its pool of experienced unemployed workers has been depleted will tend to transform the increased demand for output into rising wages, costs, and prices.

We have described how an increase in aggregate demand reduces waiting unemployment as well as search unemployment and creates inflationary pressures, in part by causing labor costs to increase. Moreover, a general increase in demand will also cause the prices the firms pay for other inputs to rise. As costs increase, firms not only will try to raise prices commensurately but also will find it less attractive to maintain production above normal, or full-employment, levels. The higher prices firms are able to obtain for their output will be offset by rising prices of inputs. Thus, as the economy reaches the new 10 percent rate of inflation—which we have assumed is to be maintained by government actions—production and desired employment return to their normal levels. Some recently hired workers will be laid off, and firms will cease trying to raid the labor forces of their competitors. The unemployment rate will rise back to its normal level, but the rate of inflation will continue at its new rate—10 percent per year.

As the economy's rate of inflation increases toward 10 percent, firms may not initially need to increase the pay of all workers at an equal rate. The speed with which a firm increases the wage rates of experienced employees, who are already earning more than they would in other firms because of their investments in firm-specific OJT, will depend on implicit contracts covering layoffs, quits, and the degree to which unanticipated increases in prosperity or the rate of inflation are to be shared with senior employees in the form of higher rates of wage increases. Eventually, however, such contracts will require that real wages must be maintained. When workers and firms have decided that the long-term rate of inflation has become 10 percent, then the wages of experienced employees will be adjusted upward by the same annual amount, over and above increases that would have been called for at a zero rate of inflation. In the long term, *real* wage rates and real wage growth will be unaffected by the rate of inflation.

The relationship between the rate of inflation and waiting unemployment is qualitatively similar to that depicted in Figure 12-16. An increase in aggregate demand causes firms and workers to adjust in ways they would not choose if they immediately perceived the new long-term rate of inflation. Ultimately, the normal unemployment rate is unaffected by the rate of inflation, although a negative relationship is observed between unemployment and inflation before the rate of inflation is fully anticipated by firms and workers. When inflation is reduced, the process we have just described will reverse itself.

The length of time that elapses before the rate of unemployment returns to its normal level—point C in Figure 12-16—depends on the speed with which the inflationary pressures are transmitted through the economy and on how rapidly anticipations adjust. As we have seen, the adjustment of workers' and firms' expectations regarding the future course of prices will be conditioned by the past. If the economy has been inflation-prone, expectations will probably adjust upward rather rapidly if excess demand increases, and the period during which there is a gain from inflation in the form of increased production and reduced unemployment may be quite short. Conversely, if the government wishes to eliminate inflation, it can do so. When the basic causes of inflation are reversed, aggregate demand declines, sales and production fall, layoffs increase, and unemployment rises temporarily. Unfortunately, "temporary" may imply a politically and economically uncomfortable length of time after the rate of increase of prices begins to slow down.

Evidence on Inflation and Unemployment

Our analysis of the relationship between inflation and unemployment explains what is commonly known as the **Phillips curve,**[41] named after the economist who popularized the short-term negative relationship between unemployment and inflation we have described. The use of the word "curve" is unfortunate, since it connotes a stable relationship between unemployment and inflation—perhaps akin to a supply curve or even a kind of budget constraint that describes the economy's available choices between unemployment and inflation. This is misleading, because our analysis of the relationship between unemployment and inflation implies that over the long term, the economy cannot choose between low unemployment and a high rate of inflation on the one hand or higher unemployment and price stability on the other. Rather, society's long-term choice lies only between different rates of inflation, since unemployment will always tend toward u^*.

Just think of it—a stable Phillips curve would mean that we could permanently reduce scarcity simply by adopting sufficiently expansionary monetary and fiscal policies. Failure to recognize the fallacy of a stable long-term Phillips curve exposes us not only to the risk of ever-increasing inflation and the attendant real costs of increased uncertainty in the economy, but also to the even greater danger that, frustrated in its efforts to overcome inflation through contractionary monetary and fiscal policies, the government will ultimately resort to direct wage and price controls.

Evidence on the relationship between unemployment and inflation is contained in dozens of empirical studies, and we could not possibly summarize them all here. Figure 12-17 shows graphically the relationship between the annual percentage

---

[41] A. W. Phillips, "The Relationship between Unemployment and the Rate of Change of Money Wage Rates in the United Kingdom, 1861–1957," *Economica*, 25 (November 1958), 283–99.

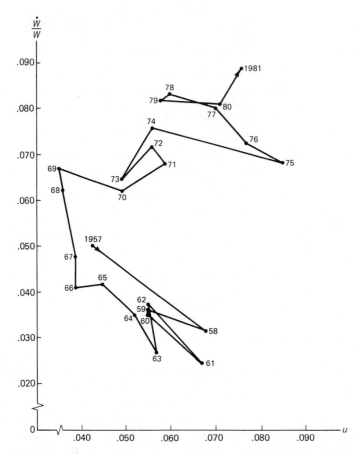

FIGURE 12-17. A Phillips Curve for the United States, 1957–1981

Source: *Economic Report of the President,* 1980, Table B-33, Unemployment Rate, and B-38, Average Weekly Hours and Hourly Earnings.

change in wages (average hourly earnings in the total private nonfarm sector) and unemployment for the United States between 1957 and 1981. The arrows should help you see how the inflationary periods of the late 1960s and 1970s only *temporarily* reduced unemployment. The "big picture" shows unemployment revolving around a normal rate that has tended to rise over time (as we have seen).

CONCLUSION

One of our goals in this chapter has been to point out the diverse dimensions of unemployment. We saw that most unemployment arises because information about job opportunities is scarce and individuals must search for their best alternative. In this regard, unemployment is a form of investment in human capital arising because workers (and firms) have incomplete labor market information. We also saw that in some instances unemployment is characteristic of jobs in cyclically sensitive industries; such unemployment arises because firms and workers have incomplete information about the future, but it is not really a search phenomenon. Although firms will attempt to lower their labor costs by offering "income insurance" to their workers in the form of a lower, but more steady, stream of wage payments, they will not *completely* offset the uncertainties of the marketplace. Thus, layoffs, and the resulting unemployment, are one of the risks workers must take in the course of their jobs, just as they risk industrial injuries and diseases.

Another goal in this chapter has been to evaluate demographic differences in unemployment rates in the United States. We saw that the primary such difference is between the young and the old. Less severe are racial differences in unemployment rates; sex differences in unemployment rates are small. In the course of our analysis we saw the value of understanding the economics of job search in helping us to sort out the social and economic forces behind the relatively high unemployment rates of youth and blacks.

We noted that total unemployment can be thought to consist of frictional, structural, and cyclical unemployment. The first two comprise so-called normal unemployment, the portion of total unemployment that is independent of the business cycle and reflects the typical amount of search and income insurance in the economy. We saw that the normal unemployment rate will vary with demographic composition of the labor force, the types of goods produced, the desire for income insurance, the efficiency of search activity, and so on. We attempted to identify the historical trend of the normal unemployment rate in the United States as well as the factors primarily responsible for that trend, paying special attention to the role played by public policy.

An important message of this chapter is that the relationship between the unemployment rate and social welfare is not as clear-cut as one might at first believe. For example, a reduction in unemployment may reflect an improvement in the operation of the labor market in the sense that workers and jobs are matched more quickly. This might result from reduced information costs, due, say, to improved transportation and communications systems. Alternatively, an increase in unemployment does not necessarily reflect a deterioration in job opportunities confronting an individual; if individuals choose to search more carefully before accepting jobs, this may result in an increase in their economic well-being in the long run because they find positions that are more suitable for their tastes and skills. In this regard more unemployment is better for a worker just as more schooling is better for a worker.

Finally, in this chapter we related the behavior of unemployment to the process of inflation. Our analysis explains much about the difficulties we have encountered in the United States in controlling the inflation that has troubled our economy throughout the past decade. Casual observation of macroeconomic events during this period has led many observers to conclude that efforts to hold inflation to a "reasonable" level (say, below 5 percent per year) are futile unless we are willing to pay for relative price-level stability by tolerating extraordinarily high unemployment. It is true that once inflationary expectations become entrenched, a period of severe excess supply in both goods and labor markets may be required if inflation is to be quickly reduced. Incomes policies in their various forms of formal or "voluntary" limits on wage and price increases, "jawboning," appeals to patriotism, and the like can be viewed as attempts to soften the impact on unemployment of reducing inflation.

Our analysis of the inflationary process allows us to see how incomes policies *might* be effective. By altering expectations of future inflation, an incomes policy might succeed in inducing workers and firms to use "restraint" in seeking wage and price increases, thus softening the impact of restrictive monetary and fiscal policies on unemployment. The difficulty in obtaining such cooperation, however, is a fundamental principle of economics. No *individual* worker or firm will reap the benefit of a reduced rate of inflation unless *all* workers and *all* firms act as if they expect the rate of inflation to decline. Thus, each individual, acting in his or her own best interest, has a strong incentive to ignore appeals to cooperate in antiinflation efforts. Voluntary incomes policies are therefore almost certainly doomed to failure, and governments are frequently tempted to impose mandatory wage and price controls when they are afraid to face the political difficulties of controlling inflation through more effective means.

Since the cure for inflation is almost inevitably difficult, prevention would definitely seem to be in order. Once again the root problem of scarcity must be recognized and respected if inflation is to be avoided. If government attempts to deceive the public into believing that wars can be fought, defense maintained, and social programs continued and enlarged without reducing private consumption expenditures, then the tax of inflation is sure to result.

REFERENCES AND SELECTED READINGS

AKERLOFF, GEORGE A., "The Economics of 'Tagging' as Applied to the Optimal Income Tax, Welfare Programs, and Manpower Planning," *American Economic Review*, 68:1 (March 1978), 8–19.

AZARIADAS, COSTAS, "Implicit Contracts and Underemployment Equilibria," *Journal of Political Economy*, 83:6 (December 1975), 1183–1202.

BAILY, MARTIN NEIL, "Wages and Employment Under Uncertain Demand," *Review of Economic Studies*, 41:1 (January 1974), 37–50.

BECKER, JOSEPH, *Experience Rating in Unemployment Insurance.* Baltimore: Johns Hopkins University Press, 1971.

BLACK, MATTHEW, "An Empirical Test of the Theory of On-the-Job Search," *Journal of Human Resources,* 16 (Winter 1981), 129–40.

————, "The Pecuniary Implications of On-the-Job Search and Quit Activity," *Review of Economics and Statistics,* 62 (May 1980), 222–29.

BRECHLING, FRANK, "The Incentive Effects of the U.S. Unemployment Insurance Tax," in *Research in Labor Economics,* ed. Ronald G. Ehrenberg, Vol. 1. Greenwich, Conn.: JAI Press, 1977, pp. 41–102.

————, "Unemployment Insurance Taxes and Labor Turnover: Summary of Theoretical Findings," *Industrial and Labor Relations Review,* 30 (July 1977), 483–92.

CHISWICK, BARRY, "The Effect of Unemployment Compensation on a Seasonal Industry: Agriculture," *Journal of Political Economy,* 84 (June 1976), 591–602.

COUNCIL OF ECONOMIC ADVISORS, *Economic Report of the President,* 1975, 123.

FELDSTEIN, MARTIN, "Temporary Layoffs in the Theory of Unemployment," *Journal of Political Economy,* 84:5 (September–October 1976), 937–57.

————, "The Unemployment Caused by Unemployment Insurance," *Proceedings of the Industrial Relations Research Association 28th Annual Winter Meetings,* 1975, 225–33.

FLEISHER, BELTON M., AND GEORGE F. RHODES, JR., "Labor Force Participation of Married Men and Women: A Simultaneous Model," *Review of Economics and Statistics,* 58 (November 1976), 398–406.

FRIEDMAN, SHELDON, DENNIS C. BERNSTEAD, AND ROBERT T. LUND, "Inverse Seniority as an Aid to Disadvantaged Groups," *Monthly Labor Review,* 99:4 (April 1976), 36–37.

GORDON, DONALD F., "A Neoclassical Theory of Keynesian Unemployment," *Economic Inquiry,* 12:4 (December 1974), 431–59.

GORDON, ROBERT J., *Macroeconomics,* 2d ed. Boston: Little, Brown & Co., 1981, Appendixes B and C.

————, "Structural Unemployment and the Productivity of Women," in *Stabilization of Domestic and International Economy,* eds. Karl Brunner and Allan Meltzer, Vol. 5 of a supplementary series to the *Journal of Monetary Economics,* 1977, 189–93.

————, "Why U.S. Wage and Employment Behavior Differs from that in Britain and Japan," *Economic Journal,* 92 (March 1982), 13–44.

HALL, ROBERT E., "Turnover in the Labor Force," *Brookings Papers on Economic Activity,* No. 3 (1972), 709–756.

HAMERMESH, DANIEL S., "Entitlement Effects, Unemployment Insurance, and Employment Decisions," *Economic Inquiry,* 17:3 (July 1979), 317–32.

————, *Jobless Pay and the Economy,* Policy Studies in Employment and Welfare, No. 29. Baltimore: Johns Hopkins University Press, 1977.

————, "Social Insurance and Consumption: An Empirical Inquiry," *American Economic Review,* 72:1 (March 1982), 101–113.

————, "Transfers, Taxes and the NAIRU," in *Supply-Side Effects of Economics Policy,* Proceedings of the 1980 Economics Policy Conference. St. Louis: The Center for the Study of American Business, Washington University in St. Louis, and the Federal Reserve Bank of St. Louis, 1981.

————, "Unemployment Insurance and Labor Supply," *International Economic Review,* 21:3 (October 1980), 517–27.

KIEFER, NICHOLAS M., AND GEORGE R. NEUMANN, "An Empirical Job-Search Model, With a Test of the Constant Reservation-Wage Hypothesis," *Journal of Political Economy,* 87:1 (February 1979), 87–109.

————, AND ————, "Individual Effects in a Nonlinear Model: Explicit Treatment of Heterogeneity in the Empirical Job-Search Model," *Econometrica,* 49:4 (July 1981), 965–80.

————, AND ————, "Structural and Reduced Form Approaches to Analyzing Unemployment Duration and Reemployment Wages," in *Studies in Labor Markets,* ed. Sherwin Rosen. Chicago: University of Chicago Press, 1981.

LILIEN, DAVID, "The Cyclical Pattern of Temporary Layoffs in United States Manufacturing," *Review of Economics and Statistics,* 62:2 (February 1980), 24–31.

LIPPMAN, STEVEN A., AND JOHN J. McCALL, "The Economics of Job Search: A Survey, Part I," *Economic Inquiry,* 14:2 (June 1976), 155–89.

LUCAS, ROBERT E., JR., "Econometric Testing of the Natural Rate Hypothesis," in Otto Eckstein, ed., *Econometrics of Price Determination,* Federal Reserve Board of Governors and Social Science Research Council Conference Papers, October 30–31, 1970, Washington, D.C.

MATTILA, PETER J., "An Analysis of the Rising Rates of Teenage Employment and Unemployment," Department of Economics, Iowa State University, June 1982.

MINCER, JACOB, "Labor Force Participation and Unemployment: A Review of Recent Evidence," in *Prosperity and Unemployment,* ed. R. A. and M. S. Gordon. New York: John Wiley, 1966, pp. 91–98.

————, "The Unemployment Effects of Minimum Wage," *Journal of Political Economy,* 84:4, part II (August 1976), S87–S104.

MOY, JOANNA, "Recent Labor Market Trends in Nine Industrial Nations," *Monthly Labor Review,* 102:5 (May 1979), 8–16.

National Bureau of Economic Research, "Why U.S. Wage and Employment Behavior Differs from that in Britain and Japan," Working Paper No. 809, Cambridge, Mass., November, 1981.

NBC White Paper, *America Works When America Works,* Aired June 25, 1981.

NEUMANN, GEORGE R., "The Labor Market Adjustments of Trade Displaced Workers: The Evidence from the Trade Adjustment Assistance Program," in *Research in Labor Economics,* ed. Ronald G. Ehrenberg, Vol. 2. Greenwich, Conn.: JAI Press, 1978, pp. 353–81.

OI, W. Y., "Labor as a Quasi-Fixed Factor," *Journal of Political Economy,* 70:6 (December 1961), 538–55.

PARSONS, DONALD O., "Models of Labor Market Turnover: A Theoretical and

Empirical Survey,'' in *Research in Labor Economics,* ed. Ronald G. Ehrenberg, Vol. 1. Greenwich, Conn.: JAI Press, 1977, pp. 185–223.

————, "Specific Human Capital: An Application to Quit Rates and Layoff Rates," *Journal of Political Economy,* 80:6 (November–December 1972), 120–43.

PERLOFF, JEFFREY M., AND MICHAEL L. WACHTER, "A Production Function-Nonaccelerating Inflation Approach to Potential Output; Is Measured Potential Output Too High?" in *Three Aspects of Policy and Policymaking,* ed. Karl Brunner and Allan H. Meltzer, Vol. 10 of a supplementary series to the *Journal of Monetary Economics,* 1979, pp. 133–34.

PHILLIPS, A. W., "The Relationship between Unemployment and the Rate of Change of Money Wage Rates in the United Kingdom, 1861–1957," *Economica,* 25 (November 1953), 283–99.

REDER, MELVIN, "The Coming Demise of Unemployment," *Proceedings of the American Philosophical Society,* 122:3 (June 1978), 139–44.

ROSEN, SHERWIN, "Short Run Employment Variation in Class I Railroads in the U.S., 1947–1963," *Econometrica,* 36:3–4 (July–October 1968), 511–29.

SHAVELL, STEVEN, AND LAWRENCE WEISS, "The Optimal Payment of Unemployment Insurance Benefits Over Time," *Journal of Political Economy,* 87:6 (December 1979), 1347–62.

STEIN, HERBERT, "Full-Employment at Last?" *The Wall Street Journal,* September 14, 1977, p. 22.

STIGLER, GEORGE J., "Information in the Labor Market," *Journal of Political Economy,* 70 (October 1962), Supplement, 94–105.

U.S. DEPARTMENT OF COMMERCE, *Long Term Economic Growth, 1860–1970,* 1973, Series B-1 and B-2.

————, *Statistical Abstract of the United States,* 1981.

U.S. DEPARTMENT OF LABOR, *Comparison of State Unemployment Laws,* 1971.

————, Bureau of Labor Statistics, *Employment and Earnings,* March 1981, Table 11-5.

————, and U.S. Department of Health and Human Services, *Employment and Training Report of the President,* 1980, Tables A-16, A-20, A-21, A-23, A-27, A-30 and A-31.

WACHTER, MICHAEL L., "The Changing Cyclical Responsiveness of Wage Inflation Over the Postwar Period," *Brookings Papers on Economic Activities,* No. 1 (1976), 115–67.

EXERCISES

Choose whether statements 1, 2, and 3 are *True, False,* or *Uncertain* (whether true or false depends on unspecified circumstances). Justify your answer. Your justification is the most important part of your answer.

1. An increase in unemployment may represent an increase in economic well-being for a worker.

2. An increase in the legal minimum wage will increase the unemployment rate of teenagers.
3. The Phillips curve for the United States shows that in the 1970s, increasing inflation was associated with growing unemployment.
4. The annual unemployment rate for the economy (u) is approximated by the relationship

$$u \cong \left(\frac{\text{number of individuals entering job search}}{\text{civilian labor force}}\right) \times (\text{average duration of search})$$

   (a) Why is this an approximation rather than an exact relation?
   (b) When the unemployment rate is relatively high, is the average duration of search relatively long or relatively short? (Data to answer this question may be found in a recent *Economic Report of the President.*)
   (c) When the unemployment rate is relatively high, is the proportion of the labor force searching for jobs relatively large or relatively small? (Data to answer this question may also be found in a recent *Economic Report of the President.*)
   (d) Of what practical importance for economic policy is the information contained in the answers to (b) and (c)?
   (e) Name some government policies that influence the average duration of search. Explain briefly.
   (f) Name some government policies that influence the proportion of the labor force searching for jobs. Explain briefly.
*5. Listed below are estimates for four local labor markets (for the month of May) from regressions of the form

$$u(\text{area})_t = \beta_0 + \beta_1 u(\text{national})_t + \beta_2 \text{Tr}$$

where $u(\text{area})_t \equiv$ the local area unemployment rate during year t
$u(\text{national})_t \equiv$ the national unemployment rate during year t
$\text{Tr} \equiv$ annual time trend variable (0, 1, 2, 3, . . .).

Labor Market	$\hat{\beta}_0$	$\hat{\beta}_1$	$\hat{\beta}_2$
Altoona, Pa.	−1.212	2.015	−0.105
	(1.23)	(7.69)	(7.34)
Baton Rouge, La.	4.235	0.044	0.051
	(7.70)	(0.30)	(6.37)
Lowell, Mass.	−4.213	2.530	0.004
	(6.89)	(15.59)	(0.41)
Seattle, Wash.	−8.80	2.933	0.070
	(12.69)	(15.93)	(7.57)

Note: Absolute t values are in parentheses.

Source: Robert Fearn, Department of Economics, North Carolina State University.

   (a) Which labor markets exhibit sensitivity to aggregate economic fluctuations?
   (b) Which labor markets seem to be experiencing structural unemployment difficulties?
   (c) For those labor markets experiencing structural unemployment difficulties,

---

* Represents a more difficult exercise.

calculate the number of years before they increase the unemployment rate by half a percentage point.

(d) Suppose you are director of the labor market development agency for Altoona. Your agency will receive a large grant from the federal government if in five years Altoona's unemployment rate (for May) exceeds 7.5. Five years from now, the national unemployment rate is predicted to be 5 (percent). Should you expect to receive the grant?

6. When analyzing the economics of job search, we considered a number of simple (one-dimensional) economic policies designed to influence unemployment rates. Suppose that the government introduces a policy *package* of progressive taxes and job training subsidies that results in both a higher average wage and a smaller dispersion in wage rates available to job searchers. What effect does such a policy package have on searchers' acceptance wages, duration of search, and labor market unemployment rates?

7. Suppose you were hired to manage a firm with a high seasonal and/or cyclical variation in sales. What are the problems you would face in adjusting compensation and the firm's production schedules to accommodate both your needs to increase profits and your workers' desire for a steady income? How would your decisions be affected by introduction of a UI tax and UI benefits that were exactly equal?

8. Consider two countries that are identical except for the fact that in one the consumer price index is kept a secret and in the other it is published in the daily newspaper. Using the tools developed in this chapter, discuss the long-run and short-run relationships between $\dot{W}$ and the unemployment rate in the two countries. Specifically, are they alike and how should they differ? What is the implication of this for economic policy?

9. Suppose that society dislikes both inflation and unemployment (both are social "bads"). Draw a set of social indifference curves reflecting this fact. Be sure to explain carefully the economic meaning of their slopes and positioning. Draw the long-run Phillips curve suggested by the theoretical analysis of this section. Using the above set of indifference curves and the Phillips curve, indicate and discuss society's optimal combination of unemployment and inflation.

INDEX